CONCISE EDITION

WORLDS TOGETHER,
WORLDS APART

Volume 2

WORLDS TOGETHER, WORLDS APART

Volume 2: From 1000 CE to the Present

Elizabeth Pollard | **Clifford Rosenberg** | **Robert Tignor**

with Jeremy Adelman, Stephen Aron, Peter Brown, Benjamin Elman,
Stephen Kotkin, Xinru Liu, Susanne Marchand, Holly Pittman,
Gyan Prakash, Brent Shaw, Michael Tsin

W. W. Norton & Company · New York · London

W. W. NORTON & COMPANY has been independent since its founding in 1923, when William Warder Norton and Mary D. Herter Norton first published lectures delivered at the People's Institute, the adult education division of New York City's Cooper Union. The firm soon expanded its program beyond the Institute, publishing books by celebrated academics from America and abroad. By midcentury, the two major pillars of Norton's publishing program—trade books and college texts—were firmly established. In the 1950s, the Norton family transferred control of the company to its employees, and today—with a staff of four hundred and a comparable number of trade, college, and professional titles published each year—W. W. Norton & Company stands as the largest and oldest publishing house owned wholly by its employees.

Editor: Jon Durbin
Associate Editor: Justin Cahill
Editorial Assistant: Penelope Lin
Developmental Editor: Ann Shin
Project Editor: Diane Cipollone
Marketing Manager, History: Sarah England
Manuscript Editor: Nancy Green
Managing Editor, College: Marian Johnson
Managing Editor, College Digital Media: Kim Yi
Production Manager: Andy Ensor
Media Editor: Lisa Moore
Media Project Editor: Penelope Lin
Media Editorial Assistant: Chris Hillyer
Design Director: Jillian Burr
Photo Editor: Nelson Colón
Permissions Manager: Megan Jackson
College Permissions Associate: Bethany Salminen
Composition: Cenveo® Publisher Services
Manufactured in the United States by LSC Communications

Permission to use copyrighted material is included on p. C-1.

The Library of Congress has cataloged the full edition as follows:

Tignor, Robert L.
    Worlds together, worlds apart : a history of the world from the beginnings of humankind to the present /
by Robert Tignor, Jeremy Adelman, Stephen Aron, Peter Brown, Benjamin Elman, Stephen Kotkin, Xinru Liu,
Suzanne Marchand, Holly Pittman, Gyan Prakash, Brent Shaw, and Michael Tsin. — Fourth edition.
        pages cm
    Includes bibliographical references and index.
    ISBN 978-0-393-92207-3 (hardcover : alk. paper) — ISBN 978-0-393-12376-0 (pbk. : alk. paper) 1. World
history. I. Title.
    D21.T53 2013
    909—dc23

                        2013038525

ISBN: 978-0-393-91848-9 (pbk.)

W. W. Norton & Company, Inc., 500 Fifth Avenue, New York, N.Y. 10110
www.wwnorton.com

W. W. Norton & Company Ltd., 15 Carlisle Street, London W1D 3BS

3 4 5 6 7 8 9 0

Contents in Brief

Contents

Chapter 10
BECOMING "THE WORLD," 1000–1300 CE   **341**

Chapter 11
CRISES AND RECOVERY IN AFRO-EURASIA, 1300–1500   **383**

Chapter 12
CONTACT, COMMERCE, AND COLONIZATION, 1450–1600   **419**

Chapter 14
CULTURES OF SPLENDOR AND POWER, 1500–1780   **497**

Chapter 15
REORDERING THE WORLD, 1750–1850   **531**

Chapter 16
ALTERNATIVE VISIONS OF THE NINETEENTH CENTURY   571

Chapter 17

NATIONS AND EMPIRES, 1850–1914   607

Chapter 18
AN UNSETTLED WORLD, 1890–1914   645

Chapter 21
GLOBALIZATION, 1970–2000   763

Current Trends in World History

Analyzing Global Developments

Global Themes and Sources

Maps

Preface

Worlds Together, Worlds Apart has set the standard for four editions for instructors who want to teach a globally integrated world history survey course. As the dynamic field of world history has evolved, so too has Worlds Together, Worlds Apart. Building on the successes of the full text, new co-authors Elizabeth Pollard (San Diego State University) and Clifford Rosenberg (City College of New York) and original author Robert Tignor (Princeton University) have created the new Concise Edition of Worlds Together, Worlds Apart. A full third shorter than its parent text and written with clear accessible prose and explanations, the Concise Edition continues to offer a coherent, cutting-edge survey of the field built around world history stories of significance. This concise globally integrated, chronological approach makes it possible for students to readily make connections and comparisons across time and place, and makes the teaching of the course more manageable for instructors. Some of the major stories dealt with in the chapters of the Concise edition are the spread of humans across the planet, the first global agricultural revolution, the creation of empires, the building of the Silk Roads, the spread of the Black Death across Afro-Eurasia, the impact of New World silver on global trade, alternative ways to organize societies during the rise of nineteenth-century capitalism, and the rise of the nation state.

HIGHLIGHTS OF THE CONCISE EDITION

The new Concise Edition is designed to be easy for students to read. It features a brand-new suite of pedagogical and media tools built around new Core Objectives, which are designed to guide students' reading and to aid them and their instructor in assessing their understanding of the material and concepts. Each of the book's 21 chapters begins with the innovative Before You Read This Chapter pedagogy, which highlights the Global Storylines and Core Objectives that students need to comprehend while reading the chapter. New Comparison Flags appear in the margins throughout the chapter to remind students of the Core Objectives while they read and to help them begin to make comparisons and connections on their own. The After

You Read This Chapter pedagogy includes Tracing the Global Storylines, which shows the impact of the chapter's main storyline on each region of the world. The new Thinking About Global Connections questions highlight major themes that unify the book's global approach, and new Study Questions place the chapter's Key Terms into a historical context.

The new Concise Edition also provides students with new features that are designed to encourage critical thinking and to help them develop historical thinking skills. Chief among these is the new Global Themes and Sources feature, which gathers at the end of each chapter a new collection of primary source documents. This includes Competing Perspectives, which invites students to compare several documents on one of the themes discussed in the chapter; and a new Interpreting Visual Evidence activity that allows students to probe a world historical theme reaching across regions.

Within the narrative of each chapter appear two unique features that also encourage critical thinking and the development of historical thinking skills. The new Analyzing Global Developments feature engages students with real historical data, much of it the result of recent scholarship, and the new Current Trends in World History feature, which presents new research trends, demonstrates how historical research remains relevant to our world today.

The Concise Edition's compelling and unique focus on world history stories, themes, and Core Objectives is further reinforced in our new online and digital support materials for students and instructors. Lead author for media Alan Karras (University of California, Berkeley) has brought together a tremendous media team to create InQuizitive—Norton's new formative, adaptive learning program—and digital materials for the Norton Coursepack to support the text (see page xxxvii for information about student and instructor resources). This exciting new authorial team has worked together closely to ensure the tightest integration possible between the main text and the media materials to help students and instructors succeed in their world history course.

OUR MAJOR THEMES

The primary organizing framework of *Worlds Together, Worlds Apart*—one that runs through the chapters and connects the different parts of the volume—is the theme of **interconnection and divergence**. While describing movements that facilitated global connectedness, this book also shows how different regions developed their own ways of handling or resisting connections and change.

Themes that stand out in *Worlds Together, Worlds Apart* highlight the importance of trade and culture exchange through the recurring efforts of people at **crossing borders—religious, political, and cultural—that brought the world together**. Merchants and educated men and women traded goods and ideas. Whole communities, in addition to select groups, moved to safer or more promising environments. This transregional crossing of ideas, goods, and peoples produced **transformations and conflicts**—a second important theme. The movement of ideas, peoples, products, and germs over long distances upset the balance of power across the world and within individual societies. Such movements changed the relationship of different population groups with other peoples and areas of the world and led over time to dramatic shifts in the ascendancy of regions. **Changes in power arrangements** within and between regions explain which parts of the world and regional groups benefited from integration and which resisted it. Finally, we highlight **the important roles that gender and the environment play in shaping the evolution of societies**. These themes (trade and cultural exchange, transformation and conflict, gender and the environment, and alterations in the balance of power) weave themselves through every chapter of this work. While we highlight major themes throughout, we tell the stories of the people caught in these currents of exchange, conflict, and changing power relations, paying particular attention to the role that gender and the environment play in shaping the evolution of societies.

OVERVIEW OF VOLUME ONE

Volume One of *Worlds Together, Worlds Apart* deals with the period from the beginnings of human history through the Mongol invasions of the thirteenth century and the spread of the Black Death across Afro-Eurasia. It is divided into eleven chapters, each of which marks a distinct historical period. Hence, each chapter has an overarching theme or small set of themes that hold otherwise highly diverse material together.

Chapter 1, "Becoming Human," presents biological and cultural perspectives on the way that early hominids became truly human. We believe that this chapter is important in establishing the global context of world history. We believe too that our chapter is unique in its focus on a range of creation narratives that explain how humans became humans. We discuss how early humans became bipedal and how they developed complex cognitive processes such as language and artistic abilities. Recent research indicates that *Homo sapiens* originated in Africa, probably no more than 200,000 years ago. These early men and women walked out of the African landmass sometime between 120,000 and 50,000 years ago, gradually populating all regions of the world. What is significant in this story is that the different population groups around the world, the so-called races of humankind, have only recently broken off from one another. Also in this chapter, we describe the domestication of plants and animals and the founding of the first village settlements around the globe.

Chapter 2, "Rivers, Cities, and First States, 3500–2000 BCE," covers the period during which five of the great river basins experienced extraordinary breakthroughs in human activity. On the flood plains of the Tigris and Euphrates in Mesopotamia, the Nile in Egypt, the Indus valley in modern-day northern India and Pakistan, and the Yellow and Yangzi rivers in China, men and women mastered annual floods and became expert in seeding and cultivating foodstuffs. In these areas, populations became dense. River-basin cultures had much in common. They had highly developed hierarchical political, social, and cultural systems, priestly and bureaucratic classes, and organized religious and cultural systems. But they also differed greatly, and these differences were passed from generation to generation. The development of these major complex societies certainly is a turning point in world history.

Extensive climatic and technological changes serve as major turning points for **Chapter 3, "Nomads, Territorial States, and Microsocieties, 2000–1200 BCE."** Drought, environmental degradation, and political instability brought the first river-basin societies to a crashing end around 2000 BCE. When aridity forced tribal and nomadic peoples living on the fringes of the settled populations to move closer to settled areas, they brought with them an insurmountable military advantage. They had become adept at yoking horses to war chariots, and hence they were in a position to subjugate or intermarry with the peoples in the settled political organizations in the river basins. Around 2000 BCE these peoples established new territorial kingdoms in Mesopotamia, Egypt, the Indus valley, and China, which gave way a millennium later (1000 BCE) to even larger, militarily and politically more powerful states. In the Americas, the Mediterranean, sub-Saharan Africa, and the Pacific worlds, microsocieties arose as an alternative form of political organization in which peoples lived in much smaller-scale societies that showcased their own unique and compelling features.

Chapter 4, "First Empires and Common Cultures in Afro-Eurasia, 1250–325 BCE," describes the different ways in which larger-scale societies grew and became unified. In the case of the world's first empires, the neo-Assyrian and Persian, political power was the main unifying element. Both states established different models that future empires would emulate. The Assyrians used brutal force to intimidate and subjugate different groups within their societies and neighboring states. The Persians followed a pattern that relied less on coercion and more on tributary relationships, while permitting cultural diversity. The Zhou state in China offered yet a third way of political unity, basing its rule on the doctrine of the mandate of heaven, which legitimated its rulers' succession as long as they were able to maintain stability and order. Vedic society in South Asia offers a dramatically different model in which religion and culture were the main unifying forces.

The last millennium before the common era witnessed some of the most monumental developments in human history. In the six and half centuries discussed in **Chapter 5, "Worlds Turned Inside Out, 1000–350 BCE,"** teachers and thinkers, rather than kings, priests, and warriors, came to the fore. Confucius, the Buddha, Plato, and Aristotle, to name only the best known of this brilliant group, offered new insights into the natural world and provided new guidelines for how to govern justly and live ethically. In this era, small-scale societies, benefiting from more intimate relationships, took the place of the first great empires, now in decline. These highly individualistic cultures developed new strategies for political organization, even including experimenting with a democratic polity. In Africa, the Bantu peoples spread across sub-Saharan Africa, and the Sudanic peoples of Meroe created a society that blended Egyptian and sub-Saharan influences. These were all dynamic hybrid societies building on existing knowledge. Equally dramatic transformations occurred in the Americas, where the Olmec and Chavín peoples were creating hierarchical societies of the like never before seen in their part of the world.

Chapter 6, "Shrinking the Afro-Eurasian World, 350 BCE–100 CE," describes two major forces that simultaneously integrated large segments of the Afro-Eurasian landmass culturally and economically. First, Hellenism, whose leading figure, Alexander the Great, paved the way in North Africa and Southwest and central Asia for the first transregional cultural system in world history. Second, a trading network known as the Silk Roads, stretching from Palmyra in the west to central Asia in the east, came into being. Buddhism was the first religion to seize on the Silk Roads' more formal existence as its followers moved quickly with the support of the Mauryan Empire to spread their ideas into central Asia.

Chapter 7, "Han Dynasty China and Imperial Rome, 300 BCE–300 CE," compares Han China and the Roman Empire, the two political, economic, and cultural systems that dominated much of the Afro-Eurasian landmass from 200 BCE to 200 CE. Both the Han Dynasty and the Roman Empire ruled effectively in their own ways, providing an instructive comparative case study. Both left their imprint on Afro-Eurasia, and rulers for centuries afterward tried to revive these glorious empires and use them as models of greatness. This chapter also discusses the effect of state sponsorship on religion, as Christianity came into existence in the context of the late Roman Empire and Buddhism was introduced to China during the decline of the Han.

Out of the crumbling Roman Empire new political systems and a new religion emerged, the major topic of **Chapter 8, "The Rise of Universal Religions, 300–600 CE."** The Byzantine Empire, claiming to be the successor state to the Roman Empire, embraced Christianity as its state religion. The Tang rulers patronized Buddhism to such a degree that Confucian statesmen feared it had become the state religion. Both Buddhism and Christianity enjoyed spectacular success in the politically fragmented post-Han era in China and in the feudal world of western Europe. These dynamic religions represent a decisive transformation in world history. Christianity enjoyed its eventual successes through state sponsorship via the Roman and Byzantine empires and by providing spiritual comfort and hope during the chaotic years of Rome's decline. Buddhism grew through imperial sponsorship and significant changes to its fundamental beliefs, when adherents to the faith deified the Buddha and created notions of an afterlife. In Africa a wide range of significant developments and a myriad of cultural practices existed; yet large common cultures also arose. The Bantu peoples spread throughout the southern half of the landmass, spoke closely related languages, and developed similar political institutions based on the prestige of individuals of high achievement. In the Americas the Olmecs established their own form of the city-state, while the Mayans owed their success to a decentralized common culture built around a strong religious belief system and a series of spiritual centers.

In **Chapter 9, "New Empires and Common Cultures, 600–1000 CE,"** in a relatively remote corner of the Arabian Peninsula, another world religion, Islam, exploded with world-changing consequences. The rise of Islam provides a contrast to the way in which universalizing religions and political empires interacted. Islam and empire arose in a fashion quite different from Christianity and the Roman Empire. Christianity took over an already existing empire—the Roman—after suffering persecution at its hands for several centuries. In contrast, Islam created an empire almost at the moment of its emergence. By the time the Abbasid Empire came into being in the middle of the eighth century, Islamic armies, political leaders, and clerics exercised power over much of the Afro-Eurasian landmass from southern Spain, across North Africa, all the way to central Asia. The Tang Empire in China, however, served as a counterweight to Islam's power both politically and intellectually. Confucianism enjoyed a spectacular recovery in this period. With the Tang rulers, Confucianism slowed the spread of Buddhism and further reinforced China's development along different, more secular pathways. Japan and Korea also enter world history at this time, as tributary states to Tang China and as hybrid cultures that mixed Chinese customs and practices with their own. The Christian world split in this period between the western Latin church and the eastern Byzantine church. Both branches of Christianity played a role in unifying societies, especially in western Europe, which lacked strong political rule.

In the three centuries from 1000 to 1300 (**Chapter 10, "Becoming 'The World,' 1000–1300 CE"**) Afro-Eurasia experienced an unprecedented rise in prosperity and population that even spread into West and East Africa. Just as importantly, the world in this period divided into regional zones that are recognizable today. And trade grew rapidly. A view of the major trading cities of this time demonstrates how commerce transformed cultures. Sub-Saharan Africa also underwent intense regional integration via the spread of the Mande-speaking peoples and the Mali Empire. The Americas witnessed their

first empire in the form of the Chimu peoples in the Andes. This chapter ends with the Mongol conquests of the twelfth and thirteenth centuries, which brought massive destruction. The Mongol Empire, however, once in place, promoted long-distance commerce, scholarly exchange, and travel on an unprecedented scale. The Mongols brought Eurasia, North Africa, and many parts of sub-Saharan Africa into a new connectedness. The Mongol story also underscores the important role that nomads played throughout the history of the early world.

The Black Death brought Afro-Eurasia's prosperity and population growth to a catastrophic end as discussed in **Chapter 11, "Crises and Recovery in Afro-Eurasia, 1300–1500."** The dying and destruction of the fourteenth century saw traditional institutions give way and forced peoples to rebuild their cultures. The political systems that came into being at this time and the intense religious experimentation that took place effected a sharp break with the past. The bubonic plague wiped out as much as two-thirds of the population in many of the densely settled locations of Afro-Eurasia. Societies were brought to their knees by the Mongols' depredations as well as by biological pathogens. In the face of one of humanity's grimmest periods, peoples and societies demonstrated tremendous resilience as they looked for new ways to rebuild their communities, some turning inward and others seeking inspiration, conquests, and riches elsewhere. Volume One concludes on the eve of the "Columbian Exchange," the moment when "old" worlds discovered "new" ones and a vast series of global interconnections and divergences commenced.

OVERVIEW OF VOLUME TWO

The organizational structure for Volume Two reaffirms the commitment to write a decentered, global history of the world. Christopher Columbus is not the starting point, as he is in so many modern world histories. Rather, we begin in the eleventh and twelfth centuries with two major developments in world history: the Mongols and the Black Death. The first, set forth in **Chapter 10, "Becoming 'The World,' 1000–1300 CE,"** describes a world that was divided for the first time into regions that are recognizable today. This world experienced rapid population growth, as is shown by a simple look at the major trading cities from Asia in the east to the Mediterranean in the west. Yet nomadic peoples remain a force as revealed in the Mongol invasions of Afro-Eurasia.

Chapter 11, "Crises and Recovery in Afro-Eurasia, 1300–1500," describes how the Mongol warriors, through their conquests and the integration of the Afro-Eurasian world, spread the bubonic plague, which brought death and depopulation to much of Afro-Eurasia. Both these stories set the stage for the modern world and are clear-cut turning points in world history. The primary agents of world connection described in this chapter were dynasts, soldiers, clerics, merchants, and adventurers who rebuilt the societies that disease and political collapse had destroyed.

The Mongols joined the two hemispheres, as we describe in **Chapter 12, "Contact, Commerce, and Colonization, 1450–1600,"** bringing the peoples and products of the Western Hemisphere into contact and conflict with Eurasia and Africa. It is the collision between the Eastern and Western Hemispheres that sets in motion modern world history and marks a distinct divide or turning point between the premodern and the modern. Here, too, disease and increasing trade linkages were vital. Unprepared for the advanced military technology and the disease pool of European and African peoples, the Amerindian population experienced a population decline even more devastating than that caused by the Black Death.

Europeans sailed across the Atlantic Ocean to find a more direct, less encumbered route to Asia and came upon lands, peoples, and products that they had not expected. One item, however, that they had sought in every part of the world and that they found in abundance in the Americas was precious metal. **Chapter 13, "Worlds Entangled, 1600–1750,"** discusses how New World silver from Mexico and Peru became the major currency of global commerce, facilitating the long-distance trading networks that had been revived after the Black Death. The effect of New World silver on the world economy was so great that it, even more than the Iberian explorations of the New World, brought the hemispheres together and marked the true genesis of modern world history. Sugar also linked the economies and polities of western Europe, Africa, and the Americas and was a powerful force in a triangular trade centered on the Atlantic Ocean. This trade involved the shipment of vast numbers of African captives to the Americas, where they toiled on sugar, tobacco, cotton, and rice slave plantations.

Chapter 14, "Cultures of Splendor and Power, 1500–1780," investigates Ottoman scientists, Safavid and Mughal artists, and Chinese literati, as well as European thinkers, whose notable achievements were rooted in their own cultures but tempered by awareness of the intellectual activities of others. This chapter looks closely at how culture is created as a historical process and describe how the massive increase in wealth during this period, growing out of global trade, led to one of the great periods of cultural flourishing in world history. Around 1800, transformations reverberated outward from the Atlantic world and altered economic and political relationships in the rest of the world.

Chapter 15, "Reordering the World, 1750–1850," discusses political revolutions in the Americas and Europe, focusing on new ideas about how to trade and labor. It contends that a powerful rhetoric of freedom and universal rights underlay the beginning of "a great divide" between peoples of European descent and those who were not. These forces of laissez-faire capitalism, industrialization, the nation-state, and republicanism not only attracted diverse groups around the world; they also threatened groups that put forth alternative visions. New ideas of freedom, as manifested in trading relations, labor, and political activities, clashed with older notions of inherited rights and statuses and further challenged the way men and women had lived in earlier times. These political, intellectual, and economic reorderings changed the way people around the world saw themselves and thus represent something quite novel in world history.

These new ways of envisioning the world did not go unchallenged, as **Chapter 16, "Alternative Visions of the Nineteenth Century,"** makes clear. Here, intense resistance to evolving modernity reflected the diversity of peoples and their hopes for the future. Wahabbism in Islam, the strongman movement in Africa, Indian resistance in the United States and Mexico, socialism and communism in Europe, the Taiping Rebellion in China, and the Indian Mutiny in South Asia catapulted to historical prominence prophets and leaders whose visions often drew on earlier traditions and led these individuals to resist rapid change.

Chapter 17, "Nations and Empires, 1850–1914," deals with the political, economic, military, and ideological power that thrust Europe and North America to the fore of global events and led to an era of nationalism and modern imperialism, new forces in world history. Yet this period of seeming European supremacy was to prove short-lived.

As **Chapter 18, "An Unsettled World, 1890–1914,"** demonstrates, even before World War I shattered Europe's moral certitude, many groups at home (feminists, Marxists, and unfulfilled nationalists) and abroad (anticolonial nationalists) had raised a chorus of complaints about European and North American dominance. As in Chapter 14, this chapter looks at the processes by which specific cultural movements rose and reflected the concerns of individual societies. Yet here, too, syncretistic movements emerged in many cultures and reflected the sway of global imperialism, which by then had become a dominant force.

Chapter 19, "Of Masses and Visions of the Modern, 1910–1939," briefly covers World War I and then discusses how, from the end of World War I until World War II, different visions of being modern competed around the world. The development of modernism and its effects on multiple cultures integrate the diverse developments discussed in this chapter. In the decades between the world wars, proponents of liberal democracy struggled to defend their views and often to impose their will on authoritarian rulers and anticolonial nationalists.

Chapter 20, "The Three-World Order, 1940–1975," presents World War II as new adversaries arose after the war. A three-world order came into being—the First World, led by the United States and extolling capitalism, the nation-state, and democratic government; the Second World, led by the Soviet Union and favoring authoritarian polities and economies; and the Third World, made up of former colonies seeking an independent status and alternative routes to modernity for themselves in world affairs. The rise of this three-world order dominates the second half of the twentieth century and constitutes another major theme of world history.

Chapter 21, "Globalization, 1970–2000," explains that, at the end of the Cold War, the modern world, while clearly more unified than before, still had profound cultural differences and political divisions. At the beginning of the twenty-first century, capital, commodities, peoples, and ideas moved rapidly over long distances. But cultural tensions and political impasses continued to exist. The rise of this form of globalism represented a vital new element as humankind headed into a new century and millennium.

The Epilogue, 2001–The Present, tracks developments since the turn of the millennium. These last few years have brought profound changes to the world order, yet we hope readers of *Worlds Together, Worlds Apart* will see more clearly how this most recent history is, in fact, entwined with trends of much longer duration that are the chief focus of this book.

MEDIA ANCILLARIES

New lead author for media and pedagogy Alan Karras has helped us gather a team of innovative world history instructors, including Shane Carter, Wendy Eagan, Theresa Quindlen, and Sally West. Together, this team has ensured that the Concise Edition of *Worlds Together, Worlds Apart* is supported by an array of digital media with tools faculty need to meet course goals—in the classroom and online—and activities for students to develop core skills in reading comprehension, writing, and analysis, and to better understand the geography and contexts in world history surveys.

FOR STUDENTS

InQuizitive

Quizzing to Learn

InQuizitive, Norton's new adaptive quizzing platform, uses interactive questions and guided feedback to motivate students to read and understand the text. Varied question types—featuring images, maps, and sources—prompt critical and analytical thinking on each of the chapter's Core Objectives. Robust grading functionality helps instructors track their students' progress on learning outcomes.

Student Site

This free site offers students access to additional primary source documents and images, Office Hour videos with the authors, and iMaps. It is ideal for instructors interested in granting students access to additional material without creating or administering online assignments.

Norton Ebooks

Norton Ebooks lets students access the entire book and much more: they can search, highlight, and take notes with ease, as well as collaborate and share their notes with instructors and classmates. Ebooks can be viewed on any device—laptop, tablet, phone, even a public computer—and will stay synced between devices.

FOR INSTRUCTORS

Norton Coursepacks

Free Norton Coursepacks (downloadable in Blackboard, WebCT, D2L, and Moodle; additional formats can be provided upon request), includes:

- **New Gradable Assignments** allow you to assign quizzes based on questions from the text including Assessing the Global Storylines, Competing Perspectives, and Interpreting Visual Evidence.
- **NEW Primary Source Exercises** include several primary sources from across cultures with a brief multiple choice exam and a short answer question.
- **Guided Reading Exercises,** keyed to each chapter's Core Objectives, instill the three-step Note-Summarize-Assess pedagogy. Each chapter has one exercise built around passages from the text.
- **Review Quizzes** include targeted feedback that highlights Core Objective, page reference, and difficulty. *Chrono-Quizzes* end each chapter quiz with a matching question.
- **Online Reader** provides over 100 primary-source documents and images.
- **Map Resources** include *iMaps*, where students can peel back each layer to highlight the information they want to see, *StoryMaps* where complex maps are broken into five annotated slides that focus on the *story* behind the *geography. World History Tours*, powered by Google Earth that are dynamic, interactive primary sources that trace global developments over time. *Map Worksheets* provide each map without labels for offline relabeling and quizzing.
- **Forum Prompts** for online and hybrid courses are a set of topics that can be used to launch discussions.
- **Key Term Flash Cards** allow students to self-study historical vocabulary.
- Links to **InQuizitive** for each chapter.

Classroom Presentation Tools

- **Lecture PowerPoints and Art PowerPoints** feature photographs and maps from the book, retouched for in-class presentation.
- *Story Maps* break complex maps into a sequence of five annotated screens that focus on the story behind the geography. Ten maps include such topics as The Silk Road, The Spread of the Black Death, and Population Growth and the Economy.

Instructor's Manual (Sharon Cohen)

The Instructor's Manual for *Worlds Together, Worlds Apart* Concise Edition has everything instructors need to prepare lectures and classroom activities: lecture outlines, lecture ideas, classroom activities. Our new Popular Fallacy section provides an exercise that helps to dispel common misconceptions students may have about each chapter.

Test Bank (Ryba Epstein)

The Test Bank features multiple-choice, true/false, and essay questions aligned with the chapter's Core Objectives and classified according to level of difficulty and Bloom's Taxonomy, offering multiple avenues for content and skill assessment. All Norton test banks are available with ExamView Test Generator software, allowing instructors to easily create, administer, and manage assessments.

ACKNOWLEDGMENTS

The quality and range of reviews on this project were truly exceptional. The final version of the manuscript was greatly influenced by the thoughts and ideas of numerous instructors.

Concise Edition Reviewers

Andreas Agocs, University of the Pacific
Anthony Barbieri-Low, University of California, Santa Barbara
Brett Berliner, Morgan State University
Carolyn Noelle Biltoft, Georgia State University
Gayle Brunelle, California State University, Fullerton
Grace Chee, West Los Angeles College
Stephen Colston, San Diego State University
Paula Devos, San Diego State University
Alan Karras, University of California, Berkeley
Elaine MacKinnon, University of West Georgia
Harold Marcuse, University of California, Santa Barbara
Eva Moe, Modesto Junior College
Alice Pate, Kennesaw State University
Chandrika Paul, Shippensburg University
Jared Poley, Georgia State University
Dana Rabin, University of Illinois
Masako Racel, Kennesaw State University
Charles Reed, Elizabeth City State University
Alice Roberti, Santa Rosa Junior College
Steven Rowe, Chicago State University
Lynn Sargeant, California State University, Fullerton
Robert Saunders, Farmingdale State College
Sharlene Sayegh-Canada, California State University–Long Beach
Jeffrey Shumway, Brigham Young University
Greg Smay, University of California, Berkeley
Lisa Tran, California State University, Fullerton
Michael Vann, California State University, Sacramento
Theodore Weeks, Southern Illinois University
Krzysztof Ziarek, University of Buffalo

For the Concise Edition we have some familiar and new friends at Norton to thank. Chief among them is Jon Durbin, who once again played a major role in bringing this edition to publication. Ann Shin, our developmental editor, did a remarkable job in helping to address reviewers' comments and streamline the whole book. Sarah England has put together a creative marketing plan for the book. Jillian Burr is responsible for the book's beautiful and effective new design. Justin Cahill and Penelope Lin have been invaluable with their work on the maps, illustrations, and new feature boxes. Lisa Moore, Tacy Quinn, and Chris Hillyer have done a masterful job strengthening the media support materials to meet the ever more complex classroom and assessment needs of instructors. Diane Cipollone, our project editor, and Andrew Ensor, our production manager, have done a great job getting the book published on time with a very tight schedule. Nancy Green did an assiduous job with the copyediting, turning the chapters around quickly to meet our schedule. A special shout out goes to Debra Morton-Hoyt and her team of cover designers. *Worlds Together, Worlds Apart* has always been incredibly creative and distinctive looking, and the Concise Edition covers are even more eye-catching and memorable than the first four editions. Last, but far from least, we thank the authors of the full edition for their participation in this Concise Edition work, while allowing the new authors considerable leeway to have their own input. Bravo!

Finally, and most importantly, we recognize that while this project often kept us apart from family members, their love and understanding holds our worlds together.

About the Authors

ELIZABETH POLLARD (*Ph.D. University of Pennsylvania*) is associate professor of history at San Diego State University. Her research expertise focuses on women accused of witchcraft in the Roman world and on the exchange of goods and ideas between the Mediterranean and the Indian Ocean. Her pedagogical interests include the effectiveness of web-based technology and world history in teaching, learning, and writing about ancient history.

CLIFFORD ROSENBERG (*Ph.D. Princeton University*) is associate professor of European history at City College and the Graduate Center, CUNY. He specializes in the history of modern France and its empire and is the author of *Policing Paris: The Origins of Modern Immigration Control Between the Wars*. He is working now on the spread of tuberculosis between France and Algeria since the mid-nineteenth century.

ROBERT TIGNOR (*Ph.D. Yale University*) is professor emeritus and the Rosengarten Professor of Modern and Contemporary History at Princeton University and the three-time chair of the history department. With Gyan Prakash, he introduced Princeton's first course in world history nearly twenty years ago. Professor Tignor has taught graduate and undergraduate courses in African history and world history and written extensively on the history of twentieth-century Egypt, Nigeria, and Kenya. Besides his many research trips to Africa, Professor Tignor has taught at the University of Ibadan in Nigeria and the University of Nairobi in Kenya.

ALAN KARRAS (*Ph.D. University of Pennsylvania*) is the Associate Director of International & Area Studies at the University of California, Berkeley, and has served as chair of the College Board's test development committee for world history and as co-chair of the College Board's commission on AP history course revisions. He studies the eighteenth-century Atlantic world and global interactions more broadly concerning illegal activities like smuggling.

JEREMY ADELMAN (*D.Phil. Oxford University*) is currently the Director of the Council for International Teaching and Research at Princeton University and the Walter S. Carpenter III Professor of Spanish Civilization and Culture. He has written and edited five books, including *Republic of Capital: Buenos Aires and the Legal Transformation of the Atlantic World*, which won the best book prize in Atlantic history from the American Historical Association, and most recently *Sovereignty and Revolution in the Iberian Atlantic*. Professor Adelman is the recent recipient of a Guggenheim Memorial Foundation Fellowship and the Frederick Burkhardt Award from the American Council of Learned Societies.

STEPHEN ARON (*Ph.D. University of California, Berkeley*) is professor of history at the University of California, Los Angeles, and executive director of the Institute for the Study of the American West, Autry National Center. A specialist in frontier and Western American history, Aron is the author of *How the West Was Lost: The Transformation of Kentucky from Daniel Boone to Henry Clay* and *American Confluence: The Missouri Frontier from Borderland to Border State*. He is currently editing the multivolume *Autry History of the American West* and writing a book with the tentative title *Can We All Just Get Along: An Alternative History of the American West*.

PETER BROWN (*Ph.D. Oxford University*) is the Rollins Professor of History at Princeton University. He previously taught at London University and the University of California, Berkeley. He has written on the rise of Christianity and the end of the Roman Empire. His works include *Augustine of Hippo, The World of Late Antiquity, The Cult of the Saints, Body and Society, The Rise of Western Christendom*, and *Poverty and Leadership in the Later Roman Empire*. He is presently working on issues of wealth and poverty in the late Roman and early medieval Christian worlds.

BENJAMIN ELMAN (*Ph.D. University of Pennsylvania*) is professor of East Asian studies and history at Princeton University. He is currently serving as the chair of the Princeton East Asian Studies Department. He taught at the University of California, Los Angeles, for over fifteen years. His teaching and research fields include Chinese intellectual and cultural history, 1000–1900; the history of science in China, 1600–1930; the history of education in late imperial China; and Sino-Japanese cultural history, 1600–1850. He is the author of five books: *From Philosophy to Philology: Intellectual and Social Aspects of Change in Late Imperial China; Classicism, Politics, and Kinship: the Ch'ang-chou School of New Text Confucianism in Late Imperial China; A Cultural History of Civil Examinations in Late Imperial China; On Their Own Terms: Science in China, 1550–1900;* and *A Cultural History of Modern Science in China.* He is the creator of Classical Historiography for Chinese History at www.princeton.edu/~classbib/, a bibliography and teaching website published since 1996.

STEPHEN KOTKIN (*Ph.D. University of California, Berkeley*) is professor of European and Asian history as well as international affairs at Princeton University. He formerly directed Princeton's program in Russian and Eurasian studies (1996–2009). He is the author of *Magnetic Mountain: Stalinism as a Civilization, Uncivil Society: 1989 and the Implosion of the Communist Establishment,* and *Armageddon Averted: The Soviet Collapse, 1970–2000.* He is a coeditor of *Mongolia in the Twentieth Century: Landlocked Cosmopolitan.* Professor Kotkin has twice been a visiting professor in Japan.

XINRU LIU (*Ph.D. University of Pennsylvania*) is associate professor of early Indian history and world history at the College of New Jersey. She is associated with the Institute of World History and the Chinese Academy of Social Sciences. She is the author of *Ancient India and Ancient China, Trade and Religious Exchanges, AD 1–600; Silk and Religion, an Exploration of Material Life and the Thought of People, AD 600–1200; Connections across Eurasia, Transportation, Communication, and Cultural Exchange on the Silk Roads,* coauthored with Lynda Norene Shaffer; and *A Social History of Ancient India* (in Chinese). Professor Liu promotes South Asian studies and world history studies in both the United States and the People's Republic of China.

SUZANNE MARCHAND (*Ph.D. University of Chicago*) is professor of European and intellectual history at Louisiana State University, Baton Rouge. Professor Marchand also spent a number of years teaching at Princeton University. She is the author of *Down from Olympus: Archaeology and Philhellenism in Germany, 1750–1970* and *German Orientalism in the Age of Empire: Religion, Race and Scholarship.*

HOLLY PITTMAN (*Ph.D. Columbia University*) is professor of art history at the University of Pennsylvania, where she teaches art and archaeology of Mesopotamia and the Iranian Plateau. She also serves as curator in the Near East Section of the University of Pennsylvania Museum of Archaeology and Anthropology. Previously she served as a curator in the Ancient Near Eastern Art Department of the Metropolitan Museum of Art. She has written extensively on the art and culture of the Bronze Age in the Middle East and has participated in excavations in Cyprus, Turkey, Syria, Iraq, and Iran, where she currently works. Her research investigates works of art as media through which patterns of thought, cultural development, and historical interactions of ancient cultures of the Near East are reconstructed.

GYAN PRAKASH (*Ph.D. University of Pennsylvania*) is professor of modern Indian history at Princeton University and a member of the Subaltern Studies Editorial Collective. He is the author of *Bonded Histories: Genealogies of Labor Servitude in Colonial India, Another Reason: Science and the Imagination of Modern India,* and *Mumbai Fables.* Professor Prakash edited *After Colonialism: Imperial Histories and Postcolonial Displacements* and *Noir Urbanisms,* coedited *The Space of the Modern City* and *Utopia/Dystopia,* and has written a number of articles on colonialism and history writing. He is currently working on a history of the city of Bombay. With Robert Tignor, he introduced the modern world history course at Princeton University.

BRENT SHAW (*Ph.D. Cambridge University*) is the Andrew Fleming West Professor of Classics at Princeton University, where he is director of the Program in the Ancient World. He was previously at the University of Pennsylvania, where he chaired the Graduate Group in Ancient History. His principal areas of specialization as a Roman historian are Roman family history and demography, sectarian violence and conflict in Late Antiquity, and the regional history of Africa as part of the Roman Empire. He has published *Spartacus and the Slaves Wars*; edited the papers of Sir Moses Finley, *Economy and Society in Ancient Greece*; and published in a variety of books and journals, including the *Journal of Roman Studies*, the *American Historical Review*, the *Journal of Early Christian Studies*, and *Past & Present*.

MICHAEL TSIN (*Ph.D. Princeton*) is associate professor of history and international studies at the University of North Carolina at Chapel Hill. He previously taught at the University of Illinois at Chicago, Princeton University, Columbia University, and the University of Florida. Professor Tsin's primary interests include the histories of modern China and colonialism. He is the author of *Nation, Governance, and Modernity in China: Canton, 1900–1927*. He is currently writing a social history of the reconfiguration of Chinese identity in the twentieth century.

THE GEOGRAPHY OF THE ANCIENT AND MODERN WORLDS

Today, we believe the world to be divided into continents, and most of us think that it was always so. Geographers usually identify six inhabited continents: Africa, North America, South America, Europe, Asia, and Australia. Inside these continents they locate a vast number of subcontinental units, such as East Asia, South Asia, Southeast Asia, the Middle East, North Africa, and sub-Saharan Africa. Yet this geographical understanding would have been completely alien to premodern men and women, who did not think that they inhabited continents bounded by large bodies of water. Lacking a firm command of the seas, they saw themselves living on contiguous landmasses, and they

thought these territorial bodies were the main geographical units of their lives. Hence, in this volume we have chosen to use a set of geographical terms, the main one being Afro-Eurasia, that more accurately reflect the world that the premoderns believed that they inhabited.

The most interconnected and populous landmass of premodern times was Afro-Eurasia. The term Eurasia is widely used in general histories, but we think it is in its own ways inadequate. The preferred term from our perspective must be Afro-Eurasia, for the interconnected landmass of premodern and indeed much of modern times included large parts of Europe and Asia and significant regions in Africa. The major African territories that were regularly joined to Europe and Asia were Egypt, North Africa, and even parts of sub-Saharan Africa.

Only gradually and fitfully did the divisions of the world that we take for granted today take shape. The peoples inhabiting the northwestern part of the Afro-Eurasian landmass did not see themselves as European Christians, and hence as a distinctive cultural entity, until the Middle Ages drew to a close in the twelfth and thirteenth centuries. Islam did not arise and extend its influence throughout the middle zone of the Afro-Eurasian landmass until the eighth and ninth centuries. And, finally, the peoples living in what we today term the Indian subcontinent did not feel a strong sense of their own cultural and political unity until the Delhi Sultanate of the thirteenth and fourteenth centuries and the Mughal Empire, which emerged at the beginning of the sixteenth century, brought political unity to that vast region. As a result, we use the terms South Asia, Vedic society, and India in place of Indian subcontinent for the premodern part of our narrative, and we use Southwest Asia and North Africa to refer to what today is designated as the Middle East. In fact, it is only in the period from 1000 to 1300 that some of the major cultural areas that are familiar to us today truly crystallized.

WORLDS TOGETHER,
WORLDS APART

Volume 2

Before You Read This Chapter

- Advances in maritime technology lead to increased sea trade, transforming coastal cities into global trading hubs and elevating Afro-Eurasian trade to unprecedented levels.

- Intensified trade and religious integration shape four major cultural "spheres": the Islamic world, India, China, and Europe.

- Sub-Saharan Africa is drawn into Eurasian exchange resulting in a true Afro-Eurasia–wide network, while the Americas experience more limited political, economic, and cultural integration.

- The Mongol Empire integrates many of the world's major cultural spheres.

- **IDENTIFY** technological advances of this period, especially in ship design and navigation, and **EXPLAIN** how they facilitated the expansion of Afro-Eurasian trade.

- **DESCRIBE** the varied social and political forces that shaped the Islamic world, India, China, and Europe, and **EVALUATE** the degree to which these forces integrated cultures and geographic areas.

- **COMPARE** both the internal integration and external interactions of sub-Saharan Africa with those of the Americas.

- **ASSESS** the impacts that the Mongol Empire had on Afro-Eurasian peoples and places.

CHAPTER

10

Becoming "The World"

1000–1300 CE

KEY TERMS

Cahokia p. 366

Chimú Empire p. 364

Delhi Sultanate p. 350

entrepôts p. 343

flying cash p. 352

jizya p. 345

Mali p. 362

manorialism p. 357

Sufism p. 347

Toltecs p. 366

In the late 1270s two Christian monks, Bar Sāwmā and Markōs, voyaged into the heart of the Islamic world. They were not Europeans. They were Uighurs, a Turkish people of central Asia, many of whom had converted to Christianity centuries earlier. The monks hoped to make pilgrimage to Jerusalem in order to visit the tombs of the martyrs.

On their journey westward, Bar Sāwmā and Markōs traveled a world bound together by economic and cultural exchange. The two monks lingered at the magnificent trading hub of Kashgar in what is now western China, where caravan routes converged in a market for jade, exotic spices, and precious silks. Unable to continue on to Jerusalem due to the route's dangers (including murderous robbers), at Baghdad the monks parted ways. Bar Sāwmā was appointed an ambassador by the Buddhist Mongol il-Khan of Persia to drum up support among European leaders for an attack on Jerusalem to wrest it from Muslim control. He visited Constantinople (where the Byzantine emperor gave him gold and silver), Rome (where he met with the pope at the shrine of Saint Peter), and Paris (where he saw that city's vibrant university). In the end, neither monk ever reached Jerusalem or returned to China. Bar Sāwmā ended his days in Baghdad and Markōs became patriarch of the Nestorian branch of Christianity, centered in modern-day Iran.

COMPARISON

IDENTIFY technological advances of this period, especially in ship design and navigation, and **EXPLAIN** how they facilitated the expansion of Afro-Eurasian trade.

Yet their voyages exemplified the crisscrossing of people, money, goods, and ideas along the trade routes and sea-lanes that connected the world's regions.

Three related themes dominate the period from 1000 to 1300 CE. First, trade along sea-based routes increased and coastal trading cities began to expand dramatically. Second, greater trade and religious integration generated the world's four major cultural "spheres," whose inhabitants were linked by shared institutions and beliefs: the Islamic world, India, China, and Europe. During this period sub-Saharan Africa and the Americas also thrived; however, they remained more fragmented, experiencing more limited political and economic integration. Third, the Mongol Empire, stretching from China to Persia and as far as eastern Europe, ruled over huge swaths of land in many of the world's major cultural spheres. Each of these three themes contributes to an understanding of how Afro-Eurasia became a "world" unified through trade, migration, and even religious conflict.

Development of Maritime Trade

By the tenth century CE, sea routes were becoming more important than land networks for long-distance trade. Improved navigational aids, better mapmaking, refinements in shipbuilding, and new political support for shipping made seaborne trade easier and slashed its cost. These developments also fostered the growth of maritime commercial hubs (called anchorages), which further facilitated the expansion of maritime trade.

A new navigational instrument spurred this boom: the magnetic needle compass. This Chinese invention initially identified promising locations for houses and tombs, but eleventh-century sailors from Guangzhou (Canton) used it to find their way on the high seas. The use of this device eventually spread among navigators. Not only did the compass allow sailing under cloudy skies, but it also improved mapmaking.

An array of new ship types—dhows, junks, and cogs—allowed for more impressive mastery of the seas. Maximizing monsoon trade winds on the Arabian Sea and the wider Indian Ocean were dhows, ships with triangular sails, called lateens. Sailing the South China seas were junks, large, flat-bottomed ships with internal sealed bulkheads, stern-mounted rudders, as many as four decks, six masts with a dozen sails, and the space to carry as many as 500 men. And, in the Atlantic, cogs, with their single mast and square sail, linked Genoa to locations as distant as the Azores and Iceland. The numbers testify to the power of the maritime revolution: while a porter could carry about 10 pounds over long distances, and animal-drawn wagons could move 100 pounds of goods over small distances, the Arab dhows could transport up to 5 tons of cargo, Atlantic cogs as much as 200 tons, and Chinese junks more than 500 tons.

Maritime traders enjoyed the protection of political authorities such as the Song rulers in China, who maintained a standing navy that protected traders and lighthouses that guided trading fleets in and out of harbors. The Fatimid

Antique Chinese Compass Chinese sailors from Canton started to use magnetic needle compasses in the eleventh century. By the thirteenth century, magnetic needle compasses were widely used on ships in the Indian Ocean and were starting to appear in the Mediterranean.

Dhow This modern dhow in the harbor of Zanzibar displays the characteristic triangular sail. The sail can make good use of the trade monsoon and thus has guided dhows on the Arabian Sea since ancient times.

caliphate in Egypt profited from maritime trade and defended merchant fleets from pirates, using armed convoys of ships to escort commercial fleets and regulate the ocean traffic. The system of protection soon spread to North Africa and southern Spain.

Long-distance trade spawned the growth of commercial cities. These cosmopolitan **entrepôts** where ships could drop anchor served as transshipment centers, located between borders or in ports, where traders exchanged commodities and replenished supplies. Beginning in the late tenth century CE, several regional centers became major anchorages of the maritime trade: in the west, the Egyptian port city of Alexandria on the Mediterranean (and Cairo, just up the Nile); near the tip of the Indian subcontinent, the port of Quilon (now Kollam); in the Malaysian Archipelago, the city of Melaka; and in the east, the Chinese city of Quanzhou (see Map 10.1) These hubs thrived under the political stability of powerful rulers who recognized that trade would generate wealth for their regimes.

Cairo and Alexandria were the Mediterranean's main maritime commercial centers. Cairo was home to numerous Muslim and Jewish trading firms, and Alexandria was their lookout post on the Mediterranean. The Islamic legal system prevalent in Egypt promoted a favorable business environment. Through Alexandria, Europeans acquired silks from China, especially the coveted *zaytuni* (satin) fabric from Quanzhou. But the Egyptian anchorage handled much more: from the Mediterranean, olive oil, glassware, flax, corals, and metals; from India, gemstones and aromatic perfumes; and from elsewhere, minerals and chemicals for dyeing or tanning, and raw materials such as timber and bamboo. Paper and books (including hand-copied Bibles, Talmuds, and Qurans) traveled along this network as well.

In south India during the tenth century CE, the Chola dynasty supported the port of Quilon, which was the nerve center of maritime trade between China and the Red Sea and the Mediterranean. Trade through Quilon continued to flourish long after the Chola golden age passed away. Personal relationships were key to trade at this anchorage as elsewhere; for instance, when striking a deal with a local merchant, a Chinese trader would mention his Indian neighbor in Quanzhou and that family's residence in Quilon. At Quilon, dhows arrived laden not only with goods from the Red Sea and Africa but

MAP 10.1 | Afro-Eurasian Trade, 1000–1300

During the early second millennium, Afro-Eurasian merchants increasingly turned to the Indian Ocean to transport their goods. Locate the global hubs of Quilon, Alexandria, Cairo, Melaka, and Quanzhou on this map.

• What regions do each of these global hubs represent?

• Based on the map, why would sea travel have been preferable to overland travel?

• According to the text, what revolutions in maritime travel facilitated this development?

also with traders, sojourners, and fugitives. Chinese junks unloaded silks and porcelain, and picked up passengers and commodities for East Asian markets. Muslims, the largest foreign community in Quilon, lived in their own neighborhoods and shipped horses from Arab countries to India and the southeast islands, where kings viewed them as symbols of royalty. There was even trade through Quilon in elephants and cattle from tropical countries, though the most common goods were spices, perfumes, and textiles.

East of Quilon, across the Bay of Bengal, Melaka became a key cosmopolitan entrepôt because of its strategic location and proximity to Malayan tropical produce. Indian, Javanese, and Chinese merchants and sailors spent months in such ports selling their goods, purchasing return cargo, and waiting for the winds to change so they could reach their next destination. During peak season, Southeast Asian ports were crowded with colorfully dressed foreign sailors, local Javanese artisans who produced finely textured batik handicrafts, and traders eager for profit. The traders converged from all over Asia to flood the markets with their merchandise and to search for pungent herbs, aromatic spices, and agrarian staples such as quick-ripening strains of rice to ship out.

In China, the Song government set up offices of seafaring affairs in its three major ports: Quanzhou, Guangzhou (Canton), and a third near present-day Shanghai. In return for a portion of the taxes, these offices registered cargoes, sailors, and traders, while guards kept a keen eye on the traffic. All foreign traders in Song China were guests of the governor, who doubled as the chief of seafaring affairs. Every year, the governor conducted a wind-calling ritual. Traders of every origin—Arabs, Persians, Jews, Indians, and Chinese—witnessed the ceremony, then joined together for a sumptuous banquet. Although most foreign merchants did not reside apart from the rest of the city, they did maintain buildings for religious worship according to their faiths. A mosque from this period still stands on a busy street in Quanzhou. Hindu traders living in Quanzhou worshipped in a Buddhist shrine where statues of Hindu deities stood alongside those of Buddhist gods. Each bustling port teemed with a cosmopolitan mix of peoples, goods, and ideas that flowed through the growing maritime networks thanks to improved ships and better navigational tools.

COMPARISON

DESCRIBE the varied social and political forces that shaped the Islamic world, China, and Europe, and **EVALUATE** the degree to which these forces integrated cultures and geographic areas.

The Islamic World in a Time of Political Fragmentation

While the number of Muslim traders began to increase in commercial hubs from the Mediterranean to the South China Sea, it was not until the ninth and tenth centuries CE that Muslims became a majority within their own Abbasid Empire (see Chapter 9), and even then rulers struggled to unite the diverse Islamic world. From the outset, Muslim rulers and clerics dealt with large non-Muslim populations, even as these groups were converting to Islam. Rulers accorded non-Muslims religious toleration as long as the non-Muslims accepted Islam's political dominion. Jewish, Christian, and Zoroastrian communities within Muslim lands were free to choose their own religious leaders and to settle internal disputes in their own religious courts. They did, however, have to pay a special tax, the *jizya*, and defer to their rulers. While tolerant, Islam was an expansionist, universalizing faith. Intense proselytizing—especially by Sufi missionaries—carried the sacred word to new frontiers and, in the process, reinforced the spread of Islamic institutions that supported commercial exchange.

POLITICAL DIVISIONS

As the Islamic faith increased its reach across Afro-Eurasia, its political institutions had begun to fragment. From 950 to 1050, it appeared that Shiism would be the vehicle for uniting the Islamic world. The Fatimid Shiites had established their authority over Egypt and much of North Africa (see Chapter 9), and the Abbasid state in Baghdad was controlled by a Shiite family, the Buyids. Each group created

Slave Market Slaves were a common commodity in the marketplaces of the Islamic world. Turkish conquests during the years from 1000 to 1300 put many prisoners on the slave market.

MAP 10.2 | The Islamic World, 900–1200

The Islamic world experienced political disintegration in the first centuries of the second millennium.

- According to the map key, what were the two major types of Muslim states in this period and what were the two major empires?
- What were the sources of instability in this period according to the map?
- As Islam continued to expand in this period, what challenges did it face?

universities, in Cairo and Baghdad respectively, ensuring that leading centers of higher learning were Shiite. But divisions also sapped Shiism, as Sunni Muslims began to challenge Shiite power and establish their own strongholds. In Baghdad, the Shiite Buyid family surrendered to a group of Sunni strongmen in 1055. A century later, the last of the Shiite Fatimid rulers gave way to a new Sunni regime in Egypt (see Map 10.2).

The new strongmen were mainly Turks. Their people had been migrating into the Islamic heartland from the Asian steppes since the eighth century CE, bringing superior military skills and an intense devotion to Sunni Islam. Once established in Baghdad, they founded outposts in Syria and Palestine, and then moved into Anatolia after defeating Byzantine forces in 1071. But this Turkish state also crumbled, as tribesmen quarreled for preeminence.

By the thirteenth century the Islamic heartland had fractured into three regions. In the east (central Asia, Iran, and eastern Iraq), the remnants of the old Abbasid state persevered, with a succession of caliphs claiming to speak for all of Islam yet deferring to their Turkish military commanders. In the core of the Islamic world—Egypt, Syria, and the Arabian Peninsula—where Arabic was the primary language, military men of non-Arab origin held the reins of power. Farther west in North Africa, Arab rulers prevailed, but the influence of Berbers, some from the northern Sahara, was extensive. Islam was a vibrant faith, but its polities were splintered.

THE SPREAD OF SUFISM

Even in the face of this political splintering, Islam's spread was facilitated by a popular form of the religion, highly mystical and communal, called **Sufism**. The term *Sufi* comes from the Arabic word for wool (*suf*), which many of the early mystics wrapped themselves in to mark their penitence. Seeking closer union with God, Sufis performed ecstatic rituals such as repeating over and over again the name of God. In time, groups of devotees gathered to read aloud the Quran and other religious tracts. Sufi mystics' desire to experience God's love found ready expression in poetry. Most admired of Islam's mystical love poets was Jalal al-Din Rumi (1207–1273), spiritual founder of the Mevlevi Sufi order that became famous for the ceremonial dancing of its whirling devotees, known as dervishes.

Although many *ulama* (scholars) despised the Sufis and loathed their seeming lack of theological rigor, the movement spread with astonishing speed and offered a unifying force within Islam. Sufism's emotional content and strong social bonds, sustained in Sufi brotherhoods, added to its appeal for many. Sufi missionaries carried the universalizing faith to India, to Southeast Asia, across the Sahara Desert, and to many other distant locations. It was from within these brotherhoods that Islam became truly a religion for the people. As trade increased and more converts appeared in the Islamic lands, urban and peasant populations came to understand the faith practiced by the political, commercial, and scholarly upper classes even while they remained attached to their Sufi brotherhood ways. Over time, Islam became even more accommodating, embracing Persian literature, Turkish ruling skills, and Arabic-language contributions in law, religion, literature, and science.

WHAT WAS ISLAM?

Buoyed by Arab dhows on the high seas and carried on the backs of camels, following commercial networks, Islam had been transformed from Muhammad's original goal of creating a religion for Arab peoples. By 1300, its influence spanned Afro-Eurasia and reached multitudes of non-Arab converts (see Map 10.3). While Arabic remained the primary language of religious devotion, Persian became the language of Muslim philosophy and art and Turkish the language of law and administration. Islam attracted city dwellers and rural peasants alike, as well as its original audience of desert nomads. As other cities joined Cairo and Baghdad as centers of Islamic learning, Islam's extraordinary universal appeal generated an intense cultural flowering around 1000 CE.

That cultural blossoming in all fields of high learning was marked by diversity in both language and ideas. Representing the new Persian ethnic pride was Abu al-Qasim Firdawsi (920–1020), a devout Muslim who believed in the importance of pre-Islamic Sasanian traditions. In the epic poem *Shah Namah*, or Book of Kings, he celebrated the origins of Persian culture and narrated the history of the Iranian highland peoples from the dawn of time to the Muslim conquest. Indicative of the enduring prominence of the Islamic faith and the Arabic language in thought was the legendary Ibn Rushd (1126–1198), known as Averroës in the western world. Steeped in the writings of Aristotle, Ibn Rushd's belief that faith and reason were compatible even influenced the thinking of the Christian world's leading philosopher and theologian, Thomas Aquinas (1225–1274).

During this period, the Islamic world became one of the four cultural spheres that would play a major role in world history, laying the foundation for what would become

MAP 10.3 | Islamic and Hindu States and the Byzantine Empire, 1200–1300

Islam continued to expand during the thirteenth century.

• Where were Islam's largest and most important gains according to the map?

• What are some of the internal divisions within the Islamic world?

• What other religious communities existed under Islamic rule in this period? Based on the map, what might account for the location where these communities prospered?

known as the Middle East up through the middle of the twentieth century. Islam became the majority religion of most of the inhabitants of Southwest Asia and North Africa, Arabic language-use became widespread, and the Turks began to establish themselves as a dominant force, ultimately creating the Ottoman Empire, which would last into the twentieth century. The Islamic world became integral in transregional trade and the creation and transmission of knowledge.

India as a Cultural Mosaic

With its pivotal location along land- and sea-based trade routes, India became an intersection for the trade, migration, and culture of Afro-Eurasian peoples. With 80 million inhabitants in 1000 CE, it had the second-largest population in the region, not far behind China's 120 million. (See **Analyzing Global Developments: Growth in the World Population to 1340**.) Turks ultimately spilled into India as they had into the Islamic heartlands, bringing their newfound Islamic beliefs. But the Turkish newcomers encountered an ethnic and religious mix of which they were just one part (see Map 10.4).

MAP 10.4 | South Asia in 1300

As the fourteenth century began, India was a blend of many cultures. Politically, the Turkish Muslim regime of the Delhi Sultanate dominated the region. Use the map key to identify the areas dominated by the Delhi Sultanate.

- How do you suppose the trade routes helped to spread the Muslims' influence in India?

- Now use the key to find the Hindu areas. Based on your reading, what factors accounted for Hinduism's continued appeal despite the Muslims' political power?

Before the Turks arrived, India was splintered among rival chiefs called *rajas*. These leaders gained support from Brahmans by doling out land grants to them. Since much of the land was uncultivated, the Brahmans first built temples, then converted the indigenous hunter-gatherer peoples to the Hindu traditions, and finally taught the converts how to cultivate the land. In this way, Brahmans simultaneously spread their faith and expanded the agrarian tax base for themselves and the rajas. They also repaid the rajas' support by compiling elaborate genealogies for them and endowing them with lengthy and legitimizing ancestries. In return, the rajas demonstrated that they, too, were well versed in Sanskrit culture, including equestrian skills and courtly etiquette, and were prepared to patronize artists and poets.

When the Turkish warlords began entering India, the rajas had neither the will nor resources to resist them after centuries of fighting off invaders. For example, Mahmud of Ghazna (971–1030) launched many expeditions from the Afghan heartland into northern India and, eager to win status within Islam, made his capital, Ghazni, a center of Islamic learning. Later, in the 1180s, Muhammad Ghuri led another wave of Islamic Turkish invasions from Afghanistan across the Delhi region in northern India. Wars raged between

Analyzing Global Developments

Growth in the World Population to 1340

The world experienced considerable human population growth during the first millennium of the Common Era in spite of occasional downturns, such as in Asia and Europe between 200 and 600 CE that were the result of climate change, movement of peoples, and the decline of the Roman and Han empires. Overall, however, an upward trajectory occurred though it averaged out to a mere .06 percent per year. For the period from 1750 to 1950 that percentage has increased to a little more than 0.5 percent per year, and since 1950 the number has risen to 1.75 percent per year. Even so, as we will see in the next chapter, the major populations in the Afro-Eurasian landmass were terrified by the loss of life that accompanied the spread of the Black Death across this immense area. Since the Afro-Eurasian recovery from the Black Death, the world's population has been on a steady increase, spectacularly so in the twentieth century, the result of more abundant food supplies, more accurate knowledge of the spread of diseases and a resulting control of epidemic diseases, and a general rise in the standards of living.

REGIONAL HUMAN POPULATION (IN MILLIONS)						
YEAR	ASIA	EUROPE	AFRICA	AMERICAS	OCEANIA	WORLD
	97	30	17	8	1	**153**
1 CE	172	41	26	12	1	**252**
200	160	55	30	11	1	**257**
600	136	31	24	16	1	**208**
1000	154	41	39	18	1	**253**
1200	260	64	48	26	2	**400**
1340	240	88	80	32	2	**442**

Source: Massimo Livi-Bacci, *A Concise History of World Population* (2012), p. 25.

QUESTIONS FOR ANALYSIS

- Why was the rate of population growth so limited in premodern times?
- Comparing the population size of the regions in 1340, what do the numbers tell us about where the largest share of wealth and power resided? How does this compare to earlier moments in the chart?
- Why was the population of the Americas in 1340 so small considering its large territorial size?
- How do changes in global population relate to the developments tracked in this chapter: a maritime revolution; a more integrally connected Africa; a thriving Abbasid caliphate; and an expanding Mongol Empire?

the Indus and Ganges rivers until, one by one, all the way to the lower Ganges valley, the fractured kingdoms of the rajas toppled. The Turks introduced their own customs while accepting local social structures, such as the hierarchical *varna* system The Turks constructed grand mosques and built impressive libraries where scholars could toil and share their wisdom with the court.

The most powerful and enduring of the Turkish Muslim regimes of northern India was the **Delhi Sultanate** (1206–1526), whose rulers brought political integration but also strengthened the cultural diversity and tolerance that were already a hallmark of the Indian social order. Sultans recruited local artisans for numerous building projects, and palaces and mosques became displays of Indian architectural tastes adopted by Turkish newcomers. But Islam never fully dominated South Asia because the sultans did not force their subjects to convert. Nor did they display much interest in the flourishing commercial life along the Indian coast. The sultans permitted these areas to develop on their own: Persian Zoroastrian traders settled on the coast around modern-day Mumbai (Bombay) while farther south, Arab traders controlled the Malabar coast. The Delhi Sultanate was a rich and powerful regime that brought political integration but did not enforce cultural homogeneity.

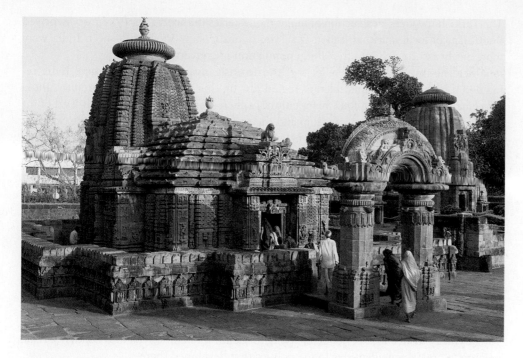

Hindu Temple When Buddhism started to decline in India, Hinduism was on the rise. Numerous Hindu temples were built, many of them adorned with ornate carvings like this small tenth-century temple in Bhubaneshwar, east India.

WHAT WAS INDIA?

During the eleventh, twelfth, and thirteenth centuries India became the most diverse and, in some respects, most tolerant region in Afro-Eurasia. India in this era arose as an impressive but fragile mosaic of cultures, religions, and ethnicities. When the Turks arrived, the local Hindu population, having had much experience with foreign invaders and immigrants, assimilated these intruders as they had done earlier peoples. Before long, the newcomers thought of themselves as Indians who, however, retained their Islamic beliefs and steppe ways. They continued to wear their distinctive trousers and robes and flaunted their horse-riding skills. At the same time, the local population embraced some of their conquerors' ways, donning the tunics and trousers that characterized Central Asian peoples.

Diversity and cultural mixing became most visible in the multiple languages that flourished in India. Although the sultans spoke Turkish languages, they regarded Persian literature as a high cultural achievement and made Persian their courtly and administrative language. Meanwhile, most of their Hindu subjects spoke local languages, adhered to the regulations of the *varna* system of hierarchies, and practiced diverse forms of Hindu worship. The rulers in India did what Muslim rulers in Southwest Asia and the Mediterranean did with Christian and Jewish communities living in their midst: they collected the *jizya* tax and permitted communities to worship as they saw fit and to administer their own communal law. Ultimately, Islam proved in India that it did not have to be an intolerant conquering religion to prosper.

Although Buddhism had been in decline in India for centuries, it, too, became part of the cultural intermixing of these centuries. As Vedic Brahmanism evolved into Hinduism (see Chapter 8), it had absorbed many Buddhist doctrines and practices, such as nonviolence (*ahimsa*) and vegetarianism. The two religions became so similar in India that Hindus simply considered the Buddha to be one of their deities—an incarnation of the great god Vishnu. Many Buddhist moral teachings mixed with and became Hindu stories. Artistic motifs reflected a similar process of adoption and adaptation. Goddesses, some beautiful and others fierce, appeared alongside Buddhas, Vishnus, and Shivas as their consorts.

The Turkish invaders' destruction of major monasteries in the thirteenth century deprived Buddhism of local spiritual leaders. Lacking dynastic support, Buddhists in India were more easily assimilated into the Hindu population or converted to Islam.

Once the initial disruptive effects of the Turkish invasions were absorbed, India remained a highly diverse and tolerant region during this period. Most importantly, India also emerged as one of the four major cultural spheres, enjoying a tremendous level of integration as Turkish-Muslim rulership and their traditions and practices were successfully intermixed with the native Hindu society, leading to a more integrated and peaceful India.

Song China: Insiders versus Outsiders

The preeminent world power in 1000 CE was still China, despite its recent turmoil. In 907 CE the Tang dynasty splintered into regional kingdoms, mostly led by military generals. In 960 CE one of these generals, Zhao Kuangyin, ended the fragmentation, reunified China, and assumed the mandate of heaven for the Song dynasty (960–1279). The following three centuries witnessed many economic and political successes, but northern nomadic tribes kept the Song dynasty from completely securing their reign (see Map 10.5 and Map 10.6). Ultimately, one of those nomadic groups, the Mongols, would bring the Song dynasty to an end; but not before Song influence had fanned out into Southeast Asia, helping to create new identities in the polities that developed there.

ECONOMIC AND POLITICAL DEVELOPMENTS

Chinese merchants, like those from India and the Islamic world, participated in Afro-Eurasia's powerful long-distance trade. Yet China's commercial successes could not have occurred without the country's strong agrarian base—especially its vast wheat, millet, and rice fields, which fed a population that reached 120 million. Crop cultivation benefited from breakthroughs in metalworking that produced stronger iron plows, which Song farmers harnessed to sturdy water buffalo to extend the agricultural frontier.

Manufacturing also flourished. With their piston-driven bellows to force air into furnaces, Song iron production in the eleventh century equaled that of European iron production in the early eighteenth century. In the early tenth century, Chinese alchemists mixed saltpeter with sulfur and charcoal to produce a product that would burn and could be deployed on the battlefield: gunpowder. Song entrepreneurs were soon inventing a remarkable array of incendiary devices that flowed from their mastery of techniques for controlling explosions and high heat. At the same time, artisans were producing increasingly light, durable, and exquisitely beautiful porcelains. Before long, their porcelain was the envy of all Afro-Eurasia (hence the modern term "china" for fine dishes). Also flowing from the artisans' skillful hands were vast amounts of clothing and handicrafts, made from the fibers grown by Song farmers. In effect, the Song Chinese oversaw the world's first manufacturing revolution, producing finished goods on a large scale for consumption far and wide.

Expanding commerce transformed the role of money and its wide circulation. By now the Song government was annually minting nearly 2 million strings of currency, each containing 1,000 copper coins. As the economy grew, the supply of metal currency could not match the demand, which fueled East Asia's desire for gold from East Africa. At the same time, merchant guilds in northwestern Shanxi developed the first letters of exchange, or paper money, which they called **flying cash**. These letters linked northern traders with their colleagues in the south. Before long, printed money became more common than minted coins for trading purposes. Eventually, the Song dynasty began to issue more notes to pay its bills—a practice that ultimately contributed to runaway inflation.

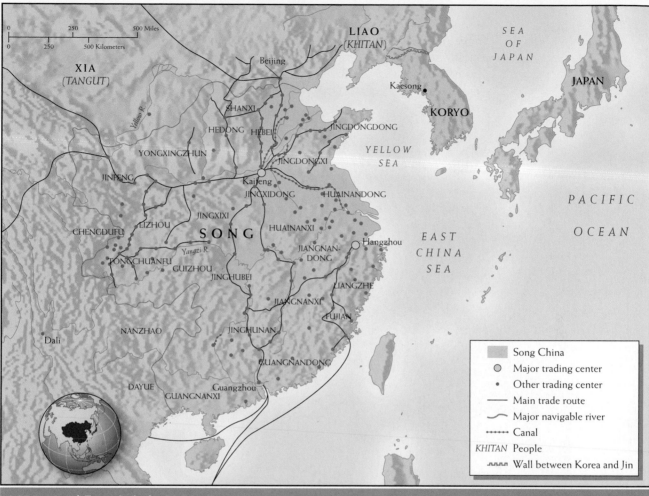

MAP 10.5 | East Asia in 1000

Several states emerged in East Asia between 1000 and 1300, but none were as strong as the Song dynasty in China. Using the key to the map, try to identify the factors that contributed to the Song state's economic dynamism.

- What external factors kept the Song dynasty from completely securing their reign?
- What factors drove the Chinese commercial revolution in this period?

Song emperors built on Tang political institutions by expanding a central bureaucracy of scholar-officials chosen even more extensively through competitive civil service examinations. Zhao Kuangyin, or Emperor Taizu (r. 960–976 CE), himself administered the final test for all who had passed the highest-level palace examination. In subsequent dynasties, the emperor was the nation's premier examiner, symbolically demanding oaths of allegiance from successful candidates. By 1100 these ranks of learned men had accumulated sufficient power to become China's new ruling elite. This expansion of the civil service examination system was crucial to a shift in power from the still significant hereditary aristocracy to a less wealthy but more highly schooled class of scholar officials.

COMPARISON

DESCRIBE the social and political forces that shaped Song China, and **EVALUATE** the degree to which they integrated the cultures of East Asia.

CHINA'S NEIGHBORS: NOMADS, JAPAN, AND SOUTHEAST ASIA

China's prosperity influenced its neighbors and its interactions with them. As Song China flourished, nomads on the outskirts eyed the Chinese successes closely. To the north, nomadic

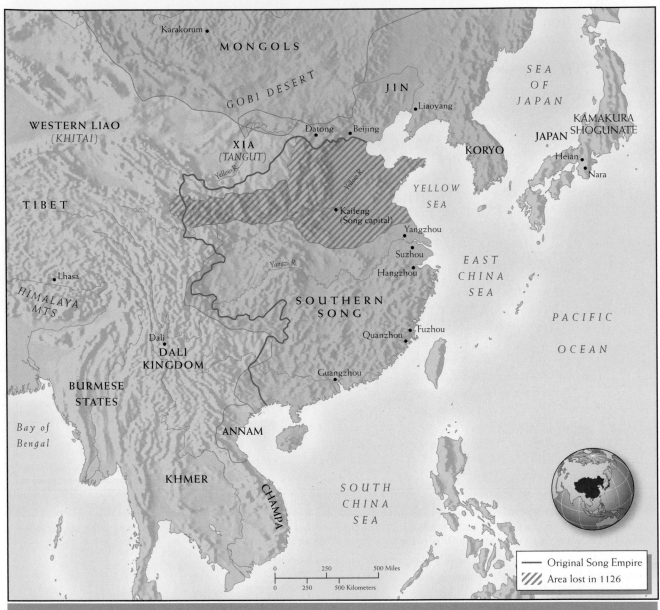

MAP 10.6 | East Asia in 1200

The Song dynasty regularly dealt with "barbarian" neighbors. What were the major "barbarian" tribes during this period?

- Approximately what percentage of Song China was lost to the Jin in 1126?
- How did the "barbarian" tribes affect the Chinese identity in this period?

societies formed their own dynasties and adopted Chinese institutions. Located within the "greater China," as defined by the Han and Tang dynasties, these non-Chinese nomads sought both to conquer and to copy China proper. Despite their sophisticated weapons, the Song army could not match their enemies on the steppe when the nomads united against them. Steel tips improved the arrows that Song soldiers shot from their crossbows, and flame throwers and "crouching tiger" catapults sent incendiary bombs streaking into their enemies' ranks. But none of these breakthroughs was secret. Warrior neighbors on the steppe mastered the new arts of war more fully than did the Song military. Consequently, China drew on its economic success (and the innovation of paper money) to "buy off" the borderlanders. This short-term solution, however, led to economic instability (particularly inflation) and military weakness, especially as the Song forces were cut off from their supply, via the steppe nomads, of horses for warfare purposes.

Feeling the pull of China's economic and political gravity, cultures around China consolidated their own internal political authority and defined their own identities in order to keep from being swallowed up by China. At the same time, they increased their commercial transactions with China. In Japan, for instance, leaders distanced themselves from Chinese influences, but they also developed a strong sense of their islands' distinctive identity. Even so, the long-standing dominance of Chinese ways remained apparent at virtually every level of Japanese society, and was most pronounced at the imperial court in the capital city of Heian (present-day Kyoto), which was modeled after the Chinese capital city of Chang'an. Outside Kyoto, however, a less China-centered way of life existed and began to impose itself on the center. Here, local notables, mainly military leaders and large landowners, began to challenge the imperial court for dominance. This challenge was accompanied by the arrival of an important new social group in Japanese society—samurai warriors. By the beginning of the fourteenth century, Japan had multiple sources of political and cultural power: an imperial family with prestige but little authority; an endangered and declining aristocracy; powerful landowning notables based in the provinces; and a rising and increasingly ambitious class of samurai.

Chinese and Barbarian After losing the north, the Han Chinese grew resentful of outsiders. They drew a dividing line between their own agrarian society and the nomadic warriors, calling them "barbarians." Such identities were not fixed, however. Chinese and so-called barbarians were mutually dependent.

During the Song period, Southeast Asia became a crossroads of Afro-Eurasian influences. The Malay Peninsula became home to many entrepôts for traders shuttling between India and China, because it connected the Bay of Bengal and the Indian Ocean with the South China Sea (see Map 10.7). Consequently, Southeast Asia was characterized by a fusion of religio-cultural influences: Vedic Brahmanism in Bali and other islands, Islam in Java and Sumatra, and Mahayana Buddhism in Vietnam and other parts of mainland Southeast Asia. Important Vedic and Buddhist kingdoms emerged in Southeast Asia. The most powerful and wealthy of these kingdoms was the Khmer Empire (889–1431), with its capital at Angkor, in present-day Cambodia. Public works and magnificent temples

Angkor Wat Mistaken by later European explorers for a remnant of Alexander the Great's conquests, the enormous temple complexes built by the Khmer people in Angkor borrowed their intricate layout and stupa (a mound-like structure containing religious relics) architecture from the Brahmanist Indian temples of the time. As the capital, Angkor was a microcosm of the world for the Khmer, who aspired to represent the macrocosm of the universe in the magnificence of Angkor's buildings and their geometric layout.

MAP 10.7 | Southeast Asia, 1000–1300

Cross-cultural influences affected Southeast Asian societies during this period.

- What makes Southeast Asia unique geographically compared to other regions of the world?
- Based on the map, why were the kingdoms of Southeast Asia exposed to so many cross-cultural influences?
- How does the system of regional kingdoms in Southeast Asia compare with that in India (Map 10.4)?

dedicated to the revived Vedic gods from India went hand in hand with the earlier influence of Indian Buddhism. One of the greatest temple complexes in Angkor—Angkor Wat—exemplified the Khmers' heavy borrowing from Vedic Indian architecture and the revival of the Hindu pantheon within the Khmer royal state. Kingdoms like the Khmer Empire functioned as political buffers between the strong states of China and India and brought stability and further commercial prosperity to the region.

WHAT WAS CHINA?

Paradoxically, the increasing exchange between outsiders and insiders within China hardened the lines that divided them and gave residents of China's interior a highly developed sense of themselves as a distinctive people possessing a superior culture. Exchanges with outsiders nurtured a "Chinese" identity among those who considered themselves true insiders and referred to themselves as Han. Song Chinese grew increasingly suspicious and resentful toward the outsiders living in their midst. They called these outsiders "barbarians" and treated them accordingly.

Print culture crystallized the distinct Chinese identity. Of all Afro-Eurasian societies in 1300, the Chinese were the most advanced in their use of printing and book publishing and circulation. Their books established classical Chinese as the common language of educated classes in East Asia. The Song government used its plentiful supply of paper to print books, especially medical texts, and to distribute calendars. The private publishing industry expanded and printing houses throughout the country produced Confucian classics, works on history, philosophical treatises, and literature—all of which figured in the civil examinations. Buddhist publications, too, were available everywhere.

China's huge population base coupled with a strong agrarian base and manufacturing innovations made it the wealthiest of the four major cultural spheres, and its common language and Confucian civil service system, which enabled a transfer of power from hereditary aristocrats to Confucian scholars, made it the most unified. China's influence on the surrounding region was tremendous.

Christian Europe

Europe, from 1000–1300, was a region of strong contrasts. Intensely localized power was balanced by a shared sense of Europe's place in the world, especially with respect to Christian identity. Some inhabitants even began to believe in the existence of something called "Europe" and increasingly referred to themselves as "Europeans" (see Map 10.8), especially in contrast to the world of Islam to the east and south.

COMPARISON

COMPARE the role that religions and migration played in forging unified identities in Europe, India, and the Islamic worlds.

LOCALIZATION OF POWER

From the agriculture-based manors of western Europe to the cities of Russia, power structures were localized. For example, in western Europe of the eleventh and twelfth centuries, the Franks became the unchallenged rulers after the collapse of Charlemagne's empire, yet they oversaw a somewhat fragmented manor-based economy and social structure. The peasantry's subjugation to this knightly class was at the heart of a system scholars have called feudalism (emphasizing the power of the local lords over the peasantry); but a more accurate term for the system is **manorialism**, which emphasizes instead the manor's role as the basic unit of economic power. The manor comprised the lord's fortified home (or castle), the surrounding fields controlled by the lord but worked by peasants (as free tenants or as serfs tied to the land), and the village in which those peasants lived. Although manorialism was driven by agriculture, limited manufacturing and trade augmented the manor economy. This system harnessed agrarian energy and helped western Europe shed its identity as a somewhat "barbarian" appendage of the Mediterranean.

Between 1100 and 1200, as many as 200,000 pioneering peasants emigrated from the regions of Belgium, Holland, and northern Germany to the frontiers of Europe (now Poland, the Czech Republic, Hungary, and the Baltic states). Despite the harsh climate and landscape, the area offered the promise of freedom from feudal lords' arbitrary justice and the imposition of forced labor that the peasants had experienced in western Europe. In a fragile balance between the native elites and liberty-seeking newcomers, castles and villages echoing the landscape of manorial France now replaced local economies that had been based on gathering honey, hunting, and the slave trade. For a thousand miles along the Baltic Sea, forest clearings dotted with new farmsteads and small towns edged inward from the coast up the river valleys.

MAP 10.8 | Latin Christendom in 1300

Catholic Europe expanded geographically and integrated culturally during this era.

• According to this map, into what areas did Western Christendom successfully expand?

• What factors contributed to the growth of a widespread common culture and shared ideas?

• How did long-distance trade shape the history of the region during this time?

Russian lands modeled themselves after Byzantium, not Rome or western Europe. A giant borderland between the steppes of Eurasia and the booming centers of Europe, Russia's cities lay at the crossroads of overland trade and migration. These cities were not agrarian centers, but hubs of expanding long-distance trade. Kiev became one of the region's greatest urban centers, a small-scale Constantinople with its own miniature Hagia Sophia. Russian Christians looked not to the Roman Catholic faith associated with the popes in Rome, but rather to Byzantium's Hagia Sophia and the Orthodoxy of the east as the source of religious authority. Russian Christianity remained that of a borderland—vivid oases of high culture set against the backdrop of vast forests and widely scattered settlements. Like the agricultural manors of western Europe, these Russian cities demonstrate the highly localized nature of power in Europe in this period.

WHAT WAS CHRISTIAN EUROPE?

Christianity in this era—primarily the Roman Catholicism of the west, but also the Orthodoxy of the east—became a universalizing faith that transformed the region becoming known as "Europe." The Christianity of post-Roman Europe had been a religion of monks, and its most dynamic centers were great monasteries. Members of the laity were expected to revere and support their monks, nuns, and clergy, but not to imitate them. By 1200, all this had changed. The internal colonization of western Europe—the clearing of woods and founding of villages—ensured that parish churches arose in all but the wildest landscapes. Now the clergy reached more deeply into the private lives of the laity. Marriage and divorce, previously considered family matters, became the domain of the church.

New understandings of religious devotion and innovative institutions for learning developed in the west. For instance, the followers of Francis of Assisi (1182–1226) emerged as an order of preachers who brought a message of repentance. Franciscans encouraged the laity—from the poorest to the elite—to feel remorse for their wrongdoings, to confess their sins to local priests, and to strive to be better Christians. At nearly the same time, intellectuals were beginning to gather in Paris to form the first European university, a sort of trade guild of scholars. These professional thinkers endeavored to prove that Christianity was the only religion that fully addressed the concerns of all rational human beings. Such was the message of Thomas Aquinas, who wrote *Summa contra Gentiles* (Summary of Christian Belief against Non-Christians) in 1264. The growing number of churches, new religious orders, and universities began to change what it meant to live in a "Christian Europe."

Crusader Kneeling, this Crusader promises to serve God (as he would serve a feudal lord) by going to fight on a Crusade (as he would fight for any lord to whom he had sworn loyalty). The two kinds of loyalty—to God and to one's lord—were deliberately confused in Crusader ideas. Both were about war. But fighting for God was unambiguously good, while fighting for a lord was not always so clear-cut.

RELATIONS WITH THE ISLAMIC WORLD

In the late eleventh century, western Europeans launched the Crusades, a wave of attacks against the Muslim world. The First Crusade began in 1095, when Pope Urban II appealed to the warrior nobility of France to put their violence to good use: they should combine their role as pilgrims to Jerusalem with that of soldiers, in order to free Jerusalem from Muslim rule. Such a just war, the clergy proposed, was a means for absolution, not a source of sin.

Starting in 1097, an armed host of around 60,000 men set out from northwestern Europe to seize Jerusalem. Crusading forces included knights in heavy armor, as well as people drawn from Europe's impoverished masses, who joined the movement to help besiege cities and construct a network of castles as the Christian knights drove their frontier forward. The fleets of Venice, Genoa, and Pisa helped transport later Crusaders and supplied the kingdoms they created as they moved eastward. Later Crusaders, especially those from the upper class, brought their wives, who found a degree of autonomy away from their homeland. There are even accounts of a children's crusade (1212), inspired by the visions of a boy. Over time, the Crusades drew together a range of peoples from varied walks of life in common purpose.

Current Trends in World History

The Crusades from Dual Perspectives

World history promotes comparative historical study, and when two cultures come together, as they did in the European crusades, their meeting offers unique opportunities to see how different societies view one another, and it provides a clear sense for their own self-identity. Such a confrontation took place during the crusades between European Christians and Muslims between 1095 and 1272.

In 1095, Pope Urban II called for the First Crusade in the following words:

Oh, race of Franks, race from across the mountains, race chosen and beloved by God, as shines forth in very many of your works, set apart from all nations by the situation of your country, as well as by your Catholic faith and the honor of the Holy Church! To you

our discourse is addressed, and for you our exhortation is intended. We wish you to know what a grievous cause has led us to your country, what peril, threatening you and all the faithful, has brought us.

The "grievous cause" was the occupation of the Holy City of Jerusalem by the Islamic empire. Formed within the complex relationship between the Byzantine Empire and the western Christian papacy and kingdoms of Europe, the religious motivation behind the Crusades became the subject of many literary renditions of the tumultuous events. It also generated emotionally stirring and argumentative writing, depicting either a Muslim or Christian enemy (depending on the work's author).

These written attacks are often passionate, harsh, and emotional. They also inspire and reinforce the conviction of fellow believers, with little concern for accuracy. Thus, some authors in the time of the Crusades were usually too biased or too misinformed to present accurate portraits of their enemies. But occasion-

ally, firsthand accounts in the form of chronicles and histories offer us unique glimpses into Christian-Muslim relations in the age of the Crusades.

Consider Usāmah ibn Munqidh (1095–1188), the learned ruler of the city of Shaizar in western Syria. Skirmishes, truces, and the ransoming of prisoners were part of his daily life, and Usāmah socialized with his Frankish neighbors as much as he fought with them. He offers a dismissive opinion of his enemies. Basically, they struck him as "animals possessing the virtues of courage and fighting, but nothing else." In particular, their medical practice appalled him. More strange, the Franks allowed their wives to walk about freely and to talk to strangers unaccompanied by male guardians. How could men be at once so brave and yet so lacking in a proper, Arab sense of honor, which would lead a man to protect his women? Unlike other Muslim authors of his time, however, Usāmah does not refer to the Franks in derogatory terms such as "infidels" or "devils." In fact, he occasionally refers to some of them as his companions and writes of a Frank who called him "my brother."

No fewer than nine Crusades were fought over the two centuries that followed Urban II's call; but none of the coalitions, in the end, created lasting Christian kingdoms in the lands they "reconquered." Most knights returned home, their epic pilgrimage completed. The remaining fragile network of Crusader lordships barely threatened the Islamic heartland. The real prosperity and the capital cities of Muslim kingdoms lay inland, away from the coast—at Cairo, Damascus, and Baghdad. The assaults' long-term effect was to harden Muslim feelings against the Franks and the millions of nonwestern Christians who had previously lived peacefully in Egypt and Syria (see **Current Trends in World History: The Crusades from Dual Perspectives**).

Other campaigns of Christian expansion, like the Iberian efforts to drive out the Muslims, were more successful. Beginning with the capture of Toledo in 1061, the Christian kings of northern Spain slowly pushed back the Muslims. Eventually they reached the heart of Andalusia in southern Iberia and conquered Seville, adding more than 100,000 square miles of territory to Christian Europe. Another force, from northern France, crossed Italy to conquer Muslim-held Sicily, ensuring Christian rule in the strategically located mid-Mediterranean island. Unlike the Crusaders' fragile foothold at the edge of the Middle East, these two conquests

Christian authors had similar interests in documenting the customs of their enemies in battle. Jean de Joinville (1224/1225–1317) was a chronicler of medieval France. During one crusade, while in the service of the king, Joinville had occasion to note the Muslims' social behavior:

Whenever the Sultan was in the camp, the men of the personal Guard were quartered all round his lodging, and appointed to guard his person. At the door of the Sultan's lodging there was a little tent for the Sultan's door-keepers, and for his musicians, who had Arabian horns and drums and kettledrums; and they used to make such a din at daybreak and at nightfall that people near them could not hear one another speak, and that they could be heard plainly all through the camp. The musicians never dared sound their instruments in the daytime unless by the order of the Chief of the Guard. Thus it was, that whenever the Sultan had a proclamation to make he used to send for the Chief of the Guard, and give him the order; and then the Chief would cause all the Sultan's instruments to be sounded; and thereupon all the host would come to hear the Sultan's commands.

Although scholars regard such literary renditions with caution, they are useful for gleaning personal details that other types of works omit. The colorful accounts by authors such as Usāmah ibn Munqidh and Joinville are invaluable resources for the social history of the Crusaders.

Jean de Joinville Joinville offering his history, in which he described the Seventh Crusade, to Louis X of France (r. 1314–1316).

QUESTIONS FOR ANALYSIS

- What customs or practices of their opponents did the Muslim and the Christian writers select to write about? Why?
- What aspects of the other side's customs does the writer seem to see as good or praiseworthy? What does that tell us about their perceptions of the strangers that they encountered?
- If a historian uses polemical written sources like this to analyze societies from the past, what can he or she say that is trustworthy about them?

Explore Further

Natasha, Hodgson, *Women, Crusading and the Holy Land in Historical Narrative* (2007).

Amin Maalouf, *The Crusades Through Arab Eyes*, trans. Jon Rothschild (1984).

Edward Peters (ed.), *The First Crusade: The Chronicle of Fulcher of Chartres and Other Source Materials* (1971).

were a turning point in relations between Christian and Muslim power in the Mediterranean. Christianity—and in particular the rise of the Roman Catholic Church, the spread of universities, and the fight against the Muslims in their native and spiritual homelands—were forces that helped create a cultural sphere known as Europe, whose peoples would become known as European, at the western end of the Afro-Eurasian landmass during this period.

Worlds Coming Together: Sub-Saharan Africa and the Americas

From 1000 to 1300, sub-Saharan Africa and the Americas became far more internally integrated—culturally, economically, and politically—than before. Islam's spread and the growing trade in gold, slaves, and other commodities brought sub-Saharan Africa more fully into the exchange networks of the Eastern Hemisphere; yet the Americas remained isolated from Afro-Eurasian networks for several more centuries.

COMPARISON

COMPARE both the internal integration and external interactions of sub-Saharan Africa with those of the Americas.

SUB-SAHARAN AFRICA COMES TOGETHER

During this period sub-Saharan Africa's relationship to the rest of the world changed dramatically. While sub-Saharan Africa had never been a world entirely apart before 1000 CE, now its integration with Eurasia became much stronger. Increasingly, interior hinterlands found themselves touched by the commercial and migratory impulses emanating from the Indian Ocean and Arabian Sea transformations (see Map 10.9).

West Africa and the Mande-Speaking Peoples Once trade routes bridged the Sahara Desert (see Chapter 9), the flow of commodities and ideas linked sub-Saharan Africa to North Africa and Southwest Asia. As the savanna region became increasingly connected to developments in Eurasia, Mande-speaking peoples became the primary agents for integration within and beyond West Africa. Exploiting their expertise in commerce and political organization, the Mande edged out rivals. The Mande homeland was a vast area, 1,000 miles wide between the bend in the Senegal River to the west and the bend of the Niger River to the east, stretching more than 2,000 miles from the Senegal River in the north to the Bandama River in the south.

By the eleventh century, Mande-speaking peoples were spreading their cultural, commercial, and political hegemony from the high savanna grasslands southward into the woodlands and tropical rain forests stretching to the Atlantic Ocean. Those dwelling in the rain forests organized small-scale societies led by local councils, while those in the savanna lands developed centralized forms of government under sacred kingships. Mande-speakers believed that their kings had descended from the gods and that they enjoyed the gods' blessing.

As the Mande broadened their territory to the Atlantic coast, they gained access to tradable items that residents of Africa's interior were eager to have—notably kola nuts and malaguetta peppers, for which the Mande exchanged iron products and manufactured textiles. Mande-speaking peoples, with their far-flung commercial networks and highly dispersed populations, dominated trans-Saharan trade in salt from the northern Sahel, gold from the Mande homeland, and slaves. By 1300 the Mande-speaking merchants had followed the Senegal River to its outlet on the coast and then pushed their commercial frontiers farther inland and down the coast. Thus, even before European explorers and traders arrived in the mid-fifteenth century, West African peoples had created dynamic networks linking the hinterlands with coastal trading hubs.

The Empire of Mali In the early thirteenth century, the empire of **Mali** became the Mande successor state to the kingdom of Ghana (see Chapter 9). The origins of the Mali Empire and its legendary founder are enshrined in *The Epic of Sundiata*. Sundiata's triumph, which occurred in the first half of the thirteenth century, marked the victory of new cavalry forces over traditional foot soldiers. Horses—which had always existed in some parts of Africa—now became prestige objects of the savanna peoples, symbols of state power.

Under the Mali Empire, commerce was in full swing. With Mande trade routes extending to the Atlantic Ocean and spanning the Sahara Desert, West Africa was no longer an isolated periphery of the central Muslim lands. The Mali king Mansa Musa (r. 1312–1332), made a celebrated hajj, or pilgrimage to Mecca, in 1325–1326, traveling through Cairo and impressing crowds with the size of his retinue—including soldiers, wives, consorts, and as many as 12,000 slaves—and his displays of wealth, especially many dazzling items made of gold. Mansa Musa's stopover in Cairo, one of Islam's primary cities, astonished the Egyptian elite and awakened much of the world to the fact that Islam had spread far below the Sahara and that a sub-Saharan state could mount such an impressive display of power and wealth.

MAP 10.9 | Sub-Saharan Africa, 1300

Increased commercial contacts influenced the religious and political dimensions of sub-Saharan Africa at this time. Compare this map to Map 9.3 (p. 314).

- Where had strong Islamic communities emerged by 1300?

- According to this map, what types of activity were affecting the Mande homeland?

- To what extent had sub-Saharan Africa "come together"?

West African Asante Gold This picture from the 1375 Catalan Atlas shows Mansa Musa, the king of Mali, on his throne, surrounded by images of gold. When Mansa Musa traveled on pilgrimage to Mecca (1324–1325), his entourage included soldiers, wives, consorts, and as many as 12,000 slaves, many wearing rich brocades woven of Persian silk. His caravan brought immense quantities of gold—nearly 100 camels each bearing 300-pound sacks of gold—and Mansa Musa distributed it lavishly. Preceding his retinue as it crossed the desert were 500 slaves, each carrying a golden staff.

The Mali Empire boasted two of West Africa's largest cities. Jenne, an entrepôt dating back to 200 BCE, was a vital assembly point for caravans laden with salt, gold, and slaves preparing for journeys west to the Atlantic coast and north over the Sahara. More spectacular was the city of Timbuktu; founded around 1100 as a seasonal camp for nomads, it grew in size and importance under the patronage of various Malian kings. By the fourteenth century it was a thriving commercial, intellectual, and religious center famed for its three large mosques, which are still standing.

Trade Between East Africa and the Indian Ocean

Africa's eastern and southern regions were also integrated into long-distance trading systems. Because of monsoon winds, East Africa was a logical end point for much of the Indian Ocean trade. Swahili peoples living along that coast became brokers for trade from the Arabian Peninsula, the Persian Gulf territories, and the western coast of India. Merchants in the city of Kilwa on the coast of present-day Tanzania brought ivory, gold, slaves, and other items from the interior and shipped them to destinations around the Indian Ocean.

Shona-speaking peoples grew rich by mining the gold ore in the highlands between the Limpopo and Zambezi rivers. By the year 1000 CE, the Shona had founded up to fifty small religious and political centers, each one erected from stone to display its power over the peasant villages surrounding it. Around 1100, one of these centers, Great Zimbabwe, stood supreme among the Shona. Built on the fortunes made from gold, its most impressive landmark was a massive elliptical building made of stones fitted so expertly that they needed no grouting.

African slaves were as valuable as African gold in shipments to Indian Ocean as well as Mediterranean markets. Although the Quran attempted to mitigate the severity of slavery, requiring Muslim slave owners to treat their slaves kindly and praising those who freed their slaves, nonetheless the African slave trade flourished under Islam. Africans became slaves either taken as prisoners of war or as criminals sold into slavery as punishment. Slaves might work as soldiers, seafarers on dhows, domestic servants, and plantation workers. One instance of plantation labor on agricultural estates of lower Iraq was so oppressive that it led, in the ninth century CE, to one of the largest slave wars documented in world history (the Zanj rebellion). Yet in this era plantation-slave labor, like that which later became prominent in the Americas in the nineteenth century, was the exception, not the rule.

THE AMERICAS

During this period, the Americas were untouched by the connections reverberating across Afro-Eurasia. Apart from limited Viking contacts in North America (see Chapter 9), navigators still did not cross the large oceans that separated the Americas from other lands. Yet, here, too, commercial and expansionist impulses fostered closer contact among peoples who lived there.

Andean States of South America Growth and prosperity in the Andean region gave rise to South America's first empire. The **Chimú Empire** developed in the early second millennium in the fertile Moche Valley bordering the Pacific Ocean (see Map 10.10). Ultimately the Moche people expanded their influence across numerous valleys and ecological zones, from pastoral highlands to rich valley floodplains to the fecund fishing grounds of the Pacific Coast. As their geographical reach grew, so did their wealth.

The Chimú economy was successful because it was highly commercialized. Agriculture was its base, and complex irrigation systems turned the arid coast into a string of fertile oases capable of feeding an increasingly dispersed population. Cotton became a lucrative export to distant markets along the Andes. Parades of llamas and porters lugged these commodities up and down the steep mountain chains that are the spine of South America. A well-trained bureaucracy oversaw the construction and maintenance of canals, with a hierarchy of provincial administrators watching over commercial hinterlands.

The Chimú Empire's biggest city, Chan Chan, held a core population of 30,000 inhabitants. A sprawling walled metropolis, covering nearly ten square miles with extensive roads circulating through neighborhoods, Chan Chan boasted ten huge palaces at its center. Protected by thick walls thirty feet high, these opulent residence halls symbolized the rulers' power. Within the compound, emperors erected burial com-

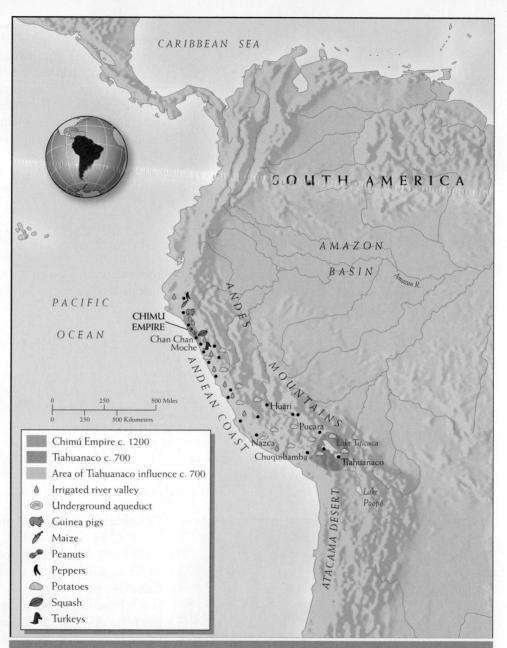

MAP 10.10 | Andean States

Although the Andes region of South America was isolated from Afro-Eurasian developments before 1500, it was not stagnant. Indeed, political and cultural integration brought the peoples of this region closer together.

- Where are the areas of the Chimú Empire and Tiahuanaco influence on the map?
- What kinds of ecological niches did they govern?
- According to your reading, how did each polity encourage greater cultural and economic integration?

plexes for storing their accumulated riches: fine cloth, gold and silver objects, splendid *Spondylus* shells, and other luxury goods. Around the compound spread neighborhoods for nobles and artisans; farther out stood rows of commoners' houses. The Chimú regime, centered at Chan Chan, lasted until Incan armies invaded in the 1460s and incorporated the Pacific state into their own immense empire.

Chan Chan The image shows what remains of Chan Chan. The city covered fifteen square miles and was divided into neighborhoods for nobles, artisans, and commoners, with the elites living closest to the hub of governmental and spiritual power.

Toltecs in Mesoamerica Additional hubs of regional trade developed farther north. By 1000 CE, Mesoamerica had seen the rise and fall of several complex societies, including Teotihuacán and the Mayans (see Chapter 8). Caravans of porters bound the region together, working the intricate roads that connected the coast of the Gulf of Mexico to the Pacific, and the southern lowlands of Central America to the arid regions of modern Texas (see Map 10.11). The **Toltecs** filled the political vacuum left by the decline of Teotihuacán and tapped into the commercial network radiating from the rich valley of central Mexico.

The Toltecs were a combination of migrant groups, farmers from the north and refugees from the south fleeing the strife that followed Teotihuacán's demise. These migrants settled northwest of Teotihuacán as the city waned, making their capital at Tula. They relied on a maize-based economy supplemented by beans, squash, and dog, deer, and rabbit meat. Their rulers made sure that enterprising merchants provided them with status goods such as ornamental pottery, rare shells and stones, and precious skins and feathers.

Tula was a commercial hub, a political capital, and a ceremonial center. While its layout differed from Teotihuacán's, many features revealed borrowings from other Mesoamerican peoples. Temples consisted of giant pyramids topped by colossal stone soldiers, and ball courts where subjects and conquered peoples alike played their ritual sport were found everywhere. The architecture and monumental art reflected the mixed and migratory origins of the Toltecs: a combination of Mayan and Teotihuacáno influences. At its height, the Toltec capital teemed with 60,000 people, a huge metropolis by contemporary European standards (if small, by Song Chinese and Abbasid Islamic world standards).

Toltec Temple Tula, the capital of the Toltec Empire, carried on the Mesoamerican tradition of locating ceremonial architecture at the center of the city. The Pyramid of the Morning Star cast its shadow over all other buildings. And above them stood columns of the Atlantes, carved Toltec god-warriors, the figurative pillars of the empire itself. The walls of this pyramid were likely embellished with images of snakes and skulls. The north face of the pyramid has the image of a snake devouring a human.

Cahokians in North America As in South America (Chan Chan of the Chimú) and Mesoamerica (Tula of the Toltecs), cities took shape at the hubs of trading networks across North America, as well. The largest was **Cahokia**, along the Mississippi River near modern-day East St. Louis. A city of about 15,000, it approximated the size of London at the time. Farmers and hunters had settled in the region around 600 CE, attracted by its rich soil, its woodlands for fuel and game, and its access to trade via the Mississippi. Eventually, fields of maize and other crops fanned out toward the horizon. The hoe replaced the trusty digging stick, and satellite towns erected granaries to hold the growing harvests.

Cahokia became a commercial center for regional and long-distance trade. The hinterlands produced staples for Cahokia's urban consumers, and in return its crafts rode inland on the backs of porters and to distant markets in canoes. Woven fabrics and ceramics from Cahokia were exchanged for mica from the Appalachian Mountains, seashells and sharks' teeth from the Gulf of Mexico, and copper from the upper Great Lakes. Cahokia became more than an

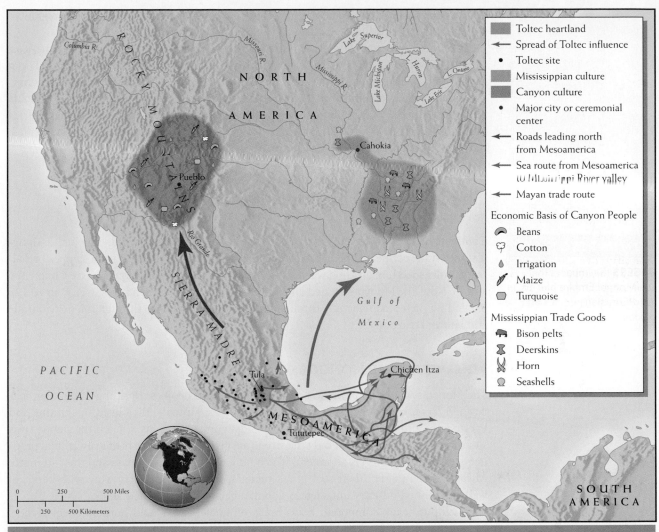

MAP 10.11 | Commercial Hubs in Mesoamerica and North America, 1000

Both Cahokia and Tula were commercial hubs of vibrant regional trade networks.

• Where are Cahokia and Tula on the map?

• According to the map, what kinds of goods circulated through these cities?

• How important do cities appear to be in North America and Mesoamerica?

importer and exporter: it was the exchange hub for an entire regional network trading in salt, tools, pottery, woven stuffs, jewelry, and ceremonial goods.

Dominating Cahokia's urban landscape were enormous earthen mounds of sand and clay (thus the Cahokians' nickname of "mound people"). It was from these artificial hills that the people honored spiritual forces. Building these types of structures without draft animals, hydraulic tools, or even wheels was labor-intensive, so the Cahokians recruited neighboring people to help. A palisade around the city protected the metropolis from marauders.

Ultimately Cahokia's success bred its downfall. As woodlands fell to the axe and soil lost nutrients, timber and food became scarce. In contrast to the sturdy dhows of the Arabian Sea and the bulky junks of the China Sea, Cahokia's river canoes could carry only limited cargoes. Cahokia's commercial networks met their limits. When the creeks that fed its water system could not keep up with demand, engineers changed their course, but to no avail. By 1350 the city was practically empty. Cahokia represented the growing networks of trade and migration, and the ability of North Americans to organize vibrant commercial societies.

Two forces contributed to greater integration in sub-Saharan Africa and the Americas, from 1000 to 1300: commercial exchange (salt, gold, ivory, and slaves in sub-Saharan Africa, and shells, pottery, textiles and metals in the Americas) and urbanization (at Jenne, Timbuktu, and Great Zimbabwe in sub-Saharan Africa, and Chan Chan, Tula, and Cahokia in the Americas). By 1300, trans-Saharan and Indian Ocean exchange had brought Africa into full-fledged Afro-Eurasian networks of exchange and, as we will see in Chapter 12, transatlantic exchange would soon bring the Americas into a global network.

The Mongol Transformation of Afro-Eurasia

COMPARISON

ASSESS the impacts that the Mongol Empire had on Afro-Eurasian peoples and places.

Commercial networks were clearly one way to integrate the world. But just as long-distance trade connected people, so could conquerors. The Inner Eurasian steppes had already unleashed horse-riding warriors such as the Kushans and Xiongnu (see Chapters 6 and 7). Now, the Mongols created an empire that straddled east and west (see Map 10.12), expanding their reach not only through brutal conquest but also through intensified trade and cultural exchange.

WHO WERE THE MONGOLS?

The Mongols were a combination of forest and prairie peoples. Residing in circular, felt-covered tents, which they shared with some of their animals, they lived by hunting and livestock herding. They changed campgrounds with the seasons. Life on the steppes was such a constant struggle that only the strong survived. Their food, primarily animal products, provided high levels of protein, which built up their muscle mass and their strength. Always on the march, their society resembled a perpetual standing army with bands of well-disciplined military units led by commanders chosen for their skill.

Wielding heavy compound bows made of sinew, wood, and horn, Mongol archers were deadly accurate at over 200 yards—even at full gallop. Their small but sturdy horses, capable of withstanding extreme cold, bore saddles with high supports in front and back, enabling the warriors to maneuver at high speeds. With their feet secure in iron stirrups, the archers could rise in their saddles to aim their arrows without stopping. These expert horsemen often remained in the saddle all day and night, even sleeping while their horses continued on. Each warrior kept many horses, replacing tired mounts with fresh ones so that the armies could cover up to seventy miles per day.

Mongol tribes solidified their conquests by extending kinship networks, building an empire out of an expanding confederation of familial tribes. Women were a vital link in those networks. Households sealed alliances by the exchange of daughters in marriage. In addition to their role in linking kinship networks, women in Mongol society were responsible for child-rearing, shearing and milking livestock, and processing pelts for clothing. But they also took part in battles. Although women could be bought and sold, Mongol wives had the right to own property and to divorce. Elite women, such as the mother and wife of the Mongol ruler Kubilai Khan, even played important political roles.

CONQUEST AND EMPIRE

The Mongols' need for grazing lands contributed to their desire to conquer the distant fertile belts and rich cities. The Mongols depended on settled peoples for grain and manufactured

Mongol Warriors This miniature painting is one of the illustrations for *History* by Rashid al Din, the most outstanding scholar under the Mongol regimes. Note the relatively small horses and strong bows used by the Mongol soldiers.

goods, including iron for tools, wagons, weapons, bridles, and stirrups. Their first expansionist forays followed caravan routes.

The Mongol expansion began in 1206 under a united cluster of tribes. These tribes were unified by a gathering of clan heads who chose one of those present as Chinggis (Genghis) Khan, or Supreme Ruler. This Chinggis (c. 1155–1227) launched a series of conquests southward across the Great Wall of China, and westward to Afghanistan and Persia. The Mongols even invaded Korea in 1231. The armies of Chinggis's sons reached both the Pacific Ocean and the Adriatic Sea. Chinggis's grandsons founded dynasties in Persia, in China, and on the southern Eurasian steppes. Thus, a realm took shape that touched all four of Afro-Eurasia's main worlds.

Mongols in Abbasid Baghdad In the thirteenth century, Mongol tribesmen were streaming out of the steppes, crossing the whole of Asia and entering the eastern parts of Europe. Mongke Khan, a grandson of Chinggis, made clear the Mongol aspiration for world domination: he commanded his brother, Hulagu, to conquer Iran, Syria, Egypt, Byzantium, and Armenia, and he appointed another brother, Kubilai, to rule over China, Tibet, and the northern parts of India.

When Hulagu reached Abbasid Baghdad in 1258, he encountered a feeble foe and a city that was a shadow of its former glorious self. Merely 10,000 horsemen faced his army of 200,000 soldiers, who were eager to acquire the booty of a wealthy city. Even before the battle had taken place, Baghdadi poets were composing elegies for their dead and mourning the defeat of Islam. The slaughter was vast. Hulagu himself boasted of taking the lives of at least 200,000 people. The Mongols hunted their adversaries in wells, latrines, and sewers and followed them into the upper floors of buildings, killing them on rooftops until, as an Iraqi Arab historian observed, "blood poured from the gutters into the streets. . . . The same happened in the mosques." In a few weeks of sheer terror, the Abbasid caliphate was demolished. Hulagu's forces showed no mercy to the caliph himself, who was rolled up in a carpet and trampled to death by horses. With Baghdad crushed, the Mongol armies pushed on to Syria, slaughtering Muslims along the way.

MAP 10.12 | Mongol Campaigns and Conquests, 1200–1300

Mongol campaigns and conquests brought Afro-Eurasian worlds together as never before. Trace the outline of the entire area of Mongol influence shaded on this map.

- What cultural groups did the Mongol armies conquer, partially conquer, or invade?
- How many different Khanates did the Mongols establish across Eurasia, and what were they?
- What role did geography play in limiting the spread of their influence?

SIBERIA

Lake Baikal

MONGOL ANCESTRAL HOMELAND

Karakorum

GOBI DESERT

CHAGATAI

Shangdu (Xanadu)
Dadu

Khanbaliq (Beijing)

KORYO

SEA OF JAPAN

KAMAKURA SHOGUNATE

JAPAN

Kyoto

Kaifeng

KHANATE OF THE GREAT KHAN (YUAN EMPIRE)

TIBET

Yangzhou
Yangzi R.
Hangzhou

MOUNTAINS

YUNNAN

BURMA

Pagan

Guangzhou

PACIFIC OCEAN

KHMER EMPIRE

ANNAM

CHAMPA

SOUTH CHINA SEA

SUMATRA

BORNEO

JAVA

Scale:
0 — 500 — 1000 Miles
0 — 500 — 1000 Kilometers

← Mongol campaigns
Mongol ancestral homeland
Mongol controlled
// Area of loose or temporary Mongol control

Mongols in China In the east, Mongol forces under Chinggis Khan had entered northern China at the beginning of the thirteenth century, defeating the Jin army that was no match for the Mongols' superior cavalry on the North China plain. Despite some serious setbacks from the climate (including malaria for the men and the death of horses from the heat), Chinggis's grandson Kubilai Khan (1215–1294) seized southern China from the Song dynasty beginning in the 1260s. The southern Song army fell before his warriors brandishing the latest gunpowder-based weapons, which the Mongols had borrowed from Chinese inventors and now used against them.

Hangzhou, the last Song capital, fell in 1276. Kubilai Khan's most able commander, Bayan, led his crack Mongol forces in seizing town after town, ever closer to the capital, while the Empress Dowager tried to buy them off, proposing substantial tribute payments, but Bayan was uncompromising. Once conquered, the Empress Dowager and Hangzhou were treated well by the Mongols. In fact, Hangzhou was still one of the greatest cities in the world when it was visited by the Venetian traveler Marco Polo in the 1280s and by the Muslim traveler Ibn Battuta in the 1340s. Both men agreed that neither Europe nor the Islamic world had anything like it.

Kubilai Khan founded his Yuan dynasty, with a capital at Dadu, present-day Beijing. The Mongol conquest both north and south changed the political and social landscape. But Mongol rule did not impose rough steppe-land ways on the "civilized" urbanite Chinese. While non-Chinese outsiders took political control, they were a conquering elite that ruled over a vast Han majority. The result was a divided ruling system in which incumbent Chinese elites governed locally, while newcomers managed the unifying central dynasty and collected taxes for the Mongols.

Southeast Asia also felt the whiplash of Kubilai Khan's conquest. Circling Song defenses in southern China, the Mongols galloped southwest and conquered states in Yunnan and in Burma. From there, in the 1270s, the armies headed directly back east into the soft underbelly of the Song state. In this sweep, portions of mainland Southeast Asia became annexed to China for the first time. Kubilai Khan used the conquered Chinese fleets to push his expansionism onto the high seas—meeting with failure during the unsuccessful 1274 and 1281 invasions of Japan from Korea. An ill-fated Javanese expedition to extend Mongol reach beyond the South China Sea in 1293 was Kubilai Khan's last.

In the end, the Mongol Empire reached its outer limits. In the west, the Egyptian Mamluks stemmed the advancing Mongol armies and prevented Egypt from falling into their hands. In the east, the waters of the South China Sea and the Sea of Japan foiled Mongol expansion into Java and Japan. Better at conquering than governing, the Mongols struggled to rule their vast possessions in makeshift states. Bit by bit, they yielded control to local administrators and rulers who governed as their surrogates. There was also frequent feuding among the Mongol rulers themselves. In China and in Persia, Mongol rule collapsed in the fourteenth century. Ultimately, the Mongols would meet a deadly adversary even more brutal than they were—the plague of the fourteenth century (see Chapter 11).

Mongol conquest reshaped Afro-Eurasia's social landscape. Islam would never again have a unifying authority like the caliphate or a powerful center like Baghdad. China, too, was divided and changed by the Mongols' introduction of Persian, Islamic, and Byzantine influences into China's architecture, art, science, and medicine. The Yuan policy of benign tolerance brought elements from Christianity, Judaism, Zoroastrianism, and Islam into the Chinese mix. The Mongol thrust also facilitated the flow of fine goods, traders, and technology from China to the rest of the world. Finally, the Mongol conquests encouraged an unprecedented Afro-Eurasian interconnectedness, surpassing even the Hellenistic connections that Alexander's conquests had brought in the late fourth century BCE (see Chapter 6).

Out of Mongol conquest and warfare would come centuries of trade, migration, and increasing contacts among Africa, Europe, and Asia.

Conclusion

Between 1000 and 1300, Afro-Eurasia was forming large cultural spheres. As trade and migration spanned longer distances, these spheres prospered and became more integrated. In central Afro-Eurasia, Islam was firmly established, and its merchants, scholars, and travelers acted as commercial and cultural intermediaries joining the landmass together, as they spread their universalizing faith. As seaborne trade expanded, India, too, became a commercial crossroads. Merchants in its port cities welcomed traders arriving from Arab lands to the west, from China, and from Southeast Asia. China also boomed, pouring its manufactures into trading networks that reached throughout Afro-Eurasia and even into Africa. Christian Europe had two centers—at Rome and at Constantinople—both of which were at war with Islam.

Neither sub-Saharan Africa nor the Americas saw the same degree of integration, but trade and migration in these areas had profound effects. Certain African cultures flourished as they encountered the commercial energy of trade on the Indian Ocean. Africans' trade with one another linked coastal and interior regions in an ever more integrated world. American peoples also built cities that dominated cultural areas and thrived through trade. American cultures shared significant features: reliance on trade, maize, and the exchange of goods such as shells and precious feathers. And larger areas honored the same spiritual centers.

By 1300, trade, migration, and conflict were connecting Afro-Eurasian worlds in unprecedented ways. When Mongol armies swept into China, into Southeast Asia, and into the heart of Islam, they applied a thin coating of political integration to these widespread regions and built on existing trade links. At the same time, most people's lives remained quite localized, driven by the need for subsistence and governed by spiritual and governmental representatives acting at the behest of distant authorities.

Still, locals noticed the evidence of cross-cultural exchanges everywhere—in the clothing styles of provincial elites, such as Chinese silks in Paris or Quetzal plumes in northern Mexico; in enticements to move (and forced removals) to new frontiers; in the news of faraway conquests or advancing armies. Worlds were coming together within themselves and across territorial boundaries, while remaining apart as they sought to maintain their own identity and traditions. In Afro-Eurasia especially, as the movement of goods and peoples shifted from ancient land routes to sea-lanes, these contacts were more frequent and far-reaching. Never before had the world seen so much activity connecting its parts. Nor within them had there been so much shared cultural similarity. By the time the Mongol Empire arose, the regions composing the globe were those that we now recognize as the cultural spheres of today's world.

After You Read This Chapter

Go to INQUIZITIVE to see what you've learned—and learn what you've missed—with personalized feedback along the way.

FOCUS ON: *Foundational Cultural Spheres*

THE ISLAMIC WORLD

- The Islamic world undergoes a burst of expansion, prosperity, and cultural diversification but remains politically fractured.

- Arab merchants and Sufi mystics spread Islam over great distances and make it more appealing to other cultures, helping to transform Islam into a foundational world.

- Islam travels across the Sahara Desert; the powerful gold- and slave-supplying empire of Mali arises in West Africa.

CHINA

- The Song dynasty reunites China after three centuries of fragmented rulership, reaching into the past to reestablish a sense of a "true" Chinese identity as the Han, through a widespread print culture and denigration of outsiders.

- Agrarian success and advances in manufacturing—including the production of both iron and porcelain—fuel an expanding economy, complete with paper money.

INDIA

- India remains a mosaic under the canopy of Hinduism despite cultural interconnections and increasing prosperity.

- The invasion of Turkish Muslims leads to the Delhi Sultanate, which rules over India for three centuries, strengthening cultural diversity and tolerance.

CHRISTIAN EUROPE

- Roman Catholicism becomes a "mass" faith and helps to create a common European cultural identity.

- Feudalism organizes the elite–peasant relationship, while manorialism forms the basis of the economy

- Europe's growing confidence is manifest in the Crusades and the reconquering of Iberia, an effort to drive Islam out of Christian lands.

CHRONOLOGY

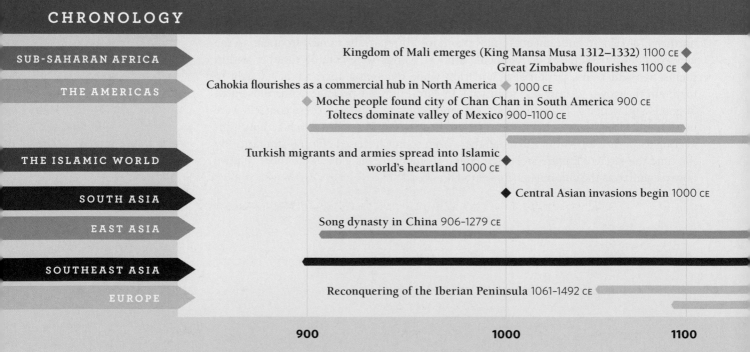

SUB-SAHARAN AFRICA

Kingdom of Mali emerges (King Mansa Musa 1312–1332) 1100 CE ◆
Great Zimbabwe flourishes 1100 CE ◆

THE AMERICAS

Cahokia flourishes as a commercial hub in North America ◆ 1000 CE
◆ Moche people found city of Chan Chan in South America 900 CE
Toltecs dominate valley of Mexico 900-1100 CE

THE ISLAMIC WORLD

Turkish migrants and armies spread into Islamic world's heartland 1000 CE

SOUTH ASIA

◆ Central Asian invasions begin 1000 CE

EAST ASIA

Song dynasty in China 906-1279 CE

SOUTHEAST ASIA

EUROPE

Reconquering of the Iberian Peninsula 1061-1492 CE

900   1000   1100

- *Thinking about* **Worlds Together, Worlds Apart** From 1000 to 1300 CE, a range of social and political developments contributed to the consolidation of four cultural spheres that still exist today: Europe, the Islamic world, India, and China. In what ways did these spheres interact with one another? In what ways was each sphere genuinely distinct from the others? To what extent were sub-Saharan Africa and the Americas folded into these spheres and with what result?

- *Thinking about* **Transformation & Conflict and Becoming the World** As the four cultural spheres of Afro-Eurasia consolidated, shocking examples of conflict between them began to take place. Whether Pope Urban II's call in 1095 to reclaim the "holy land" from Muslims or the Mongol Hulagu's brutal sack of Baghdad in 1258, this period was marked by large-scale warfare between rival cultural spheres. To what extent was such conflict inevitable? In what ways did conflict transform the groups involved?

- *Thinking about* **Crossing Borders and Becoming the World** Major innovations facilitated economic exchange in the Indian Ocean and in Song China. The magnetic needle compass, better ships, and improved maps shrank the Indian Ocean to the benefit of traders. Similarly, paper money in Song China changed the nature of commerce. How did these developments shift the axis of Afro-Eurasian exchange? What evidence suggests that bodies of water and the routes across them became more significant than overland exchange routes in binding together Afro-Eurasia? What might be the longer-term implications of these developments?

1. How did technological advances, such as the magnetic needle compass, junks, and dhows, fuel the maritime revolution in 1000–1300?

2. What political forces contributed to the fragmentation of the Islamic world in this period? What cultural forces provided a unifying force within Islam?

3. Compare raja-ruled India with that of Muslim-Turkish regimes such as the **Delhi Sultanate**.

4. How did economic and manufacturing developments, coupled with political developments, cement the power of the Song dynasty? How did Song interactions with nomads and neighbors lead to distinctive identities for both the Song and their neighbors?

5. How did developments such as **manorialism**, universities, and the Crusades contribute to Europe's identity as a fragmented yet distinctive cultural sphere?

6. Compare the trans-Saharan trade of the Mande-speaking peoples of West Africa and later **Mali** Empire that developed there with the Indian Ocean trade of the Shona-speaking peoples of East Africa. What goods were traded and what was the impact of that trade on these two regions of Africa?

7. Compare the degrees of integration in various regions of the Americas: South America (**Chimú Empire**), Mesoamerica (**Toltecs**), and North America (**Cahokia**).

8. What enabled the Mongols to conquer such huge swaths of territory across Eurasia? Contrast the expansion of Hulagu into the west with that of Kubilai Khan in the east?

Chimú Empire in South America 1000–1460

◆ Sufism spreads through Islamic world

◆ Mongol forces sack Baghdad and end Abbasid caliphate 1258

Delhi Sultanate 1206–1526

Mongol Yuan dynasty 1279–1368

Khmer state 899–1431

Crusades 1095–1272

1200   **1300**   **1400**

Competing Perspectives

"World" Travelers

The maritime revolution described in this chapter, along with the Silk Roads across Inner Eurasia, facilitated travel for trade, diplomacy, and religious pilgrimage on a scale previously unseen. Some travelers who moved between the worlds of Afro-Eurasia in this period left records of their stunning journeys.

As we saw at the start of this chapter, Bar Sāwmā traveled primarily along land routes from Yuan dynasty China all the way to modern-day France. A Nestorian Christian monk, Bar Sāwmā appears to have made his journeys with both diplomacy and religious pilgrimage in mind. The excerpt here describes his travels with his companions, which were recorded in a Syriac text shortly after his death in Baghdad in 1294.

The Venetian merchant Marco Polo was traveling at nearly the same time in the opposite direction. Long after his voyages were completed, Marco Polo recounted his twenty-four years of travel (1271–1295), including his time in the Mongol court of China. As the passage here shows, he wrote in detail about the wonders and dangers of the worlds through which he traveled.

The North African Muslim scholar Ibn Battuta traveled a combination of land and sea routes through much of Africa, Southwest Asia, Southeast Asia, and East Asia between 1325 and 1354. Writing after his travels were completed, Battuta offered details about the places he visited and their customs, as well as the hardships of travel. Battuta was particularly interested in the role and practice of Islam in each place.

The final "world" traveler represented here is the Chinese naval commander Zheng He, whose voyages came later (1405–1433; see Chapter 11) but can be usefully compared with those of Bar Sāwmā, Marco Polo, and Ibn Batutta. In a series of expeditions, Zheng He's fleet sailed from China through Southeast Asia, to Sri Lanka, into the northern Indian Ocean, and even to the Persian Gulf and the Red Sea, leaving stone inscriptions at many of the sites he visited. A trilingual inscription (in Chinese, Persian, and Tamil) was set up in 1411 by Zheng He and his companions at Sri Lanka. Included here is a translation of the Chinese portion of that inscription, which records an offering to Buddha.

PRIMARY SOURCE 10.1

Pilgrimage to Jerusalem (c. 1300), Bar Sāwmā

Chapter 3. One day they meditated, saying, "It would be exceedingly helpful to us if we were to leave this region and set out for the West, for we could then [visit] the tombs of the holy martyrs and Catholic Fathers and be blessed [by them]. And if Christ, the Lord of the Universe, prolonged our lives, and sustained us by His grace, we could go to Jerusalem, so that we might receive complete pardon for our offences, and absolution for our sins of foolishness. Now although Rabban Sâwmâ opposed Rabban Mark, and [tried to] frighten him with the toil of the journey, and the fatigue of travelling, and the terror of the ways, and the tribulations that would beset him in a foreign country, Rabban Mark burned to set out on the road. . . . And they arrived in Baghdad, and thence they went to the Great Church of Kôkê. . . . And they went to the monastery of Mâr Mârî, the Apostle, and received a blessing from the sepulchers (or relics?) of that country. And from there they turned back and came to the country of Bêth Garmai, and they received blessings from the shrine (or tomb) of Mâr Ezekiel [the prophet, near

Dâkôk], which was full of helps and healings. And from there they went to Arbîl, and thence to Mâwsil (i.e., Môṣul on the Tigris). And they went Shîgar (Sinjâr), and Nisibis, and Merdâ (Mardîn); and were blessed by the shrine [containing] the bones of Mâr Awgîn, the second Christ. And thence they went . . . and they were blessed by all the shrines and monasteries, and the religious houses, and monks, and the Fathers (i.e., Bishops) in their dioceses. . . . [W]hen they arrived there they heard from the inhabitants of the country that the road was cut because of the murders and robberies which had taken place along it.

Chapter 4. And the two monks turned back and came to Mâr Catholicus, who rejoiced [at the sight of] them, and said unto them, "This is not the time for a journey to Jerusalem. The roads are a disturbed state, and the ways are cut. Now behold, ye have received blessings from all the Houses of God, and the shrines (or relics?) which are in them, and it is my opinion that when a man visits them with a pure heart, the service thus paid to them is in no way less than that of a pilgrimage to Jerusalem.

Source: Rabban Bar Sāwmā. *The Monks of Kublai Khan, Emperor of China, or The History of the Life and Travels of Rabban Sāwmā*, trans. E. A. Wallis Budge (London: Religious Tract Society, 1928), pp. 141–43, 145–46.

Mongol Divination (c. 1300), Marco Polo

Chapter 45. Chingis-khan commanded his astrologers and magicians to declare to him which of the two armies, in the approaching conflict, should obtain the victory. Upon this they took a green reed, and dividing it lengthways into two parts, they wrote upon one the name of their master, and upon the other the name of Un-khan. They then placed them on the ground, at some distance from each other, and gave notice to the king that during the time of their pronouncing their incantations, the two pieces of reed, through the power of their idols, would advance towards each other, and that the victory would fall to the lot of that monarch whose piece should be seen to mount upon the other. The whole army was assembled to be spectators of this ceremony, and whilst the astrologers were employed in reading their books of necromancy, they perceived the two pieces begin to move and to approach, and after some small interval of time, that inscribed with the name of Chingis-khan to place itself upon the top of its adversary. Upon witnessing this, the king and his band of Tartars marched with exultation to the attack of the army of Un-khan, broke through its ranks and entirely routed it. Un-khan himself was killed, his kingdom fell to the conqueror, and Chingis-khan espoused his daughter. After this battle he continued during six years to render himself master of additional kingdoms and cities; until at length, in the siege of a castle named Thaigin, he was struck by an arrow in the knee, and dying of the wound, was buried in the mountain of Altaï.

Source: Marco Polo, *The Travels of Marco Polo, The Venetian: The Translation of Marsden Revised, with a Selection of His Notes*, ed. Thomas Wright (London: Henry G. Bohn, York Street, Convent Garden, 1854) pp. 124–25.

The Sacred Mosque of Jerusalem (c. 1360), Ibn Battuta

We then reached Jerusalem (may God ennoble her!), third in excellence after the two holy shrines of Mecca and Madína and the place whence the Prophet was caught up into heaven. Its walls were destroyed by the illustrious King Saladin and his successors, for fear lest the Christians should seize it and fortify themselves in it. The sacred mosque is a most beautiful building, and is said to be the largest mosque in the world. Its length from east to west is put at 752 "royal" cubits and its breadth at 435. . . . The entire mosque is an open court and unroofed, except the mosque al-Aqsá, which has a roof of most excellent workmanship, embellished with gold and brilliant colours. Some other parts of the mosque are roofed as well. The Dome of the Rock is a building of extraordinary beauty, solidity, elegance, and singularity of shape. It stands on an elevation in the centre of the mosque and is reached by a flight of marble steps. It has four doors. The space round it is also paved with marble, excellently done, and the interior likewise. Both outside and inside the decoration is so magnificent and the workmanship so surpassing as to defy description. The greater part is covered with gold so that the eyes of one who gazes on its beauties are dazzled by its brilliance, now glowing like a mass of light, now flashing like lightning. In the centre of the Dome is the blessed rock from which the Prophet ascended to heaven, a great rock projecting about a man's height, and underneath it there is a cave the size of a small room, also of a man's height, with steps leading down to it. Encircling the rock are two railings of excellent workmanship, the one nearer the rock being artistically constructed in iron, and the other of wood.

Source: Ibn Battúta, *Ibn Battúta: Travels in Asia and Africa, 1325–1354*, trans. and ed. H. A. R. Gibb (London: George Routledge & Sons, Ltd., 1929), pp. 55–56.

The Galle Trilingual Stone Inscription (1411), Zheng He

His Majesty, the Emperor of the Great Ming dynasty has despatched the eunuchs Ching-Ho [Zheng He], Wang Ch'ing-Lien, and others to set forth his utterance before Buddha, the World Honoured one, as follows:

"Deeply do we reverence you, Merciful and Honoured One, whose bright perfection is wide-embracing, and whose way of virtue passes all understanding, whose law enters into all human relations, and the years of whose great Kalpa (period) are like the sand of the river in number, you whose controlling influence ennobles and converts, whose kindness quickens, and whose strength discerns, whose mysterious efficacy is beyond compare! Whereas Ceylon's mountainous isle lies in the south of the ocean, and its Buddhist temples are sanctuaries of your gospel, where your miraculous responsive power imbues and enlightens. Of late, we have dispatched missions to announce our mandate to foreign nations, and during their journey over the ocean they have been favoured with the blessing of your beneficent protection. They escaped disaster or misfortune and journeyed in safety to and fro. In everlasting recognition of your supreme virtue, we, therefore, bestow offerings in recompense, and do now reverently present before Buddha, the Honoured One, oblations of gold and silver, gold embroidered jewelled banners of variegated silk, incense burners, and flower vases, silks of many colours in lining and exterior, lamps and candles with other gifts, in order to manifest the high honour of our worship. Do you, Lord Buddha, bestow on them, your regard!"

List of Alms bestowed at the shrine of the Buddhist temple in the Mountain of Ceylon as offerings:

1000 pieces of gold; 5000 pieces of silver; fifty rolls of embroidered silk in many colours; fifty rolls of silk taffeta in many colours; four pairs of jewelled banners, gold embroidered, and of variegated silk; two pairs of the same picked in red; one pair of the same in yellow; one pair in black; five antique brass incense burners; five pairs of antique brass flower vases picked in gold on lacquer, with gold stands; five pairs of yellow brass candle-sticks, picked in gold on lacquer, with gold stand; five yellow brass lamps picked in gold on lacquer, with gold stands; five incense vessels in vermilion red, lacquered gold picked on lacquer, with gold stands; six pairs of golden lotus flowers; 2500 catties of scented oil; ten pairs of wax candles; ten sticks of fragrant incense.

The date being the seventh year of Yung-Lo (1410 A.D.) marked Chi ch'ou in the sixty years' cycle, on the Chia Hsu day of the sixty days cycle in the second moon, being the first day of the month. A reverent oblation.

Source: "Appendix I. Translation of the Chinese Inscription," trans. Edmund Backhouse, in "The Galle Trilingual Stone," *Spolia Zeylanica* 8 (Issued from the Colombo Museum; Ceylon: H. M. Richards, Acting Government Printer, 1913).

QUESTIONS FOR ANALYSIS

1. Based on these excerpts, what sorts of details seem to interest each traveler? How does the form of each text (life of revered holy figure, post-trip travelogues, inscription) influence the reliability of the account?

2. What sorts of dangers are explicitly mentioned, or implied, in these texts?

3. What in the texts suggests the exchange of goods and ideas?

4. Apart from the fact that these individuals were traveling such great distances, what evidence do these texts offer for connected worlds?

Interpreting Visual Evidence

Imagining the World

During this period when Afro-Eurasia was "Becoming the World," cartographers began producing "world" maps. In 1154 al-Idrisi, a Muslim cartographer sponsored by King Roger II of Sicily, produced his *Tabula Rogeriana*. Al-Idrisi's map was accompanied by a commentary that contained information about the ten regions (numbered west to east; but note the map was drawn so that the south is at the top) and seven climate zones (numbered south to north and following the scheme set forth by the second-century-ce Greco-Roman geographer Ptolemy). In 1375, a Jewish mapmaker named Abraham Cresques, from the island of Majorca off the east coast of Spain, produced the second map included here, which is known as the *Catalan Atlas*. Cresques's map is a mixture of practical information and storytelling. The crisscrossed lines that marked compass bearings, suggestive of a nautical chart, reflect the influence of the compass on European mapmaking beginning around 1300. The ornate depictions of the Malian king Mansa Musa and the caravan of Marco Polo offer historical information. In 1459, a monk named Fra Mauro, from Venice, created his *Mappa Mundi* (Map of the World), the third map pictured here. Fra Mauro's map is striking in its detail and information. Not only does Fra Mauro's map carefully mark out shorelines, rivers, cities, and other geographical features, it also includes banners with detailed information and even drawings of the different types of ships (such as the North Atlantic cogs, Chinese junks, and Arabian dhows, discussed in this chapter) that sailed the different seas.

Al-Idrisi's Tabula Rogeriana.

Fra Mauro's Mappa Mundi.

Cresques's Catalan Atlas.

QUESTIONS FOR ANALYSIS

1. Compare these maps, in terms of their representations of land, water, perspective, and other features. What accounts for the maps' similarities and differences?

2. Based on the features and information on the maps, where did cartographers get the data to create the maps? How might these maps have been used and by whom?

3. What do these maps suggest about how these cartographers and their patrons understood the known world? Why are certain parts of the world emphasized and others left off?

Before You Read This Chapter

GLOBAL STORYLINES

- The spread of the Black Death and the collapse of the Mongol Empire sets off crises across Afro-Eurasia, with major demographic, political, economic, and cultural consequences.

- Across Afro-Eurasia, continuity in religious beliefs and cultural institutions accompanies changes in political structures in Europe, the Muslim world, and China.

- In central Eurasia, new rulers—most notably the Ottomans—rebuild dynasties in place of the Mongols, using a blend of religion, military expansion, administrative control, and cultural tolerance.

- In Western Christendom, new monarchies establish political order, and the Renaissance brings a cultural rebirth to societies devastated by plague.

- In East Asia, the Ming dynasty replaces the Mongol Yuan dynasty, using an elaborate Confucian bureaucracy to oversee infrastructure and long-distance exchange.

CORE OBJECTIVES

- **DESCRIBE** the nature and origins of the crises spanning Afro-Eurasia during the fourteenth century and **ASSESS** the magnitude of the crises' effects, locally and trans-regionally.

- **EXPLAIN** the continuities of religious belief systems from the fourteenth through the fifteenth century.

- **COMPARE** the ways in which regional rulers in post-plague Afro-Eurasia attempted to construct unified states and **ANALYZE** the extent and nature of their successes.

- **EXAMINE** the ways in which the art and/or architecture of different regions reflected political realities, and **DESCRIBE** the specific themes that communicate these messages to viewers.

- **COMPARE** the means by which the Iberian kingdoms, the Ottoman Empire, the Ming Dynasty, and European polities each extended their territory and regional influence.

CHAPTER 11

Crises and Recovery in Afro-Eurasia

1300–1500

When Mongol armies besieged the Genoese trading outpost of Caffa on the Black Sea in 1346, they not only damaged trading links between East Asia and the Mediterranean but also unleashed a devastating disease: the bubonic plague. Defeated Genoese merchants and soldiers withdrew, unknowingly taking the germs with them aboard their ships. By the time they arrived in Messina, Sicily, half the passengers were dead. The rest were dying. People waiting on shore for the ships' trade goods were horrified at the sight and turned the ships away. Desperately, the captains went to the next port, only to face the same fate. Despite these efforts at isolation, Europeans could not keep the plague (called the Black Death) from reaching their shores. As it spread from port to port, it eventually contaminated all of Europe, killing more than half of the population.

This story illustrates the disruptive effects of the Mongol invasions and the long-distance trade routes that the Mongol invasions foisted on Afro-Eurasian societies. In the thirteenth and early fourteenth centuries, Mongol armies swept into and took control of vast regions of Afro-Eurasia. Although the invasions ushered in an age of intensified cultural and political contact, the channels of exchange—the land trails and sea-lanes of human voyagers—became accidental conduits for deadly microbes. These germs devastated societies far more decisively than did Mongol warfare. They were the real "murderous hordes" of world history, infecting people from every community, class, and culture they encountered. So staggering was the Black Death's toll that population densities did not recover for 200 years. The most severely affected regions were those that the Mongols had brought together: settlements and commercial hubs along the old Silk Road and around the Mediterranean Sea and the South China Sea. While segments of the Indian Ocean trading world experienced death and disruption, South Asian societies, which had escaped the Mongol conquest, also escaped the dying and political disruptions associated with the Black Death.

This chapter explores the ways in which Afro-Eurasian peoples restored what they thought was valuable from old traditions while discarding what they thought had failed them, in favor of radically new institutions and ideas. Much of the recovery across Afro-Eurasia had striking similarities, as societies reaffirmed their most deeply held and long-standing beliefs. Chinese rulers looked to Confucian thought and well-known dynastic institutions to provide guidance going forward. In the Muslim heartland a small band of Turkish-speaking warriors—the Ottomans—channeled the energies of a revived Islam to expand their own territory and the Muslim world. Europeans also invoked their traditions. In the Iberian Peninsula political elites used a resurgent Catholicism to spread their political power and drive Muslim communities out of Europe. Europeans also created new dynastic monarchies and looked to their distant past in Greek and Roman culture for inspiration.

Radically new institutions and ideas appeared across Afro-Eurasia in the aftermath of the Black Death. Notable among these was the outburst of cultural activity that took place in western Europe. Historians have called this flourishing the Renaissance ("rebirth"), for during this era Europeans rediscovered their Greek and Roman pasts and used their inspiration drawn from classical antiquity to bring about far-reaching innovations in art, architecture, thought, and political and financial institutions. While recognizing significant changes to institutions and ideas in this period, this chapter stresses continuities. Considering how grievously people suffered and how many died, it is surprising how much of the old—particularly religious beliefs and institutions—survived the aftermath of Mongol rule and the Black Death. Rulers altered but did not transform their inherited traditions.

Collapse and Consolidation

COMPARISON

DESCRIBE the nature and origins of the crises spanning Afro-Eurasia during the fourteenth century.

Although the Mongol invasions overturned political systems, the plague devastated society itself. The pandemic killed millions, disrupted economies, and threw communities into chaos. Rulers could explain to their people the assaults of "barbarians," but it was much harder to make sense of an invisible enemy. Nonetheless, in response to the upheaval, new ruling groups moved to reorganize their states. By making strategic marriages and building powerful armies, these rulers enlarged their territories, formed alliances, and built dynasties.

THE BLACK DEATH

The spread of the Black Death was the fourteenth century's most significant historical development (see Map 11.1). Originating in Inner Asia, the disease afflicted peoples from China to Europe and killed 25 to 65 percent of infected populations.

How did the **Black Death** move so far and so fast? One explanation may lie in climatic changes. A cooler climate—scholars refer to a "Little Ice Age"—may have weakened populations and left them vulnerable to disease. In Europe, for instance, beginning around 1310, harsh winters and rainy summers shortened the growing seasons and ruined harvests. Exhausted soils no longer supplied the resources required by growing urban and rural populations, while nobles squeezed the peasantry in an effort to maintain their luxurious lifestyle. The ensuing famine lasted from 1315 to 1322, during which time millions of Europeans died of starvation or of diseases against which the malnourished population had little resistance. This climate change and famine laid the groundwork for the Black Death that soon followed. Another climate-related factor in the spread of the plague lay in the drying up of the central Asian steppe borderlands, where bubonic plague had existed for centuries. This drought may have forced rodents out of their usual dwelling places and pressed pastoral peoples, who carried the infectious strains, to move closer to settled agricultural communities. Fleas transmitted plague from rodent to rodent, and to humans. The resulting epidemic was terrifying, for its causes were unknown at the time. Infected victims died quickly—sometimes overnight—and in agony, coughing up blood and oozing pus and blood from black sores the size of eggs.

But it was the trading network that spread the germs across Afro-Eurasia into famine-struck western Europe. This wider Afro-Eurasian population was vulnerable because its members had no immunities to the disease. The first outbreak in a heavily populated region occurred in the 1320s in southwestern China. From there, the disease spread through China and then took its death march along the major trade routes. Many routes terminated at the Italian port cities, where ships with dead and dying people aboard arrived in 1347. From there, what Europeans called the Pestilence or the Great Mortality engulfed the western end of the landmass. In China, the Muslim world, and Europe, societies suffered the disastrous effects of the Black Death.

Plague Victim The plague was highly contagious and quickly led to death. Here the physician and his helper cover their noses to avoid the unbearable stench emanating from the patient. What strategies, other than medical, do you see the individuals in this image using against the plague?

Plague in China China was ripe for the plague's pandemic. Its population had increased under the Song dynasty (960 CE–1279) and subsequent Mongol rule. But by 1300, hunger and scarcity spread as resources were stretched thin. The weakened population was especially vulnerable. For seventy years, the Black Death ravaged China, reduced the size of the already small Mongol population, and shattered the Mongols' claim to a mandate from heaven. In 1331, plague may have killed 90 percent of the population in Bei Zhili (modern Hebei) province. From there it spread throughout other provinces, reaching Fujian and the coast at Shandong. By the 1350s, most of China's large cities suffered severe outbreaks.

COMPARISON

COMPARE the impact of the Black Death on China, Islam, and Europe.

SCANDINAVIA
•1349

Novgorod

NORTH SEA

Edinburgh
(1350)

BRITAIN

Dublin
(1349)

Oxford
(1348)

London
(1348)

Amiens
(1348)

Paris
(1348)

EUROPE

Bremen
(1349)

Cologne
(1349)

Lübeck
(1349)

Danzig

Moscow

MUSCOVY
•1351

Cracow

Kiev

KHANATE OF THE
GOLDEN HORDE

Rostov

New Sarai

ARAL
SEA

CASPIAN
SEA

Venice
(1347)

Buda
(1349)

BLACK

Florence
(1347)

Pisa
(1347)

Siena
(1347)

Bordeaux
(1348)

Avignon
(1347)

Marseille

Barcelona
(1348)

Naples

Madrid

Lisbon
(1349)

SPAIN
1348

Palermo
(1347)

Messina

Athens
(1347)

SEA

Constantinople
(1347)

Caffa
(1346)

Trebizond

ANATOLIA

Tabriz

Maraghan

Baghdad
(1347)

PERSIA

Bukhara

Samarkan

Silk route

IL-KHANATE

Isfahan

Ceuta

Fez

Algiers

Tunis

MEDITERRANEAN

SEA

Aleppo
(1347)

Damascus
(1347)

Jerusalem
(1347)

Basra

Shiraz

Hormuz

Marrakesh
(1349)

Tripoli
(1348)

Alexandria
(1347)

Cairo
(1347)

Medina

Mecca
(1348)

ARABIA

Persian Gulf

AFRICA

RED SEA

Aden
(1351)

ARABIAN
SEA

Mogadishu

INDIAN

ATLANTIC

OCEAN

◄── Progress of bubonic plague

─── Trade routes

• Known areas of major outbreaks

∗ Modern Chinese provincial names for
regions affected by outbreak of plague

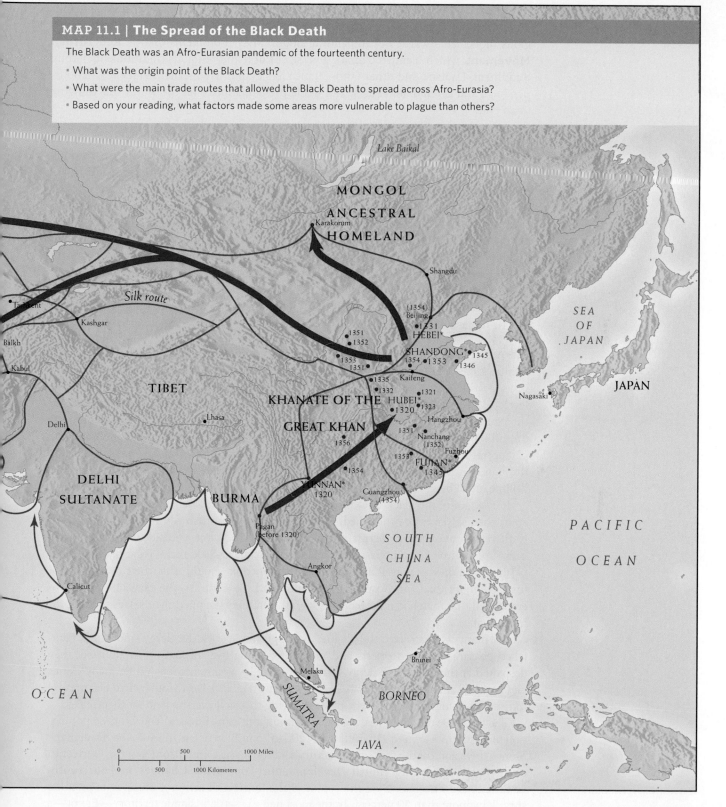

MAP 11.1 | The Spread of the Black Death

The Black Death was an Afro-Eurasian pandemic of the fourteenth century.

- What was the origin point of the Black Death?
- What were the main trade routes that allowed the Black Death to spread across Afro-Eurasia?
- Based on your reading, what factors made some areas more vulnerable to plague than others?

Even as the Black Death was engulfing China, bandit groups and dissident religious sects were undercutting the power of the last Yuan Mongol rulers. Popular religious movements warned of impending doom. Most prominent was the **Red Turban Movement**, which blended China's diverse cultural and religious traditions, including Buddhism, Daoism, and other faiths. Its leaders emphasized strict dietary restrictions, penance, and ceremonial rituals, and made proclamations that the world was drawing to an end.

Plague in the Islamic World The plague devastated parts of the Muslim world as well. The Black Death reached Baghdad by 1347. By the next year, the plague overtook Egypt, Syria, and Cyprus, with as many as 1,000 deaths a day according to a Tunisian report. Animals, too, were afflicted. One Egyptian writer commented: "The country was not far from being ruined. . . . One found in the desert the bodies of savage animals with the bubos under their arms. It was the same with horses, camels, asses, and all the beasts in general, including birds, even the ostriches." In the eastern Mediterranean, plague left much of the Islamic world in a state of near political and economic collapse. The great Arab historian Ibn Khaldun (1332–1406), who lost his mother and father and a number of his teachers to the Black Death in Tunis, underscored the desolation: "Cities and buildings were laid waste, roads and way signs were obliterated, settlements and mansions became empty, dynasties and tribes grew weak," he wrote. "The entire world changed."

Plague in Europe In Europe, the Black Death first ravaged the Italian Peninsula; then it seized France, the Netherlands, Belgium, Luxembourg, Germany, and England in its deathly grip. Overcrowded and unsanitary cities were particularly vulnerable. All levels of society—the poor, craftspeople, aristocrats—were at risk, although flight to the countryside offered some protection from infection. Nearly 50 million of Europe's 80 million perished between 1347 and 1351. After 1353, the epidemic waned, but the plague returned every seven years or so for the rest of the century, and sporadically through the fifteenth century. Consequently, the European population continued to decline, until by 1450 many areas had only one quarter the number of a century earlier.

In the face of the Black Death, some Europeans turned to debauchery, determined to enjoy themselves before they died. Others, especially in urban settings in Flanders, the Netherlands, and parts of Germany, claimed to find God's grace outside what they saw as a corrupt Church. Semimonastic orders like the Beghards held that a good layman could perform sacraments as well as a priest and that people should trust their own "interior instinct" more than the Gospel as then preached. By contrast, the Flagellants were so convinced that man had incurred God's wrath that they whipped themselves to atone for human sin.

For many who survived the plague, disappointment with the clergy smoldered. Famished peasants resented priests and monks for living lives of luxury. In addition, they despaired at the absence of clergy when they were so greatly needed. While many clerics had perished attending to their parishioners during the Black Death, others had fled to rural retreats far from the ravages of the plague, leaving their followers to fend for themselves.

The Black Death wrought devastation throughout Afro-Eurasia. The Chinese population plunged from around 115 million in 1200 to 75 million or less in 1400, the result of the Mongol invasions of the thirteenth century and the disease and disorder of the fourteenth century (see **Analyzing Global Developments: Population Changes in Fourteenth-Century Afro-Eurasia**). Over the course of the fourteenth century, Europe's population shrank by more than 50 percent. In the most densely settled Islamic territory—Egypt—a population that had totaled around 6 million in 1400 was cut in half. When farmers fell ill with the plague, food production collapsed. Famine followed and killed off the survivors.

Bubonic Plague and the Destruction of Society Bubonic plague devastated the countries of Western Christendom. Here, in Pieter Bruegel the Elder's *The Triumph of Death* (1562), we see skeletons murdering indiscriminately, rich and poor alike. Notice the role of religious imagery in this painting. Notice also the representation of social class. How does the artist convey distinctions of rank and status?

Worst afflicted were the crowded cities, especially coastal ports. Some cities lost up to two-thirds of their population. Refugees from urban areas fled their homes, seeking security and food in the countryside. The shortage of food and other necessities led to rapidly rising prices, work stoppages, and unrest. Political leaders added to their unpopularity by repressing the unrest. Everywhere, regimes trembled and collapsed. The Mongol empire, which had held so much of Eurasia together commercially and politically, disintegrated. Thus, the way was prepared for experiments in state building, religious beliefs, and cultural understandings.

REBUILDING STATES

Starting in the late fourteenth century, Afro-Eurasians began the task of reconstructing both their political order and their trading networks. By then the plague had died down, though it continued to afflict peoples for centuries. However, the rebuilding of military and civil administrations—no easy task—also required political legitimacy. With their

Analyzing Global Developments

Population Changes in Fourteenth-Century Afro-Eurasia

Famine, warfare, and disease led to vast population declines all across Afro-Eurasia in the fourteenth century. The Mongols were instrumental players in spreading disease across the landmass starting in China and moving westward along land- and sea-based trading routes towards the Mediterranean world and, ultimately, northern Europe (see Map 11.1). While the effects of these destructive forces were felt across the Afro-Eurasian landmass, some states and regions were less affected than others. The population data below come from the best historical studies of the last forty years and are based on painstaking archival research. They serve as one of the best ways for us to gain historical insight into this tumultuous century.

QUESTIONS FOR ANALYSIS

- Identify the regions or cities where population loss seems to have been lower or higher. Why might those variations in death rates have occurred?

- Compare the losses in urban areas with the losses in the region where those urban areas are located. What might that comparison suggest about the impact of fourteenth-century disasters on urban versus other populations?

- Explain why population decline was more severe and widespread in Europe than in Asia.

- Explain how the great loss of population in Europe and China marked a turning point in their histories.

LOCATION	POPULATION FIGURES	ACROSS THE 14TH CENTURY	% CHANGE
By Regions			
Europe	80M in 1346	30M in 1353	−60%
Asia	230M in 1300	235M in 1400	+2%
Islam	(regional data are not available)		
By Countries			
Spain	6M in 1346	2.5M in 1353	−60%
Italy	10M in 1346	4.5M in 1363	−55%
France	18M in 1346	7.2M in 1353	−60%
England	6M in 1346	2.25M in 1353	−62.5%
China	115M in 1200 85M in 1300	75M in 1400	−35% overall
Japan	9.75M in 1300	12.5M in 1400	+28%
Korea	3M in 1300	3.5M in 1400	+17%
India	91M in 1300	97M in 1400	+6.5%
By Cities			
London	100,000 in 1346	37,000 in 1353	−62.5%
Florence	92,000 in 1346	37,250 in 1353	−59.5%
Sienna	50,000 in 1346	20,000 in 1353	−60%
Bologna	50,000 in 1346	27,500 in 1353	−45%
Cairo	500,000 in 1300	300,000 in 1400	−40%
Damascus	80,000 in 1300	50,000 in 1400	−37%

Sources: Ole J. Benedictow, *The Black Death, 1346–1353: The Complete History* (Woodbridge, England, 2004); Michael Dols, *The Black Death in the Middle East* (Princeton, 1974): Colin McEvedy and Richard Jones, *Atlas of World Population History* (Hammondsworth, England, 1978); Ping-ti Ho, *Studies on the Population of China, 1368–1953* (Cambridge, MA, 1959).

people deeply shaken by the extraordinary loss of life, rulers needed to revive confidence in themselves and their regimes, which they did by fostering beliefs and rituals that confirmed their legitimacy and by increasing their control over subjects.

The basis for power was a political institution well known to Afro-Eurasians for centuries, the **dynasty**—the hereditary ruling family that passed control from one generation to the next. As in the past, the new dynasties sought to establish their legitimacy in three ways. First, ruling families insisted that their power derived from a divine calling: Ming emperors in China claimed for themselves what previous dynastic rulers had asserted—the "mandate of heaven"—while European monarchs claimed to rule by "divine right." From their base in Anatolia, Ottoman warrior-princes asserted that they now carried the banner of Islam. In these ways, ruling households affirmed that God or the heavens intended for them to hold power. Second, leaders prevented squabbling among potential heirs by establishing clear rules about succession to the throne. Many European states tried to standardize succession by passing titles to the eldest male heir, thus ensuring political stability at a potential time of crisis, but in practice there were countless complications and quarrels. In the Islamic world, successors could be designated by the current ruler or elected by the community; here, too, struggles over succession were frequent. Third, ruling families elevated their power through conquest or alliance—by ordering armies forcibly to extend their domains, or by marrying their royal offspring to rulers of other states or members of other elite households, a technique widely practiced in Europe. Once it established legitimacy, the typical royal family would consolidate power by enacting coercive laws and punishments and sending emissaries to govern distant territories. A ruling family would also establish standing armies and new administrative structures to collect taxes and to oversee building projects that proclaimed royal power.

As we will see in the next three sections of this chapter, the innovative state building that occurred in the wake of the plague's devastation would not have been as successful had it not drawn on older traditions. In Europe, a cultural flourishing based largely on ancient Greek and Roman models gave rise to thinkers who proposed new views of governance. The peoples of the Islamic world held fiercely to their religion as successor states, notably the Ottoman Empire, absorbed numerous Turkish-speaking groups. The Ming, having failed in their attempts to control northern Vietnam and Korea, renounced the Mongol expansionist legacy and emphasized a return to Han rulership consolidating control of Chinese lands and concentrating on internal markets rather than overseas trade. Many of these regimes lasted for centuries, promoting political institutions and cultural values that became deeply embedded in the fabric of their societies.

The Islamic Heartland

The devastation of the Black Death followed hard on the heels of the Mongol destruction of Islam's most important city, Baghdad, and Islam's old political order. Nonetheless, these two catastrophes prepared the way for new Islamic states to emerge. The old, Arabic-speaking Islamic world remained vital, still at the heart of Islam geographically, but it now had to yield authority to new rulers and religious men. These societies now included large Turkish- and Persian-speaking populations as well. The new Islamic world occupied a vast geographical triangle. It stretched from Anatolia in the west to the Khurasan region of Persia and Afghanistan in the east and to the southern point at Baghdad.

The Ottomans, the Safavids, and the Mughals emerged as the dominant states in the old Islamic world in the early sixteenth century. They exploited the rich agrarian resources of the Indian Ocean regions and the Mediterranean Sea basin, and they benefited from a brisk seaborne and overland trade. By the mid-sixteenth century the Mughals controlled the northern Indus River valley; the Safavids occupied Persia; and the Ottomans ruled Anatolia, the Arab world, and much of southern and eastern Europe. Here we will explore in depth the Ottoman Empire, which emerged first and endured the longest of the three. (See Chapter 12 for a fuller discussion of the Mughals and Chapter 14 for more on the Safavids.)

THE OTTOMAN EMPIRE

The rise of the **Ottoman Empire** owed as much to innovative administrative techniques and religious tolerance as to military strength. Although the Mongols considered Anatolia to be a borderland region of little economic importance, their military forays in the late thirteenth century opened up the region to new political forces. The ultimate victors here were the Ottoman Turks. They transformed themselves from warrior bands roaming the borderlands between Islamic and Christian worlds into rulers of a settled state and, finally, into sovereigns of a far-flung highly bureaucratic empire (see Map 11.2). Under their chief, Osman (r. 1299–1326), the Turkish Ottomans formalized a stern and disciplined warrior ethos. They triumphed over their rivals by adapting the techniques of administration from their neighbors and by attracting these groups to their rule. In time, not only did the Ottoman state win the favor of Islamic clerics, but it also became the champion of Sunni Islam throughout the Islamic world.

MAP 11.2 | The Ottoman Empire, 1300–1566

This map charts the expansion of the Ottoman state from the time of its founder, Osman, through the reign of Suleiman, the empire's most illustrious ruler. Identify the earliest part of the empire under Osman. Then identify all the areas of conquest under Suleiman.

• Against whom did the Ottomans fight between the years 1326 and 1566?

• What were the geographic limits of the empire?

• According to your reading, how did Ottoman rulers promote unity among such a diverse population?

By the mid-fourteenth century, the Ottomans had expanded into the Balkans, becoming the most powerful force in the eastern Mediterranean and western Asia. By the early sixteenth century, the state controlled a vast territory, stretching in the west to the Moroccan border, in the north to Hungary and Moldavia, in the south through the Arabian Peninsula, and in the east to the Persian border. What was impressive and new within the Islamic world was the Ottomans' elaborate administrative hierarchy, atop which stood the sultan. Below him was a military and civilian bureaucracy, whose task was to demand obedience and revenue from subjects. The bureaucracy's discipline enabled the sultan to expand his realm, which in turn forced him to invest in an even larger bureaucracy.

The empire's spectacular expansion was primarily a military affair. To recruit followers, the Ottomans promised wealth and glory to new subjects. This was an expensive undertaking, but territorial expansion generated vast financial and administrative rewards. Moreover, by spreading the spoils of conquest and lucrative administrative positions, rulers bought off potentially unhappy subordinates. Still, without military might, the Ottomans would not have enjoyed the successes associated with the brilliant reigns of Murad II (r. 1421–1451) and his appropriately named successor, Mehmed the Conqueror (r. 1451–1481).

Mehmed's most spectacular triumph was the conquest of Constantinople, an ambition for Muslim rulers ever since the birth of Islam. Mehmed left no doubt that this was his primary goal: shortly after his coronation he vowed to capture the capital of the Byzantine Empire, a city of immense strategic and commercial importance, which had withstood Muslim efforts at conquest for centuries. First he built a fortress of his own to prevent European vessels from reaching the capital. Then, by promising his soldiers free access to booty and portraying the city's conquest as a holy cause, he amassed a huge army that outnumbered the defending force of 7,000 by more than ten times. For forty days his troops bombarded Constantinople's massive walls with artillery that included enormous cannons built by Hungarian and Italian engineers. On May 29, 1453, Ottoman troops overwhelmed the surviving soldiers and took the ancient Roman and Christian capital of Byzantium—which Mehmed promptly renamed Istanbul.

The Tools of Empire Building The Ottomans adopted Byzantine administrative practices to unify their enlarged state and incorporated many of Byzantium's powerful families into it. Their dynastic power was, however, not only military; it also rested on a firm religious foundation. At the center of this empire were the sultans, who combined a warrior ethos with an unwavering devotion to Islam. Describing themselves as the "shadow of God" on earth, they claimed to be caretakers for the welfare of the Islamic faith. Throughout the empire, the sultans devoted substantial resources to the construction of elaborate mosques and to the support of Islamic schools. As self-appointed defenders of the faithful, the sultans assumed the role of protectors of the holy cities on the Arabian Peninsula and of Jerusalem, while working to unite the realm's diverse lands and peoples and constantly striving to extend the borders of Islam. During the reign of Suleiman (r. 1520–1566), the Ottomans reached the height of their territorial expansion. Under his administration, the Ottoman state ruled over 20 to 30 million people. By the time Suleiman died, the Ottoman

The Fall of Constantinople The use of heavy artillery in the forty-day siege of Constantinople was instrumental to the Ottoman victory. At the center of this Turkish miniature is one such cannon, possibly of Hungarian origin, which required hundreds of men and oxen to transport and secure outside the city walls.

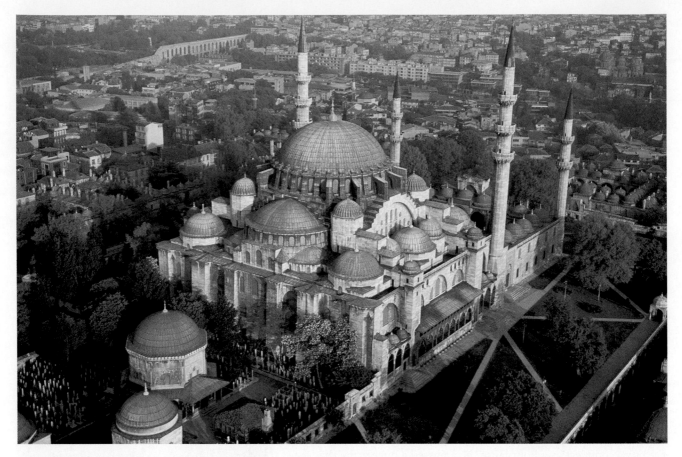

The Suleymaniye Mosque Built by Sultan Suleiman in the mid-sixteenth century to crown his achievements, the Suleymaniye Mosque was designed by the architect Sinan to dominate the city. What message do you think Suleiman was attempting to convey in building the mosque across a park from the Hagia Sophia, a formerly Christian basilica built in the sixth century by Justinian upon foundations going back 200 years earlier to the time of Constantine and his sons?

Empire bridged Europe and the Arab world. Istanbul by then was a dynamic imperial hub, dispatching bureaucrats and military men to oversee a vast domain.

Istanbul's **Topkapi Palace** exhibited the Ottomans' view of governance, the sultans' emphasis on religion, and the continuing influence of Ottoman familial traditions. Laid out by Mehmed II, the palace complex projected a vision of Istanbul as the center of the world. As a way to promote the sultan's magnificent power, architects designed the complex so that the buildings containing the imperial household were nestled behind layers of outer courtyards, in a mosaic of mosques, courts, and special dwellings for the sultan's harem. The harem had its own hierarchy of thousands of women, from the sultan's mother and consorts to the slave women who waited on them, and it became a formidable political force at the heart of Ottoman power.

The growing importance of Topkapi Palace as the command post of empire represented a crucial transition in the history of Ottoman rulers. Not only was the palace the place where future bureaucrats received their training; it was also the place where the chief bureaucrat, the grand vizier, carried out the day-to-day running of the empire. Whereas the early sultans had led their soldiers into battle personally and had met face-to-face with their kinsmen, the later rulers withdrew into the sacredness of the palace, venturing out only occasionally for grand ceremonies. Still, every Friday, subjects lined up outside the palace to introduce their petitions, ask for favors, and seek justice. If they were lucky, the

The Topkapi Palace A view of the inner courtyard of Topkapi's seraglio (sequestered living space), where the sultan and his harem lived. What does this image suggest about how the sultan used the palace to run his empire?

sultans would be there to greet them—but they did so behind grated glass, issuing their decisions by tapping on the window. The palace thus projected a sense of majestic, distant wonder, a home fit for semidivine rulers.

Diversity and Control The fact that the Ottoman Empire endured into the twentieth century owed much to the ruling elite's ability to gain the support and employ the talents of exceedingly diverse populations. After all, neither conquest nor conversion eliminated cultural differences in the empire's distant provinces. Thus, for example, the Ottomans' language policy was one of flexibility and tolerance. Although Ottoman Turkish was the official language of administration, Arabic was the primary language of the Arab provinces, the common tongue of street life. Within the empire's European corner, many people spoke their own languages. From the fifteenth century onward, the Ottoman Empire was perhaps more multilingual than any of its rivals.

In politics, as in language, the Ottomans showed flexibility and tolerance. The imperial bureaucracy permitted extensive regional autonomy. In fact, Ottoman military cadres perfected a technique for absorbing newly conquered territories into the empire by parceling them out as revenue-producing units among loyal followers and kin. Regional appointees could collect local taxes, part of which they earmarked for Istanbul and part of which they pocketed for themselves. (This was a common administrative device for many world dynasties ruling extensive domains.)

Like other empires, the Ottoman state was always in danger of losing control over its provincial rulers. Local potentates—the group that the imperial center allowed to rule in their distant regions—found that great distances enabled them to operate independently from central authority. These authorities kept larger amounts of tax revenues than Istanbul deemed proper. So, to limit their autonomy, the Ottomans established the janissaries, a corps of infantry soldiers and bureaucrats who owed direct allegiance to the sultan. The system at its high point involved a conscription of Christian youths from the empire's European lands. This conscription, called the **devshirme**, required each village to hand over a certain number of males between the ages of eight and eighteen. Uprooted from their families and villages, selected for their fine physiques and good looks, these young men were converted to Islam and sent to farms to build up their bodies and learn Turkish. A select few were moved on to Topkapi Palace to learn Ottoman military, religious, and administrative techniques. Some of these men later enjoyed exceptional careers in the arts and sciences—such as the architect Sinan, who designed the Suleymaniye Mosque. Recipients of the best education available in the Islamic world, and trained in Ottoman ways, instructed in the use of modern weaponry, and deprived of family connections, the *devshirme* recruits were prepared to serve the sultan (and the empire as a whole) rather than the interests of any particular locality or ethnic group.

Thus, the Ottomans established their legitimacy via military skill, religious backing, and a loyal bureaucracy. They artfully balanced the decentralizing tendencies of the outlying regions with the centralizing forces of the imperial capital. Relying on a careful mixture of religious faith, imperial patronage, and cultural tolerance, the sultans curried loyalty and secured political stability. Indeed, the Ottoman Empire was so strong and stable that it dominated the coveted and highly contested trading crossroads between Europe and Asia for many centuries. Thus, its consolidation had powerful consequences for European efforts to rebuild their societies after the plague; above all, it closed off traditional overland trade routes to India and China.

Western Christendom

No region suffered more from the Black Death than Western Christendom, and no region made a more spectacular comeback. From 1100 to 1300, Europe had enjoyed a surge in population, rapid economic growth, and significant technological and intellectual innovations, only to see these achievements halted in the fourteenth century by famine and the Black Death. Europeans responded by creating new political and cultural forms. New dynastic states arose, competing with one another, and a movement called the Renaissance revived Europe's connections with its Greek and Roman past and produced masterpieces of art, architecture, and other forms of thought.

THE CATHOLIC CHURCH, STATE BUILDING, AND ECONOMIC RECOVERY

In the aftermath of famine and plague, the peoples of Western Christendom, like those in the Muslim world, looked to their religious beliefs and institutions as foundations for recovery. The faith of many had been severely tested, and religious authorities had to struggle to reclaim their power. To begin with, the late medieval western church found itself divided at the top (at one point during this period there were three popes) and challenged from below, both by individuals pursuing alternative kinds of spirituality and by increasing demands on the clergy and church administration. Disappointment with the clergy smoldered. The peasantry despaired at the absence of clergy when they were so greatly needed during the famines and Black Death. With groups like the Beghards challenging the clergy's right to define religious doctrine and practices, the church fought back, identifying all that was suspect and demanding strict obedience to the true faith. This entailed the persecution of heretics, Jews, Muslims in the Iberian Peninsula, homosexuals, prostitutes, and "witches." During this period the church expanded its charitable and bureaucratic functions, providing alms to the urban poor and registering births, deaths, and economic transactions. Crucially, faced with challenges to its authority, the church associated itself with secular rulers, lending moral authority to kings who claimed to rule "by divine right."

Europe's political rulers aligned themselves with church leaders to rebuild their states and consolidate their power. One royal family, the Habsburgs, drew on their Catholic religious traditions and established a powerful, long-lasting dynasty that would rule large parts of central Europe for centuries to follow. Habsburg leaders were elected to head the

COMPARISON

COMPARE the role religious belief systems played in rebuilding Europe and Islam in the fourteenth and fifteenth centuries.

federation of states known as the Holy Roman Empire almost continuously from 1438 to 1806, and for a time they ruled Spain and its New World colonies. Yet even at the height of its power in the early sixteenth century, the Habsburg monarchy never succeeded in restoring an integrated empire to western Europe.

In 1450 Western Christendom had no central government, no official tongue, and only a few successful commercial centers, mostly in the Mediterranean basin (see Map 11.3).

MAP 11.3 | Western Christendom, 1400–1500

Europe was a region divided by dynastic rivalries during the fifteenth century. Locate the most powerful regional dynasties on the map: Portugal, Castile, Aragon, France, Burgundy, England, and the Holy Roman Empire.

• Which areas witnessed the greatest warfare during this period?

• On the basis of this map and the reading, why do you think that was the case?

• Contrast the size of political units in this map with those in Maps 11.2 and 11.4. Explain the significance of the differences.

Joan of Arc: A Charismatic Leader in a Time of Social Turmoil

The immense historical impact of a French peasant girl, Joan of Arc, demonstrates the importance of charismatic individuals—even women in male-dominated societies—during periods of social turmoil. As Europe endured plagues, famines, and war, its people sought help through the special talents of women, even in areas like warfare. Indeed, if not for Joan of Arc, the country we know today as France might not exist. Gender is also a useful approach to study the relations between men and women in a society. World historians use it as a comparative theme across cultures and time, which makes it an even more useful lens for historical analysis.

Appearing on the scene in 1429, as the English seemed to be winning the Hundred Years' War, she rallied the French against the English occupiers and turned the tide of the war. By giving religious sanction, as well as military succor, to the Valois monarch Charles VII, she made possible the consolidation of France and left Europe an inspiring image of the female warrior-saint.

The world of Joan's childhood was a chaotic one, in which English lords were laying claim to various French-speaking principalities. By 1420, Valois authority had been greatly eroded, and English armies were conquering more and more French towns. In 1428, the English laid siege to Orléans, a large town in north-central France. To contemporaries, it seemed a symbolic battle: as Orléans went, they thought, so the war would go—and so would God wish it to go.

This is the point at which the paths of a seventeen-year-old peasant girl and the monarch of France crossed. Beginning at about age thirteen, the shy girl had received visions of saints who instructed her to rescue Orléans and bring France's ruler to be crowned king at Reims Cathedral. (He had not been crowned there, in the tradition of all French kings, because the English armies controlled Reims, Paris, and northern France.) For five years Joan resisted, but at last she obeyed her celestial advisers. Granted an audience with Charles VII in 1429, Joan impressed him with her piety and her passionate devotion to the Valois crown. He concluded that God really had sent her to serve France's cause—and his own. Joan won command of 7,000 to 8,000 men; then, wearing a suit of armor and brandishing a sword, she marched to relieve Orléans. Joan directed the assault with brilliance and inspired the French forces; her charisma came not only from a tradition of female Christian "seers," but also from the peculiarity of her appearance (a young woman in male attire) and her appeal to French speakers who resented rule by English "outsiders." After driving the English from Orléans, she then pressed on to Reims; here, thanks to her military victories, Charles VII was crowned, fulfilling her visions. He was now king of France—and though the war continued, the tide now turned in favor of the French.

The tide for Joan, however, turned for the worse. Although she continued to direct the troops with remarkable savvy, she failed to force open the gates of Paris, and jealous courtiers around Charles began to question her divine authority. She was wounded, then taken prisoner. After a year in English captivity she faced the

The feudal system of a lords' control over the peasantry (see Chapter 10), which was now in decline, left a legacy of political fragmentation and enduring elite privileges, which made the consolidation of a unified Christian Europe even more difficult to achieve. Europe's linguistic diversity reflected its political fragmentation. No single ruler or language united peoples, even when they shared a religion. Latin lost ground as rulers chose various regional dialects (e.g., French, Spanish, English) to be their official state language, whereas the written literary Chinese script remained a key administrative tool for China's dynasts, and in the Islamic world Arabic was the common language of faith and Turkish the language of administration.

Those who sought to rule the emerging states faced numerous obstacles. For example, rival claimants to the throne financed threatening private armies. Also, the clergy demanded and received privileges in the form of access to land and relief from taxation; they often meddled in politics themselves, and the church became a formidable economic

Inquisition and was found guilty of heresy, on the grounds that her visions were false and misleading. On May 30, 1431, she was burned at the stake in the marketplace in the town of Rouen. Since that time she has stood as a heroic and charismatic martyr, and the French have often invoked her name to awaken patriotism against foreign threats.

The fact that this young, illiterate woman played such an important role in the history of European warfare and state formation testifies to the fact that male aristocrats, intellectuals, and clerics were not the only important actors. At the right place, at the right time, a woman could use courage, faith, and intelligence to make her visions prevail.

QUESTIONS FOR ANALYSIS

- What other heroic figures, male or female, does Joan of Arc remind you of and why?
- Why do you think Charles VII failed to rescue Joan of Arc from her English prison?

Explore Further

Régine Pernoud and Marie-Véronique Clin, *Joan of Arc: Her Story*, trans. Jeremy Adams (1999).

powerhouse. And once the printing press became available in Europe in the 1460s, printers circulated anonymous pamphlets criticizing the court and the clergy. Some states had consultative political bodies—such as the Estates General in France, the Cortes in Spain, and Parliament in England—in which princes formally asked representatives of their people for advice and, in the case of the English Parliament, for consent to new forms of taxation. Such political bodies gave no voice to common men and no representation to women. But they did allow the collective expression of grievances against overbearing policies.

Out of the chaos of famine, disease, and warfare, the diverse peoples of Europe found a political way forward. This path involved the formation of centralized dynastic monarchies. A **monarchy** is a political system in which one individual holds supreme power and passes that power on to his or her next of kin. Often in competition with the new monarchies, a handful of European city-states, in which a narrow group of wealthy and influential voters selected their leaders, survived right up to the nineteenth century and in some cases into the twentieth. Consolidation of these states occurred sometimes through strategic marriages but more often through warfare, both between princely families and with local aristocratic allies and foreign mercenaries (see **Current Trends in World History: Joan of Arc**). Political stabilization was swiftest in southern Europe, where economies rebounded through seaborne trade with Southwest Asia. The stabilization of Italian city-states such as Venice and Florence, and of monarchical rule in Portugal and Spain, led to an economic and cultural flowering known as the Renaissance. In northern and western Europe, the process took longer. In England and France, in particular, internal feuding, regional warfare, and religious fragmentation delayed recovery for decades (see Chapter 12).

POLITICAL CONSOLIDATION AND TRADE IN THE IBERIAN PENINSULA

War and overseas trade played a central role in the emergence of new dynasties in Portugal and Spain. Through the fourteenth century, Portuguese Christians devoted themselves to fighting the Moors, who were Muslim occupants of North Africa, the western Sahara, and the Iberian Peninsula. After the Portuguese crossed the Strait of Gibraltar and seized the Moorish fortresses at Ceuta, in Morocco, their ships could sail between the Mediterranean and the Atlantic without Muslim interference. With that threat diminished, the Portuguese perceived their neighbor, Castile (part of which is now Spain), as their chief foe. Under João I (r. 1385–1433) Portugal defeated the Castilians, becoming the dominant power on the Iberian peninsula. No longer preoccupied with Castilian competition, the Portuguese sought new territories and trading opportunities in the North Atlantic and along the West African coasts. João's son Prince Henrique, known later as Henry the Navigator, further expanded the royal family's domain by supporting expeditions down the coast of Africa and offshore to the Atlantic islands of the Madeiras and the Azores. The west and central coasts of Africa and the islands of the North and South Atlantic, including the Cape Verde Islands, São Tomé, Principe, and Fernando Po, soon became Portuguese ports of call.

Portuguese monarchs granted the Atlantic islands to nobles as hereditary possessions on condition that the grantees colonize them, and soon the colonizers were establishing lucrative sugar plantations. In gratitude, noble families and merchants threw their political weight behind the king. Subsequent monarchs continued to cultivate local aristocrats' support for monarchical authority, thus ensuring smooth succession to the crown for members of the royal family.

In Spain, a new dynasty also emerged, though the road was difficult. Medieval Spain comprised rival kingdoms that quarreled ceaselessly. Within those kingdoms, several religions coexisted: Muslims, Jews, and Christians lived side by side in relative harmony, and Muslim armies still occupied strategic posts in the south. Over time, marriages and the formation of kinship ties among nobles and between royal lineages yielded a new political order. One by one, the major houses of the Spanish kingdoms intermarried, culminating in the wedding of Isabella of Castile and Ferdinand of Aragon (1469). This marriage linked Castile, wealthy and populous, to Aragon, which enjoyed an extended trading network in the Mediterranean. Together, the monarchs brought unruly nobles and distant towns under their control. They topped off their achievements by marrying their children into other European royal families—especially the Habsburgs, central Europe's most powerful dynasty.

Thus, Spain's two most important provinces were joined, and Spain later became a state to be reckoned with.

The new Spanish rulers sent Christian armies south to push Muslim forces out of the Iberian Peninsula. By the mid-fifteenth century only Granada, a strategic linchpin overlooking the straits between the Mediterranean and the Atlantic, remained in Muslim hands. After a long and costly siege, Christian forces captured the fortress there in 1492. This was a victory of enormous symbolic importance, as joyous as the fall of Constantinople was depressing (for Christians).

The Inquisition and Westward Exploration Isabella and Ferdinand sought to drive all non-Catholics out of Spain. Terrified by Ottoman incursions into Europe, they launched the **Inquisition** in 1481, taking aim especially against *conversos*—converted Jews

Ferdinand and Isabella Entering Granada This altar relief, sculpted by Felipe Vigarny in the early sixteenth century, depicts the triumphant entrance of King Ferdinand and Queen Isabella into the city of Granada after their conquest of this last Muslim stronghold in Spain. Why would such an image be depicted on an altar? In what ways does the image show power and distinction among the individuals depicted?

and Muslims, whom they suspected were Christians only in name. When Granada fell, the crown ordered the expulsion of all Jews from Spain. After 1499, a more tolerant attempt to convert the Moors (Muslims) by persuasion gave way to forced conversion—or emigration. All told, almost half a million people were forced to flee the Spanish kingdoms. This lack of tolerance meant that Spain, like other European states in this era, became increasingly homogenous. With fewer groups vying for influence within their territories, rulers turned their attention outward, fueling rivalries between the various European states.

So strong was the tide of Spanish fervor by late 1491 that the monarchs listened now to a Genoese navigator whose pleas for patronage they had previously rejected. Christopher Columbus promised them unimaginable riches that could finance their military campaigns and bankroll a crusade to liberate Jerusalem from Muslim hands. Off he sailed with a royal patent that guaranteed the monarchs a share of all he discovered. Soon the Spanish economy was reorienting itself toward the Atlantic, and Spain's merchants, missionaries, and soldiers were preparing for conquest and profiteering in what had been, just a few years before, a blank space on the map.

THE RENAISSANCE

Just as the Ming harkened back to Han Chinese traditions and the Ottomans looked to Sunni Islam to point the way forward, so European elites looked to their own traditions for guidance as they rebuilt after the devastation of the plague. They found inspiration in ancient Greek and Roman institutions and ideas. Europe's extraordinary political and economic revival also involved a powerful outpouring of cultural achievements, led by Italian scholars and artists and financed by bankers, churchmen, and nobles. Much later, scholars coined the word **Renaissance** to characterize the cultural flourishing of the Italian city-states, France, the Netherlands, England, and the Holy Roman Empire in the period 1430–1550. What was being "reborn" was ancient Greek and Roman art and learning—knowledge that could help people understand an expanding world and support the rights of secular individuals to exert power in it. Although the Renaissance was largely funded by popes and Christian kings, it challenged the authority of traditional religious elites, breaking the medieval church's monopoly on answers to the big questions. The movement emphasized secular forms of learning rather than just Christian doctrine and a more human-centered understanding of the cosmos.

The Renaissance was all about new exposure to the old—to classical texts and ancient art and architectural forms. Although some Greek and Roman texts were known in Europe and the Islamic world, the use of the printing press made others accessible to western scholars for the first time. Scholars now realized that the pre-Christian Greeks and Romans had developed powerful means of representing and caring for the human body. Having studied the world directly, without the need to square their observations with biblical information, the ancients had much to teach about geography, astronomy, and architecture and about how to govern states and armies. For Renaissance scholars it was no longer enough to understand Christian doctrine and to concern themselves with the next world. One had to go back to the original, classical sources in order to understand the human condition. This in turn required the learning of languages and history. Scholarship that attempted to return to Greek and Roman sources became known as **humanism**.

Because political and religious powers were not united in Europe (as they were in China and the Islamic world), scholars and artists seeking sponsors for their work could play one side against the other, or, alternatively, could suffer both clerical and political

COMPARISON

COMPARE the way art and architecture reflected the political realities of Europe and Islam after the Black Death.

Renaissance Masterpieces Leonardo da Vinci's *The Last Supper* (*left*) depicts Christ's disciples reacting to his announcement that one of them will betray him. Michelangelo's *David* (*right*) stands over thirteen feet high and was conceived as an expression of Florentine civic ideals. In what ways do these Renaissance masterpieces draw on the principles of humanism and reflect a return to western "classics" of the Greco-Roman world?

persecution. Michelangelo (1475–1564), a leading painter, sculptor, architect, and engineer of the age, completed commissions for the famous Florentine bankers and political leaders of the Medici family, for the Florentine Wool Guild, and for Pope Julius II. Peter Paul Rubens painted for the courts of France, Spain, England, and the Netherlands, as well as selling paintings on the open market. These two painters, renowned for showing a great deal of flesh, frequently offended conservative church officials. Most support for the arts, however, came either from the church or individual clergymen, and virtually all secular donors were devout believers who commissioned works with religious themes. The Dutch scholar Desiderius Erasmus ridiculed corrupt popes and the clergy with the patronage of English, Dutch, and French supporters, while remaining a Catholic, an ordained cleric, and an opponent of Reformation doctrines. Conflicts within the Catholic Church, between the church and secular leaders, and among secular leaders and wealthy private citizens enabled artists to present challenging images and ideas with an unusual independence.

Gradually, a network of educated men and women took shape that was not wholly dependent on either the church or the state or a single princely patron. Classical knowledge gave individuals the means to challenge political, clerical, and aesthetic authority. Moreover, rivalries between Europe's relatively small states and city-states allowed many of these scholars to dodge the authorities by fleeing to neighboring communities. Of course, they could also use their learning to defend the older elites: for example, numerous lawyers and scholars continued to work for the popes in defending the papacy. At the same time, in contrast, men like Erasmus and later Martin Luther (the leading figure of the Reformation in the sixteenth century) looked to secular princes to support their critical scholarship. In Florence, Niccolò Machiavelli wrote the most famous treatise on authoritarian power, *The Prince* (1513). Machiavelli argued that political leadership required mastering the rules of modern statecraft, even if in some cases this meant disregarding moral imperatives. Holding and exercising power were vital ends in themselves, he claimed; traditional ideas of civic virtue should not deter rulers, like those of the Medici family, from maintaining control over society.

With Renaissance ideas challenging traditional authority and rulers facing a range of internal and external obstacles, the new monarchies of Europe were not all immediately successful in consolidating power and unifying peoples. In France and England, for example, the great age of monarchy had yet to dawn. Even when stable states did arise in Europe, they were fairly small compared to the Ottoman and Ming empires. In the mid-sixteenth century, Portugal and Spain, Europe's two most expansionist states, had populations of 1 million and 9 million, respectively. England, excluding Wales, was a mere 3 million in 1550. Only France, with 17 million, had a population close to the Ottoman Empire's 25 million. And these numbers paled in comparison with Ming China's population of nearly 200 million in 1550. But in Europe, small could be advantageous. Portugal's relatively small population meant that the crown had fewer groups to control. In the world of finance, the most successful merchants were those inhabiting the smaller Italian city-states and, a bit later, the cities of the northern Netherlands. The Florentines developed sophisticated banking techniques, created extensive networks of agents throughout Europe and the Mediterranean, and served as bankers to the popes. At the same time, the Renaissance—which flourished in the city-states and newly stabilized monarchies—made elite European culture more cosmopolitan and independent from government authority, even if it could not unify the states and peoples who cultivated it.

Ming China

Like the Europeans, the Chinese saw their stable worldview and political order crumble under the catastrophes of human and bacterial invasions. Moreover, like the Europeans, people in China had long regarded outsiders as "barbarians" and balked at being ruled by outsiders. Together, the Mongols and the Black Death upended the political and intellectual foundations of what had appeared to be the world's most integrated society. The Mongols brought the Yuan dynasty to power; then the plague devastated China and prepared the way for the emergence of the Ming dynasty. The Ming dynasty, ruled by ethnically Han Chinese, defined itself against its foreign predecessors. Ming emperors sought to reinforce everything Chinese. In particular, they supported China's vast internal agricultural markets in an attempt to minimize dependence on merchants and foreign trade.

RESTORING ORDER

In the chaotic fourteenth century, as plague and famine ravaged China and the Mongol Yuan dynasty collapsed, only a strong military movement capable of overpowering other groups could restore order. That intervention began at the hands of a poor young man who had trained in the Red Turban Movement: Zhu Yuanzhang.

It soon became clear that Zhu had a much grander design for China than the ambitions of most warlords. When he took Nanjing in 1356, he renamed it Yingtian ("In response to Heaven"). Lifted by subsequent successful military campaigns, Zhu (r. 1368–1398) took the imperial title of Hongwu ("expansive and martial") Emperor and proclaimed the founding of the Ming ("brilliant") dynasty in 1368. Soon thereafter, his troops met little resistance when they seized the Yuan capital of Beijing, causing the Mongol emperor to flee to his homeland in the steppe. It would, however, take Hongwu almost another twenty years to reunify the entire country.

CENTRALIZATION UNDER THE MING

Hongwu and successive Ming emperors had to rebuild a devastated society from the ground up. Although in the past China had experienced natural catastrophes, wars, and social dislocation, the plague's legacy was devastation on an unprecedented scale. It left the new rulers with the formidable challenge of rebuilding the great cities, restoring respect for ruling elites, and reconstructing the bureaucracy.

Imperial Grandeur and Kinship The rebuilding began with the Hongwu Emperor, whose capital at Nanjing reflected imperial grandeur. When the dynasty's third emperor, the Yongle ("perpetual happiness") Emperor, relocated the capital to Beijing, he flaunted an even more grandiose style, employing around 100,000 artisans and 1 million laborers to build this new capital, including its Forbidden City. The city had three separate walled enclosures. Inside the outer city walls sprawled the imperial city; within its walls lay the palace city, the Forbidden City. Traffic within the walled sections navigated through broad boulevards leading to the different gates, above which imposing towers soared. The palace compound, where the imperial family resided, had more than 9,000 rooms. Anyone standing in the front courts, which measured more than 400 yards on a side and boasted marble terraces and carved railings, would gasp at the sense of awesome power. That was precisely the effect the Ming emperors wanted, just as the Ottoman sultans did in building Topkapi Palace.

Marriage and kinship buttressed the power of the Ming imperial household, much like the dynastic strategies of Europe. The Ming dynasty's founder married the adopted daughter of a leading Red Turban rebel (her father, according to legend, was a convicted murderer), thereby consolidating his power and eliminating a threat. Empress Ma, as she was known, became Hongwu's principal wife and was praised for her compassion. Emerging as the kinder face of the regime, she tempered the harsh and sometimes cruel disposition of her spouse. He had numerous other consorts as well, including Korean and Mongol women, who bore him twenty-six sons and sixteen daughters (similar to, although on smaller scale than, the sultan's harem at Ottoman Topkapi).

COMPARISON

COMPARE the ways rulers rebuilt unified states and their levels of success in China, Islam, and Europe.

The Forbidden City The Yongle Emperor relocated the capital to Beijing, where he began the construction of the Forbidden City, or imperial palace, in the early fifteenth century. The palace was designed to inspire awe in all who saw it. In what ways do the partitions of space and the activities of people within that space appear to support imperial grandeur?

Building a Bureaucracy Faced with the challenge of reestablishing order out of turmoil, Hongwu initially sought to rule through his kinsmen—by giving imperial princes generous stipends, command of large garrisons, and significant autonomy in running their domains. However, when the princes' power began to threaten the court, Hongwu slashed their stipends, reduced their privileges, and took control of their garrisons. No longer dependent on these men, he established an imperial bureaucracy beholden only to him and to his successors. These officials won appointments through their outstanding performance on a reinstated civil service examination.

In addition, Hongwu took other steps to install a centralized system of rule. He assigned bureaucrats to oversee the manufacture of porcelain, cotton, and silk products, as well as tax collection. He reestablished the Confucian school system as a means of selecting a cadre of loyal officials (not unlike the Ottoman janissaries and administrators). He also set up local networks of villages to rebuild irrigation systems and to supervise reforestation projects to prevent flooding—with the astonishing result that the amount of land reclaimed nearly tripled within eight years. For water control, over 40,000 reservoirs underwent repairs or new construction. Historians estimate that Hongwu's reign oversaw the planting around Nanjing of about 1 billion trees, which were later used in building a maritime expedition fleet in the early fifteenth century.

Ming Deities A pantheon of deities worshipped during the Ming dynasty, demonstrating the rich religious culture of the period. In what ways does this document show Ming religious beliefs?

The imperial palace not only projected the image of a power center, it *was* the center of power. Every official received his appointment by the emperor through the Ministry of Personnel. Hongwu eliminated the post of prime minister (he executed the man who held the post) and ruled directly. Ming bureaucrats had to kneel before the emperor. The drawback of this centralized control, of course, was that the Ming emperor had to keep tabs on this immense system. Hongwu constantly moved his bureaucrats around, sometimes fortifying the administration, sometimes undermining it lest it become too autonomous. Over time, Hongwu nurtured a bureaucracy far more extensive than that of the Ottomans. The Ming thus established the most highly centralized system of government of all the monarchies of this period.

Religion under the Ming Just as the Ottoman sultans projected themselves as Muslim rulers, calling themselves the shadow of God, and European monarchs claimed to rule by divine right, so the Ming emperors enhanced their legitimacy by drawing on ancient Chinese religious traditions. Citing the mandate of heaven, the emperor revised and strengthened the elaborate rites and ceremonies that had supported dynastic power for centuries. Official rituals, such as those related to the gods of soil and grain, reinforced political and social classes, portraying the rulers as the moral and spiritual benefactors of their subjects. In lavish ceremonies, the emperor engaged in sacrificial rites, cultivating his image as mediator between the human and the spiritual worlds. The message was clear: the gods were on the side of the Ming household.

MING RULERSHIP

Conquest and defense helped establish the realm, and bureaucracy kept it functioning. The empire's scale (see Map 11.4) required complex administration. To many outsiders

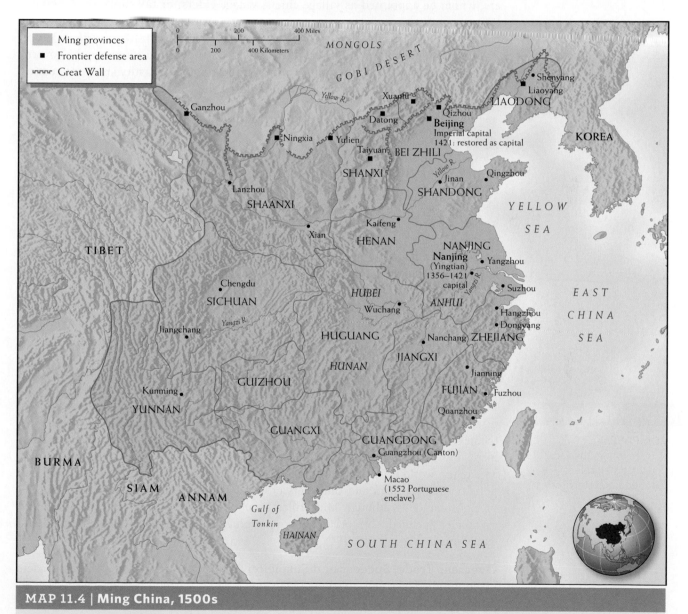

MAP 11.4 | Ming China, 1500s

The Ming state was one of the largest empires at this time—and the most populous. Using the scale, determine the length of its coastline and its internal borders.

- What were the two Ming capitals and the three main seaport trading cities and how far are they from one another?
- According to the map, where did the Ming rulers expect the greatest threat to their security?
- How did the Ming rulers view foreign contact and exchange during this period?

(especially Europeans, whose region was in a state of constant war), Ming stability and centralization appeared to be political wizardry.

Ming rulers worried in particular about maintaining the support of ordinary people in the countryside. The emperor wished to be seen as the special guardian of his subjects. He wanted their allegiance as well as their taxes and labor. But during hard times, poor farmers were reluctant to provide resources—taxes or services—to distant officials. For these reasons and because the emperor distrusted state bureaucrats, Hongwu preferred to entrust management of the rural world to local leaders, whom he appointed as village chiefs, village elders, or tax captains. A popular Chinese proverb was: "The mountain is high and the emperor is far away." Within these communities, the dynasty created a social hierarchy based on age, sex, and kinship. While women's labor remained critical for the village economy, the government reinforced a gender hierarchy by promoting women's chastity and constructing commemorative arches for widows who honored their husbands by refraining from remarrying.

Like the European and Islamic states, the Ming Empire also faced periodic unrest and rebellion. Rebels often proclaimed their own brand of religious beliefs, just as local elites resented central authority. Outright terror helped stymie threats to central authority. In a massive wave of carnage, Hongwu slaughtered anyone who posed a threat to his authority, from the highest of ministers to the lowliest of scribes. From 1376 to 1393, four of his purges condemned close to 100,000 subjects to execution. Yet, despite the emperor's immense power, the Ming Empire remained undergoverned. Indeed, as the population multiplied, there were too few loyal officials to handle local affairs. By the sixteenth and early seventeenth centuries, for example, some 10,000 to 15,000 officials shouldered the responsibility of managing a population exceeding 200 million people. Nonetheless, Hongwu bequeathed to his descendants a set of tools for ruling that drew on subjects' direct loyalty to the emperor and on the intricate workings of an extensive bureaucracy. His legacy enabled his successors to balance local sources of power with the needs of dynastic rulership.

TRADE AND EXPLORATION UNDER THE MING

COMPARISON

COMPARE the ways that the Ming, Iberian, and Ottoman rulers extended their territories and influence.

In the fourteenth century, China began its economic recovery from the devastation of disease and political turmoil. Gradually, political stability allowed trade to revive. Now the new dynasty's merchants reestablished China's preeminence in long-distance commercial exchange. Chinese silk and cotton textiles, as well as fine porcelains, ranked among the world's most coveted luxuries. When a Chinese merchant ship sailed into port, trading partners and onlookers crowded the docks to watch the unloading of precious cargoes. Although Ming rulers' support for overseas ventures wavered and eventually declined, this period saw important developments in Chinese trade and exploration.

Overseas Trade: Success and Suspicion During the Ming period, Chinese traders based in ports such as Hangzhou, Quanzhou, and Guangzhou (Canton) were as energetic as their Muslim counterparts in the Indian Ocean. These ports were home to prosperous merchants and the point of convergence for vast sea-lanes. Leaving the mainland ports, Chinese vessels carried precious wares to offshore islands, the Pescadores, and Taiwan. From there, they sailed on to the ports of Southeast Asia. As entrepôts for global goods, East Asian ports flourished. Former fishing villages developed into major urban centers.

The Ming dynasty viewed overseas expansion with suspicion, however. Hongwu feared that too much contact with the outside world would cause instability and undermine his rule. In fact, he banned private maritime commerce in 1371. But enforcement was lax, and by the late fifteenth century maritime trade once again surged. Because much of the thriving business took place in defiance of official edicts, it led to constant friction between government officials and maritime traders. Although the Ming government ultimately agreed to issue licenses for overseas trade in the mid-sixteenth century, its policies continued to vacillate. To Ming officials, unlike their counterparts in Portugal and Spain, the sea represented problems of order and control rather than opportunities.

The Expeditions of Zheng He One spectacular exception to the Ming's attitude toward maritime trade was a series of officially sponsored expeditions in the early fifteenth century. It was the ambitious third Ming emperor, the Yongle Emperor, who took the initiative. One of his loyal followers was a Muslim whom the Ming army had captured as a boy. The youth was castrated and sent to serve at the court (as a eunuch, he could not continue his family line and so theoretically owed sole allegiance to the emperor). Given the name **Zheng He** (1371–1433), he grew up to be an important military leader. The emperor entrusted him with venturing out to trade, collect tribute, and display China's power to the world.

From 1405 to 1433, Zheng He commanded the world's greatest armada and led seven naval expeditions. His larger ships stretched 400 feet in length (Columbus's Santa Maria was 85 feet), carried hundreds of sailors on four tiers of decks, and maneuvered with sophisticated rudders, nine masts, and watertight compartments. The first expedition set sail with 28,000 men aboard a flotilla of sixty-two large ships and over 200 lesser ones. Zheng He and his entourage aimed to establish tributary relations with far-flung territories—from Southeast Asia to the Indian Ocean ports, to the Persian Gulf, and to the east coast of Africa (see Map 11.5). These expeditions did not seek territorial expansion, but rather control of trade and tribute. When the Yongle Emperor died in 1424, the expeditions lost their most enthusiastic patron. Moreover, by the mid-fifteenth century, there was a revival of military threats from the north, recalling how the maritime-oriented Song

Zheng He's Ship The largest ship in Zheng He's armada had nine staggered masts and twelve silk sails, all designed to demonstrate the grandeur of the Ming dynasty. How much larger was Zheng He's ship compared to Columbus's *Santa Maria* (pictured in the foreground)? How might the differences in size and construction reflect differences in the capabilities and goals of European and Chinese seafaring?

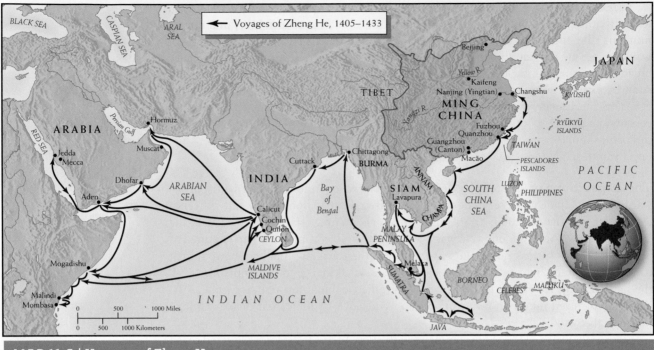

MAP 11.5 | Voyages of Zheng He, 1405–1433

Zheng He's voyages are some of the most famous in world history. Many have speculated about how history might be different if the Chinese emperors had allowed the voyages to continue.

• For how many years did Zheng's voyages go on?

• How far did Zheng go?

• Based on your reading, why did Chinese expeditions not have the same impact as European voyages of exploration toward the end of the fifteenth century, such as those of Columbus?

dynasty had been overrun by invaders from the north (see Chapter 10). Consequently, Ming officials withdrew imperial support for seagoing ventures and instead devoted their energies to overland ventures and defense.

Even though maritime commerce continued without official patronage, the Chinese decision to forgo overseas ventures was momentous. If China remained the wealthiest, most densely settled region of the world with the most fully developed state structures and thriving markets, the empire's wariness of overseas projects deprived merchants and would-be explorers of vital support in an age when others were beginning to look outward and overseas.

Conclusion

The dying and devastation that came with the Black Death caused many transformations, but certain underlying ideals and institutions endured. What changed were mainly the political regimes, which took the blame for the catastrophes. The Yuan dynasty collapsed and regimes in the Muslim world and Western Christendom were replaced by new political forms. In contrast, universal religions and cultural systems persisted even though they underwent vast transformations. A fervent form of Sunni

Islam found its champion in the Ottoman Empire. In Europe, centralizing monarchies appeared in Spain, Portugal, France, and England. The Ming dynasts in China set the stage for a long tenure by claiming the mandate of heaven and stressing China's place at the center of their universe.

The new states and empires had notable differences. These were evident in the ambition of a Ming warlord who established a new dynasty, the military expansionism of Turkish households bordering the Byzantine Empire, and the desire of various European rulers to consolidate power. But interactions among peoples also mattered; this era saw an eagerness to reestablish and expand trade networks, and a desire to convert unbelievers to "the true faith"—be it a form of Islam or an exclusive Christianity.

All of the dynasties surveyed in this chapter faced similar problems. They had to establish legitimacy, ensure smooth succession, deal with religious groups, and forge working relationships with nobles, townspeople, merchants, and peasants. Yet each state developed a distinctive identity; they all combined political innovation, traditional ways of ruling, and ideas borrowed from neighbors. European monarchies achieved significant internal unity, often through warfare with competing states. Ottoman rulers perfected techniques for ruling an ethnically and religiously diverse empire: they moved military forces swiftly, allowed local communities a degree of autonomy, and trained a bureaucracy dedicated to the Ottoman and Sunni Islamic way of life. The Ming fashioned an imperial system based on a Confucian-trained bureaucracy and intense subordination to the emperor so that it could manage a mammoth population. The rising monarchies of Europe and the Ottoman state all blazed with religious fervor and sought to eradicate or subordinate the beliefs of other groups.

The new states displayed unprecedented political and economic powers. All demonstrated military prowess, a desire for stable political and social hierarchies and secure borders, and a drive to expand. Each legitimized its rule via dynastic marriage and succession, state-sanctioned religion, and administrative bureaucracies. Each supported vigorous commercial activity. The Islamic regimes, especially, engaged in long-distance commerce and, by conquest and conversion, extended their holdings.

For Western Christendom, the Ottoman conquests were decisive. They provoked Europeans to establish commercial connections to the east, south, and west. The consequences of their new toeholds would be momentous—just as the Chinese decision to turn away from overseas exploration and commerce meant that China's contact with the outside world would be overland and eastward. As we shall see in Chapter 12, both decisions were instrumental in determining which worlds would come together and which would remain apart.

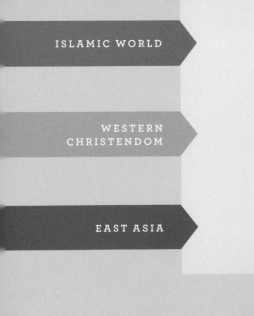

After You Read This Chapter

Go to INQUIZITIVE to see what you've learned—and learn what you've missed—with personalized feedback along the way.

FOCUS ON: *Crisis and Recovery in Afro-Eurasia*

COLLAPSE AND CONSOLIDATION

- Bubonic plague originates in Inner Asia and afflicts people from China to Europe.

- Climate change and famine leaves people vulnerable, while commerce facilitates the spread of disease.

- The plague kills 25 to 65 percent of infected populations and leaves societies in turmoil.

ISLAMIC HEARTLAND

- Ottomans overrun Constantinople and become the primary Sunni regime in the Islamic world.

- The Ottomans establish their legitimacy with military prowess, religious backing, and a loyal bureaucracy.

- Sultans manage decentralizing tendencies of outlying provinces with flexibility and tolerance, relying on religious faith, patronage, and bureaucracy.

WESTERN CHRISTENDOM

- New dynastic monarchies that claim to rule by divine right appear in Portugal, Spain, France, and England.

- The Inquisition takes aim against *conversos*—converted Jews and Muslims.

- A rebirth of classical learning, known as the Renaissance, originates in Italian city-states and spreads throughout western Europe.

MING CHINA

- The Ming dynasty replaces the Mongol Yuan dynasty and rebuilds a strong state from the ground up, claiming a mandate from heaven.

- An elaborate, centralized bureaucracy oversees the revival of infrastructure and long-distance trade.

- The emperor and bureaucracy concentrate on developing internal markets and overland trade at the expense of overseas commerce.

CHRONOLOGY

	1200	1300
ISLAMIC WORLD		Osman begins Ottoman Empire 1299 ◆
		The Black Death arrives in Baghdad 1347 ◆
WESTERN CHRISTENDOM		Black Death reaches Italian port cities 1347 ◆
EAST ASIA		Black Death begins in China 1320 ◆
		Hongwu founds Ming dynasty 1368 ◆

- *Thinking about Exchange Networks* By the fourteenth century, most of the Afro-Eurasian landmass was bound together by multiple exchange networks that functioned on many levels—political, cultural, and commercial. How did these exchange networks facilitate the spread of the plague? In what ways did the spread of the Black Death correspond with and diverge from existing political, cultural, and commercial networks?

- *Thinking about Changing Power Relationships* Fourteenth-century famine, plague, and the accompanying political, economic, and natural crises together triggered powerful, often differing, responses in western Europe, the Ottoman lands, and Ming China. How did men and women at different levels of society respond to the fourteenth-century crises? How did their responses reshape their societies? Pay special attention to the relationships among ordinary men and women, elites, and imperial bureaucracies in all three regions.

- *Thinking about Environmental Impacts* Climatic changes laid the groundwork for the devastation of the Black Death. What environmental developments in Europe, central Asia, and China set the stage for the Black Death?

1. Identify the fourteenth-century crisis that had the greatest impact throughout Afro-Eurasia and explain why: the **Black Death** (and accompanying famine of 1315 and climate change), the Mongol collapse, or political turmoil?

2. Analyze the role of philosophical and religious developments—both elite, like **humanism**, and popular movements, like the **Red Turban Movement** in China—in politics from 1300–1500 and explain how they provided both continuity and change in each society.

3. Explain how the Ottomans employed institutions such as **Topkapi Palace** and the *devshirme* system to consolidate their power?

4. Describe the ways in which regional monarchies and the **Renaissance** responded to the impact of the plague in western Europe? Analyze the role of the **Inquisition** in that process.

5. Explain how the Ming dynasty centralized power in China in the fourteenth and fifteenth centuries? What roles did emperors, bureaucrats, and ordinary people play? Compare Chinese efforts at bureaucratic centralization with those of the Ottomans.

◆ Ottoman armies conquer Constantinople 1453

Suleiman expands and consolidates
Ottoman Empire 1520-1566

◆ Castile and Aragon unite to form Spain 1469

◆ Spain conquers Granada 1492

Zheng He's voyages 1405-1433

400   1500   1600

Competing Perspectives

Cultural Responses to the Black Death

The devastation of the plague in Afro-Eurasia and the upheaval that followed were unprecedented. People desperately sought explanations, particularly religion-based ones, and responded to the turmoil in many different ways. The three primary sources brought together here exemplify radical responses to the crises of the fourteenth century. Qalandar dervishes sprang up in Damascus, Syria, and in Egypt, and renounced the world, living on alms and engaging in highly individualistic practices such as palm reading. European Flagellants also renounced the world, and whipped themselves in public until bruised, swollen, and bloody. Chinese rebels known as the Red Turbans believed that the Mongol rulers had lost the mandate of heaven and deserved to be replaced.

In the first excerpt Giovan Antonio Menavino, a European observer of Ottoman society, gives an obviously biased account of the Qalandars, whom he called the *torlaks*. In the second reading, Robert of Avesbury describes the actions of Flagellants in England during the reign of King Edward III. Finally, we see in the only surviving document written by the rebels themselves—a communiqué sent to the Koryo court in Korea in 1359—that the Red Turbans adopted the rhetoric of the dynastic authorities to establish their own political legitimacy. As you read these documents, consider not only how the groups' views and practices reflect the turmoil of the period, but also pay close attention to what perspective the authors bring to each account.

Source: Ahmet T. Karamustafa, "Dervish Groups in the Ottoman Empire, 1450–1550" from *God's Unruly Friends: Dervish Groups in the Islamic Later Middle Period, 1200–1550*, pp. 6–7. Oneworld Publications, Oxford, 2006. Reprinted with the permission of Oneworld Publications.

PRIMARY SOURCE 11.1

Qalandar Dervishes in the Islamic World (1548), Menavino

Dressed in sheepskins, the torlaks [Qalandars] are otherwise naked, with no headgear. Their scalps are always clean-shaven and well rubbed with oil as a precaution against the cold. They burn their temples with an old rag so that their faces will not be damaged by sweat. Illiterate and unable to do anything manly, they live like beasts, surviving on alms only. For this reason, they are to be found around taverns and public kitchens in cities. If, while roaming the countryside, they come across a well-dressed person, they try to make him one of their own, stripping him naked. Like Gypsies in Europe, they practice chiromancy [palm reading], especially for women who then provide them with bread, eggs, cheese, and other foods in return for their services.

Amongst them there is usually an old man whom they revere and worship like God. When they enter a town, they gather around the best house of the town and listen in great humility to the words of this old man, who, after a spell of ecstasy, foretells the descent of a great evil upon the town. His disciples then implore him to fend off the disaster through his good services. The old man accepts the plea of his followers, though not without an initial show of reluctance, and prays to God, asking him to spare the town the imminent danger awaiting it. This time-honored trick earns them considerable sums of alms from ignorant and credulous people.

PRIMARY SOURCE 11.2

Flagellants in England (1350s), Robert of Avesbury

In that same year of 1349, about Michaelmas [September 29], more than 120 men, for the most part from Zeeland or Holland, arrived in London from Flanders. These went barefoot in procession twice a day in the sight of the people, sometimes in St Paul's church and sometimes elsewhere in the city, their bodies naked except for a linen cloth from loins to ankle. Each wore a hood painted with a red cross at front and back and carried in his right hand a whip with three thongs. Each thong had a knot in it, with something sharp, like a needle, stuck through the middle of the knot so that it stuck out on each side, and as they walked one after the other they struck themselves with these whips on their naked, bloody bodies; four of them singing in their own tongue and the rest answering in the manner of the Christian litany. Three times in each procession they would all prostrate themselves on the ground, with their arms outstretched in the shape of a cross. Still singing, and beginning with the man at the end, each in turn would step over the others, lashing the man beneath him once with his whip, until all of those lying down had gone through the same ritual. Then each one put on his usual clothes and, always with their hoods on their heads and carrying their whips, they departed to their lodgings. It was said that they performed a similar penance every night.

Source: Robertus de Avesbury, "Flagellants in England" from *The Black Death*, Rosemary Horrox, trans./ed., pp. 153–54. Copyright © Rosemary Horrox 1994. Reprinted with permission of Manchester University Press.

PRIMARY SOURCE 11.3

The Red Turban Movement in China (1359)

Aggrieved that the people have long fallen under the Mongols, we have taken up the righteous cause and raised troops in order to recover the Central Plains. To the east, we have moved beyond the Shandong region; to the west, we have gone beyond Chang'an; to the south, we have passed beyond Fujian and Guandong; to the north, we have reached the Capital Region. All have joined us in good faith, like the starving who receive meat and grain or the ill who happened upon medicine. We have now ordered our generals to strictly prohibit their soldiers from disturbing the people. We will succor those people who join us; we will chastise those who resist in battle.

Source: David M. Robinson, *Empire's Twilight: Northeast Asia under the Mongols* (Cambridge, MA, 2009), p. 147.

QUESTIONS FOR ANALYSIS

1. Interpret the description of clothing in the first two documents. What does clothing tell us about the lifestyles of the dervishes and the Flagellants? What, if anything, can we tell about the authors and their views of these groups from these descriptions?

2. Explain how each of these documents characterizes setbacks within the societies. How do the members of these groups understand the period's crises, and what solutions, if any, do they offer? Pay special attention to the role of social class.

3. Identify and compare the critiques that each of the groups makes of traditional ways of behaving, whether through their own behavior or their words. What do they tell us about existing social norms?

Interpreting Visual Evidence

Marking Boundaries, Inspiring Loyalty

The fourteenth century witnessed the emergence of dynastic states across Afro-Eurasia that endured for centuries. The size of these new states and the ethnic and religious diversity of their populations posed formidable challenges to those in power. Rulers had to distinguish those who belonged to the community—and owed taxes or military service—from those who did not. They used a careful mixture of privilege and punishment to create a sense of unity among their subjects while at the same time justifying their own right to rule and reinforcing traditional social hierarchies. The three images below show different ways rulers approached this problem.

The first painting, from around 1500, is by the Spanish artist Pedro Berruguete. It portrays a scene from two centuries earlier in which Spanish authorities burned people at the stake for their alleged heretical beliefs. Notice in the foreground members of the Dominican Order, who were instrumental in the administration of the Inquisition, and soldiers loyal to the crown. The second image, a miniature painting from 1558, depicts the *devshirme* system in the Ottoman Empire. Authorities took non-Muslim children from their families in Europe as a human tribute in place of cash taxes, which the poor region could not pay. The children would then be educated in Ottoman Muslim ways and prepared for service in the sultan's civil and military bureaucracy. The final image, a painting on silk by Ch'iu Ying, represents a group of Confucian scholars waiting for the results of their civil service examination. Candidates spent three days and two nights taking examinations as they sought to enter the Ming bureaucracy.

Spanish painting by Berruguete.

The devshirme *system.*

Chinese painting by Ch'iu Ying.

QUESTIONS FOR ANALYSIS

1. Assess the combinations of privilege and punishment conveyed by these images. What kinds of assistance or special privileges did leaders grant, to whom did they offer this assistance, and what kinds of punishments did they impose?

2. Describe the original context for these images. Who might have created these images, for whom, and who might have seen them?

3. Interpret the role religion plays in these images. How does the artist present the relationship between religion and social order?

4. Explain how Berruguete's use of the past alters the relationship between royal authorities and traditional elites presented in the first painting, compared to the relationship between rulers and elites shown or implied by the other two images.

Before You Read This Chapter

Contact, Commerce, and Colonization

1450–1600

In 1519, five ships under the command of Ferdinand Magellan set out from the Spanish mainland. Nearly three years later a single vessel returned, having successfully sailed around the globe. This achievement came at a high cost: four ships had been lost, and only 18 men out of 265 had fought off scurvy, starvation, and stormy seas to complete the journey. Magellan himself had died. But the survivors had become the first true world travelers. Unlike earlier adventurers who made forays into Eurasia and Africa, Magellan's transoceanic passage connected these worlds with others that, from an Afro-Eurasian viewpoint, had been apart—the Americas.

Magellan's voyages were part of a wave of explorations that included one of the most momentous events in the narrative of world history: Christopher Columbus's voyages of discovery, which opened up worlds about which Afro-Eurasians had no previous knowledge. Although Christopher Columbus did not intend to "discover" America when he went looking for Asia, his voyages convinced Europeans that there were still new territories to exploit and peoples to convert to Christianity. For the first time since the Ice Age migrations, large numbers of people moved from Afro-Eurasian landmasses to the Americas. So did animals, plants, commercial products, and—most momentous—deadly germs.

It was enormously significant that Europeans, rather than Asians or Africans, first stumbled upon the Americas and then exploited their resources. For Europeans, too, now became empire builders—but of a different nature. Their empires were overseas. While the new colonies generated vast riches, they also brought unsettling changes to the rulers and the ruled.

Despite the significance of Europeans' activity in the Americas, most Africans and Asians were barely aware of its importance to them. Asian empires continued to flourish after recovering from the Black Death. Nor was Europe's attention exclusively on the Americas, for its royal houses competed with one another for power and territory at home. Religious revolt in the form of the Protestant Reformation intensified these rivalries. In the wake of Columbus, the drive to build and protect empires across oceans scattered peoples, splattered blood, and shattered worlds.

The Old Trade and the New

COMPARISON

DESCRIBE the broad patterns of world trade after 1450.

Well before commodities from the Americas entered Afro-Eurasian trade networks, commerce recovered from the destruction wrought by the Black Death. Just as political leaders rebuilt states by mixing traditional and innovative ideas, merchant elites revived old trade patterns while establishing new networks. Increasingly, traffic across seas supplemented the overland transportation of goods. The Indian Ocean and China seas emerged as the focal points of Afro-Eurasia's maritime commerce. Across these waters moved an assortment of goods, coordinated by Arab, Persian, Indian, and Chinese merchants who often settled in foreign lands to facilitate trade.

European mariners and traders, searching for new routes to South and East Asia, began exploring the Atlantic coast of Africa. Lured by spices, silks, and slaves, and aided by new maritime technology, Portuguese expeditions made their way around Africa and onward to India. Although Europeans still had little to offer would-be trading partners in Asia, their developing capability in overseas trade laid the foundations for a new kind of global commerce.

THE REVIVAL OF ASIAN ECONOMIES

Trade all across Afro-Eurasia benefited enormously from China's economic dynamism, which was driven primarily by China's vast internal economy. But the Chinese demand for silver fueled a revival of trade across the Indian Ocean and traditional overland routes. After the Ming dynasty relocated its capital from Nanjing in the prosperous south to the northern city of Beijing, Chinese merchants, artisans, and farmers exploited the surging domestic market. Reconstruction of the Grand Canal now opened a major artery that allowed food and riches from the economically vibrant lower Yangzi area to reach the capital region of Beijing. Urban centers, such as Nanjing with a population approaching a million and Beijing at half a million, became massive and lucrative markets. Despite official restrictions on trade, merchants thrived, and coastal cities remained active harbors. (See Map 12.5.)

Chinese Porcelain Box The shape, coloring, and texture of this Chinese porcelain writing box are a tribute to the exquisite craftsmanship that went into its production. This box was also a symbol of flourishing world trade and a typical example of what the French called "chinoiserie," the possession of which was a hallmark of taste and cultivation among the rich and the status-conscious in Europe.

What did foreign buyers have to trade with the Chinese? The answer was silver, which became essential to the Ming monetary system. Whereas their predecessors had used paper money, Ming consumers and traders mistrusted anything other than silver or gold for commercial dealings. Once the rulers adopted silver as a means of tax payment in the 1430s, it became the predominant medium for larger transactions.

China, however, did not produce sufficient silver for its booming economy. Indeed, silver and other precious metals were about the only commodities for which the Chinese would trade their precious manufactures. Through most of the sixteenth century, China's main source of silver was Japan, which one Florentine merchant called the "silver islands." After the 1570s, however, the Philippines, now under the control of the Spanish, became a gateway for silver coming from the New World. One-third of all silver mined in the Americas during the sixteenth and seventeenth centuries wound up in Chinese hands.

China's economic expansion contributed to the revival of Indian Ocean trade. Long-distance merchants developed a brisk commerce that tied the whole of the Indian Ocean together. Ports as far off as East Africa and the Red Sea enjoyed links with coastal cities of India, South Asia, and the Malay Peninsula. Muslims dominated this trade. India was the geographic and economic center of numerous trade routes. With a population expanding as rapidly as China's, its large cities (such as Agra, Delhi, and Lahore) each boasted nearly half a million residents. India's manufacturing center, Bengal, exported silk and cotton textiles and rice throughout South and Southeast Asia. Like China, India exported more than it imported, selling textiles and pepper in exchange for silver.

Overland commerce also thrived anew. One well-trafficked route linked the Baltic Sea, Muscovy, the Caspian Sea, the central Asian oases, and China. Other land routes carried goods to the ports of China and the Indian Ocean; from there, they crossed to the Ottoman Empire's heartland and went by land farther into Europe. Ottoman authorities took a keen interest in the caravan trade, since the state gained considerable tax revenue from it. To facilitate the caravans' movement, the government maintained refreshment and military stations along the route. The largest had individual rooms to accommodate the chief merchants and could provide lodging for up to 800 travelers, as well as care for all their animals. But gathering so many traders, animals, and cargoes could also attract marauders, especially desert tribesmen. To stop the raids, authorities and merchants offered cash payments to tribal chieftains as "protection money." This was a small price to pay in order to protect the caravan trade, whose revenues ultimately supported imperial expansion.

Overland Caravans and Caravanserais Muslim governments and merchants' associations constructed inns, or caravanserais, along the major trading routes. These areas were capable of accommodating a large number of traders and their animals in great comfort.

EUROPEAN EXPLORATION AND EXPANSION

COMPARISON

ANALYZE the factors that enabled Europeans to increase their trade relationships with Asian empires and **ASSESS** their significance.

The emergence of the Ottoman Empire prompted Europeans to probe unexplored links to the east in the sixteenth century. When the Ottomans took control of traditional overland trade routes from Europe to Asia, Europeans began to look south and west—and ventured across the seas. (See Map 12.1.) Taking the lead were the Portuguese, whose search for new routes to Asia led them first to Africa. Europeans had long believed that Africa was a storehouse of precious metals. In fact, a fourteenth-century map, the Catalan Atlas, had depicted a single black ruler controlling a vast quantity of gold in the interior of Africa. As the price of gold skyrocketed during and after the Black Death, ambitious men decided to venture southward in search of this commodity and its twin, silver. Having found sea routes around Africa, European merchants sought to reap the riches abounding in Asian ports, especially once Asian states were firmly established across the Indian Ocean in the seventeenth century.

Innovations in maritime technology and information from other mariners helped Portuguese sailors navigate the treacherous waters along the African coast. New vessels included the carrack, a three- or four-masted ship, developed by the Portuguese to deal with rough waters like the Atlantic Ocean and the Mediterranean. Equally important was the caravel, with specially designed triangular sails, which enabled European sailors to nose in and out of estuaries and navigate unpredictable currents and winds. By using highly maneuverable caravels and perfecting the technique of tacking (sailing into the wind rather than before it), the Portuguese advanced far along the West African coast. In addition, newfound expertise with the compass and the astrolabe helped navigators determine latitude.

Portuguese seafarers ventured from the coasts of Africa into the Indian Ocean and inserted themselves into its thriving commerce. In Asia, Portugal did not attempt to rule directly or to establish colonies. Rather, it aimed to exploit Asian commercial networks and trading systems. To do so, the Portuguese took advantage of a technology developed centuries earlier in China: gunpowder. Mounting small cannons on their warships, they bombarded ports and rival navies or merchant vessels.

The first Portuguese mariner to reach the Indian Ocean was Vasco da Gama (1469–1524). Like Columbus, da Gama was relatively unknown before his extraordinary voyage commanding four ships around the Cape of Good Hope. He found a network of commercial ties spanning the Indian Ocean, as well as skilled Muslim mariners who knew the currents, winds, and ports of call. Once established in the key ports, the Portuguese attempted to take over the trade or, failing this, to tax local merchants. From Sofala, Kilwa, and other important ports on the East African coast, Goa and Calicut in India, and Macao in southern China, the Portuguese soon dominated the most active sea-lanes of the Indian Ocean. The Portuguese did not interrupt the flow of luxuries among Asian and African elites; rather, their naval captains simply kept a portion of the profits for themselves, content to benefit from Asian prosperity without imposing Portuguese rule. Only with the

The Catalan Atlas This 1375 map shows the world as it was then known. Not only does it depict the location of continents and islands, but it also includes information on ancient and medieval tales, regional politics, astronomy, and astrology.

discovery of the Americas and the conquest of Brazil did Portugal become an empire with large overseas colonies. For this to transpire, mariners would have to traverse the Atlantic Ocean itself.

The Atlantic World

By opening new sea-lanes in the Atlantic, European explorers set the stage for a major transformation in world history: the establishment of overseas colonies. After the discovery of the Americas, Europeans conquered the native peoples and created colonies for the purpose of enriching themselves and their monarchs.

Crossing the Atlantic was a feat of monumental importance. It did not occur, however, with an aim to discover new lands. Columbus set out to open a more direct—and more lucrative—route to Japan and China. As we saw in Chapter 11, Ferdinand and Isabella hoped Columbus would bring them riches that would finance a crusade to liberate Jerusalem. Neither they nor Columbus expected he would find a "New World."

Europeans arrived in what they soon called the New World with cannons, steel weapons and body armor, horses, and, above all, deadly diseases that caused a catastrophic decline of Amerindian populations. Europeans arrived at a time of political upheaval and took advantage of divisions among the indigenous peoples. The combination of material advantages and local allies enabled Europeans to conquer and colonize the Americas, as they could not do in Asia or Africa, where long-standing patterns of trade had resulted in the development of shared immunities and stable states resisted outside incursions.

The devastation of the Amerindian population also resulted in severe labor shortages. Thus began the large-scale introduction of slave laborers imported from Africa, which led to the "Atlantic system" that connected Europe, the Americas, and Africa. The precious metals of the New World now gave Europeans something to offer their trading partners in Asia and enabled them to grow rich. In the process, they brought together peoples and ecosystems that had developed separately for thousands of years.

COMPARISON

COMPARE the practices and the impact of European explorers in Asia and the Americas.

FIRST ENCOUNTERS

Christopher Columbus set sail from Spain in early 1492, stopped in the Canary Islands for supplies and repairs, and cast off into the unknown. When he stepped onto the beach of San Salvador (in the Bahamas) on October 12, 1492, the explorer ushered in a new era in world history. Like other expansion-minded Europeans, once established in the Americas, Columbus and the other mariners aimed to Christianize the world while enriching themselves and their backers. These goals—to save souls and to make money—drove the European colonization of the Americas and the formation of an Atlantic system. They also shaped Europeans' early interactions with Amerindians and Africans captured in the slave trade.

When Columbus made landfall in the Caribbean Sea, he unfurled the royal standard of Ferdinand and Isabella and claimed the "many islands filled with people innumerable" for Spain. It is fitting that the first encounter with Caribbean inhabitants, in this case the Tainos, drew blood.

Columbus As Columbus made landfall and encountered Indians, he planted a cross to indicate the spiritual purpose of the voyage and read aloud a document proclaiming the sovereign authority of the king and queen of Spain. Quickly, he learned there was barter for precious stones and metals.

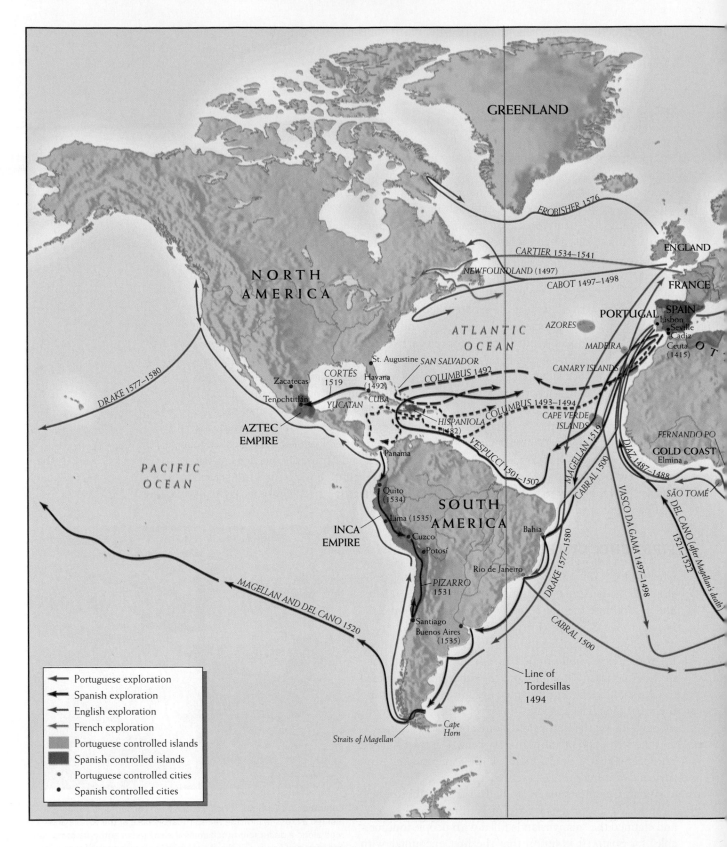

GREENLAND

NORTH AMERICA

FROBISHER 1576

CARTIER 1534–1541

ENGLAND

NEWFOUNDLAND (1497)

CABOT 1497–1498

FRANCE

PORTUGAL SPAIN
Lisbon
Seville
Cadiz
Ceuta
(1415)

ATLANTIC OCEAN

AZORES

MADEIRA

St. Augustine *SAN SALVADOR*

COLUMBUS 1492

CANARY ISLANDS

DRAKE 1577–1580

CORTÉS 1519

Zacatecas

Havana
(1492)

CUBA

COLUMBUS 1493–1494

Tenochtitlán

YUCATAN

AZTEC EMPIRE

HISPANIOLA (1492)

CAPE VERDE ISLANDS

FERNANDO PO

GOLD COAST
Elmina

Panama

VESPUCCI 1501–1502

MAGELLAN 1519

CABRAL 1500

DIAZ 1487–1488

SÃO TOMÉ

PACIFIC OCEAN

Quito (1534)

SOUTH AMERICA

Lima (1535)

INCA EMPIRE

Cuzco

Potosí

Bahia

Rio de Janeiro

PIZARRO 1531

DRAKE 1577–1580

VASCO DA GAMA 1497–1498

DEL CANO (after Magellan's death) 1521–1522

MAGELLAN AND DEL CANO 1520

Santiago
Buenos Aires
(1535)

CABRAL 1500

Line of Tordesillas 1494

Cape Horn

Straits of Magellan

Legend:
- → Portuguese exploration
- → Spanish exploration
- → English exploration
- → French exploration
- Portuguese controlled islands
- Spanish controlled islands
- • Portuguese controlled cities
- • Spanish controlled cities

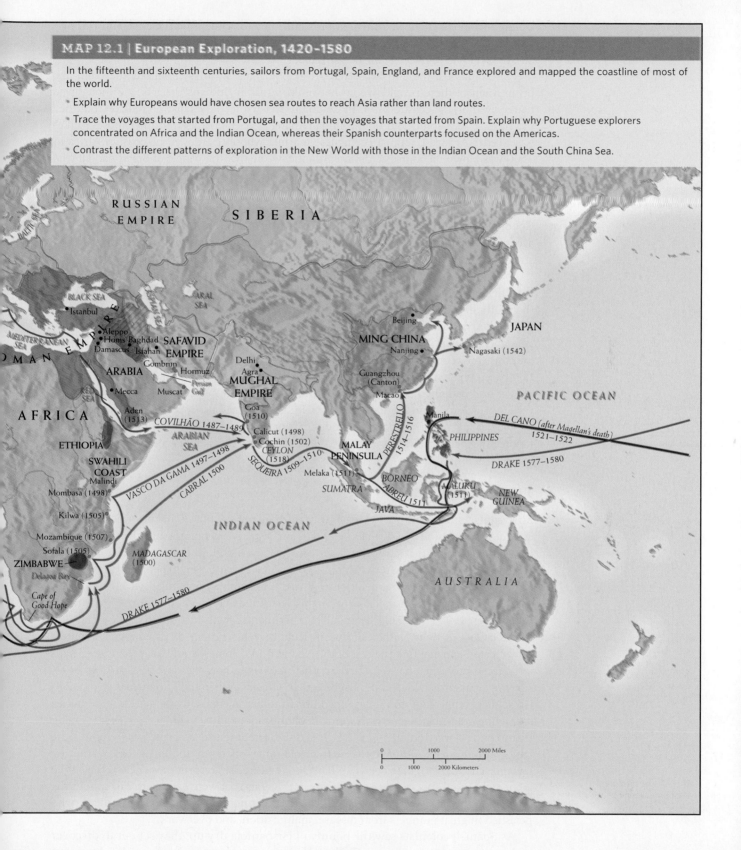

MAP 12.1 | European Exploration, 1420–1580

In the fifteenth and sixteenth centuries, sailors from Portugal, Spain, England, and France explored and mapped the coastline of most of the world.

- Explain why Europeans would have chosen sea routes to reach Asia rather than land routes.
- Trace the voyages that started from Portugal, and then the voyages that started from Spain. Explain why Portuguese explorers concentrated on Africa and the Indian Ocean, whereas their Spanish counterparts focused on the Americas.
- Contrast the different patterns of exploration in the New World with those in the Indian Ocean and the South China Sea.

RUSSIAN EMPIRE

SIBERIA

BLACK SEA
Istanbul
Aleppo
Homs Baghdad SAFAVID
Damascus Isfahan EMPIRE
Gombrun
ARABIA Hormuz
Mecca Muscat

OMAN EMPIRE

MEDITERRANEAN SEA

RED SEA

Persian Gulf

Delhi
Agra
MUGHAL EMPIRE

Beijing

MING CHINA
Nanjing

JAPAN

Nagasaki (1542)

AFRICA

Aden (1513)

COVILHÃO 1487–1489

ARABIAN SEA

Goa (1510)

Guangzhou (Canton)
Macao

PACIFIC OCEAN

ETHIOPIA

SWAHILI COAST
Malindi
Mombasa (1498)

Kilwa (1505)

Mozambique (1507)
Sofala (1505)
ZIMBABWE

Delagoa Bay

Cape of Good Hope

Calicut (1498)
Cochin (1502)
CEYLON (1518)

SEQUEIRA 1509–1510

VASCO DA GAMA 1497–1498

CABRAL 1500

MADAGASCAR (1500)

Melaka (1511)

MALAY PENINSULA

SUMATRA

BORNEO

JAVA

ABREU 1511

PERESTRELLO 1514–1516

Manila

PHILIPPINES

MALUKU (1511)

NEW GUINEA

DEL CANO (after Magellan's death) 1521–1522

DRAKE 1577–1580

INDIAN OCEAN

DRAKE 1577–1580

AUSTRALIA

0   1000   2000 Miles

0   1000   2000 Kilometers

Columbus noted, "I showed them swords and they took them by the edge and through ignorance cut themselves." The Tainos had their own weapons but did not forge steel—and thus had no knowledge of such sharp edges.

For Columbus, the Tainos' naïveté in grabbing his sword symbolized the child-like primitivism of these people, whom he would mislabel "Indians" because he thought he had arrived off the coast of Asia. In Columbus's view the Tainos had no religion, but they did have at least some gold (found initially hanging as pendants from their noses). Like-wise, Pedro Alvares Cabral, a Portuguese mariner whose trip down the coast of Africa in 1500 was blown off course across the Atlantic, wrote that the people of Brazil had all "the innocence of Adam." He also noted that they were ripe for conversion and that the soils "if rightly cultivated would yield everything." But, as with Africans and Asians, Europe-ans also developed a contradictory view of the peoples of the Americas. From the Tainos, Columbus learned of another people, the Caribs, who (according to his informants) were sav-age, warlike cannibals. For centuries, these contrasting images—innocents and savages—structured European (mis)understandings of the native peoples of the Americas.

We know less about what the Indians thought of Columbus or other Europeans on their first encounters. Certainly they were impressed with the Europeans' appearance and their military prowess. The Tainos fled into the forest at the approach of European ships, which they thought were giant monsters; others thought they were floating islands. Euro-pean metal goods, in particular weaponry, struck them as otherworldly. The Amerindians found the newcomers different not for their skin color (only Europeans drew the distinc-tion based on skin pigmentation), but for their hairiness. Indeed, the Europeans' beards, breath, and bad manners repulsed their Indian hosts. The newcomers' inability to live off the land also stood out. In due course, the Indians realized not just that the strange, hairy people bearing metal weapons were odd trading partners, but that they meant to stay and to force the local population to labor for them. The explorers had become **conquistadors** (conquerors).

FIRST CONQUESTS

First contacts between peoples gave way to dramatic conquests in the Americas; then conquests paved the way to mass exploitation of native peoples. After the first voyage, Columbus claimed that on Hispaniola (present-day Haiti and the Dominican Republic) "he had found what he was looking for"—gold. That was sufficient to persuade the Spanish crown to invest in larger expeditions. Whereas Columbus first sailed with three small ships and 87 men, ten years later the Spanish outfitted an expedition with 2,500 men.

Between 1492 and 1519, the Spanish experimented with institutions of colonial rule over local populations on the Caribbean island that they renamed Hispaniola. Ultimately they created a model that the rest of the New World colonies would adapt. But the Span-iards faced problems that would recur. The first was Indian resistance. As early as 1494, starving Spaniards raided and pillaged Indian villages. When the Indians revolted, Span-ish soldiers replied with punitive expeditions and began enslaving them to work in mines extracting gold. As the crown rewarded conquistadors with grants (*encomiendas*) giving them control over Indian labor, a rich class of *encomenderos* arose who enjoyed the fruits of the system. Although the surface gold mines soon ran dry, the model of granting favored settlers the right to coerce Indian labor endured. In return, those who received the labor rights paid special taxes on the precious metals that were extracted. Thus, both the crown and the *encomenderos* benefited. The same cannot be said of the Amerindians, who perished in great numbers from disease, malnutrition, and overwork.

As Spanish colonists saw the bounty of Hispaniola dry up, they set out to discover and conquer new territories. Finding their way to the mainlands of the American landmasses, they encountered larger, more complex, and more militarized societies than those they had overrun in the Caribbean. Great civilizations had arisen there centuries before, boasting large cities, monumental buildings, and riches based on wealthy agrarian societies. In both Mesoamerica, starting with the Olmecs (see Chapter 5), and the Andes, with the Chimú (see Chapter 10), large states had laid the foundations for subsequent Aztec and **Incan empires**. These empires were powerful. But they had evolved untouched by Afro-Eurasian developments; as worlds apart, they were unprepared for the kind of assaults that European invaders had honed. In pre-Columbian Mesoamerica and then the Andes, warfare was more ceremonial, less inclined to wipe out enemies than to make them pay tribute. As a result, the wealth and vulnerability of these empires made them irresistible to outside conquerors.

Aztec Society In Mesoamerica, the Mexicas had created an empire known to us as "Aztec." Around Lake Texcoco, Mexica cities grew and formed a three-city league in 1430, which then expanded through the Central Valley of Mexico to incorporate neighboring peoples. Gradually the **Aztec Empire** united numerous small, independent states under a single monarch who ruled with the help of counselors, military leaders, and priests. By the late fifteenth century, the Aztec realm may have embraced 25 million people. Tenochtitlán, situated on an immense island in Lake Texcoco, ranked among the world's largest cities.

Tenochtitlán spread in concentric circles, with the main religious and political buildings in the center and residences radiating outward. The city's outskirts connected a mosaic of floating gardens producing food for urban markets. Canals irrigated the land, waste served as fertilizer, and high-yielding produce found easy transport to markets. Entire households worked: men, women, and children all had roles in Aztec agriculture.

Tenochtitlán At its height, the Aztec capital Tenochtitlán was as populous as Europe's largest city. As can be seen from this map, it spread in concentric circles, with the main religious and political buildings in the center and residences radiating outward.

Extended kinship provided the scaffolding for Aztec statehood. Marriage of men and women from different villages solidified alliances and created clan-like networks. In Tenochtitlán, powerful families married their children to each other or found nuptial partners among the prominent families of other important cities. Soon a lineage emerged to create a corps of "natural" rulers. Priests legitimized new emperors in rituals to convey the image of a ruler close to the gods and to distinguish the elite from the lower orders.

Ultimately Aztec power spread though much of Mesoamerica, but the empire's constant wars and conquests deprived it of stability. In military campaigns, the Aztecs defeated their neighbors, forcing the conquered peoples to pay tribute of crops, gold, silver, textiles, and other goods that financed Aztec grandeur. Such conquests also provided a constant supply of humans for sacrifice, because the Aztecs believed that the great god of the sun required human hearts to keep on burning and blood to replace that given by the gods to moisten the earth through rain. Priests escorted captured warriors up the temple steps and tore out their hearts, offering their lives and blood as a sacrifice to the sun god.

Those whom the Aztecs sought to dominate did not submit peacefully. From 1440, the empire faced constant turmoil as subject populations rebelled. Tlaxcalans and Tarascans waged a relentless war for freedom, holding at bay entire divisions of Aztec armies. To pacify the realm, the empire diverted more and more men and money into a mushrooming military. By the time the electoral committee chose Moctezuma II as emperor in 1502, divisions among elites and pressures from the periphery placed the Aztec Empire under extreme stress.

Cortés and Conquest Not long after Moctezuma became emperor, news arrived from the coast of ships bearing pale, bearded men and monsters (horses and dogs). Here distinguishing fact from fiction is difficult. Some accounts left after the conquest by indigenous witnesses reported that Moctezuma consulted with his ministers and priests, wondering if these men were the god Quetzalcoátl and his entourage. Most historians dismiss the importance of these omens as the effort of rival elites to blame Moctezuma for their own inaction. In any case, Moctezuma sent emissaries bearing gifts, but he did not prepare for a military engagement.

Aboard one of the ships was Hernán Cortés (1485–1547), a former law student from one of the Spanish provinces. He would become the model conquistador, just as Columbus was the model explorer. For a brief time, Cortés was an *encomendero* in Cuba; but when news arrived of a potentially wealthier land to the west, he set sail with over 500 men, eleven ships, sixteen horses, and artillery. When the expedition arrived near present-day Veracruz, Cortés acquired two translators, including the daughter of a local Indian noble family, who became known as Doña Marina, also known as La Malinche. With the assistance of Doña Marina and other native allies, Cortés marched his troops to

Cortés Meets Mesoamerican Rulers *(Left)* This colonial image depicts the meeting of Cortés (second from right) and Moctezuma (seated on the left), with Doña Marina serving as an interpreter and informer for the Spanish conquistador. Notice at the bottom what are likely Aztec offerings for the newcomer. *(Right)* This detail from a twentieth-century Mexican mural depicts the meeting of Cortés and the king of Tlaxcala, enemy of the Aztecs. As Mexicans began to celebrate their mixed-blood heritage, Doña Marina (in the middle) became the symbolic mother of the first mestizos.

Tenochtitlán. Upon entering, he gasped in wonder that "this city is so big and so remarkable" that it was "almost unbelievable." One of his soldiers wrote, "It was all so wonderful that I do not know how to describe this first glimpse of things never heard of, seen or dreamed of before."

How was this tiny force to overcome an empire of many millions with an elaborate warring tradition? Crucial to Spanish conquest was their alliance, negotiated through translators, with Moctezuma's enemies—especially the Tlaxcalans. After decades of yearning for release from the Aztec yoke, the Tlaxcalans and other Mesoamerican peoples embraced Cortés's promise of help. The Spaniards' second advantage was their method of warfare. The Aztecs were seasoned fighters, but they fought to capture, not to kill. Nor were they familiar with gunpowder or sharp steel swords. Although outnumbered, the Spaniards killed their foes with abandon, using superior weaponry, horses, and war dogs. When Cortés arrived at Tenochtitlán, the Aztecs were still unsure who these strange men were and allowed Cortés to enter their city. With the aid of the Tlaxcalans and a handful of his own men, in 1519 Cortés captured Moctezuma, who became a puppet of the Spanish conqueror.

The Aztecs quickly changed their approach to fighting. When Spanish troops massacred an unarmed crowd in Tenochtitlán's central square while Cortés was away, they provoked a massive uprising. The Spaniards led Moctezuma to one of the palace walls to plead with his people for a truce, but the Aztecs kept up their barrage of stones, spears, and arrows—striking and killing Moctezuma. Cortés returned to reassert control; but realizing this was impossible, he gathered his loot and escaped. He left behind hundreds of Spaniards, many of whom were dragged up the temple steps and sacrificed by Aztec priests.

With the Tlaxcalans' help, Cortés regrouped. This time he bombarded Tenochtitlán with artillery, determined to defeat the Aztecs completely. Even more devastating was the spread of smallpox, brought by the Spanish, which ran through the Aztec soldiers and commoners like wildfire. In the end, starvation, disease, lack of artillery, and Cortes's ability to rally Amerindian allies to his side vanquished the Aztec forces. More died from disease than from fighting—the total number of Aztec casualties may have reached 240,000. As Spanish troops retook the capital, now in ruins, the Spaniards and their allies had to engage in house-to-house combat to secure control over Tenochtitlán. The Aztecs lamented their defeat in verse: "We have pounded our hands in despair against the adobe walls, for our inheritance, our city, is lost and dead." Cortés became governor of the new Spanish colony, renamed "New Spain." He promptly allocated *encomiendas* to his loyal followers and dispatched expeditions to conquer the more distant Mesoamerican provinces.

The Mexica experience taught the Spanish an important lesson: an effective conquest had to be swift—and it had to remove completely the symbols of legitimate authority. Their winning advantage, however, was disease. The Spaniards unintentionally introduced germs that made their subsequent efforts at military conquest much easier.

The Incas The other great Spanish conquest occurred in the Andes, where Quechua-speaking rulers, called Incas, had established an impressive state. Sometime around 1200, a band of Andean villagers settled into the valleys near what is now Cuzco, in Peru, which soon became the hub of South America's greatest empire. A combination of raiding neighbors and intermarrying into elite families raised the Incas to regional supremacy. Their power radiated along the valley routes that carved up the chain of great mountains until they finally ran up against the mighty warrior confederacy of the Chanca. After defeating the Chanca rivals around 1438, the Inca warrior Yupanqui renamed himself Pachacuti and began the royal line of Inca emperors. They eventually ruled a vast domain from what is now Chile to southern Colombia. At its center was the capital, Cuzco, with the magnificent fortress of Sacsayhuaman as its head. Built of huge boulders, the citadel was the nerve center of a complex network of strongholds that held the empire together.

As in most empires of the day, political power depended on a combination of tribute and commercial exchange to finance an extensive communication and military network. The empire developed an elaborate system of sending messages by runners who relayed up and down a system of stone highways carrying instructions to allies and roving armed divisions. None of this would have been possible without a wealthy agrarian base. Peasants paid tribute to village elders in the form of labor services to maintain public works, complex terraces, granaries, and food storage systems in case of drought or famine. In return, Inca rulers were obliged to shelter their people and allies in case of hardship. They oversaw rituals, festivals, and ceremonies to give spiritual legitimacy to their power. At their peak, the Incas may have governed a population of up to 6 million people. But as the empire stretched into distant provinces, especially into northern frontiers, ruling Incas lost touch with their base in Cuzco. Fissures began to open in the Andean empire as European germs and conquistadors appeared on South American shores.

When the Spaniards arrived in 1532 they found a divided empire, a situation they quickly learned to exploit. Francisco Pizarro, who led the Spanish campaign, had been inspired by Cortés's victory and yearned for his own glory. Commanding a force of about 600 men, he invited Atahualpa, the Incan ruler, to meet at the town of Cajamarca. There he laid a trap, intending to overpower the Incas and capture their ruler. As columns of Inca warriors and servants covered with colorful plumage and plates of silver and gold entered the main square, the Spanish soldiers were awed. One recalled, "many of us urinated without noticing it, out of sheer terror." But Pizarro's plan worked. His guns and horses shocked the Inca forces. Atahualpa himself fell into Spanish hands, later to be decapitated. Pizarro's conquistadors overran Cuzco in 1533 and then vanquished the rest of the Inca forces, a process that took decades in some areas.

The defeat of the New World's two great empires had enormous repercussions for world history. First, it set the Europeans on the road to controlling the human and material wealth of the Americas and opened a new frontier that the Europeans could colonize. Second, it gave Europeans a market for their own products—goods that found little favor in Afro-Eurasia. Now, following the Portuguese push into Africa and Asia (as well as a Russian push into northern Asia; see Chapter 13), the New World conquests introduced Europeans to a new scale of imperial expansion.

COMPARISON

ASSESS how European colonization of the Americas affected African and Amerindian peoples, and DESCRIBE their responses.

The Columbian Exchange The Spanish came to the Americas for gold and silver, but in the course of conquest and settlement they also learned about crops such as potatoes and corn. They brought with them horses, wheat, grapevines, and sugarcane, as well as devastating diseases. Historians call this transfer of previously unknown plants, animals, people, and products in the wake of Columbus's voyages the **Columbian exchange**. Over time, this exchange transformed environments, economies, and diets in both the new and the old worlds.

The first and most profound effect of the Columbian exchange was a destructive one: the decimation of the Amerindian population by European diseases. For millennia, the isolated populations of the Americas had been cut off from Afro-Eurasian microbe migrations. Africans, Europeans, and Asians had long interacted, sharing disease pools and gaining immunities; in this sense, in contrast, the Amerindians were indeed worlds apart. Sickness spread from almost the moment the Spaniards arrived. One Spanish soldier noted, upon entering the conquered Aztec capital, "the streets were so filled with dead and sick people that our men walked over nothing but bodies." As each wave of disease retreated, it left a population weaker than before, even less prepared for the next wave. The scale of death was unprecedented: imported pathogens wiped out up to 90 percent of the Indian population. A century after smallpox arrived

Analyzing Global Developments

The European Conquest of the Americas and Amerindian Mortality

f the fourteenth century was an age of dying across Afro-Eurasia, the sixteenth century saw even higher mortality rates in the Americas. As a result of European conquest, the exposure to virulent diseases, and the hyperexploitation of their labor under miserable conditions, the Native American populations saw their numbers reduced by 85 percent. The numbers themselves, however, are highly controversial and have sparked intense debates. Some scholars believe that no reliable numbers can be found for the population of the Americas when Europeans first arrived. Others have used a range of methods and data sources to establish population figures, including European firsthand accounts from that period, archaeological and anthropological evidence, estimates of the maximum number of people that the land could hold at that time (carrying capacity), and projections built backward from more recent censuses. These estimates vary widely from as little as 8 million to as high as more than 100 million.

AREA	POPULATION IN 1492	LATER POPULATIONS	MORTALITY RATES
The Americas	53.9 m	8 m in 1650	85%
The Caribbean			
Hispaniola	1.0 m	extinct by 1600	100%
The other islands	2.0 m	extinct by 1600	100%
Mexico	17.2 m	3.5 m in 1600	80%
The Andes	15.0 m	3.0 m in 1650	80%
Central America	5.63 m	1.12 m in 1700	80%
North America	3.79 m	1.5 m in 1700	60%
		250,000 in 1900	84%

QUESTIONS FOR ANALYSIS

- List the areas of the Americas that were most severely affected by population decline and explain why.

- Explain how the Portuguese and Spanish attempted to exploit the resources of the Americas and describe what effect this had on Amerindians and Africans.

- Explain why Native American population growth never recovered from the initial encounter with Europeans as Afro-Eurasian population growth eventually recovered from the Black Death.

Sources: Suzanne Austin Alchon, *A Pest in the Land: New World Epidemics in a Global Perspective* (2003); David Noble Cook, *Born to Die: Disease and New World Conquest, 1492 to 1650* (1998); William M. Denevan, *The Native Populations of the Americas in 1492* (1992); David Henige, *Numbers from Nowhere: The Amerindian Contact Population Debate* (1998); "La catastrophe demographique," *L'histoire,* July–August, 2007, no. 322, p. 17; Russell Thornton, *American Indian Holocaust: A Population History since 1492 (1987)*, p. xvii.

on Hispaniola in 1519, no more than 5 to 10 percent of the island's population was alive. (See **Analyzing Global Developments: The European Conquest of the Americas and Amerindian Mortality**.) Diminished and weakened by disease, Amerindians could not resist European settlement and colonization of the Americas. Thus were Europeans the unintended beneficiaries of a horrifying catastrophe.

As time passed, all sides adopted new forms of agriculture from one another. After Amerindians taught Europeans how to grow potatoes and corn, the crops became staples all across Afro-Eurasia. The Chinese found that they could grow corn in areas too dry for rice and too wet for wheat, and in Africa, corn gradually replaced sorghum, millet, and rice to become the continent's principal food crop by the twentieth century. (See **Current Trends in World History: Corn and the Rise of Slave-Supplying Kingdoms in West Africa**.) Europeans also took away tomatoes, beans, cacao, peanuts, tobacco, and squash, while importing livestock such as cattle, swine, and horses to the New World. The environmental effects of the introduction of livestock to the Americas were significant. For example, in regions of central Mexico where Native Americans had once cultivated maize

Corn and the Rise of Slave-Supplying Kingdoms in West Africa

New World varieties of corn spread rapidly throughout the Afro-Eurasian landmass soon after the arrival of Columbus in the Americas. Its hardiness and fast-ripening qualities made it more desirable than many of the Old World grain products. In communities that consumed large quantities of meat, it became the main product fed to livestock.

Corn's impact on Africa was as substantial as it was in the rest of Eurasia. Seeds made their way to western regions more quickly than to the south of the Sahara along two routes. One was via European merchants calling into ports along the coast; the second was West African Muslims returning across the Sahara after participating in the pilgrimage. The first evidence of corn cultivation in sub-Saharan Africa comes from a Portuguese navigator who identified the crop being grown on the island of Cape Verde in 1540. By the early seventeenth century, corn was replacing millet and sorghum as the main grain being grown in many West African regions and was destined to transform the work routines and diets of the peoples living in the region's tropical rain forests all the way from present-day Sierra Leone in the east to Nigeria in the west. In many ways this area, which saw the rise of a group of powerful slave-supplying kingdoms in the eighteenth century, notably Asante, Dahomey, Oyo, and Benin, owed its prosperity to the cultivation of this New World crop. (See Chapter 14 for a fuller discussion of these states.)

The tropical rain forests of West and central Africa were thick with trees and ground cover in 1500. Clearing them so that they could support intensive agriculture was exhausting work, requiring enormous outlays of human energy and man-hours. Corn, a crop first domesticated in central Mexico 7,000 years ago, made this task possible. It added much-needed carbohydrates to the carbon-deficient diets of rain-forest dwellers. In addition, as a crop that matured more quickly than those that were indigenous to the region (millet, sorghum, and rice) and required less labor, it yielded two harvests in a single year. Farmers also cultivated cassava, another New World native, which in turn provided households with more carbohydrate calories. Yet corn did more than produce more food per unit of land and labor. Households put every part of the plant to use—grain, leaves, stalks, tassels, and roots were made to serve useful purposes.

Thus, at the very time that West African groups were moving southward into the rain forests, European navigators were arriving along the coast with new crops. Corn gave communities of cultivators the caloric energy to change their forest landscapes, expanding the arable areas. In a select few of these regions, enterprising clans emerged to dominate the political scene, creating centralized kingdoms like Asante in present-day Ghana, Dahomey in present-day Benin, and Oyo and Benin in

---

and squash, Spanish settlers introduced large herds of sheep and cattle. Without natural predators, these animals reproduced with lightning speed, destroying entire landscapes with their hooves and their foraging.

As Europeans cleared trees and other vegetation for ranches, mines, or plantations, they undermined the habitats of many indigenous mammals and birds. On the islands of the West Indies, described by Columbus as "roses of the sea," the Spanish chopped down lush tropical and semitropical forests to make way for sugar plantations. Before long, nearly all of the islands' tall trees as well as many shrubs and ground plants were gone, and residents lamented the absence of birdsong. Over ensuing centuries, the plants and animals of the Americas took on an increasingly European appearance. At the same time, the interactions between Europeans and Native Americans would continue to shape societies on both sides of the Atlantic.

THE IBERIAN EMPIRES IN THE AMERICAS

The European presence in the New World went beyond the control of commercial outposts. Unlike their activities in the Indian Ocean—where they had to contend with stable, powerful states—European colonizers in the Americas controlled large amounts of territory, and ultimately the entire landmass (see Map 12.2). Those Native

Corn Plantation This nineteenth-century engraving by famed Italian explorer Savorgnan de Brazza shows women of the West African tribe Bateke working in corn plantations. Brazza would later serve as the governor general of the French colony in the Congo.

present-day Nigeria. These elites transformed what had once been thinly settled environments into densely populated states, with elaborate bureaucracies, big cities, and large and powerful standing armies.

There was much irony in the rise of these states, which owed so much of their strength to the linking of the Americas with Afro-Eurasia. The armies that they created and the increased populations that the new crops allowed were part and parcel of the Atlantic slave trade. That which the Americas gave with one hand (new crops), it took back with the other in warfare, captives, and New World slavery.

QUESTIONS FOR ANALYSIS

- What were the major effects of growing corn in West Africa?
- How did the growing of corn reshape the history of the Atlantic world during this period?

Explore Further

McCann, James, *Maize and Grace: Africa's Encounter with a New World Crop, 1500–2000* (2005).

Americans who survived the original encounters were harnessed as a means to siphon tribute payments to the new masters.

By fusing traditional tribute-taking with their own innovations, Spanish masters made villagers across their new American empire deliver goods and services. But because the Spanish authorities also bestowed *encomiendas*, those favored individuals could demand labor from their lands' Indian inhabitants—for mines, estates, and public works. Whereas Aztec and Inca rulers had used conscripted labor to build up their public wealth, the Spaniards did so for private gain.

Spanish migrants and their descendants preferred towns to the countryside. With the exception of ports, the major cities of Spanish America were the former centers of Indian empires. Mexico City took shape on the ruins of Tenochtitlán; Cuzco arose from the razed Inca capital. In their architecture, economy, and family life, the Spanish colonies adopted as much as they transformed the worlds they encountered.

Silver Silver was an important discovery for Spanish conquerors in Mesoamerica and the Andes. Conquerors expanded the customs of Inca and Aztec labor drafts to force the natives to work in mines, often in brutal conditions.

Legend:

Aztec Empire, 1519
Inca Empire, 1525
AZTEC People
Gold Commodity

Spanish settlement
To 1640
To 1750
Frontier lands 1750

Portuguese settlement
To 1640
To 1750
Frontier lands, 1750

MAP 12.2 | The Spanish and Portuguese Empires in the Americas, 1492–1750

This map examines the growth of the Spanish and Portuguese empires in the Americas over two and a half centuries.

- Identify the natural resources that led the Spaniards and Portuguese to focus their empire building where they did. What were the major export commodities from these colonized areas?

- Looking back to Map 12.1, explain why Spanish settlement covered so much more area than Portuguese settlement.

- According to your reading, describe how the production and export of silver and sugar shaped the labor systems that evolved in both empires.

The next European power to seize land in the Americas, the Portuguese, were no less interested in immediate riches than the Spanish. Disappointed by the absence of tributary systems and precious metals in the area they controlled, Brazil, they found instead abundant, fertile land, which they doled out with massive royal grants. These estate owners governed their plantations like feudal lords (see Chapter 10). Failing to find established cities, the Portuguese created enclaves along the coast and lived in more dispersed settlements than the Spanish settlers.

The problem was where to find labor to work the rich lands of Brazil. Because there was no centralized government to deal with the labor shortage, Portuguese settlers initially tried to enlist the dispersed native population; but when recruitment became increasingly coercive, Indians turned on the settlers. Some Indians fought, others fled to the vast interior. Reluctant to pursue the Indians inland, the Portuguese hugged their beachheads, extracting brazilwood (the source of a beautiful red dye) and sugar from their coastal enclaves.

Silver, Sugar, and Slaves The Iberian empires in the Americas concentrated on three commodities that would transform Europe's relationship to the rest of the world: silver, sugar, and slaves. Silver enabled Spain and Portugal to enter established trade networks in Asia. The slave trade was a big business in itself: it subsidized shipbuilding and new insurance schemes. Above all, the use of slave labor made sugar cultivation fantastically profitable, fueling economic growth and political instability around the world.

The first Europeans in the Americas hoarded vast quantities of gold and silver for themselves and their monarchs. But they also introduced precious metals into the world's commercial systems, which electrified them. In the twenty years after the fall of Tenochtitlán, conquistadors took more gold and silver from Mexico and the Andes than all the gold accumulated by Europeans over the previous centuries.

Having looted Indian coffers, the Spanish entered the business of mining directly, opening the Andean Potosí mines in 1545. Between 1560 and 1685, Spanish America sent 25,000 to 35,000 tons of silver annually to Spain. From 1685 to 1810, this sum doubled. The two mother lodes were Potosí in present-day Bolivia and Zacatecas in northern Mexico. Silver brought bounty not only to the crown but also to a privileged group of families based in Spain's colonial capitals; thus private wealth funded the formation of local aristocracies.

Colonial mines epitomized the Atlantic world's new economy. They relied on an extensive network of Amerindian labor, at first enslaved, subsequently drafted. Here again, the Spanish adopted Inca and Aztec practices of requiring labor from subjugated villages. Each year, under the *mita*, the local system for recruiting labor, village elders selected a stipulated number of men to toil in the shafts, refineries, and smelters. Under the Spanish, the digging, hauling, and smelting taxed human limits to their capacity—and beyond. Mortality rates were appalling. The system pumped so much silver into European commercial networks that it transformed Europe's relationship to all its trading partners, especially those in China and India. It also shook up trade and politics within Europe itself.

Along with silver, sugar emerged as the most valuable export from the Americas. It also was decisive in rearranging relations between peoples around the Atlantic. Cultivation of sugarcane had originated in India, spread to the Mediterranean region, and then reached the coastal islands of West Africa. The Portuguese, the Spanish, and other European settlers transported the West African model to the Americas, first, in the sixteenth century in Brazil, and then in the Caribbean. By the early seventeenth century, sugar had become a major export from the New World. Because Amerindians resisted recruitment and their numbers were greatly reduced by disease, European plantation owners began importing African slaves. By the eighteenth century, sugar production required continuous and enormous transfers of labor from Africa, and its value surpassed that of silver as an export from the Americas to Europe.

At first most sugar plantations were fairly small, employing between 60 and 100 slaves. But they were efficient enough to create an alternative model of empire, one that resulted in more complete and dislocating control of the existing population. The slaves lived in wretched conditions: their barracks were miserable, and their diets were insufficient to keep them alive under backbreaking work routines. Moreover, these slaves were disproportionately men. As they rapidly died off, the only way to ensure replenishment was to import more Africans. This model of settlement relied on the transatlantic flow of slaves.

As European demand for sugar increased, the slave trade expanded. Although African slaves were imported into the Americas starting in the fifteenth century, the first direct voyage carrying them from Africa to the Americas occurred in 1525. From the time of Columbus until 1820, five times as many Africans as Europeans moved to the Americas: approximately 2 million Europeans (voluntarily) and 10 million Africans (involuntarily) crossed the Atlantic.

Well before European merchants arrived off its western coast, Africa had known long-distance slave trading. In fact, the overall number of Africans sold into captivity in the Muslim world exceeded that of the Atlantic slave trade. Moreover, Africans maintained slaves themselves. African slavery, like its American counterpart, was a response to labor scarcities. In many parts of Africa, however, slaves did not face permanent servitude. Instead, they were assimilated into families, gradually losing their servile status.

With the additional European demand for slaves to work New World plantations alongside the ongoing Muslim slave trade, pressure on the supply of African slaves intensified. Only a narrow band stretching down the spine of the African landmass, from present-day Uganda and the highlands of Kenya to Zambia and Zimbabwe, escaped the impact of African rulers engaged in the slave trade and Asian and European slave traders.

By the late sixteenth century, important pieces had fallen into place to create a new Atlantic world, one that could not have been imagined a century earlier. This was the three-cornered **Atlantic system**, with Africa supplying labor, the Americas land and minerals, and Europeans the technology and military power to hold the system together. In time, the wealth flows to Europe and the slave-based development of the Americas would alter the world balance of power.

The Transformation of Europe

COMPARISON

ANALYZE the social and political relationships and **EXPLAIN** the sources of conflict within the Afro-Eurasian polities.

Despite the flow of American silver into Spanish coffers, most European rulers and their subjects were focused on Europe, not the New World, in the sixteenth century. The period's frequent warfare centered on purely European concerns, above all on a religious split within the Roman Catholic Church, known as the Reformation. This conflict led to profound religious rifts among states and brought additional political rivalries to the continent.

THE REFORMATION

Like the Renaissance, the **Protestant Reformation** in Europe began as a movement devoted to returning to ancient sources—in this case, to biblical scriptures. Yet returning to the sources and interpreting Christian doctrine for oneself was dangerous in the fourteenth and fifteenth centuries, for the church feared that challenges to its authority would arise if laypersons were allowed to read the scriptures as they pleased. The church was right: when Luther and his followers seized the right to read and interpret the Bible in a new way, they paved the way for a "Protestant" Reformation that split Christendom for good.

The opening challenge to the authority of the Catholic Church originated in Germany. Here a monk and a professor of theology, **Martin Luther** (1483–1546), used his knowledge of the Bible to criticize the church's ideas and practices. For Luther, God's gift of forgiveness did not depend on taking sacraments or performing good deeds. This faith was something Christians could obtain from reading the Bible—rather than by having a priest tell them what to believe. Finally, Luther concluded that Christians did not need specially appointed mediators to speak to God for them: all believers were equally bound by God's laws and obliged to minister to one another's spiritual needs.

These became the three main principles that launched Luther's reforming efforts: (1) belief that faith alone saves, (2) belief that the scriptures alone hold the key to Christian truth, and (3) belief in the priesthood of all believers. Luther also reacted against corrupt practices in the church, such as the keeping of mistresses by monks, priests, and even popes; and the selling of indulgences, certificates that would supposedly shorten the buyer's time in Purgatory. In the 1510s, clerics were hawking indulgences across Europe in an effort to raise money for the sumptuous new Saint Peter's basilica in Rome. In 1517, Luther formulated ninety-five statements, or theses, and posted them on the doors to the Wittenberg cathedral, hoping to stir up his colleagues in debate.

In response, Pope Leo X and the Habsburg emperor, Charles V, demanded that Luther take back his criticisms and theological claims. When he refused, he was declared a heretic and narrowly avoided being burned at the stake. Luther wrote many more pamphlets attacking the church and the pope, whom he now described as the anti-Christ. Luther also translated the New Testament from Latin into German so that laypersons could have direct access, without the clergy, to the word of God. This act spurred many other reformers across Europe to undertake translations of their own, and it encouraged the Protestant clergy to teach children (and adults) to read their local languages.

Spread by printed books and ardent preachers in all the common languages of Europe, Luther's doctrines and those put forward by other reformers won widespread support in some regions, particularly among urban populations. In France and Switzerland, the reformer **Jean Calvin** (1509–1564) emphasized moral regeneration through church teachings and laid out a doctrine of predestination—the notion that each person is "predestined for damnation or salvation even before birth." Those who followed the new faith of Luther and Calvin identified themselves as "Protestants." They promised that their reformed version of Christianity provided both an answer to individual spiritual needs and a new moral foundation for community life. The renewed Christian creed appealed to commoners as well as elites, especially in communities that resented rule by Catholic "outsiders." For example, Protestantism was popular among the Dutch, who resented being ruled by Philip II, an Austrian Catholic who lived in Spain. The new ideas gained a wide following, although rarely a majority before the seventeenth century, in the German states, France, Switzerland, the Low Countries, England, and Scotland (see Map 12.3).

Counter-Reformation The Catholic Church responded to Luther and Calvin by embarking on its own renovation, which became known as the **Counter-Reformation**. At the Council of Trent, whose twenty-five sessions stretched from 1545 to 1563, Catholic leaders reaffirmed the church's doctrines. But the council also enacted reforms to answer the Protestants' assaults on clerical corruption. Like the Protestants, the reformed Catholics carried their message overseas—especially through an order established by the Spaniard, Ignatius Loyola (1491–1556). Loyola founded a brotherhood of priests, the Society of Jesus, or

MAP 12.3 | Religious Divisions in Europe after the Reformation, 1590

The Protestant Reformation divided Europe religiously and politically.

• Within the formerly all-Catholic Holy Roman Empire, list the Protestant groups that took hold.

• Looking at the map, can you identify any geographic patterns in the distribution of Protestant communities.

• List the regions in which you would expect Protestant-Catholic tensions to be the most intense, and explain why.

Jesuits, dedicated to the revival of the Catholic Church. From bases in Lisbon, Rome, Paris, and elsewhere in Europe, the Jesuits opened missions as far as South and North America, India, Japan, and China. The Reformation split European society deeply as both Catholics and Protestants vigorously promoted their faiths.

RELIGIOUS WARFARE IN EUROPE

The religious revival led Europe into another round of ferocious wars. Their ultimate effect was to weaken the **Holy Roman Empire**—a loose confederation of principalities that mainly clustered in central Europe, presided over in this period by the Habsburgs (see Chapter 11)—and strengthen the English, French, and Dutch. Already in the 1520s, the circulation of books presenting Luther's ideas sparked peasant revolts across central Europe. Some peasants, hoping that Luther's assault on the church's authority would help liberate them, rose up against repressive feudal landlords. In contrast to earlier wars in which one noble's retinue fought a rival's, the defense of the Catholic mass and the Protestant Bible brought crowds of simple folk to arms. Now wars between and within central European states raged for nearly forty years.

Religious conflicts weakened European dynasties. Spain, with its massive empire and its silver mines in the New World, spent much of its new fortune waging war in Europe. Most debilitating was its costly effort to subdue recently acquired Dutch territories. After a series of wars spanning nearly a hundred years, Catholic Spain finally conceded the Protestant Netherlands its independence. Wars took their toll on the Spanish Empire, which was soon wallowing in debts; not even the riches of its American silver mines could bail out the court. In the late 1550s, Philip II could not meet his obligations to creditors, and, within two decades, Spain was declared bankrupt three times. Its decline opened the way for the Dutch and the English to extend their trading networks into Asia and the New World, and the center of power within Europe shifted to the north.

Religious conflicts also sparked civil wars. In France, the divide between Catholics and Protestants exploded in the St. Bartholomew's Day Massacre of 1572. Catholic crowds rampaged through the streets of Paris murdering Huguenot (Protestant) men, women, and children and dumping their bodies into the Seine River. The number of dead reached 3,000 in Paris and 10,000 in provincial towns. Slaughter on this scale did not break the Huguenots' spirit, but it did bring more disrepute to the monarchy for failing to ensure peace. Another round of warfare exhausted the French and brought Henry of Navarre, a Protestant prince, to the throne. To become king, Henry IV converted to Catholicism. Shortly thereafter he issued the Edict of Nantes, a proclamation that declared France a Catholic country but also tolerated some Protestant worship.

St. Bartholomew's Day Massacre An important wedding between French Catholic and Huguenot families in Paris was scheduled for August 24, 1572, St. Bartholomew's Day; but instead of reconciliation, that day saw a massacre, as Catholics tried to stamp out Protestantism in France's capital city.

As princes sought to resolve religious questions within their domains, states increasingly became identified with one or another form of Christian faith—and, for Protestants, with a local language. (Protestants translated the Bible from Latin so that more people could read it.) In this way, religious strife propelled forward the process of state building and the forming of national identities. At the same time, religious conflict fueled rivalries for wealth and territory overseas. Thus, Europe entered its age of overseas exploration as a collection of increasingly powerful yet irreconcilably competitive rival states, whose differences stemmed not just from language but from the ways they worshipped the Christian God.

Prosperity in Asia

COMPARISON

COMPARE the major features of world trade in Asia, the Americas, Africa, and Europe.

While Europe was experiencing religious warfare, Asian empires were expanding and consolidating their power, and trade was flourishing. If anything, the arrival of European sailors and traders in the Indian Ocean strengthened trading ties across the region and enhanced the political power and expansionist interests of Asia's imperial regimes. The Mughal ruler of India, Akbar, and the Ottoman sultan, Suleiman the Magnificent (see Chapter 11), were effective and esteemed rulers. The Ming dynasty's elegant manufactures enjoyed worldwide renown, and its ability to govern vast numbers of highly diverse peoples led outsiders to consider China the model imperial state.

MUGHAL INDIA AND COMMERCE

The **Mughal Empire** became one of the world's wealthiest just when Europeans were establishing sustained connections with India. These connections, however, only touched the outer layer of Mughal India, one of Islam's greatest regimes. Established in 1526, it was a vigorous, centralized state whose political authority encompassed most of modern-day India. During the sixteenth century, it had a population of between 100 and 150 million.

The Mughals' strength rested on their military power. The dynasty's founder, Babur, had introduced horsemanship, artillery, and field cannons from central Asia, and gunpowder had secured his swift military victories over northern India. Under his grandson, Akbar (r. 1556–1605), the empire enjoyed expansion and consolidation that continued (under his own grandson, Aurangzeb) until it covered almost all of India (see Map 12.4). Known as the "Great Mughal," Akbar was skilled not only in military tactics but also in the art of alliance making. Deals with Hindu chieftains through favors and intermarriage also undergirded his empire.

Mughal rulers were flexible toward their realm's diverse peoples, especially in spiritual affairs. Though its primary commitment to Islam stood firm, the imperial court also patronized other beliefs, displaying a tolerance that earned it widespread legitimacy. The contrast with Europe, where religious differences drove deep fractures within and between states, was stark. Unlike European monarchs, who tried to enforce religious uniformity, Akbar studied comparative religion and hosted regular debates among Hindu, Muslim, Jain, Parsi, and Christian theologians. His tolerance kept a multifaceted spiritual kingdom under one political roof.

During the sixteenth century, expanded trade with Europe brought more wealth to the Mughal polity, while the empire's strength limited European incursions. Although the Portuguese occupied Goa and Bombay on the Indian coast, they had little presence elsewhere and dared not antagonize the Mughal emperor. In 1578, Akbar recognized

MAP 12.5 | Trade and Production in Ming China

The Ming Empire in the early seventeenth century was the world's most populous state and arguably its wealthiest.

- According to this map, list the main items involved in China's export-import trade, and identify some of the regions that purchased its exports.
- Evaluate the relative importance of China's internal and overland trade, and contrast it with overseas commerce.
- Locate the major trading and shipbuilding centers, and then explain how important the export trade was to the Ming Empire's prosperity.

China, enabled them to participate in China's expanding import-export trade. Within five years the number of Portuguese in Macao neared 1,000 (see Map 12.5).

Seeing how much the Portuguese were earning on Asian trade, the Spanish, English, and Dutch also ventured into Asian waters. With its monopoly on American silver, Spain enjoyed a competitive advantage. In 1565, the first Spanish trading galleon reached the Philippines;

Macao This Chinese painting depicts the Portuguese enclave of Macao on the southern border of China around 1800.

in 1571, after capturing Manila and making it a colonial capital, the Spanish established a brisk trade with China. Each year, ships from Spain's colonies in the Americas crossed the Pacific to Manila, bearing cargoes of silver. They returned carrying porcelain and silks for well-to-do European consumers. Merchants in Manila also procured silks, tapestries, and feathers from the China seas for shipment to the Americas, where the mining elite eagerly awaited these imports.

The year 1571 was altogether decisive in the history of the modern world. For the first time, Spanish ships were able to circle the globe from the New World to China and from China back to Europe. Silver was the commodity that linked the world commercially, the only foreign commodity for which the Chinese had an insatiable demand. From the mother lodes of the Andes and Mesoamerica, silver made the commerce of the world go round.

Other Europeans, too, wanted their share of Asia's wealth. The English and the Dutch reached the South China Sea by 1594. Five years later, 101 English investors pooled their funds and formed a joint-stock company (an association in which each member owned shares of capital). This English East India Company soon won a royal charter granting it exclusive rights to import East Indian goods. The company displaced the Portuguese in the Arabian Sea and the Persian Gulf. Doing a brisk trade in indigo, saltpeter, pepper, and cotton textiles, the English East India Company eventually acquired control of ports on both coasts of India—Fort St. George at the coastal city of Madras (1639), Bombay (1661), and Calcutta (1690).

The Europeans' arrival in the South China Sea and the Indian Ocean hardly spelled the beginning of the end of Asian autonomy. Confined to the coasts and a limited number of trading posts, the Europeans forged very weak connections to the ruling elites of Asian societies. For the moment, the Europeans' increased presence enhanced the wealth and might of Asian dynasties.

Conclusion

In the multicentered world of the fifteenth century, Europe was a poor cousin. However, a new spirit of adventure and achievement animated its peoples, stirred up by the rediscovery of antiquity (the Renaissance), the ambitions of merchants and other elites, and the spiritual fervor of the Reformation and Counter-Reformation. Desiring Asian luxury goods, European merchants and mariners were eager to exploit trade routes leading eastward, and new navigational techniques enabled them to sail into dangerous waters. More important, Europe's location promoted expansion across the largely unknown Atlantic Ocean. With the Ottomans controlling Constantinople and the eastern Mediterranean, Atlantic sea-lanes offered an alternative route to Asia. As Europeans searched for routes around Islamic territory, they first sailed down the coast of Africa and then across the Atlantic.

Encountering the "New World" was an accident of monumental significance. In the Americas, Europeans found riches. Mountains of silver and rivers of gold gave them the currency they needed for dealing with Asian traders. Europeans also found opportunities for exchange, conquest, and colonization. Yet, establishing these transatlantic empires heightened tensions within Europe, as rivals fought over the spoils and a religious schism turned into a divisive political and spiritual struggle.

Thus two conquests characterize this age of increasing world interconnections. The Islamic conquest of Constantinople drove Europeans to find new links to Asia. In turn, the Spanish conquest of the Aztecs and the Incas gave Europeans access to silver, which bought them an increased presence in Asian trading networks.

Amerindians also played an important role, as Europeans sought to conquer their lands, exploit their labor, and confiscate their gold and silver. Sometimes Amerindians worked with Europeans, sometimes under Europeans, sometimes against Europeans—and sometimes none were left to work at all. Then Europeans brought in African laborers, compounding the calamity of the encounter with the tragedy of slavery. Out of the catastrophe of contact, a new oceanic system arose to link Africa, America, and Europe. This was the Atlantic system. Unlike the tributary and trading orders of the Indian Ocean and China seas, the Atlantic Ocean supported a system of formal imperial control and settlement of distant colonies. These would become more important to how worlds connected and collided in the following centuries.

After You Read This Chapter

Go to INQUIZITIVE to see what you've learned—and learn what you've missed—with personalized feedback along the way.

FOCUS ON: *Regional Developments in the Age of Exploration*

EUROPE

- Portugal creates a trading empire in the Indian Ocean and the South China Sea.

- Spain and Portugal establish colonies in the Americas, discover silver, and establish export-oriented plantation economies.

- The Protestant Reformation breaks out in northern and western Europe, splitting the Catholic Church.

THE AMERICAS

- Millions of Amerindians, lacking immunity to European diseases, perish in every region of the New World.

- Spanish conquest and disease destroy the two great Native American empires in Mexico (the Aztecs) and Peru (the Incas).

AFRICA

- Trade in African captives fuels the Atlantic slave trade, which furnishes labor for European plantations in the Americas.

ASIA

- Asian empires—the Mughals in India, the Ming in China, and the Ottomans in western Asia and the eastern Mediterranean—barely notice the Americas but profit economically from enhanced global trade.

CHRONOLOGY

EUROPE		Luther begins Protestant Reformation 1517 ◆
THE AMERICAS		Columbus discovers the New World 1492 ◆
		Cortés conquers Aztec Empire 1522 ◆
		Pizarro conquers Inca Empire 1533 ◆
SOUTH ASIA		Da Gama sails to India 1498 ◆
		Portuguese establish bases around Indian Ocean 1508-1511 ▬
EAST ASIA		

- ***Thinking about Exchange Networks and the Age of Exploration*** In the fifteenth and sixteenth centuries, the densest trade networks and most powerful states remained centered in Asia. How did Columbus's "discovery" of the New World alter the terms on which peoples across Afro-Eurasia interacted with one another? What commodities and trade networks brought peoples together, on what terms, and what new inequalities did those contacts create around the world?

- ***Thinking about Changing Power Relationships and the Age of Exploration*** The effort to expand empires and trading networks differed substantially across Afro-Eurasia and the Americas in the fifteenth and sixteenth centuries. How did men and women at all levels of society contribute to this expansion? How did that participation shape or reshape their societies? Pay particular attention to the relationship between lower classes and elites.

- ***Thinking about Environmental Impacts and the Age of Exploration*** The Columbian exchange led to demographic catastrophe and environmental transformation in the New World. Why did the indigenous populations of the Americas get sick so much more often than Europeans? Why did the plants and animals of the New World increasingly come to resemble those of Afro-Eurasia?

1. Describe the obstacles to consolidating power in the **Aztec** and **Inca** empires before the arrival of European **conquistadors**.

2. Describe the **Columbian exchange** and explain how it influenced the different regions of the world.

3. Compare the **Atlantic system** with European trading in Asia.

4. Analyze the influence of religion on politics in **Mughal India** and Europe, including the **Holy Roman Empire**.

5. Explain how the **Jesuits** of the **Counter-Reformation** responded to the challenge posed by **Martin Luther** and **Jean Calvin** in the **Protestant Reformation**, both in Europe and around the world.

Religious and dynastic wars 1520s–1570s

Expansion and consolidation of Mughal empire 1556–1605

Portuguese establish trading port in Macao 1557

Spanish make Manila their major port in the Pacific Ocean 1571

Competing Perspectives

Cultural Contact in the Age of Exploration

O verseas exploration and commerce brought new contacts between Amerindians, Europeans, Africans, and Asians in the fifteenth and sixteenth centuries. The primary sources brought together here document important examples of cultural contact in this era and allow us to see how people from radically different cultures perceived one another. The Florentine Codex compiled accounts of the Spanish conquest from Mexica elites a generation after the fall of Tenochtitlán. Cortés recorded his impressions of Tenochtitlán and the Aztecs in his *Letters to Charles V*, king of Spain. Nzinga Mbemba, also known as Afonso I, king of the Congo (r. c. 1506–c. 1543), writes here of his frustration with Portuguese authorities, with whom he sought a partnership. The final document, from a Ming official named He Ao (Ho Ao), also complains that Europeans (called Feringis) were untrustworthy. Such sentiments were also common among officials in subsequent centuries, even as China thrived in the commercial exchanges of an increasingly connected world.

PRIMARY SOURCE 12.1

Aztec Views of the Spaniards (ca. 16th century), Florentine Codex

And when he [Moctezuma] heard what the messengers reported, he was greatly afraid and taken aback, and he was amazed at their food. It especially made him faint when he heard how the guns went off at [the Spaniards'] command, sounding like thunder, causing people actually to swoon, blocking the ears. And when it went off, something like a ball came out from inside, and fire went showering and spitting out. And the smoke that came from it had a very foul stench, striking one in the face. And if they shot at a hill, it seemed to crumble and come apart. And it turned a tree to dust; it seemed to make it vanish, as though someone had conjured it away. Their war gear was all iron. They clothed their bodies in iron, they put iron on their heads, their swords were iron, their bows were iron, and their shields and lances were iron.

And their deer that carried them were as tall as the roof. And they wrapped their bodies all over; only their faces could be seen, very white. Their faces were the color of limestone and their hair yellow-reddish, though some had black hair. They had long beards, also yellow-reddish. [The hair of some] was tightly curled. And their food was like fasting food, very large, white, not heavy, like chaff, like dried maize stalks, as tasty as maize stalk flour, a bit sweet or honeyed, honeyed and sweet to eat.

And their dogs were huge creatures, with their ears folded over and their jowls dragging. They had burning eyes, eyes like coals, yellow and fiery. They had thin, gaunt flanks with the rib lines showing; they were very tall. They did not keep quiet, they went about panting, with their tongues hanging down. They had spots like a jaguar's, they were vari-colored.

Source: The Florentine Codex, Lockhart translation from *We People Here: Nahuatl Accounts of the Conquest of Mexico* (1993) reprinted in Stuart Schwartz, *Victors and Vanquished: Spanish and Nahua Views of the Conquest of Mexico* (2000), 97.

PRIMARY SOURCE 12.2

Approaching Tenochtitlán (1521), Cortés

This great city of Tenochtitlán is built on the salt lake. . . . It has four approaches by means of artificial causeways. . . . The city is as large as Seville or Cordoba. Its streets . . . are very broad and straight, some of these, and all the others, are one half land, and the other half water on which they go about in canoes. . . . There are bridges, very large, strong, and well constructed, so that, over many, ten horsemen can ride abreast. . . . The city has many squares where markets are held. . . . There is one square, twice as large as that of Salamanca, all surrounded by arcades, where there are daily more than sixty thousand souls, buying and selling. . . . [I]n the service and manners of its people, their fashion of living was almost the same as in Spain, with just as much harmony and order; and considering that these people were barbarous, so cut off from the knowledge of God and other civilized peoples, it is admirable to see to what they attained in every respect. . . .

It happened . . . that a Spaniard saw an Indian . . . eating a piece of flesh taken from the body of an Indian who had been killed. . . . I had the culprit burned, explaining that the cause was his having killed that Indian and eaten him, which was prohibited by Your Majesty, and by me in Your Royal name. I further made the chief understand that all the people . . . must abstain from this custom. . . . I came . . . to protect their lives as well as their property, and to teach them that they were to adore but one God . . . that they must turn from their idols, and the rites they had practised until then, for these were lies and deceptions which the devil . . . had invented. . . . I, likewise, had come to teach them that Your Majesty, by the will of Divine Providence, rules the universe, and that they also must submit themselves to the imperial yoke, and do all that we who are Your Majesty's ministers here might order them. . . .

Source: *Letters of Cortés*, translated by Francis A. MacNutt (New York: G. P. Putnam, 1908), 244, 256–57.

PRIMARY SOURCE 12.3

Letters to the King of Portugal (1526), Nzinga Mbemba

Sir, Your Highness [of Portugal] should know how our Kingdom is being lost in so many ways that it is convenient to provide for the necessary remedy, since this is caused by the excessive freedom given by your factors and officials to the men and merchants who are allowed to come to this Kingdom to set up shops with goods and many things which have been prohibited by us, and which they spread throughout our Kingdoms and Domains in such an abundance that many of our vassals, whom we had in obedience, do not comply because they have the things in greater abundance than we ourselves; and it was with these things that we had them content and subjected under our vassalage and jurisdiction, so it is doing a great harm not only to the service of God, but the security and peace of our Kingdoms and State as well.

And we cannot reckon how great the damage is, since the mentioned merchants are taking every day our natives, sons of the land and the sons of our noblemen and vassals and our relatives, because the thieves and men of bad conscience grab them wishing to have the things and wares of this Kingdom which they are ambitious of; they grab them and get them to be sold; and so great, Sir, is the corruption and licentiousness that our country is being completely depopulated, and Your Highness should not agree with this nor accept it as in your service.

Source: Trans. Basil Davidson, *The African Past: Chronicles from Antiquity to Modern Times* (Boston: Little, Brown and Co., 1964), pp. 191–92.

PRIMARY SOURCE 12.4

Commentary on Foreigners (ca. 1420), Ming Official He Ao

The Feringis are most cruel and crafty. Their arms are superior to those of other foreigners. Some years ago they came suddenly to the city of Canton, and the noise of their cannon shook the earth [these were cannon-shots fired as a salute by the fleet of Fernão Peres]. Those who remained at the post-station [places where foreigners were lodged] disobeyed the law and had intercourse with others. Those who came to the Capital were proud and struggled [among themselves?] to become head. Now if we allow them to come and go and to carry on their trade, it will inevitably lead to fighting and bloodshed, and the misfortune of our South may be boundless.

In the time of our ancestors, foreigners came to bring tribute only at fixed periods, and the law provided for precautionary measures, therefore the foreigners who could come were not many. But some time ago the Provincial Treasurer, Wu T'ing-chü, saying that he needed spice to be sent to the Court, took some of their goods no matter when they came. It was due to what he did that foreigner ships have never ceased visiting our shores and that barbarians have lived scattered in our departmental cities. Prohibition and precaution having been neglected, the Feringis became more and more familiar with our fair ways. And thus availing themselves of the situation the Feringis came into our port. I pray that all the foreign junks in our bay and the foreigners who secretly live (in our territory) be driven away, that private intercourse be prohibited and that our strategical defence be close, so that that part of our country will have peace.

Source: T'ien-Tse Chang, *Sino-Portuguese Trade from 1514 to 1644: A Synthesis of Portuguese and Chinese Sources* (Leyden: E. J. Brill, 1934), pp. 51–52. Reprinted by permission of Koninklijke Brill NV.

QUESTIONS FOR ANALYSIS

1. Identify the features of Tenochtitlán that most impressed Cortés and analyze the justification he provides for his actions.

2. Explain why the Mexica elite (of the 1550–60s) might have portrayed Moctezuma as afraid. Pay special attention to local politics before the Spaniards arrived.

3. Compare the Aztec, Congolese, and Chinese portrayals of Europeans.

4. Contrast the recommendations offered by Nzinga Mbemba and Ming Official He Ao to solve the problems posed by European intervention in their societies, and explain the significance of the differences.

Interpreting Visual Evidence

Conflict and Consent

In the fifteen and sixteenth centuries, new contacts led to conflict and, in some cases, consent. The consolidation of existing land empires, especially in Asia, required rulers to manage vast, diverse populations. They often used policies of tolerance to win the consent of their new subjects. European overseas empires, by contrast, almost immediately came into conflict with indigenous societies, decimating the Amerindian population and drafting African slaves to perform labor the remaining Amerindians refused. This resulted in societies in the Americas that initially had extremely pronounced cultural differences.

Depictions of these encounters show the dynamics between the groups involved, as well as the artist's point of view. The first image below, an anonymous Mexican painting (c. 1520), portrays Spanish soldiers in gleaming body armor with muskets firing on Amerindians, who are barely visible at the painting's edges and armed only with bows and arrows. The second, *The Conquest of the Aztecs*, was drawn by a converted Amerindian later in the sixteenth century and relied on indigenous oral histories and familiar artistic forms. It shows the Aztec warriors in full battle dress and also portrays their battles with other Amerindians who had sided with the Spanish. In the final image, *Akbar Hears a Petition*, the individuals gathered before Akbar represent the diversity of people who sought the assistance of the Mughal emperor. This miniature reflects the multiethnic and multireligious character of Akbar's empire and the tolerance required to maintain social cohesion.

Anonymous Mexican painting of Spanish conquest.

The Conquest of the Aztecs, *drawn by a converted Amerindian.*

Akbar Hears a Petition.

QUESTIONS FOR ANALYSIS

1. In the first two images, note the divisions within each camp, Spanish and Aztec. Explain how each portray the Aztec defeat. What do they present to explain the defeat, and what factors, emphasized in this chapter, do they both omit?

2. Interpret the artist's portrayal of Akbar's authority in the third image. Describe the audience presented in the painting. What can you tell about the different groups present?

3. Contrast the first two images with the third. Pay special attention to the center of each image. Describe which elements the artists privilege, in visual terms. What does that say about the social order?

4. Explain who you think was the audience for each image. Were all three produced for rulers, their court, the elite in general, a particular ethno-religious or social group, or the general public?

Before You Read This Chapter

GLOBAL STORYLINES

- Transoceanic trade networks (on an unprecedented scale) created vast wealth and new kinds of inequality.

- Silver gave Europeans a commodity to exchange with Asians and began to tilt the balance of wealth and power from Asia toward Europe.

- New World sugar also accelerated the shift of power in the Atlantic world from the Spanish and Portuguese to the British and French.

- European merchants and African leaders radically increased the volume and violence of the slave trade, destabilizing African societies.

- Asian rulers in India, China, and Japan, and Russian tsars enlarged their empires.

- The Ottoman, Safavid, and Mughal dynasties all struggled to resist European assaults.

CORE OBJECTIVES

- **IDENTIFY** and **EXPLAIN** the major steps in the integration of global trade networks in the seventeenth and eighteenth centuries, and **ANALYZE** examples of resistance to this integration.

- **ANALYZE** the consequences of the Atlantic slave trade for African societies.

- **EXPLAIN** the effects of New World silver and increased trade on the Asian empires and their response to it.

- **COMPARE** the impact of trade and religion on state power in various regions.

- **EXPLAIN** the significance of European consumption of goods (like tobacco, textiles, and sugar) for the global economy.

Worlds Entangled

1600–1750

In 1720, a financial panic engulfed Europe, making rich men into paupers and ruining many political careers. The panic arose from dashed hopes for huge profits from trade with the Americas. A group of British merchants established the South Sea Trading Company to compete with French firms and obtained privileged trading rights with all of Spanish America. Most coveted was the exclusive right to sell African slaves to Spanish colonies. As enthusiasm for such companies soared, eager investors sent share prices skyrocketing. But rumors of fantastic gains gave way to word that the original investors were dumping their shares and that the companies were worthless. Then the bubble burst. Share prices plummeted, nearly all the new companies went bankrupt, and many older firms collapsed. The so-called South Sea Bubble reflected the excitement—and the risks—of global trade and investment.

From 1600 to 1750, global trading networks propelled commerce across the world's oceans. New World silver was crucial to these networks in the early stages: it gave Europeans a commodity to exchange with Asians. From about 1600, however, other goods became as important as silver, as tobacco and then sugar flowed from Brazil and the Caribbean, spices from Southeast Asia, cotton textiles from India, and silks from China. The cumulative result was to tilt the balance of wealth and power towards Europe.

Stimulants, Sociability, and Coffeehouses

While armies, travelers, missionaries, and diseases have breached the world's main political and cultural barriers, commodities have been the least respectful of the lines that separate communities. It has been difficult for ruling elites to curtail the desire of their populations to dress themselves in fine garments, to possess jewelry, and to consume satisfying food and drink no matter where these products may originate. The history of commodities, thus, is a core area for world historical research, for products span cultural barriers and connects peoples over long distances. As the world's trading networks expanded in the seventeenth and eighteenth centuries, merchants in Europe, Asia, Africa, and the Americas distributed many new commodities. By far the most popular were a group of stimulants—coffee, cocoa, sugar, tobacco, and tea—all of which (except for sugar) were addictive and also produced a sense of well-being. Previously, many of these products had been grown in isolated parts of the world: the coffee bean in Yemen, tobacco and cocoa in the New World, and sugar in Bengal. Yet, by the seventeenth century, in nearly every corner of the world, the well-to-do began to congregate in coffeehouses, consuming these new products and engaging in sociable activities.

Coffeehouses everywhere served as locations for social exchange, political discussions, and business activities. Yet they also varied from cultural area to cultural area, reflecting the values of the societies in which they arose.

The coffeehouse first appeared in Islamic lands late in the fifteenth century. As coffee consumption caught on among the wealthy and leisured classes in the Arabian Peninsula and the Ottoman Empire, local growers protected their advantage by monopolizing its cultivation and sale and refusing to allow any seeds or cuttings from the coffee tree to be taken abroad.

Despite some religious opposition, coffee spread into Egypt and throughout the Ottoman Empire in the sixteenth century. Ottoman bureaucrats, merchants, and artists assembled in coffeehouses to trade stories, read, listen to poetry, and play chess and backgammon. Indeed, so deeply connected were coffeehouses with literary and artistic pursuits that people referred to them as schools of knowledge.

From the Ottoman territories, the culture of coffee drinking spread to western Europe. The first coffeehouse in London opened in 1652, and within sixty years the city claimed no fewer than 500 such establishments. In fact, the Fleet Street area of London had so many that the English essayist Charles Lamb commented, "[T]he man must have a rare recipe for melancholy who can be dull in Fleet Street." Although coffeehouses attracted people from all levels of society, they especially appealed to the new mercantile and

COMPARISON

IDENTIFY and **EXPLAIN** the major steps in the integration of global trade networks in the seventeenth and eighteenth centuries.

Imperial expansion and transoceanic trade now brought the world together as never before. Europeans conquered and colonized more of the Americas, the demand for African slaves to work New World plantations leaped upward, and global trade intensified. Conquest, colonization, and commerce created riches for some but also provoked bitter rivalries. In the Americas, Spain and Portugal faced new competitors—primarily England and France. With religious tensions added to the mix, the stage was set for decades of bloody warfare in Europe and the Americas. At the same time, in the East, rulers in India, China, and Japan enlarged their empires, while Russia's tsars incorporated Siberian territories into their domain. Meanwhile, the Ottoman, Safavid, and Mughal dynasties, though resisting most European intrusions, found their stability profoundly shaken by the forces that entangled the world.

Economic and Political Effects of Global Commerce

Global trade affected not only merchant groups and their sponsoring nations but also individual rulers and common people. Increasing economic ties brought new places and products into world markets. (See **Current Trends in World History: Stimulants, Sociability,** beverages in turn required liberal doses of the sweetener sugar. A smoke of tobacco topped off the experience. In this environment of pleasure, patrons of the coffeehouses indulged their addictions, engaged in gossip, conducted business, and talked politics.

QUESTIONS FOR ANALYSIS

- What factors drove the consumption of stimulants like coffee on a global scale?
- What other commodities from earlier in world history played a similar role? Were there differences in the underlying factors such as scale of consumption between the different periods?

Coffee Coffee drinkers at an Ottoman banquet (left) and in an English coffeehouse (right).

professional classes as locations where stimulating beverages like coffee, cocoa, and tea promoted lively conversations. Here, too, opponents claimed that excessive coffee drinking destabilized the thinking processes and even caused conversions to Islam. But against such opposition, the pleasures of coffee, tea, and cocoa prevailed. These bitter

Explore Further

Ralph S. Hattox, *Coffee and Coffeehouses: The Origins of a Social Beverage in the Medieval Near East* (1985).

and Coffeehouses.) Closer economic contact enhanced the power of certain states and destabilized others. It bolstered the legitimacy of England and France, and it prompted strong local support of new rulers in Japan and parts of sub-Saharan Africa. But also in England, France, Japan, Russia, and Africa, linkages led to civil wars and social unrest. In the Ottoman state, outlying provinces slipped from central control; the Safavid regime foundered and then collapsed; the Ming dynasty gave way to the Qing. In India, rivalries among princes and merchants eroded the Mughals' authority, compounding the instability caused by peasant uprisings.

COMPARISON

EXPLAIN the significance of European consumption of goods (like tobacco, textiles, and sugar) for the global economy.

EXTRACTING WEALTH: MERCANTILISM

Transformations in global relations began in the Atlantic, where the extraction and shipment of gold and silver siphoned wealth from the New World (the Americas) to the Old World (Afro-Eurasia). (See Map 13.1.) American exports were so lucrative for Spain and Portugal that other European powers wanted a share in the bounty, so they too launched colonizing ventures in the New World. Although these latecomers found few precious minerals, they devised other ways to extract wealth, for the Americas had fertile lands on which to cultivate sugarcane, cotton, tobacco, indigo, and rice.

MAP 13.1 | Trade in Silver and Other Commodities, 1650–1750

The seventeenth and eighteenth centuries were the first centuries of true global commerce. Silver was the one item that was traded all over the world.

- Can you trace the flows of silver from the Americas around the globe (by following the thick red arrows) and identify the commodities that silver was exchanged for in different parts of the world?

- Does the map provide enough information for you to conclude which of these global empires was the wealthiest and most powerful?

- According to this map, how did increased trade shape European states' territorial ambitions?

Map labels:
GREENLAND, ICELAND, ALASKA, DENMARK, NETHERLANDS, ENGLAND, Amsterdam, London, Paris, FRANCE, PORTUGAL, SPAIN, Lisbon, Seville, Cadiz, RUPERT'S LAND, NEWFOUNDLAND, Québec, NOVA SCOTIA, Boston, Philadelphia, New York, THIRTEEN COLONIES, NEW FRANCE, LOUISIANA, VICEROYALTY OF NEW SPAIN, Zacatecas, MEXICO, Mexico City, Veracruz, Acapulco, New Orleans, CURAÇAO, Cartagena, Panama, VICEROYALTY OF GRANADA, Quito, Lima, SURINAM, VICEROYALTY OF BRAZIL, DUTCH BRAZIL, Recife, Bahia, Rio de Janeiro, Potosí, VICEROYALTY OF PERU, Buenos Aires, Timbuktu, HAUSA, ASANTE, OYO, Lagos, Accra, FERNANDO PO, ATLANTIC OCEAN, PACIFIC OCEAN, Line of Tordesillas 1494

Trade commodity boxes:
Tobacco / Rice / Furs / Indigo / Meat / Timber / Grain / Taxes
From North America and Carribean
Manufactures
Sugar / Gold / Hides / Coffee / Diamonds / Calico / Taxes
From South America
Sugar / Coffee / Indigo / Cotton
Sugar / Indigo / Hides / Taxes
Slaves
Iron / Copper / Textiles / Cutlery / Firearms
Slaves
Tobacco / Sugar
Silk / Spices
Pepper / Spices / Silk / Coffee
Spices
Silk / Calico
Silk / Calico / Coffee / Pepper / Indigo / Drugs
Cape Town, Indonesia, Malaysia, Goa, China, India

ARCTIC OCEAN

RUSSIAN EMPIRE

SWEDEN
St. Petersburg
Danzig
POLAND
AUSTRIA
OTTOMAN
EMPIRE
Aleppo
Baghdad SAFAVID
Isfahan
Alexandria Suez Basra EMPIRE
ARABIA Hormuz
Muscat
ETHIOPIA
BENIN

JAPAN

Silk
Spices

PACIFIC
OCEAN

Delhi
MUGHAL
EMPIRE
Plassey BENGAL
BIHAR
Diu Calcutta
DECCAN
Bombay PLATEAU
Goa Madras
Tellicherry
Pondicherry
Cochin
CEYLON

QING CHINA

Guangzhou

Rangoon Da Nang PHILIPPINES
ANNAM Manila
(VIETNAM)

Mogadishu
Malindi
Mombasa
ZANZIBAR
Kilwa
Luanda

Melaka
SUMATRA BORNEO MALUKU
Banten NEW GUINEA
Batavia
JAVA TIMOR BANDA

Mozambique
Sofala
MADAGASCAR
MAURITIUS
RÉUNION

INDIAN
OCEAN

Delagoa Bay

Cape
Town
Cape of
Good Hope

�it Spanish territory	◀━ Silver flow
Portuguese territory	◀— Trade route
English territory	✕ Battle
French territory	Silk Commodity
Dutch territory	
Anglo-French contested area	

0   1000   2000 Miles
0   1000   2000 Kilometers

If silver quickened the pace of global trade, sugar transformed the European diet. First domesticated in Polynesia, sugar rarely appeared in European diets before the New World plantations started exporting it. Previously, Europeans had used honey as a sweetener, but they soon became insatiable consumers of sugar. Between 1690 and 1790, Europe imported 12 million tons of sugar—approximately one ton for every African enslaved in the Americas.

No matter what products they supplied, colonies were supposed to provide wealth for their "mother countries"—according to the economic theory of mercantilism, which drove European empire builders. The term **mercantilism** describes a system that saw the world's wealth as fixed, meaning that any one country's wealth came at the expense of other countries. Mercantilism further assumed that overseas possessions existed solely to enrich European motherlands. Thus, colonies should ship more "value" to the mother country than they received in return. Colonies were supposed to be closed to competitors, so that foreign traders would not drain precious resources from an empire's exclusive domain. As the mother country's monopoly over its colonies' trade generated precious metals for royal treasuries, European states grew rich enough to wage almost unceasing wars against one another. Ultimately, mercantilists believed, as did the English philosopher Thomas Hobbes (1588–1679), that "wealth is power and power is wealth."

The mercantilist system required an alliance between the state and its merchants. Mercantilists understood economics and politics as interdependent, with the merchant needing the monarch to protect his interests and the monarch relying on the merchant's trade to enrich the state's treasury. **Chartered companies**, such as the (English) Virginia Company and the Dutch East India Company were the most visible examples of the collaboration between the state and the merchant classes. European monarchs awarded these firms monopoly trading rights over vast areas.

Exchanges and Expansions in North America

As rulers in England, France, and Holland granted monopolies to merchant companies, they began to dominate the settlement and trade of new colonies in the Americas and compete with the established colonies of Spain and Portugal. (See Map 13.2.) Although the search for precious metals or water routes to Asia had initially spurred British, French, and Dutch efforts to establish New World colonies, they soon learned that only by exploiting other resources could they generate profits.

EXPANDING MAINLAND COLONIES

While the Dutch relied primarily on commerce, the British and the French exploited natural resources in their North American colonies: the British established farms in a number of ecological zones, while the French relied primarily on the fur trade, especially in the interior.

In their colonies along the Atlantic seaboard, the English established one model for new colonies in the Americas. Although these territories failed to yield precious metals or a waterway across the continent, they did boast land suitable for growing a variety of crops. Different climates and soils made for very different agricultural possibilities: wheat, rye, barley, and oats in the Middle Colonies; tobacco in Virginia and North Carolina; and rice and indigo further south. In all of England's North American colonies, population growth fed greater hunger for farmlands, which put pressure on Indian holdings. The result: a souring of relations between Native Americans and colonists, often ferocious wars

MAP 13.2 | Colonies in North America, 1607–1763

France, England, and Spain laid claim to much of North America at this time.

- Where was each of these colonial powers strongest before the outbreak of the Seven Years' War in 1756? (See p. 486 for a discussion of the Seven Years' War.)

- Which empire gained the most North American territory, and who lost the most at the end of the war in 1763?

- How do you think Native American peoples reacted to the territorial arrangements agreed to by Spain, France, and England at the Peace of Paris, which ended the war?

Woodlands Native Americans This late-sixteenth-century drawing by John White, a pioneer settler on Roanoke Island off the coast of North Carolina, depicts the Native American village of Secoton in eastern Virginia. In contrast to the great empires that the Spanish conquered in the valley of Mexico and in the Andes, the Native Americans whom English, French, and Dutch colonizers encountered in the woodlands of eastern North America generally lived in villages that were politically autonomous entities.

between natives and newcomers, and, over the course of the seventeenth and eighteenth centuries, the dispossession of Indians from lands between the Atlantic Ocean and the Appalachian Mountains.

By contrast, Dutch and French colonies rested not on the expulsion of natives, but on dependence on them. Holland's North American venture, however, proved short-lived, as the English took over New Netherland and renamed it New York in 1664. French claims were more enduring and extended across a vast swath of the continent, encompassing eastern Canada, the Great Lakes, and the Mississippi Valley. Crucial to the trade between Europeans and Native Americans in the northern parts of North America was the beaver, an animal for which Native Americans previously had little use.

The distinctive aspect of the fur trade was the Europeans' utter dependence on Native American know-how. After all, trapping required familiarity with the beavers' habits and habitats, which Europeans lacked. This reliance forced the French to adapt to Native American ways, which is evident in their pattern of exchange. Responding to Native American desires to use trade as an instrument to cement familial bonds, the French gave gifts, participated in Native American diplomatic rituals, and even married into Native American families. As a result, *métis* (French–Native American offspring) played an important role in New France as interpreters, traders, and guides. Thus, the French colonization of the Americas—owing to their reliance on Native Americans as trading partners, military allies, and mates—rested more on cooperation than conquest, especially compared to the empires built by their Spanish and English rivals.

As French (and English) traders introduced guns into the exchange networks, however, they initiated an arms race among Native Americans. To get more guns, Native Americans had to collect more skins, which resulted in the depletion of beavers in heavily trapped areas. That, in turn, pushed Native Americans to expand their hunting/trapping zones, which heightened conflicts between groups now increasingly competing for hunting territories. Alcohol, too, became a potent weapon for Europeans. It gave them a commodity that Native Americans wanted badly enough to undermine long-standing understandings of the relationship between humans and animals and to overwhelm strictures against overhunting.

The initial agricultural endeavors in the New World were modest. They relied on crops like tobacco that required relatively modest capital investments and could be profitably farmed on a small scale, with few workers. Sugar, by contrast, required major investments. It had to be processed near the cane fields, which meant mills had to be built; and it required massive amounts of labor. Produced on a large scale with slave labor, sugar was enormously profitable. From the middle of the seventeenth century, the British and French devoted their energies to replicating the Portuguese sugar plantations of Brazil on the islands they controlled in the Caribbean. All was not sweet there, however.

The Fur Trade For Europeans in northern North America, no commodity was as important as beaver skins. For the French especially, the fur trade determined the character of their colonial regime in North America. For Native Americans, it offered access to European goods, but overhunting depleted resources and provoked intertribal conflicts.

The Plantation Complex in the Caribbean

Large European plantations in the Caribbean relied on slave labor to produce sugar for export. Sugar was a killing crop. So deadly was the hot, humid environment in which sugarcane flourished (as fertile for disease as for sugarcane) that many sugar barons spent little time on their plantations. Management fell to overseers, who worked their slaves to death. Despite having immunities to yellow fever and malaria from their homeland's similar environment, the African slaves who worked on the plantations could not withstand the regimen. Inadequate food, atrocious living conditions, and a lack of sanitation added to their miseries. Moreover, plantation managers on large sugar plantations treated their slaves as nonhumans: one English gentleman commented that slaves were like cows, "as near as beasts may be, setting their souls aside."

More than disease and inadequate rations, the work itself decimated the enslaved. Average life expectancy was three years. Six days a week slaves rose before dawn, labored until noon, ate a short lunch, and then worked until dusk. At harvest time, sixteen-hour days saw hundreds of men, women, and children doubled over to cut the sugarcane and transport it to refineries, sometimes seven days per week. Under this brutal schedule, slaves occasionally dropped dead from exhaustion.

Amid disease and toil, the enslaved resisted as they could. The most dramatic expression of resistance was violent revolt. A more common form of resistance was flight. Seeking refuge from overseers, thousands of slaves took to the hills—for example, to the remote mountains of Caribbean islands or to Brazil's vast interior. Those who remained on the plantations resisted via foot dragging, pilfering, and sabotage.

Caribbean settlements and slaveholdings were not restricted to any single European power. But it was the latecomers—especially the English and the French—who concentrated on the islands of the Caribbean. (See Map 13.3.) The English took Jamaica from the Spanish and made it the premier site of Caribbean sugar by the 1740s. When the French seized half of Santo Domingo in the 1660s (renaming it Saint-Domingue, which is present-day Haiti), they created one of the wealthiest societies based on slavery of all time. This French colony's exports eclipsed those of all the Spanish and English islands combined. By 1789, French

Tobacco The cultivation of tobacco saved the Virginia colony from ruin and brought prosperity to increasing numbers of planters. The spread of tobacco plantations also pushed Native Americans off their lands and led planters to turn to Africa for a labor force.

Saint-Domingue produced nearly half of the world's supply of sugar and coffee. Its principal port city, Cap Français, was among the richest in the Atlantic world. The colony's merchants and planters built immense mansions worthy of the highest European nobles. Thus the Atlantic system benefited elite Europeans, who amassed new fortunes by exploiting the colonies' rich soil (which they eroded) and tropical climate, and the African slaves' labor.

The Slave Trade and Africa

COMPARISON

DESCRIBE the consequences of the Atlantic slave trade for African societies.

Although the slave trade began in the mid-fifteenth century, only in the seventeenth and eighteenth centuries did the numbers of human exports from Africa begin to soar. (See Map 13.4.) By 1820, four slaves had crossed the Atlantic for every European. (See **Analyzing Global Developments: The Atlantic Trade in Slaves from Africa**.) Those numbers were essential to the prosperity of Europe's American colonies. At the same time, the departure of so many inhabitants depopulated and destabilized many parts of Africa.

CAPTURING AND SHIPPING SLAVES

Merchants in Europe and the New World prospered as the slave trade grew, but their fortunes depended on trading and political networks in Africa. In fact, before the nineteenth-century discovery of quinine, European slavers could not survive in the African interior. Instead they took advantage of Africans' rivalries. Using firearms supplied by Europeans, African elites controlled the capturing of slaves; their networks linked moneylenders and traders on the coast with allies in the interior.

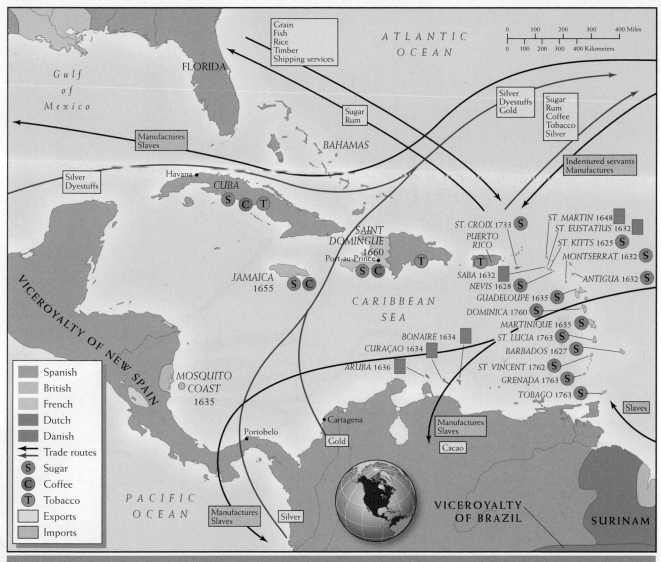

MAP 13.3 | Caribbean Colonies, 1625–1763

The Caribbean was a region of expanding trade in the seventeenth and eighteenth centuries.

- What were its major exports and imports?
- Who were its main colonizers and trading partners?
- According to your reading, how did the transformation of this region shape other societies in the Atlantic world?

Before the Europeans' arrival, Africa had an already existing system of slave commerce, mainly flowing across the Sahara to North Africa and Egypt and eastward to the Red Sea and the Swahili coast of East Africa. From the Red Sea and Swahili coast destinations, Muslim and Hindu merchants shipped slaves to ports around the Indian Ocean. However, the number of these slaves could not match the volume destined for the Americas once plantation agriculture began to spread. Indeed, 12.5 million Africans survived forcible enslavement and shipment to Atlantic ports from 1525 (the date of the first direct voyage from Africa to the Americas) until 1867 (when the last voyage took place).

Now the slave ports along the African coast became gruesome holding pens. Many slaves who perished did so before losing sight of Africa. Stuck in vast camps where disease

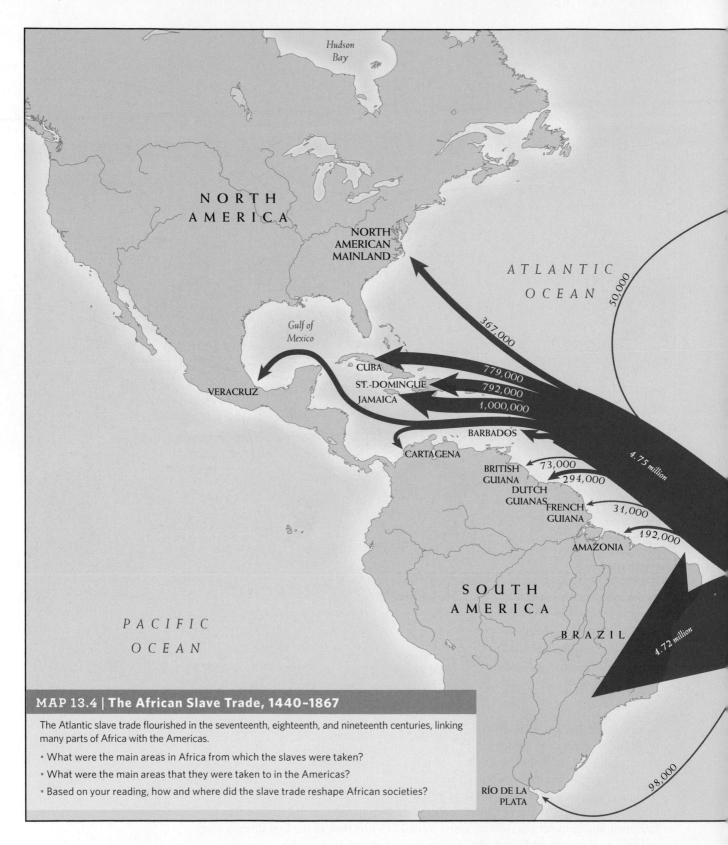

MAP 13.4 | The African Slave Trade, 1440–1867

The Atlantic slave trade flourished in the seventeenth, eighteenth, and nineteenth centuries, linking many parts of Africa with the Americas.

- What were the main areas in Africa from which the slaves were taken?
- What were the main areas that they were taken to in the Americas?
- Based on your reading, how and where did the slave trade reshape African societies?

NORTH
SEA

EUROPE

BLACK SEA

ARAL
SEA

CASPIAN SEA

ASIA

PERSIA

Persian Gulf

MEDITERRANEAN
SEA

MOROCCO

ALGERIA TUNISIA

LIBYA

EGYPT

RED SEA

ARABIA

2 million (1700–1900)

SAHARA

4.32 million

YEMEN

ETHIOPIA

892,000

ARABIAN
SEA

280,000

533,000

SENEGAMBIA

SIERRA
LEONE

WINDWARD
COAST

GOLD
COAST

ASANTE
STATE OF
BENIN

BIGHT
OF
BIAFRA

AFRICA

756,000

389,000

337,000

1.2 million

1.99 million

1.6 million

AMERICAS
12.57 million
(1501–1867)

KONGO
KINGDOM

WEST
CENTRAL
AFRICA

5.7 million

SWAHILI
COAST

INDIAN

OCEAN

SOUTHEAST
AFRICA

200,000

MADAGASCAR

MASCARENE
ISLANDS
359,000

0   500   1000   1500 Miles
0   500   1000   1500 Kilometers

Analyzing Global Developments

The Atlantic Trade in Slaves from Africa (1501–1900)

The world's leading slave traders were also the world's most important maritime powers during the period from 1501–1900. The two tables to the right focus on which countries transported these slaves and where they ended up. The Spanish and Portuguese established the first European empires in the Americas and created the model for the early slave trade. But Northern European powers like Great Britain and France, reflecting their growing strength in maritime commerce, dominated the Atlantic slave trade between 1642 and 1808. In the final phase of the Atlantic slave trade from 1808 to 1867, the Northern European powers and the United States disengaged from the slave trade, allowing the Portuguese and the Spanish to once again dominate the trade now centered largely on Cuba and Brazil.

In recent decades, scholars of the Atlantic slave trade have created the Trans-Atlantic Slave Trade Database, which can be accessed at the Voyages Web site (www.slavevoyages.org). Constructed from nearly 35,000 documented voyages during this period, this database incorporates roughly 80 percent of the slave ventures that set out for Africa to obtain slaves from all around the Atlantic world during this era. Through painstaking research historians have been able to reconstruct the Atlantic world slave trade and offer a clear insight into the experiences of all those involved and the impact of this trade on the global economy during these four centuries.

QUESTIONS FOR ANALYSIS

- Identify the countries that were the most heavily invested in the Atlantic slave trade based on the data in the first table. How do you know?

- Explain the relationship between the slave-trading countries and the colonies in the New World based on the entries in both tables.

- Why is the total number of slaves traded different from the number of slaves that disembarked? Did you expect the difference between these two numbers to be greater? If so, why?

Number of Slaves Taken from Africa to Americas by Nationality of Vessels That Carried Them (1501–1867)

VESSEL NATIONALITY	NUMBER OF SLAVES
Portugal/Brazil	5,849,300
Great Britain	3,259,900
France	1,380,970
Spain/Uruguay	1,060,900
Netherlands	555,300
United States	305,800
Baltic States	110,400
Total Atlantic World	**12,522,570**

Disembarkation of Slaves from Africa to the Americas 1501–1900

DISEMBARKING COUNTRY/COLONY	NUMBER OF SLAVES
Brazil (Portugal)	4.72 million
Smaller Caribbean Islands (mix)	1.75 million
Jamaica (Spain then Great Britain)	1.00 million
St.-Domingue (Spain then France)	792,000
Cuba (Spain)	779,000
Spanish Caribbean Mainland	390,000
United States	389,000
Dutch Guiana	294,000
Amazonia	142,000
Total	**10,703,000**

Source: David Eltis and David Richardson, Atlas of the Transatlantic Slave Trade (New Haven, 2010).

and hunger were rampant, the slaves were then forced aboard vessels in cramped and wretched conditions. These ships waited for weeks to fill their holds while their human cargoes wasted away below deck. Crew members tossed dead Africans overboard as they loaded on other Africans from the shore. When the cargo was complete, the ships set sail.

The Slave Trade (*Left*) Africans were captured in the interior and then bound and marched to the coast. Note that there is only one woman among the men (and a couple of children), reflecting the gender imbalance among those captured. (*Right*) After reaching the coast, the captured Africans would be crammed into the holds of slave vessels, where they suffered grievously from overcrowding and unsanitary conditions. Long voyages were especially deadly. If the winds failed or ships had to travel longer distances than usual, many of the captives would die en route to the slave markets across the ocean.

In their wake, crews continued to dump bodies. Most died of dehydration brought on by gastrointestinal diseases and a lack of fresh water. Smallpox and dysentery were also scourges. Either way, death was slow and agonizing.

SLAVERY'S GENDER IMBALANCE

In moving so many Africans to the Americas, the slave trade played havoc with the ratios of men to women in both places because most of the slaves shipped to the Americas were adult men. Although the numbers indicated Europeans' preferences for male laborers, they also reflected African slavers' desire to keep female slaves, primarily for household work. The gender imbalance made it difficult for slaves to reproduce in the Americas. So planters and slavers had to return to Africa to procure more captives—especially for the Caribbean islands, where slaves' death rates were so high.

Male slaves outnumbered females in the New World, but in the slave-supplying regions of Africa women outnumbered men. Female captives were especially prized in Africa because of their traditional role in the production of grains, leathers, and cotton. Moreover, the slave trade reinforced the traditional practice of polygamy—allowing relatively scarce men to take several wives, which helped minimize the loss of population.

AFRICA'S NEW SLAVE-SUPPLYING STATES

Africans did not passively let captives fall into the arms of European slave buyers; instead, local political leaders and merchants were active suppliers. This activity promoted the growth of centralized political structures, particularly in West African rain forest areas. The trade also shifted control of wealth away from households owning large herds or lands to those who profited from the capture and exchange of slaves—urban merchants and warrior elites.

The Port of Loango Partly as a result of the profits of the slave trade, African rulers and merchants were able to create large and prosperous port cities such as Loango, pictured here, which was on the west coast of south-central Africa.

In some parts of Africa, the booming slave trade created chaos as local leaders feuded over control of the traffic. In the Kongo kingdom, for example, civil wars raged for over a century after 1665, and captured warriors were sold as slaves. As members of the royal family clashed, entire provinces saw their populations vanish. Europeans fueled these conflicts and provided weapons to their African allies. Moreover, kidnapping became so prevalent that farmers worked their fields bearing weapons, leaving their children behind in guarded stockades.

As some African merchants and warlords sold other Africans, their commercial success enabled them to consolidate political power and grow wealthy. Their wealth financed additional weapons, with which they subdued neighbors and extended political control. Among the most durable new polities was the Asante state, which arose in the West African tropical rain forest in 1701 and expanded through 1750. This state benefited from its access to gold, which it used to acquire firearms (from European traders) to raid nearby communities for captives to be sold into slavery in the Americas. From its capital city at Kumasi, the state eventually encompassed almost all of present-day Ghana. Main roads spread out from the capital like spokes of a wheel, each approximately twenty days' travel from the center. Through the Asante trading networks African traders bought, bartered, and sold captives, who wound up in the hands of European merchants waiting in ports with vessels carrying manufactures and weaponry.

Slavery and the emergence of new states enriched and empowered some Africans, but they cost Africa dearly. For the princes, warriors, and merchants who organized the slave trade, their business enabled them to obtain European goods—especially alcohol, tobacco, textiles, and guns. The Atlantic system also tilted wealth away from rural dwellers and village elders and increasingly toward port cities. Across the landmass, the slave trade thinned the population. True, Africa was spared a demographic catastrophe equal to the devastation of American Indians. The introduction of American food crops—notably maize and cassava, producing many more calories per acre than the old staples of millet and sorghum—blunted the trade's depopulating aspects. Yet some areas suffered grievously from three centuries of heavy involvement in the slave trade. The Atlantic trade enhanced the warrior class, who carried out raids for captives; the dislocations, internal power struggles, and economic hardships that followed precipitated the rise and fall of West African kingdoms.

Asia in the Seventeenth and Eighteenth Centuries

Global trading networks grew as vigorously in Asia as they did in the Americas. In Asia, however, the Europeans were less dominant. Although they could gain access to Asian markets with American silver, they could not conquer Asian empires or colonize vast portions of the region. Nor were they able to enslave Asian peoples as they had Africans. The Mughal Empire continued to grow, and the Qing dynasty, which had wrested control from the Ming, significantly expanded China's borders. China remained the richest state in the world, but in some places the balance of power was tilting in Europe's direction. Not only did the Ottomans' borders contract, but by the late eighteenth century Europeans had established economic and military dominance in parts of India and much of Southeast Asia.

COMPARISON

EXPLAIN the effects of New World silver and increased trade on the Asian empires, and their responses to them.

THE DUTCH IN SOUTHEAST ASIA

In Southeast Asia the Dutch already enjoyed considerable influence by the seventeenth century. Although the Portuguese had seized the vibrant port city of Melaka in 1511 and the Spaniards had taken Manila in 1571, neither was able to monopolize the lucrative spice trade. To challenge them, the Dutch government persuaded its merchants to charter the Dutch East India Company (abbreviated as VOC) in 1602. Benefiting from Amsterdam's position as the most efficient money market with the lowest interest rates in the world, the VOC raised ten times the capital of its English counterpart—the royal chartered English East India Company. The advantages of chartered companies were evident

Attack on Bantam This engraving depicts a Dutch attack on Bantam in the late seventeenth century as part of the VOC's effort to expand its empire in Southeast Asia.

in the VOC's scale of operation: at its peak the company had 257 ships and employed 12,000 persons. Throughout two centuries it sent ships manned by a total of 1 million men to Asia.

The VOC's main impact was in Southeast Asia, where spices, coffee, tea, and teak wood were key exports (see again Map 13.1). The company's objective was to secure a trade monopoly wherever it could, fix prices, and replace the local population with Dutch planters. Under the leadership of Jan Pieterszoon Coen (who once said that trade could not be conducted without war nor war without trade), the Dutch swept into the Javanese port of Jakarta in 1619 and took over the nearby Bandanese Islands two years later. In Banda, the traditional chiefs and almost the entire population were killed outright, left to starve, or taken into slavery. Dutch planters and their slaves replaced the decimated local population and sent their produce to the VOC. The motive for such rapacious action was the huge profit to be made by buying nutmeg at a low price in the Bandanese Islands and selling it at many times that price in Europe. Although this aggressive expansion met widespread resistance from the local population and other merchants involved in the region's trade, by 1670 the Dutch had also taken Melaka from the Portuguese and controlled all of the lucrative spice trade from the Maluku islands. Next, the VOC set its sights on pepper. However, the Dutch had to share this commerce with Chinese and English competitors. Moreover, since there was no demand for European products in Asia, the Dutch had to participate more in inter-Asian trade as a way to reduce their need to make payments in precious metals.

TRANSFORMATIONS IN THE ISLAMIC HEARTLAND

Compared with Southeast Asia, the major Islamic empires did not feel such direct effects of European intrusion. They did, however, face internal difficulties, which were exacerbated by trade networks that eluded state control. From its inception, the Safavid Empire had always required a powerful, religiously inspired ruler to enforce Shiite religious orthodoxy and to hold together the realm's tribal, pastoral, mercantile, and agricultural factions. With a succession of weak rulers and declining tax revenues, the state foundered, and ultimately collapsed in 1722 (see Chapter 14). The Ottoman and Mughal empires, in contrast, remained more resilient.

The Ottoman Empire Having attained a high point under Suleiman (see Chapter 11), the Ottoman Empire ceased expanding. After Suleiman's reign, Ottoman armies and navies tried unsuccessfully to expand the empire's borders—losing, for example, on the western flank to the European Habsburgs. As military campaigns and a growing population strained the realm's limited resources, Ottoman intellectuals worried that the empire's glory was ebbing. A series of administrative reforms in the seventeenth century reinvigorated the state, but it never recaptured the vast power it enjoyed at its height.

Even as the empire's strength waned, by the seventeenth century its sultans faced a commercially more connected world. The introduction of New World silver into Ottoman networks of commerce and money lending eventually destabilized the empire. Although early Ottoman rulers had avoided trade with the outside world, the lure of silver broke through state regulations. Now Ottoman merchants established black markets for commodities that eager European buyers paid for in silver—especially wheat, copper, and wool. Because these exports were illegal, their sale did not generate tax revenues to support the state's civilian and military administration. So Ottoman rulers had to rely on loans of silver from the merchants. Some European royal houses, notably the Dutch and English, would grant those who bankrolled them a say in government, which vastly increased their credit and ultimately their power. Ottoman sultans, by contrast, feuded with their financiers, which undermined their authority.

More silver and budget deficits were a recipe for inflation. Prices tripled between 1550 and 1650. Runaway inflation caused hard-hit peasants in Anatolia, suffering from high food prices, shortages, and increasing taxes (used to pay off dynastic debts), to join together in uprisings that threatened the state's stability. Moreover, disorder at the center of the empire was accompanied by difficulties in the provinces, where breakaway regimes appeared.

The most threatening of the breakaway pressures occurred in Egypt beginning in the seventeenth century. In 1517, Egypt had become the Ottoman Empire's greatest conquest. As the wealthiest Ottoman territory, it was an important source of revenue, and its people shouldered heavy tax burdens. The group that asserted Egypt's political and commercial autonomy were military men, known as **Mamluks** (Arabic for "owned" or "possessed"), who had ruled Egypt as an independent regime until the Ottoman conquest (see Chapter 10). Although the Ottoman army had routed Mamluk forces on the battlefield, Ottoman governors in Egypt allowed the Mamluks to reform themselves. By the seventeenth century, these military men were nearly as powerful as their ancestors had been in the fifteenth century when they ruled Egypt independently. Mamluk leaders enhanced their power by aligning with Egyptian merchants and catering to the religious elites of Egypt, the *ulama*. Turning the Ottoman administrator of Egypt into a mere figurehead, this new provincial elite kept much of the area's fiscal resources for themselves at the expense not only of the imperial coffers but also of the local peasantry.

Amid new economic pressures and challenges from outlying territories, the Ottoman system also had elements of resilience—especially at the center, where decaying

Siege of Vienna This seventeenth-century painting depicts the Ottoman siege of Vienna, which began on July 14, 1683, and ended on September 12. The city might have fallen if the Polish king, John III, had not answered the pope's plea to defend Christendom and sent an army to assist German and Austrian troops in defeating the Ottomans.

leadership provoked demands for reform from administrative elites. Known as the Koprulu reforms, a combination of financial reform and anticorruption measures gave the state a new burst of energy and enabled the military to reacquire some of its lost possessions. Revenues again increased, and inflation decreased. Fired by revived expansionist ambitions, Istanbul decided to renew its assault on Christianity (see Chapter 11)—beginning with rekindled plans to seize Vienna. Although the Ottomans gathered an enormous force outside the Habsburg capital in 1683, both sides suffered heavy losses and the Ottoman forces ultimately retreated. Under the treaty that ended the Austro-Ottoman war, the Ottomans lost major European territorial possessions, including Hungary.

Thus, the Ottoman Empire began the eighteenth century dealing with serious economic challenges. Whereas in the sixteenth century rulers of the Ottoman Empire had wanted to create a self-contained and self-sufficient imperial economy, silver undermined this vision as it had elsewhere in the global economy. Indeed, the influx of silver opened Ottoman-controlled lands to trade with the rest of the world, producing breakaway regimes, widespread inflation, social discontent, and conflict between the state and its financiers that made these problems difficult to manage.

The Mughal Empire In contrast to the Ottomans' military reversals, the Mughal Empire reached its height in the 1600s. The period saw Mughal rulers extend their domain over almost all of India and enjoy increased domestic and international trade. But they, too, eventually had problems governing dispersed and resistant provinces, where many villages retained traditional religions and cultures.

Before the Mughals, India had never had a single political authority. Akbar and his successors had conquered territory in the north (see Chapter 12, Map 12.4), so now the Mughals turned to the south and gained control over most of that region by 1689. As the new provinces provided an additional source of resources, local lords, and warriors, the Mughal bureaucracy grew better at extracting services and taxes.

Imperial stability and prosperity did not depend entirely on the Indian Ocean trading system. Indeed, although the Mughals profited from seaborne trade, they never undertook overseas expansion. The main source of their wealth was land rents, which increased via incentives to bring new land into cultivation. But the imperial economy also benefited from Europeans' increased demand for Indian goods, including a sixfold rise in the English East India Company's textile purchases.

Eventually, Mughals were victims of their own success. More than a century of imperial expansion, commercial prosperity, and agricultural development placed substantial resources in the hands of local and regional authorities. As a result, local warrior elites became more autonomous. By the late seventeenth century, many regional leaders were well positioned to resist Mughal authority. As in the Ottoman Empire, then distant provinces began to challenge central rulers. Now the Indian peasants (like their counterparts in Ming China, Safavid Persia, and the Ottoman Empire) capitalized on weakening central authority. Many rose in rebellions; others took up banditry.

At this point the Mughal emperors had to accept diminished power over a loose unity of provincial states. Most of these areas accepted Mughal control in name only, administering semiautonomous regimes through access to local resources. Yet India still flourished, and landed elites brought new territories into agrarian production. Cotton, for instance, supported a thriving textile industry as peasant households focused on weaving and cloth production. Much of their production was destined for export as the region deepened its integration into world trading systems.

The Mughals themselves paid scant attention to commercial matters, but local rulers welcomed Europeans into Indian ports. As more European ships arrived, these authorities struck deals with merchants from Portugal and, increasingly, from England and Holland. Some Indian merchants formed trading companies of their own to control the sale of regional produce to competing Europeans; others established intricate trading networks that reached as far north as Russia. Mercantile houses grew richer and gained greater political influence over financially strapped emperors. Thus, even as global commercial entanglements enriched some in India, the effects undercut the Mughal dynasty.

FROM MING TO QING IN CHINA

Like India, China prospered in the seventeenth and eighteenth centuries; but here, too, growing wealth undermined central control and contributed to the fall of a long-lasting dynasty. As in Mughal India, local power holders in China increasingly defied the Ming government. Moreover, because Ming sovereigns discouraged overseas commerce and forbade travel abroad, they did not reap the rewards of long-distance exchange. Rather, such profits went to traders and adventurers who evaded imperial edicts. Together, the persistence of local autonomy and the accelerating economic and social changes brought unprecedented challenges until finally, in 1644, the Ming dynasty collapsed.

COMPARISON

ANALYZE examples of resistance in Southeast Asia and China to the growth of global trade networks.

Administrative and Economic Problems How did a dynasty that in the early seventeenth century governed the world's most economically advanced society (and perhaps a third of the world's population) fall from power? As in the Ottoman Empire, responsibility often lay with the rulers and their inadequate response to economic change. Zhu Yijun, the Wanli Emperor (r. 1573–1620) was secluded despite being surrounded by a staff of 20,000 eunuchs and 3,000 women. The "Son of Heaven" rarely ventured outside the palace compound, and when he moved within it a large retinue accompanied him, led by eunuchs clearing his path with whips. Ming emperors like Wanli quickly discovered that despite the elaborate arrangements and ritual performances affirming their position as the Son of Heaven, they had little control over the vast bureaucracy. An emperor frustrated with his officials could do little more than punish them or refuse to cooperate.

The timing of administrative breakdown in the Ming government was unfortunate, because expanding opportunities for trade led many individuals to circumvent official rules. From the mid-sixteenth century, bands of supposedly Japanese pirates ravaged the Chinese coast. Indeed, the Ming government had difficulties regulating trade with Japan and labeled all pirates as Japanese, but many of the marauders were in fact Chinese who flouted imperial authority. In tough times, the roving gangs terrorized sea-lanes and harbors. In better times, some functioned like mercantile groups: their leaders mingled with elites, foreign trade representatives, and imperial officials. What made these predators so resilient—and their business so lucrative—was their ability to move among the mosaic of East Asian cultures.

Just like in the Islamic empires, the influx of silver from the New World and Japan, while at first stimulating

Silver This seventeenth-century helmet from the Ming (1368–1633) or the Qing (1644–1911) dynasties features steel, gold, silver, and textiles, all of which were vital to the Chinese economy during this century. Silver was especially important, for its large influx from Japan and the Americas led to severe economic problems, political unrest, and the overthrow of the Ming dynasty.

the Chinese economy, led to severe economic (and, eventually, political) problems. As we saw in Chapter 12, Europeans used New World silver to pay for their purchases of Chinese goods. As a result, by the early seventeenth century silver imports exceeded domestic bullion production (uncoined gold or silver) in China by some twentyfold. Increasing monetization of the economy, which entailed silver currency becoming the primary medium of exchange, bolstered market activity and state revenues at the same time.

Yet the use of silver pressured peasants, who now needed that metal to pay their taxes and purchase goods. When silver supplies were abundant, the peasants faced inflationary prices. When supplies were low, the peasants could not meet their obligations to state officials and merchants, and they took up arms in rebellion.

The Collapse of Ming Authority By the seventeenth century, the Ming's administrative and economic difficulties were affecting their subjects' daily lives. This was particularly evident when the regime failed to cope with devastation caused by natural disasters, as in the northwestern province of Shanxi after a drop in average temperatures shortened growing seasons and reduced harvests. As the price of grain soared there in 1627–1628, the poor and the hungry fanned out to find food by whatever means they could muster. To deal with the crisis, the government imposed heavier taxes and cut the military budget. Bands of dispossessed Chinese peasants and mutinous soldiers then vented their anger at local tax collectors and officials.

Now the cycle of rebellion and weakened central authority that played out in so many other places took its predictable toll. Outlaw armies grew large under charismatic leaders. The most famous rebel leader, the "dashing prince" Li Zicheng, arrived at the outskirts of Beijing in 1644. Only a few companies of soldiers and a few thousand eunuchs were there to defend the capital's twenty-one miles of walls, so Li Zicheng seized Beijing easily. Two days later, the emperor hanged himself. On the following day, the triumphant "dashing prince" rode into the capital and claimed the throne.

News of the fall of the Ming capital sent shock waves around the empire. One hundred and seventy miles to the northeast, where China meets Manchuria, the army's commander received the news within a matter of days. His task in the area was to defend the Ming against their menacing neighbor, a group that had begun to identify itself as Manchu. Immediately the commander's position became precarious. Caught between an advancing rebel army on the one side and the Manchus on the other, he made a fateful decision: he appealed for the Manchus' cooperation to fight the "dashing prince," promising his new allies that "gold and treasure" awaited them in the capital. Thus, without shedding a drop of blood, the Manchus joined the Ming forces. After years of coveting the Ming Empire, the Manchus were finally on their way to Beijing (see Map 13.5).

The Qing Dynasty Asserts Control Despite their small numbers, the Manchus overcame early resistance to their rule and oversaw an impressive expansion of their realm. The **Manchus**—the name was first used in 1635—were descendants of a Turkic-speaking group known as the Jurchens. They emerged as a force early in the seventeenth century, when their leader claimed the title of khan after securing the allegiance of various Mongol groups in northeastern Asia, paving the way for their eventual conquest of China.

When the Manchus defeated Li Zicheng and seized power in Beijing, they numbered around 1 million. Assuming control of a domain that included perhaps 250 million people, they were keenly aware of their minority status. Taking power was one thing; keeping it was another. But keep it they did. In fact, during the eighteenth century, the Manchu

MAP 13.5 | From Ming to Qing China, 1644–1760

Qing China under the Manchus expanded its territory significantly during this period. Find the Manchu homeland and then the area of Manchu expansion after 1644, when the Manchus established the Qing dynasty.

- Where did the Qing dynasty expand? Explain what this tells us about the priorities of the ruling elite, in particular with respect to global commerce.
- Explain the significance of the chronology of Chinese expansion. Does this qualify your answer to the first question?
- What does it tell us about the evolution of the ruling elite's priorities?
- Consider the scope of Chinese territorial expansion in this period, and, based on your reading, explain the challenges this posed for central authorities.

Qing ("pure") dynasty (1644–1911) incorporated new territories, experienced substantial population growth, and sustained significant economic growth.

The key to China's relatively stable economic and geographic expansion lay in its rulers' shrewd and flexible policies. The early Manchu emperors were able and diligent administrators. They also knew that to govern a diverse population they had to adapt to local ways. At the same time, Qing rulers were determined to convey a clear sense of their own majesty and legitimacy. Rulers relentlessly promoted patriarchal values. Widows who remained "chaste" enjoyed public praise, and women in general were urged to lead a "virtuous" life serving male kin and family. To the majority Han population, the Manchu emperor represented himself as the worthy upholder of familial values and classical Chinese civilization. However, insinuating themselves into an existing order and appeasing subject peoples did not satisfy the Manchu yearning to leave their imprint. They also introduced measures that emphasized their authority, their distinctiveness, and the submission of their mostly Han Chinese subjects. For example, Qing officials composed or translated important documents into Manchu and banned intermarriage between Manchu and Han, although this proved difficult to enforce.

Manchu impositions fell mostly on the peasantry, for the Qing financed their administrative structure through taxes on peasant households. In response the peasants sought new lands to cultivate in border areas, often planting New World crops that grew well in difficult soils. This move introduced an important change in Chinese diets: while rice remained the staple of the wealthy, peasants increasingly subsisted on corn and sweet potatoes.

While officials redoubled their reliance on an agrarian base, trade and commerce flourished. Chinese merchants continued to ply the waters stretching from Southeast Asia to Japan, exchanging textiles, ceramics, and medicine for spices and rice. Although the Qing state vacillated about permitting maritime trade with foreigners in its early years, it sought to regulate external commerce more formally as it consolidated its rule. In 1720, in Canton, a group of merchants formed a monopolistic guild to trade with Europeans seeking coveted Chinese goods and peddling their own wares. Although the guild disbanded in the face of opposition from other merchants, it revived after the Qing restricted European trade to Canton. The **Canton system**, officially established by imperial decree in 1759, required European traders to have guild merchants act as guarantors for their good behavior and payment of fees.

Despite public disregard for certain imperial edicts, the Qing dynasty enjoyed a heyday during the eighteenth century. It forced Korea, Vietnam, Burma, and Nepal to pay tribute, and its territorial expansion reached far into central Asia, Tibet, and Mongolia. China, in sum, negotiated a century of upheaval without dismantling established ways in politics and economics. The peasantry continued to practice popular faiths, cultivate crops, and stay close to fields and villages. Trade with the outside world was marginal to overall commercial life; like the Ming, the Qing cared more about the agrarian than the commercial health of the empire, believing the former to be the foundation of prosperity and tranquility. As long as China's peasantry could keep the dynasty's coffers full, the government was content to squeeze the merchants when it needed funds. Some historians view this practice as a failure to adapt to a changing world order, as it ultimately left China vulnerable to outsiders—especially Europeans. But this view projects later developments onto the past. By the mid-eighteenth century, Europe still needed China more than the other way around. For the majority of Chinese, no superior model of belief, politics, or economics was conceivable. Indeed, although the Qing had taken over a crumbling empire in 1644, a century later China was enjoying a new level of prosperity.

TOKUGAWA JAPAN

Integration with the Asian trading system exposed Japan to new external pressures, even as the islands grappled with internal turmoil. But the Japanese dealt with these pressures more successfully than the mainland Asian empires (Ottoman, Safavid, Mughal, and Ming), which saw political fragmentation and even the overthrow of ruling dynasties. In Japan, a single ruling family emerged. This dynastic state, the **Tokugawa shogunate**, accomplished something that most of the world's other regimes did not: it regulated foreign intrusion. While Japan played a modest role in the expanding global trade, it remained free of outside exploitation.

Unification of Japan During the sixteenth century, Japan had suffered from political instability as banditry and civil strife disrupted the countryside. Regional ruling families, called *daimyos*, had commanded private armies of warriors known as samurai. The daimyos sometimes brought order to their domains, but no one family could establish preeminence over others. Although Japan had an emperor, his authority did not extend beyond the court in Kyoto.

Following an effort by military leaders to unify Japan, one of the daimyos, Tokugawa Ieyasu seized power. This was a decisive moment. In 1603, Ieyasu assumed the title of shogun (military ruler), retaining the emperor in name only while taking the reins of power himself. He also solved the problem of succession, declaring that rulership would be hereditary and that his family would be the ruling household. Administrative authority shifted from Kyoto to the site of Ieyasu's domain headquarters: the castle town called Edo (later renamed Tokyo; see Map 13.6). By the time Ieyasu died, Edo had become a major urban center with a population of 150,000. This hereditary Tokugawa shogunate lasted until 1867.

The Tokugawa shoguns ensured a flow of resources from the working population to the rulers and from the provinces to the capital. Villages paid taxes to the daimyos,

Edo in the Rain This facsimile of an *ukiyo-e* ("floating world") print by Hiroshige (1797–1858) depicts one of several bridges in the bustling city of Edo (later Tokyo), with Mount Fuji in the background.

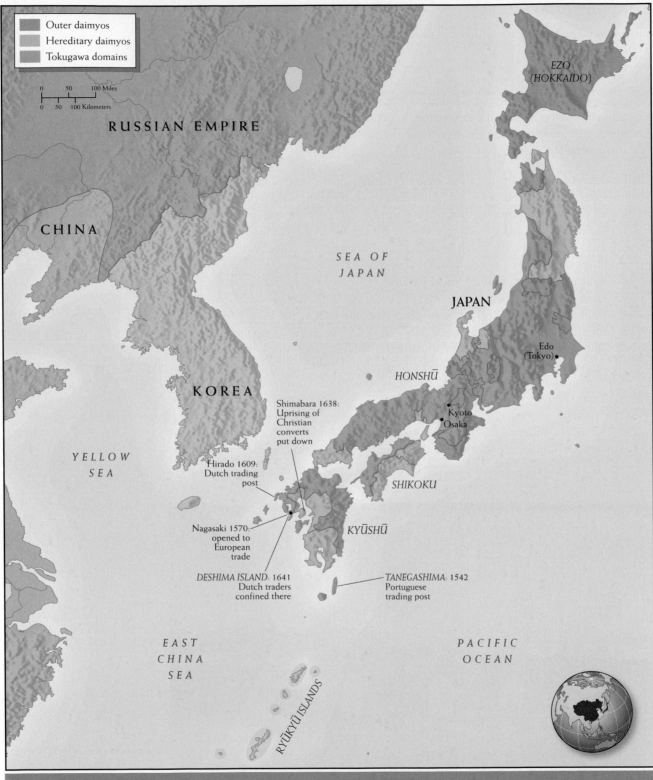

Outer daimyos
Hereditary daimyos
Tokugawa domains

0   50   100 Miles
0 50 100 Kilometers

RUSSIAN EMPIRE

CHINA

EZO
(HOKKAIDO)

SEA OF
JAPAN

JAPAN

Edo
(Tokyo)

HONSHŪ

KOREA

Shimabara 1638:
Uprising of
Christian
converts
put down

Kyoto
Osaka

YELLOW
SEA

Hirado 1609:
Dutch trading
post

SHIKOKU

Nagasaki 1570:
opened to
European
trade

KYŪSHŪ

DESHIMA ISLAND: 1641
Dutch traders
confined there

TANEGASHIMA: 1542
Portuguese
trading post

EAST
CHINA
SEA

PACIFIC
OCEAN

RYŪKYŪ ISLANDS

MAP 13.6 | Tokugawa Japan, 1603–1867

The Tokugawa shoguns created a strong central state in Japan at this time.

- According to this map, how extensive was their control?

- Based on your reading, what foreign states were interested in trade with Japan?

- How, according to the chapter, did Tokugawa leaders attempt to control relations with foreign states and other entities?

who transferred resources to the seat of shogunate authority. No longer engaged in constant warfare, the samurai became administrators. Peace brought prosperity. Agriculture thrived. Improved farming techniques and land reclamation projects enabled the country's population to grow from 10 million in 1550 to 16 million in 1600 and 30 million in 1700.

Foreign Affairs and Foreigners Internal peace and prosperity did not insulate Japan from external challenges. When Japanese rulers tackled foreign affairs, their most pressing concern was the intrusion of Christian missionaries and European traders. Initially, Japanese officials welcomed these foreigners out of an eagerness to acquire muskets, gunpowder, and other new technology. But once the ranks of Christian converts swelled, Japanese authorities realized that Christians were intolerant of other faiths, believed Christ to be superior to any authority, and fought among themselves. The government suppressed Christianity and drove European missionaries from the country.

Even more troublesome was the lure of trade with Europeans. The Tokugawa knew that trading at various Japanese ports would pull the commercial regions in various directions, away from the capital. When it became clear that European traders preferred the ports of Kyūshū (the southernmost island), the shogunate restricted Europeans to trade only in ports under Edo's direct rule in Honshū. Then, Japanese authorities expelled all European competitors. Only the Protestant (and nonproselytizing) Dutch won permission to remain in Japan, confined to an island near Nagasaki. The Dutch were allowed to unload just one ship each year, under strict supervision by Japanese authorities.

These measures did not close Tokugawa Japan to the outside world, however. Trade with China and Korea flourished, and the shogun received missions from Korea and the Ryūkyū islands. Edo also gathered information about the outside world from the resident Dutch and Chinese (who included monks, physicians, and painters). A few Japanese were permitted to learn Dutch and to study European technology, shipbuilding, and medicine (see Chapter 14). By limiting such encounters, the authorities ensured that foreigners would not threaten Japan's security.

The arrival of New World silver provided at least an initial boost to the major Asian economies. The Mughal Empire achieved its greatest influence in the seventeenth century. Despite a change in the ruling dynasty, China remained the world's center of wealth and power, although there, as elsewhere in Asia, silver caused inflation and altered relations between center and periphery. Ottoman domains shrank, and Europeans achieved important commercial footholds in parts of India and Southeast Asia.

Transformations in Europe

Between 1600 and 1750, religious conflict, commercial expansion, and the consolidation of dynastic power transformed Europe. Commercial centers shifted northward, and Spain and Portugal lost ground to England and France. To the east, the state of Muscovy expanded dramatically to become the sprawling Russian Empire.

COMPARISON

COMPARE the impact of trade and religion on state power in Europe and the Mughal Empire.

EXPANSION AND DYNASTIC CHANGE IN RUSSIA

During this period the Russian Empire expanded to become one of the world's largest-ever states. It gained positions on the Baltic Sea and the Pacific Ocean, and it established political borders with both the Qing Empire and Japan. These momentous shifts involved the elimination of steppe nomads as an independent force. Culturally, Europeans as well as Russians debated whether Russia belonged more to Europe or to Asia. The answer was both.

Muscovy Becomes the Russian Empire The principality of Moscow, or Muscovy, like Japan and China, used territorial expansion and commercial networks to consolidate a powerful state. This was the Russian Empire, the name given to Muscovy by Tsar Peter the Great around 1700. ("Tsar" was a Russian word derived from the Latin *Caesar* to refer to the Russian ruler.) Originally a mixture of Slavs, Finnish tribes, Turkic speakers, and many others, **Muscovy** spanned parts of Europe, much of northern Asia, numerous North Pacific islands, and even—for a time—a corner of North America (Alaska).

Like Japan, Russia emerged out of turmoil. Security concerns inspired the Muscovy regime to seize territory in the fifteenth and sixteenth centuries. Because the steppe, which stretches deep into Asia, remained a highway for nomadic peoples (especially descendants of the powerful Mongols), Muscovy sought to dominate the areas south and east of Moscow. Beginning in the 1590s, Russian authorities built forts and trading posts along Siberian rivers, and by 1639 the state's borders reached the Pacific. Thus, in just over a century Muscovy had claimed an empire straddling Eurasia and incorporating peoples of many languages and religions (see Map 13.7).

Much of this expansion occurred despite dynastic chaos that followed the death of Tsar Ivan IV in 1584. Ultimately, a group of prominent families reestablished central authority and threw their weight behind a new family of rulers. These were the Romanovs, court barons who set about reviving the Kremlin's fortunes. (The Kremlin was a medieval walled fortress where the Muscovite grand princes—later, tsars—resided.) Like the Ottoman and Qing dynasts, Romanov tsars and their aristocratic supporters would retain power into the twentieth century.

Absolutist Government and Serfdom In the seventeenth and eighteenth centuries, the Romanovs created an absolutist system of government. Only the tsar had the right to make war, tax, judge, and coin money. The Romanovs also made the nobles serve as state officials. Now Russia became a despotic state that had no political assemblies for nobles or other groups, other than mere consultative bodies like the imperial senate. Indeed, away from Moscow, local aristocrats enjoyed nearly unlimited authority in exchange for loyalty and tribute to the tsar.

During this period, Russia's peasantry bore the burden of maintaining the wealth of the nobility and the monarchy. Most peasant families gathered into communes, isolated rural worlds where people helped one another deal with the harsh climate, severe landlords, and occasional poor harvests. Communes functioned like extended kin networks in which members supported one another. In 1649, peasants were legally bound as serfs to the nobles and the tsar, meaning that, in principle, they had to perform obligatory services and deliver part of their produce to their lords.

Imperial Expansion and Migration A series of military victories in the eighteenth century made it possible to consolidate the empire and sparked significant population movements. The conquest of Siberia brought vast territory and riches in furs. Victory in a prolonged war with Sweden and then the incorporation of the fertile southern steppes, known as Ukraine, proved decisive. Peter the Great (r. 1682–1725) accomplished the victory in Sweden, after which he founded a new capital at St. Petersburg. Under Peter's successors, including the brilliant and ruthless Catherine the Great, Russia, already a harsh and colossal space, added even more territory. By the late eighteenth century, Russia's grasp extended from the Baltic Sea, Ukraine, and the Crimea on the Black Sea, and stretched eastward all the way to Siberia.

Many people migrated eastward to Siberia. Some were fleeing serfdom; others were being deported for rejecting religious reforms. Battling astoundingly harsh temperatures (falling to −40 degrees Centigrade/Fahrenheit) and frigid Arctic winds, these individuals traveled on horseback and trudged on foot to resettle in the east. But the difficulties of clearing forested lands or planting crops in boggy Siberian soils, combined with extraordinarily harsh

MAP 13.7 | Russian Expansion, 1462–1795

The state of Muscovy incorporated vast territories through overland expansion as it grew and became the Russian Empire.

- Using the map key, identify how many different expansions the Russian Empire underwent between 1462 and 1795 and in what directions generally.

- With what countries and cultures did the Russian Empire come into contact?

- According to the text, what drove such dramatic expansion?

winters, meant that many settlers died or tried to return. Isolation was a problem, too. There was no established land route back to Moscow until the 1770s, when exiles completed the Great Siberian Post Road through the swamps and peat bogs of western Siberia. The writer Anton Chekhov later called it "the longest and ugliest road in the whole world."

ECONOMIC AND POLITICAL FLUCTUATIONS IN CENTRAL AND WESTERN EUROPE

During this period European economies became more commercialized, especially after recovering from the Thirty Years' War. As in Asia, developments in distant parts of the world shaped the region's economic upturns and downturns. Compounding these pressures was the continuation of dynastic rivalries and religious conflicts.

The Thirty Years' War For a century after Martin Luther broke with the Catholic Church (see Chapter 12), religious warfare raged in Europe. So did contests over territory, power, and trade. The **Thirty Years' War** (1618–1648) was all three of these—a war between Protestant princes and the Catholic emperor for religious predominance in central Europe; a struggle for regional control among Catholic powers (the Spanish and Austrian Habsburgs and the French); and a bid for independence (from Spain) by the Dutch, who wanted to trade and worship as they liked.

The brutal conflict began as a struggle between Protestants and Catholics within the Habsburg Empire, but it soon became a war for preeminence in Europe. It took the lives of civilians as well as soldiers. In total, fighting, disease, and famine wiped out a third of the German states' urban population and two-fifths of their rural population. Ultimately the Treaty of Westphalia (1648) stated that as there was a rough balance of power between Protestant and Catholic states, they would simply have to put up with each other. The Dutch won their independence, but the war's enormous costs provoked severe discontent in Spain, France, and England. Central Europe was so devastated that it did not recover in economic or demographic terms for more than a century.

The Thirty Years' War The mercenary armies of the Thirty Years' War were renowned for pillaging and tormenting the civilians of central Europe. Here, the townsfolk exact revenge on some of these soldiers, hanging, as the engraving's caption claims, "damned and infamous thieves, like bad fruit, from this tree."

The Thirty Years' War transformed war making. Whereas most medieval struggles had been sieges between nobles leading small armies, centralized states fielding standing armies now waged decisive, grand-scale campaigns. The war also changed the ranks of soldiers: local enlisted men defending their king, country, and faith gave way to hired mercenaries or criminals doing forced service. Even officers, who previously obtained their stripes by purchase or royal decree, now had to earn them. Gunpowder, cannons, and muskets became standardized. By the eighteenth century, Europe's wars featured huge standing armies boasting a professional officer corps, deadly artillery, and long supply lines bringing food and ammunition to the front. The costs—material and human—of war began to soar.

Western European Economies In spite of the toll that warfare took on economic activity, the European states enjoyed significant commercial expansion in the seventeenth century. Northern Europe gained more than did the south, however. Spain, for example, started losing ground to its rivals as the costs of defending its empire soared and merchants from Northern Europe cut in on its trading networks. The weighty costs of its involvement in the Thirty Years' War dealt the Spanish economy a final, disastrous blow.

As European commercial dynamism shifted northward, the Dutch led the way with innovative commercial practices and a new mercantile elite. They specialized in shipping and in financing regional and long-distance trade. Their famous *fluitschips* carried heavy, bulky cargoes (like Baltic wood) with relatively small crews. Now shipping costs throughout the Atlantic world dropped as Dutch ships transported their own and other countries' goods. Amsterdam's merchants founded an exchange bank, established a rudimentary stock exchange, and pioneered systems of underwriting and insuring cargoes.

England and France also became commercial powerhouses, establishing aggressive policies to promote national business and drive out competitors. By stipulating that only English ships could carry goods between the mother country and its colonies, the English Navigation Act of 1651 protected English shippers and merchants—especially from the Dutch.

Economic development was not limited to port towns: the countryside, too, enjoyed breakthroughs in production. Most important was expansion in the production of food. In northwestern Europe, investments in water drainage, larger livestock herds, and improved cultivation practices generated much greater yields. Also, a four-field crop rotation involving wheat, clover, barley, and turnips kept nutrients in the soil and provided year-round fodder for livestock. As a result (and as we have seen many times before), increased agricultural output supported a growing urban population.

Production rose most where the organization of rural property changed. In England, in a movement known as **enclosure**, landowners took control of lands that traditionally had been common property serving local needs. Claiming exclusive rights to these lands, the landowners planted new crops or pastured sheep with the aim of selling the products in distant markets—especially cities. The largest landowners put their farms in the hands of tenants, who hired wage laborers to till, plant, and harvest. Thus, in England, peasant agriculture gave way to farms run by wealthy families who exploited the marketplace to buy what they needed (including labor) and to sell what they produced. In this regard, England led the way in a Europe-wide process of commercializing the countryside.

Dynastic Monarchies: France and England European monarchs had varying success with centralizing state power. In France, Louis XIII (r. 1610–1643) and especially his chief minister, Cardinal Richelieu, concentrated power in the hands of the king. Instead of sharing power with the aristocracy, much less commoners, the king and his counselors wanted him to rule free of external checks, to create an **absolute monarchy**. The ruler was not to be a tyrant, but his authority was to be complete and thorough, and his state free of bloody disorders. The king's rule would be lawful; but he, not his jurists, would dictate the last legal word. If the king made a mistake, only God could call him to account. Thus the Europeans believed in the "divine right of kings," a political belief not greatly different from imperial China where the emperor was thought to rule with the mandate of heaven.

In absolutist France, privileges and state offices flowed from the king's grace. All patronage networks ultimately linked to the king: that included financial supports the crown provided directly as well tax exemptions and a wide array of permissions—to publish a book or work in a regulated trade, from lawyers and professors to apothecaries, bookbinders, and butchers. The great palace Louis XIV built at Versailles teemed with nobles from all over France seeking favor, dressing according to the king's expensive fashion code, and attending the latest tragedies, comedies, and concerts.

The French dynastic monarchy provided a model of absolute rule for other European dynasts, like the Habsburgs of the Holy Roman Empire, the Hohenzollerns of Prussia, and the Romanovs of Muscovy. The king and his ministers controlled all public power, while other social groups, from the nobility to the peasantry, had no formal body to represent their interests. Nonetheless, French absolutist government was not as absolute as the king would have wished. Pockets of stalwart Protestants practiced their religion secretly in the plateau villages of central France, despite Louis XIV's discriminatory measures against them. Peasant disturbances continued. Criticism of court life, wars, and religious policies filled anonymous pamphlets, jurists' notebooks, and courtiers' private journals. Members of the nobility also grumbled about their political misfortunes, but since the king had suppressed the traditional advisory bodies they had dominated, they had no formal way to express their concerns.

England might also have evolved into an absolutist regime, but there were important differences between England and France. Queen Elizabeth (r. 1558–1603) and her successors used many policies similar to those of the French monarchy, such as control of patronage and elaborate court festivities. Above all, the English Parliament remained an important force. Whereas the French kings did not consult the Estates-General to enact taxes, the English monarchs had to convene Parliament to raise money.

Under Elizabeth's successors, fierce quarrels broke out over taxation, religion, and royal efforts to rule without parliamentary consent. Tensions ran high between Puritans (who preferred a simpler form of worship and more egalitarian church government) and Anglicans (who supported the state-sponsored, hierarchically organized Church of England headed by the king). Those tensions erupted in the 1640s into civil war that saw the victory of the largely Puritan parliamentary army and the beheading of the king, Charles I. Although the monarchy was restored a dozen years later, in 1660, the king's relation to Parliament and the relationship between the crown and religion remained undecided (in particular the right of Protestants to assume the throne).

Subsequent monarchs who aspired to absolute rule came into conflict with Parliament, whose members insisted on shared sovereignty and the right of Protestant succession. This dispute culminated in the Glorious Revolution of 1688–1689. In a bloodless upheaval, King James II fled to France and Parliament offered the crown to William of Orange and his wife, Mary (both Protestants). The outcome of the conflict established the principle that English monarchs must rule in conjunction with Parliament. Although the Church of England was reaffirmed as the official state church, Presbyterians and Jews were allowed to practice their religions. Catholic worship, still officially forbidden,

Versailles Louis XIV's Versailles, just southwest of Paris, was a hunting lodge that was converted at colossal cost in the 1670s–1680s into a grand royal chateau with expansive grounds. Much envied and imitated across Europe, the palace became the epicenter of a luxurious court life that included entertainments such as plays and musical offerings, state receptions, royal hunts, boating, and gambling. Thousands of nobles at Versailles vied with each other for closer proximity to the king in the performance of court rituals.

was tolerated as long as the Catholics kept quiet. By 1700, then, England's nobility and merchant classes had a guaranteed say in public affairs and assurance that state activity would privilege the propertied classes as well as the ruler. As a result, English rulers could borrow money much more effectively than their rivals.

Mercantilist Wars The rise of new powers in Europe, especially France and England, intensified rivalries for control of Atlantic trade. As conflicts over colonies and sea-lanes replaced earlier religious and territorial struggles, commercial struggles became world-wide wars. Across the globe, European empires constantly skirmished over control of trade and territory. English and Dutch trading companies took aim at Portuguese outposts in Asia and the Americas, and then at each other. Ports in India suffered repeated assaults and counterassaults. In response, European powers built huge navies to protect their colonies and trade routes and to attack their rivals.

After 1715, a series of wars occurred mainly outside Europe, as empires feuded over colonial possessions. These conflicts were especially bitter in border areas, particularly in the Caribbean and North America. Each round of warfare ratcheted up the scale and cost of fighting.

The **Seven Years' War** (known as the French and Indian War in North America) marked the culmination of this rivalry among European empires around the globe. Fought from 1756 to 1763, it saw Native Americans, African slaves, Bengali princes, Filipino militiamen, and European foot soldiers dragged into a contest over imperial possessions and control of the seas. The battles in Europe were relatively indecisive (despite being large), except in the hinterlands. After all, what sparked the war was a skirmish of British colonial troops (featuring a lieutenant colonel named George Washington) allied with Seneca warriors against French soldiers in the Ohio Valley (see Map 13.2 for North American references). In India, the war had a decisive outcome, for here the East India Company trader Robert Clive rallied 850 European officers and 2,100 Indian recruits to defeat the French (there were but 40 French artillerymen) and their 50,000 Maratha allies at Plassey. The British seized the upper hand—over everyone—in India. Not only did the British drive off the French from the rich Bengali interior, but they also crippled Indian rulers' resistance against European intruders (see Map 12.4 for India references).

The Seven Years' War changed the balance of power around the world. Britain emerged as the foremost colonial empire. Its rivals, especially France and Spain, took a pounding; France lost its North American colonies, and Spain lost Florida (though it gained the Louisiana Territory west of the Mississippi in a secret deal with France). In India, as well, the French were losers and had to acknowledge British supremacy in the wealthy provinces of Bihar and Bengal. But overwhelmingly, the biggest losers were indigenous peoples everywhere. With the rise of one empire over all others, it was harder for Native Americans to play the Europeans off against each other. Maratha princes faced the same problem. Clearly, as worlds became more entangled, the gaps between winners and losers grew more pronounced.

Conclusion

By the 1750s, the world's regions were more economically connected than they had been a century and a half earlier. The process of integrating the resources of previous worlds apart that had begun with Christopher Columbus's voyages intensified during this period. Traders shipped a wider variety of commodities—from Baltic wood to Indian cotton, from New World silver and sugar to Chinese silks and porcelain—over longer distances. People increasingly wore clothes manufactured elsewhere, consumed beverages made from products cultivated in far-off locations, and used imported guns to settle local conflicts.

Everywhere, this integration and the consumer opportunities that it made possible came at a heavy price. Nowhere was it more costly than in the Americas, where colonization and exploitation led to the expulsion of Native Americans from their lands and the decimation of their numbers. The cost was also very high for the millions of Africans forced across the Atlantic to work New World plantations and for the millions more who did not survive the journey.

Silver was the product from the Americas that most transformed global trading networks and that showed how greater entanglements could both enrich and destabilize. Although Spanish colonizers mined New World silver and shipped it to western Europe and Asia, it was Spain's main competitors in Europe that gained the upper hand in the seventeenth and eighteenth centuries. Nearly one-third of the silver from the New World ended up in China as payment for products like porcelains and silks that consumers still regarded as the world's finest manufactures. But if China's economy remained vibrant, silver did play a part in the fall of one dynasty and the rise of another. For the Ottoman and Mughal empires, the influx of silver created rampant inflation and undermined their previous economic autonomy.

Certain societies coped with increased commercial exchange and internal challenges more successfully than others. The Safavid and Ming dynasties could not withstand the pressures; both collapsed. The Spanish, Ottoman, and Mughal dynasties managed to survive but faced increasing pressure from aggressive rivals. For newcomers to the integrating world, the opportunity to trade helped support new dynasties. Japan, Russia, and England emerged on the world stage. But even in these newer regimes, commerce and competition did not erase conflict. To the contrary, while the world was more fully integrated in economic terms than ever before, greater prosperity for some hardly translated into peace for most.

After You Read This Chapter

FOCUS ON: *Regional Impact of World Trade*

THE AMERICAS

- England, France, and Holland join Spain and Portugal as colonial powers in the Americas.

- The English and French colonies in the Caribbean become the world's major exporters of sugar.

AFRICA

- The Atlantic slave trade increases to record proportions, creating gender imbalances, impoverishing some regions, and elevating the power of slave-supplying states.

SOUTHEAST ASIA

- The Dutch East India Company takes over the major islands of Southeast Asia.

THE ISLAMIC WORLD

- World trade destabilizes the Safavid, Ottoman, and Mughal empires.

EAST ASIA

- The Ming dynasty in China loses the mandate of heaven and is replaced by the Qing.

- The Tokugawa shogunate unifies Japan and limits the influence of Europeans in the country.

EUROPE

- Tsarist Russia expands toward the Baltic Sea and the Pacific Ocean and becomes the largest state in the world.

- Europe recovers from the Thirty Years' War (1618–1648), with Holland, England, and France emerging as economic powerhouses.

CHRONOLOGY

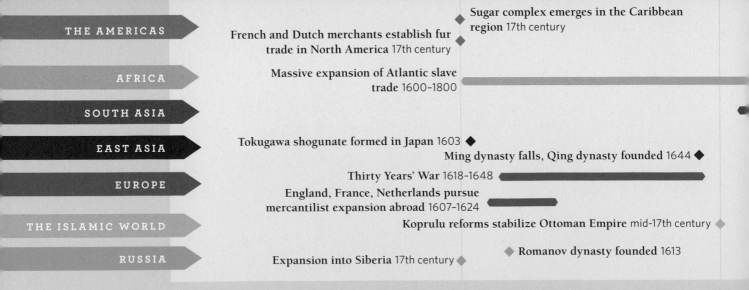

		1600	1650
THE AMERICAS	French and Dutch merchants establish fur trade in North America 17th century	Sugar complex emerges in the Caribbean region 17th century	
AFRICA	Massive expansion of Atlantic slave trade 1600–1800		
SOUTH ASIA			
EAST ASIA	Tokugawa shogunate formed in Japan 1603	Ming dynasty falls, Qing dynasty founded 1644	
EUROPE	Thirty Years' War 1618–1648 — England, France, Netherlands pursue mercantilist expansion abroad 1607–1624		
THE ISLAMIC WORLD		Koprulu reforms stabilize Ottoman Empire mid-17th century	
RUSSIA	Expansion into Siberia 17th century	Romanov dynasty founded 1613	

- ***Thinking about Exchange Networks and World Trade*** How did silver, and then sugar, transform world trade? What political and cultural forces benefited from the development of long-distance trading networks? Which groups suffered and how? Contrast the effects of long distance trade in major world regions.

- ***Thinking about Changing Power Relationships and World Trade*** The seventeenth and eighteenth centuries witnessed the rise of new powers in England, Japan, and Russia, as well as regional powers on the west coast of Africa. Several established empires continued to expand but confronted powerful new challenges to their authority. How did leaders of the Ottoman, Mughal, and Qing empires respond to challenges to their authority? What major challenges did they face? How would you characterize the new powers that emerged around the world in this period?

- ***Thinking about the Impact of World Trade on Gender Relations*** The Atlantic slave trade wreaked havoc on sex ratios both in Africa and in the slave societies of the New World because most slaves taken from Africa were men. How did this affect social life on New World plantations? What strategies did African communities utilize to mitigate the loss of so many men? Elsewhere around the world, increased trade challenged established social hierarchies. How did ruling elites mobilize gender to reinforce their authority?

1. List the commodities that most transformed world trade in the sixteenth and seventeenth centuries, and analyze their significance.

2. Explain how **chartered companies**, the **enclosure** movement, and the **Seven Years' War** influenced European economic growth in this period.

3. How did Asian leaders respond to challenges to their efforts to centralize authority? Analyze the **Tokugawa shogunate**'s treatment of foreign influences and contrast it with the Ottoman rulers' relationship to the **Mamluks** and the **Manchu**'s relationship to the Han Chinese.

4. Explain how the slave trade changed African societies both in social and political terms, and on the coast as opposed to the interior. What roles did European traders and African rulers play?

5. Define **mercantilism**. Whose interests did it serve, both in core regions and their peripheries, at whose expense? Consider both elites and common people in your answer.

British defeat French forces in North America during the Seven Years' War 1754–1761

Asante state founded 1701
Aurangzeb's expansion weakens the Mughal dynasty 1658–1707
British assume control of French interests in South Asia during Seven Years' War 1756–1763

Seven Years' War 1756–1763

Safavid dynasty collapses 1722

Peter the Great reigns 1682–1725

1700   **1750**

Competing Perspectives

Slavery in the Atlantic World

The documents gathered here present different aspects of slavery in the Atlantic world. Taught to read and write by his masters, Olaudah Equiano (c. 1745–1797) published *The Interesting Narrative of the Life of Olaudah Equiano, or Gustavus Vassa, the African* (1789) after purchasing his freedom in 1789. In the first document, Equiano describes the horrifying conditions captives endured on the African coast as they awaited the arrival of slaving ships. For African slaves, the Atlantic system was an abomination. For slave owners, merchants, and political leaders—in Africa and Europe—the slave trade was a business. Captain Thomas Phillips's 1694 account of his voyage in command of a slave ship describes the purchase of slaves at the port of Whydah (Ouidah, in present-day Benin). The author of the third document, Richard Ligon (c. 1585–1662), sought his fortune on the English island of Barbados. Here he explains the absence of slave revolts, from a European perspective.

In communities based around plantation slavery, race and enslavement (or freedom) determined how people lived. A Swiss aristocrat and explorer, the Baron de Wimpffen (1748–1819) describes the importance of race, as opposed to family lineage or nobility, in colonial society in Saint-Domingue (present-day Haiti). The final three documents show data from the 1835 household census for Santiago do Iguape, Bahia, a parish in the heart of a sugar plantation region in Brazil. They provide basic demographic statistics about the region's population, over half of whom were enslaved. Created by colonial authorities for their own purposes, the census records make it possible for historians to reconstruct the experience of people who left no written records themselves. Population pyramids are graphs that present a population's composition by age and sex, and, here, by racial classification as well. A pyramid equally divided between men and women with a wide base represents an expanding population with a large proportion of children and young adults. Iguape's free and freed populations follow this pattern but the enslaved population does not.

PRIMARY SOURCE 13.1

The Interesting Narrative of the Life of Olaudah Equiano (1789), *Olaudah Equiano*

The first object which saluted my eyes when I arrived on the coast was the sea, and a slave ship, which was then riding at anchor, and waiting for its cargo. These filled me with astonishment, which was soon converted into terror when I was carried on board. . . . When I looked round the ship too and saw a large furnace of copper boiling, and a multitude of black people of every description chained together, every one of their countenances expressing dejection and sorrow, I no longer doubted of my fate; and, quite overpowered with horror and anguish, I fell motionless on the deck and fainted. When I recovered a little I found some black people about me, who I believed were some of those who brought me on board, and had been receiving their pay; they talked to me in order to cheer me, but all in vain. I asked them if we were not to be eaten by those white men with horrible looks, red faces, and loose hair. They told me I was not . . .

In a little time after, amongst the poor chained men, I found some of my own nation, which in a small degree gave ease to my mind. I inquired of these what was to be done with us; they gave me to understand we were to be carried to these white people's country to work for them. I then was a little revived, and thought, if it were no worse than working, my situation was not so desperate: but still I feared I should be put to death, the white people looked and acted, as I thought, in so savage a manner; for I had never seen among any people such instances of brutal cruelty; and this not only shewn towards us blacks, but also to some of the whites themselves. . . .

At last, when the ship we were in had got in all her cargo, they made ready with many fearful noises, and we were all put under deck, so that we could not see how they managed the vessel. But this disappointment was the least of my sorrow. . . . The closeness of the place, and the heat of the climate, added to the number in the ship, which was so crowded that each had scarcely room to turn himself, almost suffocated us. This produced copious perspirations, so that the air soon became unfit for respiration, from a variety of loathsome smells, and brought on a sickness among the slaves, of which many died, thus falling victims to the improvident avarice, as I may call it, of their purchasers. This wretched situation was again aggravated by the galling of the chains, now become insupportable; and the filth of the necessary tubs [latrines], into which the children often fell, and were almost suffocated. The shrieks of the women, and the groans of the dying, rendered the whole a scene of horror almost inconceivable.

Source: Werner Sollors, ed., *The Interesting Narrative of the Life of Olaudah Equiano, or Gustavus Vassa, the African, Written by Himself*, A Norton Critical Edition (New York: Norton, 2001), pp. 38–41.

PRIMARY SOURCE 13.2

Buying Slaves at Whydah (1694), *Thomas Phillips*

The best goods to purchase slaves here are cowries [sea snail shells], the smaller the more esteem'd. . . .

The next in demand are brass neptunes or basons [plates], very large, thin, and flat; for after they have brought them they cut them in pieces to make anilias or bracelets, and collars for their arms legs and necks.

The other preferable goods are blue paper sletias, cambricks or lawns, caddy chints, broad ditto [various types of cloth], coral, large, smooth, and of a deep red, rangoes [beads] large and red, iron bars, [gun] powder, and brandy. . . .

[B]ut without the cowries and brass they will take none of the last goods, and but small quantities at best, especially if they can discover that you have good store of cowries and brass aboard, then no other goods will serve their turn, till they have got as much as you have; and after, for the rest of the goods they will be indifferent, and make you come to their own terms, or else lie [offshore] a long time for your slaves, so that those you have on board are dying while you are buying others ashore; therefore every man that comes here, ought to be very cautious in making his report to the king at first, of what sorts and quantities of goods he has, and be sure to say his cargo consists mostly in iron, coral, rangoes, chints, etc. so that he may dispose of those goods as soon as he can, and at last his cowries and brass will bring him slaves as fast as he can buy them. . . .

Source: Elizabeth Donnan, *Documents Illustrative of the History of the Slave Trade to America* (New York: Octagon, 1965).

PRIMARY SOURCE 13.3

A True and Exact History of the Island of Barbadoes (1673), *Richard Ligon*

It has been accounted a strange thing, that the Negroes, being more than double the number of Christians that are there, and they accounted a bloody people . . . that they should not commit some horrid massacre upon the Christians thereby to enfranchise themselves and become masters of the island. But there are three reasons that take away this wonder: the one is, they are not suffered to touch or handle any weapons; the other, that they are held in such awe and slavery as they are fearful to appear in any daring act; and seeing the mustering of our men and hearing their gun shot (which nothing is more terrible to them) their spirits are subjugated to follow a condition, as they dare not look up to any bold attempt. Besides these, there is a third reason, which stops all designs of that kind, and that is they are fetched from several parts of Africa who speak several languages, and by that means one of them understands not another.

Source: Richard Ligon, *A True and Exact History of the Island of Barbadoes* (London: Peter Parker, 1673).

PRIMARY SOURCE 13.4

A Voyage to Saint Domingue (1797), *Francis Alexander Stanislaus, Baron de Wimpffen*

The natural consequence of the order of things which prevails here, is, that all those titles of honour which are elsewhere the *pabula* [source] of emulation, of rivalry and of discord; which inspire so much pride, and create so many claims in some; so much ambition and envy in others; shrink to nothing, and entirely disappear before the sole title of WHITE. It is by your skin, however branded it may be, and not by your parchment [titles of nobility], however worm-eaten, that your pretensions to gentility are assessed. Thus you see that vanity, which on your side of the water torments and turns herself a thousand ways, to impose on the public, and usurp the tribute of respect which it accords to the claims of birth, would here lose both her time and her labor.

Each of the different classes of the inhabitants of St. Domingo has, as you will readily imagine, a turn of thinking, a style of living, more or less approximate or distinct; which, after all, has little resemblance to what you will find elsewhere; because the climate, the regimen, the manners, the wants, the occupations, the degree of reciprocal dependency, establish here connections of the slightest nature; very different from those which, with you, Sir, bind together the members of the same society.

Source: Francis Alexander Stanislaus, Baron de Wimpffen, *A Voyage to Saint Domingue, in the Years 1788, 1789, and 1790*, trans. J. Wright (London: T. Cadell, Junior, and W. Davies, 1797), 63–64.

Population Statistics of the Bahia Sugar Plantations, Brazil (1835)

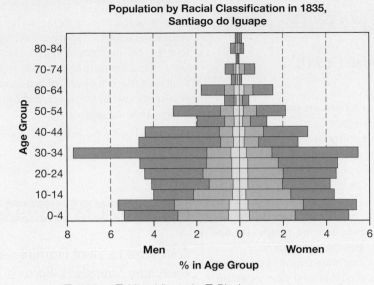

Population by Racial Classification in 1835, Santiago do Iguape

□ White   ■ Mixed (brown)   ■ Black

Free and Freed Population by Racial Classification in 1835, Santiago do Iguape

□ White   ■ Mixed (brown)   ■ Black

Enslaved Population by Place of Birth in 1835, Santiago do Iguape

Source: Katherine Holt, "Population by Racial Classification, Santiago do Iguape 1835," "Free and Freed Population by Racial Classification, Iguape 1835," and "Enslaved Population by Place of Birth, Santiago do Iguape, 1835." The Bahian History Project: The 1835 Santiago do Iguape Household Census Database. http://www.mappingbahia.org/project/.

QUESTIONS FOR ANALYSIS

1. Explain the significance of nation (or community) to Equiano.

2. Compare the perspectives of the written sources. What role does race play? Does the evidence from the graphs support or undermine the claims of those sources?

3. Compare the data for each racial group in the first graph and consider why the Brazilian state organized its records according to racial categories. How do you think the demands of sugar production shaped the racial categories Brazilian officials used to sort the local population?

4. Describe the challenges slaves would have faced in establishing families on the sugar plantations of Santiago do Iguape and contrast their experience with the freed people of different racial classifications.

Interpreting Visual Evidence

A World of Goods

As overseas trade generated new wealth, elites displayed this wealth in diverse ways. Some used new wealth to buy expensive local materials, while others displayed their power by incorporating foreign materials into local designs. Near commercial centers, opportunities for consumption and display of new goods also drew ordinary people into market activities. Ranging from the purely ornamental to the modest and practical, material objects reflected the identities of the people who bought and displayed them, as well as the identities of the producers who made them. They reinforced and sometimes altered status hierarchies as people's appreciation of these material objects, their beauty, and the skill that went into their production shaped the status of both consumers and producers.

The first object, the "Oba with Sacrificial Animals from the Ezomo's Altar of the Hand" (eighteenth–nineteenth century) was made of brass, which signified the elite status of the patron—more modest men would have requested terra-cotta or wood. In the kingdom of Benin, altars like this celebrated exceptional individuals. In addition to the materials chosen, the artist used costume and scale to show the status of the figures depicted. The king, Ehenua, dressed in full military regalia, appears in the center of a group of smaller soldiers, aids, and priests. Two rows of musketeers above the frieze include Portuguese soldiers, showing the support Europeans provided Benin's leaders. The second object is a porcelain bowl produced in China for the British market, with a painting of a cricket match by the English painter Francis Hayman (1708–1776). The third object, a Chinese lacquer plate from the 1620s, is edged with silver filigree, which was crafted in Portuguese-controlled Goa, on the coast of India. The final object, a British-manufactured teapot, was made for middle-class consumers who could not afford imported porcelain from China. This example, with a handle, was intended to match European decorative style; the factory left off the handle for "oriental" designs.

Oba from Ezomo's Altar of the Hand.

Chinese porcelain bowl, with painting by Hayman.

Chinese lacquer plate with silver filigree.

British-manufactured teapot.

QUESTIONS FOR ANALYSIS

1. Describe how these objects were used. What functions did they serve?

2. Analyze the relationship between display and function in these objects. What impression do you think these objects made on people who saw them?

3. Explain the significance of these works for the people who produced them. What roles do you think artistry, craft skill, and financial gain played for the artists and artisans who produced them?

4. How did the conditions in which these objects were produced relate to the identities consumers sought to project? Consider also the relationship between the production of commodities—such as the tea and sugar associated with the final object—with consumer identity.

Before You Read This Chapter

GLOBAL STORYLINES

- Growing global commerce enriches rulers and merchants, who express their power through patronage for the arts.
- Distinctive cultures flourish in the major regions of the world, blending new influences with local traditions to varying degrees.
- While the Islamic and Asian worlds confidently retain their own belief systems, the Americas and Oceania increasingly face European cultural pressures.

CORE OBJECTIVES

- **EXPLAIN** the connections between cultural growth and the creation of a global market.
- **DESCRIBE** and **COMPARE** how each culture in this period reflected the ideas of the states in which they were produced.
- **ANALYZE** the different responses to foreign cultures across Afro-Eurasia in the period from 1500 to 1700.
- **DESCRIBE** how hybrid cultures emerged in the Americas, and **EXPLAIN** the connection between these cultures and Enlightenment ideology.
- **ANALYZE** the role that race and cultural difference played in the process of global integration.

Cultures of Splendor and Power

1500–1780

In 1664, a sixteen-year-old girl from the provinces of New Spain asked her parents for permission to attend the university in the capital. Although she had mastered Greek logic, taught Latin, and become a proficient mathematician, she had two strikes against her: she was a woman, and her thinking ran against the grain of the Catholic Church. So keen was she to pursue her studies that she proposed to disguise herself as a man. But her parents denied her requests, and instead of attending the university she entered a convent in Mexico City, where she would spend the rest of her life. The convent turned out to be a sanctuary for her. There she studied science and mathematics and composed remarkable poetry. Sor (Sister) Juana Inés de la Cruz was her name, and she spoke for a new world where people mixed in faraway places, where new wealth created new customs, and where new ideas began to take hold.

Sor Juana's story attests to the conflicts between new ideas and old orders that occurred as commerce and the consolidation of empires intensified contact between diverse cultures. On the one hand, global commerce created riches that supported arts, architecture, and scientific ventures. On the other, experiments with new ways caused discomfort among defenders of the old order and provoked backlashes against innovation.

This chapter explores how global commerce enriched and reshaped cultures in the centuries after the Americas ceased to be worlds apart from Afro-Eurasia. As New World commodities invigorated global trade and states consolidated power, rulers and merchants on both sides of the Atlantic displayed their power by commissioning fabulous works of art and majestic palaces and sprawling plazas. These cultural splendors were meant to impress, which they surely did. They also demonstrated the growing connections between distant societies, reflecting how foreign influences could blend with domestic traditions. Book production and consumption soared, with some publications finding their way around the world. The spread of books and ideas and increasing cultural contact led to experiments in religious toleration and helped foster cultural diversity. Yet even as Europeans, who were the greatest beneficiaries of New World riches, claimed to advance new universal truths, cultures around the globe still showed the resilience of inherited traditions.

Trade and Culture

COMPARISON

EXPLAIN the connections between cultural growth and the creation of a global market.

New wealth amassed by global commerce in the aftermath of Columbus's "discovery" created the conditions for cultural dynamism from 1500 to 1800. With newfound wealth, rulers promoted learning and the arts in order to legitimize their power and show their sophistication. In Europe, monarchs known as enlightened absolutists restricted the clergy and nobility and hired loyal bureaucrats who championed the knowledge of the new age. Mughal emperors, Safavid shahs, and Ottoman sultans glorified their regimes by bringing artists and artisans from all over the world to give an Islamic flavor to their major cities and buildings. Rulers in China and Japan also looked to artists to extol their achievements. In Africa, the wealth garnered from slave trading underwrote cultural productions of extraordinary merit.

Some rulers were more eager for change than others. Moreover, certain societies—in the Americas and the South Pacific, for example—found that contact, conquest, and commerce undermined indigenous cultural life. Although Europeans and native peoples often exchanged ideas and practices, these transfers were not equal. Native Americans, for example, adapted to European missionizing by creating mixed forms of religious worship—but only because they were under pressure to do so. And as the Europeans swallowed up new territories, it was *their* culture that spread and diversified. Indeed, the Europeans absorbed much from Native Americans and African slaves but offered them little share of sovereignty or wealth in return.

Despite the unifying aspects of world trade, each society retained core aspects of its individuality. Ruling classes disseminated values based on cherished classical texts and long-established moral and religious principles. They used space in new ways to establish and project their power. They mapped their geographies and wrote their histories according to their traditional visions of the universe.

It is not surprising that in 1500 the world's most dynamic cultures remained in Asia, in areas profiting from the Indian Ocean and China Sea trades. It was in China and the Islamic world that the spice and luxury trades first flourished; here, too, rulers had successfully established political stability and centralized control of taxation, law making, and military force. Although older ways did not die out, both trade and empire building contributed to the spread of knowledge about distant people and foreign cultures.

Culture in the Islamic World

As the Ottoman, Safavid, and Mughal empires gained greater expanses of territory in the sixteenth and seventeenth centuries, they acquired new resources to fund cultural development. Rulers supported new schools and building projects, and the elite produced books, artworks, and luxury goods. Cultural life was connected to the politics of empire building, as emperors and elites sought greater prestige by patronizing intellectuals and artists.

Forged under different empires, Islamic cultural and intellectual life now reflected three distinct worlds. In place of an earlier Islamic cosmopolitanism, unique cultural patterns prevailed within each empire. Although the Ottomans, the Safavids, and the Mughals shared a common faith, each developed a relatively autonomous form of Muslim culture.

COMPARISON

DESCRIBE and **COMPARE** how each Islamic culture in this period reflected the ideas of the state in which it was produced.

THE OTTOMAN CULTURAL SYNTHESIS

By the sixteenth century, the Ottoman Empire enjoyed a remarkably rich culture that reflected a variety of mixing influences. As the Ottoman Empire absorbed more cultures and territories, its blend of ethnic, religious, and linguistic elements exceeded the diversity of previous Islamic empires. It also balanced the interests of military men and administrators with those of clerics. Finally, it allowed autonomy to the minority faiths of Christianity and Judaism. That ability to balance a wide array of local traditions and interests and yet maintain authority in the center, supported by new revenues drawn from global trade, constituted the Ottoman synthesis.

Religion and Education A sophisticated educational system was crucial for the empire's religious and intellectual integration and for its cultural achievements. Here, as in religious affairs, the Ottomans tolerated difference. They encouraged three educational systems that produced three streams of talent—civil and military bureaucrats, *ulama,* and Sufi religious masters. The administrative elite attended hierarchically organized schools that culminated in the palace schools at Topkapi (see Chapter 11). In the religious sphere, an equally elaborate system took students from elementary schools (where they learned reading, writing, and numbers) on to higher schools, or *madrasas* (where they learned law, religion, the Quran, and the natural sciences). These graduates became *ulama* who served as judges, experts in religious law, or teachers. Yet another set of schools, *tekkes*, taught the devotional strategies and religious knowledge for students to enter Sufi orders.

Science and the Arts During this period, the Ottomans integrated some foreign elements into their culture, especially in science and philosophy, while furthering their own traditions in architecture, literature, and music. Most of the foreign influences came from Europe, with which the Ottomans were in constant contact. The Ottomans' most impressive effort to spread European knowledge occurred when a Hungarian convert to Islam, Ibrahim Muteferrika, set up a printing press in Istanbul in 1729. Muteferrika published works on science, history, and geography. One included sections on geometry; others, the works of Copernicus, Galileo, and Descartes; and a plea to the Ottoman elite to learn from Europe. When his patron was killed, however, the *ulama* promptly closed off this avenue of contact with western learning.

The Ottomans and the Tulip From the earliest times, the Ottomans admired the beauty of the tulip. (*Left*) Sultan Mehmed II smelling a tulip, symbol of the Ottoman sultans. (*Right*) The Ottomans used tulip motifs to decorate tiles in homes and mosques and pottery wares, as on the plate shown here.

The Ottomans combined inherited traditions with new elements in art as well. For example, portraiture became popular after the Italian painter Gentile Bellini visited Istanbul and composed a portrait of Mehmed II. In other areas, though, the Ottomans kept their own styles. The magnificent architectural monuments built in the sixteenth through eighteenth centuries, including mosques, gardens, tombs, forts, and palaces, showed scant western influence. Nor were the Ottomans interested in western literature or music. For the most part, they believed that God had given the Islamic world a monopoly on truth and enlightenment and that their military successes proved his favor.

The Ottomans' capacity to celebrate their well-being and prosperity spread from elites to the broader public during the so-called Tulip Period, which occurred in the first half of the eighteenth century. The elite had long admired the tulip's bold colors and graceful blooms, and for centuries the flower served as the sultans' symbol. In fact, both Mehmed the Conqueror and Suleiman the Magnificent grew tulips in the most se-cluded and prestigious courtyards at Topkapi Palace in Istanbul. And many Ottoman warriors heading into battle wore undergarments embroidered with tulips to ensure victory. By the early eighteenth century, tulip designs appeared on tiles, fabrics, and public buildings, and authorities sponsored elaborate tulip festivals. Indeed, Ottoman enjoyment of luxury goods (including lemons, soap, pepper, metal tools, coffee, and wine) grew so extensive that a well-traveled diplomat looked askance at the supposed wealth of Europe. He wrote, "In most of the provinces [of Europe], poverty is wide-spread, as a punishment for being infidels. Anyone who travels in these areas must confess that goodness and abundance are reserved for the Ottoman realms." Thus, despite challenges from western Europe and fears that their best days were behind them, the Ottomans' cultural traditions flourished into the eighteenth century and beyond.

SAFAVID CULTURE, SHIITE STATE

If global trade ultimately strengthened Safavid rivals both within the empire and without (see Chapter 13), it also provided the wherewithal for a period of spectacular artistic and architectural creativity, especially at the height of Safavid power in the seventeenth century. The Safavid Empire in Persia (1501–1722) was not as long-lived as the Ottoman Empire, but it was significant for giving the Shiite branch of Islam a home base and a location for displaying Shiite culture. The brilliant culture that emerged during the Safavid period provided a unique blend of Shiism and Persia's distinctive historical identity.

The Safavids created a mixed political and religious system based on Shiism and loyalty to the royal family. The most effective architect of a cultural life based on Shiite religious principles and Persian royal absolutism was Shah Abbas I (r. 1587–1629). The location that he chose to display the wealth and royal power of his state, its Persian and Shiite heritages, and its artistic sensibility was Isfahan, the capital city from its creation in 1598 until the empire's end in 1722.

Architecture and the Arts The Safavid shahs were unique among Afro-Eurasian rulers of this era, for they sought to project both absolute authority and accessibility. Their dwellings were unlike those of other rulers—such as Topkapi Palace in Istanbul, the Citadel in Cairo, and the Red Forts of the Mughals. Those were enclosed and fortified buildings, designed to enhance rulers' power by concealing them from their subjects. In contrast, the buildings of Isfahan were open to the outside, demonstrating the Safavid rulers' desire to connect with their people. Isfahan's centerpiece was the great plaza next to the royal palace and the royal mosque at the heart of the capital.

Other aspects of intellectual life reflected the elites' aspirations, wealth, and commitment to Shiite principles. Safavid artists perfected the illustrated book, the outstanding example being *The King's Book of Kings*, which contained 250 miniature illustrations. Here, artists demonstrated their mastery of three-dimensional representation and their ability to harmonize different colors. Weavers produced ornate silks and carpets for trade throughout the world; artisans painted tiles in vibrant colors and created mosaics that adorned mosques and other buildings. Moreover, the Safavids developed an elaborate calligraphy that was the envy of artists throughout the Islamic world. All of these works celebrated Shiite visions of the sacred while at the same time reinforcing the authority and prestige of the empire's ruling elite.

POWER AND CULTURE UNDER THE MUGHALS

Like the Safavids and the Ottomans, the Mughals fostered a lavish high culture, supported primarily by taxes on agriculture but reliant on silver for its currency and, at its high point, open to global trade. Because the Mughals ruled over a large non-Muslim population, the culture they developed in South Asia was initially broad and open, welcoming non-Muslims into its circle. Thus, while Islamic traditions dominated the empire's political and judicial systems, Hindus shared with Muslims the flourishing of learning, music, painting, and architecture, especially from the middle of the sixteenth century to the middle of the seventeenth.

Religion, Architecture, and the Arts In the sixteenth and early seventeenth centuries, Mughal culture mixed diverse elements from within South Asia and the broader Islamic world. The promise of an open Islamic high culture found its greatest fulfillment under the

Akbar Leading Religious Discussion This miniature painting from 1604 shows Akbar receiving Muslim theologians and Jesuits. The Jesuits (in the black robes on the left) hold a page relating, in Persian, the birth of Christ. A lively debate will follow the Jesuits' claims on behalf of Christianity.

Mughal emperor Akbar (r. 1556–1605). This skillful military leader was also a popular ruler who allowed common people as well as nobles from all ethnic groups to converse with him at court. His quest for universal truths outside the strict *sharia* led him to develop a religion of his own, which incorporated many aspects of Hindu belief and ritual practice (see Chapter 12).

In architecture, too, the Mughals produced masterpieces that blended styles. This was already evident as builders combined Persian, Indian, and Ottoman elements in tombs and mosques built by Akbar's predecessors. But Akbar enhanced this mixture in the elaborate city he built at Fatehpur Sikri, beginning in 1571. The buildings included residences for nobles (whose loyalty Akbar wanted), gardens, a drinking and gambling zone, and even an experimental school devoted to studying language acquisition in children.

Akbar's descendant Shah Jahan was also a lavish patron of architecture and the arts. In 1630, Shah Jahan ordered the building in Agra of a magnificent white marble tomb for his beloved wife, Mumtaz Mahal. Like many other women in the Mughal court, she had been an important political counselor. Designed by an Indian architect of Persian origin, this structure, the **Taj Mahal**, took twenty years and 20,000 workers to build. The forty-two-acre complex included a main gateway, a garden, minarets, and a mosque. The translucent marble mausoleum lay squarely in the middle of the structure, enclosed by four identical facades and crowned by a majestic central dome rising to 240 feet. The stone inlays of different types and hues, organized in geometrical and floral patterns, and featuring Quranic verses inscribed in Arabic calligraphy, gave the surface an appearance of delicacy and lightness. Blending Persian and Islamic design with Indian materials and motifs, this poetry in stone represented the most splendid example of Mughal high culture and the combining of cultural traditions.

Foreign Influences versus Islamic Culture Although later emperors were less tolerant than Akbar, Mughal culture remained vibrant. Well into the eighteenth century, the Mughal nobility lived in unrivaled luxury. The presence of foreign scholars and artists enhanced the courtly culture, and the elite eagerly consumed exotic goods from China and Europe. Foreign trade also brought in more silver, advancing the money economy and supporting the nobles' sumptuous lifestyles. In addition, the Mughals assimilated European military technology: they hired Europeans as gunners and military engineers in their armies, employed them to forge guns, and bought guns and cannons from them.

For all their openness to outside influences, the Mughals, like the Ottomans, remained supremely confident of their own traditions. The centers of the Islamic world were still Istanbul, Cairo, and Delhi. Even while incorporating a few new European elements into their cultural mix, most Muslims regarded Europeans as rude barbarians. Elites in Persia, India, and the Ottoman Empire looked to China and the east, not to Europe and the west, for inspiration.

Culture and Politics in East Asia

In East Asia, prosperity, facilitated by China's vast importation of silver from Japan and the Americas, promoted cultural dynamism in the sixteenth through eighteenth centuries. Still, it was China's booming internal market, more than global trade, that fueled a Chinese culture inspired mainly by its own traditions. China had long been a renowned center of learning, with its emperors and elites supporting artists, poets, musicians, scientists, and teachers. But in late Ming and early Qing China, a growing population and extensive commercial networks propelled the circulation of ideas as well as goods.

In Japan, too, economic growth supported elite and popular culture. Because of its giant neighbor across the sea, the Japanese people had always been aware of outside influences. Like the Chinese government, the Tokugawa shogunate tried to promote Confucian notions of a social hierarchy organized on the basis of social position, age, gender, and kin. It also tried to shield the country from egalitarian ideas that would threaten the strict social hierarchy. But the forces that undermined governmental control of knowledge in China proved even stronger in Japan.

COMPARISON

ANALYZE the different responses to foreign cultures across Afro-Eurasia in the period from 1500–1700.

CHINA: THE CHALLENGE OF EXPANSION AND DIVERSITY

While China had become increasingly connected with the outside world in the sixteenth and seventeenth centuries, the sources for its cultural flourishing during the period came primarily from within. The circulation of books spread ideas among the literate, and religious rituals instilled cultural values among the broader population. Advances in cartography reflected the distinctive worldview of Chinese elites.

Publishing and the Transmission of Ideas The decentralization of book production and the domestic market helped circulate ideas within China. Woodblock and moveable type printing had been present in China for centuries. Although initially the state had spurred book production by printing Confucian texts, before long the economy's increasing commercialization weakened government controls over what got printed. Even as officials clamped down on unorthodox texts, there was no centralized system of censorship, and unauthorized opinions circulated freely.

By the late Ming era, a burgeoning publishing sector catered to the diverse social, cultural, and religious needs of educated elites and urban populations. European visitors admired the vast collections of printed materials housed in Chinese libraries, describing them as "magnificently built" and "finely adorn'd." Perhaps more important, books and other luxury goods were now more affordable. Increasingly, publishers offered a mix of wares: guidebooks for patrons of the arts, travelers, or merchants; handbooks for performing rituals, choosing dates for ceremonies, or writing proper letters; almanacs and encyclopedias; morality books; medical manuals; and, above all, study guides.

Study aids for the civil service examination dominated the literary marketplace. In 1595, Beijing reeled with scandal over news that the second-place graduate had reproduced verbatim several model essays published by commercial printers. Ironically, then, the increased circulation of knowledge led critics to bemoan a decline in real learning; instead of mastering the classics, they charged, examination candidates were simply memorizing the work of others.

Elite women also joined China's literary culture. Anthologies of women's poetry were especially popular, not only in the market but when issued in limited circulation to

Current Trends in World History

The Political Uses of Space

The use of space for political purposes is a theme we can trace across world history. In the early modern period, many kings and emperors opted to build grand palaces to create lavish power centers, from which they could project their influence over their kingdoms; petitioners and potential rivals would have to come to *them* to ask for favors or to complete their business. Monarchs sculpted these environments, creating a series of spaces, each of them open to a smaller and smaller number of the king's favorites. Both palaces and their surrounding grounds were ornate and splendid, were expensive to construct, and involved the best craftsmen and artists available, which often meant borrowing ideas and designs from neighboring cultures. Palace complexes of this type, built in Beijing, in Istanbul, in Isfahan, and just outside of Paris, used space to project the rulers' power and to show who was boss.

The **Forbidden City of Beijing** was the earliest of these impressive sites of royal power (see illustration on p. 405). Its construction took about four years—from 1416 to 1420—although the actual name "Forbidden City" did not appear until 1576.

The entrance of the City was straddled by the Meridian Gate, the tallest structure of the entire complex, which towered over all other buildings at more than thirty-five meters above the ground. It was from this lofty position that the emperor extended his gaze toward his empire, as he oversaw various court ceremonies, including the important annual proclamation of the calendar that governed the entire country's agricultural and ritual activities. Foreign emissaries received by the court were also often allowed to use one of the passageways through the gate, where they were expected to be duly awed. As for the officials' daily audience with the emperor, they had to line up outside the Meridian Gate around three a.m. before proceeding to the Hall of Supreme Harmony. It was typical of the entire construction project that this impressive hall with vermilion walls and golden tiles was built at considerable cost. For the columns of the hall, fragrant hardwood had to be found in the tiger-ridden forests of the remote southwest, while the mountain forests of the south and southwest were searched for other timbers that eventually made their way to the capital through the Grand Canal.

The Topkapi Palace in Istanbul, capital of the Ottoman Empire, began to take shape in 1458 under Mehmed II and underwent steady expansion over the years (see illustration on p. 395. Topkapi projected royal authority in much the same way as the Forbidden City emphasized Chinese emperors' power: governing officials worked enclosed within massive walls, and monarchs rarely went outside their inner domain.

More than two centuries later, in the 1670s and 1680s, the French monarch Louis XIV built the **Palace of Versailles** on the site of a royal hunting lodge eleven miles from Paris, the French capital (see illustration on p. 485). This enormously costly complex was built to house Louis's leading clergymen and nobles, who were obliged to visit at least twice a year. Louis hoped that by taking wealthy and powerful men and women away from their local power bases, and by diverting them with entertainments, he could keep them from plotting new forms of religious schism or challenging his right to rule. Going to Versailles also allowed him to escape the pressures and demands of the population of Paris. Many European monarchs—including Russia's Peter the Great—would build palace complexes modeled on Versailles.

If in China, the Ottoman Empire, and France, emperors built what were essentially private spaces in which to conduct and dominate state business, Shah Abbas (r. 1587-1629) of the Safavid Empire chose to create a great new public space instead. In the early seventeenth century,

---

celebrate the refinement of the writer's family. Men of letters soon recognized the market potential of women's writings; some also saw women's less regularized style (usually acquired through family channels rather than state-sponsored schools) as a means to challenge stifling stylistic conformity. On rare occasions, women even served as publishers themselves.

Although elite women enjoyed success in the world of culture, the period brought increasing restrictions on their lives. The practice of footbinding (which elite women first adopted at least as far back as the twelfth century) continued to spread among common people, as small, delicate feet came to signify femininity and respectability. The thriving

Shah Abbas oversaw the construction of the **great plaza at Isfahan**, a structure that reflected his desire to bring trade, government, and religion together under the authority of the supreme political leader. An enormous public mosque, the Shah Abbas Mosque, dominated one end of the plaza, which measured 1,667 feet by 517 feet. At the other end were trading stalls and markets. Along one side sat government offices; the other side offered the exquisite Mosque of Shaykh Lutfollah. If the other rulers of this era devoted their (considerable) income to creating rich *private* spaces, Shah Abbas used the vast open space of the plaza to open up his city to all comers, keeping only the Mosque of Shaykh Lutfollah for his personal use.

The royal use of space says a great deal about how monarchs in this era wished to be seen and remembered, and about how they wanted to rule. While some wanted to retreat from the rest of society, Shah Abbas wanted to create an open space for trade and the exchanging of ideas. World history is full of palaces and plazas (the Piazza San Marco in Venice might be compared to the royal plaza at Isfahan); we can still visit and admire them. But when we do, we should also remember that space, and the architecture that either opens up to the public or sets aside privileged spaces, has always had political as well as cultural functions.

Isfahan On the great plaza at Isfahan, markets and government offices operated in close proximity to the public Shah Abbas Mosque, shown here, and the shah's private mosque. This structure represented Shah Abbas's desire to unite control of trade, government, and religion under one leader.

QUESTIONS FOR ANALYSIS

- Choose one of the places discussed in this feature. Explain how the architectural layout shaped the political power exercised by that space.
- Contrast private spaces, like the palace at Versailles, with public spaces, like the great plaza at Isfahan. What political goals could be accomplished by each?

Explore Further

Babaie, Sussan, *Isfahan and Its Palaces: Statecraft, Shi'ism and the Architecture of Conviviality in Early Modern Iran* (2008).

Necipoğlu, Gülru, *Architecture, Ceremonial, and Power: The Topkapi Palace in the Fifteenth and Sixteenth Centuries* (1991).

publishing sector indirectly promoted stricter morality by printing plays and novels that echoed the government's conservative attitudes.

Popular Culture and Religion Important as the book trade was, it had only an indirect impact on most men and women in late Ming China. Those who could not read well or at all absorbed cultural values through oral communication, ritual performance, and daily practices.

Villagers participated in various religious and cultural practices, such as honoring local guardian spirits, patronizing Buddhist and Daoist temples, or watching performances

Footbinding Two images of bound feet: (*left*) as an emblem of feminine respectability when wrapped and concealed, as on this well-to-do Chinese woman; (*right*) as an object of curiosity and condemnation when exposed for the world to see.

by touring theater groups. At the grassroots level, there was little distinction among Buddhist, Daoist, and local cults. The Chinese believed in cosmic unity, and although they celebrated spiritual forces, they did not consider any of them to be a Supreme Being who favored one sect over another. They believed it was the emperor, rather than any religious group, who held the mandate of heaven. (See **Current Trends in World History: The Political Uses of Space**.) Unless sects posed an obvious threat, the emperor had no reason to regulate their spiritual practices. This situation promoted religious tolerance and avoided the sectarian warfare that plagued post-Reformation Europe.

Technology and Cartography Belief in cosmic unity did not prevent the Chinese from devising technologies to master nature's operations in this world. For example, the magnetic compass, gunpowder, and the printing press were all Chinese inventions. Chinese astronomers also compiled accurate records of eclipses, comets, novas, and meteors. In part, the emperor's needs drove their interest in astronomy and calendrical science. It was the emperor's job as the Son of Heaven, and thus mediator between heaven and earth, to determine the best dates for planting, holding festivities, scheduling mourning periods, and convening judicial court sessions.

Convinced that their sciences were superior, Christian missionaries in China tried to promote their own knowledge in areas such as astronomy and cartography (mapmaking).

In 1583, the Jesuit missionary Matteo Ricci brought European maps to China, hoping to impress the elite with European learning. Challenging their belief that the world was flat, his maps demonstrated that the earth was spherical—and that China was just one country among many others. Chinese critics complained that Ricci treated the Ming Empire as "a small unimportant country." As a concession, he placed China closer to the center of the maps and provided additional textual information. Still, his maps had a negligible impact, as neither the earth's shape nor precise scale was particularly important to most Chinese geographers.

Before the nineteenth century, the Chinese had fairly incomplete knowledge about foreign lands despite a long history of contact. Chinese writers, for example, often identified groups of other people through distinctive and, to them, odd physical features. A Ming geographical publication portrayed the Portuguese as "seven feet tall, having eyes like a cat, a mouth like an oriole, an ash-white face, thick and curly beards like black gauze, and almost red hair." Chinese elites glorified their "white" complexions against the peasants' dark skin; against the black, wavy-haired "devils" of Southeast Asia; and against the Europeans' "ash-white" pallor. Qing authors in the eighteenth century confused France with the Portugal known during Ming times, and they characterized England and Sweden as dependencies of Holland. During this period of cultural flourishing, in short, most Chinese did not feel compelled to revise their view of the world.

CULTURAL IDENTITY AND TOKUGAWA JAPAN

The culture that developed in Japan in this period drew on local traditions and, increasingly, foreign influences from China and Europe. Chinese cultural influence had long crossed the Sea of Japan, but under the Tokugawa shogunate there was also interest in European culture. This interest grew via the Dutch presence in Japan and limited contacts with Russians. At the same time, there was a surge in the study of Japanese traditions and culture. Thus, Tokugawa Japan engaged in a three-cornered conversation among time-honored Chinese ways, European teachings, and distinctly Japanese traditions.

Native Arts and Popular Culture Elite and popular culture featured elements that were distinctly Japanese. Until the seventeenth century, the main patrons of Japanese culture were the imperial court in Kyoto, the hereditary shogunate, religious institutions, and a small upper class. These groups developed an elite culture of theater and stylized painting. Samurai (former warriors turned bureaucrats) and daimyo (regional lords) favored a masked theater, called Nō, and an elegant ritual for making tea and engaging in contemplation.

Alongside the elite culture arose a rougher urban one that artisans and merchants patronized. Urban dwellers could purchase works of fiction and colorful prints made from carved wood blocks, and they could enjoy the company of female entertainers known as geisha. These women were skilled (*gei*) in playing the three-stringed instrument (*shamisen*), storytelling, and performing; some were also prostitutes. Geisha worked in the cities' pleasure quarters, which were famous for their geisha houses, public baths, brothels, and theaters. Kabuki—a type of theater that combined song, dance, and skillful staging to dramatize conflicts between duty and passion—became wildly popular. This art form featured dazzling acting, brilliant makeup, and sumptuous costumes.

Much popular entertainment chronicled the world of the common people rather than politics or high society. The urbanites' pleasure-oriented culture was known as "the floating world" (*ukiyo*), and the woodblock prints depicting it as *ukiyo-e* (*e* meaning

Artist and Geisha at Tea The erotic, luxuriant atmosphere of Japan's urban pleasure quarters was captured in a new art form, the *ukiyo-e*, or "pictures from a floating world." In this image set in Tokyo's celebrated Yoshiwara district, several geisha flutter about a male artist.

"picture"). Here, the social order was temporarily turned upside down. Those who were usually considered inferior—actors, musicians, courtesans, and others seen as possessing low morals—became idols.

Literacy in Japan now surged, especially among men. The most popular novels sold 10,000 to 12,000 copies. In the late eighteenth century, Edo had some sixty booksellers and hundreds of book lenders. In fact, the presence of so many lenders allowed books to spread to a wider public that previously could not afford to buy them. By the late eighteenth century, as more books circulated and some of them criticized the government, officials tried to censor certain publications. The government's response testified to the uncommon power wielded by people of modest means and the relative significance of popular culture in Japan.

Religion and Chinese Influence In the realm of higher culture and religion, China loomed large in the Tokugawa world. Japanese scholars wrote imperial histories of Japan in the Chinese style, and Chinese law codes and other books attracted a significant readership. Some Japanese traveled south to Nagasaki to meet Zen Buddhist masters and Chinese residents there. Buddhism originally came to Japan from China and remained associated with Chinese monks. A few of those monks even won permission to found monasteries outside Nagasaki and to give lectures and construct temples in Kyoto and Edo.

Although Buddhist temples grew in number, they did not displace the native Japanese practice of venerating ancestors and worshipping gods in nature. Later called Shintō ("the way of the gods"), this practice boasted a network of shrines throughout the country. Shintō developed from time-honored beliefs in spirits, or *kami*, who were associated with places (mountains, rivers, waterfalls, rocks, the moon) and activities (harvest, fertility). Seeking healing or other assistance, adherents appealed to these spirits in nature and daily life through incantations and offerings. Some women under Shintō served as *mikos*, a kind of shaman with special divinatory powers.

Reacting to the influence of Chinese Buddhism and desiring to honor their own country's greatness, some thinkers promoted intellectual traditions from Japan's past. These efforts stressed "native learning," Japanese texts, and Japanese uniqueness. In so doing, they formalized a Japanese religious and cultural tradition, and they denounced Buddhism as a foreign contaminant.

European Influences Not only did Chinese intellectual influences compete with revived native learning, but by the late seventeenth century Japan was also tapping other sources of knowledge. By 1670 a guild of Japanese interpreters in Nagasaki who could speak and read Dutch accompanied Dutch merchants on trips to Edo. As European knowledge spread to high circles in Edo, in 1720 the shogunate lifted its ban on foreign books. Thereafter European ideas, called "Dutch learning," circulated more openly.

Scientific, geographical, and medical texts appeared in Japanese translations and in some cases displaced Chinese texts. A Japanese-Dutch dictionary appeared in 1745, and the first official school of Dutch learning followed. Students of Dutch and other European teachings remained a limited segment of Japanese society, but the demand for translations intensified.

Japan's internal debates about what to borrow from the Europeans and the Chinese illustrate the changes that the world had undergone in recent centuries. A few hundred years earlier, products and ideas generally did not travel beyond coastal regions and had only a limited effect (especially inland) on local cultural practices. By the eighteenth century, though, expanded networks of exchange and new prosperity made the integration of foreign ideas feasible and, sometimes, desirable. The Japanese did not consider the embracing of outside influences as a mark of inferiority or subordination, particularly when they could put those influences to good use. This was not the case for the cultures that thrived within the great Asian land-based empires, which were eager lenders but hesitant borrowers.

African Cultural Flourishing

The wealth that spurred artistic achievement and displays of power in Asia and the Islamic world did not bypass African states. Proceeds from the slave trade enabled African upper classes to fund cultural activities and invigorate strong artisanal and artistic traditions that dated back many centuries. African artisans, like those in East Asia, maintained local forms of cultural production, such as woodcarving, weaving, and metalworking.

Cultural traditions in Africa varied from kingdom to kingdom, but there were patterns among them. For example, all West African elites encouraged craftsmen to produce carvings, statues, masks, and other objects that would glorify the power and achievements of rulers. (Royal patrons in Europe, Asia, and the Islamic world did the same with architecture and painting.) There was also a widespread belief that rulers and their families had the blessing of the gods. Arts and crafts not only celebrated royal power but also captured the energy of a universe that people believed was suffused with spiritual beings. Starting in the 1500s and continuing through the eighteenth century when the slave trade reached its peak, African rulers who benefited from that trade had even more reason—and means—to support cultural pursuits.

COMPARISON

DESCRIBE and **COMPARE** how Chinese, African, and Japanese cultures in this period reflected the ideas of the state in which it was produced.

THE ASANTE, OYO, AND BENIN CULTURAL TRADITIONS

The kingdom of Asante led the way in cultural attainments, and the Oyo Empire and Benin also promoted rich artistic traditions.

The Asante kingdom's access to gold and the revenues that it derived from selling captives made it the richest state in West Africa, perhaps even in the whole of sub-Saharan Africa. The citizens of Asante accorded the highest respect to entrepreneurs who made money and were able to surround themselves with retainers and slaves. The adages of the age were inevitably about becoming rich: "money is king" or "nothing is as important as money" or "money is what it is all about."

Asante's artisans celebrated these traditions through the crafting of magnificent seats or stools coated with gold as symbols of authority; the most ornate were reserved for the head of the Asante federation, the Asantehene, who ruled this far-flung empire

Brass Oba Head The brass head of an Oba, or king, of Benin. The kingdom's brass and bronze work was among the finest in all of Africa.

from the capital city of Kumasi. By the eighteenth century, these monarchs ventured out from the secluded royal palace only on ceremonial and feast days, when they wore sumptuous silk garments featuring many dazzling colors and geometric patterns all joined together in interwoven strips. Known as Kente cloth, this fabric could be worn only by the rulers. Kings also had a golden elephant tail, which was carried in front of them. It symbolized the highest level of wealth and power. Also held aloft on these celebratory occasions were maces, spears, staffs, and other symbols of power fashioned from the kingdom's abundant gold supplies. These reminded the common people of the Asantehene's connection to the gods.

Equally resplendent were rulers of the Oyo Empire and Benin, located in the territory that now constitutes Nigeria. Elegant, refined metalwork in the form of West African bronzes reflects these rulers' power and their peoples' high esteem. In the Oyo Empire, the Yoruba people drew on craft and artistic traditions dating back to the first millennium CE. The bronze heads of Ife, capital city of the Yoruba Oyo Empire, are among the world's most sophisticated pieces of art. According to one commentator, "little that Italy or Greece or Egypt ever produced could be finer, and the appeal of their beauty is immediate and universal." Artisans fashioned the best known of these works in the thirteenth century (before the slave-trade era), but the tradition continued and became more elaborate in the seventeenth and eighteenth centuries.

Stunning bronzes were produced in Benin as well. Although historical records have portrayed Benin as one of Africa's most brutal slave-trading regimes, it produced art of the highest order. Whether Benin's reputation for brutality was deserved or simply part of Europeans' desire to label African rulers as "savage" in order to justify their intervention in African affairs, it cannot detract from the splendor of its artisans' creations.

Although supported by funds from the Atlantic slave trade, the cultural traditions of western Africa remained little influenced by intellectual and artistic influences from the wider world. African culture during this period was relatively autonomous, even as Africa became increasingly entangled in the global webs of economic exchange and political domination.

The Enlightenment in Europe

An extraordinary cultural flowering also blossomed in Europe during the seventeenth and eighteenth centuries, driven by trade and internal commerce. Often the **Enlightenment** is defined purely in intellectual terms as the spreading of faith in reason and in universal rights and laws, but this era encompassed broader developments, such as the expansion of literacy, the spread of critical thinking, and the decline of religious persecution. Contact between Europe and the wider world after the fifteenth century played a formative role in Europeans' view of the world and their place in it. They quickly became eager consumers of other people's goods and practices. From Amerindian trapping methods to African slaves' cultivation techniques, from Chinese porcelain to New World tobacco and chocolate, contact with others influenced Europe in the seventeenth and eighteenth centuries. The more they learned, the more European intellectuals became convinced not only that their culture was superior—for that was hardly rare—but that they had discovered a set of universal laws that applied to everyone, everywhere around the world.

Abandoning the Christian belief in divine intervention, Enlightenment thinkers sought universal, objective knowledge that did not reflect any particular religion, political view, class, gender, or culture. These scholars struggled to formulate universal, natural laws, although most of these thinkers were unaware of how culture-bound their vision was. They ignored the extent to which European, upper-class male perspectives colored their "objective" knowledge.

THE NEW SCIENCE

Interest in scientific discoveries increased gradually over the seventeenth and eighteenth centuries. While the sixteenth century had brought new prosperity, the seventeenth century produced civil and religious wars, dynastic conflicts, and famines that devastated central Europe. These events bankrupted the Spanish, caused chaos in France, led to the execution of the English king, and saw the Dutch break free from Spanish control. They also contributed to the spread of Protestantism in Europe. At the same time, the crises made some intellectuals wish to turn their backs on religious strife and develop useful ways for understanding and improving *this* world—by imposing order on the chaos and instability they saw around them. By 1750, in some western countries, a significant minority of the population was eager to join in these discussions, which concentrated on the natural sciences, especially physics and astronomy.

The search for new, testable knowledge began centuries before the Enlightenment, in the efforts of Nicolaus Copernicus (1473–1542) and Galileo Galilei (1564–1642) to understand the behavior of the heavens. These men were both astronomers and mathematicians. Making their own mathematical calculations and observations of the stars and planets, they came to conclusions that contradicted age-old assumptions. This entailed considerable risk: when Galileo confirmed Copernicus's claims that the earth revolved around the sun, he was tried for heresy.

In the seventeenth century, a small but influential group of scholars committed themselves, similarly, to experimentation, calculation, and observation. They adopted a method for "scientific" inquiry laid out by the philosopher Sir Francis Bacon (1561–1626), who claimed that real science entailed the formulation of hypotheses that could be tested in carefully controlled experiments. Bacon was chiefly wary of classical and medieval authorities, but his principle also applied to traditional knowledge that European scientists were encountering in the rest of the world. Confident of their calculations performed according to the new **scientific method**, scientists like Isaac Newton (1642–1727) sought universal laws that applied to all matter and motion; they criticized older conceptions of nature (from Aristotelian ideas to folkloric and foreign ones) as absurd and obsolete. Thus, in his *Principia Mathematica* Newton set forth the laws of motion—including the famous law of gravitation, which simultaneously explained falling bodies on earth and planetary motion.

Most historians no longer call these changes a scientific revolution, for European thinking did not change overnight. Only gradually did thinkers come to see the natural world as operating according to inviolable laws that experimenters could figure out, like gravity and inertia. But by the late seventeenth century many rulers had developed a new interest in science, and they established royal academies to encourage research. This patronage, of course, had a political function. By incorporating the British Royal Society in 1662, for example, Charles II hoped to show not only that the crown backed scientific progress but also that England's great minds backed the crown. Similar reasoning lay behind Louis XIV's founding of the French Royal Academy of Sciences.

Gradually, the new science expanded beyond the court to gain popularity among elite circles. Marquise de Chatelet-Lomont built a scientific laboratory in her home and translated Newton's *Principia* into French, which her lover, Voltaire, one of the most influential of the Enlightenment figures, popularized. By about 1750, even artisans and journalists were applying Newtonian mechanics to their practical problems and inventions. In Italy, numerous female natural philosophers emerged, and the genre of scientific literature for "ladies" took hold. A consensus emerged among proponents of the new science that useful knowledge came from collecting data and organizing them into universally valid systems, rather than from studying revered classical texts.

By no means, however, did the scientific worldview dominate European thinking. Most people still understood their relationships with God, nature, and fellow humans via Christian doctrines and local customs. Although literacy was increasing, it was far from universal; schools remained church-governed or elite, male institutions. All governments employed censors and punished radical thinkers, peasants still suffered under arbitrary systems of taxation, and judicial regimes were as harsh as during medieval times. Nonetheless, the promise of universal scientific truths inspired Enlightenment thinkers, who in turn held them out as an ideal.

ENLIGHTENMENT THINKERS

Enlightenment thinkers, called **philosophes** in France, applied scientific reasoning to human interaction, to society as opposed to nature. Such thinkers included the French writers Voltaire (1694–1778) and Denis Diderot (1713–1784) and the Scottish moral philosopher and political economist Adam Smith (1723–1790). These writers also called attention to the evils and flaws of human society: Voltaire criticized the torture of criminals, Diderot denounced the despotic tendencies of the French kings Louis XIV and Louis XV, and Smith exposed the inefficiencies of mercantilism. Other Enlightenment thinkers, similarly, criticized contemporary European conditions, and they often suffered imprisonment or exile for writing about what they considered to be superstitious beliefs and corrupt political structures.

The Enlightenment touched all of Europe, but the extent of its reach varied. In France and Britain, enlightened learning spread widely; in Spain, Poland, and Scandinavia, enlightened circles were small and had little influence on rulers or the general population. Enlightened thought flourished in commercial centers like Amsterdam and Edinburgh and in colonial ports like Philadelphia and Boston. (See **Analyzing Global Developments: How Can We Measure the Impact of an Idea?**)

Popular Culture In the emerging marketplace for new books and new ideas, some of the most popular works were not from high intellectuals. Pamphlets charging widespread corruption, fraudulent stock speculation, and insider trading circulated widely. Sex, too, sold well. Works like *Venus in the Cloister, or the Nun in a Nightgown* racked up as many sales as the now-classic works of the Enlightenment. Bawdy and irreligious, these vulgar best-sellers exploited consumer demand—but they also seized the opportunity to mock authority figures, such as nuns and priests. Some even dared to go after the royal family, portraying Marie Antoinette as having sex with her court confessor. Such works displayed the seamier side of the Enlightenment, but they also revealed a willingness on the part of high- and low-brow intellectuals alike to challenge established beliefs and institutions and to undermine royal authority.

The reading public itself helped generate new cultural institutions and practices. In Britain and Germany, book clubs and coffeehouses sprang up to cater to sober men of business and learning; here, aristocrats and well-to-do commoners could read news sheets or discuss stock prices, political affairs, and technological novelties. The same sort of noncourtly socializing occurred in Parisian salons, where aristocratic women presided. The number of female readers, and writers, soared, and the relatively new genre of the novel, as well as specialized women's journals, appealed especially to them. A public sphere emerged that was radically democratic and beyond the control of kings or any corporate body: all it took to participate was the ability to read and the willingness to debate the issues of the day.

Challenges to Authority and Tradition Even though they took the aristocracy's money, many Enlightenment thinkers tried to overturn the status distinctions that characterized European society. They emphasized merit rather than birth as the basis for status. In his *Treatise on Human Understanding* (1690), John Locke claimed that man was born with a mind that was a clean slate (*tabula rasa*) and acquired all his ideas through experience. Locke stressed that cultural differences were not the result of unequal natural abilities, but of unequal opportunities to develop one's abilities. Similarly, in *The Wealth of Nations,* Adam Smith remarked that there was little difference (other than education) between a philosopher and a street porter: both were born, he claimed, with the ability to reason, and both should be free to rise in society according to their talents. Yet Locke and Smith still believed that a mixed set of social and political institutions was necessary to regulate relationships among ever-imperfect humans. Moreover, they did not believe that women could act as independent, rational individuals in the same way that all men, presumably, could. Although educated women like Mary Wollstonecraft and Olympe de Gouges took up the pen to protest these inequities (see Chapter 15 for further discussion), the Enlightenment did little to change the subordinate status of women in European society.

Universal Laws and Religious Tolerance Efforts to discover the "laws" of human behavior linked up with criticism of existing governments. Explaining the laws of economic relations was chiefly the work of Adam Smith, whose book *The Wealth of Nations* described universal economic principles. According to Smith, all people have what he called the propensity to truck, barter, and exchange—an innate desire to trade with one another. He objected that mercantilist controls and guild restrictions stifled economic growth and argued instead that a division of labor, spurred on by free and fair competition, provided the best conditions for producing wealth (though he did not advocate completely free, unregulated markets). Assuming that all people, everywhere shared Protestant notions of thrift and discipline, Smith claimed that by pursuing their own rational self-interest, virtuous individuals would advance the common good without meaning to do so—as if, as he put it, by an "invisible hand." Smith was conscious of growing economic gaps between "civilized and thriving" nations and "savage" ones. Yet he believed that until the poorer nations learned to abide by nature's laws and behaved virtuously, they could not expect a happy fate.

One of the most controversial areas for applying universal laws was religion. Although few Enlightenment thinkers were atheists (people who do not believe in any god), most of them called for religious toleration. They insisted that the use of reason, not force, was the best way to create a community of believers and morally good people. Governments often reacted by censoring books or exiling writers who criticized the authority of the church, but the arguments managed to persuade some rulers. Thus, in the late eighteenth century, governments from Denmark to Austria passed acts offering religious minorities some freedom of worship. However, toleration did not mean full civil rights—especially for Catholics in England or Jews anywhere in Europe. Religious minorities enjoyed much greater freedom in this period in the Ottoman Empire than they did in any European country.

Analyzing Global Developments

How Can We Measure the Impact of an Idea?

The single most important work of the European Enlightenment, which set out to provide an objective compendium of all human knowledge, Denis Diderot's *Encyclopédie* was very French. Of its more than 130 authors, only sixteen were foreign, and, of those sixteen, seven came from the French-speaking city of Geneva, just across the border. All of them were men. Within France, the authors came primarily from the north, especially from Paris. Noble and clerical authors weighed more heavily on the list of authors than in society at large (this had to do with literacy rates, which were much higher among the elite); most of Diderot's authors came from the Third Estate. None of those bourgeois authors had much to do with capitalism, nor did the aristocratic authors have much to do with feudalism. There were large contingents of doctors, lawyers, government officials, and skilled artisans.

We know very little about the production and diffusion of the first edition of the *Encyclopédie*, produced from 1751 to 1772 under Diderot's direction. The first four editions, in fact, were expensive luxury items, relatively unimportant in terms of diffusion. The great mass of *Encyclopédies* that circulated in prerevolutionary Europe came from cut-rate quarto and octavo editions published between 1777 and 1782, when the final, revised version, the *Encyclopédie méthodique*, began to appear. For these later editions, thorough records have survived, raising far-reaching questions about how ideas circulated and where during the Enlightenment, at least within Europe. (We know very little about the circulation of the *Encyclopédie* beyond Europe.) Where did the writers come from, where did their ideas go, and how, if at all, did their origins influence the content and ultimate significance of their project? We include a table of key words and their classification in thematic categories from the original edition, to give a sense of its contents and priorities.

TERMS	WORD COUNT	PRINCIPAL CATEGORIES
Commerce	5,713	Commerce, Geography
Science	2,095	[Multiple Categories]
Christ	1,821	Theology, Holy Scripture
African	1,772	Geography, History, Natural History, Botany
Slavery	238	Natural Law, Ethics, Religion, Ancient History
African Slavery (*La traite des nègres*)	15	Commerce
Negro	536	Natural History, Commerce
Saint-Domingue	96	Geography, Botany
China	957	Agriculture, Chemistry, History, Natural History, Geography, Metaphysics, Tapestry
Turk or Turkey	701	Geography, History
Muhammad	356	Theology, History, Philosophy

QUESTIONS FOR ANALYSIS

- What does the diffusion of the *Encyclopédie* within France and across Europe tells us about its influence? How should we evaluate the influence of a book?

- Do you think the *Encyclopédie*'s local origins compromise its universal ambitions?

- How do you think the social origins of the contributors shaped the kinds of topics covered by the *Encyclopédie*?

Source: Robert Darnton, *The Business of the Enlightenment: A Publishing History of the Encyclopédie, 1775–1800* (1979).

Seeking Universal Knowledge The Enlightenment produced numerous works that attempted to encompass universal knowledge. Most important was the French *Encyclopédie*, which ultimately comprised twenty-eight volumes containing essays by nearly 200 intellectuals. It was popular among the elite despite its political, religious, and intellectual radicalism. Its purpose was "to collect all the knowledge scattered over the face of the earth" and to make it useful to men and women in the present and future. Indeed, the

The *Encyclopédie* Originally published in 1751, the *Encyclopédie* was the most comprehensive work of learning of the French Enlightenment. The title page (*left*) features an image of light and reason being dispersed throughout the land. The title itself identifies the work as a dictionary, based on reason, that deals not just with the sciences but also with the arts and occupations. It identifies two of the leading men of letters (*gens de lettres*), Denis Diderot and Jean le Rond d'Alembert, as the primary authors of the work. Contributors to the *Encyclopédie* included craftsmen as well as intellectuals. The detailed illustrations of a pin factory and the processes and machinery employed in pin making shown below are from a plate in the fourth volume of the *Encyclopédie* and demonstrate its emphasis on practical information.

Encyclopédie offered a wealth of information about the rest of the world, including more than 2,300 articles on Islam. Here, the authors typically praised Arab culture for preserving and extending Greek and Roman science—and in doing so, preparing the way for scientific advances in Europe. But at the same time the authors portrayed Islam with the same ill will that they applied to other organized religions, condemning Muhammad for promoting a bloodthirsty religion and Muslim culture in general for not rejecting superstition.

COMPARISON

ANALYZE the role that race and cultural difference played in the process of global integration.

The Enlightenment and the Origins of Racial Thought The Enlightenment introduced new ways of thinking about human difference. Scientists sought objective, rational ways to classify peoples and cultures in the same way that botanists classified plants—indeed, many leaders in this field were botanists. To do so, they relied on new concepts of race.

Before the eighteenth century, the word *race* referred to a swift current in a stream or a test of speed; sometimes it meant a family lineage (mainly that of a royal or noble family). The Frenchman François Bernier, who had traveled in Asia, may have been the first European to attempt to classify the peoples of the world. He used a variety of criteria, including those that were to become standard from the late eighteenth century down to the present, such as skin color, facial features, and hair texture. Bernier published these views in his *New Division of the Earth by the Different Groups or Races Who Inhabit It* (1684). In addition, the Swedish naturalist Carolus Linnaeus (1707–1778), the French scholar Georges Louis LeClerc, the comte de Buffon (1707–1788), and the German anatomist Johann Friedrich Blumenbach (1752–1840) also were among the first to use racial principles to classify humankind.

In his *Systema Naturae* (first published in 1735), Europe's most accomplished naturalist, Carolus Linnaeus, identified five subspecies of *Homo sapiens*, or wise man. He gave each of the continents a subspecies: there was *Homo europaeus*; *Homo americanus*; *Homo afar*; and *Homo asiaticus*, to which he added a fifth category, *Homo monstrosus*, for "wild" men and "monstrous" types. He believed that each of these groups was marked by distinctive social and intellectual characteristics, contrasting light-skinned Europeans, who he believed were governed by laws, to "sooty" Asians, who were governed by opinion. Custom governed copper-skinned Americans, while only personal whim ruled Africans, whom he consigned to the lowest rung of the human ladder.

Linnaeus thought these categories were malleable, both under environmental pressure and mixing to create new species. Skin color, facial features, and hair type did not directly and permanently correlate to intelligence or morality—this was far removed from the racial thought that emerged a century later. But the idea that human beings could be classified in a few large groups proved enormously influential both in scientific discourse and popular opinion, and the categories he devised were profoundly marked by the biases of his European upbringing.

The Enlightenment quest for universal knowledge spread the idea of liberty far and wide. In many ways its message implied that all people—rich and poor, men and women, slave and free—were created equal and therefore enjoyed the same moral status, deserved the same ability to make claims on one another and receive a fair hearing in return. It opened the possibility that all people might someday be treated as equals. The problem was that although Enlightenment thinkers used universal language, they did not intend it to be applied universally. Voltaire famously argued that equality was natural, but he also contended that, in practice, there would always be classes of people that commanded and classes called upon to obey. Some strands of Enlightenment thought justified European expansion overseas and new kinds of racism, while at the same time the movement provided powerful critiques of all kinds of exploitation.

Creating Hybrid Cultures in the Americas

As European empires expanded in the Americas, mingling between colonizers and native peoples, as well as African slaves, produced hybrid cultures. But the mixing of cultures grew increasingly unbalanced as Europeans imposed authority over more of the Americas. In addition to guns and germs, many European colonizers brought Bibles, prayer books, and crucifixes. With these, they set out to Christianize and "civilize" Amerindian and African populations in the Americas. Yet missionary efforts produced uneven and often unpredictable outcomes. Even as Amerindians and African slaves adopted Christian beliefs and practices, they often retained older religious practices too.

European colonists likewise borrowed from the peoples they subjugated and enslaved. This was especially true in the sixteenth and seventeenth centuries, when the colonists' survival in the New World often depended on adapting. New sorts of hierarchies emerged, and elites in Latin America and North America increasingly followed the tastes and fashions of European aristocrats. Yet, even as they imitated Old World ways, these colonials forged identities that separated them from Europe.

COMPARISON

DESCRIBE how hybrid cultures emerged in the Americas, and **EXPLAIN** the connection between these cultures and Enlightenment ideology.

SPIRITUAL ENCOUNTERS

Although the Jesuits had little impact in China and the Islamic world, Christian missionaries in the Americas had armies and officials to back up their insistence that Native Americans and African slaves abandon their own deities and spirits for Christ. Nonetheless, their attempts to force conversions were rarely a complete success, and some European settlers became interested in Amerindian culture.

European missionaries, especially Catholics, used numerous techniques to bring Amerindians within the Christian fold. They smashed idols, razed temples, and whipped backsliders. Catholic orders (principally Dominicans, Jesuits, and Franciscans) also learned what they could about Indian beliefs and rituals—and then exploited that knowledge to make converts to Christianity. For example, many missionaries found it useful to demonize local gods, subvert indigenous spiritual leaders, and transform Indian iconography into Christian symbols.

Neither gentle persuasion nor violent coercion produced the results that missionaries desired. When conversions did occur, the Christian practices that resulted were usually syncretic: mixed forms in which indigenous deities and rituals merged with Christian ones. Those who did convert saw Christian spiritual power as an addition to, not a replacement for, their own religions.

Europeans also attempted to Christianize slaves from Africa, though many slave owners doubted the wisdom of converting persons they regarded as mere property. Sent forth with the pope's blessing, Catholic priests targeted slave populations in the American colonies of Portugal, Spain, and France. Applying many of the same techniques that missionaries used with Indian "heathens," these priests produced similarly mixed results.

More distressing to missionaries than the blending of beliefs or outright defiance were the Amerindians' successes in assimilating captured colonists. It deeply troubled the missionaries that quite a few captured colonists adjusted to their situation, accepted adoptions into local societies, and refused to return to colonial society when given the chance. Moreover, some Europeans voluntarily chose to live among the Amerindians. Comparing the records of cultural conversion, one eighteenth-century colonist suggested that "thousands of Europeans are Indians," yet "we have no examples of even one of those Aborigines having from choice become European." (Aborigines are original, native inhabitants of a region, as opposed to invaders, colonizers, or later peoples of mixed ancestry.)

Racial Mixing (*Left*) This image shows racial mixing in colonial Mexico—the father is Spanish, the mother Indian, and the child a mestizo. This is a well-to-do family, illustrating how Europeans married into the native aristocracy. (*Right*) Here too we see a racially mixed family. The father is Spanish, the mother black or African, and the child a mulatto. Observe, however, the less aristocratic and markedly less peaceful nature of this family.

While this calculation was no doubt exaggerated, it shows that despite the missionaries' intentions, cultural exchange went in more than one direction.

INTERMARRIAGE AND CULTURAL MIXING

In the early stages of colonization, Europeans mixed with Amerindians in part because there were many more men than women among the colonists. Almost all the early European traders, missionaries, and settlers were men (although the British North American settlements saw more women arrive relatively early on). In response to the scarcity of women and as a way to help Amerindians accept the newcomers' culture, the Portuguese crown authorized intermarriage between Portuguese men and local women. These relations often amounted to little more than rape, but longer-lasting relationships developed in places where Amerindians kept their independence—as among French fur traders and Amerindian women in Canada, the Great Lakes region, and the Mississippi Valley. Whether by coercion or consent, sexual relations between European men and Amerindian women resulted in offspring of mixed ancestry. In fact, the mestizos of Spanish colonies and the *métis* of French outposts soon outnumbered settlers of wholly European descent.

The increasing numbers of African slaves in the Americas complicated the mix of New World cultures even further. Unlike marriages between fur traders and Indian women, in which the women held considerable power because of their connections to Indian trading partners, sexual intercourse between European men and enslaved African women was almost always forced. Children born from such unions swelled the ranks of mixed-ancestry people in the colonial population, contributing to the new cultural mix that was emerging.

FORMING AMERICAN IDENTITIES

Over time, as European colonies in the Americas became more securely established, the colonists developed a sense of their own distinctive "American" identities. The colonization of the Americas brought Europeans, Africans, and Indians into sustained contact, though the nature of the colonies and the character of the contact varied considerably. Where European dominance was most secure, colonists imposed their ways on subjugated populations and imported what they took to be the chief cultural and institutional attributes of the countries they had left behind. Yet Europeans were not immune to cultural influences from the groups they dispossessed and enslaved.

The Creole Identity In Spanish America, ethnic and cultural mixing produced a powerful new class, the **creoles**—people born in the Americas. By the late eighteenth century, creoles increasingly resented the control that **peninsulares**—men and women born in Spain or Portugal but living in the Americas—had over colonial society. Creoles especially resented the exclusive privileges given to peninsular rulers, like those that forbade creoles from trading with other colonial ports. Also, they disliked the fact that royal ministers gave most official posts to peninsulares.

In many cities of the Spanish and Portuguese empires, reading clubs and salons hosted energetic discussions of fresh Enlightenment ideas and contributed to the growing creole identity. The Spanish crown, recognizing the role of printing presses in spreading troublesome ideas, strictly controlled the number and location of printers in the colonies. In Brazil, royal authorities banned them altogether. Nonetheless books, pamphlets, and simple gossip allowed new notions of science, history, and politics to circulate among literate creoles.

Anglicization In one important sense, wealthy colonists in British America were similar to the creole elites in Spanish and Portuguese America: they, too, copied European ways. For example, they constructed "big houses" (in Virginia and elsewhere—especially the Caribbean) modeled on the country estates of English gentlemen and imported opulent furnishings and fashions from the finest British stores. Imitating the British also involved tightening patriarchal authority. In seventeenth-century Virginia, men had vastly outnumbered women, which gave women some power (widows in particular gained greater control over property and more choices when they remarried). During the eighteenth century, however, sex ratios became more equal, and women's property rights diminished as British customs took precedence.

Intellectually, too, British Americans were linked to Europe. Importing enormous numbers of books and journals, these Americans played a significant role in the Enlightenment as producers and consumers of political pamphlets, scientific treatises, and social critiques. Indeed, drawing on the words of numerous Enlightenment thinkers, American intellectuals created the most famous of enlightened documents: the Declaration of Independence. It announced that all men were endowed with equal rights and were created to pursue worldly happiness. In this way Anglicized Americans showed themselves, like the creole elites of Latin America, to be products of both European and New World cultures.

The Influence of European Culture in Oceania

In the South Pacific as in the Americas, European influence had powerful consequences in the eighteenth century. Though in centuries past Hindu, Buddhist, and Islamic missionaries and Chinese traders had traveled to Malaysia and nearby islands, they had not ventured beyond Timor (see Map 14.1). Europeans began to do so in the years after 1770, turning their sights on **Oceania** (Australia, New Zealand, and the islands of the southwest Pacific). Using their new wealth to fund voyages with scientific and political objectives, Europeans invaded these remaining unexplored areas. The results were mixed: while some islands maintained their autonomy, the biggest prize, Australia, underwent thorough Anglicization.

Until Europeans colonized it in the late eighteenth century, Australia was, like the Americas before Columbus, truly a world apart. Separated by water and sheer distance from other regions, Australia's main features were harsh natural conditions and a sparse population. At the time of the European colonization, the island was home to around 300,000 people, mostly hunter-gatherers. Now the intrusion into Oceania presented Europeans with a previously unknown region that could serve as a laboratory for studying other peoples and geographical settings.

THE SCIENTIFIC VOYAGES OF CAPTAIN COOK

In Oceania and across the South Pacific, Europeans experimented with a scientific form of imperialism. The story of the region's most famous explorer, Captain James Cook (1728–1779), shows how closely related science and imperialist ventures could be. Cook's voyages and his encounter with the South Sea Islanders opened up the Pacific, and particularly Australia, to European colonizers.

Captain Cook has become a legendary figure in European cultural history, portrayed as one of the saintly scientists of enlightened progress. His first voyage had two objectives. The Royal Society charged him with the scholarly task of observing the movement of the planet Venus from the Southern Hemisphere, and the British government assigned him the secret mission of finding and claiming "the southern continent" for Britain. Cook set sail in 1768, and his voyage was so fruitful that he subsequently undertook two more scientific-imperial adventures.

The Voyages of Captain James Cook During his celebrated voyages to the South Pacific, Cook (*left*) kept meticulous maps and diaries. Although he had little formal education, he became one of the great exemplars of enlightened learning through experience and experiment. (*Right*) Kangaroos were unknown in the West until Cook and his colleagues encountered (and ate) them on their first visit to Australia. This engraving of the animal (which unlike most animals, plants, and geographical features actually kept the name the Aborigines had given it) from Cook's 1773 travelogue, *A Voyage Round the World in the Years 1768-1771,* lovingly depicts the kangaroo's environs and even emotions.

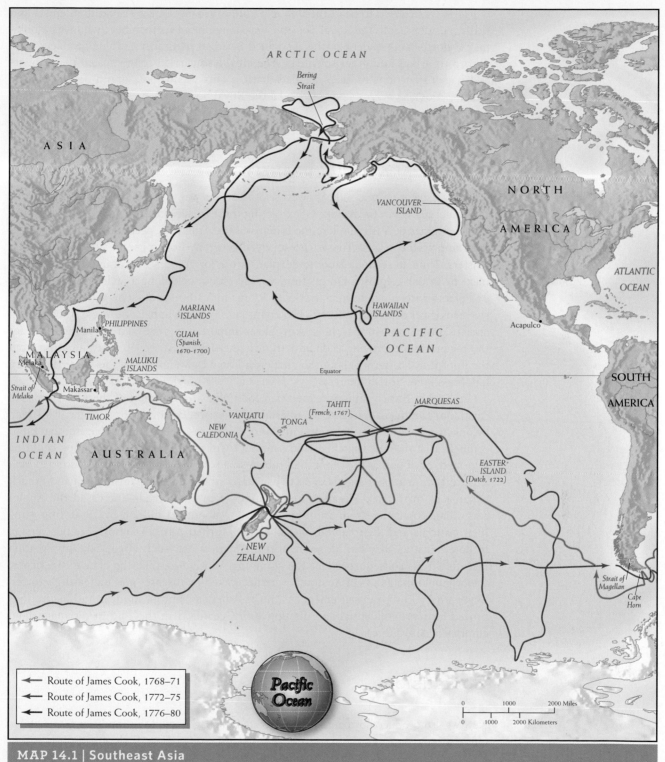

ARCTIC OCEAN

Bering
Strait

ASIA

NORTH

AMERICA

VANCOUVER
ISLAND

ATLANTIC
OCEAN

MARIANA
ISLANDS

PHILIPPINES

Manila

HAWAIIAN
ISLANDS

Acapulco

PACIFIC
OCEAN

GUAM
(Spanish,
1670–1700)

MALAYSIA

Melaka

MALUKU
ISLANDS

SOUTH

Strait of
Melaka

Makassar

Equator

AMERICA

TIMOR

INDIAN
OCEAN

AUSTRALIA

VANUATU

NEW
CALEDONIA

TONGA

TAHITI
(French, 1767)

MARQUESAS

EASTER
ISLAND
(Dutch, 1722)

NEW
ZEALAND

Strait of
Magellan

Cape
Horn

← Route of James Cook, 1768–71
← Route of James Cook, 1772–75
← Route of James Cook, 1776–80

Pacific
Ocean

0   1000   2000 Miles

0   1000   2000 Kilometers

MAP 14.1 | Southeast Asia

Captain Cook's voyages throughout the Pacific Ocean symbolized a new era in European exploration of other societies.

• According to this map, how many voyages did Cook take?

• Where did Cook explore, and what peoples did he encounter?

• Contrast the routes Cook selected for his three voyages. How do they differ? What does that tell us about his project?

Cook was chosen to head the first expedition because of his scientific interests and skills. Besides Cook, the Royal Society sent along one of its members who was a botanist; a doctor and student of the renowned Swedish naturalist Carolus Linnaeus; and numerous artists and other scientists. The crew also carried sophisticated instruments and had instructions to keep detailed diaries. This was to be a grand data-collecting journey. Cook's voyages surpassed even the Royal Society's hopes. The scientists made approximately 3,000 drawings of Pacific plants, birds, landscapes, and peoples never seen in Europe.

ECOLOGICAL AND CULTURAL EFFECTS

More than science was at stake, however, for Australia was intended to supply Britain with raw materials. As in the Americas, extracting those materials required a labor force, and the Aborigines of Australia, like the Indians of the Americas, perished in great numbers from imported diseases. Those who survived generally fled to escape control by British masters. Thus, to secure a labor force, plans arose for grand-scale conquest and resettlement by British colonists. On his third voyage, Cook took along a wide array of animals and plants with which to turn the South Pacific into a European-style garden, with massive ecological consequences. His lieutenant later brought apples, quinces, strawberries, and rosemary to Australia; the seventy sheep imported in 1788 laid the foundations for the region's wool-growing economy. In fact, the domestication of Australia arose from the Europeans' certainty about their superior know-how and a desire to make the entire landmass serve British interests.

In 1788, a British military expedition took official possession of the eastern half of Australia. The intent was, in part, to establish a prison colony far from home. This plan belonged as well to the realm of "enlightened" dreams: removing people from an environment that did not suit them and sending them to new climes where they could be reformed, or, if not, at least limiting problems back home. The intent was also to exploit Australia for its timber and flax and to use it as a strategic base against Dutch and French expansion. In the next decades, immigration—free and forced—increased the Anglo-Australian population from an original 1,000 to about 1.2 million by 1860. Importing their customs and their capital, British settlers turned Australia into a frontier version of home, just as they had done in British America. Yet, such large-scale immigration had disastrous consequences for the surviving Aborigines. Like the Native Americans, the original inhabitants of Australia were decimated by diseases and increasingly forced westward by European settlement. As in the Americas, European ideas and institutions proved far more influential and disruptive in Oceania than they did in the major land empires of Afro-Eurasia.

Conclusion

New wealth produced by commerce and state building created the conditions for a global cultural renaissance in the sixteenth, seventeenth, and eighteenth centuries. It began in the Chinese and Islamic empires and then stretched into Europe, Africa, and previous worlds apart in the Americas and Oceania. Experiments in religious toleration encouraged cultural exchange; book production and consumption soared; grand new monuments took shape; luxury goods became available for wider enjoyment.

Although the Islamic and Chinese worlds confidently retained their own systems of knowing, believing, and representing, the Americas and Oceania increasingly faced

European cultural pressures. Here, while hybrid practices became widespread by the late eighteenth century, European beliefs and habits took over as the standards for judging degrees of "civilization." African cultures largely escaped this influence, though their homelands felt the impact of European expansionism because of the slave trade.

From a commercial standpoint, the world was more integrated than ever before. But the exposure and cultural borrowing that global trade promoted did not obliterate established cultural traditions. The Chinese, for instance, still believed in the superiority of their traditional knowledge and customs. Muslim rulers, confident of the primacy of Islam, allowed others to form subordinate cultural communities within their realm and adopted the Europeans' knowledge only when it served their own imperial purposes.

Only the Europeans were constructing knowledge that they believed was both universal and objective, enabling mortals to master the world of nature and all its inhabitants. This view would prove consequential, as well as controversial, in the centuries to come.

After You Read This Chapter

Go to INQUIZITIVE to see what you've learned—and learn what you've missed—with personalized feedback along the way.

FOCUS ON: *The Flourishing of Regional Cultures*

THE ISLAMIC WORLD

- The Ottomans' unique cultural synthesis accommodates not only mystical Sufis and ultraorthodox *ulama* but also military men, administrators, and clerics.

- The Safavid state proclaims the triumph of Shiism and Persian influences in the sumptuous new capital, Isfahan.

- Mughal courtly culture values art and learning and, at its high point, welcomes non-Muslim contributions.

EAST ASIA

- China's cultural flourishing, coming from within, is evident in the broad circulation of traditional ideas, publishing, and mapmaking.

- Japan's imperial court at Kyoto develops an elite culture of theater, stylized painting, tea ceremonies, and flower arranging.

EUROPE

- Cultural flourishing known as the Enlightenment yields a faith in reason and a belief in humans' ability to fathom the laws of nature and human behavior.

- European thinkers articulate a belief in unending human progress.

- Europeans expand into Australia and the South Pacific.

AFRICA

- Slave-trading states such as Asante, Oyo, and Benin celebrate royal power and wealth through art.

THE AMERICAS

- Even as Euro-Americans participate in the Enlightenment, their culture reflects Native American and African influences.

CHRONOLOGY

	1500	1550	1600
THE ISLAMIC WORLD		Shah Abbas builds Isfahan 1587–1629	
AFRICA		Oyo and Asante kingdoms produce vibrant artistic works 1600s	
EUROPE			
EAST ASIA		Growing circulation of books and ideas in China 1600s	
		Floating Worlds appear in Japanese cities 1600s	
THE AMERICAS		Hybrid cultures appear 1600s	

- ***Thinking about Exchange Networks and Cultural Change*** How did increased exchanges of goods and ideas change established traditions? What institutions and ideas proved most hospitable to foreign influence, even in established cultures, and why? Which fields proved more resistant to outside ideas? Why were some regions more receptive to foreign influences than others? Consider religion, natural science, and art.

- ***Thinking about Changing Power Relationships and Cultural Change*** How did established cultures respond to the inclusion of the Americas into an increasingly integrated world? Which cultures flourished, and why? What relationship(s) can you see between new wealth and cultural change?

- ***Thinking about Environmental Impacts and Cultural Change*** The isolation of the Americas and Oceania paved the way for ecological catastrophe when Europeans arrived. How, in turn, did ecological catastrophes leave indigenous cultures vulnerable? Consider the nature of religious change in the Americas and the Afro-Eurasian core regions and population movements in Australia.

1. Explain how wealth and trade shaped cultural traditions. Where did established high cultures remain vibrant? Where did they come under attack? Where did innovations occur? What made innovation possible?

2. Define the **Enlightenment** and contrast it to the other cultural developments in this chapter. In what ways was it unique?

3. Explain the relationship between **creoles** and **peninsulares** and, more broadly, between the various social groups in the Spanish empire.

4. Compare different uses of monumental architecture as instruments of rule. Consider the **Forbidden City of Beijing**, the **great plaza at Isfahan**, the **Palace of Versailles**, and the **Taj Mahal**.

5. Analyze the relationship between the **scientific method**, concepts of racial difference, and established social hierarchies. Pay particular attention to Captain Cook's expedition to **Oceania**.

Taj Mahal built in Mughal Dynasty 1630–1650

Tulip Period in Ottoman Empire 1720s

◆ Isaac Newton publishes *Principia Mathematica* 1687
◆ Enlightenment philosophy spreads among educated elites 1700s
◆ Carolus Linnaeus publishes *Systema Naturae* 1735
Adam Smith publishes *The Wealth of Nations* 1776 ◆
Voyages of Captain Cook 1768–1779

◆ Enlightenment philosophy spreads among colonial elites 1700s

| 1650 | 1700 | 1750 | 1800 |

Competing Perspectives

What is Enlightenment?

The German philosopher Immanuel Kant (1724–1804) famously answered this question with the Latin *Sapere aude!*—Dare to know! The European Enlightenment was an ambitious cultural project to spread reason, to change contemporaries' worldviews, and to transform political and social institutions. Enlightenment thinkers sought change within Europe, but also, at least implicitly, around the world. (In Chapters 15 and 16 we will look at sources from within the West and other cultures around the world that challenge this European Enlightenment worldview.)

The movement stressed universal laws and objective knowledge. There were, however, several different currents of Enlightenment thought. In addition to Kant's famous essay, the sources reproduced here include selections from Voltaire on tolerance, taking his fellow Europeans to task; Adam Smith on the "invisible hand" of the market and its propensity to support the common good; countered by Jean-Jacques Rousseau's critique of private property and his views on the central importance of community and on the state's ability to force people to be free.

PRIMARY SOURCE 14.1

"What is Enlightenment?" (1784), Immanuel Kant

Enlightenment is the human being's emergence from his self-incurred minority. Minority is inability to make use of one's own understanding without direction from another. This minority is *self-incurred* when its cause lies not in lack of understanding but in lack of resolution and courage to use it without direction from another. *Sapere aude!* Have courage to make use of your *own* understanding! is thus the motto of enlightenment.

It is because of laziness and cowardice that so great a part of humankind, after nature has long since emancipated them from other people's direction (*naturaliter maiorennes*), nevertheless gladly remains minors for life, and that it becomes so easy for others to set themselves up as their guardians. It is so comfortable to be a minor! If I have a book that understands for me, a spiritual advisor who has a conscience for me, a doctor who decides upon a regimen for me, and so forth, I need not trouble myself at all. I need not think, if only I can pay; others will readily undertake the irksome business for me. That by far the greatest part of humankind (including the entire fair sex) should hold the step toward majority to be not only troublesome but also highly dangerous will soon be seen to by those guardians who have kindly taken it upon themselves to supervise them; after they have made their domesticated animals dumb and carefully prevented these placid creatures from daring to take a single step without the walking cart in which they have confined them, they then show them the danger that threatens them if they try to walk alone. Now this danger is not in fact so great, for by a few falls they would eventually learn to walk.

Source: Immanuel Kant, "What is Enlightenment?," from *Practical Philosophy* (*The Cambridge Edition of the Works of Immanuel Kant*), edited by Mary J. Gregor (Cambridge University Press, 1999).

PRIMARY SOURCE 14.2

"What is Tolerance?" (1764), Voltaire

What is tolerance? It is the natural attribute of humanity. We are all formed of weakness and error: let us pardon reciprocally each other's folly. That is the first law of nature.

It is clear that the individual who persecutes a man, his brother, because he is not of the same opinion, is a monster. There is no difficulty here. . . .

Madmen, who have never been able to worship the God who made you! . . . Look at the Great Turk. He governs Guebres, Banians, Greek Christians, Nestorians, Romans. The first who tried to stir up tumult would be impaled; and everyone is at peace.

Of all the religions, the Christian is without doubt the one which should inspire tolerance most, although up to now the Christians have been the most intolerant of all men.

Source: Voltaire, *Philosophical Dictionary* (1764) in Ben Ray Redman, ed., *The Portable Voltaire* (New York: Penguin, 1949), 212–13.

PRIMARY SOURCE 14.3

On the Invisible Hand (1776), Adam Smith

As every individual, therefore, endeavours as much as he can, both to employ his capital in the support of domestic industry, and so to direct that industry that its produce may be of the greatest value; every individual necessarily labours to render the annual revenue of the society as great as he can. He generally, indeed, neither intends to promote the public interest, nor knows how much he is promoting it. By preferring the support of domestic to that of foreign industry, he intends only his own security; and by directing that industry in such a manner as its produce may be of the greatest value, he intends only his own gain; and he is in this, as in many other cases, led by an invisible hand to promote an end which was no part of his intention. Nor is it always the worse for the society that it was no part of it. By pursuing his own interest, he frequently promotes that of the society more effectually than when he really intends to promote it.

Source: Adam Smith, *An Inquiry into the Nature and Causes of the Wealth of Nations* (London: W. Strahan and T. Cadell, 1776), BK. 4, Ch. 2, p. 35.

PRIMARY SOURCE 14.4

On Inequality (1755), Jean-Jacques Rousseau

The first man who, having enclosed a piece of ground, bethought himself of saying *This is mine*, and found people simple enough to believe him, was the real founder of civil society. From how many crimes, wars and murders, from how many horrors and misfortunes might not any one have saved mankind, by pulling up the stakes, or filling up the ditch, and crying to his fellows, "Beware of listening to this impostor; you are undone if you once forget that the fruits of the earth belong to us all, and the earth itself to nobody." But there is great probability that things had then already come to such a pitch, that they could no longer continue as they were; for the idea of property depends on many prior ideas, which could only be acquired successively, and cannot have been formed all at once in the human mind. Mankind must have

made very considerable progress, and acquired considerable knowledge and industry, which they must also have transmitted and increased from age to age before they arrived at this last point of the state of nature.

Source: Jean-Jacques Rousseau, *Rousseau's Political Writings*, A Norton Critical Edition, trans. Julia Conaway Bondanella (New York: W. W. Norton & Company, 1988), 34.

PRIMARY SOURCE 14.5

On the Claims of Community (1762), Jean-Jacques Rousseau

In fact, each individual, as a man, may have a particular will contrary or dissimilar to the general will which he has as a citizen. His particular interest may speak to him quite differently from the common interest: . . . he may wish to enjoy the rights of citizenship without being ready to fulfill the duties of a subject. The continuance of such an injustice could not but prove the undoing of the body politic.

In order then that the social compact may not be an empty formula, it tacitly includes the undertaking, which alone can give force to the rest, that whoever refuses to obey the general will shall be compelled to do so by the whole body. This means nothing less than that he will be forced to be free; for this is the condition which, by giving each citizen to his country, secures him against all personal dependence. In this lies the key to the working of the political machine; this alone legitimizes civil undertakings, which, without it, would be absurd, tyrannical, and liable to the most frightful abuses.

Source: Jean-Jacques Rousseau, *Rousseau's Political Writings*, A Norton Critical Edition, trans. Julia Conaway Bondanella (New York: W. W. Norton & Company, 1988), 34.

QUESTIONS FOR ANALYSIS

1. Describe the language used in these documents. Is it neutral, couched in universal terms that apply everywhere?

2. Identify the common assumptions about human nature, society, and the natural world in these documents. What do they all share?

3. Explain what these authors mean by progress. What forces support progress, in their views, and what forces hinder or jeopardize it?

4. Assess the role of government—what it is or what it ought to be—indicated in these passages.

Interpreting Visual Evidence

Envisioning the World

Although maps give the impression of objectivity and geographic precision, the arrangement of names and locations, as well as the areas placed at the center and the margins, reveal the mapmakers' views of the world. In most cultures, official maps located their own major administrative and religious sites at the center of the universe and reflected local elites' ideas about how the world was organized.

There were, however, important differences. For example, Chinese maps, like the first two below, typically devoted more attention to textual explanations with moral and political messages than to locating places accurately. The Codex Xolotl presents a cartographic history, showing mountains and waterways and using hieroglyphic place-names for sites in the Valley of Mexico, marking historic conquests of an Aztec group, the Acolhuas of Texcoco. The Iranian map presents an unabashedly Islamic vision, with a grid that measures the distances from any location in the Islamic world to Mecca. The Japanese map shows Dutch influence, with much information about distant lands both in the map and in the two-person images to the left. Finally, the European maps (the Waldseemüller map and the Mercator projection) appear objective at first glance, but they too group the rest of the world around their own territory, which they distort to make appear disproportionately large.

The Huayi tu *map, 1136.*

Chinese wheel map, 1760s.

Codex Xolotl, early sixteenth century.

Iranian map, seventeenth century.

Japanese map of the world, 1761.

Waldseemüller map, 1507.

Mercator projection, 1569.

QUESTIONS FOR ANALYSIS

1. Describe the organizing principles, and therefore priorities, of each map.

2. Compare the maps. How are they different from one another?

3. Evaluate the relative awareness each map shows of distant cultures and territories.

Before You Read This Chapter

GLOBAL STORYLINES

- A new era based on radically new ideas of freedom and the nation-state emerges in the Atlantic world.

- The industrious and industrial revolutions transform communities and the global economy.

- The worldwide balance of power shifts decisively towards northwestern Europe.

CORE OBJECTIVES

- **DESCRIBE** the new ideas of freedom and **EXPLAIN** how they differed from earlier understandings of this term.

- **COMPARE** political and economic developments in the Atlantic world with regions elsewhere around the globe during the period 1750–1850.

- **IDENTIFY** and **EXPLAIN** the key developments that constituted the Industrial Revolution.

- **EXPLAIN** patterns of global trade and economic growth and **CONNECT** them to political changes during the period 1750–1850.

- **COMPARE** the groups of people who held power in each of the regions in 1750 and then in 1850, and **EXPLAIN** the changes that took place during this period in these societies.

Reordering the World

1750–1850

In 1798, the French commander Napoleon Bonaparte invaded Egypt. At the time, Europeans regarded this territory as the cradle of a once-great culture, a land bridge to the Red Sea and trade with Asia, and an outpost of the Ottoman Empire. Occupying the country would allow Napoleon to introduce some of the principles of the French Revolution and to seize control of trade routes to Asia. Napoleon also hoped that by defeating the Ottomans, who controlled Egypt, he would augment his and France's historic greatness. But events did not go as Napoleon planned, for his troops faced a resentful Egyptian population. Although Napoleon soon returned to France and his dream of a French Egypt was short-lived, his invasion challenged Ottoman rule and threatened the balance of power in Europe. Indeed, Napoleon's actions in Africa, the Americas, and Europe, combined with the principles of the American and French revolutions, laid the foundations for a new era—one based on a radically new understanding of freedom as the absence of constraint, the opposite of privileges handed down by a lord or master.

That new idea of freedom first rang out across western Europe and the Americas and reverberated around the world. It destroyed the American colonial domains of Spain, Portugal, Britain, and France;

brought new nations to the stage; and challenged established elites everywhere, leading in some cases to the expansion of colonial rule. The impulse for change was a belief that governments should enact laws that apply to all people, though in practice there were significant exceptions (slaves, women, and colonized subjects). Free speech, free markets, free labor, and governments freely chosen by freeborn men, it was thought, would benefit everyone. In Europe and the Americas, though not elsewhere, the era also witnessed the emergence of the nation-state. This new form of political organization derived legitimacy from its inhabitants, often referred to as citizens, who, in theory, if not always in practice, shared a common culture, ethnicity, and language.

Yet, freedom in some corners of the globe set the stage for depriving people of freedom elsewhere and led inexorably to changes in the worldwide balance of power. Even as western European countries lost their New World colonies, they gained economic and military strength, which further challenged Asian and African governments.

Revolutionary Transformations and New Languages of Freedom

COMPARISON

DESCRIBE the new ideas of freedom and **EXPLAIN** how they differed from earlier understandings of this term.

In the eighteenth century, the circulation of goods, people, and ideas created pressures for reform around the Atlantic world. As economies expanded, many people felt that the restrictive mercantilist system prevented them from sharing in the new wealth and power. Similarly, an increasingly literate public called for their states to adopt just practices, including the abolition of torture and the accountability of rulers. In several places, power holders could not stamp out these demands before they became full-scale revolutions.

Reformers wanted to expand the franchise, to enable property holders to vote. Claims of **popular sovereignty**, the idea that political power depends on "the people," became rooted in the idea of the nation: people who shared a common language, common culture, and common history. This in turn gave rise to the nation-state as a form of political organization. Over the course of the nineteenth century, political movements began to emphasize nationalism, the idea that a fully fledged nation should have a state of its own, and democracy, the idea that the people, the *demos*, should choose their own representatives and be governed by them (see Chapter 16). In this chapter, we concentrate on the first expressions of this new thinking, in thirteen of Britain's North American colonies and in France. In both places, the "nation" and the "people" toppled their former rulers.

This chapter also concentrates on far-reaching economic developments that came in tandem with revolutionary political change. Economic reformers argued that unregulated economies would produce faster economic growth. Going well beyond the work of Adam Smith, they called for **free trade** (or **laissez-faire**), unencumbered by tariffs, quotas, and fees; free markets, which would be unregulated; and free labor, which meant using paid rather than slave labor. They insisted that these economic freedoms would yield more just and more efficient societies, ultimately benefiting everyone, everywhere in the world.

Yet, the same European and Euro-American elites who wanted a freer world often exploited slaves, denied women equal treatment, restricted colonial economies, and tried forcibly to open Asia's and Africa's markets to European trade and investment. In Africa, idealistic upheavals did not lead to free and sovereign peoples, but to greater enslavement.

Political Reorderings

Late in the eighteenth century, revolutionary ideas spread across the Atlantic world (see Map 15.1) following the trail of Enlightenment ideas about freedom and reason. As more newspapers, pamphlets, and books circulated in European countries and American colonies, readers began to discuss their societies' problems and to believe they had the right to participate in governance.

The slogans of independence, freedom, liberty, and equality seemed to promise an end to oppression, hardship, and inequities. In the North American colonies and in France, revolutions ultimately brought down monarchies and blossomed into republics. The examples of the United States and France soon encouraged other people in the Caribbean and Central and South America to reject the rule of monarchs. In these revolutionary environments, new institutions—such as written constitutions and permanent parliaments—claimed to represent the people.

COMPARISON

COMPARE political and economic developments in the Atlantic world with regions elsewhere around the globe during the period 1750–1850.

THE NORTH AMERICAN WAR OF INDEPENDENCE, 1776–1783

The American Revolution ended British rule in North America. It was the first of a series of revolutions to shake the Atlantic world, inspired by new ideas of freedom.

By the mid-eighteenth century, Britain's colonies in North America swelled with people and prosperity. Bustling port cities like Charleston, Philadelphia, New York, and Boston saw inflows of African slaves, European migrants, and manufactured goods, while agricultural staples flowed out. A "genteel" class of merchants and landowning planters dominated colonial affairs.

Land was a constant source of dispute. Planters struggled with independent farmers (yeomen). Sons and daughters of farmers, often unable to inherit or acquire land near their parents, moved westward, where they came into conflict with Amerindian peoples. To defend their lands, many Amerindians allied with Britain's rival, France. After losing the Seven Years' War (see Chapter 13), however, France ceded its Canadian colony to Britain to secure the return of its much more lucrative Caribbean colonies, especially Saint-Domingue. This left many Indians no choice but to turn to the British government to help them resist the aggressive advances of land-hungry colonists. British officials did make some concessions to Indian interests, but they did not have the troops or financial strength to enforce them.

Asserting Independence from Britain Despite these tensions, Britain stood supreme in the Atlantic world in the mid-1760s, with its greatest foes defeated and its empire expanding. Political revolution in North America seemed unimaginable. And yet, a decade later, that is what occurred.

The spark came from the government of King George III, which insisted that colonists contribute to the crown that protected them, notably in the Seven Years' War (known in North America as the French and Indian War). The king's officials imposed taxes on a variety of commodities and tried to put an end to smuggling by colonists who sought to evade mercantilist restrictions on trade. To the king's surprise and dismay, colonists objected to the new measures and protested having to pay taxes when they lacked political representation in the British Parliament.

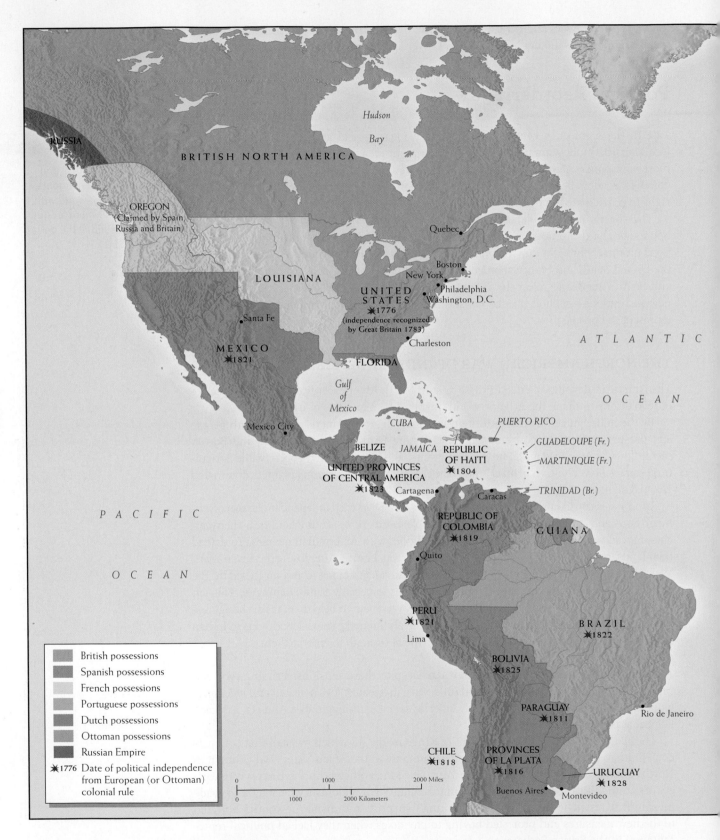

RUSSIA

BRITISH NORTH AMERICA

Hudson Bay

OREGON
(Claimed by Spain, Russia and Britain)

LOUISIANA

Quebec

Boston
New York
Philadelphia
Washington, D.C.

UNITED STATES
✳1776
(independence recognized
by Great Britain 1783)

Santa Fe

MEXICO
✳1821

Charleston

FLORIDA

Gulf of Mexico

Mexico City

CUBA

PUERTO RICO

GUADELOUPE (Fr.)

BELIZE *JAMAICA* REPUBLIC OF HAITI
✳1804

MARTINIQUE (Fr.)

UNITED PROVINCES
OF CENTRAL AMERICA
✳1823

Cartagena

Caracas

TRINIDAD (Br.)

REPUBLIC OF
COLOMBIA
✳1819

G U I A N A

P A C I F I C

Quito

O C E A N

PERU
✳1821

Lima

B R A Z I L
✳1822

BOLIVIA
✳1825

PARAGUAY
✳1811

Rio de Janeiro

CHILE
✳1818

PROVINCES
OF LA PLATA
✳1816

URUGUAY
✳1828

Buenos Aires Montevideo

A T L A N T I C

O C E A N

British possessions
Spanish possessions
French possessions
Portuguese possessions
Dutch possessions
Ottoman possessions
Russian Empire

✳1776 Date of political independence
from European (or Ottoman)
colonial rule

0   1000   2000 Miles
0   1000   2000 Kilometers

MAP 15.1 | Revolutions of National Independence in the Atlantic World, 1776–1829

Influenced by Enlightenment thinkers and the French Revolution, colonies gained independence from European powers (and in the case of Greece, from the Ottoman Empire) in the late eighteenth and early nineteenth centuries.

- Which European powers granted independence to their colonial possessions in the Americas during this period?

- What were the first two colonial territories to become independent in the Americas?

- Based on the chronology presented here and on your reading, consider the relative importance of European influence and local developments in the Americas in accounting for the timing of independence in different countries. Why, in particular, did colonies in Spanish and Portuguese America obtain political independence decades after the United States won its independence?

The Boston Massacre Paul Revere's idealized view of the Boston Massacre of March 5, 1770. In the years after the Seven Years' War, Bostonians grew increasingly disenchanted with British efforts to enforce imperial regulations. When British troops fired on and killed several members of an angry mob in what came to be called the "Boston Massacre," the resulting frenzy stirred revolutionary sentiments among the populace.

In 1775, resistance in the form of petitions and boycotts turned into open warfare between a colonial militia and British troops in Massachusetts. Once blood was spilled, more radical voices came to the fore. Previously, leaders of the protest had claimed to revere the British Empire. Now calls for severing the ties to Britain became more prominent. Thomas Paine, a recent immigrant from England, captured the new mood in a pamphlet he published in 1776, arguing that it was "common sense" for people to govern themselves. Later that year, the Continental Congress (in which representatives from thirteen colonies gathered) adapted part of Paine's popular pamphlet for the Declaration of Independence.

Drawing on Enlightenment themes (see Chapter 14), the declaration written by Thomas Jefferson stated the people's "natural right" to govern themselves. It also drew inspiration from the writings of the British philosopher John Locke, notably the idea that governments should be based on a **social contract** in which the law binds both ruler and people. Locke had written nearly a century earlier that the people had the right to rebel against their government if it broke the contract and infringed on their rights. With the Declaration of Independence, the rebels announced their right to rid themselves of the English king and form their own government.

The Declaration's assertion that "all men are created equal" overturned former social hierarchies in the thirteen colonies (now calling themselves states). Thus, common men no longer automatically deferred to gentlemen of higher rank. Many women claimed that their contributions to the revolution's cause (by managing farms and shops in their husbands' absence) earned them greater equality in marriage, including property rights. However, the political arrangements Americans designed during their War of Independence gave voting rights only to white, male property owners—not women, not slaves, not Amerindians, not poor white men without property. Indeed, many slaves sided against the revolution, for it was the British who offered them freedom—most directly in exchange for military service. Their hopes for freedom were thwarted when Britain conceded the loss of its rebellious American colonies. With the Treaty of Paris (1783), the United States gained its independence.

Building a Republican Government With independence, the former colonists had to build a new government. They generally agreed that theirs was not to be a monarchy. But what it *was* to be remained through the 1780s a source of much debate, involving heated words and sometimes heated action. As a loose confederation of relatively autonomous states, the new national state struggled to deal with local rebellions, foreign relations, and crushing levels of debt. To save the young nation from falling into "anarchy," propertied men convened the Constitutional Convention in Philadelphia in 1787.

This gathering aimed to forge a document that would create a more powerful national government and a more unified nation. After fierce debate, the convention drafted a charter for a republican government in which power would rest with representatives of the people—not with a king. When it went before the states for approval, the Constitution was controversial. Its critics, known as anti-Federalists, feared the growth of a potentially tyrannical national government and insisted on including a Bill of Rights to protect individual liberties from abusive government intrusions. Ultimately the Constitution was ratified by the states and then amended by the Bill of Rights.

Ratification of the Constitution and the addition of the Bill of Rights did not end arguments about the scope and power of the national government of the United States. Some Americans called for the national government to abolish slavery. However, many others—especially leaders in the south, where slavery was a mainstay of the economy—argued that the national government did not have the power to do so. In an uneasy truce, political leaders agreed not to let the debate over whether to abolish slavery escalate into a cause for disunion. As the frontier pushed westward, however, the question of which new states would or would not allow slavery again sparked debates. Initially the existence of ample land postponed a confrontation. In 1800, Thomas Jefferson's election as the third president of the United States marked the triumph of a model of sending pioneers out to new lands in order to reduce conflict on old lands. In the same year, however, a Virginia slave named Gabriel Prosser raised an army of slaves to seize the state capital at Richmond and won support from white artisans and laborers for a more inclusive republic. His dream of an egalitarian revolution fell victim to white terror and black betrayal, though: twenty-seven slaves, including Prosser, went to the gallows. With them, for the moment, died the dream of a multiracial republic in which all men were truly created equal.

In the larger context of the Atlantic world, the successful defiance of Europe's most powerful empire and the establishment of a nonmonarchical, republican form of government sent shock waves through the Americas and Europe and even into distant corners of Asia and Africa. It also helped pave the way for other revolts over the next several decades.

THE FRENCH REVOLUTION, 1789–1799

Partly inspired by the American Revolution, French men and women soon began to call for liberty too—and the result profoundly shook Europe's dynasties and social hierarchies. Its impact, though, reached well beyond Europe, for the French Revolution, even more than the American, inspired rebels and terrified rulers around the globe.

Origins and Outbreak The French king himself opened the door to revolution. Eager to weaken his rival, England, Louis XVI spent huge sums in support of the American rebels—and thereby overloaded the state with debt. To restore his credit, Louis needed to raise taxes on the privileged classes; to do so, he was forced to convene the Estates-General, a medieval advisory body that had not met for over a century. Like the American colonists, French nobles argued that taxation gave them the right of representation.

When the delegates assembled in 1789, however, a procedural dispute spun out of control. The delegates of the clergy (the First Estate) and the aristocracy (the Second Estate) hoped to vote by estate and overrule the delegates representing everyone else (the Third Estate). But the Third Estate, which had more representatives than the first two estates combined, refused to be outvoted. It demanded that all delegates sit together in one chamber and vote as individuals. Soon delegates of the Third Estate declared themselves to be the "National Assembly," the body that should determine France's future.

Afraid that the King would crush the reform movement, a Parisian crowd attacked a medieval armory in search of weapons on July 14, 1789. Not only did this armory—the Bastille—hold gunpowder, but it was also an infamous prison for political prisoners.

The "Tennis Court Oath" Locked out of the chambers of the Estates-General, the deputies of the Third Estate reconvened at a nearby indoor tennis court in June 1789; there they swore an oath not to disband until the king recognized the sovereignty of a national assembly.

The crowd stormed the prison and murdered the commanding officer, then cut off his head and paraded it through the streets of Paris. On this day (Bastille Day), the king made the fateful decision not to call out the army, and the capital city belonged to the crowd. As news spread to the countryside, peasants torched manor houses and destroyed municipal archives containing records of feudal dues, payments they owed to landlords of specially designated properties. Barely three weeks later, the French National Assembly abolished the privileges of the nobility and the clergy. It declared a new era of liberty, equality, and fraternity. Liberty, like freedom, now meant the absence of constraint rather than a special privilege granted by the king.

Revolutionary Transformations The French Revolution connected the concept of a people more closely with a nation. The "Declaration of the Rights of Man and Citizen" (1789) echoed the Americans' Declaration of Independence, but in more radical terms. It guaranteed all citizens of the French nation inviolable liberties and gave all men equality under the law. It also proclaimed that "the principle of all sovereignty rests essentially in the nation." Both the rhetorical and the real war against old-regime privileges threatened to end dynastic and aristocratic rule in Europe.

Social relations changed too, as women felt that the new principles of citizenship should include women's rights. In 1791, a group of women demanded the right to bear arms to defend the revolution, but they stopped short of claiming equal rights for both sexes. In their view, women would become citizens by being good revolutionary wives and mothers, not because of any natural rights. In the same year, Olympe de Gouges composed the "Declaration of the Rights of Woman and Citizen," proposing rights to divorce, hold property in marriage, be educated, and have public careers. The all-male assembly did not take up these issues, believing that a "fraternity" of free *men* composed the nation.

As the revolution gained momentum, deep divisions emerged. In 1790, all clergy had to take an oath of loyalty to the new state—an action that bitterly divided the country. The most divisive, destructive turn in the revolution came in 1792, when the French declared a preemptive war against Austria, and then Prussia, Britain, and Russia. They soon had foreign armies on their soil and a civil war to contend with, when peasants outraged by the loyalty oath and city dwellers in major provincial cities rose up against the Revolutionary government and its wartime demands.

The Terror In response to this self-induced crisis, elite reformers made common cause with urban radicals in Paris, who demanded price controls, direct democracy, and the violent suppression of dissent. Together, they launched the Reign of Terror. The Committee of Public Safety, including the lawyer Maximilien Robespierre, oversaw the execution of as many as 40,000 so-called enemies of the people—mostly peasants and laborers who had taken up arms against them—justified in terms of defending the Republic. If most victims were of modest means, the term *aristocrat* was often equated with treason. Even before terror was declared as government policy, Louis XVI and his wife, Marie Antoinette, had lost their heads to the guillotine (itself a novel and supposedly rational, enlightened way to execute prisoners painlessly).

By 1794 France's army numbered some 800,000 soldiers, making it the world's largest. Most French officers now came from the middle classes, some even from the lower class. Foot soldiers identified with the French fatherland. Having vowed to wage a defensive war, they now pushed foreign armies off French soil and waged a war to "liberate" the disenfranchised from their rulers across Europe.

When the military emergency ended, enthusiasm for Robespierre's measures lost popular support, and Robespierre himself went to the guillotine on 9 Thermidor (according to the new, Revolutionary calendar, or July 28, 1794). His execution marked the end of the Terror but did not restore order. Several years later, following yet more political turmoil, a coup d'état brought to power a thirty-year-old general from the recently annexed Mediterranean island of Corsica.

The general, **Napoleon Bonaparte** (1769–1821), put security and order ahead of social reform. His regime retained significant revolutionary changes, especially those associated with more efficient state government. He eased religious tensions by working out an accord with the Vatican. However, Napoleon was determined not only to reform France but also to prevail over its enemies, and he retreated from republican principles. Taking the title Emperor of the French, he centralized government administration and established a system of rational tax collection. Most important, he created a civil legal code—the "Code Napoleon"—that applied throughout all of France (and the French colonies).

THE NAPOLEONIC ERA, 1799–1815

Determined to extend the reach of French influence, Napoleon launched a series of military campaigns in an effort to build a vast empire. He had his armies trumpet the principles of liberty, equality, and fraternity wherever they went. Many local populations initially embraced the French, regarding them as liberators from the old order. Although Napoleon thought the entire world would take up his cause, this was not always the case.

In Portugal, Spain, and Russia, French troops faced fierce popular resistance. Portuguese and Spanish soldiers and peasants formed bands of resisters called guerrillas, and British troops joined them to fight the French in the Peninsular War (1808–1813).

MAP 15.2 | Napoleon's Empire, 1812

Early in the first decade of the nineteenth century, Napoleon controlled almost all of Europe.

• What major states were under French control? What countries were allied to France?

• Compare this map with the European part of Map 15.1, and explain how Napoleon redrew the map of Europe. What major country was not under French control?

• According to your reading, how was Napoleon able to control and build alliances with so many states and kingdoms?

In Germany and Italy, as local inhabitants grew tired of paying tribute, many looked to their past for inspiration to oppose the French. Now they discovered something they had barely recognized before: *national* traditions and borders. One of the ironies of Napoleon's attempt to bring all of Europe under French rule was that it laid the foundations for nationalist strife.

In Europe, Napoleon extended his empire from the Iberian Peninsula to the Austrian and Prussian borders. (See Map 15.2.) By 1812, when he invaded Russia, however, his forces were too overstretched and undersupplied to survive the harsh winter. After his failed attack on Russia, all the major European powers united against him. At the Battle of

Waterloo in Belgium in 1815, armies from Prussia, Austria, Russia, and Britain crushed his troops as they made their last stand. The stage was now set for a century-long struggle on the continent between those who wanted to restore society as it was before the French Revolution and those who wanted to guarantee a more liberal order based on individual rights, limited government, and free trade.

REVOLUTION IN SAINT-DOMINGUE (HAITI)

France also saw colonies break away in this age of new freedoms, notably Saint-Domingue. Unlike most of British North America, revolution here came from the bottom rungs of the social ladder: slaves. In this Caribbean colony, freedom therefore meant not just liberation from Europe, but emancipation from white planters. It posed a powerful question: how universal were these new rights?

At the outset of the French Revolution the island's black slave population numbered 500,000, compared with 40,000 white French settlers and about 30,000 free "people of color" (individuals of mixed black and white ancestry, as well as freed black slaves). Almost two-thirds of the slaves were relatively recent arrivals, brought to the colony to toil on its renowned sugar plantations, which were exceptional in their brutality. The slave population was an angry majority without local ties, producing wealth for rich absentee landlords of a different race.

Revolution in Saint-Domingue In 1791, slaves took up arms against white planters. This engraving was based on a German report on the uprising and reflects white fears of slave rebellion as much as the actual events themselves.

The breakdown of authority in France unleashed conflict in Saint-Domingue, where local tensions were already high. White settlers sought self-government; they wanted to break free of the exclusive trade arrangement with France and to control the island themselves. Free blacks wanted to end racial discrimination among property holders without, initially, calling slavery into question. Slaves, by contrast, invoked revolutionary language to denounce their masters and air long-standing grievances. As civil war erupted, slaves fought French forces that had arrived to restore order. In 1793, the National Convention in France abolished slavery. In part, the motive was to declare the universality of liberty, equality, and fraternity within the French nation, which included colonies. In part, it was to restore order to the colony. Once liberated, the former slaves took control of the island. (See **Current Trends in World History: Two Case Studies in Political Change and Environmental Degradation**.)

The specter of a free country ruled by former slaves sent shudders across the Western Hemisphere, and above all in Britain and Spain, which had neighboring colonies. A version of martial law was declared in Venezuela. Thomas Jefferson, author of the Declaration of Independence and U.S. president at the time, refused to recognize Haiti. Like other American slave owners, he worried that the example of a successful slave uprising might inspire similar revolts in the United States and elsewhere in the Americas.

REVOLUTIONS IN SPANISH AND PORTUGUESE AMERICA

Revolutionary enthusiasm also spread through Spanish and Portuguese America. As in Haiti, subordinated people of color took advantage of the period's political instability;

Two Case Studies in Political Change and Environmental Degradation

Overthrowing slavery and colonial domination did not necessarily halt environmental degradation. In fact, in two important New World countries, the new nations of Haiti and Brazil, the transition to independence aggravated environmental problems created by former colonial regimes.

Two hundred and fifty years ago, Haiti, which was under French colonial rule at that time and known as Saint-Domingue, was the richest colony in the Americas, perhaps even the richest colony in the world, accounting for two-thirds of France's worldwide investment. Saint-Domingue's extraordinary wealth came from large, white-owned sugar plantations that used a massive and highly coerced slave population. The slaves' lives were short and brutal, lasting on average only fifteen years; hence the wealthy planter class had to replenish their labor supplies from Africa at frequent intervals.

White planters on the island were eager to amass quick fortunes so that they could sell out and return to France. Vastly outnumbered by enslaved Africans at a time when abolitionist sentiments were gaining ground in Europe and even circulating among slaves in the Americas, the planters' families knew that their prosperity was unlikely to last. They gave little thought to sustainable growth and were not troubled that they were destroying their environment.

The planters greeted the onset of the French Revolution in 1789 with enthusiasm. They saw an opportunity to assert their independence from France, to engage in wider trading contacts with North America and the rest of the world, and thus to become even richer. They ignored the possibility that the ideals of the French Revolution—especially its slogan of liberty, equality, and fraternity—could inspire the island's free blacks, free mulattoes, and slaves. Indeed, no sooner had the white planters thrown in their lot with the Third Estate in France than a slave rebellion broke out in Saint-Domingue. From its beginnings in 1791, it led, after great loss of life to African slaves and French soldiers, to the proclamation of an independent state in Haiti in 1804, ruled by African Americans. Haiti became the Americas' second independent republican government. Although the revolt brought political independence to its black population, it only intensified the land's environmental deterioration. Not only did sugarcane fields become scorched battlefields, but freed slaves rushed to stake out independent plots on the old plantations and in wooded areas. In both places, the new peasant class energetically cleared the land. The small country became even more deforested, and intensive cultivation increased erosion and soil depletion. Haiti fell into a more vicious cycle of environmental degradation and poverty.

The second case study of political change leading to the destruction of the environment comes from the independent Brazilian state where the ruling elite, having achieved autonomy from Portugal, expanded the agrarian frontier. Landowners oversaw the clearing of ancient hardwood forests so that slaves and squatters could plant coffee trees. The clearing process had begun with sugarcane in the coastal regions, but it accelerated with coffee plantings in the hilly regions of São Paulo.

In fact, coffee was a worse threat to Brazil's forests than any other invader in the previous 300 years. Coffee trees thrive on soils that are neither soggy nor overly dry. Therefore planters razed the virgin forest,

they mobilized European ideas against European colonizers and challenged the established order. (See Map 15.3.)

Even before the French Revolution, Andean Indians rebelled against Spanish colonial authority. In a major uprising in the 1780s, they demanded freedom from forced labor and compulsory consumption of Spanish wares. After an army of 40,000 to 60,000 Andean Indians besieged the ancient capital of Cuzco and nearly vanquished Spanish armies, it took Spanish forces many years to eliminate the insurgents.

After this uprising, Iberian American elites who feared their Indian or slave majorities renewed their loyalty to the Spanish or Portuguese crown. Ultimately, however, the French Revolution and Napoleonic wars shattered the ties between Spain and Portugal and their American colonies.

Brazil and Constitutional Monarchy Brazil was a prized Portuguese colony whose path to independence saw little political turmoil and no social revolution. In 1807, French troops stormed Lisbon, the capital of Portugal, but not before the royals and their associates

Slaves Cutting Cane Sugar was the preeminent agricultural export from the New World for centuries. Owners of sugarcane plantations relied almost exclusively on African slaves to produce the sweetener. Labor in the fields was especially harsh, as slaves worked in the blistering sun from dawn until dusk.

which contained a balanced variety of trees and undergrowth, and Brazil's once-fertile soil suffered rapid depletion by a single-crop industry. Within one generation the clear-cutting led to infertile soils and extensive erosion, which drove planters farther into the frontier to destroy even more forest and plant more coffee groves. The environmental impact was monumental: between 1788 and 1888, when slavery was abolished, Brazil produced about 10 million tons of coffee and lost 300 million tons of ancient forest biomass (the accumulated biological material from living organisms).

QUESTIONS FOR ANALYSIS

- Who intensified the deforestation and degradation in each case, and why did they do it?
- Why do you think deforestation increased in intensity after Haitians and Brazilians gained their autonomy/independence?

Explore Further

David Geggus (ed.), *The Impact of the Haitian Revolution in the Atlantic World* (2001).

Jared Diamond and James A. Robinson (eds.), *Natural Experiments of History* (2010).

---

fled to Rio de Janeiro, then the capital of Brazil. There they settled down, enacting reforms in administration, agriculture, and manufacturing and establishing schools, hospitals, and a library. Brazil now became the center of the Portuguese empire. Furthermore, the royal family willingly shared power with the local planter aristocracy, so the economy prospered, and slavery expanded.

When the King returned to Portugal in 1821, his son Pedro remained. Fearing an uprising among local elites, Pedro declared Brazil an independent state and established a constitutional monarchy. Local elites soon embraced Pedro's rule and cooperated to minimize conflict, lest a slave revolt erupt. By the 1840s, Brazil had achieved a political stability unmatched in the Americas.

Mexico's Independence When Napoleon occupied Spain, he sparked a crisis in the Spanish empire that eventually led Mexico to secede. Because the ruling Spanish monarchy fell captive to Napoleon in 1807, colonial elites in Buenos Aires (Argentina), Caracas (Venezuela), and Mexico City (Mexico) found themselves without an emperor.

MAP 15.3 | Latin American Nation Building

Creating strong, unified nation-states proved difficult in Latin America. The map shows where boundaries were drawn in Mexico, the United Provinces of Central America, and the Republic of Colombia. In each case, the governments' territorial and nation-building ambitions failed to some degree.

• During what period did a majority of the colonies in Latin America gain independence?

• Which European countries lost the most in Latin America during this period?

• Why did all these colonies gain their independence during this time?

After Napoleon's defeat, locally born creoles resented the fact that Spain reinstated *peninsulares* (people born in Spain) as colonial officials with the help of the royal army. Inspired by Enlightenment thinkers and chafing at the efforts to restore Iberian authority, the creoles wanted to keep their privileges and get rid of the peninsulares.

Mexico's creoles identified themselves more as Mexicans than as Spanish Americans, and as the Spanish king appeared less and less able to govern effectively, Mexican generals (with support of the creoles) proclaimed Mexican independence in 1821. Unlike the situation in Brazil, Mexican secession did not lead to stability.

Other South American Revolutions The loosening of Spain's grip on its colonies was more prolonged and militarized than Britain's separation from its American colonies. Venezuela's Simón Bolívar (1783–1830), the son of a merchant-planter family, who was educated on Enlightenment texts, dreamed of a land governed by reason. He revered Napoleonic France as a model state built on military heroism and constitutional proclamations. So did the Argentine leader General José de San Martín (1778–1850). Men like Bolívar, San Martín, and their many generals waged extended wars of independence against Spanish armies and their allies between 1810 and 1824.

What started in South America as a political revolution against Spanish colonial authority escalated into a social struggle among Indians, mestizos, slaves, and whites. The armed populace threatened the planters and merchants; rural folk battled against aristocratic creoles; Andean Indians fled the mines and occupied great estates. Popular armies, having defeated Spanish forces by the 1820s, fought civil wars over the new postcolonial order.

New states and collective identities of nationhood now emerged. A narrow elite led these political communities, and their guiding principles were often contradictory. Bolívar, for instance, urged his followers to become "American," to overcome their local identities. He wanted the liberated countries to form a Latin American confederation, urging Peru and Bolivia to join Venezuela, Ecuador, and Colombia in the "Gran Colombia." But local identities prevailed, giving way to unstable national republics. Bolívar died surrounded by opponents; San Martín died in exile. The real heirs to independence were local military chieftains, who often forged alliances with landowners. Thus the legacy of the Spanish American revolutions was contradictory and echoed developments elsewhere around the world: the triumph of wealthy elites under a banner of liberty, yet often at the expense of poorer, nonwhite, and mixed populations.

Change and Trade in Africa

Africa also was swept up in revolutionary tides, as increased domestic and world trade—including the selling of African slaves—shifted the terms of state building across the continent. The main catalyst for Africa's political shake-up was the rapid growth and then the demise of the Atlantic slave trade.

ABOLITION OF THE SLAVE TRADE

Even as it enriched and empowered some Africans and many Europeans, the slave trade became a subject of fierce debate in the late eighteenth century. Some European and American revolutionaries argued that slave labor was inherently less productive than free wage labor and ought to be abolished. At the same time, another group favoring abolition of the slave trade insisted that traffic in slaves was immoral. In London they created committees, often led by Quakers, to lobby Parliament for an end to the slave trade. Quakers in Philadelphia did likewise. Pamphlets, reports, and personal narratives denounced the traffic in people.

In response to abolitionist efforts, North Atlantic powers moved to prohibit the slave trade. Denmark acted first in its Caribbean colonies in 1803, Great Britain followed in 1807, and the United States joined the campaign in 1808. Over time, the British persuaded the French and other European governments to do likewise. To enforce the ban, Britain posted a naval squadron off the coast of West Africa to prevent any slave trade above the equator and compelled Brazil's emperor to end slave imports. After 1850, Atlantic slave-shipping dropped sharply, though slavery did not end for several decades due to the continued profitability of cotton in the southern United States, sugar in the Caribbean, and coffee in Brazil.

NEW TRADE WITH AFRICA

Even as the Atlantic slave trade died down, Europeans promoted commerce with Africa. Now they wanted Africans to export raw materials and to purchase European manufactured goods. What Europeans liked to call "legitimate" trade aimed to raise the Africans' standards of living by substituting trade in produce for trade in slaves. West Africans responded by exporting palm kernels and peanuts. The real bonanza was in vegetable oils to lubricate machinery and make candles and in palm oil to produce soap. European merchants argued that by becoming vibrant export societies, Africans would earn the wealth to profitably import European wares.

The new trade gave rise to a generation of successful West African merchants. There were many rags-to-riches stories, like that of King Jaja of Opobo (1821–1891). Kidnapped and sold into slavery as a youngster, he started out paddling canoes carrying palm oil to coastal ports. Ultimately becoming the head of a coastal canoe house, he founded the port of Opobo and could summon a flotilla of war canoes on command. Another freed slave, a Yoruba, William Lewis, made his way back to Africa and in 1828 settled in Sierra Leone (a British colony for freed slaves, notably Black Loyalists from the United States). Starting with a few utensils and a small plot of land, he became a successful merchant who sent his son Samuel to England for his education. Samuel eventually became an important political leader in Sierra Leone.

However, the rise of free labor in the Atlantic world and the dwindling foreign slave trade had an unanticipated effect. It strengthened slavery within Africa. In some areas, by the mid-nineteenth century slaves accounted for more than half the population. No longer did they comfortably serve in domestic employment; instead, they toiled on palm oil plantations or, in East Africa, on clove plantations. They also served in the military forces, bore palm oil and ivory to markets as porters, or paddled cargo-carrying canoes along rivers leading to the coast. In 1850, northern Nigeria's ruling class had more slaves than independent Brazil, and almost as many as the United States. As Africa ceased to be the world's supplier of slaves, it became in time the world's largest slave-holding region.

Economic Reordering

COMPARISON

IDENTIFY and **EXPLAIN** the key developments that constituted the Industrial Revolution.

Behind the political and social upheavals, profound changes were occurring in the world economy. Until the middle of the eighteenth century, global trade touched only the edges of most societies, which produced for their own subsistence. Surpluses of special goods, from porcelains to silks, entered trade arteries but did not change the cultures that produced

New Farming Technologies Although major technological changes in agriculture only emerged late in this period, the spread of more intensive cultivation led to increased yields.

them. A century later, by the middle of the nineteenth century, global trade networks had expanded their reach. The desire for cash, for silver or gold, drove market relations much further than they had ever reached before. People increasingly worked to produce goods they could sell, which transformed social relations in agricultural hinterlands as well as bustling urban centers.

AN INDUSTRIOUS REVOLUTION

Many of these developments took place first in northwestern Europe and British North America. Here, as elsewhere in the world, households had always produced mainly for themselves and made available for marketplaces only meager surpluses of goods and services. But dramatic changes occurred when family members, including wives and children, decided to work harder and longer in order to produce more for the market and purchase more in the market. In these locations, households devoted less time to leisure activities and more time to working, using the additional income from hard work to purchase products produced elsewhere. Scholars recently have come to call this change an **industrious revolution**. Beginning in the second half of the seventeenth century, it gained speed in the eighteenth century and laid the foundations for the industrial revolution of the late eighteenth and early nineteenth centuries.

The willingness on the part of families to work more and an eagerness to eat more diverse foods, to wear better clothes, and to consume products that had once been available as luxuries only to the wealthy classes led in turn to a large expansion in trade. Sugar and silver were the pioneering products. But by the eighteenth century, other staples joined the long-distance trading business, including tea: its leaves came from China, the sugar to cut its bitterness from the Caribbean, the slaves to harvest the sweetener from Africa, and the ceramics to serve a proper cup from the English Midlands. Even ordinary people could purchase imported goods with their earnings. Thus, the poor began to enjoy coffee, tea, and sugar. European artisans and farmers purchased tools, furnishings, and home decorations. Slaves and colonial laborers also used their meager earnings to buy imported cotton cloth made in Europe from the raw cotton they themselves had picked several seasons earlier.

The expansion of global trade had important social and political consequences. As new goods flowed from ever more distant corners of the globe, immense fortunes grew. To support their enterprise, traders needed new services in insurance, bookkeeping, and the recording of legal documents. Trade supported the growth of the liberal professions—accountants and lawyers. The new cities of the commercial revolution, hubs like Bristol, Bombay, and Buenos Aires, provided the homes and flourishing neighborhoods for the growing class of men and women known as the **bourgeoisie**: urban businessmen, financiers, and other property owners without aristocratic origins.

THE INDUSTRIAL REVOLUTION

Trade and finance repositioned western Europe's relationship with the rest of the world. So did the emergence of manufacturing. Like agricultural production, output of industrial commodities surged. The heart of this process was a gradual accumulation and diffusion of technical knowledge. Lots of little inventions, their applications, and their spread across the Atlantic world gradually built up a stock of technical knowledge and practice. Historians have traditionally called these changes the **industrial revolution**.

Nowhere was this industrial revolution more evident than in Britain. Britain had access to waterways, constructed a network of canals, and had large supplies of coal and iron—key materials used in manufactured products. It also had a political and social environment that allowed merchants and industrialists to invest heavily while also expanding their internal and international markets. Among their investments was the application of steam power to textile production, which enabled Britain's manufacturers to produce cheaper goods in larger quantities. Finally, Britain had access to New World lands as sources of financial investment, raw materials, and markets for manufactured goods. These factors' convergence promoted self-sustaining economic growth.

Consider the relationship between inventor and investor in the advent of the steam engine. Such engines burned coal to boil water, and the resulting steam drove mechanized devices. There were several tinkerers working on such an engine. But the most famous was James Watt (1736–1819) of Scotland, who managed to separate steam condensers from piston cylinders so that pistons could stay hot and run constantly; he joined forces with the industrialist Matthew Boulton, who marketed the steam engine and set up a laboratory where Watt could refine his device. The steam engine catalyzed a revolution in transportation. Steam-powered engines also improved sugar refining, pottery making, and other industrial processes, generating more products at lower cost than when workers had made them by hand.

Textile production was critical. Most raw cotton for the British cloth industry had come from colonial India until 1793, when the American inventor Eli Whitney (1765–1825) patented a "cotton gin" that separated cotton seeds from fiber. After that, cotton farming spread so quickly in the southern United States that by the 1850s it was producing more than 80 percent of the world's cotton supply. In turn, every black slave in the Americas and many Indians in British India were consumers of cheap, British-produced cotton shirts. The price of cotton cloth declined by nearly 50 percent between 1780 and 1850, as textiles became the

A Cotton Textile Mill in the 1830s The region of Lancashire became one of the major industrial hubs for textile production in the world. By the 1830s, mills had made the shift from artisanal work to highly mechanical mass production. Among the great breakthroughs was the discovery that cloth could be printed with designs, such as paisley or calico (as in this image), and marketed to middle-class consumers.

world's most dynamic industry. England became the world's largest cloth producer, driving most of the other centers of textile production, notably those in the Indian subcontinent, out of business.

Wherever the industrial revolution took hold, it allowed societies to outdistance rivals in manufacturing and elevated them to a new place in the emerging global economic order. (See Map 15.4.) But why did this revolution cluster mainly in the Atlantic world? This is an important question, because the unequal distribution of global wealth, the gap between the haves and have-nots, really took off in this era of revolutions. In much of Asia and Africa, technical change altered modes of production and business practices, but it was not followed by a continuous cascade of changes. The great mystery was China, the home of astronomical water clocks and gunpowder. Why did China not become the epicenter of the industrial revolution?

There are two reasons. China did not foster experimental science of the kind that allowed Watt to stumble onto the possibility of steam, or Whitney the cotton gin. Experimentation, testing, and the links between thinkers and investors were a distinctly Atlantic phenomenon. The Qing, like the Mughal and Ottoman dynasties, swept the great minds into the bureaucracy and reinforced the old agrarian system based on peasant exploitation and tribute. Second, Chinese, Mughal, and Ottoman rulers did not support overseas expansion and trade that helped create the commercial revolution in the Atlantic world. The agrarian dynasties of China and India neither showered favors on local merchants nor effectively shut out interlopers. This made them vulnerable to cheap manufactured imports from European traders backed by their governments extolling the virtues of free trade.

The effects were profound. Historically, Europe had a trade imbalance with partners to the east—furs from Russia, and spices and silks from Asia. It made up for this with silver from the Americas. But the new economic order meant that by the nineteenth century, western Europe not only had manufactures like cotton textiles to export to Asia, it

MAP 15.4 | Industrial Europe around 1850

By 1850 much of western Europe was industrial and urban, with major cities linked to one another through a network of railroads.

• According to this map, what natural resources contributed to the growth of the industrial revolution? What effects did it have on urban population densities?

• Compare the course of major rivers with those of the railways.

• According to your reading, why were the effects of the industrial revolution more rapidly apparent in Great Britain and in north-central Europe?

also had capital. One of Europe's biggest debtors was none other than the sultan of the Ottoman Empire, whose tax system could not keep up with the spending necessary to keep the realm together. More and more, Asian, African, and American governments found themselves borrowing from Europe's financiers just as their people were buying industrial products from Europe and selling their primary products to European consumers and producers.

WORKING AND LIVING

The industrial revolution brought more demanding work routines—not only in the manufacturing economies of western Europe and North America but also on the farms and plantations of Asia and Africa.

Urban Life and Work Routines Increasingly, Europe's workers made their livings in cities. London, Europe's largest city in 1700, saw its population nearly double over the next century to almost 1 million. By the 1820s, population growth was even greater in the industrial hubs of Leeds, Glasgow, Birmingham, Liverpool, and Manchester. (See **Analyzing Global Developments: Town and Countryside, Core and Periphery in the Nineteenth Century**.)

For most urban dwellers, cities were not healthy places. Water that powered the mills, along with chemicals used in dyeing, went directly back into waterways that provided drinking water. Overcrowded tenements shared just a few outhouses. Most European cities as late as 1850 had no running water, no garbage pickup, no underground sewer system. The result was widespread disease. (In fact, no European city at this time had as clean a water supply as the largest towns of the ancient Roman Empire once had.)

Changes in work affected the understanding of time. Whereas most farmers' workloads had followed seasonal rhythms, after 1800 industrial settings imposed a rigid concept of work discipline. To keep the machinery operating, factory and mill owners installed huge clocks and used bells or horns to signify the workday's beginning and end. Employers also measured output per hour and compared workers' performance.

Industrialization imposed numbing work routines and paltry wages. Worse, however, was having no work at all. As families abandoned their farmland and depended on wages, being idle meant having no income. Periodic downturns in the economy put wage workers at risk, and many responded by organizing protests.

Social Protest and Emigration While entrepreneurs accumulated private wealth, the effects of the industrial revolution on working-class families raised widespread concern, sometimes leading to protests or emigration. In the 1810s in England, groups of jobless craftsmen, called Luddites, smashed the machines that had left them unemployed. Social advocates sought protective legislation for workers, including curbing child labor, limiting the workday, and, in some countries, legalizing prostitution for the sake of monitoring the prostitutes' health.

Some people, however, could not wait for legislative reform. The period saw unprecedented emigration, as unemployed workers or peasants abandoned their homes to seek their fortunes in America, Canada, and Australia. During the Irish Potato Famine of 1845–1849, at least 1 million Irish citizens left their country (and a further million or so died) when fungi attacked their subsistence crop. Desperate to escape starvation, they booked cheap passage to North America on ships so notorious for disease and malnutrition that they earned the name "Coffin Ships."

Analyzing Global Developments

Town and Countryside, Core and Periphery in the Nineteenth Century

The textile industry was by far the most dynamic sector of the world economy in the nineteenth century. It was dependent on cotton, whose production was labor-intensive but required relatively little capital investment and benefited little from economies of scale. In the first half of the century, cotton was primarily produced by slaves in the southern United States. By the late 1850s, the United States accounted for 77 percent of the cotton consumed in Britain, for 90 percent in France, and for about 92 percent in Russia. After the U.S. Civil War and subsequent slave emancipations, sharecroppers continued to produce the crop, though cotton production began to flourish in Brazil, Egypt, West Africa, and India.

Wheat, on the other hand, was the basic staple of European and Mediterranean diets well into the nineteenth century, and it remains vitally important. Before the advent of railroads, most wheat was consumed locally. In the second half of the century, however, vast quantities of wheat came onto world markets as railroads spread through the midwest of the United States and the plains of central and eastern Europe. Grown on large, capital-intensive farms, that wheat—as well as rye, corn, millet, and other grains—fed radically expanding European and American industrial cities and factory towns, linking them to rich agricultural hinterlands and contributing unwittingly to the economic volatility of the nineteenth century. Here we chart the fortunes of two of the most important commodities of the nineteenth-century world—cotton and wheat—against the growth of cities and railroads.

QUESTIONS FOR ANALYSIS

- Which countries appear to be the most dynamic? Pay attention to relative change over time—not only in the biggest cities and most extensive rail networks but also in those growing the fastest.
- How does the growth of railroads and cities vary by country? What does this tell us about the relationship between economic core regions and their peripheries, and about patterns of inequality more generally?
- How did the extension of railroads, and the economic integration they fostered, influence patterns of inequality worldwide?

POPULATION OF MAJOR CITIES (IN THOUSANDS)

	1800	1830	1850	1880	1900
Alexandria	15		60	231	320
Delhi		150	152	173	209
Rio de Janeiro	43	125	166	360	523
London	1,117		2,685	4,770	6,586
Paris	576		1,053	2,269	2,714
Moscow	250		365	748	989
New York City	60	161	340	847	1,478
Tokyo	457			824	1,819

POPULATION ESTIMATES (IN THOUSANDS)

	1800	1825	1850	1875	1900
Egypt	3,854	4,541	4,752	6,961	10,186
India	255,000	257,000	285,000	306,000	
Brazil			7,678	9,930	17,438
England	8,893	12,000	17,928	22,712	32,528
France	27,349	30,462	35,783	36,906	38,451
Russia	35,500	52,300	68,500	90,200	132,900
America	5,297	11,252	23,261	45,073	76,094
Japan	25,622	26,602	27,201	25,037	44,359

OUTPUT OF COTTON (IN THOUSAND METRIC TONS)

	1800	1825	1850	1875	1900
Egypt				132	293
India			12	533	536
America	17	121	484	1,050	2,120

WHEAT PRODUCTION (IN THOUSAND METRIC TONS)

	1825	1850	1875	1900
France	4,580	6,600	7,550	8,860
Russia			53	136
America		2,722	8,546	16,302

LENGTH OF OPEN RAILWAY LINES (IN KILOMETERS)

	1825	1850	1875	1900
Egypt		1,184	1,410	2,237
India		32	10,527	39,834
Brazil		14	1,801	15,316
England	43	9,797	23,365	30,079
France	17	2,915	19,351	38,109
Russia	27	501	19,029	53,234
America	37	14,518	119,246	311,160
Japan		29	62	6,300

Sources: S. Beckert, "Emancipation and Empire: Reconstructing the Worldwide Web of Cotton Production in the Age of the American Civil War," *The American Historical Review* 109, no. 5 (December 2004): 1405–1438; B. R. Mitchell, *International Historical Statistics: Africa, Asia, and Oceania, 1750–2005, International Historical Statistics: The Americas, 1750–2005,* and International Historical Statistics: Europe, 1750–2005 (London: Palgrave Macmillan, 2007).

The industrial revolution produced wealth on an unprecedented scale, but that wealth was distributed unevenly. Enormous inequalities resulted, both within societies and between them. Free trade resulted, in the long run, not in the proliferation of ever-more-productive small workshops but in massive industrial concentration, a concentration that would prove dynamic, creative, and unstable.

Persistence and Change in Afro-Eurasia

Western Europe's military might, its technological achievements, and its economic strength represented a threat to the remaining Afro-Eurasian empires. Western European merchants and industrialists sought closer economic and (in some cases) political ties. They did so in the name of gaining "free" access to Asian markets and products. Rulers in Russia, the Ottoman Empire, India, and China all sought to borrow from the ideas and institutions emerging from western Europe, but they did so on their own terms, intent on defending the core of their social and political traditions.

COMPARISON

COMPARE the groups of people who held power in each of the regions in 1750 and then in 1850, and **EXPLAIN** the change that took place during this period in these societies.

REVAMPING THE RUSSIAN MONARCHY

Russian rulers responded to the pressures by strengthening their traditional authority through modest reforms and the suppression of domestic opposition. Tsar Alexander I (r. 1801–1825) was fortunate that Napoleon committed several blunders and lost his formidable army in the Russian snows. Yet the French Revolution and its massive armies struck at the heart of Russian political institutions, which rested upon a huge peasant population laboring as serfs. The tsars could no longer justify their absolutism by claiming that enlightened despotism was the most advanced form of government, since a new model, rooted in popular sovereignty and the concept of the nation, had arisen.

In December 1825, when Alexander died unexpectedly and childless, there was a question over succession. Some Russian officers launched a patriotic revolt. The Decembrists, as they were called, came primarily from elite families and were familiar with western European life and institutions. Some called for a constitutional monarchy to replace Russia's despotism; others favored a tsar-less republic and the abolition of serfdom. Their conspiracy failed to win over conservatives or the peasantry, who still believed in the tsar's divine right to rule. Nicholas (r. 1825–1855) became tsar and brutally suppressed the insurrectionists.

Still, Alexander's successors faced a world in which powerful European states had constitutions and national armies of citizens, not subjects. In trying to maintain absolutist rule, Russian tsars portrayed the monarch's family as the ideal historical embodiment of the nation with direct ties to the people. Nicholas himself prevented rebellion by expanding the secret police, enforcing censorship, conducting impressive military exercises, and maintaining serfdom. And in the 1830s he introduced a conservative ideology that stressed religious faith, hierarchy, and obedience. For the time being, the influence of the French Revolution was quashed in Russia.

REFORMING EGYPT AND THE OTTOMAN EMPIRE

Unlike Russia, where Napoleon's army had reached Moscow, the Ottoman capital in Istanbul never faced a threat by French troops. Still, Napoleon's invasion of Egypt shook the Ottoman Empire. Even before this trauma, Ottoman authorities faced the challenge posed by increased trade with Europe—and the greater presence of European merchants and missionaries. In addition, many non-Muslim religious communities in the sultan's empire wanted the European powers to advance their interests. In the wake of Napoleon, who had promised to remake Egyptian society, reformist energies swept from Egypt to the center of the Ottoman domain.

COMPARISON

EXPLAIN patterns of global trade and economic growth and **CONNECT** them to political changes during the period 1750–1850.

Reforms in Egypt In Egypt, far-reaching changes came with the rule of **Muhammad Ali**. After the French withdrawal in 1801, Muhammad Ali (r. 1805–1848) won a chaotic struggle for supreme power in Egypt and aligned himself with influential Egyptian families. Yet he looked to revolutionary France for a model of modern state building. As with Napoleon (and with Simón Bolívar in Latin America), the key to his hold on power was the army.

Muhammad Ali also made reforms in education and agriculture. He established a school of engineering and opened the first modern medical school in Cairo under the supervision of a French military doctor. And his efforts in the countryside made Egypt one of the world's leading cotton exporters. A summer crop, cotton required steady watering when the Nile's irrigation waters were in short supply. So Muhammad Ali's Public Works Department, advised by European engineers, deepened the irrigation canals and constructed a series of dams across the Nile. These efforts transformed Egypt, making it the most powerful state in the eastern Mediterranean and alarming the Ottoman state (which still controlled Egypt) and the great powers in Europe. At the same time, European merchants pressed for free access to Egyptian markets, just as they did in Latin America and Africa.

Ottoman Reforms Under political and economic pressures like those facing Muhammad Ali in Egypt, Ottoman rulers also made reforms. Indeed, military defeats and humiliating treaties with Europe were painful reminders of the sultans' vulnerability. In 1805 Sultan Selim III tried to create a new infantry, trained by western European officers. But before he could bring this force up to fighting strength, the janissaries stormed the palace, killed its officers, and deposed Selim in 1807. Over the next few decades, janissary military men and clerical scholars (*ulama*) cobbled together an alliance that thwarted reformers.

Why did reform falter in the Ottoman state before it could be implemented? Reform was possible only if the forces opposed to reform—especially in the military—were weak and the reformers strong. In the Ottoman Empire, the janissary class had grown powerful, providing the main resistance to change. Ottoman authority depended on clerical support, and the Muslim clergy also resisted change. Blocked at the top, Ottoman rulers hesitated to appeal for popular support. Such an appeal, in the new age of popular sovereignty and national feeling, would be dangerous for an unelected dynast in a multiethnic and multireligious realm.

Mahmud II (r. 1808–1839) broke the political deadlock, shrewdly manipulating his conservative opponents. Like Muhammad Ali in Egypt, Mahmud brought in European officers to advise his forces. Here, too, military reform spilled over into nonmilitary areas. The Ottoman modernizers created a medical college, then a school of military sciences. To understand Europe better and to create a first-rate diplomatic corps, the Ottomans schooled their officials in European languages and had European classics translated into Turkish. As Mahmud's successors extended reforms into civilian life, this era—known as the Tanzimat, or Reorganization period—saw legislation that guaranteed equality for all Ottoman subjects, regardless of religion.

The reforms, however, stopped well short of revolutionary change. Reform relied too much on the personal whim of rulers, and the bureaucratic and religious infrastructure

MAP 15.5 | The British in India, 1767–1857

Starting from locations in eastern and northeastern India, the British East India Company extended its authority over much of South Asia prior to the outbreak of the Indian Rebellion of 1857.

- What type of location did the British first acquire in India?
- According to your reading, how did the company expand into the interior of India and administer these possessions?
- Why did it choose a strategy of direct rule over some areas and indirect rule over other areas in India?

remained committed to old ways. Any effort to reform the rural sector met resistance by the landed interests. Finally, the merchant classes profited from business with a debt-ridden sultan. By preventing the empire's fiscal collapse through financial support to the state, bankers lessened the pressure for reform and removed the spark that had fired revolutions in Europe.

COLONIAL REORDERING IN INDIA

Europe's most important colonial possession in Asia between 1750 and 1850 was British India. Unlike in North America, the changes that the British fostered in Asia did not lead to political independence. Instead, India was increasingly dominated by the **East India Company**, which the crown had chartered in 1600. The company's control over India's imports and exports in the eighteenth and nineteenth centuries, however, contradicted British claims about their allegiance to a world economic system based on "free trade."

The East India Company's Monopoly In enforcing the East India Company's monopoly on trade, the British soon took control of much of the region. Initially, the British tried to control India's commerce by establishing trading posts along the coast without taking complete political control. After conquering the state of Bengal in 1757, the company began to fill its coffers and its officials began to amass personal fortunes. In spite of violent opposition, the British secured the right for the East India Company to collect tax

Indian Resistance to Company Rule Tipu Sultan, the Mysore ruler, put up a determined resistance against the British. This painting by Robert Home shows Cornwallis, the East India Company's governor, receiving Tipu's two sons as hostages after defeating him in the 1792 war. The boys remained in British custody for two years. Tipu returned to fighting the British and was killed in the war of 1799.

revenues in Bengal, Bihar, and Orissa and to trade free of duties throughout Mughal territory. In return, the Mughal emperor would receive a hefty annual pension. The company went on to annex other territories, bringing much of South Asia under its rule by the early 1800s. (See Map 15.5.)

To rule with minimal interference required knowing the conquered society. This led to orientalist scholarship: British scholar-officials wrote the first modern histories of South Asia, translated Sanskrit and Persian texts, identified philosophical writings, and compiled Hindu and Muslim law books. Through their efforts, the company-state presented itself as a force for revitalizing authentic Hinduism and recovering India's literary and cultural treasures. However, although the orientalist scholars admired Sanskrit language and literature, they still supported British colonial rule and did not necessarily agree with local beliefs.

Effects in India Company rule and booming trade altered India's urban geography. By the early nineteenth century, colonial cities like Calcutta, Madras, and Bombay became the new centers at the expense of older Mughal cities like Agra, Delhi, Murshidabad, and Hyderabad. As the colonial cities attracted British merchants and Indian clerks, artisans, and laborers, their populations surged. Calcutta's reached 350,000 in 1820; Bombay's jumped to 200,000 by 1825. In these cities, Europeans lived close to the company's fort and trading stations, while migrants from the countryside clustered in crowded quarters called "black towns."

India now became an importer of British textiles and an exporter of raw cotton—a reversal of its traditional pattern of trade. In the past, India had been an important textile manufacturer, exporting fine cotton goods throughout the Indian Ocean and to Europe.

But its elites could not resist the appeal of cheap British textiles. As a result, India's industrial sector declined. In addition, the import of British manufactures caused unfavorable trade balances that changed India from a net importer of gold and silver to an exporter of these precious metals.

Led by evangelical Christians and liberal reformers, the British did more than alter the Indian economy; they also advocated far-reaching changes in Indian culture. For example, they sought to stop the practice of *sati,* by which women burned to death on the funeral pyres of their dead husbands. Now the mood swung away from the orientalists' respect for India's classical languages, philosophies, cultures, and texts. In 1835, when the British poet, historian, and Liberal politician Lord Macaulay was making recommendations on educational policies, he urged that English replace Persian as the language of administration and that European education replace Oriental learning. The result, reformers hoped, would be a class that was Indian in blood and color but English in tastes and culture.

This was a new colonial order, but it was not stable. Most wealthy landowners resented the loss of their land and authority. Peasants, thrown to the mercy of the market, moneylenders, and landlords and subject to high taxation, were in turmoil. The non-Hindu forest dwellers and roaming cultivators, faced with the hated combination of a colonial state and moneylenders, revolted. Dispossessed artisans stirred up towns and cities. And merchants and industrialists chafed under the British-dominated economy. As freedom expanded in Europe, exploitation expanded in India.

PERSISTENCE OF THE QING EMPIRE

The remote Chinese empire was largely unaffected by the upheavals in Europe and America until the first Opium War (1839–1842) forced the Chinese to acknowledge their military weaknesses. The Qing dynasty, which had taken power in 1644, was still enjoying prosperity and territorial expansion as the nineteenth century dawned. Their sense of imperial splendor continued to rest on the political structure and social order inherited from the Ming (see Chapter 11). However, they could not resist European demands for access to their resources and markets.

The Qing had a talent for extending the empire's boundaries and settling frontier lands. Before 1750, they conquered Taiwan (the stronghold of remaining Ming forces), pushed westward into central Asia, and annexed Tibet. To secure these territorial gains, the Qing encouraged settlement of frontier lands like Xinjiang. New crops from the Americas aided this process—especially corn and sweet potatoes, which grow well in less fertile soils.

Like their European counterparts, Chinese peasants were on the move. But migration occurred in Qing China for different reasons. The state-sponsored westward movement into Xinjiang, for example, aimed to secure a recently pacified frontier region through military colonization, after which civilians would follow. So peasants received promises of land, tools, seed, and the loan of silver and a horse—all with the dual objectives of producing enough food to supply the troops and relieving pressure on the poor and arid northwestern part of the country. These efforts brought so much land under cultivation by 1840 that the region's ecological and social landscape completely changed.

Despite their success in expanding the empire, the Qing faced nagging problems. As a ruling minority, they looked warily at innovation, and only late in the eighteenth century did they deal with their rapidly expanding population. On the one hand, the tripling of China's population since 1300 demonstrated the realm's prosperity; on the other, a population of over 300 million severely strained resources—especially soil for growing crops and wood for fuel. In the late eighteenth and early nineteenth centuries, uprisings inspired by mystical beliefs in folk Buddhism, and at times by the idea of restoring the Ming, engulfed northern China.

By the mid-nineteenth century, extraordinary changes had made western European powers stronger than ever before, and the Qing could no longer dismiss their demands. The first clear evidence of an altered global balance of power was not the rise of Napoleon, but a British-Chinese war over a narcotic. Indeed, the **Opium War** exposed China's vulnerability in a new era of European ascendancy.

The Opium War and the "Opening" of China Europeans had been selling staples and intoxicants in China for a long time, and by the late eighteenth century opium, which had previously been used as a medicine or an aphrodisiac, was being smoked in long-stemmed pipes at every level of Chinese society. Sensing opium's economic potential, the East India Company established a monopoly over the export of opium from India in 1773 to help pay for a rapid growth in the company's purchase of tea from China. Because the Chinese showed little taste for British goods, the British had been financing their tea imports with exports of silver to China. But by the late eighteenth century, the company's tea purchases had become too large to finance with silver. Fortunately for the company, the Chinese were eager for Indian cotton and opium, and then mostly just opium.

Opium's impact on China's balance of trade was devastating. In a reversal from earlier trends, silver began to flow out of instead of into China. Once silver shortages occurred, the peasants' tax burden grew heavier. Consequently, long-simmering unrest in the countryside gained momentum. At the Qing court, some officials wanted to legalize the opium trade so as to eliminate corruption and boost revenues. (After all, as long as opium was an illegal substance, the government could not tax its traffic.) In 1838 the emperor sent

Opium (*Left*) A common sight in late Qing China was establishments catering specifically to opium smoking. Taken from a volume condemning the practice, this picture shows opium smokers idling their day away. (*Right*) Having established a monopoly in the 1770s over opium cultivation in India, the British greatly expanded their manufacture and export of opium to China to balance their rapidly growing import of Chinese tea and silk. This picture from the 1880s shows an opium warehouse in India where the commodity was stored before being transported to China.

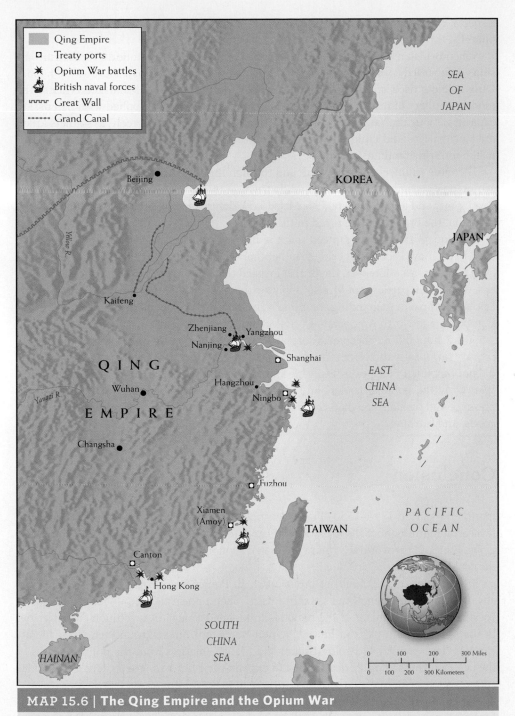

MAP 15.6 | The Qing Empire and the Opium War

The Opium War demonstrated the superiority of British military technology. Their victory granted the British control of Hong Kong and established a series of treaty ports, which gave Europeans access to Chinese trade and which were subject to the laws of designated European countries.

• How many treaty ports were there after the Opium War? What was their significance?

• How were the treaty ports distributed along China's coastline?

• According to the text, how did the Opium War change relations between China and the western powers?

a special commissioner to Canton, the main center of the trade, to eradicate the influx of opium.

When British merchants in Canton resisted, war broke out. In June 1840, British warships bombarded coastal regions near Canton and sailed upriver for a short way. On land, Qing soldiers used spears, clubs, and a few imported matchlock muskets against the modern artillery of British troops, many of whom were Indians supplied with percussion cap rifles. Along the Yangzi River, outgunned Qing forces fought fiercely, as soldiers killed their own wives and children before committing suicide themselves. But they were no match for British military technology.

The Qing ruling elite capitulated, and through the 1842 Treaty of Nanjing, the British acquired the island of Hong Kong and the right to trade directly with the Chinese in five treaty ports and to reside there. (See Map 15.6.) They also forced the Chinese to repay the costs that the British had incurred in the war.

Subsequent treaties guaranteed that the British and other foreign nationals would be tried in their own courts for crimes, rather than in Chinese courts, and would be exempt from Chinese law. Moreover, the British insisted that any privileges granted through treaties with other parties would also apply to them. Other western nations followed the British example in demanding the same right, and the arrangement thus guaranteed all Europeans and North Americans a privileged position in China.

Still, China did not become a formal colony. To the contrary, in the mid-nineteenth century Europeans and North Americans were trading only on its outskirts. Most Chinese did not encounter Europeans. Daily life for most people went on as it had before the Opium War. Only the political leaders and urban dwellers were beginning to feel the foreign presence and wondering what steps China might take to acquire European technologies, goods, and learning.

Conclusion

During the period 1750–1850, changes in politics, commerce, industry, and technology reverberated throughout the Atlantic world and, to varying degrees, elsewhere around the globe. By 1850, the world was more integrated economically, with Europe increasingly at the center.

In the Americas, colonial ties broke apart. In France, the people toppled the monarchy. Dissidents threatened the same in Russia. Such upheavals introduced a new public vocabulary—the language of the nation—and made the idea of revolution empowering. In the Americas and parts of Europe, nation-states took shape around redefined hierarchies of class, gender, and color. Britain and France emerged from the political crises of the late eighteenth century determined to expand their borders. Their drive forced older empires such as Russia and the Ottoman state to make reforms.

As commerce and industrialization transformed economic and political power, European governments compelled others (including Egypt, India, and China) to expand their trade with European merchants. Ultimately, such countries had to participate in a European-centered economy as exporters of raw materials and importers of European manufactures. By the 1850s, many of the world's peoples became more industrious, producing less for themselves and more for distant markets. Through changes in manufacturing, some areas of the world also made more goods than ever before. With its emphasis on free trade, Europe began to force open new markets—even to the point of colonizing them. Gold and silver now flowed out of China and India to pay for European products like opium and textiles.

However, global reordering did not mean that Europe's rulers had uncontested control over other people, or that the institutions and cultures of Asia and Africa ceased to be dynamic. Some countries became dependent on Europe commercially; others became colonies. China escaped colonial rule but was forced into unfavorable trade relations with the Europeans. In sum, dramatic changes combined to unsettle systems of rulership and to alter the economic and military balance between western Europe and the rest of the world.

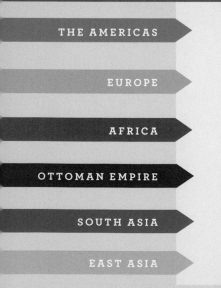

After You Read This Chapter

Go to INQUIZITIVE to see what you've learned—and learn what you've missed—with personalized feedback along the way.

FOCUS ON: *The Global Effects of the "New Ideas"*

THE ATLANTIC WORLD

- North American colonists revolt against British rule and establish a nonmonarchical, republican form of government.

- In the wake of the American Revolution, the French citizenry proclaims a new era of liberty, equality, and fraternity and executes opponents of the revolution, notably the king and queen of France.

- Napoleon's French empire extends many principles of the French Revolution throughout Europe.

- In the midst of the French Revolution, Haitian slaves throw off French rule, abolish slavery, and create an independent state.

- Napoleon's invasion of Iberia frees Portuguese and Spanish America from colonial rule.

- The British lead a successful campaign to abolish the Atlantic slave trade and promote new sources of trade with Africa.

- An industrial revolution spreads outward from Britain to a few other parts of the Atlantic world.

AFRICA, INDIA, AND ASIA

- In Egypt, a military leader, Muhammad Ali, modernizes the country and threatens the political integrity of the Ottoman Empire.

- The British East India Company increasingly dominates the Indian subcontinent.

- The Qing Empire persists despite major European encroachments on its sovereignty.

CHRONOLOGY

	1700	1750
THE AMERICAS		
EUROPE		James Watt invents the steam engine 1769 ◆
AFRICA		
OTTOMAN EMPIRE		
SOUTH ASIA		
EAST ASIA		

- *Thinking about Exchange Networks and Sociopolitical Change* How did established dynasties respond to pressures created by increased exchanges of goods, ideas, and peoples? To what degree did established elites respond by forging a partnership with "the people"? Who defined "the people," on what terms?

- *Thinking about Changing Power Relationships and Sociopolitical Change* What new kinds of political organizations emerged in this period? Where did new political systems take root, and where did established elites resist most successfully?

- *Thinking about Environmental Impacts and Sociopolitical Change* Although new technologies only gradually transformed agriculture—by far the most common economic activity in the world—the spread of more intensive cultivation demanded considerable capital investment. How did the relationship between town and countryside change as a result? How did living conditions change in cities as their populations swelled?

1. Describe the political and social revolutions that occurred in the Atlantic world between 1750 and 1850. What ideas inspired these changes? Pay special attention to **free trade**, **popular sovereignty**, the **social contract**, and republican government. Who was included and who was excluded from revolutionary measures?

2. Explain how the Atlantic world's political and social revolution led to the end of the Atlantic slave trade. What economic, social, and political consequences did this development have on sub-Saharan Africa?

3. Explain the relationship between industrialization and the **industrious revolution**. How did industriousness spur economic growth? Where did the decisive changes take place, both in geographical terms but also in social terms? That is, which social groups were most important in effecting change? What role did the **bourgeoisie** play?

4. Evaluate how the **industrial revolution** altered the societies that began to industrialize during this time. What impact did this process have on the environment? How were gender roles and family relationships altered?

5. Compare responses to European influence in Egypt under **Muhammad Ali**; in India, under the rule of the **East India Company**; and in China during the **Opium War**.

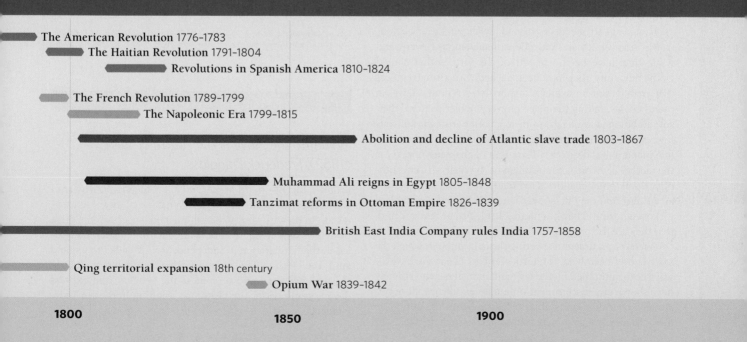

The American Revolution 1776–1783
The Haitian Revolution 1791–1804
Revolutions in Spanish America 1810–1824

The French Revolution 1789–1799
The Napoleonic Era 1799–1815

Abolition and decline of Atlantic slave trade 1803–1867

Muhammad Ali reigns in Egypt 1805–1848
Tanzimat reforms in Ottoman Empire 1826–1839

British East India Company rules India 1757–1858

Qing territorial expansion 18th century
Opium War 1839–1842

1800   1850   1900

Competing Perspectives

Revolution for Whom?

Although Enlightenment *philosophes* argued that the laws of reason applied to everyone and the American Declaration of Independence declared that all men are created equal, their ideas immediately provoked a wide range of opposition. In Europe and the United States, women and the enslaved protested their exclusion, while elites in territories occupied by Western colonizers pointed to the hypocrisy of the occupiers' egalitarian rhetoric.

The documents in this section present a range of critiques of Enlightenment ideas. One of the founding figures of modern feminism, Mary Wollstonecraft argues that the superiority of men—an assumption that was accepted by most Enlightenment thinkers—was as arbitrary as the divine right of kings, for which one critic called her a "hyena in petticoats." The author of the second document, Frederick Douglass, spent the first twenty years of his life as a slave, before becoming a leading abolitionist. In an address delivered on July 5, 1852, Douglass contrasts the freedoms and natural rights championed in the Declaration of Independence and celebrated on the Fourth of July with the substantial lack of freedom endured by African American slaves. The Cairo scholar Abd al-Rahman al-Jabarti provides a clearly expressed commentary on Napoleon Bonaparte's attempt to win local support for his 1798 invasion of Egypt. Napoleon portrayed himself as a liberator, invoking the ideals of the French Revolution, but Egyptians saw the French forces quite differently. Finally, the section of the Haitian Constitution included here celebrates the expulsion of "this nation of executioners"—a reference to revolutionary France.

PRIMARY SOURCE 15.1

On the Rights of Women (1792), Mary Wollstonecraft

I love man as my fellow; but his sceptre, real or usurped, extends not to me, unless the reason of an individual demands my homage; and even then the submission is to reason, and not to man. In fact, the conduct of an accountable being must be regulated by the operations of its own reason; or on what foundation rests the throne of God?

It appears to me necessary to dwell on these obvious truths, because females have been insulated, as it were; and while they have been stripped of the virtues that should clothe humanity, they have been decked with artificial graces that enable them to exercise a short-lived tyranny. Love, in their bosoms, taking the place of every nobler passion, their sole ambition is to be fair, to raise emotion instead of inspiring respect; and this ignoble desire, like the servility in absolute monarchies, destroys all strength of character. Liberty is the mother of virtue, and if women be, by their very constitution, slaves, and not allowed to breathe the sharp invigorating air of freedom, they must ever languish like exotics, and be reckoned beautiful flaws in nature. Let it also be remembered, that they are the only flaw.

As to the argument respecting the subjection in which the sex has ever been held, it retorts on man. The many have always been enthralled by the few; and monsters, who scarcely have shown any discernment of human excellence, have tyrannized over thousands of their fellow-creatures. Why have men of superior endowments submitted to such degradation? For, is it not universally acknowledged that kings, viewed collectively, have ever been inferior, in abilities and virtue, to the same number of men taken from the common mass of mankind—yet have they not, and are they not still treated with a degree of reverence that is an insult to reason? China is not the only country where a living man has been made a God. *Men* have submitted to superior strength to enjoy with impunity the pleasure of the moment; *women* have only done the same, and therefore till it is proved that the courtier, who servilely resigns the birthright of a man, is not a moral agent, it cannot be demonstrated that woman is essentially inferior to man because she has always been subjugated.

Source: Mary Wollstonecraft, *A Vindication of the Rights of Woman*, A Norton Critical Edition, edited by Deirdre Shauna Lynch (New York. W. W. Norton & Company, 2009): 40–41.

PRIMARY SOURCE 15.2

"What to the Slave Is the Fourth of July?" (1852), Frederick Douglass

Fellow-Citizens—pardon me, and allow me to ask, why am I called upon to speak here to-day? What have I, or those I represent, to do with your national independence? Are the great principles of political freedom and of natural justice, embodied in that Declaration of Independence, extended to us? and am I, therefore, called upon to bring our humble offering to the national altar, and to confess the benefits, and express devout gratitude for the blessings, resulting from your independence to us? . . .

But, such is not the state of the case. I say it with a sad sense of the disparity between us. I am not included within the pale of this glorious anniversary! Your high independence only reveals the immeasurable distance between us. The blessings in which you this day rejoice, are not enjoyed in common. The rich inheritance of justice, liberty, prosperity, and independence, bequeathed by your fathers, is shared by you, not by me. The sunlight that brought life and healing to you, has brought stripes and death to me. This Fourth of July is *yours*, not *mine*. *You* may rejoice, *I* must mourn. . . .

Must I undertake to prove that the slave is a man? That point is conceded already. Nobody doubts it. The slaveholders themselves acknowledge it in the enactment of laws for their government. They acknowledge it when they punish disobedience on the part of the slave. There are seventy-two crimes in the state of Virginia, which, if committed by a black man (no matter how ignorant he be) subject him to the punishment of death; while only two of these same crimes will subject a white man to the like punishment. What is this but the acknowledgment that the slave is a moral, intellectual, and responsible being. The manhood of the slave is conceded. It is admitted in the fact that southern statute books are covered with enactments forbidding, under severe fines and penalties, the teaching of the slave to read or write. When you can point to any such laws, in reference to the beasts of the field, then I may consent to argue the manhood of the slave. When the dogs in your streets, when the fowls of the air, when the cattle on your hills, when the fish of the sea, and the reptiles that crawl, shall be unable to distinguish the slave from a brute, then will I argue with you that the slave is a man!

Source: Frederick Douglass, *Narrative of the Life of Frederick Douglass, an American Slave, Written by Himself,* A Norton Critical Edition, edited by William L. Andrews and William S. McFeely (New York: W. W. Norton & Company): 123–125.

PRIMARY SOURCE 15.3

An Egyptian Reaction to French Occupation (1798), Abd al-Rahman al-Jabarti

On Monday news arrived that the French had reached Damanhur and Rosetta [in the Nile Delta]. . . . They printed a large proclamation in Arabic, calling on the people to obey them. . . . In this proclamation were inducements, warnings, all manner of wiliness and stipulations. Some copies were sent from the provinces to Cairo and its text is:

In the name of God, the Merciful, the Compassionate. There is no God but God. He has no son nor has He an associate in His Dominion.

On behalf of the French Republic which is based upon the foundation of liberty and equality, General Bonaparte, Commander-in-Chief of the French armies makes known to all the Egyptian people that for a long time the Sanjaqs [its Mamluk rulers] who lorded it over Egypt have treated the French community basely and

contemptuously and have persecuted its merchants with all manner of extortion and violence. Therefore the hour of punishment has now come.

Unfortunately, this group of Mamluks . . . have acted corruptly for ages in the fairest land that is to be found upon the face of the globe. However, the Lord of the Universe, the Almighty, has decreed the end of their power.

O ye Egyptians . . . I have not come to you except for the purpose of restoring your rights from the hands of the oppressors and that I more than the Mamluks serve God. . . .

And tell them also that all people are equal in the eyes of God and the only circumstances which distinguish one from the other are reason, virtue, and knowledge. . . . Formerly, in the lands of Egypt there were great cities, and wide canals and extensive commerce and nothing ruined all this but the avarice and the tyranny of the Mamluks.

[Jabarti then challenged the arguments in the French proclamation and portrayed the French as godless invaders, inspired by false ideals.] They follow this rule: great and small, high and low, male and female are all equal. Sometimes they break this rule according to their whims and inclinations or reasoning. Their women do not veil themselves and have no modesty. . . . Whenever a Frenchman has to perform an act of nature he does so where he happens to be, even in full view of people, and he goes away as he is, without washing his private parts after defecation. . . .

His saying "[all people] are equal in the eyes of God" the Almighty is a lie and stupidity. How can this be when God has made some superior to others as is testified by the dwellers in the Heavens and on Earth? . . .

So those people are opposed to both Christians and Muslims, and do not hold fast to any religion. You see that they are materialists, who deny all God's attributes. . . . May God hurry misfortune and punishment upon them, may He strike their tongues with dumbness, may He scatter their hosts, and disperse them.

Source: Abd al-Rahman al-Jabarti, *Napoleon in Egypt: al-Jabarti's Chronicle of the French Occupation, 1798,* translated by Shmuel Moreh (Princeton, NJ: Markus Wiener Publishing, 1993), pp. 24–29.

PRIMARY SOURCE 15.4

The Haitian Declaration of Independence (1804)

Citizens:

It is not enough to have expelled the barbarians who have bloodied our land for two centuries; it is not enough to have restrained those ever-evolving factions that one after another mocked the specter of liberty that France dangled before you. We must, with one last act of national authority, forever assure the empire of liberty in the country of our birth; we must take any hope of re-enslaving us away from the inhuman government that for so long kept us in the most humiliating torpor. In the end we must live independent or die.

Independence or death . . . let these sacred words unite us and be the signal of battle and of our reunion.

Citizens, my countrymen, on this solemn day I have brought together those courageous soldiers who, as liberty lay dying, spilled their blood to save it; these generals who have guided your efforts against tyranny have not yet done enough for your happiness; the French name still haunts our land.

Everything revives the memories of the cruelties of this barbarous people: our laws, our habits, our towns, everything still carries the stamp of the French. Indeed! There are still French in our island, and you believe yourself free and independent of that Republic which, it is true, has fought all the nations, but which has never defeated those who wanted to be free.

What! Victims of our [own] credulity and indulgence for 14 years; defeated not by French armies, but by the pathetic eloquence of their agents' proclamations; when will we tire of breathing the air that they breathe? What do we have in common with this nation of executioners? The difference between its cruelty and our patient moderation, its color and ours the great seas that separate us, our avenging climate, all tell us plainly that they are not our brothers, that they never will be, and that if they find refuge among us, they will plot again to trouble and divide us. . . .

Swear, finally, to pursue forever the traitors and enemies of your independence.

Source: Laurent Dubois and John Garrigus, *Slave Revolution in the Caribbean, 1789–1804: A Brief History with Documents* (2006).

QUESTIONS FOR ANALYSIS

1. Identify the influence of Enlightenment ideas in these texts. What role do they play?

2. Do these documents challenge those Enlightenment ideas or seek to apply them more fully? Do they reject the Enlightenment tradition or contend that its values have not been fully realized?

3. Evaluate the degree to which these documents make universal arguments and the degree to which their claims are rooted in local traditions and beliefs.

Interpreting Visual Evidence

Framing the Subject

Important currents of Enlightenment thought (which fed into classical liberalism in the nineteenth century—see Chapter 16) stressed the autonomy of the individual. All men were thought to be created equal, endowed with reason and the ability to master nature and the world around them. European liberals celebrated individual initiative, self-control, and material success through hard work as signs of virtue. They also drew from the Enlightenment a faith that the natural world follows observable laws. This faith gave rise, as we have seen, to advances in the natural sciences and then the social sciences. In the arts, that faith corresponded to a renewed interest in representing the external world in precise, objective terms, called realism. Painters sought to capture and reflect an independent, external, stable reality—this in a period before photography. It was a confident but also a self-centered view of the world.

Here we consider efforts to represent the individual in portraiture. Jean-Auguste-Dominique Ingres painted the French newspaper baron and businessman Louis-François Bertin, in a portrait from 1832. Bertin's *Journal des Débats* served as the recognized organ of the opposition to the Bourbon Restoration in early nineteenth-century France and helped put the constitutional July Monarchy, in power. The painter Édouard Manet described Bertin as "the Buddha of the self-satisfied, well-to-to, triumphant bourgeoisie." Unlike Ingres, who painted a real historical figure, Jean-Léon Gérôme painted a model dressed in garments made of textiles he had acquired on a trip to the Near East, to represent the unpaid, irregular mercenary soldiers who lived from plunder and fought in Ottoman armies, in his "Bashi-Bazouk" (1868–69). Gérôme conceived and executed this painting of an Ottoman soldier in a European studio. In the "Study for Portrait of an Indian," French artist Anne-Louis Girodet-Trioson painted a man in Ottoman clothing. Finally, the "Portrait of the Imperial Bodyguard Zhanyinbao" was probably sketched by a (European) Jesuit artist in the Chinese court and then transferred to a silk scroll by a Chinese master.

Ingres, *Louis-François Bertin.*

Gérôme, *Bashi-Bazouk.*

Girodet-Trioson, *Study for Portrait of an Indian.*

Portrait of the Imperial Bodyguard Zhanyinbao.

QUESTIONS FOR ANALYSIS

1. Create a psychological profile for each portrait. What clues does the artist give you about the men, their values, and their standing in the world?

2. What is the effect of the sparse backgrounds and the intricate detail in the foreground? What do you think the artists left out of these portraits that might influence your profiles?

3. Do the painters create coherent images of their subjects? What contradictions can you see, for example between violent aggression and delicate refinement, between order and disorder, with respect to discipline and control?

4. Compare the two "orientalist" paintings—the *Portrait of an Indian* and *Bashi-Bazouk*—with the other two. What does orientalist mean in this context? How, in particular, do they differ from the *Portrait of the Imperial Bodyguard*?

Before You Read This Chapter

GLOBAL STORYLINES

- Protest movements challenge the nineteenth-century order based on industrial capitalism, the nation-state, and colonization.

- Led by prophets, political radicals, and common people, the movements arise among marginal groups and regions and express visions of ideal, utopian futures.

- The movements differ markedly depending on distance from the centers of change (Europe and the Americas) and reflect local circumstances.

- Although most movements are defeated, they give voice to the views of peasants and workers and have a lasting effect on the policies of ruling elites.

CORE OBJECTIVES

- **DESCRIBE** the challenges to the ideals of industrial capitalism, colonialism, and nation-states in this period.

- **COMPARE** the utopian goals, immediate outcomes, and long-term influence of rebel movements around the world.

- **ANALYZE** the connection between nineteenth-century protest movements and organized religion.

- **ASSESS** the role religion played in these alternate social visions.

CHAPTER 16

Alternative Visions of the Nineteenth Century

By the late nineteenth century, territorial expansion in the United States confined almost all Native Americans to reservations. The buffalo that once supported many tribes disappeared: white settlers built towns, farms, and railroads throughout the buffalo's natural habitat, and Native Americans overhunted the shrinking herds. Across the American West, many Native Americans fell into despair. One was a Paiute Native American named Wovoka. But in 1889, he had a vision of a much brighter future. In his dream, the "Supreme Being" told Wovoka that if Native Americans lived harmoniously, shunned white ways (especially alcohol), and performed the cleansing Ghost Dance, then the buffalo would return, and Native Americans, including the dead, would be reborn to live in eternal happiness.

As word spread of Wovoka's vision, Native Americans from hundreds of miles around made pilgrimages to the lodge of this new prophet. Many proclaimed him the Native Americans' messiah or the "Red Man's Christ," an impression fostered by scars on his hands. Soon, increasing numbers joined in the ritual Ghost Dance, hoping it would restore the good life that European colonialism in the Americas had extinguished. Among the hopefuls was Sitting Bull, a revered Sioux chief who was himself famous for his visions. Yet, less than two years after Wovoka's vision, Sitting Bull died at the hands of police forces on a Sioux reservation. A few days later, on December 29, 1890, the U.S. Seventh Cavalry Regiment massacred Sioux Ghost Dancers at a South Dakota creek called Wounded Knee.

Though it failed, this movement was one of many prophetic crusades that challenged an emerging nineteenth-century order. The ideals of the French and American revolutions in politics—equality before the law, and government for and by property-holding citizens in a world of nation-states—now provided the dominant answers to age-old questions of who should govern and how. Emerging from the industrial revolution, the ideas of free-market (laissez-faire) capitalism, in which private owners competed against one another to maximize profits using new technologies and industrial organizations, provided the dominant answers to questions about how productive activity should be organized. But these political and economic answers were not powerful enough entirely to stamp out other views. A diverse assortment of political radicals, charismatic prophets, peasant rebels, and anticolonial insurgents put forward striking counterproposals to those that capitalists, colonial modernizers, and nation-state builders had developed. The people making these counterproposals were motivated by the impending loss of their existing worlds and were energized by visions of ideal, utopian futures.

This chapter presents the voices and visions of those who opposed a nineteenth-century world in which capitalism, colonialism, and nation-states held sway. It puts the spotlight on challengers who shared a dislike of global capitalism and European (and North American) colonialism. Beyond that similarity, these challengers differed in significant ways, for the alternatives they proposed reflected the local circumstances in which each of them developed. Although many of these challengers suffered devastating defeats, like the Ghost Dancers at Wounded Knee, the dreams that aroused their fervor did not always die with them. Some of these alternative visions of the nineteenth century endured to propel the great transformations of the twentieth.

Reactions to Social and Political Change

COMPARISON

ANALYZE the connections between nineteenth-century protest movements and organized religion in Islam, China, and the Americas.

The alternatives to the emerging order of the nineteenth century varied considerably. Some rebels and dissidents called for the revitalization of traditional religions; others wanted to strengthen village and communal bonds; still others imagined a society where there was no private property and where people shared goods equally. The actions of these dissenters depended on their local traditions and the degree of contact they had with the effects of industrial capitalism, European colonialism, and centralizing nation-states.

This era of rapid social change, when differing visions of power and justice vied with one another, offers unique opportunities to hear the voices of the lower orders—the peasants and workers, whose perspectives the elites often ignored or suppressed. While there are few written records that capture the views of the illiterate and the marginalized, we do have traditions of folklore, dreams, rumors, and prophecies. Handed down orally from generation to generation, these resources illuminate the visions of common people.

Prophecy and Revitalization in the Islamic World and Africa

In regions that experienced European and North American influence but not direct colonial rule, alternative perspectives were strongest far from the main trade and cultural routes. People outside the emerging capitalist world order led these movements. In the

Islamic world and Africa, leaders on the margins were especially important in articulating alternative views.

Even though much of the Islamic world and non-Islamic Africa had not been colonized and was only partially involved with European-dominated trading networks, these regions had reached turning points. By the late eighteenth century, the era of Islamic expansion and cultural flowering under the Ottomans, Safavids, and Mughals was over. Their empires had extended Muslim trading orbits, facilitated cross-cultural communication, and promoted common knowledge over vast territories. Their political and military decline, however, brought new challenges to the faithful. The sense of alarm intensified as Christian Europe's power spread from the edges of the Islamic world to its centers. While this perception of danger motivated military men in Egypt and the Ottoman sultans to modernize their states (see Chapter 15), it also bred religious revitalization movements that sought to recapture the glories of past traditions. Led by prophets who feared that the Islamic faith was in trouble, these movements spoke the language of revival and restoration as they sought to establish new religiously based governments across lands in which Muslims ruled and Islamic law prevailed.

Prophecy also exerted a strong influence in non-Islamic Africa, where long-distance trade and population growth were upending the social order. Just as Muslim clerics and political leaders sought solutions to unsettling changes by rereading Islamic classics, African communities looked to charismatic leaders who drew strength from their peoples' spiritual and magical traditions. Often uniting disparate groups behind their dynamic visions, prophetic leaders and other "big men" gained power because they were able to resolve local crises—mostly caused by drought, a shortage of arable land, or some other issue related to the harsh environment.

ISLAMIC REVITALIZATION

Movements to revitalize Islam took place on the peripheries—at a certain remove from trade networks and the changes wrought by global capitalism. (See Map 16.1.) Here, religious leaders rejected the westernizing influences they felt encroaching on their authority and way of life. Revitalization movements looked back to Islamic traditions and modeled their revolts on the life of Muhammad. But even as they looked to the past, they attempted to establish something new: full-scale theocracies. These reformers conceived of the state as the primary instrument of God's will and as the vehicle for purifying Islamic culture. (See **Current Trends in World History: Islam: An Enduring Alternative in Algeria**.)

Wahhabism One of the most powerful reformist movements arose on the Arabian Peninsula, the birthplace of the Muslim faith. In the Najd region, an area surrounded by mountains and deserts, a religious cleric named Muhammad Ibn abd al-Wahhab (1703–1792) galvanized the population by attacking what he regarded as lax religious practices. His message found a ready response among local inhabitants, who felt threatened by the new commercial activities and fresh intellectual currents swirling around them. Abd al-Wahhab demanded a return to the pure Islam of Muhammad and the early caliphs.

Although Najd was far removed from the centers of the expanding world economy, Abd al-Wahhab himself was not. Having been educated in Iraq, Iran, and the Hijaz (a region on the western end of modern Saudi Arabia, on the Red Sea), he believed that Islam had fallen into a degraded state, particularly in its birthplace. He railed against the polytheistic beliefs that had taken hold of the people, complaining that in defiance of Muhammad's tenets men and women were worshipping trees, stones, and tombs and making sacrifices to false images. Abd al-Wahhab's movement stressed the absolute oneness of Allah and severely criticized Sufi sects for extolling the lives of saints over the worship of God.

As **Wahhabism** swept across the Arabian Peninsula, the movement threatened the Ottomans' hold on the region. Wahhabism gained a powerful political ally in the Najdian

Islam: An Enduring Alternative in Algeria

Many of the alternative movements featured in this chapter derived their impetus from deeply held religious beliefs. Religion played a role in the Indian mutiny and in the visions that spurred the Taiping rebels. In Muslim locations far from the main currents of Western influence, like the Arabian Peninsula and northern Nigeria, it generated revivalist movements. But elsewhere it became a political force, and one that developed a palpably anti-European nature as well as the power to endure long beyond the victory of European invaders. World historians like to study political and social movements because they bring into relief the relationship between the colonizer and the colonized and, in the case of these alternative movements, the relationship between peoples living on the peripheries of empires and those living in the center who are part of the ruling elite, including indigenous elites.

This was the case in particular along the old Ottoman periphery, one of the major targets for European colonization. Strikingly, in the first decades of the nineteenth century, in the Ottomans' Balkan domains of Serbia and Greece, Christianity had linked together opponents against the empire. In the decades to follow, as Ottoman power receded, it left behind it Islamic groups who also used religion as the glue that bound together otherwise diverse peoples. The example below highlights the importance of Islam in galvanizing resistance to French imperialism in Algeria. But it would also be possible to cite examples from the Caucasus Mountains, another Ottoman periphery, where Islam linked together Chechen and other groups in opposition to Russian colonization in the 1840s and 1850s; in the early twentieth century, Libyans attempted to oppose Italian colonization by rallying behind the green flag of the prophet. Unquestionably, the more Europeans sought to dominate lands inhabited by Muslims, the more they called forth in reaction Islamic alternatives and a politicized form of Islamic resistance.

In 1830, through a series of mishaps and miscalculations the French found themselves in possession of the Regency of Algiers, a territory of 60,000 square miles where previously 10,000 Ottoman Turks had ruled over 3 million Arab and Berber tribesmen. The French invasion had been an ill-considered adventure, designed to divert attention from the fact that the backward-looking French king, Charles X, had lost his legitimacy at home. In 1830, Charles was toppled by the so-called July Revolution, but his successor, King Louis Philippe, (r. 1830–1848), decided to pursue France's adventure abroad. This was a risky and in the long run costly plan, however, as the French controlled only a few costal enclaves and the capital city of Algiers; in 1831, the European civilian population was a mere 3,228. Moreover, although the French had driven out the Turks, they had emboldened Arab tribes in the western part of the land to found their own independent state.

In seeking a leader to unite them, the Arab tribes turned to Abd al-Qadir (1807–1883), a charismatic and domineering personality even though only twenty-five years of age. His father, head of the most important Sufi Brotherhood in Algeria, had groomed his son to be a leader, and taught him to despise the Ottoman overlords. Abd al-Qadir and his followers had already committed themselves to overthrowing the Ottomans; but once the French arrived, they were even more determined to rid their area of invaders they regarded as infidels, intent on seizing their lands and imposing their way of life on them. In organizing resistance to the French, it mattered greatly that Abd al-Qadir was also known as a holy man and a scholar, rather than as merely the head of one of the tribes. In preparation

House of Saud, a leading family whose followers, inspired by the Wahhabis' religious zeal, undertook a militant religious campaign in the final years of the eighteenth century. Frightened by the Wahhabi challenge, the Ottoman sultan persuaded the provincial ruler of Egypt to send troops to the Arabian Peninsula to suppress the movement. The Egyptians defeated the Saudis in 1818, but Wahhabism and the House of Saud continued to represent a pure Islamic faith that attracted clerics and ordinary people throughout the Muslim world.

Usman dan Fodio and the Fulani In West Africa, Muslim revolts erupted from Senegal to Nigeria in the early nineteenth century, partly in response to increased trade with the outside world and the circulation of religious ideas from across the Sahara Desert. In this region, the Fulani people were decisive in religious uprisings that sought, like the Wahhabi movement, to re-create a supposedly purer Islamic past. The majority were cattle-keepers, practicing a for battle, he called on his soldiers to follow him in a holy war (*jihad*) against Christian invaders, promising those who joined him in battle that "anyone of you who dies, will die a martyr; those of you who survive will gain glory and live happily." Tribes that might not have fought together, or fought together so long, did so because they were united by their loyalty to a religious as well as a political leader; Abd al-Qadir succeeded in part because he was a forceful personality, but in part, too, because he stood for Islam, something that the native Algerians shared, whatever their kinship ties or their loyalties to local leaders.

For fifteen years, Abd al-Quadir's forces held out, only surrendering to a massive French force of 108,000 men in 1847. Although often defeated in pitched battles, Abd al-Qadir used his superior knowledge of the terrain and his ability to wait in ambush for French columns to frustrate the French. The French government was finally compelled to send its most accomplished military man, Marshal Thomas Robert Bugeaud, and to provide him with one-third of its entire military force, to finish the job of "pacifying" Algeria.

The French conquest of Algeria marks one of the bloodiest episodes in the his-

Abd al-Qadir Polish artist Stanislaw Chlebowski painted Abd al-Qadir in 1866 during his exile in Constantinople.

tory of those two lands. No fewer than 300,000 Algerians perished during these years. Although the French portrayed Abd al-Qadir as a Muslim fanatic, determined to take his people back to a dark age, their message fell on deaf ears. The Algerians extolled him for resisting the French and later made him an iconic figure of the nationalist movement. One of the first acts carried out by the independent Algerian government in 1962 was to tear down the statue of Marshal Bugeaud

and to replace it with one of Abd al-Qadir. The religiously motivated resistance leader had prevailed over the secular political conquerors after all.

QUESTIONS FOR ANALYSIS

- What impact did Algeria's geographic location play in determining its role in these revolutionary events?
- How did the native Algerians view their former Ottoman rulers compared to the French Europeans? What was their ultimate goal?

Explore Further

Julia Clancy-Smith, *Rebel and Saint: Muslim Notables, Populist Protest, Colonial Encounter (Algeria and Tunisia, 1800–1904)* (1994).

Raphael Danziger, *Abd al-Qadir: Resistance to the French and Internal Consolidation* (1977).

John Ruedy, *Modern Algeria: The Origins and Development of a Nation* (2005).

---

pastoral and nomadic way of life. But some were sedentary, living in settled communities, and people in this group converted to Islam, read the Islamic classics, and communicated with holy men of North Africa, Egypt, and the Arabian Peninsula. They concluded that West African peoples were violating Islamic beliefs and engaging in irreligious practices.

The most powerful of these reform movements flourished in what is today northern Nigeria. Its leader was a Fulani Muslim cleric, **Usman dan Fodio** (1754–1817), who ultimately created a vast Islamic empire. Dan Fodio's movement had all the trappings of the Islamic revolts of this period. It sought inspiration in the life of Muhammad and demanded a return to early Islamic practices. It attacked false belief and urged followers to wage holy war (*jihad*) against unbelievers.

Dan Fodio blamed local leaders for what he saw as their failure to respect Islamic law. He won the support of devout Muslims in the area, who agreed that the people were

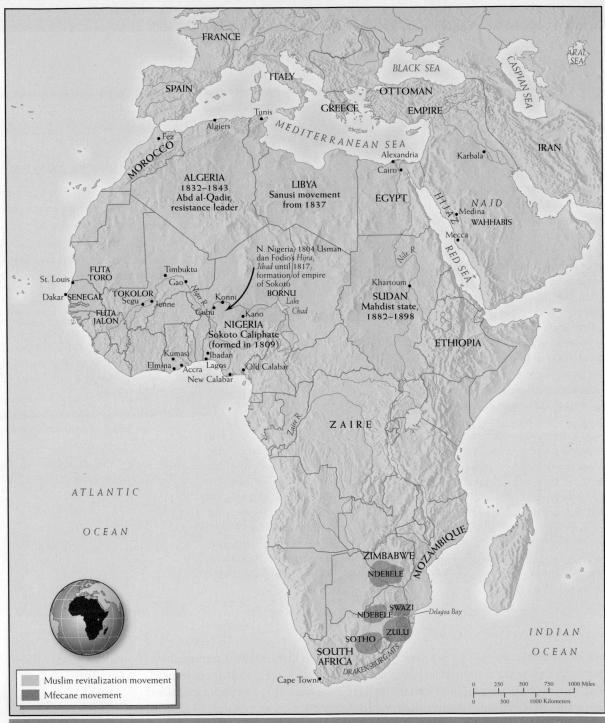

FRANCE

SPAIN

ITALY

GREECE

BLACK SEA

OTTOMAN

EMPIRE

CASPIAN SEA

ARAL SEA

IRAN

MOROCCO

Fez

Algiers

Tunis

MEDITERRANEAN SEA

Alexandria

Cairo

Karbala

ALGERIA
1832–1843
Abd al-Qadir,
resistance leader

LIBYA
Sanusi movement
from 1837

EGYPT

HIJAZ

Medina

Mecca

RED SEA

NAJD

WAHHABIS

N. Nigeria, 1804 Usman
dan Fodio's *Hijra*,
Jihad until 1817;
formation of empire
of Sokoto

FUTA
TORO

St. Louis

Dakar SENEGAL

Timbuktu

Gao

TOKOLOR

Segu   Jenne

Niger R.

Konni

Gubu

FUTA
JALON

Kano

NIGERIA
Sokoto Caliphate
(formed in 1809)

BORNU

Lake
Chad

Khartoum

SUDAN
Mahdist state,
1882–1898

Nile R.

ETHIOPIA

Kumasi

Elmina

Accra

Ibadan

Lagos

Old Calabar

New Calabar

ATLANTIC

OCEAN

ZAIRE

Zaire R.

ZIMBABWE

NDEBELE

MOZAMBIQUE

NDEBELE

SWAZI

Delagoa Bay

SOTHO

ZULU

SOUTH
AFRICA

DRAKENSBURG MTS.

Cape Town

INDIAN

OCEAN

| Muslim revitalization movement |
| Mfecane movement |

0   250   500   750   1000 Miles

0   500   1000 Kilometers

MAP 16.1 | Muslim Revitalization Movements in the Middle East and Africa and the *Mfecane* Movement in Southern Africa

During the nineteenth century, a series of Muslim revitalization movements took place throughout the Middle East and North Africa.

• According to this map, in how many different areas did the revitalization movements occur?

• Based on their geographic location within their larger regions, did these movements occur in central or peripheral areas?

• According to your reading, were any of the same factors that led to Islamic revitalization involved in the *Mfecane* developments in southern Africa?

not properly practicing Islam. He also gained the backing of his Fulani tribes and many Hausa-speaking peasants, who had suffered under the rule of the Hausa landlord class. The revolt, initiated in 1804, resulted in the overthrow of the Hausa rulers and the creation of a confederation of Islamic emirates, almost all of which were in the hands of the Fulani allies of dan Fodio.

Fulani women of northern Nigeria made critical contributions to the success of the religious revolt. Although dan Fodio and other male leaders of the purification movement expected women to obey the *sharia* (Islamic law), being modest in their dress and their association with men outside the family, they also expected women to support the community's military and religious endeavors. In this effort, they cited women's important role in the first days of Islam. The best known of the Muslim women leaders was Nana Asma'u (1793–1864), daughter of dan Fodio. Fulani women of the upper ranks acquired an Islamic education, and Asma'u was as astute a reader of Islamic texts as any of the learned men in her society. Like other Muslim Fulani devotees, she accompanied the warriors on their campaigns, encamped with them, prepared food for them, bound up their wounds, and provided daily encouragement. According to many accounts, Asma'u inspired the warriors at their most crucial battle, hurling a burning spear into the midst of the enemy army. Her poem "Song of the Circular Journey" celebrates the triumphs of military forces that trekked thousands of miles to bring a reformed Islam to the area.

Usman dan Fodio considered himself a cleric first and a political and military man second. Although his political leadership was decisive in the revolt's success, thereafter he retired to a life of scholarship and writing. He delegated the political and administrative functions of the new empire to his brother and his son. An enduring decentralized state structure, which became known as the Sokoto caliphate in 1809, developed into a stable empire that helped spread Islam through the region. In 1800, on the eve of dan Fodio's revolt, Islam was the faith of a small minority of people living in northern Nigeria; a century later, it had become the religion of the vast majority, thanks to dan Fodio's military prowess and success in creating a stable political structure, and the increasing Fulani contacts with the broader Islamic world.

CHARISMATIC MILITARY MEN IN NON-ISLAMIC AFRICA

Non-Islamic Africa saw revolts, new states, and prophetic movements arise from the same combination of factors that influenced the rest of the world—particularly long-distance trade and population increase. Local communities here also looked to religious traditions and, as was so often the case in African history, expected charismatic clan leaders, known as "big men," to provide political leadership.

In southern Africa, early in the nineteenth century, a group of political revolts reordered the political map. Collectively known as the ***Mfecane*** ("the crushing" in Zulu) **movement**, its epicenter was a large tract of land lying east of the Drakensberg Mountains, an area where growing populations and land resources existed in a precarious balance (see again Map 16.1). Many branches of Bantu-speaking peoples had inhabited the southern part of the African landmass for centuries. At the end of the eighteenth century, however, their political organizations still operated on a small scale. These tiny polities could not cope with the competition for land that now dominated southern Africa. That competition intensified with the arrival of British colonizers, who fought both with Dutch settlers and indigenous African communities over natural resources. The import of European goods that flowed into southern Africa from Delagoa Bay also was a destabilizing factor. A branch of the Nguni, the Zulus, produced a fierce war leader, Shaka (1787–1828), who created a ruthless warrior state. It drove other populations out of the region and forced a shift from small clan communities to large, centralized monarchies throughout southern and central Africa.

Shaka and His Zulu Regiments (*Left*) This illustration, the only one from the time, may be an exaggeration, but it does not exaggerate the view that many had of the awesome strength and power of Shaka, the leader who united the Zulu peoples into an invincible warrior state. (*Right*) Shaka's Zulu state owed its political and military successes to its young warriors, who were deeply loyal to their ruler and whose training and discipline were exemplary. Shown here is a regimental camp in which the warriors slept in huts massed in a circular pattern and trained in military drill and close combat in the inside circle.

Shaka was the son of a minor chief who emerged victorious in the struggle for cattle-grazing and farming lands that arose during a severe drought. A physically imposing figure, Shaka used terror to intimidate his subjects and to overawe his adversaries. His enemies knew that the price of opposition would be a massacre, even of women and children. Nor was he kinder to his own people. Following the death of his beloved mother, he executed those who were not properly contrite and did not weep profusely. Reportedly, it took 7,000 lives to assuage his grief.

Shaka built a new Zulu state around his military and organizational skills and the fear that his personal ferocity produced. He drilled his men relentlessly in the use of short stabbing spears and in discipline under pressure. Like the Mongols, he had a remarkable ability to incorporate defeated communities into the state and to absorb young men into his military. His army of 40,000 men comprised regiments that lived, studied, and fought together. Forbidden from marrying until they were discharged from the army, Shaka's warriors developed an intense esprit de corps and regarded no sacrifice as too great in the service of the state. So overpowering were these forces that other peoples of the region fled from their home areas, and Shaka claimed their estates for himself and his followers. Peoples in nearby areas who weren't absorbed into the Zulu state adopted many of Shaka's military and political innovations, at first to defend themselves and then to take over new land as they fled their old areas. The new states of the Ndebele in what later became Zimbabwe and the Sotho of South Africa came into existence in this way in the mid-nineteenth century.

In turning southern Africa from a region of smaller polities into an area with larger and more powerful states, Shaka seemed very much a man of the modern, nineteenth-century world. Yet he was, in his own unique way, a familiar kind of African leader. He shared a charismatic and prophetic style with others who emerged during periods of acute social change. His new state built an enduring Zulu community and established its traditions against encroachments by outside, European forces.

Prophecy and Rebellion in China

In the mid-nineteenth century, China experienced an explosive popular rebellion that incorporated Christian beliefs into its long tradition of peasant revolts. Whereas movements promoting alternative visions in the Islamic world and Africa appeared in areas distant from western influences and drew substantially on their own traditions, China was no longer isolated. In fact, it had been conducting a brisk trade in opium with Europe. Until 1842, the Chinese had confined trade with Europeans to the port city of Canton. After the Opium War, however, westerners forced Qing rulers to open up a number of other ports to trade.

As in the Islamic world and other parts of sub-Saharan Africa, population increases in China—from 250 million in 1644 to around 450 million by the 1850s—were putting considerable pressure on land and other resources. Moreover, the rising consumption of opium, grown in India and brought to China by British traders, produced further social instability and financial crisis. As banditry and rebellions spread, the Qing rulers turned to the landed elites, the gentry, to maintain order in the countryside. But as the gentry raised its militia to suppress these troublemakers, it whittled away at the authority of the Qing Manchu rulers. Faced with these changes, the Qing dynasty struggled to maintain control.

Searching for an alternative present and future, hundreds of thousands of disillusioned peasants joined what became known as the Taiping Rebellion. Beginning in 1850, the uprising drew on China's long history of peasant revolts. Traditionally, these rebellions ignited within popular religious sects whose visions were egalitarian or **millenarian** (convinced of the imminent coming of a just and ideal society). Moreover, in contrast to orthodox institutions, here women played important roles. Inspired by Daoists, who revered a past golden age before the world was corrupted by human conventions, or by Buddhist sources, these sects threatened the established order.

THE DREAM OF HONG XIUQUAN

The story of the rebellion begins with a complex dream that inspired its founding prophet, Hong Xiuquan (1813–1864). A native of Guangdong province in the southernmost part of the country (see Map 16.2), Hong first encountered Christian missionaries in the 1830s. He was then trying, unsuccessfully, to pass the civil service examination. After failing the exam for the third time, Hong suffered a strange "illness" in which he had visions of combating demons; these dreams included a mysterious "Old Father" and an "Elder Brother." He also began proclaiming himself the Heavenly King. Relatives and neighbors thought he might have gone mad, but Hong gradually returned to his normal state.

In 1843, after failing the exam for the fourth time, Hong immersed himself in a Christian tract entitled *Good Words for Exhorting the Age*. Reportedly, reading this tract enabled Hong to realize the full significance of his earlier visions. All the pieces suddenly fell into place, and he began to grasp their meaning. The "Old Father," he concluded, was the Lord Ye-huo-hua (a Chinese rendering of "Jehovah"), the creator of heaven and earth. His visions of cleansing rituals in heaven foretold Hong's baptism. The "Elder Brother" was Jesus the Savior, the son of God. He, Hong Xiuquan, was the younger brother of Jesus—God's other son. Just as God had previously sent Jesus to save mankind, Hong thought that God was now sending *him* to rid the world of evil. What was once a series of dreams now became a prophetic vision.

THE REBELLION

Hong's prophecy tapped into a millenarian tradition, inspiring a movement that spread rapidly from southern China. Unlike earlier sectarian leaders whose plots for rebellion were

MAP 16.2 | The Taiping Rebellion in China, 1851–1864

The Taiping Rebellion started in the southwestern part of the country. The rebels, however, went on to control much of the lower Yangzi region and part of the coastal area.

- What cities did the rebels' march start and end in?
- Why do you think the Taiping rebels were so successful in southern China and not in northern regions?
- How did western powers react to the Taiping Rebellion? Would they have been as concerned if the rebellion took place farther to the north or west?

secret before exploding onto the public arena, Hong chose a more audacious path. Once convinced of his vision, he began to preach his doctrines openly, baptizing converts and destroying Confucian idols and ancestral shrines. Such assaults on the establishment testified to his conviction that he was carrying out God's will. Hong's message of revitalization of a troubled land and restoration of the "heavenly kingdom," imagined as a just and egalitarian order, appealed to the subordinate classes caught in the flux of social change. Drawing on a largely rural social base and asserting allegiance to Christianity, the **Taiping** ("Great Peace") **Rebellion** (1850–1864) claimed to herald a new era of economic and social justice.

Many early followers came from the margins of local society—those whose anger at social and economic dislocations caused by the Opium War was directed not at the Europeans, but at the Qing government. The Taiping identified the ruling Manchus as the "demons" and as the chief obstacle to realizing God's kingdom on earth. Taiping policies were strict: they prohibited the consumption of alcohol, the smoking of opium, or any indulgence in sensual pleasure. Men and women were segregated for administrative and residential purposes. At the same time, in a drastic departure from dynastic practice, women joined the army in segregated units.

By 1850, Hong's movement had amassed a following of over 20,000, giving Qing rulers cause for concern. When they sent troops to arrest Hong and other rebel leaders, Taiping forces repelled them and then took their turmoil beyond the southwestern part of the country. In 1851, Hong declared himself Heavenly King of the "Taiping Heavenly Kingdom" (or "Heavenly Kingdom of Great Peace"). By 1853, the rebels had captured major cities. Upon capturing Nanjing, the Taiping cleansed the city of "demons" by systematically killing all the Manchus they could find—men, women, and children. Then they established their own "heavenly" capital in the city.

But the rebels could not sustain their vision. Several factors contributed to the fall of the Heavenly Kingdom: struggles within the leadership, an excessively rigid code of conduct, and the rallying of Manchu and Han elites around the embattled dynasty. Disturbed by the Taiping's rejection of Confucianism and wanting to protect their property, landowning gentry led militias against the Taiping. Moreover, western governments also opposed the rebellion, claiming that its doctrines represented a perversion of Christianity. Thus, a mercenary army led by foreign officers took part in suppressing the rebellion. Hong himself perished as his heavenly capital fell in 1864. All told, at least 20 million people died in the Taiping Rebellion.

Taiping Rebellion A painting depicting the Taiping rebels attacking a town. Had the Taiping succeeded in overthrowing the Qing, it would have changed the course of Chinese history and profoundly affected the rest of the world.

Like their counterparts in the Islamic world and Africa, the Taiping rebels promised to restore lost harmony. Despite all the differences of cultural and historical background, what Abd al-Wahhab, dan Fodio, Shaka, and Hong had in common was the perception that the present world was unjust. Thus, they sought to reorganize their communities—an endeavor that involved confronting established authorities. In this regard, the language of revitalization used by prophets in Islamic areas and China was crucial, for it provided an alternative vocabulary of political and spiritual legitimacy. By mobilizing masses eager to return to an imagined golden age, these prophets and charismatic leaders gave voice to those dispossessed by global change, while producing new, alternative ways of organizing society and politics.

Socialists and Radicals in Europe

Europe and North America were the core areas of economic growth, based on the industrial revolution and free trade, nation-state building, and colonial expansion. But there, too, the main currents of thought and activity encountered challenges. Prophets of all stripes—political, social, cultural, and religious—voiced antiestablishment values and dreamed of alternative arrangements. Radicals, liberals, utopian socialists, nationalists, abolitionists, and religious mavericks made plans for better worlds to come.

COMPARISON

DESCRIBE the challenges to the ideals of industrial capitalism and nation states in this period in Europe and the Americas.

RESTORATION AND RESISTANCE

The social and political ferment of the efforts to restore the old order, known as the Restoration period (1815–1848) owed a great deal to the ambiguous legacies of the French Revolution and the Napoleonic wars. (See Map 16.3.) Kings had been toppled and replaced by republics, and then by Napoleon and his relatives; these experiments gave Restoration-era states and radicals many political options from which to choose in the years between Napoleon's downfall in 1815 and the revolutions of 1848.

This period has often been called the Age of Ideology because revolutionary upheavals forced everyone, even those in power, to justify their vision of the social order. Appeals to tradition no longer sufficed. Those called reactionaries or conservatives wanted a return to the world that existed before the French Revolution; they rejected change. Liberals, by contrast, accepted the French Revolution's overthrow of aristocratic privilege. They wanted to hold on to the principles of 1789—above all free trade and equality before the law—without accepting the price controls and political violence of the Terror. Free markets rather than government controls, they believed, would make the most sensible decisions. These proponents of **liberalism** insisted on the individual's right to think, speak, act, and vote as he or she pleased without government interference, so long as no harm came to people or property. Both reactionaries and liberals could find elements to their taste in all the states of the post-Napoleonic world. Much more threatening to the ruling elite were the radicals who believed that the French Revolution had not gone far enough. They longed for a grander revolution that would sweep away the Restoration's political *and* economic order.

RADICAL VISIONS

Reactionaries and liberals did not form the only alternative groups of importance at this time. Most discontented of all—and most determined to effect grand-scale change—were the radicals.

The term *radicals* refers to those who favored the total reconfiguration of the old regime's state system: going to the root of the problem and continuing the revolution, not reversing it or stopping reform. In general, radicals shared a bitter hatred for the status quo and an insistence on popular sovereignty, but beyond this consensus much disagreement remained. If some radicals demanded the equalization or abolition of private property, others—like Serbian, Greek, Polish, and Italian nationalists—were primarily interested in throwing off the oppressive overlordship of the Ottoman and Austrian empires and creating their own nation-states. It was the radicals' threat of a return to revolutions that ultimately reconciled both liberals and reactionaries to preserving the status quo.

Nationalists In the period before the revolutions of 1848, nationalism was a cause dear to both liberals and radicals, and it threatened conservative rulers who claimed to rule by divine right. The idea of popular sovereignty spread, especially during and after Napoleon's occupation of the continent, but who exactly were "the people"? The "people," or the nation, were generally considered to be those who shared a common language, culture, and history, but nationalists fought bitterly over which people counted and who decided. All nationalists believed that governments

Congress of Vienna Following the French Revolution and Napoleon's defeat, European kings and aristocrats revived most of their former powers. At the Congress of Vienna in 1815, the Austrian prime minister Clemens von Metternich took the lead in drafting a peace settlement that would balance power among the states of Europe.

Foreign intervention to put down revolutions
- ← Austrian
- ← British
- ← Egyptian
- ← French
- ← Russian

— German Confederation
✳ Revolutionary activity

MAP 16.3 | Civil Unrest and Revolutions in Europe, 1819–1848

Civil unrest and revolutions swept Europe after the Congress of Vienna established a peace settlement at the end of the French Revolution and Napoleon's conquests. Conservative governments had to fight off liberal rebellions and demands for change.

- How many sites of revolutionary activity can you locate on this map?

- What parts of Europe appear to have been politically stable, and what parts rebellious? Based on your reading and the map, can you explain the stability of some parts of Europe and the instability of others?

should represent the "people" and that each people—or, at least, their people—should have a state of their own.

Each fledgling nationalist movement—whether Polish, Czech, Greek, Italian, or German—had different contours, but they all drew backers from the liberal aristocracy and the well-educated, commercially active middle classes. Most nationalist movements were, at first, weak and easily crushed, such as attempted Polish uprisings inside tsarist Russia in 1830–1831 and 1863–1864. Unable to win political power, the movements' leaders instead pursued educational and cultural programs to arouse and unite their nation for eventual statehood. By contrast, the Greeks, inspired by religious revivalism and enlightened ideas, managed to wrest independence from the Ottoman Turks after a years-long series of skirmishes, in 1832.

Other nationalist movements were suppressed or at least slowed down with little bloodshed. In places like the German principalities, the Italian states, and the Hungarian parts of the Habsburg Empire, secret societies of young men—students and intellectuals—gathered to plan bright, republican futures. Regrettably for these patriots, however, organizations like Young Italy, founded in 1832 to promote national unification and renewal, had little popular or foreign support. Censorship and a few strategic executions suppressed them. Yet many of these movements ultimately succeeded in the century's second half, when conservatives and liberals alike in western Europe employed nationalist fervor to advance their own ambitions. Kings, aristocrats, and bourgeois businessmen realized that they could mobilize popular support in their capacity as Germans, Frenchmen, or Italians, even as they limited poor people's political rights. However, in central Europe, nationalism pitted many claimants for the same territories against one another, like the Czechs, Serbs, Slovaks, Poles, and Ruthenians (Ukrainians). They did not understand why they could not have a nation-state too. Indeed the term "nation," like that of the people, was so abstract and vague that it unleashed a series of competing claims that were incompatible with one another and would prove enormously destructive in the twentieth century.

Socialists and Communists Early socialists and communists (the terms were more or less interchangeable in the nineteenth century) insisted that political reforms offered no effective answer to the more pressing "social question": what was to be done about the inequalities so powerfully magnified by industrial capitalism? The socialists worried in particular about two things. One was the growing gap between impoverished workers and newly wealthy employers. The other concern was that the division of labor—that is, the dividing up and simplifying of tasks so that each worker performs most efficiently—might make people into soulless, brainless machines. Socialists believed that the whole free-market economy, not just the state, had to be transformed to save the human race from self-destruction. Liberty and equality, they insisted, could not be separated; liberal capitalism and free markets belonged on history's ash heap, in their view, along with aristocratic privilege.

No more than a handful of radical prophets hatched revolutionary plans in the years after 1815, but they were not the only participants in strikes, riots, peasant uprisings, and protest meetings. Indeed, ordinary workers, artisans, domestic servants, and women employed in textile manufacturing all joined in attempts to answer the "social question" to their satisfaction. A few socialists and feminists—like the English thinker John Stuart Mill and his wife, Harriet—campaigned for social and political equality of the sexes. In Britain in 1819, Manchester workers at St. Peter's Field demonstrated peacefully for increased representation in Parliament, but panicking guardsmen fired on the crowd, leaving 11 dead and 460 injured in an incident later dubbed the Peterloo Massacre. In 1839 and 1842, nearly half the adult population of Britain signed the People's Charter, which called for universal suffrage for all adult males, the secret ballot, equal electoral districts, and annual parliamentary elections. This mass movement, known as Chartism, like most such endeavors, ended in defeat. Parliament rejected the charter in 1839, 1842, and 1848.

Fourier and Utopian Socialism Despite their many defeats, the radicals kept trying. Charles Fourier's **utopian socialism** was perhaps the most visionary and influential of all Restoration-era alternative movements.

Fired by the egalitarian hopes and the cataclysmic failings of the French Revolution, Fourier (1772–1837) believed himself to be the scientific prophet of the new world to come. He was an imaginative, self-taught man who earned his keep in the cloth trade, an occupation that gave him an intense hatred for merchants and middlemen. Convinced that the division of labor and repressive moral conventions were destroying mankind's natural talents and passions, Fourier concluded that a revolution grander than that of 1789 was needed. But this utopian transformation of economic, social, and political conditions, he thought, could occur through organization, not through bloodshed. Indeed, by 1808 Fourier believed that the thoroughly corrupt world was on the brink of giving way to a new and harmonious age, of which he was the oracle.

First formulated in 1808, his "system" envisioned the reorganization of human communities into what he called phalanxes. In these harmonious collectives of 1,500 to 1,600 people, diversity would be preserved but efficiency maintained; best of all, work would become enjoyable. All members of the phalanx, rich and poor, would work, though not necessarily at the same tasks. All would work in short spurts of no more than two hours, so as to make labor more interesting and sleep, idleness, and overindulgence less attractive. Truly undesirable jobs, like sweeping out stables or cleaning latrines, would fall to young adolescents, who, Fourier argued, actually liked mucking about in filth.

Fourier's writings gained popularity in the 1830s, appealing to radicals who supported a variety of causes. In France, women were particularly active in spreading his ideas. Longing for social and moral reforms that would address problems such as prostitution, poverty, illegitimacy, and the exploitation of workers (including women and children), some women saw in Fourier's ideas a higher form of Christian communalism. By reshaping the phalanx to accommodate monogamous families and Christian values, women helped to make his work more respectable to middle-class readers. In Russia, Fourier's works inspired the imaginations of the young writer Fyodor Dostoevsky. He and fourteen others in the radical circle to which he belonged were sentenced to death for their views (though their executions were called off at the last minute). The German thinker Karl Marx read Fourier with great care, and there are many remnants of utopian thought in his work. In *The German Ideology* Marx describes life in an ideal communist society; in a postrevolutionary world, he predicts, people would no longer have to commit to a single profession or sphere of activity. Everyone could develop their talents in a range of areas. A well-ordered society would make it possible, as he put it in a famous phrase, "for me to do one thing today and another tomorrow, to hunt in the morning, fish in the afternoon, rear cattle in the evening, [and] criticize after dinner."

Marxism University-educated and philosophically radical, Karl Marx (1818–1883) elaborated what he called a scientific socialism. After being expelled from the university for

The Phalanx The Phalanx, as one of Fourier's German followers envisioned it. In this rendering, the idealized home for the residents of the cooperative social system is represented as a building architecturally similar to the home of the French kings, the Louvre.

Karl Marx The author (with Friedrich Engels) of *The Communist Manifesto*, Karl Marx argued that the exploitation of wage laborers would trigger a proletarian revolution and would lead to socialism supplanting capitalism.

his radical views, Marx took up a career in journalism. In that capacity, he covered legislative debates over property rights and taxation and developed an interest in economics. His understanding of capitalism, a term he was instrumental in popularizing, deepened through his collaboration with Friedrich Engels (1820–1895). Engels was a German-born radical who, after observing conditions in the factories owned by his wealthy father in Manchester, England, published a devastating indictment of industrial wage labor entitled *The Condition of the Working Class in England*.

Together, Marx and Engels developed what they called "scientific socialism," which they contrasted with the "utopian socialism" of others like Fourier. Scientific socialism was rooted, they argued, in a materialist theory of history: what mattered in history were the production of material goods and the ways in which society was organized into classes of producers and exploiters. History, they claimed, consisted of successive forms of exploitative production and rebellions against them. Capitalist exploitation of the wage worker was only the latest, and worst, version of class conflict, Marx and Engels contended. In industrialized societies, capitalists owned the means of production (the factories and machinery) and exploited wage workers. Marx and Engels were confident that the clashes between industrial wage workers with nothing to sell but their labor—or **proletarians**—and capitalists would end in a colossal transformation of human society and would usher in a new world of true liberty, equality, and fraternity. These beliefs constituted the fundamentals of **Marxism**. For Marx and Engels, history moved through stages: from feudalism to capitalism, and then, finally, to socialism (or communism).

From these fundamentals, Marx and Engels issued a comprehensive critique of post-1815 Europe. They identified a whole class of the exploited—the working class. They believed that more and more people would fall into this class as industrialization proceeded and that the masses would not share in the rising prosperity that capitalists monopolized. Marx and Engels predicted that there would be overproduction, and underconsumption of goods would lead to lower profits for capitalists and, consequently, to lower wages or unemployment for workers—which would ultimately spark a proletarian revolution. This revolution would result in a "dictatorship of the proletariat" and the end of private property. With the destruction of capitalism, the men claimed, exploitation would cease and the state would wither away.

After a decade of hardship across Europe known as the hungry forties, revolutions erupted in 1848 in France, Austria, Russia, Italy, Hungary, and the German states. After hearing that revolution had broken out in France, Marx and Engels published *The Communist Manifesto*, calling on the workers of all nations to unite in overthrowing capitalism. These were not proletarian revolutions. Modern industry had not developed beyond a few key locations by midcentury, mostly in northern and western Europe. Instead the revolutions were cross-class affairs, lead by an uneasy coalition of liberal doctors, lawyers, and university professors; often radical students and urban artisans; and a mass of poor peasants. As a group, they shared little more than a frustration with old elites and a desire for independent nations. Marx and Engels were sorely disappointed (not to mention exiled) by the reactionary crackdowns that quickly crushed the 1848 revolutions. The failure of those revolutions, however, did not doom their prophecy itself or diminish commitment to alternative social landscapes.

Insurgencies against Colonizing and Centralizing States

COMPARISON

DESCRIBE the challenges to the ideals of industrial capitalism in India and the Americas.

Outside Europe, for Native Americans and for Britain's colonial subjects in India, the greatest threat to traditional worlds was colonialism. While European radicals looked back to revolutionary legacies in imagining a transformed society, Native Americans insurgents and rebels in British India drew on their traditional cultural and political resources to imagine local alternatives to foreign impositions. Like the peoples of China, Africa, and the Middle East, native groups in the Americas and India met the period's challenges with prophecy, charismatic leadership, and rebellion. The insurgents all sought to defend their cultures and looked to an idealized past free from outside influences, but the new worlds they envisioned bore unmistakable marks of the present as well.

NATIVE AMERICAN PROPHETS

Like other native peoples threatened by imperial expansion, the Native Americans of North America dreamed of a world in which intrusive colonizers disappeared. Taking such dreams as prophecies, many Native Americans in the Ohio Valley flocked in 1805 to hear the revelations of a Shawnee Native American named Tenskwatawa. Facing a dark present and a darker future, they enthusiastically embraced the Shawnee Prophet's visions, which (like that of the Paiute prophet Wovoka nearly a century later) foretold how invaders would vanish if Native Americans returned to their customary ways and traditional rites.

Early Calls for Resistance and a Return to Tradition Tenskwatawa's visions—and the anticolonial uprising they inspired—drew on a long tradition of visionary leaders. Often these prophets inspired their followers not only to engage in cleansing ceremonies but also to cooperate in violent, anticolonial uprisings. In the 1760s, for example, the preachings of the Delaware shaman Neolin encouraged Native Americans of the Ohio Valley and Great Lakes to take up arms against the British, leading to the capture of several British military posts. Although the British put down the uprising, imperial officials learned a lesson from the conflict: they assumed a less arrogant posture toward Ohio Valley and Great Lakes Native Americans, and they forbade colonists from trespassing on lands west of the Appalachian Mountains. The British, however, were incapable of restraining the flow of settlers across the mountains, and the problem became much worse for the Native Americans once the American Revolution ended. With the Ohio Valley transferred to the new United States, American settlers crossed the Appalachians and flooded into Kentucky and Tennessee.

Despite the settlers' considerable migration, much of the territory between the Appalachian Mountains and the Mississippi River, which Americans referred to as the "western country," remained a Native American country. North and south of Kentucky and Tennessee, Native American warriors more than held their own against American forces. But in 1794 Native American warriors failed to repel invading American armies, and their leaders had to surrender lands in what is now the state of Ohio to the United States. (See Map 16.4.)

Tenskwatawa: The Shawnee Prophet The Shawnees, who lost most of their land, were among the most bitter—and bitterly divided—of Native American peoples living in the Ohio Valley. Some Shawnee leaders concluded that their people's survival now required that they cooperate with American officials and Christian missionaries. This strategy, they realized, entailed wrenching changes in Shawnee culture. European reformers, after all, insisted that Native American men give up hunting and take up farming, an occupation that the Shawnees and their neighbors had always considered "women's work." Moreover, the Shawnees were pushed to abandon communal traditions in favor of private property rights.

Among the demoralized Shawnees was **Tenskwatawa** (1775–1836), whose story of overcoming personal failures through religious visions and embracing a strict moral code has parallels with that of Hong Xiuquan, the Taiping leader. In his first thirty years, Tenskwatawa could claim few accomplishments. He had failed as a hunter and as a medicine man, had blinded himself in one eye, and had earned a reputation as an obnoxious braggart. All this changed in the spring of 1805, however, after he fell into a trance and experienced a vision. In this dream, Tenskwatawa encountered a heaven where the virtuous enjoyed the traditional Shawnee way of life and a hell where evildoers suffered punishments. Additional revelations followed, and Tenskwatawa soon stitched these together into a new social gospel that urged disciples to abstain from alcohol and return to traditional customs.

Like other prophets, Tenskwatawa exhorted Native Americans to avoid contact with outside influences, to reduce their dependence on European trade goods and to sever their connections to Christian missionaries. If Native Americans obeyed these dictates, Tenskwatawa promised, the deer, which "were half a tree's length under the ground," would come back in abundant numbers to the earth's surface. Likewise, he claimed, Native Americans killed in conflict with colonial intruders would be resurrected, while evil Americans would depart from the country west of the Appalachians.

Like the Qing's response to Hong's visions, American officials grew concerned as the Shawnee Prophet gathered followers. The spread of Tenskwatawa's message raised fears of a pan-Native American confederacy. Hoping to undermine the Shawnee Prophet's claims to supernatural power, territorial governor William Henry Harrison challenged Tenskwatawa to make the sun stand still. But Tenskwatawa one-upped Harrison. Having learned

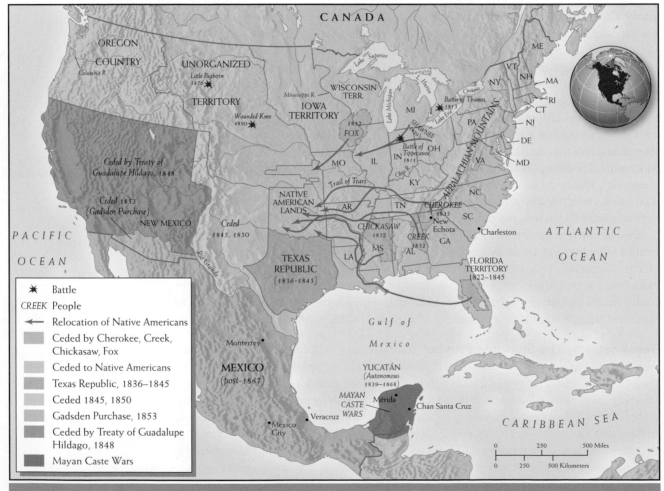

MAP 16.4 | Native American Revolts in the United States and Mexico

The new world order of expanding nation-states and industrial markets strongly affected indigenous peoples in North America.

• According to this map, where did the fiercest resistance to centralizing states and global market pressures occur?

• What regions of the United States were Native Americans forced to leave?

• According to your reading, to what extent, if any, did the natives' alternative visions create or preserve an alternative to the new emerging order?

of an impending eclipse from white astronomers, Tenskwatawa assembled his followers on June 16, 1806. Right on schedule, and as if on command, the sky darkened. Claiming credit for the eclipse, Tenskwatawa saw his standing soar, as did the ranks of his disciples.

At the same time, however, Tenskwatawa had made plenty of enemies among his fellow Native Americans. His visions consigned drinkers to hell and singled out those who cooperated with colonial authorities for punishment in this world and the next. Indeed, Tenskwatawa condemned as witches those Native Americans who rejected his preaching in favor of the teachings of Christian missionaries and American authorities. (To be sure, Tenskwatawa's damnation of Christianized Native Americans was somewhat paradoxical, for missionary doctrines obviously influenced his vision of a burning hell for sinners and his crusade against alcohol.)

Tecumseh and the Wish for Native American Unity Although Tenskwatawa's accusations alienated some Native Americans, his prophecies gave heart to many more. This was particularly the case once his brother, Tecumseh (1768–1813), helped circulate the message of Native American renaissance among Native American villages from the Great Lakes to the Gulf Coast. On his journeys after 1805, Tecumseh did more than spread his brother's visions; he also wedded them to the idea of an enlarged Native American confederation. Moving around the Great Lakes and traveling across the southern half of the western country, Tecumseh preached the need for Native American unity. Always, he insisted that Native Americans resist any American attempts to get them to sell more land. In response, thousands of followers renounced their ties to colonial ways and prepared to combat the expansion of the United States.

By 1810, Tecumseh had emerged, at least in the eyes of American officials, as even more dangerous than his brother. Impressed by Tecumseh's charismatic organizational talents, William Harrison warned that this new "Indian menace" was forming "an Empire that would rival in glory" that of the Aztecs and the Incas. In 1811, while Tecumseh was traveling among southern tribes, Harrison had his troops attack Tenskwatawa's village, Prophet's Town, on the Tippecanoe River in what is now the state of Indiana. The resulting battle was evenly fought, but the Native Americans eventually gave ground and American forces burned Prophet's Town. That defeat discredited Tenskwatawa, who had promised his followers protection from destruction at American hands. Spurned by his former disciples, including his brother, Tenskwatawa fled to Canada. Tecumseh soldiered on, supporting the British in the War of 1812 in the hope that a British victory would check American expansionism. But in 1813, with the war's outcome still in doubt and the pan-Native American confederacy still fragile, he perished at the Battle of the Thames, north of Lake Erie.

Native American Removals The discrediting of Tenskwatawa and the death of Tecumseh damaged the cause of Native American unity; then British betrayal dealt it a fatal blow. Following the war's end in 1814, the British withdrew their support and left the Native Americans south of the Great Lakes to fend for themselves against land-hungry American settlers and the armies of the United States. By 1815, American citizens outnumbered Native Americans in the western country by a seven-to-one margin, and this gap dramatically widened in the next few years. Recognizing the hopelessness of military resistance, Native Americans south of the Great Lakes resigned themselves to relocation. During the 1820s, most of the peoples north of the Ohio River were removed to lands west of the Mississippi River. During the 1830s, the southern tribes were cleared out, completing what amounted to an ethnic cleansing of Native American peoples from the region between the Appalachians and the Mississippi.

In the midst of these final removals, Tenskwatawa died, though his dream of an alternative to American expansion had faded for his people years earlier. Through the rest of the

Visions of Native American Unification (*Left*) A portrait of Tenskwatawa, the "Shawnee Prophet," whose visions stirred thousands of Native Americans in the Ohio Valley and Great Lakes to renounce dependence on colonial imports and resist the expansion of the United States. (*Right*) A portrait of his brother, Tecumseh, who succeeded in building a significant pan-Native American confederation, although it unraveled following his death at the Battle of the Thames in 1813 and the end of warfare between the United States and Britain the following year.

nineteenth century, however, other Native American prophets emerged, and their visions continued to inspire followers with the hope of an alternative to life under the colonial rule of the United States. But like Wovoka and the Ghost Dancers in 1890, these dreams failed to halt the expansion of the United States and the contraction of Native American lands.

THE CASTE WAR OF THE YUCATAN

As in North America, the Spanish establishment of an expansionist nation-state in Mexico sparked widespread revolts by indigenous peoples. The most protracted was the Mayan revolt in the Yucatan peninsula. The revolt started in 1847, and its flames were not finally doused until the full occupation of the Yucatan by Mexican national troops in 1901.

The strength and endurance of the Mayan revolt stemmed in large measure from the unusual features of the Spanish conquest in southern Mesoamerica. Because this area lacked precious metals and fertile lands, Spain and its rivals focused elsewhere—on central and northern Mexico and the Caribbean islands. As a result, the Mayan Indians escaped forced recruitment for silver mines or sugar plantations. This does not mean that global processes sidestepped the Mayan Indians. In fact, the production of dyes and foodstuffs for shipment to other regions drew the Yucatan into long-distance trading networks. Nonetheless, cultivation and commerce were much less disruptive to indigenous lives in the Yucatan than elsewhere in the New World.

Growing Pressures from the Sugar Trade Local developments, however, encroached on the Mayan world in the nineteenth century. First, regional elites—mainly white, but often with the support of mixed race (mestizo) populations—bickered for supremacy so long as the central authority of Mexico City remained weak. Weaponry flowed freely through the peninsula, and some combatants even appealed for Mayan support. At the same time, regional and international trade spurred the spread of sugar estates, which threatened traditional corn cultivation in the Yucatan. Over the decades, plantations encroached on Mayan properties. Planters used several devices to lure independent Mayans to work, especially in the harvest. The most important device, debt peonage, involved giving small cash advances to Indian families, which obligated fathers and sons to work for meager wages to pay off the debts. In addition, Mexico's costly wars, culminating in a showdown with the United States in 1846, drove tax collectors and army recruiters into villages in search of revenues and soldiers.

The combination of material and physical threats was explosive. When a small band of Mayans, fed up with rising taxes and ebbing autonomy, used firearms to drive back white intruders in 1847, they sparked a war that took a half century to complete. The rebels were primarily free Mayans who had not yet been absorbed into the sugar economy. They wanted to dismantle old definitions of Indians as a caste—a status that deprived the Indians of legal and political equality with whites and that also subjected the Indians to special taxes. Thus, local Mayan leaders, like Jacinto Pat and Cecilio Chi, upheld a republican model in the name of formal equality of all political subjects and devotion to a spiritual order that did not distinguish between Christians and non-Christians. "If the Indians revolt," one Mayan rebel explained, "it is because the whites gave them reason; because the whites say they do not believe in Jesus Christ, because they have burned the cornfield."

The Caste War Horrified, the local white elites reacted to the uprising with vicious repression and dubbed the ensuing conflict a **caste war**. In their view, the bloody conflict was a struggle between forward-looking liberals and backward-looking Indians. At first, whites and mestizos were no match for the determined Mayans, whose forces seized town after town. They especially targeted symbols of white power. With relish they demolished the whipping posts where Indians had endured public humiliation and punishment.

In the end, fortune, not political savvy, saved the Yucatan's whites. Settlement of the war with the United States in 1848 enabled Mexico City to rescue local elites in the Yucatan. With the help of a $15 million payment from Washington for giving up its northern provinces, Mexico could spend freely to build up its southern armies. The Mexican government soon fielded a force of 17,000 soldiers and waged a scorched-earth campaign to drive back the depleted Mayan forces.

By 1849, the confrontation had entered a new phase in which Mexican troops engaged in mass repression of the Mayans. Mexican armies set Indian fields and villages ablaze. Between 30 and 40 percent of the Mayan population perished in the war and its repressive aftermath. The inhabitants of entire Mayan cities pulled up stakes and withdrew to isolated districts protected by fortified villages. War between armies degenerated into guerrilla warfare between an occupying Mexican army and mobile bands of Mayan squadrons, inflicting a gruesome toll on the invaders. As years passed, the war ground to a stalemate, especially once the U.S. funds ran out and Mexican soldiers began deserting in droves.

Reclaiming a Mayan Identity Warfare prompted a spiritual transformation that reinforced a purely Mayan identity against the Mexican invaders' efforts to create a strong, centralized state. Thus, a struggle that began with

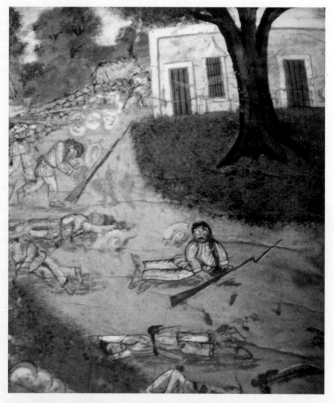

Caste War in the Yucatan The ruthless slaughter of Maya farmers by Mexican troops is captured in this 1850 painting. The intimacy of the bloodstained straw hats strewn on the road suggest this work was an eyewitness account.

demands for legal equality and relative cultural autonomy became a crusade for spiritual salvation and the complete cultural separation of the Mayan Indians. A particularly influential group under José María Barrera retreated to a hamlet called Chan Santa Cruz. There, at the site where he found a cross shape carved into a mahogany tree, Barrera had a vision of a divine encounter. Thereafter, people in a swath of Yucatan villages around Chan Santa Cruz refashioned themselves as moral communities. Leaders created a polity, with soldiers, priests, and tax collectors pledging loyalty to the Speaking Cross. Like the followers of Hong in China's Taiping Rebellion, Indian rebels forged an alternative religion: it blended Christian rituals, faiths, and icons with Mayan legends and beliefs. At the center was a stone temple, Balam Na ("House of God"), 100 feet long and 60 feet wide. Through pilgrimages to Balam Na and the secular justice of Indian judges, the Mayans soon governed their domain in the Yucatan autonomously, almost completely cut off from the rest of Mexico.

The Mexican government threw its weight behind the strong-arm ruler General Porfirio Díaz (r. 1876–1911). The general sent one of his veteran commanders, Ignacio Bravo, to do what no other Mexican could accomplish: vanquish Chan Santa Cruz. When General Bravo finally entered the town, he found the once imposing temple Balam Na covered in vegetation. Nature was reclaiming the territories of the Speaking Cross. Hunger and Bravo's soldiers finally drove the Mayans to work on white Mexican plantations; the alternative vision was vanquished. A combination of declining economic conditions and the soldiers under Ignacio Bravo brought an end to the Mayan revolt.

THE REBELLION OF 1857 IN INDIA

COMPARISON

DISTINGUISH the long-term influence of protest movements from their immediate political accomplishments in Asia, Islam, and Africa.

Like Native Americans, the peoples of nineteenth-century India had a long history of opposition to colonial domination. Armed revolts had occurred since the onset of rule by the British East India Company (see Chapter 15). Nonetheless, the uprising of 1857 was unprecedented in its scale, and it posed a greater threat than had any previous rebellion. (See **Analyzing Global Developments: Alternative Movements in Asia and Africa**.)

India under Company Rule During the first half of the nineteenth century the British rulers of India had dismantled most of the traditional powers of the nobility and the rights of peasants. Believing that the princely powers and landed aristocracies were out of date, the company instituted far-reaching changes in administration. Lord Dalhousie, upon his appointment as governor-general in 1848, immediately began annexing what had been independent princely domains and stripping native aristocrats of their privileges. Swallowing one princely state after another, the British removed their former allies.

The government also decided to collect taxes directly from peasants, displacing the landed nobles as intermediaries. In disarming the landed nobility, the British threw the retainers and militia of the notables into unemployment, and by demanding high taxes from peasants, the British forced them to rely on moneylenders, who could take ownership of land when peasant proprietors failed to pay. Meanwhile, the company transferred judicial authority to an administration that was insulated from the Indian social hierarchy.

The most prized object for annexation was the kingdom of Awadh in northern India (see Map 16.5). Founded in 1722 by an Iranian adventurer, it was one of the first successor states to have gained a measure of independence from the Mughal ruler in Delhi. With access to the fertile resources of the Ganges Plain, its opulent court in Lucknow was one place where Mughal splendor still survived. In 1765, the company imposed a treaty on Awadh under which the ruler paid an annual tribute for British troops stationed in his territory to "protect" his kingdom from internal and external enemies.

Analyzing Global Developments

Alternative Movements in Asia and Africa

During the nineteenth century, five uprisings of global significance occurred in Africa and Asia, two of which were carried out on a massive scale (the Taiping Rebellion and the Indian Rebellion of 1857) while the other three involved much smaller numbers. The two large-scale uprisings did not last as long as the three movements in sub-Saharan Africa and the Arabian Peninsula and were put down with great loss of life. In contrast, the Wahhabi revolt in the Arabian Peninsula, Shaka's Zulu state in southern Africa, and the Fulani revolt in northern Nigeria were immensely successful right from the start, and their political and cultural successes can be seen clearly even to this day.

QUESTIONS FOR ANALYSIS

- How would you assess the influence of Europe on the uprisings discussed in this chapter and their role in shaping the outcomes?
- Although all five movements suffered stinging military defeats (the Fulani at the hands of the British in 1900, the Zulu state at the hands of the British in 1878, the Wahhabis at the hands of Egyptian troops at the beginning of the nineteenth century, the Taiping rebels at the hands of the Qing rulers, and the Indian rebels by British soldiers), were their long-term consequences markedly different?
- Is there anything that holds these diverse movements together and allows us to represent them as alternatives to the main developments under way in western Europe and North America, where rapid economic growth, nationhood, and the beginnings of democracy came to the fore?

Explore Further

William Dalrymple, *The Last Mughal: The Fall of a Dynasty: Delhi, 1857* (2007).

Carolyn Hamilton (ed.), *The Mfecane Aftermath: Reconstructive Debates in Southern African History* (1995).

Mervyn Hiskett, *The Sword of Truth: The Life and Times of the Shehu Usman dan Fodio* (1994).

Jonathan Spence, *God's Chinese Son: The Taiping Heavenly Kingdom of Hong Xiuquan* (1996).

MOVEMENT/LEADER	SHORT-TERM CONSEQUENCES	LONG-TERM CONSEQUENCES
Smaller-Scale Uprisings		
The Fulani Revolt Northern Nigeria (1804–1817) Usman dan Fodio (1754–1817)	• Created largest state in sub-Saharan Africa • Occupied two-thirds of present day Nigeria • British conquered it in early twentieth century	• Gained independence in 1960 • Fulani elite families who worked with British now rule over present-day Nigeria
Shaka's Zulu State Shaka (1787–1828)	• Created an army of 40,000 warriors • Created Zulu State covering 11,500 sq. miles in South Africa	• British conquered Zulu in 1878 • Zulu maintained their identity through apartheid • Population of 11 million today
The Wahhabi Rebellion Arabian Peninsula (1744–1818) Ibn Abd al-Wahhab (1703–1792)	• Ruled over much of the Arabian Peninsula • Defeated by Egyptian army in 1812	• Created the House of Saud, which rules over Saudi Arabia today • Retains commitment to Wahhab principles today
Larger-Scale Uprisings		
The Taiping Rebellion (1851–1864) Hong Xiuquan (1813–1864)	• Half a million members • Leader Hong and rebels ruled over central and southern China from Nanjing for 11 years	• Rebellion caused 20 million deaths by 1853 • Nearly toppled Qing Dynasty Mao viewed it as precursor to peasant-led Communist movement. Now viewed as threat to social order due to large-scale violence
The Indian Rebellion (1857–1858) Geographic Leaders, no monolithic figure	• Indian sepoys of East India Company started • Sepoys pledged support to Mughal emperor • Revolt included sepoys, peasants, small landholders; and religious leaders across north India	• British crown ended company rule after suppressing rebellion brutally • Laid the foundation for later Indian populist and nationalist resistance

Treaty Violations and Annexation In 1856, citing misgovernment and deterioration in law and order, the East India Company violated its treaty obligations and sent its troops to Lucknow to take control of the province. Nawab Wajid Ali Shah, the poet-king of Awadh, whom the British saw as weak and immoral, refused to sign the treaty ceding control to the British.

The annexation of princely domains and the abolition of feudal privileges formed part of the developing practices of European imperialism. To the policy of annexation, Dalhousie added an ambitious program of building railroads, telegraph lines, and a postal network to unify the disjointed territory into a single "network of iron sinew" under British control. Dalhousie saw these infrastructures as key to developing India into a productive colony—a supplier of raw materials for British industry, and a market for its manufactures.

A year after Dalhousie's departure in 1856, India went up in flames. The spark that ignited the simmering discontent into a furious rebellion—the Rebellion of 1857—was the "greased cartridge" controversy. At the end of 1856, the British army, which consisted of many Hindu and Muslim recruits (sepoys) commanded by British officers, introduced the new Enfield rifle to replace the old-style musket. To load the rifle, soldiers had to bite the cartridge open. Although manufacturing instructions stated that linseed oil and beeswax be used to grease the cartridge, a rumor circulated that cow and pig fat had been used. Biting into cartridges greased with animal fat meant violating the Hindu and Muslim sepoys' religious traditions. The sepoys became convinced that there was a plot afoot to defile them and to compel their conversion to Christianity. So a wave of rebellion spread among the 270,000 Indian soldiers, who greatly outnumbered the 40,000 British soldiers employed to rule over 200 million Indians.

Rebellion Breaks Out The mutiny broke out on May 10, 1857, at the military barracks in Meerut. The revolt soon turned from a limited military mutiny into a widespread civil rebellion that involved peasants, artisans, day laborers, and religious leaders. While the insurgents did not eliminate the power of the East India Company, which managed to retain the loyalty of princes and landed aristocrats in some places, they did throw the

The Indian Sepoys Pictured here are Indian soldiers, or sepoys, who were armed, drilled, and commanded by British officers. The sepoys were drawn from indigenous groups that the British considered to be "martial races." This photograph shows the Sikhs, designated as one such "race."

MAP 16.5 | Indian Rebellion of 1857

The Indian Rebellion of 1857 broke out first among the Indian soldiers of the British army. Other groups soon joined the struggle.

- According to this map, how many centers of rebellion were located in British territory and how many in dependent states?

- Why do you think the rebellion occurred in the interior of the subcontinent rather than along the coasts?

- In what way was the company's expansion into formerly autonomous areas during the first half of the nineteenth century a factor in the rebellion?

company into a crisis. Before long, the mutineers in Delhi issued a proclamation declaring that because the British were determined to destroy the religion of both Hindus and Muslims, it was the duty of the wealthy and the privileged to support the rebellion. To promote Hindu-Muslim unity, rebel leaders asked Muslims to refrain from killing cows in deference to Hindu sentiments.

Although the dispossessed aristocracy and petty landholders led the rebellion, leaders also appeared from the lower classes. Bakht Khan, who had been a junior noncommissioned officer in the British army, became commander-in-chief of the rebel forces in Delhi, replacing one of the Mughal emperor's sons. And Devi Singh, a wealthy peasant, set himself up as a peasant king. Dressed in yellow, the insignia of Hindu royalty, he constituted a government of his own, modeling it on the British administration. While his imitation of company rule showed his respect for the British bureaucracy, he defied British authority by leading an armed peasantry against the hated local moneylenders. The call to popular forces also marked the rebel career of Maulavi Ahmadullah Shah, a Muslim theologian. He stood at the head of the rebel forces in Lucknow, leading an army composed primarily of ordinary soldiers and people from the lower orders. Claiming to be an "Incarnation of the Deity," and thus inspired by divine will, he emerged as a prophetic leader of the common people. He voiced his undying hatred of the British in religious terms, calling on Hindus and Muslims to destroy British rule and warning his followers against betrayal by landed authorities.

Participation by the Peasantry The presence of popular leadership points to the important role of the lower classes. Although feudal chieftains often brought them into the rebellion, the peasantry made it their own. The organizing principle of their uprising was the common experience of oppression. Thus, they destroyed anything that represented the authority of the company: prisons, factories, police posts, railway stations, European bungalows, and law courts. Equally significant, the peasantry attacked native moneylenders and local power-holders who were seen as benefiting from company rule.

Vigorous and militant as the popular rebellion was, it was limited in its territorial and ideological horizons. To begin with, the uprisings were local in scale and vision. Peasant rebels attacked the closest seats of administration and sought to settle scores with their most immediate and visible oppressors. They generally did not carry their action beyond the village or collection of villages. Their loyalties remained intensely local, based on village attachments and religious, caste, and clan ties. Nor did popular militants seek to undo traditional hierarchies of caste and religion.

British Response Convinced that the rebellion was the result of plotting by a few troublemakers, the British reacted with brutal vengeance. Villages were torched, and rebels were tied to cannons and blown to bits to teach Indians a lesson in power.

By July 1858, the vicious campaign to restore British control had achieved its goal. Yet, in August, the British Parliament abolished company rule and the company itself, and transferred responsibility for the governing of India to the crown. In November, Queen Victoria issued a proclamation guaranteeing religious toleration, promising improvements, and allowing Indians to serve in the government. She promised to honor the treaties and agreements with princes and chiefs and to refrain from interfering in religious matters. The insurgents had risen up not as a nation, but as a multitude of communities acting independently; their determination to find a new order shocked the British and threw them into a panic. Having crushed the uprising, the British resumed the work of transforming India into a modern colonial state and economy. But the desire for radical alternatives and traditions of popular insurgency, though vanquished, did not vanish.

Conclusion

The nineteenth century was a time of turmoil and transformation. While powerful forces reconfigured the world as a place for capitalism, colonialism, and nation-states, so too did prophets, charismatic leaders, radicals, peasant rebels, and anticolonial insurgents arise to offer alternatives. Reflecting local circumstances and traditions, the struggles of these men and women for a different future opened up spaces for the ideas and activities of lower classes.

Conventional historical accounts either neglect these struggles or fail to view them as a whole. These individuals were not just romantic, last-ditch resisters, as some scholars have argued. Even after defeat, their messages remained alive within their communities. Nor were their actions isolated and atypical events, for when viewed on a global scale they bring to light a world that looks very different from the one that became dominant. To see the Wahhabi movement in the Arabian Peninsula together with the Shawnee Prophet in North America, the utopians and radicals in Europe with the peasant insurgents in British India, and the Taiping rebels with the Mayans in the Yucatan is to glimpse a world of marginalized regions and groups. It was a world that more powerful groups endeavored to suppress but could not erase.

In this world, prophets and rebel leaders usually cultivated power and prestige locally; the emergence of an alternative political or social movement in one region did not impinge on communities and political organizations in others. As much as these individuals had in common, they envisioned widely different kinds of futures. Even Karl Marx, who called the workers of the world to unite, was acutely aware that the call for a proletarian revolution applied only to the industrialized countries of Europe. Other dissenters had even more localized horizons. A world fashioned by movements for alternatives meant a world with multiple centers and different historical timelines.

What gave force to a different mapping of the world was the fact that common people were at the center of these alternative visions, and their voices, however muted, gained a place on the historical stage. The quest for various forms of equality defined efforts to reconstitute alternative worlds. In Islamic regions, the emphasis on equality in revitalization movements was evident in their mobilization of all Muslims, not just the elites. Likewise, charismatic military leaders in Africa, for all their use of raw power, used the framework of community to build new polities. The Taiping Rebellion distinguished itself by seeking to establish an equal society of men and women in service of the Heavenly Kingdom. Operating under very different conditions, European radicals imagined a society free from aristocratic privileges and bourgeois property. Anticolonial rebels and insurgents depended on local solidarities and proposed alternative moral communities. In so doing, these movements compelled ruling elites to adjust the way they governed. The next chapter explores this challenge.

After You Read This Chapter

FOCUS ON: *Regional Variations in Alternative Visions*

EUROPE

- European socialists and radicals envision a world free of exploitation and inequalities, while nationalists work to create new independent nation-states.

THE AMERICAS

- Native American prophets in the United States imagine a world restored to its customary ways and traditional rites.

- Mayans in the Yucatan defy the central Mexican government in a rebellion known as the Caste War.

THE ISLAMIC WORLD AND AFRICA

- Revivalist movements in the Arabian Peninsula and West Africa demand a return to traditional Islam.

- A charismatic warrior, Shaka, creates a powerful state in southern Africa.

SEMI-COLONIAL CHINA

- An inspired prophetic figure, Hong Xiuquan, leads the Taiping Rebellion against the Qing dynasty and European encroachment on China.

COLONIAL INDIA

- Indian troops mutiny against the British and attempt to restore Mughal rule.

CHRONOLOGY

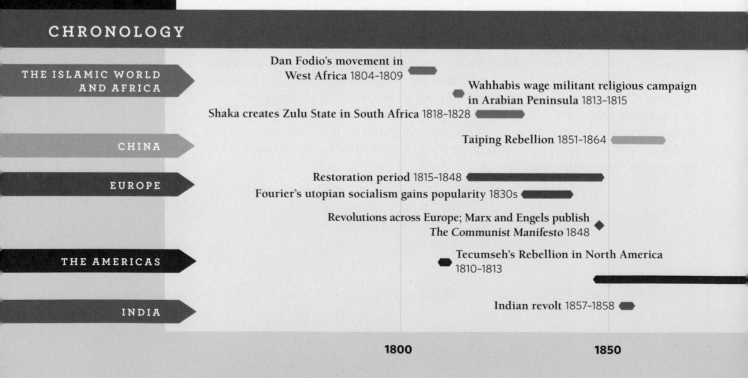

	1800	1850
THE ISLAMIC WORLD AND AFRICA	Dan Fodio's movement in West Africa 1804–1809 · Shaka creates Zulu State in South Africa 1818–1828	Wahhabis wage militant religious campaign in Arabian Peninsula 1813–1815
CHINA		Taiping Rebellion 1851–1864
EUROPE	Restoration period 1815–1848 · Fourier's utopian socialism gains popularity 1830s	Revolutions across Europe; Marx and Engels publish The Communist Manifesto 1848
THE AMERICAS	Tecumseh's Rebellion in North America 1810–1813	
INDIA		Indian revolt 1857–1858

- *Thinking about Exchange Networks and Alternative Visions* How did people around the world respond to the major changes of the French, American, and Industrial Revolutions? What difference did proximity to the European and American "core" make?

- *Thinking about Changing Power Relationships and Alternative Visions* What kind of challenges did the new order provoke? What kinds of traditions did those challenges draw on, and what kind of success did they have?

- *Thinking about Gender and Alternative Visions* Describe the role women played in millenarian protest movements during the nineteenth century, and explain the significance of gender to those movements.

1. Describe the global order that emerged in the nineteenth century, and identify its core values.

2. Explain the goals of Islamic revitalization movements such as **Wahhabism** in the Arabian Peninsula and **Usman dan Fodio's** movement in West Africa. How were these regions affected by the new world order? What alternative did Islamic revitalization propose?

3. Compare the **millenarian** aspirations of the **Taiping Rebellion**, and the Shawnee rebellion of **Tenskwatawa**.

4. Compare the role of state centralization in the *Mfecane movement* and the **Caste War** in the Yucatan, Mexico.

5. Explain the relationship between **liberalism**, **utopian socialism**, and **Marxism**.

Caste War in Yucatan, Mexico 1847-1901
Ghost Dance movement in North America 1889-1890

Competing Perspectives

Envisioning Alternatives to Nineteenth-Century Capitalism

While European capitalism and colonialism drove transformative changes in the nineteenth century, protest movements around the world envisioned a future based on other values. These selections provide radically different visions for the future—different from European capitalism and colonialism, and different from one another. In the first decade of the nineteenth century, the Shawnee Native American leader Tenskwatawa recalled an earlier, happier time for the Native American peoples of the United States's Great Lakes and Ohio Valley, a time before the arrival of the Europeans. In the passage below, Tenskwatawa urges people to spurn the ways of white Americans and return to the authentic, pure ways of a precolonial past. The Islamic scholar and poet Nana Asma'u was the daughter of Usman dan Fodio, the leader of the Fulani revolt in northern Nigeria. Many of her poems conveyed religious inspiration and demonstrated how much the Fulani revolt was inspired by the life and message of the Prophet Muhammad.

Europeans also envisioned alternatives to the dominant capitalist system. In January 1848, Karl Marx and Friedrich Engels prepared a party program for the Communist League, a German worker's association. Published in February 1848, *The Communist Manifesto* foretold the inevitable overthrow of bourgeois-dominated capitalism by the working classes and the transition to socialism.

In Asia like the Americas, protest movements invoked ideas of cultural purity to challenge Western influence. Inspired by their understanding of Christianity, the Taiping leadership confronted the central role of the family and ancestral worship in Chinese society by urging all its followers to regard themselves as belonging to a single family in this excerpt from 1854. They also advocated the segregation of the sexes, despite striving to improve women's lives in other ways. The Indian leaders of the rebellion of 1857 issued numerous proclamations. Bahadur Shah issued the Azamgarh Proclamation in August 1857 on behalf of the rebels who had seized the garrison town of Azamgarh, sixty miles north of Benares. The proclamation attacks the British for subverting Indian traditions and calls on the rebellion's followers to restore the pre-British order—in this case, the Mughal Empire.

PRIMARY SOURCE 16.1

Visions of the Great Good Spirit (1810), Tenskwatawa

Our Creator put us on this wide, rich land, and told us we were free to go where the game was, where the soil was good for planting. That was our state of true happiness. We did not have to beg for anything. Our Creator had taught us how to find and make everything we needed, from trees and plants and animals and stone. We lived in bark, and we wore only the skins of animals.

Thus were we created. Thus we lived for a long time, proud and happy. We had never eaten pig meat, nor tasted the poison called whiskey, nor worn wool from sheep, nor struck fire or dug earth with steel, nor cooked in iron, nor hunted and fought with loud guns, nor ever had diseases which soured our blood or rotted our organs. We were pure, so we were strong and happy.

For many years we traded furs to the English or the French, for wool blankets and guns and iron things, for steel awls and needles and axes, for mirrors, for pretty things made of beads and silver. And for liquor. This was foolish, but we did not know it. We shut our ears to the Great Good Spirit. We did not want to hear that we were being foolish.

But now those things of the white men have corrupted us, and made us weak and needful. Our men forgot how to hunt without noisy guns. Our women don't want to make fire without steel, or cook without iron, or sew without metal awls and needles, or fish without steel hooks. Some look in those mirrors all the time, and no longer teach their daughters to make leather or render bear oil. We learned to need the white men's goods, and so now a People who never had to beg for anything must beg for everything! . . .

And that is why Our Creator purified me and sent me down to you full of the shining power, to make you what you were before!

No red man must ever drink liquor, or he will go and have the hot lead poured in his mouth! . . .

Do not eat any food that is raised or cooked by a white person. It is not good for us. Eat not their bread made of wheat, for Our Creator gave us corn for our bread. . . .

The Great Good Spirit wants our men to hunt and kill game as in the ancient days, with the silent arrow and the lance and the snare, and no longer with guns.

If we hunt in the old ways, we will not have to depend upon white men, for new guns and powder and lead, or go to them to have broken guns repaired. Remember it is the wish of the Great Good Spirit that we have no more commerce with white men! . . .

Our Creator told me that all red men who refuse to obey these laws are bad people, or witches, and must be put to death. . . .

The Great Good Spirit will appoint a place to be our holy town, and at that place I will call all red men to come and share this shining power. For the People in all tribes are corrupt and miserable! In that holy town we will pray every morning and every night for the earth to be fruitful, and the game and fish to be plentiful again.

Source: Words of Tenskwatawa, in *Messages and Letters of William Henry Harrison*, edited by Logan Esarey (Indianapolis: Indiana Historical Commission, 1922).

PRIMARY SOURCE 16.2

A Female Muslim Voice in Africa (1838–39), Nana Asma'u

I give thanks to the King of Heaven, the One God. I invoke blessings on the Prophet and set down my poem.

The Lord made Heaven and earth and created all things, sent prophets to enlighten mankind.

Believe in them for your own sake, learn from them and be saved, believe in and act upon their sayings.

I invoke blessings on the Prophet who brought the Book, the Qur'an: he brought the *hadith* to complete the enlightenment.

Muslim scholars have explained knowledge and used it, following in the footsteps of the Prophet.

It is my intention to set down Bello's characteristics and explain his ways.

For I wish to assuage my loneliness, requite my love, find peace of mind through my religion.

These are his characteristics: he was learned in all branches of knowledge and feared God in public and in private.

He obeyed religious injunctions and distanced himself from forbidden things: this is what is known about him.

He concentrated on understanding what is right to know about the Oneness of God.

He preached to people and instructed them about God: he caused them to long for Paradise.

He set an example in his focus on eternal values: he strove to end oppression and sin.

He upheld the *shari'a*, honored it, implemented it aright, that was his way, everyone knows.

And he made his views known to those who visited him: he said to them "Follow the *shari'a*, which is sacred."

He eschewed worldly things and discriminated against anything of ill repute; he was modest and a repository of useful knowledge.

He was exceedingly level-headed and generous, he enjoyed periods of quietude: but was energetic when he put his hand to things.

He was thoughtful, calm, a confident statesman, and quick-witted.

He honored people's status: he could sort out difficulties and advise those who sought his help.

He had nothing to do with worldly concerns, but tried to restore to a healthy state things which he could. These were his characteristics.

He never broke promises, but faithfully kept them: he sought out righteous things. Ask and you will hear.

He divorced himself entirely from bribery and was totally scrupulous: He flung back at the givers money offered for titles.

One day Garange [chief of Mafora] sent him a splendid gift, but Bello told the messenger Zitaro to take it back.

He said to the envoy who had brought the bribe, "Have nothing to do with forbidden things."

And furthermore he said, "Tell him that the gift was sent for unlawful purposes; it is wrong to respond to evil intent."

He was able to expedite matters: he facilitated learning, commerce, and defense, and encouraged everything good.

He propagated good relationships between different tribes and between kinsmen. He afforded protection; everyone knows this.

When strangers came he met them, and taught about religious matters, explaining things: he tried to enlighten them.

He lived in a state of preparedness, he had his affairs in order and had an excellent intelligence service.

He had nothing to do with double agents and said it was better to ignore them, for they pervert Islamic principles.

He was a very pleasant companion to friends and acquaintances: he was intelligent, with a lively mind.

He fulfilled promises and took care of affairs, but he did not act hastily.

He shouldered responsibilities and patiently endured adversities.

He was watchful and capable of restoring to good order matters which had gone wrong.

He was resourceful and could undo mischief, no matter how serious, because he was a man of ideas.

He was gracious to important people and was hospitable to all visitors, including non-Muslims.

He drew good people close to him and distanced himself from people of ill repute.

Those are his characteristics. I have recounted a few examples that are sufficient to provide a model for emulation and benefit.

May God forgive him and have mercy on him: May we be united with him in Paradise, the place we aspire to.

For the sake of the Prophet, the Compassionate, who was sent with mercy to mankind.

May God pour blessings on the Prophet and his kinsmen and all other followers.

May God accept this poem. I have concluded it in the year 1254 AH [after *hijra*, the Muslim dating system].

Source: "Gikku Bello" from *One Woman's Jihad: Nana Asma'u, Scholar and Scribe* by Beverly B. Mack and Jean Boyd. Copyright © 2000 by Beverly B. Mack and Jean Boyd. Reprinted by permission of Indiana University Press.

Bourgeoisie and Proletariat (1848), Karl Marx and Friedrich Engels

A spectre is haunting Europe—the spectre of Communism. . . .

The history of all hitherto existing society is the history of class struggles.

Freeman and slave, patrician and plebian, lord and serf, guild-master and journeyman, in a word, oppressor and oppressed, stood in constant opposition to one another, carried on an uninterrupted, now hidden, now open fight, a fight that each time ended, either in a revolutionary re-constitution of society at large, or in the common ruin of the contending classes.

In the earlier epochs of history, we find almost everywhere a complicated arrangement of society into various orders, a manifold gradation of social rank. In ancient Rome we have patricians, knights, plebeians, slaves; in the Middle Ages, feudal lords, vassals, guild-masters, journeymen, apprentices, serfs; in almost all of these classes, again, subordinate gradations. . . .

Our epoch, the epoch of the bourgeoisie, possesses, however, this distinctive feature: it has simplified the class antagonisms: Society as a whole is more and more splitting up into two great hostile camps, into two great classes directly facing each other: Bourgeoisie and Proletariat. . . .

The bourgeoisie . . . has put an end to all feudal, patriarchal, idyllic relations. It has pitilessly torn asunder the motley feudal ties that bound man to his "natural superiors," and has left remaining no other nexus between man and man than naked self-interest, than callous "cash payment. . . ."

The bourgeoisie cannot exist without constantly revolutionizing the instruments of production, and thereby the relations of production, and with them the whole relations of society. . . . Constant revolutionizing of the production, uninterrupted disturbance of all social conditions, everlasting uncertainty and agitation distinguish the bourgeois epoch from all earlier ones. All fixed, fast-frozen relations, with their train of ancient and venerable prejudices and opinions, are swept away. . . .

The need of a constantly expanding market for its products chases the bourgeoisie over the whole surface of the globe. It must nestle everywhere, settle everywhere, establish connexions everywhere. . . .

The bourgeoisie, by the rapid improvement of all instruments of production, by the immensely facilitated means of communication, draws all, even the most barbarian, nations into civilisation. The cheap prices of its commodities are the heavy artillery with which it batters down all Chinese walls, with which it forces the barbarians' intensely obstinate hatred of foreigners to capitulate. . . .

The weapons with which the bourgeoisie felled feudalism to the ground are now turned against the bourgeoisie itself.

But not only has the bourgeoisie forged the weapons that bring death to itself; it has also called into existence the men who are to wield those weapons—the modern working class—the proletarians. . . . These labourers, who must sell themselves piece-meal, are a commodity, like every other article of commerce, and are consequently exposed to all the vicissitudes of competition, to all the fluctuations of the market. . . .

But with the development of industry the proletariat not only increases in number; it becomes concentrated in greater masses, its strength grows, and it feels that strength more. . . . Thereupon the workers begin to form combinations (Trades Unions) against the bourgeois; they club together in order to keep up the rate of wages; they found permanent associations in order to make provision beforehand for these occasional revolts. Here and there the contest breaks out into riots.

Now and then the workers are victorious, but only for a time. The real fruit of their battles lies, not in the immediate result, but in the ever-expanding union of the workers. . . .

What the bourgeoisie, therefore, produces, above all, is its own grave-diggers. Its fall and the victory of the proletariat are equally inevitable.

Source: Karl Marx and Friedrich Engels, *The Communist Manifesto,* in *The Marx-Engels Reader,* 2nd ed., edited by Robert C. Tucker (New York: W. W. Norton and Company, 1978), pp. 473–83, 490–91, 500.

The Principles of the Heavenly Nature (1854), Taiping Heavenly Kingdom

We brothers and sisters, enjoying today the greatest mercy of our Heavenly Father, have become as one family and are able to enjoy true blessings; each of us must always be thankful. Speaking in terms of our ordinary human feelings, it is true that each has his own parents and there must be a distinction in family names; it is also true that as each has his own household, there must be a distinction between this boundary and that boundary.

Yet we must know that the ten thousand names derive from the one name, and the one name from one ancestor. Thus our origins are not different. Since our Heavenly Father gave us birth and nourishment, we are of one form though of separate bodies, and we breathe the same air though in different places. This is why we say, "All are brothers within the four seas." Now, basking in the profound mercy of Heaven, we are of one family. . . .

We brothers, our minds having been awakened by our Heavenly Father, joined the camp in the earlier days to support our Sovereign, many bringing parents, wives, uncles, brothers, and whole families. It is a matter of course that we should attend to our parents and look after our wives and children, but when one first creates a new rule, the state must come first and the family last, public interests first and private interests last.

Moreover, as it is advisable to avoid suspicion [of improper conduct] between the inner [female] and the outer [male] and to distinguish between male and female, so men must have male quarters and women must have female quarters; only thus can we be dignified and avoid confusion. There must be no common mixing of the male and female groups, which would cause debauchery and violation of Heaven's commandments. Although to pay respects to parents and to visit wives and children occasionally are in keeping with human nature and not prohibited, yet it is only proper to converse before the door, stand a few steps apart and speak in a loud voice; one must not enter the sisters' camp or permit the mixing of men and women. Only thus, by complying with rules and commands, can we become sons and daughters of Heaven.

Source: *The Principles of the Heavenly Nature*, in *Sources of Chinese Tradition*, 2nd ed., vol. 2, compiled by Wm. Theodore de Bary and Richard Lufrano (New York: Columbia University Press, 2000), pp. 229–30.

PRIMARY SOURCE 16.5

The Azamgarh Proclamation (1857), Bahadur Shah

It is well known to all, that in this age the people of Hindoostan, both Hindoos and Mohammedans, are being ruined under the tyranny and oppression of the infidel and treacherous English. It is therefore the bounden duty of all the wealthy people of India, especially of those who have any sort of connection with any of the Mohammedan royal families, and are considered the pastors and masters of their people, to stake their lives and property for the well being of the public. . . .

Several of the Hindoo and Mussalman chiefs, who have long since quitted their homes for the preservation of their religion, and have been trying their best to root out the English in India, have presented themselves to me, and taken part in the reigning Indian crusade. . . . Parties anxious to participate in the common cause, but having no means to provide for themselves, shall receive their daily subsistence from me;

and be it known to all, that the ancient works, both of the Hindoos and the Mohammedans, the writings of the miracle-workers and the calculations of the astrologers, pundits, and rammals, all agree in asserting that the English will no longer have any footing in India or elsewhere. . . .

Section I—Regarding Zemindars [large landholders, responsible for collecting land taxes for the government]. It is evident, that the British Government in making zemindary settlements have imposed exorbitant *Jumas* [revenue assessments], and have disgraced and ruined several zemindars. . . . Such extortions will have no manner of existence in the Badshahi Government; but on the contrary, the *Jumas* will be light, the dignity and honour of the zemindars safe, and every zemindar will have absolute rule in his own zemindary. . . .

Section II—Regarding Merchants. It is plain that the infidel and treacherous British Government have monopolized the trade of all the fine and valuable merchandise, such as indigo, cloth, and other articles of shipping, leaving only the trade of trifles to the people, and even in this they are not without their share of the profits, which they secure by means of customs and stamp fees, &c. in money suits, so that the people have merely a trade in name. . . . When the Badshahi Government is established, all these aforesaid fraudulent practices shall be dispensed with, and the trade of every article, without exception, both by land and water, shall be open to the native merchants of India. . . .

Section IV—Regarding Artisans. It is evident that the Europeans, by the introduction of English articles into India, have thrown the weavers, the cotton dressers, the carpenters, the blacksmiths, and the shoemakers, &c., out of employ, and have engrossed their occupations, so that every description of native artisan has been reduced to beggary. But under the Badshahi Government the native artisan will exclusively be employed in the services of the kings, the rajahs, and the rich. . . .

Section V—Regarding Pundits, Fakirs and other learned persons. The pundits and fakirs being the guardians of the Hindoo and Mohammedan religions respectively, and the Europeans being the enemies of both the religions, and as at present a war is raging against the English on account of religion, the pundits and fakirs are bound to present themselves to me, and take their share in the holy war.

Source: "Proclamation of Emperor Bahadur Shah," in *India in 1857: The Revolt against Foreign Rule,* edited by Ainslie T. Embree (Delhi: Chanakya Publications, 1987), pp. 3–6.

QUESTIONS FOR ANALYSIS

1. Identify the values and assumptions that all of these documents share.

2. Explain the relationship between internal and external forces in each document. To what degree do the authors blame broad changes affecting their communities from the outside? To what degree do they identify the most pressing problems as internal to their communities and as deviations from authentic traditions?

3. Analyze the role commodities play in these documents.

4. Explain the significance of the ideas of "barbarism" and "civilization" in these documents. How are they defined, whether implicitly or explicitly? How does each document mark the boundaries of its community?

Interpreting Visual Evidence

The Gender of Nations

Nations are abstractions. They have no material form. The scholar Benedict Anderson famously referred to them as "imagined communities," groups of people who have never met, who may not even speak the same language or worship the same god(s), and yet who come to think of themselves as sharing something profound in common, such as being an American, or an Egyptian, or Chinese. In order to create this sort of community, nationalists have had to represent their nations visually, often in human form and more often as women than as men. For every John Bull (England) or Uncle Sam (the United States), there were several Mariannes (France) or Ranis of Jhansi (India). Especially in areas where few people could read, images and iconography played a vital role in spreading the idea of nationalism to the masses.

The attributes of the chosen figures provide insight into different nationalist movements. The figures' ties to real or invented historical traditions often reflect how these movements defined themselves in opposition to established authorities. In the first image, *Liberty Leading the People* (1830), the French Romantic painter Eugène Delacroix represents a barefoot, bare-chested woman, Marianne, leading a cross-class group of rebels against King Charles X. She wears a Phrygian bonnet, which had become popular during the Revolution of 1789–1799. Influenced by Delacroix, the Brazilian painter Manoel Lopes Rodrigues painted the *Efígie da República* (1896), which soon became a symbol for the newly formed First Brazilian Republic (1889–1930). In the 1890s, an Egyptian Jew named Ya'qub Sanu'a published a nationalist journal in Paris called *Abu Naddara*, which helped introduce Egypt to cartoons. In one issue he presents a veiled Egypt, with France and Russia by her side, confronting Great Britain. Finally, the Rani of Jhansi was the queen of the Maratha-ruled state of Jhansi in the north-central part of India and a leading figure in the rebellion of 1857. She later became a nationalist icon, as the twentieth-century watercolor here illustrates, as a symbol of heroic resistance against the British.

Delacroix, *Liberty Leading the People*.

Rodrigues, *Efígie da República*.

Sanu'a, cartoon in *Abu Naddara*.

The Rani of Jhansi.

QUESTIONS FOR ANALYSIS

1. Why do you think nationalists in all of these countries, unlike those in Great Britain and the United States, used female symbols for the nation? What kind of established political authority did they challenge, and how did that challenge differ from the British and American cases?

2. Why do you think Rodrigues, like other artists around the world, borrowed French imagery so explicitly? What does that tell us about Brazilian politics, the challenges the Brazilian people faced, and their reservoirs of strength?

3. Why do you think Sanu'a, a cosmopolitan liberal who had criticized the subordination of women, presented Egypt as a fully covered, veiled woman? To whom do you think he was appealing?

4. To what extent does the image of the Rani of Jhansi look backward and invoke history, at least implicitly? To what extent does it look forward and make claims about the nature of contemporary India?

Before You Read This Chapter

GLOBAL STORYLINES

- Nation-state building and imperial expansion change the map of the world.
- Industrialization, science, and technology enable states in North America and western Europe—and, to a lesser extent, Japan—to overpower other regions politically, militarily, and economically.
- European, American, and Japanese imperialists encounter significant opposition in Africa and Asia.

CORE OBJECTIVES

- **IDENTIFY** the institutions that enabled elites in western Europe, the Americas, and Japan to consolidate nation-states, and **ANALYZE** the degree to which they succeeded during this period.
- **EXPLAIN** the roles that industrialization, science, and technology played in the expansion of powerful states into the rest of the world.
- **COMPARE** the reactions to imperialism in Africa and Asia, and **EVALUATE** how effective these responses were.
- **ANALYZE** the extent to which colonies contributed to the wealth and political strength of the nation-states that controlled them.

CHAPTER 17

Nations and Empires

1850–1914

In 1895, the Cuban patriot José Martí launched a rebellion against the last Spanish holdings in the Americas. The anti-Spanish struggle continued until 1898, when Spain withdrew from Cuba and Puerto Rico. Martí hoped to bring freedom to a new Cuban nation and equality to all Cubans. But even as he helped secure freedom from the declining Spanish empire, he could not prevent military occupation and political domination of Cuba by the world's newest imperial power, the United States. Martí's hopes and frustrations found parallels around the world.

After 1850, the building of nation-states in Europe, the Americas, and Oceania and the expansion of their empires changed the map of the world, exhilarating some peoples and frustrating others. Those who benefited most were Europeans and peoples of European descent. During these decades the nation-states of Europe, now locked in intense political and economic rivalry, projected their power across the entire world. Much of the rivalry among European states intensified through disruptions in the European balance of power, caused by the unification of two new states (Italy and Germany). Across the Atlantic, the United States abandoned its anticolonial origins and annexed overseas possessions. Yet imperial expansion did not go unchallenged. It encountered resistance from communities being incorporated into the new empires. In Asia and Africa resisters struggled to repel their invaders, often demanding the right to govern themselves.

The second half of the nineteenth century witnessed the simultaneous—and entwined—advance of nationalism and imperialism. These decades also saw the further expansion of industrialization. Taken together, the era's political and economic developments allowed western Europe and the United States to attain primacy in world affairs. But tensions inside these states and their empires, as well as within other states, made the new world order anything but stable.

Consolidating Nations and Constructing Empires

COMPARISON

IDENTIFY the institutions that enabled elites in western Europe, the Americas, and Japan to consolidate nation-states.

During the second half of the nineteenth century, the idea of building nation-states engulfed the globe, and nationalism became closely linked to imperialism. Enlightenment thinkers had emphasized the importance of nations, defined as peoples who shared a common past, territory, culture, and traditions. To many people it seemed natural that once absolutist rulers had fallen, governments should draw their power and legitimacy from those who lived within their borders and that the body of institutions governing each territory should be uniquely concerned with promoting the welfare of that particular people. This seemed such a natural process that little thought was given to the relationship between "nation" and "state," between the people and their government; national states were simply supposed to well up from the people's longing for liberty and togetherness.

BUILDING NATIONALISM

More often than not, however, local elites created nations. They did so by compelling diverse groups of people and regions to accept a unified network of laws, a central administration, time zones, national markets, and a single regional dialect as the "national" language. To overcome strong regional identities, state administrators broadened public education in the national language and imposed universal military service to build a national army. In this way, dominant elites spread their values and institutions outward to regions throughout each nation and beyond their borders. While a handful of nation-states were already well established in the mid-nineteenth century, two of the most important—Italy and Germany—were newly created in this period, forged through strategic military contests.

EXPANDING THE EMPIRES

The processes of nation building also required the acquisition of new territories, often overseas, a development that was called **imperialism.** Rulers measured national strength not only by their people's unity but also by their economic power and the conquest of new territories. Thus, Germany, France, the United States, Russia, and Japan challenged Britain's leadership in overseas trade by developing their industries and seizing new territories.

Imperial rule facilitated a widespread movement of labor, capital, commodities, and information. As scholars studied previously unknown tribes and races, new schools taught colonized peoples the languages, religions, scientific practices, and cultural traditions of their colonizers. Publications and products from the "mother country" circulated widely among indigenous elites. Yet colonies were seen as subordinate to the mother country and were given little or no representation in home governments. In this sense, nation and empire were in tension with one another.

Expansion and Nation Building in the Americas

Once freed from European control, the elites of the Americas set about creating political communities of their own. By the 1850s they shared a desire both to create widespread loyalty to their political institutions and to expand territorial domains. This also meant finding ways to settle hinterlands that previously belonged to indigenous populations.

Although nation-states took shape throughout the world, the Americas saw the most complete assimilation of new possessions. Instead of treating outlying areas as colonial outposts, American nation-state builders turned them into new provinces. With the help of rifles, railroads, schools, and land surveys, frontiers became staging areas for the expanding populations of North and South American societies. For indigenous peoples, however, such national expansion meant the loss of traditional lands on a vast scale, and many lost lives.

THE UNITED STATES

Military might, diplomacy, and the power of numbers enabled the United States to claim territory that spanned the North American continent (see Map 17.1). At its independence, the new country established a barely united confederation of states. Native American resistance and Spanish and British rivalry hemmed in the Americans of European descent. At the same time, the disunited states threatened to break apart, as questions of states' rights and of slavery versus free labor intruded into national politics. Yet, rallying to the rhetoric of **Manifest Destiny**, which maintained that it was God's will for the United States to "overspread" North America, American whites pushed their territorial claims and boundaries westward. They acquired territories via purchase agreements and treaties with France, Spain, and Britain, and via warfare and treaties with diverse Native American nations and Mexico.

Civil War and States' Rights Westward expansion proved the undoing of the American nation. The question was whether newly acquired lands would be open to slavery or restricted to free labor. Following the 1860 election of Abraham Lincoln, who pledged to halt the expansion of slavery, the United States divided between North and South and plunged into a gruesome Civil War (1861–1865).

The bloody conflict led to the abolition of slavery, and the struggle to extend voting and citizenship rights to male freed slaves qualified the Civil War as a second American Revolution. Abraham Lincoln had promised a new model of freedom for a state reborn out of bloodshed. Its cornerstone would be the incorporation of freed slaves as citizens of the United States. Yet experiments in biracial democracy during the Reconstruction period (1867–1877) were short-lived. In the decades after the Civil War, counter-revolutionary pressure led to the denial of voting rights to African Americans and the restoration of (white, patriarchal) planter rule in the southern states. This pressure was spearheaded by the terrorism of some former Confederates who sought to reverse African Americans' legal and political gains and to restore white planters to power in the South.

COMPARISON

ANALYZE the degree to which elites in the Americas succeeded in consolidating nation-states.

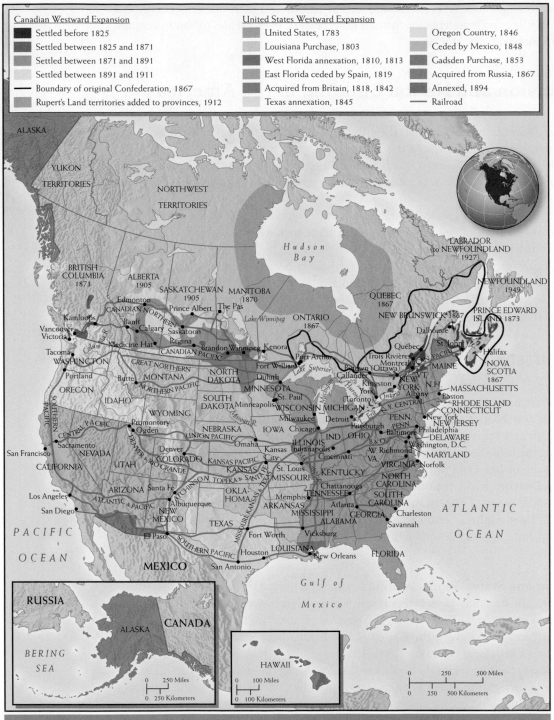

Canadian Westward Expansion
- Settled before 1825
- Settled between 1825 and 1871
- Settled between 1871 and 1891
- Settled between 1891 and 1911
- ⎯⎯ Boundary of original Confederation, 1867
- Rupert's Land territories added to provinces, 1912

United States Westward Expansion
- United States, 1783
- Louisiana Purchase, 1803
- West Florida annexation, 1810, 1813
- East Florida ceded by Spain, 1819
- Acquired from Britain, 1818, 1842
- Texas annexation, 1845
- Oregon Country, 1846
- Ceded by Mexico, 1848
- Gadsden Purchase, 1853
- Acquired from Russia, 1867
- Annexed, 1894
- ⎯⎯ Railroad

MAP 17.1 | U.S. and Canadian Westward Expansion, 1803–1912

Americans and Canadians expanded westward in the second half of the nineteenth century, aided greatly by railways.

- How many railroad lines ultimately reached the western borders of Canada and the United States?

- By what years were the territorial expansions of Canada and the United States complete? How did territorial expansion strengthen Canadian and American nationalism?

- What were the major events that led to the annexation of the western half of the United States?

African American Gains and Losses In the immediate aftermath of the American Civil War, "Radical Republicans" asserted political control by passing laws and constitutional amendments ending slavery, guaranteeing equal rights, and enfranchising freed slaves, known as freedmen. One result was the election of African Americans (*above*) to the U.S. Congress. During the 1870s, however, white leaders retreated from the commitment to black rights, allowing ex-Confederates to reassert control over southern politics. (*Right*) The Ku Klux Klan terrorized African Americans in the post–Civil War South. Klan violence reversed many of the legal and political gains made by freedmen and helped restore planters to power in the South.

Nonetheless, the war brought enduring changes across the United States. The defeat of the South established the preeminence of the national government. After the Civil War, Americans learned to speak of their nation in the singular ("the United States is" in contrast to "the United States are"). With an invigorated nationalism came a stronger national government.

Economic and Industrial Development Even more dizzying were social and economic changes that followed the Civil War. Within ten years of the war's end, the industrial output of the United States had climbed by 75 percent. Americans made such impressive industrial gains that the United States soon joined Britain and Germany atop the list of economic giants.

A potent instrument of capital accumulation appeared at this time—the **limited-liability joint-stock company**. Firms such as Standard Oil and U.S. Steel attracted money from well-to-do investors via a stock market. These investors, called shareholders, in theory owned the company; nonetheless they left the running of these enterprises to paid managers. Intermediaries, like J. Pierpont Morgan, the New York financial giant who became the world's wealthiest man, loaned money and brokered big deals on the New York Stock Exchange. So great were the fortunes amassed by leading financiers and industrialists that by 1890 the richest 1 percent of Americans owned nearly 90 percent of the nation's wealth.

The expansion of railroad lines symbolized American economic and territorial growth. In 1865, the United States boasted 35,000 miles of track. By 1900, nearly 200,000 miles of track connected the Atlantic to the Pacific and crisscrossed the American territory in between. Americans continued their migrations west. Joined by throngs of immigrants from Europe, they were attracted by homestead acts promising nearly free acreage to settlers and by promoters from the railroads.

By now the United States had become a major world power. It boasted an economy that, despite troubles in the 1890s, had expanded rapidly over the last decades of the nineteenth century. It also was a more integrated nation after the Civil War, with an amended constitution that claimed to uphold the equality of all members of the American nation, even those men who were not white. But there was disagreement on what that equality should involve (for example, should it include women as voters?) or how the country would adjust to a new century in which the nation's "destiny" had already been fulfilled.

CANADA

Canadians also built a new nation, enjoyed economic success, and followed an expansionist course. Like the United States, Canada had access to a vast frontier prairie for growing agricultural exports. And as in the United States, these lands became the homes and farms of more European immigrants. However, whereas the United States had waged a war to gain independence, Canada's separation from Britain was peaceful. From the 1830s to the 1860s, Britain gradually passed authority to the colony, leaving Canadians to grapple with the task of creating a shared national community.

Building a Nation Sharp internal divisions made that task especially difficult. For one thing, there was a well-established French population. Wanting to keep their villages, their culture, their religion, and their language intact, these French Canadians did not feel integrated into the emerging Canadian national community. Nor were they eager to join the English-speaking population in settling new areas, lest such migration dilute their French-Canadian presence.

The English-speakers were equally unenthusiastic about creating an independent Canadian state. Fear of being absorbed into the American republic reinforced these Canadians' loyalty to the British crown and made them content with colonial status. Indeed, when Canada finally gained its independence in 1867, it was by an Act of Parliament in London and not by revolution.

Territorial Expansion Lacking cultural and linguistic unity, Canadians used territorial expansion to build an integrated state. In response to the U.S. purchase of Alaska from Russia in 1867 and the movement of settlers onto the American plains, Canadian leaders realized that they had to incorporate their own western territories, lest these, too, fall into American hands.

The Canadian state also faced friction with indigenous peoples. Frontier warfare threatened to drive away investors and settlers, who could always find property south of the border instead. To prevent the kind of bloodletting that characterized the United States' westward expansion, the Canadian government signed treaties with indigenous peoples to ensure strict separation between natives and newcomers.

The Canadian government acquired significant powers to intervene in, regulate, and mediate social conflict between Anglo and French residents, and among both groups and the Native American population. These powers, in fact, were fuller than those of the U.S. government. But even though the state was relatively strong, the sense of a national identity was comparatively weak. Expansionism helped Canada remain an autonomous state, but it did not solve the question of what it meant to belong to a Canadian nation.

LATIN AMERICA

Latin American elites also engaged in nation-state building and expanded their territorial borders. But unlike in the United States and Canada, expansion did not always create homesteader frontiers that could help expand democracy and forge national identities. Instead, civil conflict fractured certain countries in the region (see Chapters 15 and 16), although a few, most notably Brazil and Mexico, remained united.

Much of Latin America shared a common social history. Far more than in North America, the richest lands in Latin America went to large estate holders producing exports such as sugar, coffee, or beef. As a result, privileged elites monopolized power more than in North America's young democracies.

Amerindian and peasant uprisings were a major worry in new Latin American republics. Fearing insurrections, elites devised governing systems that protected private property while limiting the political rights of the poor. Likewise, the specter of slave revolts, driven home not just by earlier, brutal events in Haiti (see Chapter 15) but also by daily rumors of rebellions, kept elites in a state of alarm. Creating strong states, it seemed to many Latin American elites, required excluding large groups of people from power.

Brazil's "Exclusive" Nation-State Brazil illustrates the process by which Latin American rulers built nation-states that excluded much of the population from both the "nation" and the "state." Through the nineteenth century, rulers in Rio de Janeiro defused political conflict by allowing planters to retain the reins of power.

The official prohibition of the slave trade in 1830, coupled with slave resistance, began to choke the planters' system by driving up the price of slaves within the region. Thereafter, Brazilian elites retained some former slaves as gang-workers or sharecroppers (who received tools and seeds in return for a share of the crop), and they also imported new workers—especially from Italy, Spain, and Portugal—as seasonal migrant workers or indentured tenant farmers. Indeed, European and even Japanese migration to Brazil helped planters preserve their holdings in the post-slavery era. In all, 2 million Europeans and some 70,000 Japanese moved to Brazil.

The Brazilian state was deliberately exclusive. As in the United States, elites imposed severe restrictions on suffrage and set rules that reduced political competition. However, given the greater share of the black population in Brazil, restrictions there excluded a larger share of the potential electorate than in the United States.

Brazilian Expansion and Economic Development

Like Canada and the United States, the Brazilian state extended its reach to distant areas and incorporated them as provinces. The largest land-grab occurred in the Amazon River basin, the world's largest drainage watershed and tropical forest. Here, the Brazilian state gave giant concessions to local capitalists to extract rubber latex. When combined with sulfur, rubber was a key raw material for tire manufacturing in European and North American bicycle and automobile industries.

For a time, Brazil became the world's exclusive exporter of rubber; as a result, its planters, merchants, and workers prospered. Rich merchants became lenders and financiers, not only to workers but also to landowners. The mercantile elite of Manaus, the capital of the Amazon region, designed and decorated their city to reflect their new fortunes. Although the streets were still paved with mud, the town's elite built a replica of the Paris Opera House, and Manaus

Opera House in Manaus The turn-of-the-century rubber boom brought immense wealth to the Amazon jungle. As in many boom-and-bust cycles in Latin America, the proceeds flowed to a small elite and diminished when the rubber supply outstripped the demand. But the wealth produced was sufficient to prompt the local elite to build temples of modernity in the midst of the jungle. Pictured here is the Opera House in the rubber capital of Manaus. Like other works built by Latin American elites of the period, this one emulated the original in Paris.

became a regular stopover for European opera singers on the circuit between Buenos Aires and New York. Rubber workers also benefited from the boom. Mostly either Amerindians or mixed-blood people, they sent their wages home to families elsewhere in the Amazon jungle or on the northeastern coast of Brazil.

One problem was the ecosystem. Such a diversified biomass could not tolerate a regimented form of production. Cultivating rubber trees at the expense of other vegetation made the forest vulnerable to nonhuman predators. Leaf blights and ferocious ants destroyed all experiments at creating more sustainable rubber plantations.

The Brazilian rubber boom, moreover, soon went bust. As competition led to increased supplies and reduced prices, Brazilian producers went bankrupt. Merchants called in their loans, landowners forfeited their titles, and rubber workers returned to their small subsistence farms. Tropical vines crept over the Manaus Opera House, and it gradually fell into disrepair.

Throughout the Americas, nineteenth-century elites, working with outdated ideas of who should wield power, nonetheless attempted to satisfy popular demands for inclusion. While the ideal was to construct nation-states that could reconcile differences among their citizens and pave the way for economic prosperity, political autonomy did not bring prosperity, or even the right to vote, to all. As each nation-state expanded its territorial boundaries, many inhabitants were left out of the political realm.

Consolidation of Nation-States in Europe

COMPARISON

COMPARE the challenges elites within Europe faced to those in the Americas in consolidating their nation-states and the degree to which they succeeded.

In Europe, no "frontier" existed into which new states could expand. Instead, nation-states took shape out of older monarchies and empires, and their borders were determined by diplomats or by battles. In the wake of the French Revolution, the idea caught on that "the people" should form the basis for the nation and that nations should share a common culture—but no one could agree on who "the people" should be. Yet, over the course of the nineteenth century, as literacy, cities, industrial production, and the number and prosperity of property owners expanded, ruling elites had no choice but to share power with a wider group of citizens. These citizens, in turn, increasingly defined themselves as, say, French or German, rather than as residents of Marseilles or subjects of the King of Bavaria.

DEFINING "THE NATION"

For a very long time, in most places, "the nation" was understood to comprise kings, clergymen, nobles—and occasionally rich merchants or lawyers—and no one else. Although some peoples, such as the English and the Spanish, were already self-conscious about their unique histories, only in the late eighteenth century were the crucial building blocks of European nationalism put in place.

Cultural changes laid the foundations of the nation. Increasingly literate urban populations met in coffee houses and other public places to discuss the issues of the day. Their collective debates—public opinion—weighed for the first time on the decisions of kings and statesmen. During the nineteenth century, a huge expansion of the periodical press made it possible for people all across Europe to read books and newspapers in their own languages. The emerging industrial economy made merchants anxious to standardize laws, taxation policies, and weights and measures. States invested huge sums in building roads and then railroads—and these linked provincial towns and bigger cities, laying the foundations for a closer political integration.

But who were the people, and what constituted a viable nation-state? For some, the nation was a collection of all those who spoke one language; for others, it was all those who

MAP 17.2 | Italian Unification and German Unification, 1815–1871

Italian unification and German unification altered the political map of Europe.

- What were the names of the two original states that grew to become Italy and Germany?
- Who were the big losers in these territorial transfers?
- According to your reading, what problems did the new Italian and German states face in creating strong national communities?

lived in a certain territory and who shared a common religious heritage. This was a particularly acute problem in multiethnic central and southeastern Europe, where many people were multilingual, rich and poor alike. But some who shared the same language objected to being lumped into one nation-state. The Irish, for example, spoke English but were predominately Catholics and wanted to be free from Anglican rule.

UNIFICATION IN GERMANY AND ITALY

Two of Europe's fledgling nation-states came into being when the dynastic states of Prussia and Piedmont-Sardinia incorporated their smaller, linguistically related neighbors, creating the German and Italian nation-states (see Map 17.2). In both regions, conservative prime ministers—Count Otto von Bismarck of Prussia and Count Camillo di Cavour of Piedmont—exploited liberal, nationalist sentiment to rearrange the map of Europe.

Building Unified States The unification of Germany and Italy posed all the familiar problems of who should be included in the new nation-states. To begin with, German-speakers were spread all across central and eastern Europe; for centuries they had lived in many different states. Similarly, Italians had lived separately in city-states and small kingdoms on the Italian peninsula and spoke a range of dialects. The historical experiences and economic developments had made Bavarian Germans (Catholic) quite different from Prussian Germans (Protestant); likewise, the Milanese (who lived in a wealthy urban industrial center) shared little, language included, with the typical Sardinian peasant. But liberal nationalists had made the case that their high culture—especially their literary, musical, and theatrical traditions—overrode these differences, and emotional appeals by poets, composers, and orators convinced many people that this was indeed the case. Bismarck and Cavour merged this nationalist rhetoric with clever diplomacy—and the use of military force in a series of small conflicts—to forge united German and Italian nation-states.

These "unified" states rejected democracy. In the new Italy, which was a constitutional monarchy, less than 5 percent of the 25 million people could vote. The new German empire (the Second Reich) had an assembly elected by all adult males (the Reichstag), but it had little power. The country was ruled by a combination of aristocrats and bureaucrats under a monarch. Liberals dominated in many localities, but only the emperor (the Kaiser) could depose the prime minister. In fact, Bismarck continued to dominate Prussian politics for twenty-eight years, until fired in 1890 by Kaiser Wilhelm II. By that time, unification had yielded brisk economic growth both in Italy and especially Germany, but conflict between regions and political groups continued.

NATION BUILDING AND ETHNIC CONFLICT IN THE AUSTRO-HUNGARIAN EMPIRE

Bismarck's unification of Germany came at the expense of Habsburg supremacy in central Europe and (as we will see in the next section) of French territory and influence in the west. After Germany won a victory over the Austrian army in 1866, the Hungarian nobles who controlled the eastern Habsburg Empire forced the weakened dynasts to grant them home rule. In the Compromise of 1867, the Habsburgs agreed that their state would officially be known as the Austro-Hungarian Empire. But this move did not solve Austria-Hungary's nationality problems. In both the Hungarian and the Austrian halves of the dual state, Czechs, Poles, and other Slavs now began to clamor for their own power-sharing "compromise" or autonomous national homelands. They would, however, have to wait until the end of World War I.

DOMESTIC DISCONTENTS IN FRANCE AND BRITAIN

Although already unified as nation-states, Britain and France faced major difficulties. For the French, dealing with defeat at the hands of the Germans was the primary national concern in the decades leading up to World War I. For the British, issues of Irish separatism, the rise of the working class, and feminists' demands troubled the political arena.

Destabilization in France The Franco-Prussian War of 1870–1871 completed the unification of Germany. Germany took the French provinces of Alsace and Lorraine, and its victory destabilized France. The German siege of Paris, which lasted for more than three months, devastated the capital. Unprepared, Parisians had no food stocks and were compelled to eat all sorts of things, including two zoo elephants. Under terrible conditions and without effective leadership, the French capital resisted until January 1871, when the government signed a humiliating peace treaty. The Germans left in place a weak provisional French government. Refusing the negotiated peace, furious Parisians vented their rage and established their own government, proclaiming the city a utopia for workers. The leftist commune they established lasted until the provisional national government's army stormed Paris a few months later. At least 25,000 Parisians died in the bloody mop-up that followed. A "Third Republic" took the place of Napoleon III's empire, but it struggled to achieve stability. In the years following the Franco-Prussian war, France saw increasing conflict between classes and the rise of anti-German nationalism.

Irish Nationalism in Great Britain Although the English had long thought of themselves as a nation, the idea that all British people belonged in the same state was much more problematic. The kingdom of England—which was originally composed of England, clearly the dominant state, and Wales—became the kingdom of Great Britain when it united with Scotland in 1707 and Ireland in 1801. It was home to peoples whose historical experiences, religious backgrounds, and economic opportunities were very different. In the nineteenth century, British leaders wrestled in particular with demands for independence from Irish nationalists and lower-class agitation, especially in England. Beginning in 1832, England responded to class conflict at home by extending political rights to most men but not women. England finally established universal suffrage for all adult males after World War I, in 1918; roughly one quarter of British women gained the right to vote at that time and the rest a decade later.

Yet Ireland remained Britain's Achilles' heel. The British government was widely condemned for its failure to relieve Irish suffering during the potato famine of 1845–1849 (see Chapter 15); even though millions of poor Irish and Scottish workers made their way to England, seeking either passage to North America or work in the English mill towns, they did not assimilate easily and often got the lowliest jobs. All of this, on top of 300 years of repressive English domination, fueled a mass movement for Irish home rule that continued into the twentieth century.

Born in opposition to the old monarchical regimes, European nationalism by the end of the nineteenth century had become a means used by liberal and conservative leaders alike to unite the people behind them. But just what they meant by "the people" remained bitterly contested. Continental powers increasingly resorted to an aggressive foreign policy and imperial expansion to maintain popular support without granting political power to ordinary people. France alone, of the European great powers, had a parliamentary democracy elected by universal manhood suffrage.

Industry, Science, and Technology

A powerful combination of industry, science, and technology shaped the emerging nation-states in North America and western Europe. It also reordered the relationships among different parts of the world. One critical factor was that after 1850 western Europe and North America experienced a new phase of industrial development—essentially a second industrial revolution. Japan, too, joined the ranks of industrializing nations as its state-led program of industrial development started to pay dividends. These changes transformed the global economy and intensified rivalries among industrial societies.

COMPARISON

EXPLAIN the roles that industrialization, science, and technology played in expansion of powerful states into the rest of the world.

NEW TECHNOLOGIES, MATERIALS, AND BUSINESS PRACTICES

New technologies and materials drove economic development in the late nineteenth century and led to new business practices. This period witnessed major technological changes with the arrival of new organic sources of power (like oil) and new ways to get old organic sources (like coal) to processing plants. These changes freed manufacturers from having to locate their plants close to their fuel sources. Not only did the most important new source of energy—electricity—permit factories to arise in areas with plenty of skilled workers, but it also slashed production costs. **Steel**, now cheaply produced because of technical innovations, became essential for shipbuilding and railways. They were part of a bundle of innovations that included chemicals and pharmaceuticals, which together transformed northwestern Europe, the United States, and Japan.

The breakthroughs of the second industrial revolution ushered in new business practices, especially mass production and the giant integrated firm. No longer would modest investments suffice, as they had in Britain a century earlier. Now large banks were the major providers of funds. In Europe, limited-liability joint-stock companies were as wildly successful in raising capital on stock markets as they were in the United States. Companies like Standard Oil, U.S. Steel, and Siemens mobilized investments from large numbers of shareholders. The scale of these firms was awesome. U.S. Steel alone produced over half of the world's steel ingots, castings, rails, and heavy structural shapes—and nearly half of all its steel plates and sheets, which were vital in the construction of buildings, railroads, ships, and the like.

INTEGRATION OF THE WORLD ECONOMY

Not only did industrial change concentrate power in North Atlantic societies, but it also reinforced their power on the world economic stage and created a more integrated global economy. Europe and the United States increased their exports in new products; they also grew eager to control the importation of tropical commodities such as cocoa and coffee. While the North Atlantic societies were still largely self-sufficient in coal, iron, cotton, wool, and wheat (the major commodities of the first industrial revolution), the second industrial revolution bred a need for rubber, copper, oil, and bauxite (an ore used to make aluminum), which were not available domestically. Equally important, large pools of money became available for investing overseas.

Movements of Labor and Technology Vast movements of workers took place to satisfy the labor demands of an increasingly integrated world economy. Indians moved thousands of miles from Asia to work on sugar plantations in the Caribbean, Mauritius, and Fiji, to labor in South African mines, and to build railroads in East Africa. Chinese workers constructed railroads in the western United States and toiled on sugar plantations in Cuba. The Irish, Poles, Jews, Italians, and Greeks flocked to North America to fill its burgeoning factories. Italians also moved to Argentina to harvest wheat and corn.

With steam-powered gunboats and breech-loading rifles, Europeans opened new territories for trade and conquest. At home and in their colonial possessions, imperial powers constructed networks of railroads that carried people and goods from hinterlands to the coasts. From there, steamships bore them across the seas. Completion of the Suez Canal in 1869 shortened ship voyages between Europe and Asia and lowered the costs of interregional trade. Information moved even faster than cargoes, thanks to the laying of telegraph cables under the oceans, supplemented by overland telegraph lines.

Charles Darwin and Natural Selection Although machines were the most visible evidence that humans could master the universe, perhaps the most momentous shift in the conception of nature derived from the travels of one British scientist: **Charles Darwin** (1809–1882).

Darwin's theory, articulated in his *Origin of Species* (1859), laid out the principles of **natural selection**. Inevitably, he claimed, populations grew faster than the food supply; this condition

Charles Darwin This image depicts Darwin testing the speed of a tortoise in the Galapagos Islands. It was during his visit to these islands that Darwin developed many of the ideas that he would put forth in his 1859 *Origin of Species*.

created a "struggle for existence" among species. In later work he showed how the passing on of individual traits was also determined by what he called sexual selection—according to which the "best" mates are chosen for their strength, beauty, or talents and the less fit fail to reproduce at comparable rates. Although Darwin's book dealt exclusively with animals (and mostly with birds), his readers immediately wondered what his theory implied for humans.

A passionate debate began among scientists and laymen, clerics and anthropologists. Some read Darwin's doctrine of natural selection to mean that it was natural for the strong nations to dominate the weak, or justifiable to allow disabled persons to die—something Darwin explicitly rejected. As more groups (mis)interpreted Darwin's theory to suit their own objectives, a set of beliefs known as social Darwinism legitimated the suffering of the underclasses in industrial society. In subsequent years Europeans would repeatedly suggest that they had evolved more than Africans and Asians. Extending Darwinian ideas far beyond the scientist's intent, some Europeans came to believe that therefore nature itself gave them the right to rule others.

Global Expansionism and an Age of Imperialism

Increasing rivalries among nations and social tensions within them produced an expansionist wave late in the nineteenth century. Although Africa became the primary focus of interest, a frenzy of territorial conquest overtook Asia as well. In China's territories, competition by foreign powers to establish spheres of influence heated up in the 1890s. And in India, imperial ambitions provoked the British to conquer Burma (present-day Myanmar). Moreover, Britain and Russia competed for preeminence from their respective outposts in Afghanistan and central Asia. In the Americas, new territories were usually incorporated as provinces of the expansionist state, making them integral parts of the nation. In Asia and Africa, however, European and American imperialism turned far-flung territories into colonial possessions.

COMPARISON

COMPARE the different western colonial models used in various regions of the world and the responses of those regions.

The Raj Strengthens Control
(*Top*) In the aftermath of the Indian Rebellion of 1857, the British government, called the Raj (meaning "rule" in Hindi), intervened much more actively in India. It built an extensive system of railroads to develop India as a profitable colony and to maintain military security. This engraving shows the East India Railway around 1863. (*Bottom*) The British allowed several native princes to remain as long as they accepted imperial hegemony. This photograph shows a road-building project in one such princely state. Officials of the Muslim princely ruler and British advisers supervise the workers.

The inhabitants of these colonial possessions were generally designated as subjects of the empire without the rights and privileges of citizens.

INDIA AND THE IMPERIAL MODEL

Britain's rule in India provided a model for other imperialist governments by developing the colony's infrastructure in order to maximize British profits from trade. Having suppressed the Indian Rebellion of 1857 (see Chapter 16), authorities revamped the colonial administration. From the British point of view, Indians were not to be appeased—and certainly not brought into British public life. But they did have to be governed, and the economy had to be revived. So, after replacing the East India Company's rule by crown government in 1858, the British set out to make India into a more secure and productive colony. This period of British sovereignty was known as the **Raj** ("rule").

The most urgent tasks facing the British in India were those of modernizing its transportation and communication systems and transforming the country into an integrated colonial state. These changes had begun under the governor-general of the East India Company, Lord Dalhousie, who oversaw the development of India's modern infrastructure. After the British suppressed the revolt, they took up the construction of public works with renewed vigor.

Railways were a key element both in the pacification, shuttling troops to danger zones, and in the later reform project. The first railway line opened in 1853, and by 1910 India had 30,627 miles of track in operation—the fourth largest railway system in the world.

Construction of other public works followed. Engineers built dams across rivers to tame their force and to irrigate lands; workers installed a grid of telegraph lines that opened communication between distant parts of the region. These public works served imperial and economic purposes: India was to become a consumer of British manufactures and a supplier of primary staples such as cotton, tea, and wheat. On the hillsides of the island of Ceylon and the northeastern plains of India, the British established vast plantations to grow tea—which was then marketed in England as a healthier alternative to Chinese green tea. India also became an important consumer of British manufactures, especially textiles, in an ironic turnaround to its centuries-old tradition of exporting its own cotton and silk textiles.

The reform efforts of the Raj made India into a unified territory and enabled its inhabitants to begin to regard themselves as "Indians." These were the first steps to becoming a "nation" like Italy and the United States, but there were profound differences. Above all, as colonial subjects Indians did not enjoy basic civic and human rights, and even elites lacked the vote. Other European powers followed the British example in trying to modernize and integrate their colonies economically without welcoming colonial peoples into the life of the nation.

COLONIZING AFRICA

No region felt the impact of European colonialism more powerfully than Africa. In 1880, the only two large European colonial possessions there were French Algeria and two British-ruled South African states, the Cape Colony and Natal. But within a mere thirty years, seven European states had carved almost all of Africa into colonial possessions.

Partitioning the African Landmass In the context of heightened international rivalries, Portugal called for an international conference to discuss claims to Africa. Meeting in Berlin between 1884 and 1885, delegates from Europe, the United States, and the Ottoman Empire agreed to carve up Africa and to recognize the claims of the first European power that claimed control of a given territory. Colonizers rushed to plant their flags as widely as possible, lest they be outmaneuvered by their rivals (see Maps 17.3a and 17.3b).

The consequences for Africa were devastating. Nearly 70 percent of the newly drawn borders failed to correspond to older demarcations of ethnicity, language, culture, and commerce—for Europeans knew little of the landmass beyond its coast and rivers. They based their new colonial boundaries on European trading centers rather than on the location of African population groups (see Map 17.4).

MAP 17.3A | Senegal and Gambia

MAP 17.3B | Mandara Peoples

MAP 17.4 | Partition of Africa, 1880–1914

The partition of Africa took place between the early 1880s and the outbreak of World War I.

- Which two European powers gained the most territory in Africa?

- Which two African states managed to remain independent? What kind of economic and political gain did European powers realize through the colonization of Africa? Did any of the European states realize their ambitions in Africa?

Europeans in Africa (*Left*) Henry Morton Stanley was one of the most famous of the nineteenth-century explorers in Africa. He first made his reputation when he located the British missionary-explorer David Livingstone, feared dead, in the interior of Africa, uttering the famous words, "Dr. Livingstone, I presume." Stanley worked on behalf of King Leopold, establishing the Belgian king's claims to territories in the Congo and often using superior weaponry to cow African opponents. (*Right*) The ardent British imperialist Cecil Rhodes endeavored to bring as much of Africa as he could under British colonial rule. He had an ambition to create a swath of British-controlled territory that would stretch from the Cape in South Africa to Cairo in Egypt, as this cartoon shows.

Several motives led the European powers into their frenzied partition of Africa. Although European businesses were primarily interested in Egypt and South Africa, where their investments were lucrative, small-scale traders and investors harbored fantasies of great treasures locked in the vast uncharted interior. Politicians, publicists, and the reading public also took an interest. The writings of explorers like David Livingstone (1813–1873), a Scottish doctor and missionary, and Henry Morton Stanley (1841–1904), an adventurer in the pay of the *New York Herald*, excited readers with accounts of Africa as a continent of unlimited economic potential.

The most determined of the African empire builders was Leopold II (r. 1865–1909), king of the Belgians. (See **Current Trends in World History: Africa's Newest Hunters and Gatherers** for Leopold's activities in central Africa and their effects on Africans and the environment.) In southern Africa, the British champion of imperialism Cecil Rhodes (1853–1902) brought the Rhodesias, Nyasaland, Bechuanaland, the Transvaal, and the Orange Free State into the British Empire as part of a design to have British territories stretching all the way from the Cape of Good Hope in South Africa to Cairo in Egypt.

Other Europeans saw Africa as a grand opportunity for converting souls to Christianity. In fact, Europe's civilizing mission was an important motive in the scramble for African

Africa's Newest Hunters and Gatherers: Greed, Environmental Degradation, and Resistance

Africa was the birthplace of hunting and gathering (see Chapter 1). Ironically, although the European colonizers justified their partition of Africa on the grounds of bringing civilization to a benighted people, in fact, in their quest to enrich themselves, the first generation of colonizers exploited the most available resources of the continent, enslaved and killed huge numbers of people, and returned parts of the continent to a hunting-and-gathering mode of production. The most driven and greediest of these figures was Leopold II, king of the Belgians, who was determined, in spite of sweet-sounding rhetoric, to do whatever it took to line his pockets and make himself a formidable figure in European politics. King Leopold's story and others like it fascinate world historians because it conveys in the starkest detail the nature of the relationship between the rulers and the Africans that they ruled. It also provides a strong point of comparison for the different models of ruling that each European power instituted in their colonies.

Even before ascending the throne in 1865, Leopold cast about for ways to become more than the constitutional monarch of a small, recently established, and neutral state. A voracious reader on colonialism, he was struck forcefully by one book: *How the Dutch Ruled Java*, published in 1861. By demonstrating how the Dutch colonial state had expropriated money from the East Indies (today called Indonesia) to spend on projects at home, the book fired his imagination. Could he not do the same? Could he not stake out a colony, take money from it to swell his own exchequer, and use some of it on public works at home—to beautify the cities of Belgium the way Paris had been beautified in the 1850s and 1860s?

Fixing his gaze on central Africa, in the 1880s Leopold manipulated the other European states into recognizing him as the sovereign head of a "Congo Free State," in which he lead a European effort to "civilize" (and especially to exploit) the Congo River basin. Leopold hired the world-famous explorer, Henry Stanley, to "pacify" the country and ready it for economic development.

But how to make these lands pay off? They were almost entirely unexplored and unsurveyed, and though in time they would yield some of the richest mineral deposits in the world, these prospects were unknown to Leopold and his administrators at first. What the rain forests of Africa had was wild products, especially rubber and ivory. But how to get Africans, who at that point hardly participated in world trade, to tap wild rubber vines and hunt elephants? The solution here and elsewhere in similar African environments was to create large armies (known in Leopold's state as the *Force Publique*), fix quotas for districts to procure, and compel villagers to bring in baskets of rubber and elephant tusks.

For Leopold the results were little short of astonishing. He extracted vast sums from the Congo, spending lavishly on himself and on Belgium. He sank millions

territory. In Uganda, northern Nigeria, and central and western Africa, missionaries went ahead of European armies, begging the European statesmen to follow their lead.

African Resistance Africans faced two unappealing options: they could capitulate to the Europeans and negotiate to limit the loss of their autonomy, or they could fight to preserve their sovereignty. Only a few chose to negotiate. Lat Dior, a Muslim warlord in Senegal, refused to let the French build a railway through his kingdom. "As long as I live, be well assured," he wrote the French commandant, "I shall oppose with all my might the construction of this railway. I will always answer no, no, and I will never make you any other reply. Even were I to go to rest, my horse, *Malay,* would give you the same answer." Conflict was inevitable, and Lat Dior lost his life in a battle with the French in 1886. Most Africans who resisted were unaware of the Europeans' superior military technology, and even those who adapted their tactics to meet the challenge were unable to keep the Europeans out indefinitely.

Only Menelik II of Ethiopia successfully repulsed the Europeans, for he knew how to play rivals off one another. By doing so, he procured weapons from the French, British, Russians, and Italians. He also had a united, loyal, and well-equipped army. In 1896, his of francs into making the seaside city of Ostend one of the finest resorts in the world. At Tervuren, while a choir sang the new Congo anthem, Leopold laid the foundation stone of a world college for overseas colonial administration. In Brussels he spent over $5 million renovating royal palaces and constructing parks, avenues, casinos, and racecourses.

For the Congolese, Leopold's state was nothing more than a reign of terror. Forced to roam farther and farther from their home villages in search of rubber and elephants to keep pace with ever-escalating quotas, villagers suffered an immense loss of life through famine and conflicts with the *Force Publique*. Perhaps as many as 10 million Africans perished in a population that had been roughly 20 million before Leopold's agents arrived.

Leopold's brutality did not go unobserved, however. Already in 1899, the writer Joseph Conrad took the Congo as his model of rapacious European imperialism in his novella, *Heart of Darkness*. African villagers rebelled, though unsuccessfully, and, by the first decade of

King Leopold Despite the inhumane way in which he funded his vast array of public buildings, Leopold is sometimes called, not unaffectionately, the "Builder King" by Belgians today.

the twentieth century, rumors and then detailed reports painted a stark picture of terror and environmental degradation as the villagers rooted out almost all of the wild rubber and began the hunt for elephants that would ultimately render them an endangered species. In 1908, just a year before his death, Leopold was

compelled, against his wishes, to turn the administration of the Congo over to the Belgian parliament.

QUESTIONS FOR ANALYSIS

- Why was King Leopold such an important figure in the European partition of Africa?
- While the Congo story is arguably one of the most brutal of all stories of colonial exploitation and environmental degradation, which other episodes in world history does it remind you of and why?

Explore Further

Herbst, Jeffrey, *States and Power in Africa: Comparative Lessons in Authority and Control* (2000).

Hochschild, Adam, *King Leopold's Ghost* (New York, 1998).

---

troops routed Italian forces at the Battle of Adwa, after which Adwa became a celebrated moment in African history. Its memory inspired many of Africa's later nationalist leaders.

Colonial Administrations in Africa Once the Europeans' euphoria over the gains of the partition and conquest had worn off, the power to rule the colonies fell to "men on the spot"—military adventurers, settlers, and entrepreneurs whose main goal was to get rich quick. As these individuals established little kingdoms in some areas, Africans (like Amerindians on the other side of the Atlantic) found themselves confined to territories where they could barely provide for themselves.

Eventually, these rough-and-ready systems led to violent revolts from aggrieved Africans, and in their aftermath the colonial rulers had to create more efficient administrations, dedicated to providing health care and education for the colonized. As in India, colonial powers in Africa laid the foundations for future nation-state organizations. Once information trickling out of Africa revealed that the imperial governments were not realizing their goal of bringing "civilization" to the "uncivilized" and creating easy profits, each European power implemented a new form of colonial rule, stripping the strongman conquerors of their absolute powers,

COMPARISON

ANALYZE the extent to which colonies contributed to the wealth and political strength of the nation-states that controlled them.

Battle of Adwa Portrait of King Menelik, who defeated the Italian forces at the battle of Adwa in 1896, thus saving his country from European colonization.

monitoring them more closely and assuming greater responsibility for the colonized peoples.

Eventually, stabilized colonies began to deliver on their economic promise. Whereas early imperialism in Africa had relied on the export of ivory and wild rubber, after these resources became depleted the colonies pursued other exports. From the rain forests came cocoa, coffee, palm oil, and palm kernels. From the highlands of East Africa came tea, coffee, sisal (used in cord and twine), and pyrethrum (a flower used to make insecticide). Another important commodity was long-staple, high-quality cotton, grown in Egypt and the Anglo-Egyptian Sudan. Indeed, tropical commodities from all across Africa (as from India and Latin America) flowed to industrializing societies. (See **Analyzing Global Developments: Imperialism and the African Trade Revolution**.)

Thus, European colonial administrators saw Africa as fitting into the world economy in the same way that British administrators viewed India—as an exporter of raw materials and an importer of manufactures. They expected Africa to profit from this role. But, in truth, African workers gained little from participating in colonial commerce, while the price they paid in disruption to traditional social and economic patterns was substantial.

To observers, the European empires in Africa seemed solid and durable, but in fact European colonial rule there was fragile. For all of British Africa, the only all-British force was 5,000 men garrisoned in Egypt. Elsewhere, European officers depended on African military and police forces. And prior to 1914, the number of British administrative officers available for the whole of northern Nigeria was less than 500. These were hardly strong foundations for colonial rule. It would not take much to destabilize the European order in Africa.

THE AMERICAN EMPIRE

The United States, like Europe, was drawn into the mania of overseas expansion and empire building. Echoing the earlier rhetoric of Manifest Destiny, the expansionists of the 1890s claimed that Americans still had a divine mission to spread their superior civilization and their Christian faith around the globe. However, America's new imperialists followed the European model of colonialism from Asia and Africa: colonies were to provide harbors for American vessels, supply raw materials to American industries, and purchase the surplus production of American farms and factories. These new territorial acquisitions were not intended for American settlement or statehood. Nor were their inhabitants to become American citizens, for nonwhite foreigners were considered unfit for incorporation into the American nation.

The pressure to expand came to a head in the late 1890s, when the United States declared war on Spain and invaded the Philippines, Puerto Rico, and Cuba. The United States annexed Puerto Rico after minimal protest, but Cubans and Filipinos resisted becoming colonial subjects. Bitterness ran particularly high among Filipinos, to whom American leaders had promised independence if they joined in the war against Spain. Betrayed, Filipino rebels launched a war for independence in the name of a Filipino nation. In two years of fighting, over 5,000 Americans and perhaps 200,000 Filipinos perished. The outcome: the Philippines became a colony of the United States.

Analyzing Global Developments

Imperialism and the African Trade Revolution

The colonial period initiated a trade revolution in Africa, which, as we have seen, had been a supplier of human labor to the Americas from the fifteenth century until the middle of the nineteenth century (see Chapter 13). Even as the Europeans endeavored to eradicate the African institution of slavery and slave trading within the continent, they also promoted the reintegration of African economies into the world economy. African exports included new cash crops like cocoa from West Africa and significant minerals like gold and diamonds from South Africa, while imports were mainly European manufactures. To promote trade, the colonial powers financed railways and deepened harbors. Already by the outbreak of World War I, West Africa had become the world's leading exporter of cocoa, South Africa the leading exporter of diamonds and gold, and Egypt, along with the United States, the leading exporter of high-quality cotton.

QUESTIONS FOR ANALYSIS

- Is there a correlation between the increase in the length of railway lines built and the quantity of natural resources taken out of Africa? If so, how can you tell?
- During what period were the largest increases in the construction of the railroads and the exportation of cocoa and gold, and why was this so?
- What, then, can we assume about the economic impact of colonial rule in this period, and who were the beneficiaries of the increased trade between Africa and the rest of the world?

LENGTH OF RAILWAY LINE OPENED (IN KILOMETERS)

Year	Africa
1880	4,579
1885	6,813
1890	9,202
1895	11,962
1900	16,319
1905	25,574
1910	37,768
1915	47,624

COCOA EXPORTS FROM THE GOLD COAST AND NIGERIA (IN TONS)

Year	Gold Coast	Nigeria
1900	536	202
1905	5,090	470
1910	22,600	2,932
1915	77,300	9,105
1920	125,000	17,155

UNION OF SOUTH AFRICA GOLD MINES (IN OUNCES)

Year	Total Output	Estimated % of World Output
1897	2,744	24%
1907	6,451	32.4%
1913	8,799	39.3%
1916	9,297	42.3%
1921	8,129	50.9%

Sources: B. R. Mitchell, *International Historical Statistics: Africa, Asia, and Oceania, 1750–2005* (2007), pp. 713–18; Polly Hill, *The Gold Coast Cocoa Farmer: A Preliminary Survey* (1965), p. 132; Sara Berry, *Cocoa, Custom and Socio-Economic Change in Western Nigeria,* Oxford Studies in African Affairs (1975), p. 221; S. Herbert Frankel, *Capital Investment in Africa: Its Course and Effects* (1938), pp. 83–84.

Colonies in the Philippines and Puerto Rico laid the foundations for a revised model of U.S. expansionism. The earlier pattern had been to turn Native American lands into privately owned farmsteads and to extend the Atlantic market across the continent. But now, in this new era, the nation's largest corporations (with government support) aggressively intervened in the affairs of neighbors near and far. Following the Spanish-American

War, the United States repeatedly sent troops to many Caribbean and Central American countries. The Americans preferred to turn these regimes into dependent states, rather than making them part of the United States itself (as with Alaska and Hawaii) or converting them into formal colonies (as the Europeans had done in Africa and Asia).

IMPERIALISM AND CULTURE

Europeans and Americans set out to bring "civilization" to the peoples of their colonies. At least since the Crusades, Europeans had regularly written and thought about others. These images and ideas had grown more numerous and varied as commerce and colonialism in Asia and the Atlantic world increased; they served various purposes, including those of informing, entertaining, flattering, and criticizing European culture. As Europeans and Americans grew more and more confident in their achievements, they became convinced that their arts and sciences were superior—and curiosity often turned to disdain. In time Europeans presumed that the only true modern civilization was their own; other peoples might have reigned over great empires in antiquity, but had since fallen into decadence and decline. Artists and writers portrayed nonwestern peoples as exotic, sensuous, and economically backward in a genre scholars have come to call "orientalism."

If Darwin remained ambivalent about the nature of race, his followers embraced the idea of stable racial differences that evolved only on the longest of time horizons, at a glacial pace, over thousands of years rather than decades or centuries. They ratified a view of "lower" and "higher" races, the former stuck in the past and the latter anointed by God (or in the case of social Darwinists, by nature itself) to define and dictate civilization's future. Europeans' relationship to others might now be one of condescending sympathy or of ruthless exploitation, but

The Women of Algiers in Their Apartment An oil painting by Eugène Delacroix (1798–1863) of Algerian women being attended by a black servant. European painters in the nineteenth century often used images of women to portray Arab Muslim society.

the result was that it was up to white Europeans and Americans to create modern culture. The darker people, social Darwinists argued, were not nearly as fully "evolved" as the Europeans, and could not hope to catch up. At best they could be taught European languages, sciences, and religions, and perhaps be made to evolve more quickly. It is telling that French colonial subjects who did well at French schools were known as *evolués*, "the evolved ones."

Celebrating Imperialism Especially in middle- and upper-class circles, Europeans celebrated their imperial triumphs. After the invention of photographic film and the Eastman Kodak camera in 1888, imperial images surfaced in popular forms such as postcards and advertisements. Imperial themes also decorated packaging materials; tins of coffee, tea, tobacco, and chocolates featured pictures highlighting the commodities' colonial origins. Cigarettes often had names like "Admiral," "Royal Navy," "Fighter," and "Grand Fleet." Some of this served as propaganda, produced by investors in imperial commodities or by colonial pressure groups.

Propaganda promoted imperialism abroad but also inspired changes at home. For example, champions of empire argued that if the British population did not grow fast enough to fill the world's sparsely settled regions, then the population of other nations would. Population was power, and the number of healthy children provided an accurate measure of global influence. "Empire cannot be built on rickety and flat-chested citizens," warned a British member of Parliament in 1905. Empire and imperialism carried European, American, and, to a lesser extent, Japanese power and culture throughout the world. In terms of the size of the populations they ruled, this era was the high point of European and Euro-American predominance.

Pressures of Expansion in Japan, Russia, and China

The challenge of integrating political communities and extending territorial borders was a problem not just for western Europe and the United States. Other societies also aimed to overcome domestic dissent and establish larger domains. Japan, Russia, and China provide three contrasting models; their differing forms of expansion eventually led them to fight over possessions in East Asia.

JAPAN'S TRANSFORMATION AND EXPANSION

Starting in the 1860s, Japanese rulers tried to recast their country less as an old dynasty and more like a modern nation-state. Since the early seventeenth century, the Tokugawa Shogunate had kept outsiders within strict limits and thwarted internal unrest. But after an American naval officer, Commodore Matthew Perry, entered Edo Bay in 1853 with a fleet of steam-powered ships, other Americans, Russians, Dutch, and British followed in his wake. These outsiders forced the Tokugawa rulers to sign humiliating treaties that opened Japanese ports, slapped limits on Japanese tariffs, and exempted foreigners from Japanese laws. Younger Japanese, especially among the military (samurai) elites, felt that Japan should respond by adopting, not rejecting, Western practices.

In 1868, a group of reformers toppled the Tokugawa Shogunate and promised to return Japan to its mythic greatness. Then Emperor Mutsuhito—the Meiji ("Enlightened Rule") Emperor—became the symbol of a new Japan. His reign (1868–1912) was called the **Meiji Restoration**. By founding schools, initiating a propaganda campaign, and revamping the army to create a single "national" fighting force, the Meiji government promoted a political

COMPARISON

COMPARE the challenges elites faced in Japan, China, and Russia in consolidating nation-states to those faced by western elites.

Perry arrives in Japan A Japanese wood-block print portraying the uninvited arrival into Edo (Tokyo) Bay on August 7, 1853, of a tall American ship, which was commanded by Matthew Perry. This arrival marked the end of Japan's ability to fully control the terms of its interactions with foreigners.

community that stressed linguistic and ethnic homogeneity, as well as superiority compared to others. In this way the Meiji leaders overcame age-old regional divisions, subdued local political authorities, and mobilized the country to face the threat from powerful Europeans.

Economic Development One of the Meiji period's remarkable achievements was the nation's economic transformation. After 1871, when the government banned the feudal system and allowed peasants to become small landowners, farmers improved their agrarian techniques and saw their standard of living rise. The energetic new government unified the currency around the yen, created a postal system, introduced tax reforms, and established an advanced civil service system. In 1889, the Meiji government introduced a constitution (based largely on the German model). The following year, 450,000 people—about 1 percent of the population—elected Japan's first parliament, the Imperial Diet.

As the government sold valuable enterprises to the people who had provided strong support, it created private economic dynasties. The new large companies (such as Sumitomo, Yasuda, Mitsubishi, and Mitsui) were trusted family organizations. Fathers, sons, cousins, and uncles ran different parts of large integrated corporations—some in charge of banks, some running the trade wing, some overseeing factories. Women played a crucial role, not just as custodians of the home but also as cultivators of important family alliances, especially among potential marriage partners. In contrast to American limited-liability firms, which issued shares on stock markets to anonymous buyers, Japan's version of large-scale managerial capitalism was a personal affair.

Expansionism and Conflict with Neighbors As in many other emerging nation-states, expansion was a tempting prospect to the Japanese. It offered the promise of more markets for selling goods and obtaining staples, and it was a way to burnish the image of national superiority and greatness. The Meiji moved first to take over the kingdom of the Ryūkyūs, southwest of Japan (see Map 17.5). A small show of force, only 160 Japanese soldiers, was enough to establish the new Okinawa Prefecture there in 1879. The Japanese regarded the people of the Ryūkyūs as an ethnic minority and refused to incorporate them into the nation-state on

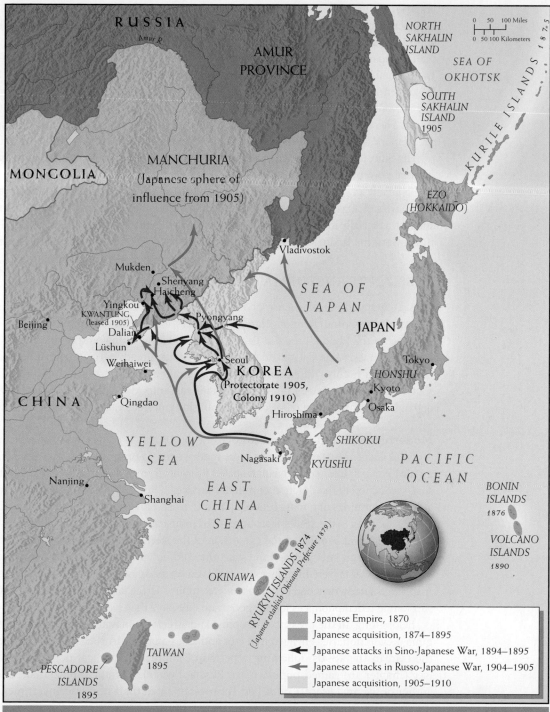

MAP 17.5 | Japanese Expansion, 1870–1910

Under the Meiji Restoration, the Japanese state built a strong national identity and competed with foreign powers for imperial advantage in East Asia.

- According to the map, what were the first areas that the Japanese Empire acquired as it started to expand?

- What two empires' spheres of influence were affected by Japan's aggressive attempts at expansion?

- According to your reading, what were the new Japanese state's objectives? How were they similar to or different from European expansionism of the same period?

equal terms. In contrast with the British in India or the Americans in Puerto Rico, the Japanese conquerors refused to train a native Ryūkyūs governing class. Meiji intellectuals insisted that the "backward" Okinawans were unfit for local self-rule and representation.

The Japanese fixed upon Korea, which put their plans on a collision course with China. In a formal treaty, the Japanese recognized Korea as an independent state (expected to be no longer dominated by China), opened Korea to trade, and won the right to apply Japanese law in Korea. As a result, the Chinese worried that soon the Japanese would try to take over Korea. These fears were well founded, for Japanese designs on Korea eventually sparked the Sino-Japanese War of 1894–1895, in which the Chinese suffered a humiliating defeat.

The Sino-Japanese War accelerated Japan's rapid transformation into a nation-state and a colonial power with no peer in Asia. Having lost the war, China ceded the province of Taiwan to the Japanese. Japan also annexed Korea in 1910 and converted Taiwan and Korea into the twin jewels of its young empire. Like the British in India, the Japanese regarded their colonial subjects as racially inferior and unworthy of the privileges of citizenship. And like other imperial powers, the Japanese expected their possessions to serve the metropolitan center.

RUSSIAN TRANSFORMATION AND EXPANSION

Russia expanded out of a sense of a civilizing mission and a need to defend against other countries expanding along its immense borders. Facing an emerging Germany, a British presence in the Middle East and Persia, a consolidating China, and an increasingly powerful Japan, Russia knew it would have to extend its already large territorial domain. So it established a number of expansionist fronts simultaneously: southwest to the Black Sea, south into the Caucasus and Turkestan, and east into Manchuria (see Map 17.6). Success depended on annexing territories and establishing protectorates over conquered peoples.

Modernization and Internal Reform In the 1860s, Tsar Alexander II launched a wave of "Great Reforms" to make Russia more modern and to preserve its status as a great power. In 1861, for example, a decree emancipated peasants from serfdom. Other changes included a sharp reduction in the duration of military service, a program of education for the conscripts, and the beginnings of a mass school system to teach children reading, writing, and Russian culture. Starting in the 1890s, state-sponsored industrialization led to the building of railroads and factories and stimulated the expansion of the steel, coal, and petroleum industries. But while the reforms strengthened the state, they did not enhance the lives of common people. Workers in Russia were brutally exploited, even by the standards of the industrial revolution. Also, large landowners had kept most of the empire's fertile land, and the peasants had to pay substantial redemption fees for the poorer-quality plots they received.

Before long, in the press, courtrooms, and streets, men and women denounced the regime. Revolutionaries engaged in terror and assassination. In 1881, a terrorist bomb killed the tsar. In the 1890s, following a period of famine, the radical doctrines of Marxism (see Chapter 16) gained popularity in Russia. Even aristocratic intellectuals, such as the author of *War and Peace*, Count Leo Tolstoy, lamented their despotic government.

Territorial Expansion Yet the critics of internal reform did not hold back the Russian expansionists, who believed they had to take over certain lands to keep them out of rivals' hands. So they conquered the highland people of the Caucasus Mountains to prevent Ottomans and Persians from encroaching on Russia's southern flank. And they battled the British over areas between Turkestan and British India, such as Persia (Iran) and Afghanistan. Although some Russians moved to these lands, they never became a majority there. The new provinces were multiethnic, multireligious communities that were only partially integrated into the Russian nation.

MAP 17.6 | Russian Expansion, 1801–1914

The Russian state continued to expand in the nineteenth century.

- According to this map, what lands did Russia acquire during the period 1796–1855? What lands did it acquire next?
- Compare this map of Russian expansion with Map 13.7 (p. 481). How did the direction of Russia's expansion change in the nineteenth century?
- Which states did the expanding Russian Empire more resemble in this era, western Europe (such as Great Britain) or American states (such as the United States)?

Perhaps the most impressive Russian expansion occurred in East Asia, where the Amur River basin offered rich lands, mineral deposits, and access to the Pacific Ocean. The Chinese also wanted to colonize this area, which lay just north of Manchuria. After twenty years of struggle, Russia claimed the land north and south of the Amur River and in 1860 founded Vladivostok, a port on the Pacific Ocean whose name signified "Rule the East." Deciding to focus on these areas in Asia, the Russian government sold its one territory in North America (Alaska) to the United States. Then, to link central Russia and the western part of the country to its East Asian spoils, the government began construction of the Trans-Siberian Railroad. When it was completed in 1916, the new railroad bridged the east and the west.

Governing a Diverse Empire Russia was a huge empire whose rulers were only partially effective at integrating its diverse parts into a political community. Unlike the United States, which displaced or slaughtered native populations during its expansion across an entire continent, Russia tolerated and taxed many of the new peoples. The state's approach ranged from outright repression (of Poles and Jews) to favoritism (toward Baltic Germans and Finns), although the beneficiaries of favoritism often later lost favor if they became too strong. Further, unlike the United States, which managed to pacify borders with its weaker neighbors, Russia faced the constant suspicions of Persians and Ottomans and the menace of British troops in Afghanistan. In East Asia, a clash with expansionist Japan loomed on the horizon.

CHINA UNDER PRESSURE

While the Russians and Japanese scrambled to copy European models of industrialism and imperialism, the Qing were slower to mobilize against threats from the west. Even as the European powers were dividing up China into spheres of influence, Qing officials were much more worried about internal revolts and threats from their northern borders than European incursions.

Adopting Western Learning and Skills A growing number of Chinese officials recognized the superior armaments and technology of rival powers and were deeply troubled by the threat posed by European military might. Starting in the 1860s, reformist bureaucrats sought to adopt elements of western learning and technological skills—but with the intention of keeping the core Chinese culture intact.

This so-called **Self-Strengthening movement** included a variety of new ventures: arsenals, shipyards, coal mines, a steamship company to contest the foreign domination of coastal shipping, and schools for learning foreign ways and languages. Most interesting was the dispatch abroad of about 120 schoolboys under the charge of Yung Wing. The first Chinese graduate of an American college (Yale University, 1854), Yung believed that western education would greatly benefit Chinese students, so he took his charges to Connecticut in the 1870s to attend school and live with American families. Conservatives at the Qing court were soon dismayed by reports of the students' interest in Christianity and aptitude for baseball. In 1881, after the U.S. government refused to admit the boys into military academies, they summoned the students home.

Yung Wing's abortive educational mission was not the only setback for the Self-Strengthening movement, for skepticism about western technology was rife among conservative officials. Some insisted that the introduction of machinery would lead to unemployment; others worried that railways would facilitate western military maneuvers and lead to an invasion; still others complained that the crisscrossing tracks disturbed the harmony between humans and nature. The first short railway track ever laid in China was torn up in 1877 shortly after being built, and the country had only 179 miles of track prior to 1895.

Although they did not acknowledge the railroad's usefulness, the Chinese did adopt other new technologies to access a wider range of information. For example, by the early 1890s there were about a dozen Chinese-language newspapers (as distinct from the foreign-language press) published in major cities, with the largest ones having a circulation of 10,000 to 15,000. To avoid government intervention, these papers sidestepped political controversy; instead, they featured commercial news and literary contributions. In 1882, the newspaper *Shenbao* made use of a new telegraph line to publish dispatches within China.

Internal Reform Efforts China's defeat by Japan in the Sino-Japanese War (1894–1895), sparked by quarrels over Korea, prompted a more serious attempt at reform by the Qing. Known as the Hundred Days' Reform, the episode lasted only from June to September 1898. The force behind it was a thirty-seven-year-old scholar named Kang Youwei and his twenty-two-year-old student Liang Qichao. Citing rulers such as Peter the Great of Russia and the Meiji Emperor of Japan as their inspiration, the reformers urged Chinese leaders to develop a railway network, a state banking system, a modern postal service, and institutions to foster the development of agriculture, industry, and commerce. The reform failed when a group of conservative leaders placed the Dowager Cixi on the throne, rescinded the reformist laws, and executed six of the reform movement's major leaders. They did not, however, capture Kang Youwei, who fled to Japan.

But, in truth, the reforms of the Self-Strengthening movement were ineffectual, too modest and poorly implemented. Very few Chinese acquired new skills. Despite talk of modernizing, the civil service examination remained based on Confucian classics and still opened the only doors to government service. Governing elites were not yet ready to reinvent the principles of their political community, and they adhered instead to the traditional dynastic structure.

By the late nineteenth century, the success of the Qing regime in expanding its territories a century earlier seemed like a distant memory, as various powers repeatedly forced it to make economic and territorial concessions. Unlike Japan or Russia, however, the Qing government resisted comprehensive social reforms (until after the turn of the twentieth century), and its policies left the country vulnerable to both external aggression and internal instability.

Conclusion

Between 1850 and 1914, most of the world's people lived not in nation-states but in land empires or in the overseas colonies of nation-states. But leaders in colonial territories, often responding to popular upheavals and destabilizing economic changes, began to see independent nation-states as the most desirable form of governance for their regions.

Although the ideal of "a people" united by territory, history, and culture grew increasingly popular worldwide, it was not easy to make it a reality. Official histories, national heroes, novels, poetry, and music helped, but central to the process of nation formation were the actions of bureaucrats. Asserting sovereignty over what it claimed as national territory, the state "nationalized" diverse populations by creating a unified system of law, education, military service, and government.

Colonization beyond borders was another part of nation building in many societies. In these efforts, territorial conquests took place under the banner of nationalist endeavors. In Europe, the Americas, Japan, and to some extent Russia, the intertwined processes of nation building and territorial expansion were most effective. Expansion abroad consolidated national identities at home.

However, the integrating impulses of imperialist nation-states did not wipe out local differences, mute class antagonisms, or eliminate gender inequalities. Even as Europeans and Americans came to see themselves as chosen—by God or by natural selection—to rule the rest, they suffered deep divisions. Not everyone identified with the nation-state or the empire, or agreed on what it meant to belong or to conquer. But by the century's end, racist advocates and colonial lobbyists seem to have convinced many that their interests and destinies were bound up with their countries' unity, prosperity, and global clout.

Ironically, imperial expansion had an unintended consequence, for self-determination could also apply to racial or ethnic minorities at home and in the colonies. Armed with the rhetoric of progress and uplift, colonial authorities tried to subjugate distant people, but colonial subjects themselves often asserted the language of "nation" and accused imperial overlords of betraying their own lofty principles. As the twentieth century opened, Filipino and Cuban rebels used Thomas Jefferson's Declaration of Independence to oppose American invaders, Koreans defined themselves as a nation crushed under Japanese heels, and Indian nationalists made colonial governors feel shame for violating British standards of "fair play."

FOCUS ON: *Nationalism, Imperialism, and Technological Innovations*

THE AMERICAS AND EUROPE: CONSOLIDATING NATIONS

- Residents of the United States claim territory across the North American continent after fighting a bloody civil war to preserve the union and abolish slavery.

- Canadians also build a new nation and expand across the continent.

- Brazilians create a prosperous nation-state that excludes much of the population from the privileges of belonging to the "nation" and the "state."

- The dynastic states of Prussia and Sardinia-Piedmont create German and Italian nation-states at the expense of France and the Austrian Empire.

INDUSTRY, SCIENCE, AND TECHNOLOGY ON A GLOBAL SCALE

- Continued industrialization transforms the global economy.

- New technologies of warfare, transportation, and communication lead to greater global economic integration.

- Charles Darwin's *Origin of Species* overturns previous conceptions of nature, arguing that present-day life forms evolved from simpler ones over long periods.

EMPIRES

- After suppressing the Indian Rebellion of 1857, the British reorganize their rule in India, providing a model for other imperialist powers.

- European powers partition the entire African continent (except for Ethiopia and Liberia) despite intense African resistance.

- Americans win the Spanish-American War, annex Puerto Rico, and establish colonial rule over the Philippines.

- The expansionist aims of Japan, Russia, and China lead to clashes over possessions in East Asia, with Russia gaining much territory and Japan defeating the Chinese.

- Colonial rule spurs nationalist sentiments among the colonized.

After You Read This Chapter

Go to INQUIZITIVE to see what you've learned—and learn what you've missed—with personalized feedback along the way.

CHRONOLOGY

	1800	1850
THE AMERICAS		U.S. Civil War 1861–1865 Canada gains self-rule 1867
EUROPE		*On the Origin of Species* published 1859
EAST ASIA AND SOUTHEAST ASIA		Commodore Perry "opens" Japan 1853
AFRICA AND THE MIDDLE EAST		
SOUTH ASIA		
RUSSIA		Crimean War 1853–1856 Great Reforms to modernize Russia 1860s

- *Thinking about* **Worlds Together, Worlds Apart** *and Nations & Empires* Compare the eighteenth century empires of Spain, Portugal, and Britain with the new empires arising in Africa at the end of the nineteenth century. What were the sources of their wealth and power? How and to what degree were colonial territories and economies integrated with their imperialist states?

- *Thinking about Changing Power Relationships and Nations & Empires* How did the growth of Western influence and Japanese power lay the basis for opposition movements in Africa and Asia? How did people respond to imperialism? Where was resistance most effective?

- *Thinking about Environmental Impacts and Nations & Empires* Describe the the second industrial revolution and explain how it differed from the first industrial revolution. Pay special attention to the new technologies used in the late nineteenth century and especially to the sources of power and new materials that were used.

1. Compare **Manifest Destiny** in the United States with European **imperialism** in Africa. What common influences shaped both kinds of expansion? How did they differ?

2. Describe the challenges that mass nationalism and economic expansion posed for the multiethnic, multireligious empires of Austria-Hungary and Russia.

3. Compare the **Meiji Restoration** with China's **Self-Strengthening movement**. What values did they share? Can you explain their differences?

4. Explain the significance of **steel** and **limited-liability joint-stock companies** to the second industrial revolution.

5. Analyze the cultural impact of imperialist ambitions on imperialist nations. How did notions of race and ethnicity shape the colonial mentality of Europeans, Americans, and Japanese?

Brazil abolishes slavery 1888 ◆   ◆ Spanish-American War 1898
Unifications of Germany and Italy 1870–1871

Meiji Era in Japan 1868–1912
Sino-Japanese War 1894–1895

European expansion in sub-Saharan Africa 1870s–1890s
◆ British occupation of Egypt 1882

British Raj 1858–1947

Construction of Trans-Siberian Railroad 1890s

1900   **1950**

Competing Perspectives

Evolution and Imperialism

In the second half of the nineteenth century, a handful of nation-states, most of them in Europe, renewed their competition for overseas colonies. Class conflict at home and resistance to their efforts overseas diminished Europeans' faith, inherited from Enlightenment thinkers, in the harmony of the natural world. A new, conflictual vision emerged around the world that stressed competition and struggle in nature as well as human affairs. Doubts arose about the progressive nature of the changes ushered in by the era of the French and industrial revolutions, in particular the idea that granting more people the vote and spreading free markets would lead to peace and prosperity for everyone. Colonizers increasingly believed that they must control ever-greater expanses of territory or risk defeat by rival powers.

Major scientific work on evolution shaped thinking about politics in general, and especially imperialism. In *On the Origin of Species* (1859), Charles Darwin examines the evolution of different species in nature. In addressing the question "How and why are new species created?" Darwin describes the process of natural selection, in which nature creates overabundance so that the "fittest" species survive and adapt themselves to their environments. Although his book says nothing about human beings and Darwin himself was appalled by human suffering and the exploitation of imperialism, many of his contemporaries used Darwin's ideas as a justification for imperial expansion.

The other three documents provide material from imperialists influenced, directly or indirectly, by Darwin's work as well as a reaction of the Indian anticolonial leader, Mohandas Gandhi. In the second selection, New York newspaper editor John L. O'Sullivan coins the term "Manifest Destiny" in 1845, to explain how the "manifest design of Providence" supported the territorial expansion of the United States. Okuma's *Fifty Years of New Japan* (1907–1908) explores the sources of Meiji Japan's power and the role of competition with the West. Finally, Gandhi calls into question the degree to which material wealth and physical force will determine the outcome of global competition. As you read these excerpts, consider how they relate to the aggressive competition for imperial expansion at the turn of the twentieth century.

PRIMARY SOURCE 17.1

On the Origin of Species *(1859), Charles Darwin*

Again, it may be asked, how is it that varieties, which I have called incipient species, become ultimately converted into good and distinct species, which in most cases obviously differ from each other far more than do the varieties of the same species? How do those groups of species, which constitute what are called distinct genera, and which differ from each other more than do the species of the same genus, arise? All these results . . . follow inevitably from the struggle for life. Owing to this struggle for life, any variation, however slight and from whatever cause proceeding, if it be in any degree profitable to an individual of any species, in its infinitely complex relations to other organic beings and to external nature, will tend to the preservation of that individual, and will generally be inherited by its offspring. The offspring, also, will thus have a better chance of surviving, for, of the many individuals of any species which are periodically born, but a small number can survive. I have called this principle, by which each slight variation, if useful, is preserved, by the term of Natural Selection, in order to mark its relation to man's power of selection. We have seen that man by selection can certainly produce great results, and can adapt organic beings to his own uses, through the accumulation of slight but useful variations, given to him by the hand of Nature. But Natural Selection, as we shall hereafter see, is a power incessantly ready for action, and is as immeasurably superior to man's feeble efforts, as the works of Nature are to those of Art.

We will now discuss in a little more detail the struggle for existence. . . . I should premise that I use the term Struggle for Existence in a large and metaphorical sense, including dependence of one being on another, and including (which is more important) not only the life of the individual, but success in leaving progeny. Two canine animals in a time of dearth, may be truly said to struggle with each other which shall get food and live. But a plant on the edge of a desert is said to struggle for life against the drought, though more properly it should be said to be dependent on the moisture. . . .

A struggle for existence inevitably follows from the high rate at which all organic beings tend to increase. Every being, which during its natural lifetime produces several eggs or seeds, must suffer destruction during some period of its life, and during some season or occasional year, otherwise, on the principle of geometrical increase, its numbers would quickly become so inordinately great that no country could support the product. Hence, as more individuals are produced than can possibly survive, there must in every case be a struggle for existence, either one individual with another of the same species, or with the individuals of distinct species, or with the physical conditions of life. . . . Although some species may be now increasing, more or less rapidly, in numbers, all cannot do so, for the world would not hold them.

It may be said that natural selection is daily and hourly scrutinising, throughout the world, every variation, even the slightest; rejecting that which is bad, preserving and adding up all that is good; silently and insensibly working, whenever and wherever opportunity offers, at the improvement of each organic being in relation to its organic and inorganic conditions of life. We see nothing of these slow changes in progress, until the hand of time has marked the long lapses of ages, and then so imperfect is our view into long past geological ages, that we only see that the forms of life are now different from what they formerly were.

Source: Charles Darwin, *On the Origin of Species*, ed. Philip Appleman (New York: W. W. Norton and Company, 2002), Chapters 3 and 4.

PRIMARY SOURCE 17.2

"Manifest Destiny" (1845), John L. O'Sullivan

Texas has been absorbed into the Union in the inevitable fulfilment of the general law which is rolling our population westward; the connexion of which with that ratio of growth in population which is destined within a hundred years to swell our numbers to the enormous population of *two hundred and fifty millions* (if not more), is too evident to leave us in doubt of the manifest design of Providence in regard to the occupation of this continent. It was disintegrated from Mexico in the natural course of events, by a process perfectly legitimate on its own part, blameless on ours; and in which all the censures due to wrong, perfidy and folly, rest on Mexico alone. And possessed as it was by a population which was in truth but a colonial detachment from our own, and which was still bound by myriad ties of the very heart strings to its old relations, domestic and political, their incorporation into the Union was not only inevitable, but the most natural, right and proper thing in the world. . . .

California will, probably, next fall away from the loose adhesion which, in such a country as Mexico, holds a remote province in a slight equivocal kind of dependence on the metropolis. Imbecile and distracted, Mexico never can exert any real governmental authority over such a country. The impotence of the one and the distance of the other, must make the relation one of virtual independence. . . . The Anglo-Saxon foot is already on its borders. Already the advance guard of the irresistible army of Anglo-Saxon emigration has begun to pour down upon it, armed with the plough and the rifle, and marking its trail with schools and colleges, courts and representative halls, mills and meeting-houses. A population will

soon be in actual occupation of California, over which it will be idle for Mexico to dream of dominion. They will necessarily become independent.

Source: John L. O'Sullivan, "Manifest Destiny," *Democratic Review* (July 1845), pp. 7–10, in Clark C. Spence, ed., *The American West: A Source Book* (New York: Thomas Y. Crowell Company, 1966), pp. 108–9.

PRIMARY SOURCE 17.3

Fifty Years of New Japan *(1910), Okuma*

By comparing the Japan of fifty years ago with the Japan of today, it will be seen that she has gained considerably in the extent of her territory, as well as in her population, which now numbers nearly fifty million. Her government has become constitutional not only in name, but in fact, and her national education has attained to a high degree of excellence. In commerce and industry, the emblems of peace, she has also made rapid strides, until her import and export trades together amounted in 1907 to the enormous sum of 926,000,000 yen. Her general progress, during the short space of half a century, has been so sudden and swift that it presents a rare spectacle in the history of the world. This leap forward is the result of the stimulus which the country received on coming into contact with the civilization of Europe and America, and may well, in its broad sense, be regarded as a boon conferred by foreign intercourse. Foreign intercourse it was that animated the national consciousness of our people, who under the feudal system lived localized and disunited, and foreign intercourse it is that has enabled Japan to stand up as a world power. We possess today a powerful army and navy, but it was after Western models that we laid their foundations by establishing a system of conscription in pursuance of the principle "all our sons are soldiers," by promoting military education, and by encouraging the manufacture of arms and the art of shipbuilding. We have reorganized the systems of central and local administration, and effected reforms in the educational system of the empire. All this is nothing but the result of adopting the superior features of Western institutions. That Japan has been enabled to do so is a boon conferred on her by foreign intercourse, and it may be said that the nation has succeeded in this grand metamorphosis through the promptings and the influence of foreign civilization. For twenty centuries the nation has drunk freely of the civilizations of Korea, China, and India, being always open to the different influences impressed on her in succession. Yet we remain politically unaltered under one Imperial House and sovereign, that has descended in an unbroken line for a length of time absolutely unexampled in the world. We have welcomed Occidental civilization while preserving their old Oriental civilization. They have attached great importance to Bushido, and at the same time held in the highest respect the spirit of charity and humanity. They have ever made a point of choosing the middle course in everything, and have aimed at being always well-balanced. We are conservative simultaneously with being progressive; we are aristocratic and at the same time democratic; we are individualistic while also being socialistic. In these respects we may be said to somewhat resemble the Anglo-Saxon race.

Source: From Okuma, *Fifty Years of New Japan* (Kaikoku Gojunen Shi), 2d Ed., (London: Smith, Elder, 1910).

PRIMARY SOURCE 17.4

Excerpts on the Struggle for Existence (1907), Gandhi

Darwin was a great Englishman of the last century who made great scientific discoveries. His memory and his power of observation were amazing. He has written some books that deserve to be read and pondered. With a mass of evidence and arguments, he has shown how man came into being; how he has evolved from a particular kind of monkey. After a large number of experiments and much sifting of evidence, he realized that there was not much difference between the anatomy of man and that of the ape. Whether this conclusion is correct or not has not much to do with ethics. Besides this, Darwin has also shown how ideas of morality affect mankind. . . .

The question now arises: Does the influence of environment lead us to be moral? Or can it be that the forces that surround us are indifferent to morality?

At this point it becomes necessary to consider Darwin's views. Though Darwin did not write as a moral philosopher, he has shown how close the connection is between morality and environment. Those who think that morality is unimportant and that physical strength and mental capacity are the only things that matter should read Darwin.

According to him, there is an instinct of self-preservation in men as in other creatures. He also says that those who survive the struggle for existence may be regarded as successful, that is, those who are unfit to tend to extinction, but that the issue of the struggle does not depend on mere physical force.

Source: Gandhi, *Collected Works*, 100 vols. (Delhi, 1969–1994), 6: 316–17.

QUESTIONS FOR ANALYSIS

1. Identify the aspects of Darwin's thought that his contemporaries drew on to justify imperialism. Do you think Darwin's text supports their views or not?

2. Explain the relationship between Darwin's text and the Enlightenment tradition. Pay special attention to his views of nature and his use of the scientific method.

3. Contrast the sources of the nation's strength as identified in the second two documents. What barriers, if any, stand in the way of expansion?

4. How do you think Gandhi would reply to O'Sullivan and Okuma?

Interpreting Visual Evidence

Occidentalism: Representing Western Influence

Ever since the publication of Edward Said's landmark work *Orientalism* (1978), scholars have carefully examined European and American efforts to represent nonwestern peoples in disciplines ranging from art, languages, and literature to law, biology, and philosophy. The field of postcolonial studies that emerged in Said's wake has emphasized the degree to which Western descriptions of "orientals" were really efforts to describe themselves—as the rational, disciplined opposite of the supposedly sensual Orient—and to affirm their own values. More recently, scholarly attention has turned to different peoples' efforts to make sense of European and American influences on their societies—representations that we might call "Occidentalism" (the "Occident" meaning the West).

Here we consider a range of visual materials that both reflected and shaped ordinary people's views of Western influence. These depictions circulated widely; notice the combination of text and images, for those who could not read. While Japan was not colonized, the Meiji Restoration relied heavily on European models for its constitution and economic plans. In the *Engine of Progress* (1880s–1890s), Kawanabe Kyosai depicts a struggle between traditional Japanese goods and Western imports, with the smoke from a locomotive's engine billowing in the background. In the second image (1908-1909), in the aftermath of the Young Turk revolution in the Ottoman Empire—which deposed the sultan and replaced monarchic institutions with constitutional ones—the Ottoman province of Egypt remained under British control. The artist presents Great Britain as a greedy giant, relaxing on Egypt's pyramids while young Egyptians protest, emulating the Young Turks at the center of the empire. In the final image, the Mexican caricaturist José Guadalupe Posada mocks American influence in *The American Mosquito* (1910-1913). Whether the mosquitos in question represent American tourists, the Americans brought in by Mexico's President Diaz to manage railroads and mines, or the American dollar remains unclear.

Engine of Progress.

Ottoman cartoon: Britain as a greedy giant, leaning on the pyramids on page 466 of the *Encyclopedia of the Ottoman Empire*.

The American Mosquito.

QUESTIONS FOR ANALYSIS

1. Compare the representation of foreign influences in each work. Are those influences purely oppressive? Do any local actors appear to find outside influence appealing? What is the greater threat, according to these images, internal weakness or a coercive foreign intervention?

2. Analyze the relationship between local traditions and progress in these works. Do these images present a vision of progress? From the perspective of the artists, what is the relationship, if any, between foreign influence and progress?

3. Do the artists present a homegrown vision of progress, or is progress something that comes from abroad? Is it possible to be Japanese, Egyptian, or Mexican and modern at the same time?

4. What messages do these works convey about their own societies? Do the artists present their own people as powerless victims, as vulnerable and divided, as caught between their own autocratic rulers and outside invaders, or perhaps as unified and defiant?

Before You Read This Chapter

- Numerous factors lead to global instability: vast population movements, worldwide financial crises, class conflict, the rise of women's consciousness, and hatred of colonial domination.

- Class conflict, economic instability, and great power rivalry within Europe combine with growing protest from overseas to undermine Europe's dominant position in world affairs.

- New scientific thinking and artistic expression, known as cultural modernism, challenge the dominant Western view of progress and open Europe and North America to the cultural achievements of nonwestern societies.

- **EXPLAIN** the connections between migration and the development of nationalism in this period.

- **COMPARE** Chinese responses to imperialism with responses to imperialism in Africa.

- **IDENTIFY** and **DESCRIBE** political, economic, and social crises that swept through the world in this period, and **ANALYZE** the impact they had on different regions of the world.

- **EXPLAIN** the ways in which new cultural forms at the turn of the century reflected challenges to the world order as it then existed.

- **EVALUATE** the ways in which race, nation, and religion unified populations but also made societies more difficult to govern and economies more difficult to manage.

An Unsettled World

1890–1914

In 1905 a young African man, Kinjikitile Ngwale, began to move among various ethnic groups in German East Africa, spreading a message of opposition to German colonial authorities. In the tradition of visionary prophets (see Chapter 16), Kinjikitile claimed that by anointing his followers with blessed water (*maji* in Swahili), he could protect them from European bullets and drive the Germans from East Africa. Kinjikitile's reputation spread rapidly, drawing followers from across 100,000 square miles of territory. Although German officials soon executed Kinjikitile, they could not prevent a broad uprising, called the Maji-Maji Revolt. The Germans brutally suppressed the revolt, killing between 200,000 and 300,000 Africans.

The Maji-Maji Revolt and its aftermath revealed the intensity of opposition to the world of nations and their empires. In Europe and North America, critics who felt deprived of the full benefits of industrializing nation-states—especially women, workers, and frustrated nationalists—demanded far-reaching reforms. In Asia, Africa, and Latin America, anticolonial critics and exploited classes protested European domination. In the face of so much unrest from within their nations and from their colonies, Europeans' faith in the idea of progress and the superiority of their "civilization" was shaken. Ironically, this occurred at the very moment when Europeans and people of European descent seemed to have established preeminence in world affairs.

This chapter tackles the anxieties and insecurities that unsettled the world around the turn of the twentieth century. It ties them in particular to several key factors: (1) the uprooting of millions of people from countryside to city and from one continent to another, (2) discontent with the poverty that many suffered even as economic production increased, and (3) resentment of and resistance to European domination. Around the globe, this tumult caused a questioning of established ideas that led to a flowering of new thinking and fresh artistic expression under the label of "modernism." This unsettling movement was a defining feature of the era.

Progress, Upheaval, and Movement

COMPARISON

EXPLAIN the connections between migration and the development of nationalism in this period.

Rapid economic progress in the decades leading up to 1914 brought challenges to the established order and the people in power. In Europe and the United States, radicals and middle-class reformers agitated for political and social change. In areas colonized by European countries and the United States, resentment focused on either colonial rulers or indigenous elites. Even in nations such as China, which had not been formally colonized but which faced repeated intrusions, popular discontent targeted domination by Europeans. At the same time, millions of people migrated to cities and different countries in search of a better life.

In the late nineteenth century, whole new industries fueled economic growth, especially in the industrial countries and in territories that exported vital raw materials to Europe and the United States. But industrial capitalism also spurred inequalities within industrial countries and, especially, between the world's industrial and nonindustrial regions. Periodic economic downturns left thousands out of work. This led, in some cases, to organized opposition to authoritarian regimes or to the free market system; it also provoked new critiques of the new industrial order and the values that supported it.

In Europe and North America, a generation of young artists, writers, and scientists broke with older conventions and sought new ways of seeing and describing the world. In Asia, Africa, and South America as well, many of these innovators were energized by the idea of moving beyond traditional forms of art, literature, music, and science. But this generation's exuberance worried those who were not ready to give up their cultural traditions and institutions.

PEOPLES IN MOTION

If the world was being *unsettled* by political, economic, and cultural changes, it was also being *resettled* by mass emigration (see Map 18.1). The emigration of throngs of Europeans to temperate zones in the Americas and Oceania began after the Napoleonic wars and gathered momentum in the 1840s, when the Irish fled their starving communities to seek better lives in North America. After 1870, the flow of Europeans became a torrent. The United States was the favored destination, with six times as many European immigrants arriving there as in Argentina (the second-place receiving country) between 1871 and 1920. The high point occurred between 1901 and 1910, when over

6 million Europeans entered the United States. This was nothing less than a demographic revolution.

Emigration, Immigration, Internal Migration Europeans were not the only peoples on the move. Between the 1840s and the 1940s, 29 million South Asians migrated into the Malay Peninsula and Burma (British colonies), the Dutch Indies (Indonesia), East Africa, and the Caribbean. Most were recruited to labor on plantations, railways, and mines in British-controlled territories. Meanwhile, the Chinese, too, emigrated in massive numbers. Between 1845 and 1900, population pressure, a shortage of cultivable land, and social turmoil drove 800,000 Chinese to seek new homes in North and South America, New Zealand, Hawaii, and the West Indies. Nearly four times as many settled in Southeast Asia. Moreover, industrial changes caused millions to migrate *within* their own countries or to neighboring ones, seeking employment in the burgeoning cities or other opportunities in frontier regions.

From the 1860s until 1914, governments imposed almost no controls on immigration or emigration. In China, the Qing government failed in its effort to restrict emigration into the dominant Manchus' northeastern homelands. The United States allowed entry to anyone who was not a prostitute, a convict, or a "lunatic"; but in 1882, racist reactions spurred legislation that barred entry to almost all Chinese. Travel within Europe required no passports or work permits; foreign-born criminals were subject to deportation, but that was the extent of immigration policy. (See **Analyzing Global Developments: Migration and the Origin of Border Control Policies**.)

Urban Life Cities boomed, with both positive and negative effects. Tokyo's population climbed from 500,000 in 1863 to 1,750,000 in 1908, and London's passed 6.5 million.

Urban Transportation (*Left*) Streetcars in Tokyo, Japan's capital, are watched over by sword-bearing patrolmen in 1905, during the Russo-Japanese War. The first electric streetcar began running in Japan in 1895. Note the elevated electricity lines, which dated from the 1880s. (*Right*) Heavy traffic in London, about 1910, points to an urban population on the move. Note the many kinds of transportation—motor buses as well as horse-drawn wagons; the railings in the foreground mark the entrance to the Underground, or subway.

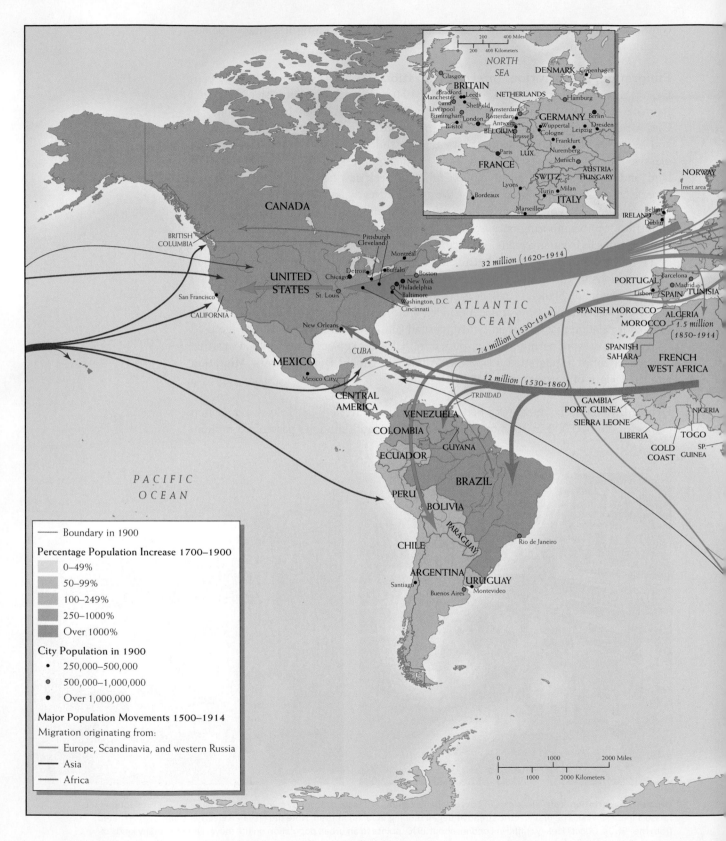

NORTH SEA

DENMARK Copenhagen

Glasgow

BRITAIN
Bradford
Manchester and
Leeds
Liverpool
Birmingham
Bristol
Sheffield
London

NETHERLANDS
Amsterdam
Rotterdam
Antwerp
BELGIUM
Brussels
Hamburg

GERMANY
Berlin
Wuppertal
Cologne
Frankfurt
Nuremberg
Leipzig
Dresden

LUX.
Paris FRANCE

SWITZ
AUSTRIA-HUNGARY

Lyons
Bordeaux
Turin Milan
ITALY
Marseilles

0   200   400 Miles
0   200   400 Kilometers

Inset area

CANADA

BRITISH COLUMBIA

Pittsburgh
Cleveland
Montréal

Detroit
Chicago
Buffalo
Boston

San Francisco

UNITED STATES

St. Louis

New York
Philadelphia
Baltimore
Washington, D.C.
Cincinnati

CALIFORNIA

ATLANTIC OCEAN

32 million (1620-1914)

NORWAY

IRELAND
Belfast
Dublin

PORTUGAL
Lisbon

SPAIN
Madrid
Barcelona

TUNISIA

New Orleans

MEXICO

CUBA

Mexico City

7.4 million (1530-1914)

SPANISH MOROCCO
MOROCCO

ALGERIA
1.5 million (1850-1914)

SPANISH SAHARA

FRENCH WEST AFRICA

CENTRAL AMERICA

TRINIDAD

12 million (1530-1860)

GAMBIA
PORT. GUINEA
SIERRA LEONE

NIGERIA

VENEZUELA

COLOMBIA

GUYANA

LIBERIA

GOLD COAST

TOGO
SP. GUINEA

ECUADOR

PACIFIC OCEAN

PERU

BRAZIL

BOLIVIA

PARAGUAY

CHILE

Rio de Janeiro

ARGENTINA

URUGUAY

Santiago

Buenos Aires
Montevideo

—— Boundary in 1900

Percentage Population Increase 1700–1900

- 0–49%
- 50–99%
- 100–249%
- 250–1000%
- Over 1000%

City Population in 1900

- • 250,000–500,000
- • 500,000–1,000,000
- • Over 1,000,000

Major Population Movements 1500–1914

Migration originating from:

—— Europe, Scandinavia, and western Russia

—— Asia

—— Africa

0   1000   2000 Miles
0   1000   2000 Kilometers

MAP 18.1 | Nineteenth-Century Migration

The nineteenth century witnessed a demographic revolution in terms of migration, urbanization patterns, and population growth. The world's population also rose from roughly 625 million in 1700 to 1.65 billion in 1900 (a two-and-a-half-fold increase).

- To what areas did most of the migrants from Europe go? What about the migrants from China, India, and Africa?

- What four areas saw the greatest population increase by 1900?

- How were migration flows and urbanization connected? What factors most accounted for these global population changes? Was internal growth more important than external migration in the case of the world's population growth? In what countries was population growth most affected by external or internal migration?

Analyzing Global Developments

Migration and the Origin of Border Control Policies

The movement of large numbers of people within and across regions—namely, the spread of the Mongols, the Atlantic slave trade, and nineteenth-century migrations from Europe and Asia to the Americas—is not a new phenomenon in world history. What is relatively more recent to world history is the effort over the last 150 years to increase border control and identity documentation of these people(s) on the move. Historian Adam McKeown in a recent work has demonstrated that the origins of the effort to regulate and document border control go back to late-nineteenth-century America and the efforts to substantially restrict the number of Asian immigrants trying to enter the United States. The earlier argument was that modern-day border control grew out of long-standing sovereignty practices of states and countries dating back to even earlier centuries.

In the first table below, we see a comparison of the rates of population growth from 1850 to 1950 between the major regions of the world.

In the second table, we see more concretely the number of people on the move in terms of their points of origin and destinations.

World Population Growth, 1850–1950 (in millions)

	1850 POPULATION	1950 POPULATION	AVERAGE ANNUAL GROWTH (%)
Receiving			
Americas	59	325	1.72
North Asia	22	104	1.57
Southeast Asia	42	177	1.45
Sending			
Europe	265	515	0.67
South Asia	230	445	0.66
China	420	520	0.21
Africa	81	205	0.93
World	1,200	2,500	0.74

Global Long-Distance Migration, 1840–1940

DESTINATION	ORIGINS	MIGRANTS (MILLIONS)	AUXILIARY ORIGINS
Americas	Europe	55–58	2.5 million from India, China, Japan, Africa
Southeast Asia, Indian Ocean Rim, Australasia	India S. China	48–52	5 million from Africa, Europe, NE Asia, Middle East
Manchuria, Siberia, Central Asia, Japan	NE Asia Russia	46–51	

These data were compiled from port and customs statistics at major entry points to major countries. What we see in the data is that the receiving nations' populations grew by a factor of 4.0–5.5 during this 100-year period, and that their overall growth was more than twice that of the sending regions during this time. Not only was the population growth rate of the receiving nations much more dramatic during this period, but the redistribution of the world's population was equally dramatic. In 1850 10 percent of the world's population lived in the receiving areas, but by 1950 nearly 25 percent of the world's population lived in those areas.

QUESTIONS FOR ANALYSIS

- The number of immigrants from Asia to the America's was only about 3 percent of the total. Why do you think such a relatively small number of people would cause a dramatic change in border and identification control?
- Why do you think that the populations in the sending areas also continued to grow at substantial rates during this period?
- Why do you think so many people were on the move from South China and India to other parts of the Indian Ocean world? From northeast Asia to East Asia and Inner Asia?

Sources: Adam McKeown, *Melancholy Order: Asian Migration and the Globalization of Borders* (2008); Colin McEvedy and Richard Jones, *Atlas of World Population History* (1978); Adam McKeown, "Global Migration, 1846–1940," *Journal of World History* 15 (2004), p. 156.

Major cities faced housing shortages, despite governments' massive rebuilding and beautification projects. This was the era in which city planning came into its own—to widen and regularize thoroughfares for train and streetcar traffic, and to make crowded city life attractive to new inhabitants. City governments in New York, Cairo, Buenos Aires,

Bombay, and Brussels spent lavishly on opera houses, libraries, sewers, and parks, hoping to ward off disease and crime and to impress others with their modernity. And yet, for all those efforts, cholera and tuberculosis remained major killers, and suicide and alcoholism became growing problems. Population movement and the growth of cities were distinct features of the later nineteenth century all over the world, opening up new opportunities to become rich or to sink into poverty.

Discontent with Imperialism

In the decades before the Great War, opposition to European domination in Asia and Africa gathered strength. During the nineteenth century, as Europeans touted imperialism as a "civilizing mission," local prophets had voiced alternative visions contesting European supremacy (see Chapter 16). While imperialists consolidated their hold, suppression of unrest in the colonies required ever more force and bloodshed. As the cycle of resistance and repression escalated, many Europeans back home, mainly on the left and out of power, questioned the harsh means of controlling their colonies. By 1914, these questions were intensifying as colonial subjects across Asia and Africa challenged imperial domination.

COMPARISON

COMPARE Chinese responses to imperialism with responses to imperialism in Africa.

UNREST IN AFRICA

Africa witnessed many anticolonial uprisings in the first decades of colonial rule (see Map 18.2). Violent conflicts embroiled not only the Belgians and the Germans, who paid little attention to African political traditions, but also the British, whose colonial system left traditional African rulers in place. These uprisings made Europeans uneasy. Why, they wondered, were Africans resisting regimes that had huge advantages in firepower and transport and that were bringing medical skills, literacy, and other fruits of European civilization? Some Europeans concluded that Africans were too stubborn or unsophisticated to appreciate Europe's generosity. Others, shocked by colonial cruelty, called for reform. A few radicals even demanded an end to imperialism.

The Anglo-Boer War The continent's most devastating anticolonial uprising occurred in South Africa. This unique struggle pitted two white communities against each other: the British in the Cape Colony and Natal against the Afrikaners, descendants of original Dutch settlers who lived in the Transvaal and the Orange Free State (see Map 18.2 inset). Although two white regimes were the main adversaries, the Anglo-Boer War (1899–1902) involved the area's 4 million black inhabitants as fully as its 1 million whites.

The war's origins lay in the discovery of gold in the Transvaal in the mid-1880s. As the area rapidly became Africa's richest state, the prospect that Afrikaner republics might become the powerhouse in southern Africa was more than British imperialists could accept. Fearing that war was inevitable, the president of the Transvaal launched a preemptive strike against the British. In late 1899, Afrikaner forces crossed into South Africa. Fighting a relentless guerrilla campaign, Afrikaners waged a war that would last three years and cost Britain 20,000 soldiers and £200 million.

In a frustrated effort to respond to Afrikaner hit-and-run tactics, the British instituted a terrifying innovation: the concentration camp. At one moment in the war, at least 155,000 captured men, women, and children were held in camps surrounded by barbed wire. The British rounded up Afrikaners and Africans, whom they feared would side with the "anticolonial" Dutch descendants. Ultimately, the British won the war, bringing the Transvaal and the Orange Free State—with their vast gold reserves—into their empire.

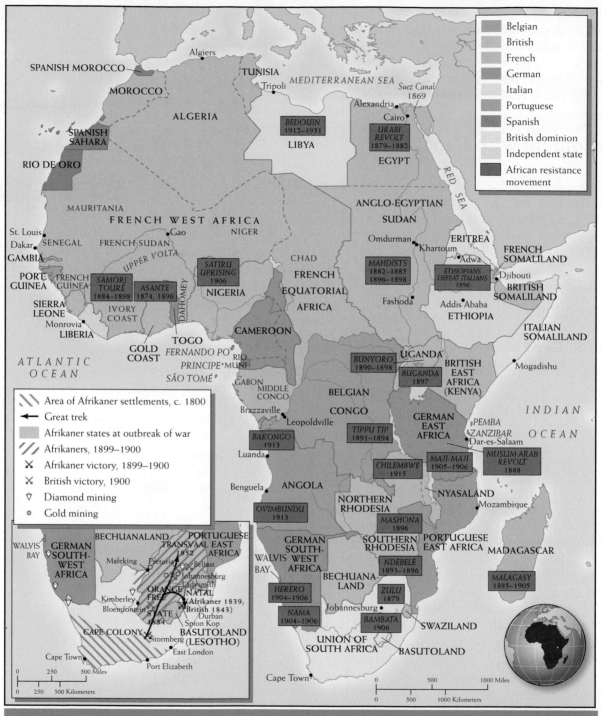

Legend:
- Belgian
- British
- French
- German
- Italian
- Portuguese
- Spanish
- British dominion
- Independent state
- African resistance movement

SPANISH MOROCCO
MOROCCO
Algiers
TUNISIA
Tripoli
MEDITERRANEAN SEA
Suez Canal 1869
Alexandria
Cairo
ALGERIA
SPANISH SAHARA
RIO DE ORO
BEDOUIN 1912–1931
LIBYA
URABI REVOLT 1879–1882
EGYPT
MAURITANIA
FRENCH WEST AFRICA
NIGER
St. Louis
Dakar
SENEGAL
FRENCH SUDAN
Gao
UPPER VOLTA
GAMBIA
PORT. GUINEA
FRENCH GUINEA
SAMORI TOURÉ 1884–1898
SATIRU UPRISING 1906
ASANTE 1874, 1896
NIGERIA
CHAD
FRENCH EQUATORIAL AFRICA
ANGLO-EGYPTIAN SUDAN
RED SEA
Omdurman
Khartoum
ERITREA
Adwa
FRENCH SOMALILAND
Djibouti
BRITISH SOMALILAND
MAHDISTS 1882–1885 1896–1898
ETHIOPIANS DEFEAT ITALIANS 1896
Fashoda
Addis Ababa
ETHIOPIA
SIERRA LEONE
Monrovia
LIBERIA
IVORY COAST
DAHOMEY
GOLD COAST
TOGO
FERNANDO PO
PRINCIPE
SÃO TOMÉ
RIO MUNI
CAMEROON
GABON
MIDDLE CONGO
Brazzaville
Leopoldville
BELGIAN CONGO
BUNYORO 1890–1898
UGANDA
BUGANDA 1897
BRITISH EAST AFRICA (KENYA)
Mogadishu
ITALIAN SOMALILAND
ATLANTIC OCEAN
BAKONGO 1913
Luanda
TIPPU TIP 1891–1894
GERMAN EAST AFRICA
PEMBA
ZANZIBAR
Dar-es-Salaam
INDIAN OCEAN
CHILEMBWE 1915
MAJI-MAJI 1905–1906
MUSLIM ARAB REVOLT 1888
Benguela
ANGOLA
NORTHERN RHODESIA
NYASALAND
Mozambique
OVIMBUNDU 1913
MASHONA 1896
SOUTHERN RHODESIA
PORTUGUESE EAST AFRICA
MADAGASCAR
MALAGASY 1885–1905
WALVIS BAY
GERMAN SOUTH-WEST AFRICA
HERERO 1904–1906
BECHUANALAND
NDEBELE 1893–1896
NAMA 1904–1906
Johannesburg
ZULU 1879
BAMBATA 1906
SWAZILAND
BASUTOLAND
UNION OF SOUTH AFRICA
Cape Town

South Africa inset legend:
- Area of Afrikaner settlements, c. 1800
- Great trek
- Afrikaner states at outbreak of war
- Afrikaners, 1899–1900
- ✕ Afrikaner victory, 1899–1900
- ✕ British victory, 1900
- ▽ Diamond mining
- ● Gold mining

WALVIS BAY
GERMAN SOUTH-WEST AFRICA
BECHUANALAND
PORTUGUESE EAST AFRICA
TRANSVAAL 1852
Mafeking
Pretoria
Belfast
Johannesburg
Ladysmith
ORANGE FREE STATE 1854
NATAL (Afrikaner 1839; British 1843)
Kimberley
Bloemfontein
Durban
Spion Kop
CAPE COLONY
BASUTOLAND (LESOTHO)
Stormberg
East London
Cape Town
Port Elizabeth

0   250   500 Miles
0   250   500 Kilometers

0   500   1000 Miles
0   500   1000 Kilometers

MAP 18.2 | Uprisings and Wars in Africa

The European partition and conquest of Africa were violent affairs.

- How many separate African resistance movements can you count on this map?
- Where was resistance the most prolonged?
- According to your reading, why were Ethiopians, who sustained their autonomy, able to do what other African opponents of European armies were not?

But the horrors of the war traumatized the British, who regarded themselves as Europe's most enlightened and efficient colonial rulers.

Other Struggles in Colonized Africa The disgust that some Europeans felt toward imperial violence deepened after Germany's activities in Africa also went brutally wrong. Germany had established colonies in Southwest Africa (present-day Namibia), Cameroon, and Togo in 1884 and in East Africa in 1885. In German Southwest Africa, the Herero and San people resisted the Germans, and in German East Africa (modern-day Tanzania), the Muslim Arab peoples rebelled. Between 1904 and 1906, fighting in German Southwest Africa escalated to such an extent that the German commander issued an extermination order against the Herero population.

According to those who favored European imperialism, however, the atrocities of the Boer War and German Southwest Africa, like the horrors of Leopold's Belgian Congo (see Chapter 17), were exceptions to what they considered their enlightened rule. Portraying Africans as either accepting subjects or childlike primitives—as in the Maji-Maji Revolt in German East Africa, described at the beginning of this chapter—Europeans redoubled their efforts to impose colonial order. The problem, in their view, was that they

Extermination of the Herero The Germans carried out a campaign of near-extermination against the Herero population in German Southwest Africa in 1904–1906. Nearly 90 percent of the Herero were killed.

had not tried hard enough to bring civilization. In many cases, the number of officials stationed in the colonies increased.

THE BOXER UPRISING IN CHINA

Although not formally colonized, China too struggled against European intrusions. As the population swelled to over half a billion and outstripped the country's resources, problems of landlessness, poverty, and peasant discontent (long-standing concerns in China's modern history) left the established order vulnerable to internal revolts and foreign intervention.

The breakdown of dynastic authority originated largely with foreign pressure. For one thing, China's defeat in the Sino-Japanese War of 1894–1895 (see Chapter 17) was deeply humiliating. Japan acquired Taiwan as its first major colony, and European powers demanded that the weakened Qing government grant them specific areas within China as their respective "spheres of influence" (see Map 18.3). The United States argued instead for maintaining an "open door" policy in China that would keep access available to all traders, while supporting missionary efforts to spread Christianity.

Unrest and Revolt The most explosive reaction to these pressures, the **Boxer Uprising**, started within the peasantry. Like colonized peoples in Africa, the Boxers violently resisted European meddling. And like the Taiping Rebellion decades earlier (see Chapter 16), the story of the Boxers was tied to missionary activities. Whereas in earlier centuries Jesuit missionaries had sought to convert the court and the elites, by the mid-nineteenth century the missionary goal was to convert commoners. After the Taiping Rebellion, Christian missionaries had streamed into China, impatient to make new converts in the hinterlands and confident of their governments' backing.

MAP 18.3 | Foreign Spheres of Influence in China, 1842–1907

While technically independent, the Qing dynasty could not prevent foreign penetration and domination of its economy during the nine-teenth century.

• Which five powers established spheres of influence in China?

• At what time was the greatest number of treaty ports established?

• According to your reading, what did the foreign powers hope to achieve within their spheres of influence? What kinds of local opposition did the foreign influence inspire?

The Boxers rejected claims of Western superiority. Especially in regions suffering from natural disasters and economic hardship, activists provided assistance to the dis-possessed. Women played a prominent role. The so-called Red Lanterns were mostly teenage girls and unmarried women who announced their loyalty by wearing red garments. Although segregated from the male Boxers—Red Lanterns worshipped at their own altars and practiced martial arts at separate boxing grounds—they were important to the movement in counteracting the influence of Christian women. Indeed, one of the Boxers' greatest fears was that cunning Christian women would use their guile to weaken the Boxers' spirits. They claimed that the "purity" of the Red Lanterns could counter this threat. The Red Lanterns were supposedly capable of incredible feats: they could walk on water or fly through the air. Belief in their magical powers provided critical assistance for the uprising.

As the movement gained momentum, the Qing vacillated between viewing the Boxers as a threat to order and embracing them as a force to check foreign intrusion. Early in 1900, Qing troops clashed with the Boxers in an escalating cycle of violence. By spring, however, the Qing could no longer control the tens of thousands of Boxers roaming the vicinities of Beijing and Tianjin. Embracing the Boxers' cause, the empress dowager declared war against the foreign powers in June 1900.

Acting without any discernible plan or leadership, the Boxers attacked Christian and foreign symbols and persons. They harassed and sometimes killed Chinese Christians in parts of northern China, destroyed railroad tracks and telegraph lines, and attacked owners of foreign objects such as lamps and clocks. In Beijing, the Boxers besieged foreign embassy compounds where diplomats and their families cowered in fear. The Boxers also reduced the Southern Cathedral to ruins and then besieged the Northern Cathedral, where more than 3,000 Catholics and 40 French and Italian marines had sought refuge.

Foreign Involvement and Aftermath In August 1900, a foreign army of 20,000 troops crushed the Boxers. About half came from Japan; the rest came primarily from Russia, Britain, Germany, France, and the United States. Thereafter, the victors forced the Chinese to sign the punitive Boxer Protocol. It required the regime to pay an exorbitant compensation in gold (about twice the empire's annual income) for damages to foreign life and property. The protocol also authorized western powers to station troops in Beijing.

Even in defeat, the Boxers' antiwestern uprising showed how much had changed in China since the Taiping Rebellion. Although the Boxers were primarily peasants, even they had felt the unsettledness generated by European inroads into China. Indeed, the Europeans' commercial and spiritual reach, once confined to elites and port cities, had extended across much of China. Whereas the Taiping Rebellion had mobilized millions against the Qing, the Boxers remained loyal to the dynasty and focused their wrath on foreigners and Chinese Christians. The Boxer Rebellion, like the Maji-Maji Revolt in East Africa, revealed the widespread political opposition to westernization and the willingness of disaffected populations to resist western programs.

Worldwide Insecurities

COMPARISON

IDENTIFY and **DESCRIBE** political, economic, and social crises that swept through the world in this period, and **ANALYZE** the impact they had on different regions of the world.

While news of unrest in the distant colonies and in China generally did not lead Europeans to question their ways, conflicts closer to home tore at European confidence in this era. The rise of a European-centered world deepened rivalries within Europe. Numerous factors fostered conflict, including France's smoldering resentment at its defeat in the Franco-Prussian War (see Chapter 17), and led to a buildup of military forces, especially in Britain, Germany, and France. Tensions also increased as the European states competed for raw materials and colonial footholds. Not everyone, however, supported vast expenditures on the military. Many Europeans disapproved of spending on massive steam-powered warships. Others warned that the arms race would end in a devastating war. At the same time, the booms and busts of expanding industrial economies, challenges about the proper roles of women, and problems of uncontrolled urbanization shook the established order and had an impact across the globe (see again Map 18.1). These changes and insecurities transformed Europe and swept through the world.

FINANCIAL, INDUSTRIAL, AND TECHNOLOGICAL CHANGE

Economic developments helped make powers "great," but they could also unsettle societies. Indeed, pride about wealth and growth coincided with laments about changes in national and international economies. To begin with, Americans and Europeans recognized that the small-scale, laissez-faire capitalism championed by Adam Smith (see Chapter 14) was giving way to an economic order dominated by huge, heavily capitalized firms. Gone, it seemed, was Smith's vision of many small producers in vigorous competition with one another, all benefiting from efficient—but not exploitative—divisions of labor.

Instead of smooth progress, the economy of Europe and North America in the nineteenth century bounced between booms and busts: long-term business cycles of rapid growth followed by countercycles of stagnation. Late in the century, the pace of economic change accelerated. Large-scale steel production, railroad building, and textile manufacturing expanded at breakneck speed, while waves of bank closures, bankruptcies, and agricultural crises ruined many small property owners, including farmers. By the century's end, European and North American economies were dominated as never before by a few large-scale firms, such as John D. Rockefeller's Standard Oil and the large banking institutions in France, Britain, Germany, and the United States. The same was true in Japan, where *zaibatsu*—large companies with banking subsidiaries for finance and industrial wings dominating different sectors of the market—like Sumitomo, Mitsui, and Mitsubishi were the engine of Japan's extraordinary economic growth.

Financial Integration and Crises These were years of heady international financial integration. More and more countries joined the world system of borrowing and lending; more and more countries were linked financially through global loans and the fact that all of the major national currencies in the world, such as the American dollar, the British pound, and the French franc were exchanged at reliable rates. At the hub of this world system were the banks of London, which since the Napoleonic wars had been a major source of capital for international borrowers.

The rise of giant banks and huge industrial corporations caused alarm, for it seemed to signal an end to free markets and competitive capitalism. Rather than longing for the return of truly free markets, many critics sought reforms that would protect people from economic instability. The solution, many economists and politicians thought, was for the state to manage the national economies.

Banking especially seemed in need of closer government supervision. Many industrial societies already had central banks (banks that issued national currencies, fixed underlying interest rates, and in general controlled monetary policy); London's Bank of England had long since overseen local and international money markets. But governments did not have the resources to protect all—or even most—investments during times of crisis. Between 1890 and 1893, 550 American banks collapsed, and only the intervention of J. P. Morgan prevented the depletion of the nation's reserves of gold that stood behind the dollar.

The road to regulation of banking and finance, however, was hardly smooth. In 1907, a more serious crisis threatened. A panic on Wall Street led to a run on the banks. Once again, J. P. Morgan rescued the American economy from financial panic—by compelling financiers to commit unprecedented funds (eventually $35 million) to protect banks and trusts against depositors' panic. Morgan himself lost $21 million and emerged from the bank panic convinced that some sort of public oversight was needed. By 1913, the U.S. Congress ratified the Federal Reserve Act, creating boards to monitor the supply and demand of the nation's money. The crisis of 1907 also showed how national financial matters could quickly become international affairs as panicked American investors withdrew their funds from other countries, many of which relied on American capital.

Industrialization and the Modern Economy Backed by big banks, industrialists extended their enterprises to new places. For example, with loans from European investors, Russia built railways, telegraph lines, and factories. By 1900, Russia was producing half of the world's oil and a considerable amount of steel. Yet industrial development remained uneven: southern Europe and the American South continued to lag behind northern regions. The gap was even more pronounced in colonial territories, which contained few industrial enterprises aside from railroad building and mining.

By 1914, the factory and the railroad had become global symbols of the modern economy—and of its positive and negative effects. Everywhere, the coming of the railroad to one's town or village was a big event: for some, it represented an exhilarating leap into the modern world; for others, a terrifying abandonment of the past. Ocean liners, automobiles, and airplanes likewise could be both dazzling and disorienting.

For ordinary people, the new economy brought benefits and drawbacks. Factories produced cheaper goods, but they belched clouds of black smoke. Railways offered faster transport, but they ruined small towns unlucky enough to be left off the branch line. Machines (when operating properly) were more efficient than human and animal labor, but workers who used them felt reduced to machines themselves. Indeed, the American Frederick Winslow Taylor proposed a system of "scientific management" to make human bodies perform more like machines, maximizing the efficiency of workers' movements. But workers did not want to be managed or to cede control of the pace of production to employers. Labor's resistance to "Taylorization" led to numerous strikes. For strikers, as for those left out of the new economy, the course of progress had taken an unsettling turn.

THE "WOMAN QUESTION"

Complicating the situation was turmoil about the "woman question." In the West, female activists demanded that women be given more rights as citizens; more radical voices called for fundamental changes to the family and the larger society. At the same time, imperialists claimed that colonial rule was bringing great improvements to women in Asia and Africa. But the "woman question" was no more easily settled there than elsewhere.

Women's Issues in the West In western countries, for most of the nineteenth century, a belief in "separate spheres" had supposedly confined women to domestic matters, while leaving men in charge of public life and economic undertakings. (In practice, only women from middle- and upper-class families avoided working outside the home for wages.) However, as economic developments created new jobs for women and greater access to education, women increasingly found work as teachers, secretaries, typists, department store clerks, social workers, and telephone operators. These jobs offered greater economic and social independence. Some educated women spearheaded efforts to improve conditions for the urban poor and to expand the government's role in regulating economic affairs. Nonetheless much of the population continued to think that higher education and public activism were not suitable for women.

In one important change, many women began to assert control over reproduction. Although in numerous countries the use of contraceptive devices was illegal, women still found a variety of ways to limit the number of children they bore. In addition to marrying late and sleeping apart, some used spermicidal herbs, which sometimes worked but sometimes killed the woman; others relied a variety of sponges and other barriers; condoms; or insisted on the practice of *coitus interruptus* (withdrawal). When contraception failed, many women turned to abortion, even though it was illegal. Successful contraception, by whatever means, depended on cooperation and communication and tended to be more effective as educational levels increased.

Early in the twentieth century, the birthrate in America was half of what it had been a century before. By having fewer children, families could devote more income to education, food, housing, and leisure activities. Declining birthrates, along with improved medicine, also meant that fewer women died in childbirth; more would see their children reach adulthood.

Still, changes in women's social status did not translate into full political rights at the national level, such as the vote. By the mid-nineteenth century, women's suffrage movements had appeared in several countries, but these campaigns bore little immediate fruit. In 1868, women received the right to vote in local elections in Britain. Within a few years, Finland, Sweden, and some American states allowed single, property-owning women the right to cast ballots—again, only in local elections. Women obtained the right to vote in national elections in New Zealand in 1893, in Australia in 1902, in Finland in 1906, and in Norway in 1913.

Despite these gains, male alarmists portrayed women's suffrage and women's rights as the beginning of civilization's end. Among women, views on feminism varied. Most middle-class women in Europe and the Americas were not seeking to make women equal to men. Indeed, many bourgeois women recoiled from the close relationships between socialism and feminism. In Latin America, for example, anarchists championed a version of feminism arguing that the abolition of private property would liberate women from their misery and that the traditional family was a bourgeois convention. Other women feared becoming too "mannish," and a few worried that equality would destroy female sensuality. Most, probably, looked to reform less in terms of voting rights and more in terms of better treatment within families and local communities.

Women's Status in Colonies In the colonial world, the woman question was also a contentious issue—but it was mainly argued among men. European authorities liked to boast that colonial rule improved women's status. Citing examples of traditional societies' treatment of women, they criticized the veiling of women in Islamic societies, the binding of women's feet in China, widow burning (*sati*) in India, and female genital mutilation in Africa. Europeans believed that prohibiting such acts was a justification for colonial intervention.

And yet, colonialism only added to women's burdens. As male workers headed into the export economy, formerly shared agricultural work fell exclusively on women's shoulders. In Africa, for example, the opening of vast gold and diamond mines drew thousands of men away to work in the mines, leaving women to tend to the farmstead and to do colonial tasks that men once did. Similarly, the rise of European-owned agricultural estates in Kenya and Southern Rhodesia depleted surrounding villages of male family members, who went to work on the estates. In these circumstances, women kept the local, food-producing economy afloat.

Nor did colonial "civilizing" rhetoric improve women's political or cultural circumstances. In fact, European missionaries preached a message of domesticity to Asian and African families, emphasizing that women's place was in the home raising children and that women's education should be different from men's. Thus, males overwhelmingly dominated the new schools that Europeans built. Moreover, the chiefs who collaborated with colonial officials consistently favored men. As a result, African women often lost landholding and other rights that they had enjoyed before the Europeans' arrival.

CLASS CONFLICT

As capitalism's volatility shook confidence in free market economies and sharpened conflicts between classes, the tone of political debate was transformed as new voices called for radical change. Although living conditions for European and North American workers improved over time, widening inequalities in income and the slow pace of reform bred frustration. Most workers remained committed to peaceful agitation, but some radicals favored violence against the state and its agents.

Strikes and Revolts In the Americas and in Europe, radicals adopted numerous tactics for asserting the interests of the working class. In Europe, the franchise was gradually expanded in hopes that the lower classes would prefer voting to revolution—and indeed, most of the new political parties that catered to workers had no desire to overthrow the state. But conservatives feared them anyway, especially as they gained electoral clout. The Labour Party, founded in Britain in 1900, quickly boasted a large share of the vote. By 1912, the German Social Democratic Party was the largest party in the Reichstag though it lacked power since the Reichstag was only an advisory body. It was not the legally sanctioned parties that sparked violent street protests and strikes in the century's last decades. A whole array of **syndicalists** (labor activists), **anarchists** (who opposed government altogether), royalists, and socialists sprang up in this period, making work stoppages everyday affairs.

Although the United States had similar radical groups, they were few and small. Nonetheless, American workers were organizing. The labor movement's power burst forth

Labor Disputes The late nineteenth century witnessed a surge in industrial strife, worker strikes, and violent suppression of labor movements. (*Left*) One of the deadliest confrontations in the United States occurred in May 1892, when a strike against the Carnegie Steel Company escalated into a gunfight, which left ten dead and many more wounded. Here, a group of striking workers keeps watch over the steel mill in Homestead, Pennsylvania. (*Right*) Striking dockworkers rally in London's Trafalgar Square, 1911. By this time, residents of European cities were used to seeing crowds of protesters pressing for improved working conditions or political reform.

dramatically in 1894. Spawned by wage cuts and firings following an economic downturn, the Pullman strike (directed against the maker of railway sleeping cars, George Pullman) involved approximately 3 million workers. The strike's conclusion, however, revealed the enduring power of the status quo. After hiring replacement workers to break the strike, Pullman requested federal troops to protect his operation. After its leaders were jailed, the strike collapsed. Although strikes and protests in the United States and Europe often failed to achieve their immediate goals, they worried those in power and ultimately led to important changes.

Revolution in Mexico Perhaps the most successful turn-of-the-century revolution occurred in Mexico. This peasant uprising thoroughly transformed the country. Fueled by the unequal distribution of land and by disgruntled workers, the **Mexican Revolution** erupted in 1910 when political elites split over the succession of General Porfirio Díaz after decades of his strong-arm rule. Dissidents balked when Díaz refused to step down, and peasants and workers rallied to the call to arms.

From the north (led by the charismatic Pancho Villa) to the south (under the legendary Emiliano Zapata), peasants, farmers, and other rural workers helped topple the Díaz regime. In the name of providing land for farmers and ending oligarchic rule, peasant armies defeated Díaz's troops and proceeded to destroy many large estates. The fighting lasted for ten brutal years, during which almost 10 percent of the country's population perished.

Thereafter political leaders had to accept popular demands for democracy, respect for the sovereignty of peasant communities, and land reform. The revolution's most lasting legacy was perhaps the creation of rural communes for Mexico's peasantry. These communal village holdings, called *ejidos*, looked back to a precolonial heritage. The revolution spawned a set of new national myths based on the heroism of rural peoples, Mexican nationalism, and a celebration of the Aztec past.

Preserving Established Orders Although the Mexican Revolution succeeded in toppling the old elite, elsewhere in Latin America the ruling establishment remained united against assaults from below. Already, in 1897, the Brazilian army had mercilessly suppressed a peasant movement in the northeastern part of the country. Moreover, in Cuba, the Spanish and then the American armies crushed tenant farmers' efforts to reclaim land from sugar estates. In Guatemala, Mayan Indians lost land to coffee barons.

In Europe and the United States, the preservation of established orders did not rest on repression alone. Here, elites also grudgingly agreed to gradual change. Indeed, by the century's end, left-wing agitators, muckraking reporters, and middle-class reformers began to win meaningful social improvements. Unable to suppress the socialist movement, Otto von Bismarck, the German chancellor, defused the appeal of socialism by enacting social welfare measures in 1883–1884, insuring workers against illness, accidents, and old age and establishing maximum working hours. In the United States, it took lurid journalistic accounts of unsanitary practices in Chicago slaughterhouses (including tales of workers falling into lard vats and being rendered into cooking fat) to spur the federal government into action. (See **Current Trends in World History: Industrialization and Its Antidotes**.) In 1906, President Theodore Roosevelt signed a Meat Inspection Act that provided for government supervision of meatpacking operations. In other cases (banking, steel production, railroads), the federal government's enhanced supervisory authority served corporate interests as well.

These consumer and family protection measures reflected a broader reform movement, one dedicated to creating a more efficient society and correcting the undesirable consequences of urbanization and industrialization. At local and state levels, these **progressive reformers** attacked corrupt city governments that had allegedly fallen into the hands of immigrant-dominated "political machines." The progressives also attacked other vices, such as gambling, drinking, and prostitution—all associated with industrialized, urban settings. The creation of city parks preoccupied urban planners, who hoped parks' green spaces would serve as the city's "lungs" and offer healthier forms of entertainment than houses of prostitution, gambling dens, and bars. From Scandinavia to California, the proponents of old-age pensions and public ownership of utilities put pressure on lawmakers. Thousands of associations took shape against capitalism's harsher effects, and they occasionally succeeded in changing state policies. Indeed, the period leading up to World War I was one of rapid change, in which financial crises reverberated across the globe, European and American women pressed for their rights and also agitated for the rights of Asian and African women, and elites were forced to make reforms, though they tended to be limited, in the colonial and colonializers' worlds.

Cultural Modernism

As revolutionaries and reformers wrestled with the problems of progress, intellectuals, artists, and scientists struggled to make sense of change in their own societies and beyond. What we call **modernism**—the sense of having broken with tradition—came to prominence in many fields, from physics to architecture, from painting to the social sciences.

COMPARISON

EXPLAIN how European modernism drew on Afro-Asian influences and represented uncertainty about ideas inherited from the Enlightenment.

Industrialization and Its Antidotes: Conservation and Regulation

As the impact of industrialization spread during the late nineteenth century, a few individuals, including those who championed rapid economic development, recognized that this progress brought unwanted consequences. A new awareness dawned that while industrialization allowed production to increase dramatically, it also resulted in the depletion of natural resources and the degradation of the quality of life for humans. Awakened to the ecological costs of economic progress, these environmentalist pioneers tried to reverse a trend, which we have highlighted throughout this study, of humankind's growing tendency to pollute the environment, overgraze marginal areas, and exploit resources to their exhaustion.

One of the first world leaders to take seriously industrialization's threats to the environment—and to national character—was President Theodore Roosevelt. A man who delighted in hunting, riding, and testing himself against the elements, Roosevelt worried that as the United States became an increasingly industrialized and urbanized society, the American people would lose the courage, the fitness, and the "rugged individualism" that the taming of wildernesses had supposedly imbued in them. In understanding the problem and formulating a response to it, he was especially struck by George Perkins Marsh's 1864 Man and Nature, which explored the ways in which the use and depletion of forests and other natural resources had determined the rise and fall of civilizations around the ancient Mediterranean. If the United States failed to curb its destruction of woodlands, that book suggested, it faced a collapse similar to Greece and Rome. Although several "national" parks and forests had been founded before Roosevelt became U.S. president in 1901, he was extremely active in pushing forward legislation to conserve more land, especially in the west. By offering visitors the opportunity to experience wilderness conditions, the national parks were to provide a partial antidote to what Roosevelt saw as the effeminizing tendencies of modern society.

In setting aside lands as national forests and parks, Roosevelt wanted to prevent what he feared might be the degeneration of the American character. But Roosevelt had other objects in view too in pressing the state to take a more activist role in the economy. Noting that on the European continent, "progressives" and urban-based reformers were augmenting the reach and power of the state to combat economic inequalities and to build infrastructures that benefited all, Roosevelt pushed for a departure from the laissez-faire principles that had dominated American political-economic discourse in the last decades of the nineteenth century. With European state-funded projects like the straightening of the Rhine River in mind, Roosevelt argued that the state should itself tackle projects that were too large to be built by private enterprises.

In yet another area, Roosevelt created a national, regulatory solution to a problem that the market could not solve by itself. In the decade or so before he came into office, newspaper reporters had exposed hundreds of schemes by sellers of home remedies such as Mrs. Winslow's Soothing Syrup to get rich by promising consumers that their "patent" medicines would cure any disease. In truth, many of these "medicines" contained alcohol, cocaine, or just cod-liver oil; some were

Modernist movements were notably international. Egyptian social scientists read the works of European thinkers, while French and German painters flocked to museums to inspect artifacts from Egypt and artworks from other parts of Africa, Asia, and Oceania. As education spread and political reforms enfranchised more Americans and Europeans, changes in the meaning of culture occurred, causing it to be less elitist and more popular. Yet European elites did not give up their opera houses and paintings in favor of arts and entertainments that were appealing to urban workers or colonized peoples. Instead, the arts became more abstract: musicians abandoned the comfort of harmonic and diatonic sound (the eight-tone scale standard in classical western music at the time); writers and visual artists left realistic representation behind.

Above all, modernism in arts and sciences replaced the certainties of the Enlightenment with the unsettledness of the new age. Modernists challenged claims to provide complete, coherent explanations and representations of all kinds. With growing doubts harmful, others were simply useless. Other investigators, such as the novelist Upton Sinclair, exposed horrors in the meatpacking industry. Sinclair's realist novel, *The Jungle* (1906), for example, contained reports of extremely unsanitary workplace conditions and of workers falling into fat-rendering machines and being canned along with the beef. In the same year that Sinclair's hugely influential novel appeared, Roosevelt oversaw the creation of the Food and Drug Administration and the passage of the Pure Food and Drug Act. The FDA's charge was to implement this act, and to look after public health—something that did not concern profit-hungry corporations—by regulating food and medicines against contamination. In the wake of the banking panic of 1907 (see Financial Integration and Crises, p. 657), too, Americans came to accept that they needed banking regulations as well, and in 1913 Congress enacted the Federal Reserve Act. Americans were not alone in beginning to temper capitalism with regulation, and industrialization with conservation. Europeans at last began to enact legislation to protect workers from dangerous workplaces and to create large green spaces

Patent Medicines Like Mrs. Winslow's Soothing Syrup, Hamlin's Wizard Oil claimed to cure anything from headaches to cancer, in humans and animals alike.

in cities so that the industrialized world might have "lungs" with which to breathe. In Argentina, many were drawn to mountainous regions to escape becoming too

"soft" in urban surroundings, and a conservationist movement began that would hit its stride in the 1930s. Although such developments only moderated—slightly— the industrialized world's contributions to environmental degradation and the exploitation of mass consumers, they did signal the reality that some, at least, had begun to recognize that progress, too, had its price.

QUESTION FOR ANALYSIS

- Who benefited from Roosevelt's national parks and the Pure Food and Drug Act? Who may have suffered from these regulations?
- Roosevelt considered courage, fitness, and "rugged individualism" vital to the American identity. Why did he choose these traits specifically, and are these traits as vital today? Explain.

Explore Further

Douglas Brinkley, *Wilderness Warrior: Theodore Roosevelt and the Crusade to Save America* (2010).

Edmund Morris, *Theodore Rex* (2002).

about civilizing missions or urban and industrial "progress," artists and scientists struggled to understand a world in which human reason seamed inadequate.

POPULAR CULTURE COMES OF AGE

From the late eighteenth to the late nineteenth century, production and consumption of the arts, books, music, and sports changed dramatically. The change derived mainly from new urban settings, technological innovations, mass education, and increased leisure time. Middle-class art lovers eagerly purchased mass-produced engravings; millions attended dance halls and vaudeville shows (entertainment by singers, dancers, and comedians). For the first time, sports attracted mass followings. Soccer in Europe, baseball in the United States, and cricket in India had wildly devoted middle- and working-class fans. Thus did a truly **popular culture** emerge, delivering affordable and accessible forms of art and entertainment to "the masses."

Impressionism was an artistic movement, radical in its day, which emerged in Paris in the last third of the nineteenth century. Its members broke away from the conventional art community and its official, academic salons. With small, visible brushstrokes, the impressionists stressed the changing qualities of light, the passage of time, and movement. Rather than compete with photography and present a facsimile of a stable, static, coherent external reality, they sought to capture perceptions of a world in rapid flux. These two paintings, Claude Monet's *The Gare St-Lazare* (*left*) and Camille Pissarro's *Sunset over the Boieldieu Bridge at Rouen* (*right*), exemplify the impressionists' ambivalent view of nineteenth-century progress.

By the nineteenth century's close, the press stood as a major form of popular entertainment and information. This was partly because publishers were offering different wares to different classes of readers and partly because many more people could read, especially in Europe and the Americas. By that time, the English *Daily Mail* and the French *Petit Parisien* boasted circulations of over 1 million. In the United States, urban dwellers, many of them immigrants, avidly read newspapers—some in English, others in their native languages. Banner headlines, sensational stories, and simple language drew in readers with little education or poor English skills.

By now the kind of culture one consumed had become a reflection of one's real (or desired) status in society. For many Latin American workers, for example, reading one's own newspaper or comic strip was part of being a worker. Argentina's socialist newspaper, *La Vanguardia*, was one of Buenos Aires's most prominent periodicals, read and debated at work and in the cafés of working-class neighborhoods. Anyone seen reading the bourgeois paper, *La Prensa*, faced heckling and ridicule by fellow workers. As the community of cultural consumers broadened, and as ideas from across the globe flooded in, writers, artists, and scholars struggled to adapt.

MODERNISM IN EUROPEAN CULTURE

In intellectual and artistic terms, Europe at the turn of the twentieth century experienced perhaps its richest age since the Renaissance. Artists' work reflected their doubts about the modern world, as represented by the railroad, the big city, and the factory. While the artists and writers of the mid-nineteenth century had largely celebrated progress, the painters and novelists of the century's end took a darker view. They turned away from reason, which the Enlightenment had championed, and descriptive prose as they searched for meanings that came from instinct and emotion. The primitive came to symbolize both Europe's lost innocence and the forces that reason could not control, such as sexual drives, religious fervor, or brute strength.

New Forms of Subjectivity Jean-Auguste-Dominique Ingres, one of the great realist artists of the nineteenth century, was one of Pablo Picasso's idols. The portrait of the newspaper baron Louis-François Bertin (*left*) embodies the artist's confidence in his own ability to represent an external reality just as it appears. Picasso refined his technique by copying Ingres's works at the Louvre. He clearly used Ingres as a model for his 1910 portrait of his own art dealer, Ambroise Vollard (*right*), which built on the work of the impressionists, in an effort to challenge the two-dimensional realism of his master.

Europeans began to see the world in a fundamentally different way, aided by the experience of nonwestern visual arts. The painter who led the way in incorporating nonwestern themes into modern art was Pablo Picasso (1881–1973), who found in African art forms a radically new way of expressing human sentiments that was shocking to most European and American observers. Other artists were inspired by the sleekness and syncopation of machines, or by the irrational content of dreams. And painting was not the only art form that displayed a modern style. Arnold Schönberg (1874–1951) composed the first piece of music that rejected traditional western tonality. World-famous dancers like Isadora Duncan (1877–1927) pioneered the expressive, free-form movements that laid the foundations for modern dance.

However, the arts alone did not undermine older views of the world. Even science, in which the Enlightenment had placed so much faith, challenged the idea that the world functioned according to easily understood natural laws. After 1900, pioneering physicists and mathematicians like Albert Einstein (1879–1955) challenged the idea that a single scientific theory, like Newton's, could explain everything. They took apart the Enlightenment's conviction that man could achieve full knowledge of, and control over, nature. In a series of papers published between 1905 and 1915, Einstein worked out the special and general theories of relativity, which demonstrated that measurements of speed and gravitational pull were not purely objective, but always conditioned by the relative position and conditions of the observer. Although most scientists continued to collect data, feeling certain that they could plumb nature's depths, some of their colleagues began to question the arrogance of this view.

From the time of the Enlightenment, Europeans had prided themselves in their "reason." To be rational was to be civilized and to master irrational urges; respectable, middle-class nineteenth-century men were thought to embody these virtues. But in the late nineteenth century, faith in rationality began to falter. Perhaps reason was *not* man's highest attainment, said some; perhaps reason was impossible for man to sustain, said others. Friedrich Nietzsche (1844–1900) claimed that conventional European attempts to assert The Truth— including science and Judeo-Christian moral codes—were nothing more than life-destroying quests for power. Sigmund Freud (1856–1939) began to excavate layers of the human subconscious, where irrational desires and fears lay buried. For Freud, human nature was not as simple as it had seemed to Enlightenment thinkers. Instead, he asserted, humans were driven by sexual longings and childhood traumas. Neither Nietzsche nor Freud was well loved among nineteenth-century liberal elites. But in the new century, Nietzsche would become the prophet for many antiliberal causes, from nudism to Nazism; and Freud's dark vision would become central to the twentieth century's understanding of the self.

CULTURAL MODERNISM IN CHINA

What it meant to be modern sparked debate beyond western Europe. Europeans provided one set of answers; thinkers elsewhere offered quite different answers. Chinese artists and scientists at the turn of the century selectively engaged western ideas and transformed them. Indeed, some scholars have described the late Qing period as a time of competing cultural *modernities*, in contrast to the post-Qing era, which pursued a single, western-oriented *modernity*. These forms of modernity involved critical reflection on Chinese traditions and mixed reactions to Western culture.

As in the West, Chinese writers now had a wider readership. By the late nineteenth century, more than 170 presses in China were serving a potential readership of 2 to 4 million concentrated mostly in the urban areas. These cities were more economically and culturally vibrant than the hinterlands. Not only was there an expanding body of readers, but newly rich beneficiaries of the treaty-port economy now patronized the arts.

Painters from the lower Yangzi region, collectively known as the **Shanghai School**, adopted elements from both indigenous and foreign sources. Although classically trained, they appropriated new western techniques into their art.

Similarly, fantasy novels drew on both western science and indigenous supernatural beliefs. Some experimental writers explicitly addressed Chinese–western relations. Depicting China at war with western powers, the novel *New Era* (1908) celebrated conventional military themes but also introduced western inventions such as electricity-repellent clothing and bulletproof satin.

Although steamships, telegraphs, and railroads captured public attention, there was little interest in changing fundamental Chinese beliefs. Indeed, even as Chinese intellectuals recognized new modes of knowledge, many of the elite insisted that Chinese learning remain the principal source of all knowledge. What kind of balance should exist between western thought and Chinese learning, or even whether the ancient classics should keep their fundamental role, was an issue that would haunt generations to come. In this respect, the Chinese dilemma reflected a worldwide challenge to accepting the impulses of modernism.

Modernism arose at a time when intellectuals began to question the values that had sustained Europe and North America throughout most of the nineteenth century. It reflected discontent with industrialization, income inequality, and colonial repression. Even though modernism had its origins and most profound impact in Europe, in many ways, especially in art, it drew upon nonwestern traditions and spread its influence throughout Asia and Africa among the educated classes.

Rethinking Race and Reimagining Nations

Ironically, at this time of huge population transfers and shared technological modernization, many European and American elites embraced the idea that the identities of peoples and nations were deeply rooted and unchangeable and were based on physical and cultural characteristics. By the century's close, racial roots had become a crucial part of identity. People wanted to know who they (and their neighbors) were—especially in terms of *biological* ancestry. Now the idea of inheritance took on new weight, in both cultural and biological forms. Nationalists spoke of the uniqueness of the Slavic soul, the German mind, Hindu spirituality, the Hispanic race.

Nationalist and racial ideas were different in different parts of the world. In Europe and America, debates about race and national purity reflected several concerns: above all, fear of being overrun by the brown, black, and yellow peoples beyond the borders of "civilization." By contrast, in India these ideas were part of the anticolonial debate, and they helped to mobilize people politically. This was also the case in China, Latin America, and the Islamic world, where discussions of identity went hand in hand with opposition to western domination and corrupt indigenous elites.

As we will see, these new impulses produced a variety of national movements, from China's anti-Qing campaign to India's Swadeshi movement. At the same time, pan-ethnic movements looked beyond the nation-state, envisioning communities based on ethnicity. Behind these movements was the notion that political communities should be built on racial purity.

COMPARISON

EVALUATE the ways in which race, nation, and religion unified populations but also made societies more difficult to govern.

NATION AND RACE IN NORTH AMERICA AND EUROPE

Americans and Europeans greeted the end of the century with a combination of pride and pessimism, and this mood influenced attitudes about national identity, race, and religion. In the early 1890s, for example, Americans flocked to extravagant commemorations of the four-hundredth anniversary of Christopher Columbus's discovery. Yet, at the same time, Americans—like many Europeans—feared for their future.

Regulating the Environment and Immigration Americans especially worried that the United States had exhausted its supposedly infinite supply of new land and resources—as evidenced by the disappearance of the buffalo, the erosion of soils, and the depletion of timber stands by aggressive logging companies. Conservationists' alarm grew more intense with the Census Bureau's 1890 announcement that the American frontier had "closed." When Theodore Roosevelt became president of the United States in 1901, he translated concerns about conserving natural resources into government policy. The market, insisted Roosevelt and like-minded conservationists, could not be trusted to protect "nature." Instead, federal regulation was necessary. This led to the creation in 1905 of the National Forest Service to manage the development of millions of acres of permanent public lands.

Another issue troubled the Americans: the need to maintain the dominance of persons of European descent. As a result, the government initiated new forms of racial discrimination where old forms (like slavery) had broken down. In the American West, animosity toward Chinese workers led to the 1882 Exclusion Act, which prohibited almost all immigration from China. In the American South, where most of the nation's 7 million African Americans resided, a system of "Jim Crow" laws upheld racial segregation and inequality.

Americans from western Europe grew even more anxious as throngs of "swarthy" immigrants entered the United States from southern and eastern Europe. Even more threatening were darker peoples who were colonial subjects in the Philippines, Puerto Rico, and Cuba. Talk of the end of white America fueled support for more restrictive immigration policies.

Across the North Atlantic, European elites engaged in similar discussions. For them, the final divvying up of Africa was in many respects equivalent to the closing of the American frontier. The Germans and Italians, in particular, complained about the lack of new territories on which to plant their flags. The French and British, by contrast, worried about how to preserve their overseas empires in a period of intense international competition.

New Social Issues in Europe Darwinist theory provoked new anxieties about inherited diseases, racial mixing, and the dying out of white "civilizers." Sexual relations between European colonizers and indigenous women—and their mixed offspring—had always been a part of European expansionism, but as racial identities hardened, many saw racial mixing as harmful to the supposedly superior white races. In addition, medical attention focused on homosexuality, regarding it as a disease and a threat to civilization.

Some people debated whether Jews—defined by religious practice or, increasingly, by ethnicity—could be fully assimilated into European society. Even though Jews had gained rights as citizens in most European countries by the late nineteenth century, powerful prejudices persisted. In the 1880s and 1890s, violent attacks known as pogroms, often involving police complicity, targeted the large Jewish populations in the Russian Empire's western territories and pushed the persecuted farther westward. These emigrants' presence, in turn, stirred up fear and resentment, especially in Austria, Germany, and France. Rumors circulated about Jewish bankers' conspiratorial powers, and anxieties over the "pollution" of the European races became widespread.

RACE-MIXING AND THE PROBLEM OF NATIONHOOD IN LATIN AMERICA

In Latin America, debates about identity chiefly addressed ethnic intermixing and the legacy of a system of government that, unlike much of the North Atlantic world, excluded rather than included most people. Social hierarchies reaching back to the sixteenth century ranked whites born in Spain and Portugal at the top, creole elites in the middle, and indigenous and African populations at the bottom. Thus, the higher on the social ladder, the more likely people were to be white.

Contested Mixtures and Invented Traditions "Mixing" did not lead to a shared heritage. Nor did it necessarily lead to homogeneity. In fact, the "racial" order did not stick, since some Iberians occupied the lower ranks, while a few people of color managed to ascend the social ladder. Moreover, starting in the 1880s, the racial hierarchy saw further disruption by the deluge of poor European immigrants; they flooded into prospering Latin American countrysides or into booming cities like Buenos Aires in Argentina and São Paulo in Brazil. Latin American societies, then, did not easily become homogeneous "nations."

Latin American leaders began to exalt bygone glories as a way to promote national identity and foster unity. Inventing successful myths could make a government seem

Diego Rivera's History of Mexico This is one of the most famous works of Mexican art, a portrait of the history of Mexico by the radical nationalist painter Diego Rivera. In this chapter, and in previous chapters, we have shown parts of this mural. In stepping back to view the whole work, which is in the National Palace in Mexico City, we can see how Rivera envisioned the history of his people generally. Completed in 1935, this work seeks to show a people fighting constantly against outside aggressors, from their glorious preconquest days (lower center), winding like a grand epic through the conquest, colonial exploitation, the revolution for independence, nineteenth-century invasions from France and the United States, to the popular 1910 revolution. It culminates in an image of Karl Marx, framed by a "scientific sun"—pointing to a future of progress and prosperity for all, as if restoring a modern Tenochtitlán of the Aztecs. This work captured many Mexicans' efforts to return to the indigenous roots of the nation and to fuse them with modern scientific ideas.

more legitimate—as the heir to a rightful struggle of the past. In Mexico, many parades celebrated Aztec grandeur, thereby creating a mythic arc from the greatness of the Aztec past to the triumphal story of Mexican independence. As the government glorified the Aztecs with pageants, statues, and pavilions, however, it continued to ignore modern Aztec descendants, who lived in squalor. Thus, race in Latin America was a more fluid category than it was in North America and Europe.

SUN YAT-SEN AND THE MAKING OF A CHINESE NATION

Just as Latin Americans celebrated their past, Chinese writers emphasized the power and depth of Chinese culture—in contrast to the Qing Empire's failing political and social strength. Here, writers used race to emphasize the superiority of the Han Chinese. Here, too, the pace of change generated a desire to trace one's roots back to secure foundations. Moreover, traditions were reinvented in the hope of saving Chinese culture threatened by modernity.

Among those who thought most intensely about the future of China was **Sun Yat-sen** (1866–1925), whose life story symbolized the challenge of nation building. Sun was part of an emerging generation of critics of the old regime. Like his European counterparts, Sun dreamed of a political community reshaped along national lines. Born into a modest rural household in southern China, he studied medicine in the British colony of Hong Kong and then turned to politics during the Sino-Japanese War. When the Qing government rejected his offer of service to the Chinese cause, he became convinced that China's rulers were out of touch with the times. Subsequently he established an organization based in Hawaii to advocate the Qing downfall and the cause of republicanism. The cornerstone of his message was Chinese—specifically, Han—nationalism. Sun blasted the feeble rule by outsiders, the Manchus, and trumpeted a sovereign political community of "true" Chinese.

Replacing the Qing and Reconstituting a Nation Realizing that reforms were necessary, the Manchu court began overhauling the administrative system and the military in the aftermath of the Boxer Uprising. Yet these changes came too late. The old elites grumbled, and the new class of urban merchants, entrepreneurs, and professionals (who often benefited from business with westerners) regarded the government as outmoded. Peasants and laborers resented the high cost of the reforms, which seemed to help only the rulers.

A mutiny, sparked in part by the government's nationalization of railroads and its low compensation to native Chinese investors, broke out in the city of Wuchang in central China in 1911. As it spread to other parts of the country, Sun Yat-sen hurried home from traveling in the United States. Few people rallied to the emperor's cause, and the Qing dynasty collapsed—an abrupt end to a dynastic tradition of more than 2,000 years.

China was soon be reconstituted, and Sun's ideas, especially those regarding race, played a central role. The original flag of the republic, for example, consisted of five colors representing the citizenry's major racial groups: red for the Han, yellow for the Manchus, blue for the Mongols, white for the Tibetans, and black for the Muslims. But Sun had reservations about this multiracial flag, believing there should be only one Chinese race. The existence of different groups in China, he argued, was the result of incomplete assimilation—a problem that the modern nation now had to confront.

NATIONALISM AND INVENTED TRADITIONS IN INDIA

British imperial rule persisted in India, but the turn of the century saw cracks in its stranglehold. Four strands had woven the territory together: the consolidation of colonial administration, the establishment of railways and telegraphs, the growth of western education and ideas, and the development of colonial capitalism. Now it was possible to speak of India as a single unit. It was also possible for anticolonial thinkers to imagine seizing and ruling India by themselves. Thus a new form of resistance emerged, different from peasant rebellions of the past. Now, dissenters talked of Indians as "a people" who had both a national past and national traditions.

A Modernizing Elite Leaders of the nationalist opposition were western-educated intellectuals from colonial cities and towns. Although a tiny minority of the Indian population, they gained influence through their access to the official world and their familiarity with European knowledge and history. This elite group used their knowledge to develop modern cultural forms. For example, they turned colloquial languages (such as Hindi, Urdu, Bengali, Tamil, and Malayalam) into standardized, literary forms for writing novels and dramas. Now the publication of journals, magazines, newspapers, pamphlets, novels, and dramas surged, facilitating communication throughout British India.

Along with print culture came a growing public sphere where intellectuals debated social and political matters. By 1885, voluntary associations in big cities had united to establish a political party, the Indian National Congress. Lawyers, prominent merchants, and local notables dominated its early leadership. The congress demanded greater representation of Indians in administrative and legislative bodies, criticized the government's economic policies, and encouraged India's industrialization.

Underlying this political nationalism, embodied by the Indian National Congress, was cultural nationalism. The nationalists claimed that Indians might not be a single race but were at least a unified people, because of their unique culture and common colonial history.

Rewriting Traditions The recovery of traditions became a way to establish a modern Indian identity without acknowledging the recent subjugation by British colonizers. So Indian intellectuals (like those in Latin America) turned to the past and rewrote the histories of ancient empires and kingdoms. In this way, Indian intellectuals promoted the idea of India as a nation-state.

To portray Indians as a people with a unifying religious creed, intellectuals reconfigured Hinduism so that it resembled western religion. This was no easy task, for traditional Hinduism did not have a supreme textual authority, like the Bible or the Quran, a monotheistic God, an organized church, or an established creed. Nonetheless, nationalist Hindu intellectuals combined various philosophical texts, cultural beliefs, social practices, and Hindu traditions into a mix that they labeled the authentic Hindu religion. While fashioning hybrid forms, revivalists also narrowed the definition of Indian traditions. As Hindu intellectuals looked back, they identified Hindu traditions and the pre-Islamic past as the only sources of India's culture. Other contributors to the region's mosaic past were forgotten; the Muslim past, in particular, had no prominent role.

Hindu Revivalism Hindu revivalism became a powerful political force in the late nineteenth century, when the nationalist challenge to the colonial regime took a militant turn. New leaders rejected constitutionalism and called for militant agitation. The British decision to partition Bengal in 1905 into two provinces—one predominantly Muslim, the other Hindu—drew militants into the streets to urge the boycott of British goods. Rabindranath Tagore, a famous Bengali poet and future Nobel laureate, composed stirring nationalist poetry. Activists formed voluntary organizations, called Swadeshi ("one's own country") Samitis, which championed indigenous enterprises for manufacturing soap, cloth, medicine, iron, and paper, as well as schools for imparting nationalist education. Although few of these ventures succeeded, the efforts reflected the nationalist desire to assert Indians' autonomy as a people.

Unlike the insurgents of 1857, nationalist leaders in India at the turn of the twentieth century imagined a modern national community. Invoking religious and ethnic symbols, they formed modern political associations to operate in a national public arena. They did not seek a radical alternative to the colonial order; instead, they fought for the political rights of Indians as a secular, national community. In these new nationalists, British rulers discovered an enemy not so different from themselves.

THE PAN MOVEMENTS

India and China were not the only places where activists dreamed of founding new states. Across the globe, groups had begun to imagine new communities based on ethnicity or, in some cases, religion. **Pan movements** (from the Greek *pan*, "all") sought to link people across state boundaries. The grand aspiration of all these movements—which included pan-Asianism, pan-Islamism, pan-Africanism, pan-Slavism, pan-Turkism, pan-Arabism, pan-Germanism, and Zionism—was the rearrangement of borders in order to unite dispersed communities. But such remappings posed a threat to rulers of the Russian, Austrian, and Ottoman empires, as well as to overseers of the British and the French colonial empires.

Pan-Islamism Within the Muslim world, intellectuals and political leaders begged their fellow Muslims to put aside their differences and unite under the banner of Islam in opposition to European incursions. The leading spokesman for pan-Islamism was the well-traveled Jamal al-Din al-Afghani (1839–1897). Born in Iran and given a Shiite upbringing, he nonetheless called on Muslims worldwide to overcome their Sunni and Shiite differences so that they could work together against the West. Afghani called for unity and action, for an end to corruption and stagnation, and for acceptance of the true principles of Islam.

The pan-Islamic message only added to Muslims' confusion as they confronted the West. Indeed, Arab Muslims living as Ottoman subjects had many calls on their loyalties.

Religion and Reform Efforts in the Ottoman Empire Sultan Abdul Hamid bestows a constitution on the Ottoman Empire. The Sultan sponsored pan-Islamic sentiment in order to hold the empire together.

Should they support the Ottoman Empire to resist European encroachments? Or should they embrace the Islamism of Afghani? Most decided to work within the fledgling nation-states of the Islamic world, looking to a Syrian or Lebanese identity, for example, as the way to deal with the West and gain autonomy. But Afghani and his disciples had struck a chord in Muslim culture, and their Islamic message has long retained a powerful appeal.

Pan-Germanism and Pan-Slavism Pan-Germanism found followers across central Europe, where it often competed with a pan-Slavic movement that sought to unite all Slavs against their Austrian, German, and Ottoman overlords. This area had traditionally been ruled by German-speaking elites, who owned the land farmed by Slavic peasants. German elites began to feel increasingly uneasy as Slavic nationalisms (spurred by the midcentury revivals of traditional Czech, Polish, Serbian, and Ukrainian languages and cultures) became more popular. Even more threatening was the fact that the Slavic populations were growing faster than the German population. As pogroms in the Russian Empire's borderlands in the 1880s, as well as economic opportunities, drove crowds of eastern European Jews westward, German resentment toward these newcomers also increased.

The rhetoric of pan-Germanism inspired mass, grassroots political activism. It motivated central Europeans to think of themselves as members of a German *race*, their identities determined by blood rather than defined by state boundaries. This, too, was the lesson of pan-Slavism. Both movements led extremists to take actions that were dangerous to existing states. The organization of networks of radical southern Slavs, for example, unsettled Bosnia and Herzegovina (annexed by the Austrians in 1908). Indeed, it was a Serbian proponent of plans to carve an independent Slav state out of Austrian territory in the Balkans who assassinated the heir to the Habsburg throne in June 1914. By August, the whole of Europe had descended into mass warfare, bringing much of the rest of the world directly or indirectly into the conflict as well. Eventually, the war would fulfill the pan-Slav, pan-German, and anti-Ottoman Muslim nationalist longing to tear down the Ottoman and Habsburg empires. Intellectuals articulated the pan movements, but aspiring political leaders and secret societies took up their ideologies, leaving Europe and much of Asia at the end of the nineteenth century boiling with ideas of how to change the borders of states and the dominance of France and Britain.

Conclusion

Ever since the Enlightenment, Europeans had put their faith in "progress." Through the nineteenth century, educated, secular elites took pride in booming industries, bustling cities, and burgeoning colonial empires. Yet by the century's end, urbanization and industrialization seemed more disrupting than uplifting, more disorienting than reassuring.

Moreover, colonized people's resistance to the "civilizing mission" fueled doubts about the course of progress.

The realization that "the people" were developing ways to unseat them terrified ruling elites. In colonial settings, nationalists learned how to mobilize large populations. In Europe, socialist and right-wing leaders likewise challenged liberals by appealing to the idea of popular sovereignty. A politics that relied on closed-door negotiations between "rational" gentlemen was unprepared to deal with modern ideas and identities.

Nor were elites able to control the scope of change, for the expansion of empires had drawn ever more people into an unbalanced global economy. Everywhere, disparities in wealth appeared. Moreover, the size and power of industrial operations threatened small firms and made individuals seem insignificant. Even some cities seemed too big and too dangerous. All these social and economic challenges stretched the capacities of gentlemanly politics.

They also stimulated creative energy. Western artists borrowed nonwestern images and vocabularies; nonwestern intellectuals looked to the West for inspiration, even as they formulated antiwestern ideas. The upheavals of modern experience propelled scholars to study the past and to fabricate utopian visions of the future.

Even as these changes unsettled the European-centered world, they intensified rivalries among Europe's powers themselves. Although the world had become a smaller place and travel was easier and quicker, at least for those who had wealth and came from powerful societies, this increasing global integration had its limitations and contradictions. At its center—Europe—the global order was unstable. And in the massive conflict that destroyed this era's faith in progress, Europe would ravage itself. The Great War (described in Chapter 19) would yield an age of even more rapid change—with even more violent consequences.

After You Read This Chapter

Go to INQUIZITIVE to see what you've learned—and learn what you've missed—with personalized feedback along the way.

FOCUS ON: *Sources of Global Anxieties and Expressions of Cultural Modernism*

GLOBAL TRENDS

- Mass migrations and unprecedented urban expansion challenge national identities.

AFRICA AND CHINA: ANTI-COLONIALISM

- The Anglo-Boer War and violent uprisings against colonial rule in Africa call Europe's imperializing mission into question.

- The Chinese rise up against European encroachments in the Boxer Uprising.

EUROPE AND NORTH AMERICA: MOUNTING TENSIONS

- Intense political rivalries, financial insecurities and crises, rapid industrialization, feminism, and class conflict roil Europe and spread to the rest of the world.

MEXICO: RESENTMENT TOWARD ELITES

- The most widespread revolution from below takes place in Mexico.

CULTURAL MODERNISM

- Increased earning power gives workers in wealthy nations the leisure to enjoy music, vaudeville shows, sports, and other forms of popular culture and to read mass-circulation newspapers.

- Elite culture explores new forms in painting, architecture, music, literature, and science in order to break with the past and differentiate itself more dramatically from popular culture.

- New ideas of race emerge, as does a renewed emphasis on the nation-state and nationalism.

CHRONOLOGY

	1870	1880	1890
AFRICA			
THE AMERICAS		Jim Crow laws in the United States 1890s	
		Labor unrest 1880s–1910s	
EUROPE			
SOUTH ASIA		Indian National Congress founded 1885 ◆	
EAST ASIA			

- **Thinking about Crossing Borders and an Unsettled World** How did mobility of different kinds unsettle established certainties in this period? Think in particular of the massive flight of farmers towards cities, and the erosion of traditional social hierarchies; the prevalence of steamships and rail travel, making long-distance journeys easier than ever before; and the emergence of the telephone and telegraph, which revolutionized communications.

- **Thinking about Changing Power Relationships and an Unsettled World** To what extent were challenges to western influence internal to the western tradition, the product of growing doubts and contradictions within the Enlightenment project, articulated by Europeans like Nietzsche and Freud? To what degree were they external to that tradition, a reaction against the massive concentration of wealth and power centered in the West and the values that supported western dominance?

- **Thinking about Women and Gender in an Unsettled World** To what degree did the economic and technological breakthroughs of the nineteenth century improve women's lives? To what extent were women able to make claims on governments in different parts of the world? How did ordinary women take control of their bodies and their lives, and how did feminists challenge patriarchal cultures?

1. Identify different understandings of the term *progress* in Europe and the United States. What did the term mean and what were its sources for competing social and political groups? What were the views of **progressive reformers**, **anarchists**, and **syndicalists**.

2. Compare the challenges to the West posed by the **pan movements** and **Sun Yat-sen**.

3. Describe new forms of **popular culture** that emerged in this period and explain their significance.

4. Explain the significance of race and nation in this period.

5. Compare the goals and methods of revolutionary and reform movements in Latin America (especially the **Mexican Revolution**) and China (especially the **Boxer Uprising**) during this era.

6. To what extent did the challenges **modernism** posed grow out of the Enlightenment tradition and to what extent were they external to that tradition?

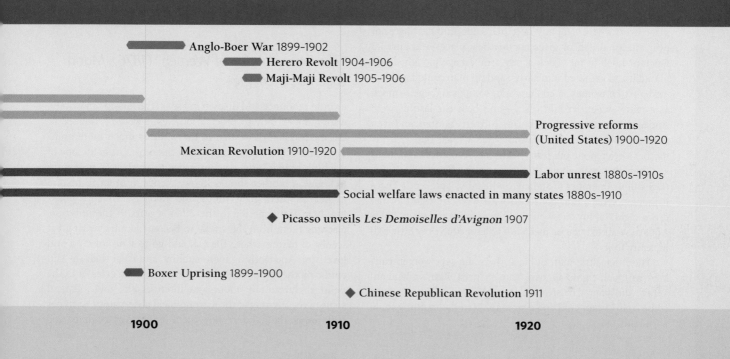

Anglo-Boer War 1899–1902

Herero Revolt 1904–1906

Maji-Maji Revolt 1905–1906

Progressive reforms (United States) 1900–1920

Mexican Revolution 1910–1920

Labor unrest 1880s–1910s

Social welfare laws enacted in many states 1880s–1910

Picasso unveils *Les Demoiselles d'Avignon* 1907

Boxer Uprising 1899–1900

Chinese Republican Revolution 1911

| 1900 | 1910 | 1920 |

Competing Perspectives

Global Feminisms

The word "feminist" first entered common usage in French in the 1890s, in English shortly thereafter, and then in a wide array of languages. Demands for women's rights, however, emerged long before that, as we have seen, and they did so around the world.

Here we present a range of women's voices on women's rights. Born a slave in New York State, Sojourner Truth gained her freedom in 1827 and became well known as an abolitionist speaker and advocate of women's rights. In an extemporaneous speech to a women's convention in Akron, Ohio, in 1851, Truth insisted that women's rights were inseparable from racial equality and social justice. In Argentina, the young writer María Eugenia Echenique (1851–1878) advocated scientific education for women. She presented her views in a leading women's newspaper, *La Ondina del Plata*, in July 1876, in reply to a critic who celebrated women's role as mothers, responsible for the home, who could only be corrupted by public life. In the third excerpt, Qiu Jin compares the treatment of Chinese women to slavery and ties the nation's future to the fate of women. Finally, in a 1909 lecture in Cairo open only to women, an educated, upper-class Egyptian woman, Bahithat al-Badiya, insisted that female veiling in public was unnatural, absurd, and counterproductive.

PRIMARY SOURCE 18.1

"Ain't I A Woman?" (1851), Sojourner Truth

Well, children, where there is so much racket there must be something out of kilter. I think that 'twixt the negroes of the South and the women at the North, all talking about rights, the white men will be in a fix pretty soon. But what's all this here talking about?

That man over there says that women need to be helped into carriages, and lifted over ditches, and to have the best place everywhere. Nobody ever helps me into carriages, or over mud-puddles, or gives me any best place! And ain't I a woman? Look at me! Look at my arm! I have ploughed and planted, and gathered into barns, and no man could head me! And ain't I a woman? I could work as much and eat as much as a man—when I could get it—and bear the lash as well! And ain't I a woman? I have borne thirteen children, and seen most all sold off to slavery, and when I cried out with my mother's grief, none but Jesus heard me! And ain't I a woman?

Then they talk about this thing in the head; what's this they call it? [member of audience whispers, "intellect"] That's it, honey. What's that got to do with women's rights or negroes' rights? If my cup won't hold but a pint, and yours holds a quart, wouldn't you be mean not to let me have my little half measure full?

Then that little man in black there, he says women can't have as much rights as men, 'cause Christ wasn't a woman! Where did your Christ come from? Where did your Christ come from? From God and a woman! Man had nothing to do with Him.

If the first woman God ever made was strong enough to turn the world upside down all alone, these women together ought to be able to turn it back, and get it right side up again! And now they is asking to do it, the men better let them.

Obliged to you for hearing me, and now old Sojourner ain't got nothing more to say.

Sojourner Truth, "Ain't I a Woman?" *History of Woman Suffrage*, vol. 1, 2nd edition, eds. Elizabeth Cady Stanton, Susan B. Anthony, and Matilda Joslyn Gage (Rochester, N.Y.: Charles Mann, 1889), 116.

PRIMARY SOURCE 18.2

"The Emancipation of Women" (1876), Maria Eugenia Echenique

I would renounce and disown my sex if the mission of women were reduced only to procreation, yes, I would renounce it; but the mission of women in the world is much more grandiose and sublime, it is more than the beasts', it is the one of teaching humankind, and in order to teach it is necessary to know. A mother should know science in order to inspire in her children great deeds and noble sentiments, making them feel superior to the other objects in the universe, teaching them from the cradle to become familiar with great scenes of nature where they should go to look for God and love Him. And nothing more sublime and ideal than the scientific mother who, while her husband goes to cafes or to the political club to talk about state interests, she goes to spend some of the evening at the astronomical observatory, with her children by the hand to show them Jupiter, Venus, preparing in that way their tender hearts for the most legitimate and sublime aspirations that could occupy men's minds. This sacred mission in the scientific mother who understands emancipation—the fulfillment of which, far from causing the abandonment of the home, causes it to unite more closely—instead of causing displeasure to her husband, she will cause his happiness.

Source: Maria Eugenia Echenique, "The Emancipation of Women," trans. Francisco Manzo Robledo, in *Reading About the World*, vol. 2, ed. Paul Brians et al. (Boston, Mass.: Harcourt Brace College Publishing, 1999).

PRIMARY SOURCE 18.3

Injustices to Chinese Women (early twentieth century), Qiu Jin

Alas! The greatest injustice in this world must be the injustice suffered by our female population of two hundred million. If a girl is lucky enough to have a good father, then her childhood is at least tolerable. But if by chance her father is an ill-tempered and unreasonable man, he may curse her birth: "What rotten luck: another useless thing." Some men go as far as killing baby girls while most hold the opinion that "girls are eventually someone else's property" and treat them with coldness and disdain. In a few years, without thinking about whether it is right or wrong, he forcibly binds his daughter's soft, white feet with white cloth so that even in her sleep she cannot find comfort and relief until the flesh becomes rotten and the bones broken. What is all this misery for? Is it just so that on the girl's wedding day friends and neighbors will compliment him, saying, "Your daughter's feet are really small"? Is that what the pain is for?

But that is not the worst of it. When the time for marriage comes, a girl's future life is placed in the hands of a couple of shameless matchmakers and a family seeking rich and powerful in-laws. A match can be made without anyone ever inquiring whether the prospective bridegroom is honest, kind, or educated. On the day of the marriage the girl is forced into a red and green bridal sedan chair, and all this time she is not allowed to breathe one word about her future. . . .

When Heaven created people it never intended such injustice because if the world is without women, how can men be born? Why is there no justice for women? We constantly hear men say, "The human mind is just and we must treat people with fairness and equality." Then why do they greet women like black slaves from Africa?

How did inequality and injustice reach this state? . . .

I hope that we all shall put aside the past and work hard for the future. Let us all put aside our former selves and be resurrected as complete human beings. Those of you who are old, do not call yourselves old and useless. If your husbands want to open schools, don't stop them; if your good sons want to study abroad, don't hold them back. Those among us who

are middle-aged, don't hold back your husbands lest they lose their ambition and spirit and fail in their work. After your sons are born, send them to schools. You must do the same for your daughters and, whatever you do, don't bind their feet. As for you young girls among us, go to school if you can. If not, read and study at home. Those of you who are rich, persuade your husbands to open schools, build factories, and contribute to charitable organizations. Those of you who are poor, work hard and help your husbands. Don't be lazy, don't eat idle rice. These are what I hope for you. You must know that when a country is near destruction, women cannot rely on the men any more because they aren't even able to protect themselves. If we don't take heart now and shape up, it will be too late when China is destroyed.

Sisters, we must follow through on these ideas!

Source: Qiu Jin, "An Address to Two Hundred Million Fellow Countrywomen." Reprinted with the permission of The Free Press, a division of Simon & Schuster, Inc., from *Chinese Civilization: A Sourcebook*, Second Edition, revised and expanded by Patricia Buckley Ebrey. Copyright © 1993 by Patricia Buckley Ebrey. All rights reserved.

PRIMARY SOURCE 18.4

Industrialization and Women's Freedom in Egypt (1909), Bahithat al-Badiya

Men say when we become educated we shall push them out of work and abandon the role for which God created us. But isn't it rather men who have pushed women out of work? Before, women used to spin and to weave cloth for clothes for themselves and their children, but men invented machines for spinning and weaving and put women out of work. . . . Since male inventors and workers have taken away a lot of our work should we waste our time in idleness or seek other work to occupy us? Of course, we should do the latter. . . . Obviously, I am not urging women to neglect their home and children to go out and become lawyers or judges or railway engineers. But if any of us wish to work in such professions our personal freedom should not be infringed. . . .

Men say to us categorically, "You women have been created for the house and we have been created to be breadwinners." Is this a God-given dictate? How are we to know this since no holy book has spelled it out? Political economy calls for a division of labor but if women enter the learned professions it does not upset the system. The division of labor is merely a human creation. . . . If men say to us that we have been created weak we say to them, "No it is you who made us weak through the path you made us follow." After long centuries of enslavement by men, our minds rusted and our bodies weakened. . . .

Men criticize the way we dress in the street. They have a point because we have exceeded the bounds of custom and propriety. . . . [But:] veiling should not prevent us from breathing fresh air or going out to buy what we need if no one can buy it for us. It must not prevent us from gaining an education nor cause our health to deteriorate. When we have finished our work and feel restless and if our house does not have a spacious garden why shouldn't we go to the outskirts of the city and take the fresh air that God has created for everyone and not just put in boxes exclusively for men.

Source: Bahithat al-Badiya, "A Public Lecture for Women Only in the Club of the Umma Party," from "Industrialization and Women's Freedom in Egypt," in *Opening the Gates: A Century of Arab Feminist Writing*, ed. Margot Badran and Miriam Cooke. Copyright © 1990. Reprinted with permission of Indiana University Press.

QUESTIONS FOR ANALYSIS

1. Explain what women's rights means to these authors. What supports rights, in their view, and what stands in their way? Do the authors' views agree or disagree with one another?

2. What social classes did these women represent? Explain the significance of class in each document.

3. Compare the opinions of marriage and motherhood expressed in these documents.

4. Compare the distinction each text draws between the private and public life.

Interpreting Visual Evidence

Global Modernism

Modernism was an international cultural movement that reacted against established traditions and sought to mark a break between the old and the new. In Europe, the movement's center, modernists challenged the Enlightenment belief in stable, universal truth. They criticized realism—the attempt to reproduce the natural world and human interactions faithfully, like a photograph—as naïve and superficial, compressing a three-dimensional reality into two and leaving out the passions and often irrational urges that motivate human behavior.

When the Franco-Spanish artist Pablo Picasso first showed his painting, *Les Demoiselles d'Avignon* (The Courtesans of Avignon; 1907), his friends accused him of wasting his talents, and outraged critics likened the canvas to a broken pane of glass. Picasso broke all the rules of the art academies. He abandoned perspective and proportion, distorted shapes, and borrowed from what at the time were considered primitive cultures in order to criticize the hypocrisies of bourgeois European culture. Rather than idealizing the human form of nymphs or classical goddesses, Picasso rendered it in jagged, jarring terms, presenting five common prostitutes in a brothel.

Influenced by Europe, modernists elsewhere challenged a different set of established traditions, but they too set out to redefine what it meant to be modern. For them, the problem was how to be Bengali, Chinese, or Egyptian, for example, and modern at the same time. In the self-portrait shown here (1850s), the Shanghai School artist Ren Xiong relied on old conventions in Chinese art, but the subject's pose, facial expression, the physicality of his uncovered shoulder, and engagement with the viewer all pointed in a new direction, as if to contrast the artist's experience with the established traditions of Chinese art.

The Indian artist Abanindranath Tagore painted a number of works that drew inspiration from Mughal art. His best known work, *Bharat Mata* (Mother India; 1905), presents a young woman with four arms, in the manner of Hindu gods, holding symbols of India's national aspirations—a book, sheaves of rice, Hindu prayer beads, and a white cloth—in an effort to create national feeling in Indians across the subcontinent.

Picasso, *Les Demoiselles d'Avignon.*

Ren Xiong, *Self-Portrait.*

Tagore, *Bharat Mata.*

QUESTIONS FOR ANALYSIS

1. Identify similarities in these works. Do you see connections in terms of the use of color or other artistic techniques? What characteristics, if any, do they share?

2. Who do you think made up the audience for these works? With whom were the artists trying to communicate? To whom were they responding? How broad do you think they imagined their public was, compared to the broadsides reproduced in the Interpreting Visual Evidence section of Chapter 17?

3. What do you think each artist understood by the term "modern," and how is it reflected in his work?

Before You Read This Chapter

GLOBAL STORYLINES

- The Great War (World War I) engulfs the globe, exhausts Europe, and promotes production and consumption on a mass scale.

- The harsh terms of the peace settlement produce resentment in Germany and contribute to global economic problems.

- European countries' efforts to rebuild their economies after the Great War by cutting expenses and returning to the gold standard cause the Great Depression, which directly affects the entire global economy.

- Three strikingly different visions for building a better world arise: liberal democracy, authoritarianism, and anticolonialism.

CORE OBJECTIVES

- **IDENTIFY** the causes for World War I, and **ANALYZE** the effects of the war on regions both within and outside of Europe.

- **EXPLAIN** how the development of modern, mass societies both caused and were affected by the Great Depression.

- **COMPARE** the ideologies of liberal democracy, authoritarianism, and anticolonialism, and **EVALUATE** the success of each in this period.

- **EXPLAIN** how access to consumer goods and other aspects of mass society influenced political conflict in Asia, Africa, and Latin America.

Of Masses and Visions of the Modern

1910–1939

Raging from August 1914 to November 1918, the Great War (World War I) shook the foundations of the European-centered world. Although most major battles occurred on European soil, multitudes of American, African, and Asian soldiers were ferried across oceans to join the war effort. Campaigns also bloodied the soil in Turkey, Egypt, Syria, and sub-Saharan Africa. The war's impact was thoroughly global. In addition to involving countless soldiers from Europe's colonies, it spread notions of freedom and self-determination and a growing disillusionment with European rule. Elsewhere, nations grappled with competing visions for building stable governments and strong economies.

This chapter deals with the Great War and its global impact. First, because the war was fought on a worldwide scale and to utter exhaustion in Europe, it required the resources of a large part of the world. It prompted production and consumption on a mass scale. Wartime leaders also used new media such as radio and film to promote national loyalties and to discredit enemies—and thereby helped to spread a mass culture. Second, the harsh terms of the peace settlement contributed to the outbreak of the Great Depression. Third, political turmoil surrounding the war inflamed disputes over how to manage mass societies and build a better world. To this end, three distinct visions arose:

liberal democracy, authoritarianism, and anticolonialism. These ideologies competed for preeminence in the decades leading up to World War II.

The Quest for the Modern

When people spoke of "being modern" in the 1920s and 1930s, they disagreed about what it meant. For culture and the arts (see Chapter 18), the term "modernism" has a fairly precise meaning. It emerged in the late nineteenth century as a challenge to the supposedly conservative values of realism in Europe, and to established artistic traditions elsewhere. In other fields, however, there was much less agreement. Reformers have always distinguished their ideas as modern or progressive while opposing accepted norms as backward or traditional. In the early twentieth century, most people agreed that in economic terms modernity involved mass production and mass consumption. In the West, for example, the automobile, the gramophone (record player), the cinema, and the radio reflected the benefits of economic progress and mass culture. In politics, being modern meant the involvement of the masses. Everywhere people favored strong leadership to reinvigorate their societies; some wanted more democracy to replace monarchical and colonial rule while others favored more authoritarian solutions.

The first political vision of being or becoming modern—the *liberal democratic* one—confronted economic failings that beset this period, such as the Great Depression, without sacrificing market economies or representative democracy. It widened participation in politics but also gave greater power to regulatory bureaucracies. After the Great Depression spread hard times and unemployment, this predominantly American and western European model linking capitalism and democracy no longer seemed so promising. Although many countries rejected the liberal perspective, the system survived in the United States, parts of western Europe, and several Latin American nations.

For many observers, liberal democracies failed to match the astonishing dynamism of a second perspective—*authoritarianism*. Authoritarian regimes rejected democracy, subordinated the individual to the state, managed and often owned most industries, used censorship and terror to enforce loyalty, and exalted an all-powerful leader. During this period, authoritarianism was evident in both right-wing dictatorships (including Fascist Italy, Nazi Germany, dictatorial Spain and Portugal, and militaristic Japan) and a left-wing dictatorship (the Soviet Union).

The third vision—*anticolonialism*—also questioned the liberal democratic order, primarily because of its connection to colonialism. However, many anticolonialists did not reject representative democracy, private property, or free markets. Resentful of European rulers who preached democracy but practiced despotism, anticolonial leaders sought to oust their colonial rulers and then find their own path to modernity, their own vision of progress. They generally favored mixing Western ideas with indigenous traditions.

Authoritarian and anticolonial visions of modernity both embraced technology and economic dynamism. They sought to take advantage of economic growth and mass support and redefine what freedom meant, while rejecting what they considered the hypocrisy and weakness of liberal democracy.

The Great War

Few events were more decisive in drawing men and women worldwide into national and international politics than the **Great War**. For over four years, millions of soldiers from Europe, as well as from its dominions and colonies, killed one another. The war's carnage

COMPARISON

IDENTIFY the causes for World War I, and **ANALYZE** the effects of the war on regions both within and outside of Europe.

shook the hierarchies of prewar society around the world. Above all, the war made clear how much the power of the state now depended on the support of the people.

The war's causes were complex. At the heart of the European tensions, however, were nationalist rivalries, which pitted Britain and France against a rising Germany, and Austria-Hungary and Russia against each other as the Ottoman Empire began to crumble. Through most of the nineteenth century, Britain had been the preeminent power. By the century's end, however, German industrial output had surpassed Britain's, and Germany had begun building a navy. For the British, who controlled the world's seas, the German navy was an affront; for the Germans, it was a logical step in their expanding ambitions. This Anglo-German antagonism drew in the other powers in rival alliances. Germany joined Austria-Hungary to form the Central Powers; Britain affiliated itself with France and Russia in the Triple Entente (later called the Allied Powers after Italy joined).

THE FIGHTING

Despite hopes for a swift resolution, the war became infamous for its duration and horrors. Well-armed and secretly pledged to defend their partners in 1914, the rivals lacked only a spark to ignite open hostilities. That came in August, when the heir to the Habsburg throne was assassinated in Sarajevo, the capital of Austrian Bosnia. The assassin hoped to trigger an independence movement that would detach South-Slav territories from the Austro-Hungarian Empire (see Chapter 18) and unite them with independent Serbia. Russia backed the Serbs against Austria-Hungary, and the British, French, and Germans were drawn into the conflict to support their partners. The world war that followed dragged in Europe's colonies, too. For those who expected a short war, the fighting did not go as expected.

Stalemate The initial German offensive stalled thirty miles outside Paris at the First Battle of the Marne, in September 1914 (see Map 19.1). A stalemate ensued. Vast land armies dug trenches along the Western Front—from the English Channel through Belgium and France to the Alps—installing barbed wire and setting up machine-gun posts.

Trenches in World War I
The expectation of a short, decisive war turned out to be an illusion; instead, armies dug trenches and filled them with foot soldiers and machine guns. To advance entailed walking into a hail of machine-gun fire. Life in the trenches meant cold, dampness, rats, disease, and boredom.

Western Front
- ← Allied advance
- ← German advance
- — The Western Front, November 1914
- •••• German offensive, spring 1918
- –·– The Western Front, March 1918
- — Armistice Line, November 1918
- ✳ Major battle

Eastern Front
- ← Russian advance
- ← German advance
- — Limit of Russian advance, 1914–1915
- –·– Limit of Austro-German advances, 1915–1916
- — German penetration into Russia, June 1918
- ✳ Major battle

- Allies and colonies
- Neutral nations that joined Allies
- Central Powers
- Neutral nations and empires that joined Central Powers and colonies
- Neutral nations
- ← Allied advance
- ← Central Powers' advance
- –·– Maximum German Advance, 1918
- — Armistice line, Nov. 11, 1918
- — Armistice line, Treaty of Brest-Litovsk, 1918

MAP 19.1 | World War I: The European and Middle Eastern Theaters

Most of the fighting in World War I, despite its designation as a world war, occurred in Europe. Although millions of soldiers fought on both sides, the territorial advances were relatively small. Look at the maps above, and identify all the countries where the Allies and Central Powers made advances.

- Which countries had to fight a two-front war?
- Did the armies of the Central Powers or the Allies gain the most territory during the war?
- According to your reading, how did those territorial gains affect the war's outcome?

Anything but glorious, life in the trenches mixed boredom, dampness, dirt, vermin, and disease, punctuated by the terror of being ordered to "go over the top" to attack the enemy's entrenched position. Doing so meant running across a "no man's land" in which machine guns mowed down almost all attackers. The war also witnessed new instruments of warfare, including poison gas; submarines; military aircraft, used primarily for reconnaissance; and, in the latter stages, tanks.

The death toll forced governments to call up more men than ever before. More than 70 million men worldwide fought in the war, including almost all of Europe's young adult males. From 1914 to 1918, 13 million served in the German army. In Russia, more than 15 million men took up arms. The British Empire mobilized nearly 9 million soldiers, and the 5.25 million troops of the United Kingdom (England, Scotland, Wales, and Ireland) constituted almost half the prewar population of men aged fifteen to forty-nine. In France around 8 million served, roughly 80 percent of men aged fifteen to forty-nine, a greater proportion than in any other major power. Over half of all the men mobilized for World War I were killed, injured, taken prisoner, or unaccounted for. (See **Analyzing Global Developments: Measuring Casualties in World War I**.)

Mass mobilization also undermined traditional gender boundaries. Tens of thousands of women served at or near the front as doctors, nurses, and technicians. Even more women mobilized on the "home front," taking on previously male occupations—especially in munitions plants. But women could also turn against the state. Particularly in central Europe and Russia, the war's demands for soldiers and supplies left farms untended and caused food shortages. Bread riots and peaceful protests by women, traumatized by loss and desperate to feed their children, put states on notice that their citizens expected compensation for their sacrifices. Indeed, civilian pressure forced many states to make promises they would have to fulfill after the war, in the form of welfare provisions, expanded suffrage, and pensions for widows and the wounded.

Empire and War The war's horrors reached around the globe (see Map 19.2). In 1915–1916, Ottoman forces (allied with the Central Powers) massacred or deported 1.3 million Armenians, who were accused as a group of collaborating with the Russians. Many analysts regard these attacks as the world's first genocide, the intentional elimination of a whole people. To increase their forces, the British and the French conscripted colonial subjects: India provided 1 million soldiers; over 1 million Africans fought in Africa and Europe for their colonial masters, and another 3 million transported war supplies. Even the sparsely populated British dominions of Australia, New Zealand, and Canada dispatched over a million young men to fight for the empire.

The Russian Revolution The war destroyed entire empires. The first to go was Romanov Russia. In February 1917, Tsar Nicholas II stepped down under pressure from his generals. They wanted to quash the mass unrest in the capital, St. Petersburg, which, they believed, threatened the war effort along the Eastern Front. Some members of the Russian parliament formed a provisional government; at the same time, grassroots councils (soviets) sprang up in factories,

Women's War Effort With armies drafting nearly every able-bodied man, women filled their places in factories, especially in those that manufactured war materials, such as the French plant pictured here in 1916.

Analyzing Global Developments

Measuring Casualties in World War I

You would think that tabulating historical data would be a fairly easy thing to do. At different points in this text, however, we have seen that it takes painstaking efforts on the part of historians and demographers first to figure out the best way to collect the data and second to accurately categorize and count the data. Figuring out the number of Africans that left on slave ships and where they embarked and disembarked during the Atlantic slave trade is a great example of this kind of work. Historian Jay Winter and others have worked tirelessly during the last thirty years to come up with accurate death tolls for the soldiers and civilians in World War I. In a landmark book, *The Great War and the British People*, Winter used a range of archival sources from government agencies' data and mortality rate tables from major insurance companies to estimate and calculate the number of deaths among people in Britain and Ireland. While the carnage in World War I seems beyond measure, Winter, in one paradoxical finding, demonstrated that death rates among civilians actually went down during World War I in Britain and Ireland. Winter suggests that the best explanation for this development was the efforts of the state to mobilize the civilian population, to provide health insurance, and, most importantly, to improve nutrition.

The table below builds on Winter's early efforts and shows the best estimates for the military death tolls across all the major participants in World War I.

QUESTIONS FOR ANALYSIS

- Based on data provided in the table, did the mobilization for the war have a greater impact on the societies of the Central Powers or the Allied Powers? Please justify your answer.
- While the Allies mobilized nearly twice as many men as the Central Powers, the latter suffered greater casualty rates. Why?
- The United States played a major role in World War I, but why were the number of its dead, wounded, and missing/POW so low compared to the other major combatants?

Military participation and military losses in World War I

COUNTRY	MOBILIZED	DEAD	WOUNDED	POW/MISSING	TOTAL CASUALTIES	% CASUALTIES
Allied Powers						
Russia	15,798,000	1,800,000	4,950,000	2,500,000	9,250,000	59
France	7,891,000	1,375,800	4,266,000	537,000	6,178,800	78
GB, Emp. and Dom.	8,904,467	908,371	2,090,212	191,652	3,190,235	36
Italy	5,615,000	578,000	947,000	600,000	2,125,000	38
USA	4,273,000	114,000	234,000	4,526	352,526	8
Japan	800,000	300	907	3	1,210	0
Romania	1,000,000	250,706	120,000	80,000	450,706	45
Serbia	750,000	278,000	133,148	15,958	427,106	57
Belgium	365,000	38,716	44,686	34,659	118,061	32
Greece	353,000	26,000	21,000	1,000	48,000	14
Portugal	100,000	7,222	13,751	12,318	33,291	33
Montenegro	50,000	3,000	10,000	7,000	20,000	40
Total	**45,899,467**	**5,380,115**	**12,380,704**	**3,984,116**	**22,194,935**	**46**
Central Powers						
Germany	13,200,000	2,037,000	4,216,058	1,152,800	7,405,858	56
Austria-Hungary	900,000	1,100,000	3,620,000	2,200,000	6,920,000	77
Turkey	2,998,000	804,000	400,000	250,000	1,454,000	48
Bulgaria	400,000	87,500	152,390	27,029	266,919	67
Total	**25,598,000**	**4,028,500**	**8,388,448**	**3,629,829**	**16,046,777**	**63**
Grand Total	**71,497,467**	**9,408,615**	**21,219,152**	**7,613,945**	**38,241,712**	**53**

Sources: John Horne (ed.), *A Companion to World War I* (2010); Tucker Spencer (ed.), *The European Powers in the First World War: An Encyclopedia* (1996); J. M. Winter, *The Great War and the British People* (1985).

The Russian Revolution (*Above*) The July 1917 demonstrations in Petrograd were among the largest in the Russian Empire during that turbulent year of war and revolution. In this photo, marchers carry banners, "Down with the Ministers-Capitalists" and "All Power to the Soviets of Worker, Soldier and Peasant Deputies." (*Left*) Vladimir Lenin died just six years and three months after the October 1917 revolution, but he lived on in his writings and images, such as in this painting by Pavel Kuznetsov. Artists and propagandists helped make Lenin an icon of the new Soviet order.

garrisons, and towns. The irony of Russia's February Revolution, which brought an end to the monarchy, was that the military and civilian elites wanted to restore order, not encourage a revolution. With the tsar removed, millions of peasants seized land, soldiers and sailors abandoned the front, and borderland non-Russian groups declared autonomy from the crumbling Russian Empire.

In October 1917, left-wing Socialists calling themselves **Bolsheviks** seized power. Led by Vladimir Lenin and Leon Trotsky, the Bolsheviks drew support among radicalized soldiers, sailors, and factory workers organized in the soviets. Arresting provisional government members and claiming power in the name of the soviets, the Bolsheviks proclaimed a socialist revolution to overtake the February "bourgeois" revolution. Several months later, Soviet Russia signed the Treaty of Brest-Litovsk, acknowledging German victory on the Eastern Front as the Russian army collapsed. For protection, the Bolshevik leadership relocated the capital to Moscow and set up a dictatorship. Lenin insisted on accepting the peace treaty and the loss of vast territories to safeguard the socialist revolution.

The Fall of the Central Powers On April 2, 1917, the United States declared war on Germany. This occurred after German submarines sank several American merchant ships and after a secret telegram came to light in which German officials sought Mexican support by promising to help Mexico regain territories it had lost to the United States in 1848.

With American support, the Allies turned the tide at the Second Battle of the Marne in July 1918 and forced the Germans to retreat into Belgium. German troops then began to surrender, and some announced a soldiers' strike as hunger and influenza became unbearable. Before long, Germany tottered on the edge of civil war as the Allied blockade caused food shortages. Faced with defeat and civil strife, the Central Powers fell one after

GREENLAND

CANADA

UNITED STATES

FINLAND

NORWAY SWEDEN

DENMARK

BALTIC SEA

UNITED KINGDOM

GERMANY

POLAND

FRANCE

AUSTRIA-HUNGARY

ITALY

ROMANIA

SERBIA

BLACK SEA

CAUCASUS

PORTUGAL SPAIN

MONTENEGRO

ALBANIA

BULGARIA

GREECE

OTTOMAN EMPIRE

IRAQ

TUNISIA

MOROCCO

ALGERIA

LIBYA

EGYPT

ARABIA

ATLANTIC OCEAN

BAHAMAS

RIO DE ORO

BRITISH HONDURAS

CUBA

JAMAICA

WEST INDIES

ANGLO-EGYPTIAN SUDAN

HONDURAS

NICARAGUA

BRITISH GUIANA

DUTCH GUIANA

FRENCH GUIANA

GAMBIA

GUINEA

SIERRA LEONE

NIGERIA

ETHIOPIA

COSTA RICA

PANAMA

VENEZUELA

COLOMBIA

GOLD COAST

TOGO

CAMEROON

UGANDA

BRITISH EAST AFRICA

ECUADOR

PERU

BRAZIL

GERMAN EAST AFRICA

PACIFIC OCEAN

BOLIVIA

PARAGUAY

NORTHERN RHODESIA

CHILE

GERMAN SOUTH-WEST AFRICA

SOUTHERN RHODESIA

ARGENTINA

URUGUAY

SOUTH AFRICA

Allied Powers, colonies and allies

Central Powers and colonies

Neutral nations throughout the war

← Troop movements

0   1000   2000 Miles

0   1000   2000 Kilometers

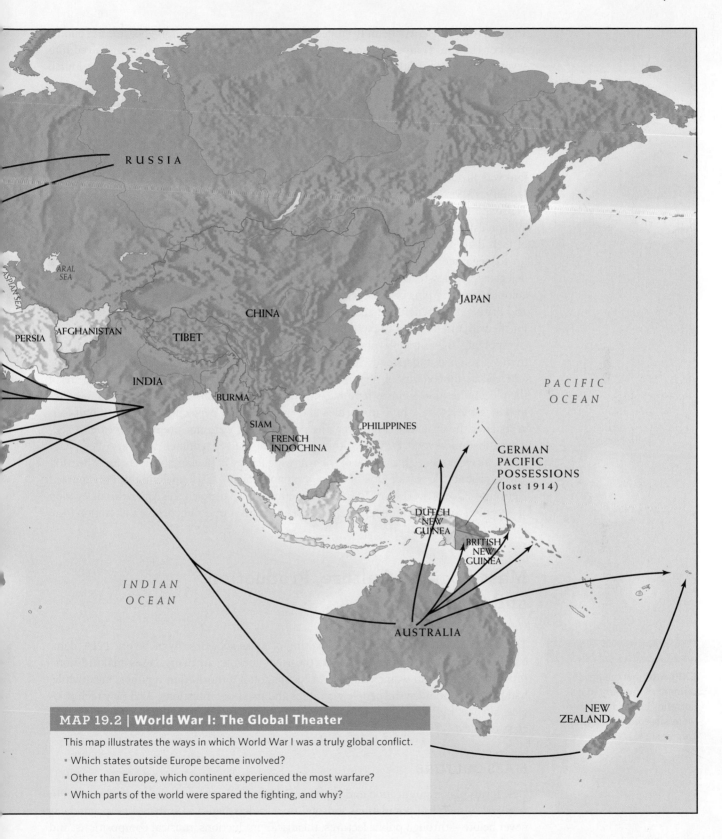

RUSSIA

ARAL SEA

CASPIAN SEA

PERSIA AFGHANISTAN

INDIA TIBET CHINA

JAPAN

BURMA

SIAM

FRENCH INDOCHINA

PHILIPPINES

PACIFIC OCEAN

GERMAN PACIFIC POSSESSIONS (lost 1914)

DUTCH NEW GUINEA

BRITISH NEW GUINEA

INDIAN OCEAN

AUSTRALIA

NEW ZEALAND

MAP 19.2 | World War I: The Global Theater

This map illustrates the ways in which World War I was a truly global conflict.

• Which states outside Europe became involved?

• Other than Europe, which continent experienced the most warfare?

• Which parts of the world were spared the fighting, and why?

another. After Kaiser Wilhelm II slipped into exile, the German empire became a republic. The last Habsburg emperor also gave up the throne, and Austria-Hungary dissolved into several new states. With the collapse of the Ottoman Empire, the war claimed a fourth dynasty among its casualties.

THE PEACE SETTLEMENT AND THE IMPACT OF THE WAR

To decide the fate of vanquished empires and the future of the modern world, the victors convened five peace conferences, one for each of the Central Powers. Most important was the conference to negotiate peace with Germany, held at Versailles, France, in January 1919. Delegates drew many of their ideas from American president Woodrow Wilson's "Fourteen Points," a blueprint he had devised for making peace in Europe. Wilson especially insisted that postwar borders be redrawn by following the principle of "self-determination of nations" and that an international League of Nations be set up to negotiate further quarrels. Such high-minded ideas were appealing, but once delegates got down to the business of carving up Europe and doling out Germany's colonies, negotiations became tense and difficult. Over the objections of the Americans and British, the French insisted on a punitive treaty that assigned Germany sole blame for the war and forced it to pay reparations.

Applying the principle of self-determination was much more difficult in practice than Wilson had understood. Suddenly, 60 million people in central and eastern Europe emerged as inhabitants of new nation-states (see Map 19.3). The patchwork nature of the old multiethnic empires here meant that as many as 25 million now lived in states in which they were ethnic minorities and vulnerable to persecution in the tumultuous years after the armistice. Moreover, the peacemakers were not prepared to extend self-determination beyond Europe. Although political elites negotiated the Versailles peace treaty, its effects as well as those of the war were felt by anticolonial leaders and their followers around the world. One of them, a photographer's assistant living in Paris named Nguyen Ai Quoc, the future Ho Chi Minh, famously challenged the American delegation at Versailles to take their own principles seriously and support his people's liberation from French rule, to no avail.

Mass Society: Culture, Production, and Consumption

COMPARISON

EXPLAIN how the development of modern, mass societies both caused and were affected by the Great Depression.

The war dramatically extended the making of mass societies. Even before 1914, democratic regimes had begun to extend the right to vote, in many cases making non–property holders and women eligible to cast ballots. Authoritarian regimes, meanwhile, had begun to mobilize the people via rallies and mass organizations. And new technologies, such as radio, were helping to create mass cultures that spanned geographic and class divides.

MASS CULTURE

New forms of communication and entertainment contributed to the new mass culture. In an effort to mobilize populations for total war, leaders had disseminated propaganda as never before—through public lectures, theatrical productions, musical compositions, and (censored) newspapers. Indeed, the war's impact had politicized cultural activities while broadening the audience for nationally oriented information and entertainment.

Republic of Turkey after Treaty of Lausanne 1923
French territory
French mandate
French protectorate
British mandate
British colony
British influence
Italian colony

MAP 19.3 | Outcomes of World War I in Europe, North Africa, and Some of the Middle East

The political map of Europe and the Middle East changed greatly after the peace treaty of 1919.

- Comparing this map with Map 19.1, which shows the European and Middle Eastern theaters of war, identify the European countries that came into existence after the war.

- What happened to the Ottoman Empire, and what powers gained control over many territories of the Ottoman state?

- What states emerged from the Austro-Hungarian Empire?

Josephine Baker Reacting to the Great War's carnage, many Europeans looked longingly for supposedly pristine worlds that their own corrupting civilization had not destroyed. The African American entertainer Josephine Baker was a sensation on the stage in Paris after the war. Many of her shows exoticized or even caricatured her African descent.

Postwar *mass culture* was distinctive. First, it differed from elite culture (opera, classical music, paintings, literature) because it reflected the tastes of the working and the middle classes, who now had more time and money to spend on entertainment. Second, mass culture relied on new technologies, especially film and radio, which could reach an entire nation's population and consolidate their sense of being a single state.

Radio Radio entered its golden age after World War I. Invented early in the twentieth century, it made little impact until the 1920s, when powerful transmitters permitted stations to reach much larger audiences—often with nationally syndicated programs. Radio "broadcasts" gave listeners a sense of intimacy with newscasters and stars, addressing consumers as personal friends and drawing them into the lives of serial heroes.

Radio also was a way to mobilize the masses, especially in authoritarian regimes. The Italian dictator Benito Mussolini pioneered the radio address to the nation; later, Soviet and Nazi propagandists used it to great effect, as did the right-wing Japanese government. But even dictatorships could not exert total control over mass culture. For example, although the Nazis regarded jazz as racially inferior music and the Soviets regarded it as "bourgeois," neither could prevent young or old from tuning in to foreign radio broadcasts, smuggling gramophone records over the borders, or creating their own jazz bands.

Film and Advertising Film, too, had profound effects. For traditionalists, Hollywood by the 1920s signified vulgarity and decadence because the silver screen prominently displayed modern sexual habits. Like radio, film served political purposes. Here, again, antiliberal governments took the lead. German filmmaker Leni Riefenstahl's movie of the Nazi Nuremberg rally of 1934, *Triumph of the Will,* is a key example of propagandistic cinema. Nazi-era films were comedies, musicals, melodramas, detective films, and adventure epics—sometimes framed by racial stereotypes and political goals. Soviet film studios also produced Hollywood-style musicals alongside didactic pictures about socialist triumphs.

In market economies, radio and film grew into big businesses, and with expanded product advertising they promoted other enterprises as well. Especially in the United States, advertising became a major industry, with radio commercials shaping national consumer tastes. Increasingly, too, American-produced entertainment, radio programs, and cinematic epics reached an international audience. Thanks to new media, America and the world began to share mass-produced images and fantasies.

MASS PRODUCTION AND MASS CONSUMPTION

The same factors that promoted mass culture also enhanced production and consumption on a mass scale. In fact, World War I had relied on industrial might, for machine technologies produced war materials with abundant and devastating effect.

Never before had armies had so much firepower at their disposal. Whereas in 1809 Napoleon's artillery had discharged 90,000 shells over two days during the largest battle waged in Europe to that point, by 1916 German guns were firing 100,000 rounds of shells per hour for twelve hours at a time in the Battle of Verdun. To sustain military production, millions of men and women worked in factories at home and in the colonies. Producing huge quantities of identical guns, gas masks, bandage rolls, and boots, these factories reflected the modern world's demands for greater volume, faster speed, reduced cost, and standardized output—key characteristics of *mass production*.

The war reshuffled the world's economic balance of power, boosting the United States as an economic powerhouse. As the United States' share of world industrial production climbed above one-third in 1929 (roughly equal to that of Britain, Germany, and Russia combined), people around the globe regarded it as a "working vision of modernity" in which not only production but also consumption boomed.

The Automobile Assembly Line The most outstanding example of the relationship between mass production and consumption in the United States was the motor car. Before World War I, the automobile had been a rich man's toy. Then came Henry Ford, who founded the Ford Motor Company in 1903. Seeking to make more cars more quickly and cheaper, Ford used mechanized conveyors to send the auto frame along a track, or assembly line, where each worker performed one simplified task. By standardizing the manufacturing process and substituting machinery for manual labor, Ford's assembly line brought a new efficiency to the mass production of automobiles.

By the 1920s, a finished car rolled off Ford's assembly line every ten seconds. Although workers complained about becoming "cogs" in a depersonalized labor process, the system boosted output and reduced costs. Altogether, nearly 4 million jobs related directly or indirectly to the automobile—an impressive total in a labor force of 45 million workers.

After World War I, automobile ownership became more common among Americans. Ford further expanded the market for cars by paying his own workers $5 per day— approximately twice the average manufacturing wage in the United States. He understood that without *mass consumption*, increased purchasing power in the middle classes, and appetite for goods there could be no mass production. Whereas in 1920 Americans owned 8 million motor cars, a decade later they owned 23 million. The automobile's rapid spread seemed to demonstrate that mass production worked.

The Great Depression However, it was not all easy listening and smooth motoring in countries where mass societies were taking root. On October 24, 1929—Black Tuesday— the American stock market collapsed, plunging not only the American economy and its consumers, heavily in debt, but also international financial and trading systems into crisis. This event led the world into the **Great Depression**.

The causes of the Depression went back to the Great War. The efforts by European governments to slash spending and return to the prewar gold standard (see Chapter 18) stifled growth and compromised their ability to pay their war debts. Political and economic

Triumph of the Will Though later denounced, this propaganda film of Adolf Hitler and the Nazi Party Congress won a Golden Lion at the 1935 Venice Biennale and an award at the 1937 World's Exhibition in Paris. Its poster featured the many mass rallies that projected an image of dynamism and collective will, which Hitler claimed to embody.

instability in Germany, the linchpin of the European economy, made matters even more difficult. The financial terms of the Versailles treaty required Germany to pay reparations to compensate for the costs of the war. The German government, however, was unable or unwilling to tax citizens at the rates that prevailed in victor countries, which would have enabled them to meet their treaty obligations. They opted instead to print more money. The resulting hyperinflation destroyed both the German economy and democracy.

To restore stability, Europeans borrowed heavily from the United States. Germany borrowed more from the United States than it paid in reparations, but that assistance was insufficient and short-lived. In 1928 and 1929, American banks pulled their support. Starting in central Europe, banks began to collapse. The panic then spread to the world's stock markets, which led to the Wall Street crash of 1929, which spurred more bank closures.

Financial turmoil produced a major reduction in world trade. Striving to protect workers and investors from the influx of cheap foreign goods, governments raised tariffs against imports. After the United States enacted protective tariffs, other governments abandoned free trade in favor of protectionism. Manufacturers cut back production, laid off millions of workers, and often went out of business. By 1935, world trade had shrunk to one-third of its 1929 level. The producers of raw materials, mainly found in the less developed economies, felt the harshest effects, for their international markets shut down almost completely. For example, world prices for Argentine beef, Chilean nitrates, and Indonesian sugar all dropped sharply.

The Great Depression forced people to rethink the core of laissez-faire liberalism (see Chapter 15), the idea that free markets regulate themselves and free trade leads to economic progress. By the late 1930s, the exuberant embrace of private mass production had ceded to a new conviction: state intervention to regulate the economy was critical to prevent disaster. In 1936, the British economist John Maynard Keynes published a landmark treatise, *The General Theory of Employment, Interest, and Money*. He argued that the market could not always adjust to its own failures and that sometimes the state had to stimulate it by increasing the money supply and creating jobs. Although the "Keynesian Revolution" took years to transform economic policy, many governments had doubts whether capitalism could be saved. The Great Depression did more than any other event to challenge the belief that liberal democracy and capitalism were the best way to achieve political stability and economic progress.

Mass Politics: Competing Visions for Building Modern States

COMPARISON

COMPARE the ideologies of liberal democracy, authoritarianism, and anticolonialism, and **EVALUATE** the success of each in this period.

In the aftermath of World War I, societies grappled with the question of how to build modern, prosperous states. The war upset class, gender, and colonial relations, which were already unsettled in the prewar period. On battlefronts and home fronts, countless workers, peasants, women, and colonial subjects had sacrificed and now expected to share in the fruits of peace. Many, even in victorious nations, lost confidence in traditional authorities who had failed to prevent the cataclysm and allowed it to go on so long. Amid widespread political turmoil, the states that retained some form of democracy revised the liberal vision, while authoritarianism gained in popularity and anticolonial movements gathered steam.

LIBERAL DEMOCRACY UNDER PRESSURE

The demands of fighting a total war had a profound effect on all of the European states. All of them, including the democracies in Britain and France, seized the opportunity to experiment with illiberal policies. Indeed, the war brought both the suspension of many democratic rights and an effort by governments to manage industry and distribution. States on both sides of the conflict jailed many individuals who opposed the war. Governments regulated both production and, through rationing, consumption. Above all, the war and the economic crises that followed revolutionized the size and scope of the state.

British and French Responses to Economic Crises Britain and France retained their democracies, but even here, old-fashioned liberal democracy was on the run. Strife rippled across the British Empire, and in the home isles Britain gave independence to what became the Republic of Ireland in 1922. Britain's working-class Labour Party came to power twice between 1923 and 1931; but either alone or in coalition with Liberals and Conservatives, Labour could not lift the country out of its economic crisis.

Disorder was even more pronounced in France, which had lost 10 percent of its young men and seen the destruction of vast territory. In 1932–1933, six government coalitions came and went over the course of just nineteen months. Against the threat of a rightist coup, a coalition of the moderate and radical left, including the French Communist Party, formed the Popular Front government (1936–1938). It introduced the right of collective bargaining, a forty-hour workweek, two-week paid vacations, and minimum wages.

The American New Deal In the United States, too, markets and liberalism faced challenges. When the Great Depression shattered the nation's fortunes, pressure intensified to create a more secure political and economic system.

By the end of 1930, more than 4 million American workers had lost their jobs. As President Hoover insisted that citizens' thrift and self-reliance, not government handouts, would restore prosperity, the economic situation worsened. By 1933, industrial production had dropped by a staggering 50 percent since 1929. The hard times were even worse in the countryside, where farm income plummeted by two-thirds between 1929 and 1932.

In the 1932 presidential election, a Democrat, Franklin Delano Roosevelt, won in a landslide. He promptly launched what came to be called the New Deal, a set of programs and regulations that dramatically expanded the scope of the American national

"Jim Crow" The American New Deal left most African Americans behind. In the rural American South, "Jim Crow" laws mandated racial segregation, with African Americans forced to use separate, and usually unequal, facilities, including schools, hotels, and theaters, such as this one in Mississippi.

government and its role in the nation's economic life. In his first hundred days in office, Roosevelt obtained legislation to provide relief for the jobless and to rebuild the shattered economy. Among his administration's experiments were the Federal Deposit Insurance Corporation to guarantee bank deposits up to $5,000, the Securities and Exchange Commission to monitor the stock market, and the Federal Emergency Relief Administration to help states and local governments assist the needy. Subsequently, in 1935, the Works Progress Administration put nearly 3 million people to work building roads, bridges, airports, and post offices. In addition, the Social Security Act inaugurated old-age pensions supported by the federal government.

Never before had the U.S. federal government expended so much on social welfare programs or intervened so directly in the national economy. Yet the Depression lingered, and before long unemployment again climbed—from 7 million in 1937 to 11 million in 1938.

The New Deal did not substantially redistribute national income. Privately owned enterprises continued to dominate American society. Roosevelt's aim was not to destroy capitalism, but to save it. In this regard the New Deal succeeded, for it staved off authoritarian solutions to modern problems.

During the interwar years, liberal democratic regimes respected elections and defended private property against challenges from labor movements. But they intervened in markets and regulated people's lives in ways their prewar counterparts never would have contemplated.

AUTHORITARIANISM AND MASS MOBILIZATION

Like the liberal systems they challenged, authoritarian regimes came in various stripes. Right-wing dictatorships arose in Italy, Germany, and Japan. Although differing in important respects, they all disliked the left-wing dictatorship of the Soviet Union. The Soviets, in turn, hated the Fascists.

The Soviet Union and Socialism The most dramatic blow against liberal capitalism occurred in Russia when the Bolshevik Party seized power and established a socialist regime. Fearing the spread of socialist revolutions, Britain, France, Japan, and the United States sent armies to Russia to contain bolshevism. But after executing the tsar and his family, the Bolsheviks rallied support by defending the homeland against its invaders. They also mobilized people to fight (and win) a civil war (1918–1921) in the name of defending the revolution.

To revive the economy, which had been devastated by war, revolution, and civil war, the Bolsheviks grudgingly legalized private trade and private property. In 1924, with the country still recovering from civil war, the undisputed leader of the revolution, Lenin, died. No one had done more to shape the institutions of the revolutionary regime, including creating expectations for a single ruler. After eliminating his rivals, **Joseph Stalin** (1878–1953) emerged as the new leader of the Communist Party and the

Collectivized Agriculture Soviet plans for the socialist village envisioned the formation of large collectives supplied with advanced machinery, thereby transforming peasant labor into an industrial process. The realities behind the images of smiling farmers—such as in this poster, proclaiming "Let's Achieve a Victorious Harvest"—were low productivity, enormous waste, and often broken-down machinery.

country, which soon became the Union of Soviet Socialist Republics (U.S.S.R.), or Soviet Union.

Since socialism as a fully developed social and political order did not exist anywhere in the 1920s, no one was sure how it would actually work. Stalin resolved this dilemma by defining Soviet or revolutionary socialism in opposition to capitalism. Since capitalism had "bourgeois" parliaments serving the interests of the rich, socialism, as elaborated by Stalinist leaders, would have soviets (councils) of worker and peasant deputies. Since capitalism had unregulated markets, which led to inefficiency and unemployment, socialism would have economic planning and full employment. And since capitalism relied on the "exploitation" of private ownership, socialism would outlaw private trade and private property. In short, socialism would eradicate capitalism and then invent socialist forms in housing, culture, values, dress, and even modes of reasoning.

The efforts to build a noncapitalist society required class war, and these efforts began in the heavily populated countryside. As Stalin solidified his control over the Soviet Union in the late 1920s, he sought to combine individual farms into larger units owned and worked collectively, and run by regime loyalists. Tens of thousands of urban activists

MAP 19.4 | The Soviet Union

The Union of Soviet Socialist Republics (U.S.S.R.) came into being after World War I.

- How did its boundaries compare with those of the older Russian Empire, as shown in Map 17.6 (p. 633)?

- Identify the other Soviet Socialist Republics.

- What does the large number of Soviet republics suggest about the ethnic diversity within the Soviet Union?

and Red Army soldiers led a drive to establish these collective farms and to compel farmers to sell all their grain and livestock at state-run collection points for whatever price the state was willing to pay (often very little).

In protest, many peasants burned their crops, killed their livestock, and destroyed their farm machinery. The government responded by deporting the protesters, along with many bystanders, to remote areas. Meanwhile, harvests again declined, and famine claimed millions more lives. Grudgingly, the regime allowed the collectivized peasants to have household plots. Here they could grow their own food and take some of their produce to approved markets. But few escaped the collectives, which depended on the state for seed, fertilizers, and machinery.

The year 1928 saw the beginning of a frenzied Five-Year Plan to "catch and overtake" the leading capitalist countries. As peasants were forced onto collective farms, millions of enthusiasts (as well as deported peasants) set about building a socialist urban utopia founded on advanced technology, almost all of it purchased from the Depression-mired capitalist countries. More than 10 million people helped build or rebuild hundreds of factories, hospitals, and schools. Huge hydroelectric dams, automobile and tractor factories, and heavy machine–building plants symbolized the promise of Soviet-style modernity, which eliminated unemployment during the capitalist Great Depression. Soviet authorities also started building socialism on the borderlands, and the U.S.S.R soon included several new republics (see Map 19.4), all of which acquired their own institutions—but under central rule from Moscow.

Mass Terror and Stalin's Dictatorship The Soviet political system became more ruthless as the state expanded. Police power grew the most, partly from forcing peasants into collectives and organizing mass deportations. As the party's ranks swelled, ongoing loyalty tests also led to the removal of party members, even when they professed absolute loyalty. From 1936 to 1938, trials of supposedly treasonous "enemies of the people" resulted in the execution of around 750,000 people and the arrest or deportation of several million more. They were sent to forced-labor camps, collectively known as the Gulag. Such purges decimated the loyal Soviet elite—party officials, state officials, intelligentsia, army officers, and even members of the police who had enforced the terror. Lenin and Stalin secured a communist regime based in Russia but did so through highly coercive and deeply resented methods. Nonetheless, Stalin's efforts at heavy industrialization were to pay off when Nazi Germany invaded the Soviet Union in World War II (see Chapter 20).

Italian Fascism Disillusionment with the costs of the Great War and fear of a communist takeover like that in Russia inspired violent political movements in many European countries, above all in Italy and Germany. In Italy, mass strikes, occupations of factories, and peasant land seizures swept the country in 1919 and 1920. Amid this disorder, authoritarian nationalists seized power. Their leader was **Benito Mussolini** (1883–1945), a former socialist journalist, who coined the term **fascism**. In the wake of the Russian Revolution of 1917, fascism represented a counterrevolution. It combined mass movements, which had emerged on the political left, with an aggressive, authoritarian nationalism and antisocialist and antiliberal values.

In 1919, Mussolini sought to organize alienated veterans into a mass political movement. In the early years, black-shirted vigilante squads received money from landowners and factory owners to beat up socialist leaders. Still, the Fascists presented themselves as champions of the little guy, of peasants and (nonsocialist) workers, as well as of war veterans, students, and white-collar professionals.

In 1922, Mussolini announced a march on Rome. The march was a bluff, since Mussolini had no military support, yet it intimidated the king, who opposed Fascist ruffians but feared bloodshed. So he withheld use of the army against the lightly armed marchers.

When the Italian government resigned in protest, the monarch invited Mussolini to become prime minister, despite the fact that Fascists had won only a small minority of seats in the 1921 elections. Soon a series of decrees transformed Italy from a constitutional monarchy into a dictatorship. Within a few years, all parties except that of the Fascists had been dissolved. The regime used parades, films, radio, and visions of recapturing Roman imperial grandeur to boost support during the troubled times of the Depression. Mussolini used his personal charisma to promote the idea that as *Il Duce* (the leader), he personified the power and unity of Italy.

Mussolini's dictatorship made deals with big business and the church. He left traditional elites in place and preserved their powerful institutions; thus, his regime fell short of a total social revolution. By the mid-1930s, Italian fascism had settled into a traditional form of conservatism. Nonetheless, as the first antiliberal, antisocialist alternative, the early phase of Italian fascism served as a model for other countries.

German Nazism In Germany, too, fear of bolshevism and anger over the war's outcome propelled a violent, authoritarian party to power. Here, the dictator was **Adolf Hitler** (1889–1945), backed by the nationalist workers' movement, whose name he changed to the National Socialist German Workers' Party (*Nationalsozialistische Deutsche Arbeiterpartei*, or **Nazis**).

Unlike Mussolini, the young Hitler was never a Socialist, but the Nazi's Twenty-Five Points (1920) combined nationalism with a heavy dose of anticapitalism. The party platform called for the renunciation of the Treaty of Versailles and discrimination against Jews. It was an assertion of Germany's grievances against the world and of the small man's grievances against those whom the Nazis perceived as the rich. At first, Hitler and the Nazis were unsuccessful, and Hitler himself was arrested. He was sentenced to five years in prison for treason, but served less than a year. While in prison he wrote an autobiographical and fanatically anti-Semitic treatise called *Mein Kampf* (My Struggle, 1925), which subsequently became wildly popular among Nazis.

As the Great Depression eroded popular support for the Weimar Republic (the democratic regime that came into existence after the Treaty of Versailles), conservative leaders sought to profit from Hitler's popularity. Germany's president appointed Hitler chancellor (prime minister) in 1933, even as the Nazi movement was declining as an electoral force. Like Mussolini, Hitler came to power legally, with the help of traditional elites. Yet neither leader won an electoral majority.

Hitler's first step as chancellor was to heighten fears of communist conspiracy. The burning of the Reichstag (parliament) building in Berlin gave the Nazis an opportunity to blame the fire on the Communists. They immediately suspended civil liberties, including free speech and freedom of association, and attacked and imprisoned their opponents, especially Communists. By July 1933, the Nazis were the only legal party and Hitler was dictator of Germany. Like Mussolini, Hitler relied on choreographed mass rallies, new mediums like film and radio, as well as his own personal charisma to mobilize a mass following.

Hitler also unleashed a campaign of persecution against Jews. Like many other right-wing Germans, he believed that a Jewish-socialist conspiracy had stabbed the German army in the back, causing its surrender in World War I, and that intermarriage with Jews was destroying the supposed purity of the Aryan race (which included northern, white Europeans). Hitler and the Nazis did not believe that religious practice defined Jewishness; instead, they held, it was transmitted biologically from parents to children. Hitler encouraged the use of terror against Jews, destroying their businesses, homes, and marriages with non-Jews, and ultimately eliminating all traces of Jewish life and culture in Nazi-dominated central Europe.

The Nazis won popular support for restoring order and reviving the economy, although the economic gains had more to do with timing than Nazi policy. In any case, Germany reemerged as a great power with expansionist aspirations. Just as Mussolini reached back to ancient Rome to connect fascism to the Italian past, Hitler, too, invoked history.

He called his state the Third Reich—he considered the Holy Roman Empire (or Reich) the first, and the Reich created by Bismarck in 1871 the second—to bolster its legitimacy.

Militarist Japan Unlike authoritarian regimes in Europe, the right-wing movement that emerged in Japan did not spring from wounded power and pride during World War I. In fact, because wartime disruptions reduced European and American competition, Japanese products found new markets in Asia. Although the government expanded the electorate and seemed headed towards liberal democracy in the early 1920s, Japan veered to the political right in 1926 when Emperor Hirohito came to power.

Adding Manchuria to its Korean and Taiwanese colonies (see Map 19.5), Japan established the puppet state of Manchukuo. Meanwhile, at home, "patriots" carried out a campaign of terror against uncooperative businessmen and critics of the military. Unlike Italian fascism and German Nazism, Japanese authoritarianism had an explicitly religious dimension. The state in Japan took on a sacred aura through the promotion of an official religion, Shinto, and of Emperor Hirohito's divinity. By 1940, Hirohito and his closest advisers had merged all political parties into the Imperial Rule Assistance Association, ending even the semblance of democracy, and they advocated a radical form of racial purity. The Imperial Army divided the peoples of Asia into "master races," "friendly races," and "guest races," reserving a dominant position for the Japanese "Yamato Race."

Common Features of Authoritarian Regimes All of the major authoritarian regimes of this period claimed that modern economies required state direction. In Japan, the government fostered huge business conglomerates (*zaibatsu*); in Italy, it encouraged big business to form cartels. The German state also regarded the private sector as the vehicle of economic growth, but it expected entrepreneurs to support the Nazis' racial, antidemocratic, and expansionist aims. The most thorough form of economic coordination occurred in the Soviet Union, which adopted American-style mass production while eliminating private enterprise. Instead, the Soviet state owned and managed all of the country's industry.

All of these states relied heavily on mass organizations. Russia, Italy, and Germany had single mass parties; Japan had various rightist groups until the 1940 merger. All promoted dynamic youth movements, such as the Hitler Youth and the Union of German Girls, the Soviet Communist Youth League, and the Italian squads marching to the anthem "Giovinezza" (Youth).

Three of the four adopted extensive social welfare policies. The Nazis emphasized full employment, built public housing, and provided assistance to needy Aryan families. The Italian National Agency for Maternity and Infancy provided services for unwed mothers and infant care. Soviet programs addressed maternity, disability, sickness, and old age. Although Japan did not enact innovative social welfare legislation, its Home Affairs Ministry enlisted helpmates among civic groups, seeking to raise savings rates and improve child-rearing practices.

All of these regimes, except the Soviet Union, were ambivalent about women in public roles. Even the Soviets, who claimed to support gender equality, eventually restricted abortion and rewarded mothers who had many children. Officials were eager to honor new mothers as a way to repair the loss of so many young men during the Great War. Yet many more women were also entering professional careers, and some were becoming their families' primary wage earners.

Finally, all the dictatorships used violence and terror as tools for remaking the sociopolitical order. The Italians and the Japanese were not shy about arresting political opponents, particularly in their colonies. However, it was the Nazis and especially the Soviets who filled concentration and labor camps with alleged enemies of the state, whether Jews or supposed counterrevolutionaries.

MAP 19.5 | The Japanese Empire in Asia, 1933

Hoping to become a great imperial power like the European states, Japan established numerous colonies and spheres of influence early in the twentieth century.

- What were the main territorial components of the Japanese Empire?

- How far did the Japanese succeed in extending their political influence throughout East Asia?

- According to your reading, what problems did the desire to extend Japanese influence in China present to Japanese leaders?

THE HYBRID REGIMES IN LATIN AMERICA

COMPARISON

EXPLAIN how access to consumer goods and other aspects of mass society influenced political conflict in Asia, Africa, and Latin America.

Latin American countries felt the same pressures that produced liberal democratic and authoritarian responses in Europe, Russia, and Japan. However, the Latin American leaders devised solutions that combined democratic and authoritarian elements.

Economic Turmoil Latin American states had stayed out of the fighting in World War I, but their export economies had suffered. As trade plummeted, popular confidence in oligarchic regimes fell, and radical agitation surged.

As in Europe, Latin American governments stepped in to manage volatile economic markets. More than in any other region, the Depression battered Latin America's trading and financial systems, as well as the standards of living of laborers, because all were so dependent on exports. Exporters of basic staples, from sugar to wheat, faced stiff competition from other exporters and evaporating demand for their commodities. The region in fact suffered doubly because it had borrowed so much money to invest in infrastructure and expansion. When the world's major banks failed, creditors called in their loans from Latin America. This move drove borrowers to default. In an effort to improve their economic prospects, Latin American governments—with enthusiastic backing from the middle classes, nationalist intellectuals, and urban workers—turned to their domestic rather than foreign markets as the main engine of growth. Here, too, the state took a much more interventionist role in market activity than the ideal of classical liberalism.

After the war, Latin American elites confronted the mass age by establishing mass parties and encouraging interest groups to associate with them. Collective bodies such as chambers of commerce, trade unions, peasant associations, and organizations for minorities like blacks and Indians all operated with state sponsorship. This form of modern politics, often labeled corporatist, used social groups to bridge the gap between ruling elites and the general population.

Corporatist Politics in Brazil Corporatist politics took hold especially in Brazil, where the old republic collapsed in 1930. In its place, a coalition led by the skilled politician Getúlio Vargas (1883–1954) cultivated a strong following by enacting socially popular reforms.

Dubbing himself the "father of the poor," Vargas encouraged workers to organize, erected monuments to national heroes, and supported the building of schools and the paving of roads. He made special efforts to appeal to Brazilian blacks, who had been excluded from public life since the abolition of slavery. Thus, he legalized many previously forbidden Afro-Brazilian practices, such as the ritual "candomblé" dance, whose African and martial overtones seemed threatening to white elites. Vargas also supported samba schools, organizations that not only taught popular dances but also raised funds for public works. Moreover, Vargas addressed maternity and housing policies and enfranchised women (although they had to be able to read, as did male voters). Although he condemned the old elites for betraying the country to serve the interests of foreign consumers and investors, he also

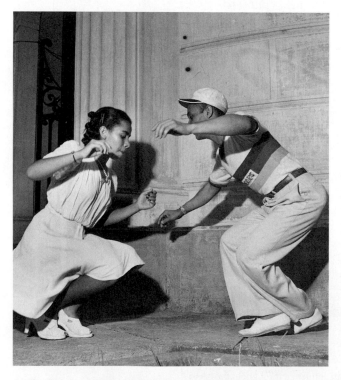

Samba dancers The dance started in the shantytowns of Rio de Janeiro and eventually became popular throughout the world, thanks to films, photographs, and long-playing records that featured samba music.

arranged foreign funding and technical transfers to build steel mills and factories. However, he took this step to create domestic industry so that Brazil would not be so dependent on imports. In these and other ways, Brazil and other Latin American governments combined democratic and authoritarian institutions and methods as a response to the economic downturn of the depression.

ANTICOLONIAL VISIONS OF MODERN LIFE

Debates over liberal-democratic versus authoritarian models engaged the world's colonial and semicolonial regions as well. But here there was a larger concern: what to do about colonial authority? Throughout Asia, most educated members of these communities wanted to roll back the European and American imperial presence. Some Asians even accepted Japanese imperialism as an antidote, under the slogan "Asia for the Asians." In Africa, however, where the European colonial presence was more recent, intellectuals still questioned the real meaning of colonial rule: were the British and the French sincerely committed to African improvement, or were they obstacles to African peoples' well-being? (See **Current Trends in World History: Population Movements**.)

In Africa as well as Asia, then, the search for the modern encompassed demands for power sharing or full political independence. To overcome the contradictions of the democratic liberalism Europeans practiced at home and the authoritarianism they exercised in colonial areas, educated Asians and Africans proposed various forms of nationalism.

Behind the Asian and African nationalist movements were profound disagreements about how best to govern nations once they gained independence and how to define citizenship. The democratic ethos of the imperial powers appealed to many intellectuals. Others liked the radical authoritarianism of fascism and communism, with their promises of rapid change. Whatever their political preferences, most literate colonial subjects also regarded their own religious and cultural traditions as sources for political mobilization. Thus Muslim, Hindu, Chinese, and African nationalist leaders used traditional values to gain the support of the rank and file. The colonial figures involved in political and intellectual movements insisted that the societies they sought to establish were going to be modern *and* at the same time retain their indigenous characteristics.

African Stirrings Africa contained the most recent territories to come under the Europeans' control, so anticolonial nationalist movements there were quite young. The region's fate remained very much in the hands of Europeans. After 1918, however, African peoples probed more deeply for the meaning of Europe's imperial presence.

There was some room (but not much) for voicing African interests under colonialism. The French had long held to a vision of assimilating their colonial peoples into French culture. In France's primary West African colony, Senegal, four coastal cities had traditionally elected one delegate (of mixed African and European ancestry) to the French National Assembly. This practice, limiting African representation to men of mixed ancestry, lasted until 1914, when Blaise Diagne (1872–1934), an African candidate, ran for office and won the seat in the French National Assembly, invoking his African origins and garnering the African vote. While the British allowed Africans to elect delegates to municipal bodies, they refused to permit colonial representatives to sit in Parliament.

Opposition was still not widespread in Africa, for protests ran up against not only colonial administrators but also western-educated African elites. Yet, even this privileged group began to reconsider its relationship to colonial authorities. In Kenya, immediately after World War I, a small contingent of mission-educated Africans called on the British to provide more and better schools and to return lands they claimed European settlers had

Population Movements: Filling Up the Empty Spaces and Spreading Capitalism

As we have seen in Chapters 12 and 13, the European discovery of the Americas resulted in a vast movement of peoples across the Atlantic Ocean from Europe and Africa into the Western Hemisphere. These population movements, among the largest in world history to that point, pale when measured against the long-distance migrations that occurred in the hundred years between 1840 and 1940. During these years, 150 million individuals of European and Asian descent filled up the less populated parts of the world, moving from Europe, South Asia, and China into the Americas, Southeast Asia, and northern Asia in unprecedented numbers and spreading a capitalist mode of production wherever they moved. A

great many of the migrants went as laborers in the factories and on the plains of the Americas and on the rubber, sugar, tea, and coffee plantations springing up in the Dutch East Indies and East and southern Africa. They were as essential to the expansion of the capitalist system in these regions as the 12 million African captives transported to the Americas during the Atlantic slave trade were for the economic expansion of the Americas. Although the new watchword in economic relations was free labor, not all of the men and women who moved were in fact free workers. Indentured servitude—that is, agreeing to work for a certain number of years, usually between three and seven, in return for transportation to the region, food, housing, and clothing—was widely used with Chinese and Indian workers.

A good example of the movement and use of semi-coerced or indentured workers in less-developed regions comes from

East Africa. There, the British and Germans were engaged in a furious political rivalry to extend their control over territories, and British officials believed that constructing a railway from the coast of East Africa at the port of Mombasa to Kisumu at Lake Victoria would enhance their territorial ambitions in East Africa. They also concluded that they would be unable to recruit a sufficient supply of African workers to accomplish the task. Not surprisingly, they looked to the government of India to assist them in providing the necessary work force.

The British government of India did more than help them. In all, it made available nearly 35,000 indentured South Asian workers on three-year contracts for the construction of what was known as the Uganda Railway, the track for which, covering a distance of 582 miles, was completed in a mere five years from 1896 to 1901. The work was arduous, the

stolen. Although defeated in this instance, the young nationalists drew important lessons from their confrontation with the authorities. Their new spokesperson, Jomo Kenyatta (1898–1978), invoked their precolonial Kikuyu traditions as a basis for resisting colonialism. These early anticolonial movements prepared the foundations for more widespread resistance to colonial rule after World War II.

Imagining an Indian Nation As Africans explored the use of modern politics against Europeans, the war and its aftermath brought full-blown challenges to British rule in India. Indeed, the Indian nationalist challenge provided inspiration for other anticolonial movements.

For over a century, Indians had heard British authorities extol the virtues of liberal democracy, yet they were excluded from participation. In 1919, the British did slightly enlarge the franchise in India and allowed more local self-government, but these moves did not satisfy Indians' nationalist longings. During the 1920s and 1930s, the nationalists, led by **Mohandas Karamchand (Mahatma) Gandhi** (1869–1948), laid the foundations for an alternative, anticolonial movement.

Gandhi and Nonviolent Resistance When Gandhi returned to India in 1915, after studying law in England and gaining a reputation for working on behalf of Indian immigrants in South Africa, he immediately became the focus of the Indian nationalist movement. He spelled out the moral and political philosophy of *satyagraha,* or nonviolent resistance, which he had developed while in South Africa. His message to Indians was simple:

The Uganda Railway Indian workers cut rock for the Uganda Railway in this 1905 photograph, taken in British East Africa.

living conditions in the work camps were horrific, yet the British official overseeing the construction concluded that had it not been for this work force, it is doubtful if the project could have been completed in less than twenty years. The building of the Uganda Railway is one of many examples where we see significant numbers of people moving to new places and regions, sometimes by their own choosing and sometimes not, to play an important role in the expansion of the capitalist system and the rivalries between colonial powers.

QUESTIONS FOR ANALYSIS

- Why do you think that in some cases, like the building of the Uganda Railway, governments had to be involved in forcibly moving workers to where they were needed rather than letting market forces draw the workers to where work was available?
- What do you see as some of the similarities and differences in the treatment of the African slaves versus the forced or indentured servants during this period?

Explore Further

Adam McKeown, *Melancholy Order: Asian Migration and the Globalization of Border* (2008).

develop your own resources and inner strength and control the instincts and activities that encourage participation in colonial economy and government, and you shall achieve *swaraj* ("self-rule"). Faced with Indian self-reliance and self-control pursued nonviolently, Gandhi claimed, the British eventually would have to leave.

Indian nationalists urged people to oppose cooperation with government officials, to boycott goods made in Britain, to refuse to send their children to British schools, and to withhold taxes. Gandhi added his voice, calling for an all-India *satyagraha*. He also formed an alliance with Muslim leaders and began turning the Indian National Congress from an elite organization of lawyers and merchants into a mass organization open to anyone who paid dues, even the illiterate and poor.

When the Depression struck India in 1930, Gandhi singled out salt as a testing ground for his ideas on civil disobedience. Every Indian used salt, whose production was a heavily taxed government monopoly. Thus, salt symbolized the Indians' subjugation to an alien government. To break the colonial government's monopoly, Gandhi began a 240-mile march from western India to the coast to gather sea salt for free. Accompanying him were seventy-one followers representing different regions and religions of India. News wire services and mass-circulation newspapers worldwide reported on the drama of the sixty-one-year-old Gandhi, wooden staff in hand, dressed in coarse homespun garments, leading the march. Thousands of people gathering en route were moved by the sight of the frail apostle of nonviolence encouraging them to embrace independence from colonial rule. By insisting

Gandhi and the Road to Independence *(Left)* Gandhi launched a civil disobedience movement in 1930 by violating the British government's tax on salt. Calling it "the most inhuman poll tax the ingenuity of man can devise," Gandhi, accompanied by his followers, set out on a month-long march on foot covering 240 miles to Dandi on the Gujarat coast. The picture shows Gandhi arriving at the sea, where he and his followers broke the law by scooping up handfuls of salt. *(Right)* Gandhi believed that India had been colonized by becoming enslaved to modern industrial civilization. Indians would achieve independence, he argued, when they became self-reliant. Thus, he made the spinning wheel a symbol of *swaraj* and handspun cloth the virtual uniform of the nation.

that Indians follow their conscience (always through nonviolent protest), by exciting the masses through his defiance of colonial power, and by using symbols like homespun cloth to counter foreign, machine-spun textiles, Gandhi instilled in the people a sense of pride, resourcefulness, and Indian national awareness.

A Divided Anticolonial Movement in India Although Gandhi gained a mass following, his program met opposition from within, for many in the Indian National Congress Party did not share his vision of community as the source of public life. Cambridge-educated Jawaharlal Nehru (1889–1964), for example, believed that only by embracing science and technology could India develop as a modern nation.

Even less enamored were radical activists who wanted a revolution, not peaceful protest. In the countryside, these radicals sought to organize peasants to overthrow colonial domination. Other activists galvanized the growing industrial proletariat by organizing trade unions. Their stress on class conflict ran against Gandhi's ideals of national unity.

Religion, too, threatened to fracture Gandhi's hope for anticolonial unity. The Hindu-Muslim alliance crafted by nationalists in the early 1920s splintered over who represented them and how to ensure their political rights. The Muslim community found an impressive leader in Muhammad Ali Jinnah, who set about making the Muslim League the sole representative organization of the Muslim community. In 1940, the Muslim League passed a resolution demanding independent Muslim states in provinces where they constituted a majority, on the grounds that Muslims were not a religious minority of the Indian nation, but a nation themselves.

In 1937, the British belatedly granted India provincial assemblies, a national legislature with two chambers, and an executive. By then, however, India's people were deeply politicized. The Congress Party, which inspired the masses to overthrow British rule, struggled to contain the different ideologies and new political institutions, such as labor unions, peasant associations, religious parties, and communal organizations. Seeking a path to economic modernization, Gandhi, on one side, envisioned independent India as an updated collection of village republics organized around the benevolent authority of male-dominated households. Nehru, on another side, hoped for a socioeconomic transformation powered by science and state-sponsored economic planning. Both believed that India's traditions of collective welfare and humane religious and philosophical practices set it apart from the modern West. By the outbreak of World War II, India was well on its way toward political independence, but British policies and India's divisions foretold a violent end to imperial rule (see Chapter 20).

Chinese Nationalism Unlike India and Africa, China was never formally colonized. But foreign powers' "concession areas" on Chinese soil compromised its sovereignty. Indeed, foreign nationals living in China enjoyed many privileges, including immunity from Chinese law. Furthermore, unequal treaties imposed on the Qing government had robbed China of its customs and tariff autonomy. Thus, the Chinese nationalists' vision of a modern alternative echoed that of the Indian nationalists: ridding the nation of foreign domination was the initial condition of national fulfillment. For many, the 1911 Revolution (as the fall of the Qing dynasty came to be known; see Chapter 18) symbolized the first step toward transforming a crumbling agrarian empire into a modern nation.

Despite high hopes, the new republic could not establish legitimacy. For one thing, factional and regional conflicts made the government little more than a loose alliance of rural elites, merchants, and military leaders. Its intellectual inspiration came from the ideas of Sun Yat-sen, founder of the nationalist political party, the Guomindang. Under the banner of anti-imperialism, the party sponsored large-scale organizations of workers' unions, peasant leagues, and women's associations that looked to students and workers as well as the Russian Revolution for inspiration.

In 1926, amid a renewed tide of anti-foreign agitation, **Chiang Kai-shek** (1887–1975) seized control of the party following Sun's death. Chiang launched a partially successful military campaign to reunify the country and established a new national government with its capital in Nanjing.

Peasant Populism in China: White Wolf For many Guomindang leaders, the peasant population represented a backward class. Thus, the leadership failed to tap into the revolutionary potential of the countryside, which was alive with grassroots movements such as that of White Wolf.

From late 1913 to 1914, Chinese newspapers circulated reports about a roving band of armed men led by a mysterious figure known as White Wolf. This figure terrified members of the elite. It is unlikely that the band, rumored to have close to a million followers, had more than 20,000 members even at its height. But the mythology surrounding White Wolf was so widespread that the movement's impact reverberated well beyond its physical presence.

Popular myth depicted White Wolf as a Chinese Robin Hood with the mission to restore order. The band's objective was to rid the country of government injustices. Raiding major trade routes and market towns, White Wolf's followers gained a reputation for robbing the rich and aiding the poor. Stories of helping the poor won the White Wolf army many followers in rural China, where local peasants joined temporarily as fighters and then returned home when the band moved on. Although the White Wolf army lacked the power to restore order in the countryside, its presence reflected the changes that had to come in China.

A Post-Imperial Turkish Nation Of all the postwar anticolonial movements, none was more successful or more committed to European models than that of **Mustafa Kemal Ataturk** (1881–1938), who helped forge the modern Turkish nation-state. Until 1914, the Ottoman Empire was a colonial power in its own right. But having fought on the losing German side, it saw its realm shrink to a part of Anatolia under the Treaty of Sèvres, which ended the war between the Allies and the Ottoman Empire.

In 1920, an Ottoman army officer and military hero named Mustafa Kemal harnessed an outpouring of Turkish nationalism into opposition to Greek troops who had been sent to enforce the peace treaty. Rallying his own troops to defend the fledgling Turkish nation, Kemal reconquered most of Anatolia and the area around Istanbul and secured international recognition for the new state in 1923 in the Treaty of Lausanne. Thereafter, a vast, forcible exchange of populations occurred. Approximately 1.2 million Greek Christians left Turkey to settle in Greece, and 400,000 Muslims relocated from Greece to Turkey.

With the Ottoman Empire gone, Kemal and his followers moved to build a state based on Turkish national identity. First they deposed the sultan. Then they abolished the Ottoman caliphate and proclaimed Turkey a republic, whose supreme authority would be an elected House of Assembly. Later, after Kemal insisted that the people adopt European-style surnames, the assembly conferred on Kemal the mythic name Ataturk, "father of the Turks."

In forging a Turkish nation, Kemal looked to construct a European-style secular state and to eliminate Islam's hold over civil and political affairs. The Turkish elite replaced Muslim religious law with the Swiss civil code, instituted the western (Christian) calendar, and abolished the once-powerful dervish religious orders. They also sought to eliminate Arabic and Persian words from Turkish, substituted Roman script for Arabic letters, forbade polygamy, made wearing the fez (a brimless cap associated in Kemal's mind with old-fashioned ways) a crime, and instructed Turks to wear European-style hats. The veil, though not outlawed, was denounced as a relic. In 1934, the government enfranchised Turkish women, granted them property rights in marriage and inheritance, and allowed them to enter the professions. Schools were taken out of the hands of Muslim clerics, placed under state control, and, along with military service, became the chief instrument for making the masses conscious of belonging to a Turkish nation. Yet, many villagers did not accept Ataturk's non-Islamic nationalism, remaining devoted to Islam and resentful of the prohibitions against dervish dancing.

In imitating Europe, Kemal also borrowed many of its antidemocratic models. Inspired by the Soviets, he inaugurated a five-year plan for the economy emphasizing centralized coordination by the government. During the 1930s, Turkish nationalists also drew on Nazi examples by advocating racial theories that celebrated central Asian Turks as the founders of all civilization. In another authoritarian move, Kemal occasionally rigged parliamentary elections, while using the police and judiciary to silence his critics. The Kemalist revolution in Turkey was the most far-reaching and enduring transformation that had occurred outside Europe and the Americas up to that point. It offered an important model for the founding of secular, authoritarian states in the Islamic world.

Nationalism and the Rise of the Muslim Brotherhood in Egypt Elsewhere in the Middle East, where France and Britain expanded their holdings at the Ottomans' expense, anticolonial movements borrowed from European models while putting their own stamp on nation-making and modernization campaigns. In Egypt, the British occupation predated the fall of the Ottoman Empire, but here, too, World War I energized the forces of anticolonial nationalism.

When the war ended, Sa'd Zaghlul (1857–1927), an educated Egyptian patriot, pressed for an Egyptian delegation to be invited to the peace conference at Versailles. He hoped to present Egypt's case for national independence. Instead, British officials arrested and exiled him and his most vocal supporters. When news of this action came out, Egypt burst into revolt. Rural rebels broke away from the central government, proclaiming local republics. Villagers tore up railway lines and telegraph wires, the symbols of British authority.

After defusing the conflict, British authorities tried to appease the Egyptian desire to control their own destiny. In 1922, Britain proclaimed Egypt independent, although it retained the right to station British troops on Egyptian soil. This provision was intended to protect traffic through the Suez Canal and foreign populations residing in Egypt, but it also enabled the British to continue to influence Egyptian politics. Two years later, elections placed Zaghlul's nationalist party, the Wafd, in office. But the British prevented the Wafd from exercising real power.

This subversion of independence and democracy provided an opening for antiliberal versions of anticolonialism in Egypt. During the Depression years, a fascist group, Young Egypt, garnered wide appeal. Much more influential and destined to have an enduring influence throughout the Arab world was an Islamic group, the Muslim Brotherhood, which attacked liberal democracy as a facade for middle-class, business, and landowning interests. The Muslim Brotherhood was anticolonial and anti-British, but its members considered mere political independence insufficient. Egyptians, they argued, must also renounce the lure of the West (whether liberal capitalism or godless communism) and return to a purified form of Islam. For the Muslim Brotherhood, Islam offered a complete way of life. A "return to Islam" through the nation-state created yet another model of modernity for colonial and semicolonial peoples.

Conclusion

The Great War and its aftermath accelerated the trend toward mass participation in a broad range of activities and the debate over how to define progress and organize the people. Because mass society meant production and consumption on a staggering scale, satisfying the populace became a pressing concern for rulers worldwide. Competing programs vied for influence in the new, broader, public domain.

Most programs fell into one of three categories: liberal democratic, authoritarian, or anticolonial. Liberal democracy defined the political and economic systems in most of western Europe and the Americas in the decade following World War I. Resting on faith in free enterprise and representative democracy (with a restricted franchise), liberal regimes had already been unsettled before the Great War. Turn-of-the-century reforms broadened electorates and brought government oversight and regulation into private economic activity. But during the Great Depression, dissatisfaction again deepened. Only far-reaching reforms, introducing greater regulation and more aggressive government intervention to provide for the citizenry's welfare, saved capitalist economies and democratic political systems in Britain, France, and North America from collapse.

Through the 1930s, liberal democracy was in retreat. Authoritarianism seemed better positioned to satisfy the masses while representing the dynamism of modernity. While authoritarians differed about the faults of capitalism, they joined in the condemnation of electoral democracy. Authoritarians mobilized the masses to put the interests of the nation above the individual. That mobilization often involved brutal repression, yet it seemed also to restore pride and purpose to a great number of people.

Meanwhile, the colonial and semicolonial world searched for ways to escape from European domination. In Asia and Africa, anticolonial leaders sought to eliminate foreign rule while turning colonies into nations and subjects into citizens. Some looked to the liberal democratic West for models of nation building, but others rejected liberalism because it was associated with colonial rule. Instead, socialism, communism, fascism, and a return to religious traditions offered more promising paths.

After You Read This Chapter

FOCUS ON: *World War I and Its Aftermath*

THE GREAT WAR

- The war destroys empires, starting with the Bolshevik Revolution against the tsarist regime in Russia, followed by the defeat and dissolution of the German, Austro-Hungarian, and Ottoman empires.

- Mass mobilization sees almost 70 million men join the fighting, undermines traditional gender boundaries, and forces states to recognize their peoples' demands for compensation afterward.

- Popular culture spreads as leaders use the new media of radio and film to promote national loyalties and discredit enemies.

THE AFTERMATH

- Liberal democracies in France, Britain, and the United States survive the Great Depression by enacting far-reaching changes in their political systems and free market economies.

- Authoritarian (communist and fascist) dictatorships with many political similarities emerge in the Soviet Union, Italy, and Germany, Spain, and Portugal.

- Latin American leaders devise hybrid solutions that combine democratic and authoritarian elements.

- Peoples living under colonial rule in Asia and Africa mobilize traditional values to oppose imperial rulers.

- Key individuals emerge in the struggle to define newly independent nations: Kenyatta, Gandhi, Chiang Kai-shek, and Ataturk.

CHRONOLOGY

	1900	1910	1920
THE AMERICAS		U.S. enters World War I 1917 ◆	
EUROPE		World War I 1914-1918 ▬▬	Mussolini takes over Italy 1922 ◆
SOVIET UNION		Bolshevik Revolution 1917 ◆ Russian civil war 1918-1921 ▬▬	
EAST ASIA			
SOUTH ASIA			
MIDDLE EAST		Mustafa Kemal creates modern Turkish nation state 1923 ◆	

- *Thinking about Transformation & Conflict and Visions of the Modern* What was the relationship between war and progress in the early twentieth century? What new political, social, and cultural movements grew out of the Great War? Think in particular of the role of former soldiers in politics; the adaptation in peacetime of production practices developed for the war effort; and governments' willingness and ability to regulate the economy and people's everyday lives.

- *Thinking about Changing Power Relationships and Visions of the Modern* What, if anything, was left in this period of the tradition of classical liberalism, which trusted markets to regulate themselves and believed progress would result from individuals pursuing their own self interest? What role did government intervention—in the economy and society—play for the three major traditions discussed in this chapter: liberal democratic, authoritarian, and anticolonial? How central was state intervention to their respective views of progress and modernity?

- *Thinking about Gender and Visions of the Modern* What role did women play in the social transformations of the early twentieth century, both as participants and as symbols? Pay special attention to the role of women workers in war production and, increasingly, in professional careers thereafter; to women consumers in an era of mass production; and to governments' commitment to the ideal of gender equality, and (faltering) willingness to abide by that ideal.

1. Explain the relationship between the **Great War** and the **Great Depression**, both in terms of origins and outcomes. What common sources did they share? What caused them? What values and assumptions did they both challenge?

2. Define the terms mass culture, mass production, and mass consumption. How, where, and why did they spread?

3. Distinguish **fascism** from traditional conservatism. Compare it to other political movements discussed in this chapter, especially **bolshevism**.

4. Explain how authoritarian leaders (**Stalin, Mussolini, and Hitler**) defined progress. What did it mean to them? What elements did they share with liberal democracy, and in what terms did they reject that tradition?

5. Contrast the visions of progress espoused by anticolonial leaders, including **Gandhi, Ataturk**, and **Chiang Kai-shek**. To what extent did they reflect borrowed elements versus local native traditions and ideas?

6. Describe how Latin American societies adjusted to economic instability. How did visions of becoming modern affect states and societies in that region of the world?

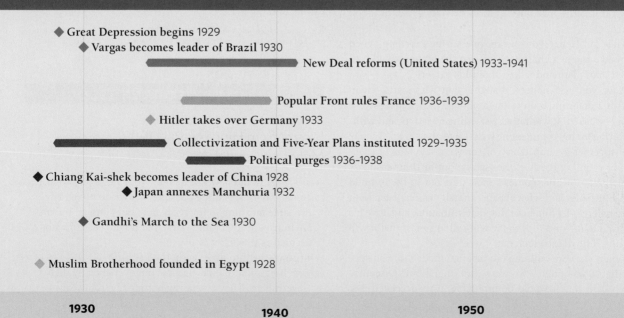

◆ Great Depression begins 1929
　◆ Vargas becomes leader of Brazil 1930
　　　　━━━━━━━━━━━━━━ New Deal reforms (United States) 1933-1941

　　　　　　━━━━━━ Popular Front rules France 1936-1939
◆ Hitler takes over Germany 1933
━━━━━━━━ Collectivization and Five-Year Plans instituted 1929-1935
　　　━━━━━ Political purges 1936-1938
◆ Chiang Kai-shek becomes leader of China 1928
　　◆ Japan annexes Manchuria 1932

　◆ Gandhi's March to the Sea 1930

◆ Muslim Brotherhood founded in Egypt 1928

1930　　　　　**1940**　　　　　**1950**

Competing Perspectives

Technology, Religion, and the Meaning of Progress

What does it mean to be modern? People have never stopped asking themselves this question, distinguishing their own lives from those who came before them. But the emergence of modern factory production and new forms of overseas imperialism in the second half of the nineteenth century profoundly reoriented the terms of debate. While we looked closely at modernism in art in the last chapter, here we consider broader efforts to make sense of what it meant to be modern in the early twentieth century. Within Europe and the United States, debates raged over its meaning. Did the Western liberal ideals of thrift, self-discipline, and the scientific method make life better for everyone, or only a tiny elite? Elsewhere around the world, reformers and intellectuals sought ways to be modern, to make material gains, and at the same time remain true to their cultures and traditions.

The documents presented here define progress and modernity in different ways. In *The Man Nobody Knows* (1925), the journalist and, later, advertising executive Bruce Barton interpreted the life and teachings of Jesus as a gospel for success in modern business. In the second excerpt, Gandhi presents modern technology and economic dynamism as threats to Indian civilization, though he embraced the idea that all Indians should be treated as equal citizens. One of Kenya's leading nationalists, Jomo Kenyatta wrote an account of his own Kikuyu community in *Facing Mount Kenya* (1937), which stressed the cohesion of precolonial society and identified destructive consequences of colonialism in Africa. Writing from within the European tradition, Wilfred Owen damned the values that drove him and the men of his generation to fight in the Great War. The title of his poem, "Dulce et Decorum Est," comes from an ode by the classical poet Horace: it is good and right to die for one's country.

PRIMARY SOURCE 19.1

The Man Nobody Knows *(1925),*
Bruce Barton

"If you're forever thinking about saving your life," Jesus said, "you'll lose it; but the man who loses his life shall find it." Because he said it and he was a religious teacher, because it's printed in the Bible, the world has dismissed it as high minded ethics but not hard headed sense. But look again! . . .

What did Henry Ford mean, one spring morning, when he tipped a kitchen chair back against the whitewashed wall of his tractor plant and talked about his career?

"Have you ever noticed that the man who starts out in life with a determination to make money, never makes very much?" he asked. It was rather a startling question; and without waiting for my comment he went on to answer it: "He may gather together a competence, of course, a few tens of thousands or even hundreds of thousands, but he'll never amass a really great fortune. But let a man start out in life to build something better and sell it cheaper than it has ever been built or sold before—let him have that determination, and, give his whole self to it—and the money will roll in so fast that it will bury him if he doesn't look out."

"When we were building our original model, do you suppose that it was money we were thinking about? Of course we expected that it would be profitable, if it succeeded, but that wasn't in the front of our minds. We wanted to make a car so cheap that every family in the United States could afford to have one. So we worked morning, noon and night, until our muscles ached and our nerves were so ragged that it seemed as if we just couldn't stand it to hear anyone mention the word automobile again. One night, when we were almost at the breaking point I said to the boys, 'Well, there's one consolation,' I said, 'Nobody can take this business away from us unless he's willing to work harder than we've worked.' And so far," he concluded with a whimsical smile, "nobody has been willing to do that."

Source: Bruce Barton, *The Man Nobody Knows: A Discovery of the Real Jesus*, in Loren Baritz, ed., *The Culture of the Twenties* (Indianapolis: Bobbs-Merrill, 1925), pp. 241–42.

PRIMARY SOURCE 19.2

Excerpt from Hind Swaraj *(1909),*
Mahatma Gandhi

READER: . . . I would now like to know your views on Swaraj. . . .

EDITOR [GANDHI]: It is quite possible that we do not attach the same meaning to the term. You and I and all Indians are impatient to obtain Swaraj, but we are certainly not decided as to what it is. . . .

Why do we want to drive away the English?

READER: Because India has become impoverished by their Government. They take away our money from year to year. The most important posts are reserved for themselves. We are kept in a state of slavery. They behave insolently towards us, and disregard our feelings.

EDITOR: Supposing we get self-government similar to what the Canadians and the South Africans have, will it be good enough?

READER: . . .We must own our navy, our army, and we must have our own splendour, and then will India's voice ring through the world.

EDITOR: . . . In effect it means this: that we want English rule without the Englishman. You want the tiger's nature, but not the tiger; that is to say, you would make India English, and, when it becomes English, it will be called not Hindustan but Englistan. This is not the Swaraj that I want.

READER: Then from your statement I deduce that the Government of England is not desirable and not worth copying by us.

EDITOR: . . . If India copies England, it is my firm conviction that she will be ruined.

READER: To what do you ascribe this state of England?

EDITOR: It is not due to any peculiar fault of the English people, but the condition is due to modern civilisation. It is a civilisation only in name. Under it the nations of Europe are becoming degraded and ruined day by day.

READER: . . . I should like to know your views about the condition of our country.

EDITOR: . . . India is being ground down not under the English heel but under that of modern civilisation. It is groaning under the monster's terrible weight. . . . India is becoming irreligious. Here I am not thinking of the Hindu, the Mahomedan, or the Zoroastrian religion, but of that religion which underlies all religions. We are turning away from God.

READER: You have denounced railways, lawyers and doctors. I can see that you will discard all machinery. What, then, is civilisation?

READER: . . . The tendency of Indian civilisation is to elevate the moral being, that of the Western civilisation is to propagate immorality. The latter is godless, the former is based on a belief in God. So understanding and so believing, it behooves every lover of India to cling to the old Indian civilisation even as a child clings to its mother's breast.

READER: . . . What, then, . . . would you suggest for freeing India?

EDITOR: . . . Those alone who have been affected by Western civilisation have become enslaved. . . . If we become free, India is free. And in this thought you have a definition of Swaraj. It is Swaraj when we learn to rule ourselves.

Source: M. K. Gandhi, *Hind Swaraj and Other Writings*, edited by Anthony J. Parel (Cambridge: Cambridge University Press, 1997), pp. 26–91.

Facing Mount Kenya *(1937), Jomo Kenyatta*

And it is the culture which he inherits that gives a man his human dignity as well as his material prosperity. It teaches him his mental and moral values and makes him feel it worth while to work and fight for liberty.

But a culture has no meaning apart from the social organisation of life on which it is built. When the European comes to the Gikuyu country and robs the people of their land, he is taking away not only their livelihood, but the material symbol that holds family and tribe together. In doing this he gives one blow which cuts away the foundations from the whole of Gikuyu life, social, moral, and economic. When he explains, to his own satisfaction and after the most superficial glance at the issues involved, that he is doing this for the sake of the Africans, to "civilize" them, "teach them the disciplinary value of regular work," and "give them the benefit of European progressive ideas," he is adding insult to injury, and need expect to convince no one but himself.

There certainly are some progressive ideas among the Europeans. They include the ideas of material prosperity, of medicine, and hygiene, and literacy which enables people to take part in world culture. But so far the Europeans who visit Africa have not been conspicuously zealous in imparting these parts of their inheritance to the Africans, and seem to think that the only way to do it is by police discipline and armed force. They speak as if it was somehow beneficial to an African to work for them instead of for himself, and to make sure that he will receive this benefit they do their best to take away his land and leave him with no alternative. Along with his land they rob him of his government, condemn his religious ideas, and ignore his fundamental conception of justice and morals, all in the name of civilisation and progress.

If Africans were left in peace on their own lands, Europeans would have to offer them the benefits of white civilisation in real earnest before they could obtain the African labour which they want so much. They would have to offer the African a way of life which was really superior to the one his fathers lived before him, and a share in the prosperity given them by their command of science. They would have to let the African choose what parts of European culture would be beneficially transplanted, and how they could be adapted. He would probably not choose the gas bomb or the armed police force, but he might ask for some other things of which he does not get so much today. As it is, by driving him off his ancestral lands, the Europeans have robbed him of the material foundations of his culture, and reduced him to a state of serfdom incompatible with human happiness. The African is conditioned, by the cultural and social institutions of centuries, to a freedom of which

Europe has little conception, and it is not in his nature to accept serfdom for ever. He realises that he must fight unceas-
ingly for his own complete emancipation; for without this he
is doomed to remain the prey of rival imperialisms, which in
every successive year will drive their fangs more deeply into
his vitality and strength.

Source: Excerpt from *Facing Mount Kenya: The Tribal Life of the Gikuyu* by Jomo Kenyatta,
published by Vintage Books, a division of Random House, Inc. Used by permission of
Alfred A. Knopf, a division of Random House, Inc.

PRIMARY SOURCE 19.4

"Dulce et Decorum Est" (1920), Wilfred Owen

Bent double, like old beggars under sacks,
Knock-kneed, coughing like hags, we cursed through sludge,
Till on the haunting flares we turn our backs,
And towards our distant rest began to trudge.
Men marched asleep. Many had lost their boots,
But limped on, blood-shod. All went lame, all blind;
Drunk with fatigue; deaf even to the hoots
Of gas-shells dropping softly behind.

Gas! GAS! Quick, boys!—An ecstasy of fumbling
Fitting the clumsy helmets just in time,
But someone still was yelling out and stumbling
And flound'ring like a man in fire or lime.—
Dim through the misty panes and thick green light,
As under a green sea, I saw him drowning.

In all my dreams before my helpless sight
He plunges at me, guttering, choking, drowning.

If in some smothering dreams, you too could pace
Behind the wagon that we flung him in,
And watch the white eyes writhing in his face,
His hanging face, like a devil's sick of sin,
If you could hear, at every jolt, the blood
Come gargling from the froth-corrupted lungs
Bitten as the cud
Of vile, incurable sores on innocent tongues,—
My friend, you would not tell with such high zest
To children ardent for some desperate glory,
The old Lie: *Dulce et decorum est
Pro patria mori.*

Source: Wilfred Owen, *Poems by Wilfred Owen* (New York: The Viking Press, 1920), p. 15.

QUESTIONS FOR ANALYSIS

1. Identify the view of technological progress expressed in
   each text and place these views on a continuum from a
   positive embrace of technological progress to a negative
   rejection. Which author is most optimistic about technological progress? Which author is most concerned about
   its negative effects?

2. Compare the critiques of European culture presented
   by Kenyatta and Gandhi. What impressed them about
   Europe and what did they criticize?

3. Contrast the role of religion in the excerpts from Gandhi
   and Barton. Did both men consider religion essential to
   becoming modern?

4. In his poem, Owen bends the traditional rules of meter
   (the number of syllables per line), rhythm, and rhyme
   used by Shakespeare, among many others. Why do you
   think he did so, and what is the effect?

Interpreting Visual Evidence

Men, Machines, and Mass Production

Mass production of consumer goods reshaped economies and societies in the early twentieth century. Powered by coal and later electricity, the modern factory transformed work, first in Europe, the United States, and Japan, and then, especially from 1950 onwards, around the world. The images gathered here provide several perspectives on mass production and its cult of efficiency—its efforts to streamline, to standardize productive activity, to maximize output and minimize cost—and its consequences for workers.

Large-scale manufacturing on assembly lines demands coordinated action. Engineers like Frederick Winslow Taylor (see Chapter 18) developed the field of "scientific management," the forerunner of ergonomics, to streamline the production process. Rather than shaping production to the needs and desires of skilled workers, Winslow tried to adapt machines and human bodies to one another. He and his followers broke down complex tasks into standardized, repeatable actions and then timed workers, imposing a predictable uniformity and minimizing accidents and error. Gone were the days when farmers organized their days by the light of the sun.

The French inventor-scientist, Étienne-Jules Marey (1830–1904), helped prepare the way for the scientific study of labor. He developed stop-action photography in 1882, with a photographic "gun" that took twelve frames per second, which helped pave the way for modern cinema. Here we look at a series of studies of human movement that would influence Taylor and facilitate the study of labor practices around the world.

Inspired by Pablo Picasso and Karl Marx, among others, the Mexican muralist Diego Rivera (1886–1957) was fascinated by labor. His Detroit mural (1923) of the Ford Motor Company depicted workers on an assembly line, celebrating the physical force of cosmopolitan groups of industrial workers. The final two images include a photograph of a Ford assembly line in Detroit and one from a Mitsubishi electric plant in Japan in the 1930s, representing iconic examples of modern factories, with standardized, streamlined production processes powered by electricity and massive machines.

Photographs by Étienne-Jules Marey.

Mural in Detroit by Diego Rivera.

Car assembly line at Ford plant.

Mitsubishi Electric Factory.

QUESTIONS FOR ANALYSIS

1. Describe the relationship between workers and machines in these images, from the point of view of the workers.

2. Explain how engineers like Taylor, who were interested in maximizing production, could also use Marey's images to improve working conditions.

3. Explain the relationship between factory production and factory workers, as depicted in these images, and mass consumption and consumers, as presented in this chapter.

4. On balance, do the images of the human body and industrial work presented here promise alienation or liberation for workers?

Before You Read This Chapter

GLOBAL STORYLINES

- World War II shatters the European-centered global order, weakening Europe and Japan, and unsettling empires.
- The United States and its liberal-democratic allies (the First World) engage in a cold war with the Soviet Union and its communist allies (the Second World).
- Decolonized states in Asia, Africa, and Latin America (the Third World) struggle to find a "third way" but find themselves caught between rival superpowers.

CORE OBJECTIVES

- **EXPLAIN** the relationship between World War II and the three-world order.
- **ANALYZE** the extent to which World War II was a global war.
- **ANALYZE** the roles that the United States and the Soviet Union played in the Cold War.
- **IDENTIFY** the goals of Third World states in this period, and **EVALUATE** the degree to which these goals were achieved.
- **COMPARE** the civil rights issues in the First, Second, and Third worlds, and **ASSESS** the ways each "world" addressed these and other basic rights.

CHAPTER 20

The Three-World Order

1940–1975

In February 1945, the three leaders of the World War II Allies—president Franklin Delano Roosevelt of the United States, prime minister Winston Churchill of Great Britain, and premier Joseph Stalin of the Soviet Union—met to prepare for the postwar world. By then, Germany, Italy, and Japan were losing the war. But the world's reordering was a source of deep contention, for the three leaders had profoundly different visions for the future. Roosevelt envisioned independent nation-states protected by an international body and had no interest in restoring the old European empires. Churchill, however, resisted decolonization of the British Empire. Stalin sought above all to secure Soviet influence in eastern Europe and to weaken Germany so that it could never again menace the Soviet Union. When the fighting stopped, the European-centered order, shocked by World War I, had been shattered by World War II. Empires lay in ruins and faced dismantling by independence movements. The nation-state had emerged as the prevailing global political organization.

With the weakening of western Europe, a new three-world order emerged. Heading the "First World," the United States championed capitalism and democracy as the best way to bring unprecedented prosperity in the decades after 1945. The United States' crucial ally

COMPARISON

EXPLAIN the relationship between World War II and the three-world order.

during World War II, the Soviet Union became its chief adversary in the decades that followed. As leader of the communist "Second World," the Soviet Union contested capitalist societies' claims and trumpeted socialism's accomplishments. As their spheres of influence expanded, the Americans and the Soviets (and their respective allies) engaged in a bitter ideological rivalry, known as the **Cold War** because no direct military conflict occurred between these two superpowers. Caught in between were formerly colonized and semicolonized people. Lumped together as the "Third World" by Western intellectuals and by Asian and African leaders who embraced the idea of an alternative to the dominant blocs, these nations emerged from the war eager to seek their own ways forward.

World War II and Its Aftermath

COMPARISON

ANALYZE the extent to which World War II was a global war.

World War II was truly a world conflict, a devastatingly total one. It grew out of unresolved problems connected to the Great War. World War I had not been, as many had prophesied, "the war to end all wars." Especially influential were the resentments bred by the harsh provisions and controversial state boundaries set out in the treaties signed at the war's end. World War II also resulted from the aggressive ambitions and racial theories of Germany and Japan. By the late 1930s, German and Japanese ambitions to become colonial powers brought these dictatorships (which along with Italy constituted the Axis powers) into conflict with France, Britain, the Soviet Union, and eventually the United States (the Allied powers). Fighting occurred in Europe, Africa, and Asia, and the Atlantic and Pacific oceans, as the warring nations mobilized millions of people and placed enormous demands on civilian populations.

THE WAR IN EUROPE

World War II began in September 1939 with Germany's invasion of Poland and the British and French decision to oppose it. Before it was all over in 1945, much of Europe, including Germany, had been leveled.

Blitzkrieg and Resistance Germany's early success was staggering. Nazi troops overran Poland, France, Norway, Denmark, Luxembourg, Belgium, and Holland. Within less than two years, the Germans controlled virtually all of Europe from the English Channel to the Soviet border (see Map 20.1). Only Britain escaped Axis control, although Nazi bombers pulverized British cities. In 1939, Germany signed a nonaggression pact with the Soviets, but in 1941 the German army broke the pact and invaded the Soviet Union with 170 divisions, 3,000 tanks, and 3.2 million men—an invasion force of a size unmatched before or since. Here, as elsewhere, the Germans fought a *blitzkrieg* ("lightning war") of tank-led assaults followed by motorized infantrymen and then foot soldiers. By October 1941, the Germans had reached the outskirts of Moscow. The Soviet Union seemed on the verge of a monumental defeat.

The Nazi war was not just a grab for land and raw materials; it was also a crusade for a new order based on race. Throughout Europe, Hitler established puppet governments that complied with deportation orders against Jews and dissidents. His new order made Europe a giant police state. It gave rise to collaborators, who worked with the Germans; resistance fighters, who opposed German occupiers for varying reasons; and a wide range

The Devastation of War (*Left*) In the Battle of Britain, Nazi warplanes strafed British cities in an effort to break British morale. But the devastating bombing raids, such as this one in Coventry in November 1940, helped rally the British, who refused to give in. (*Right*) In November 1942, Nazi troops entered Stalingrad, some 2,000 miles from Berlin. Hitler wanted to capture the city not only to exploit the surrounding wheat fields and the oil of the Caucasus but also for its very name. With handheld flamethrowers and sometimes just their fists, Soviet troops drove out the Germans in February 1943.

of options in between, as people struggled to make their way and take care of their families as best they could.

In the east, the tide turned against the Germans and their collaborators after the ferocious battles of Stalingrad in 1942–1943 and Kursk in 1943. At the battle of Stalingrad, the German army and its allies suffered 1.5 million men killed, wounded, or captured against 750,000 Soviet troops suffering the same fates. Only six months later, at the battle of Kursk, the largest tank conflict in world history, the Germans, boasting a tank force of more than 2,000, lost out to a Soviet tank force twice its size. Once the Soviet army blunted the initial German assault, it launched a massive counteroffensive. This move initiated the defeat of the German war effort on the Eastern Front, but full retreat took another two years as the Soviets drove Hitler's army slowly westward. The spectacular D-Day landing of western Allied forces in Normandy on June 6, 1944 (when the Germans had a mere 15 divisions in France, as compared with more than 300 on the Eastern Front), initiated defeat in the west. On April 30, 1945, as Soviet and Anglo-American forces converged on Berlin, Hitler committed suicide. Days later, Germany surrendered unconditionally.

The Bitter Costs of War The war in Europe had devastating human and material costs. This was particularly the case in eastern Europe, where German forces leveled more than 70,000 Soviet villages, obliterated one-third of the Soviet Union's wealth, and inflicted 7 million Soviet military deaths (by contrast, the Germans lost 3.5 million soldiers) and at least 20 million civilian deaths. German bombing of British cities, such as London, took a heavy toll on civilians and buildings, as did Allied bombing of war plants and Axis cities like Dresden and Tokyo. Tens of millions were left homeless.

Europe's Jews paid an especially high price. Hitler had long talked of "freeing" Europe of all Jews. At the war's outset, the Nazis herded Jews into ghettos and labor camps and then seized their property. As the German army moved eastward, more and more Jews came under their control.

At first the Nazi bureaucrats considered deportation but then ruled out transporting "subhumans" as too costly, and began instead to starve Jews and crowd them together in

MAP 20.1 | World War II: The European Theater

The Axis armies enjoyed great success during the early stages of World War II.

• Looking at the map, which states were within the Axis territory when World War II began in September 1939? What were the territorial boundaries when the Axis powers reached their greatest extent?

• When did the military balance begin to turn against Germany and Italy? Where do you think the outcome of the conflict was decided, eastern Europe or western Europe?

unsanitary ghettos. By the summer of 1941, special troops operating behind the army on the Eastern Front had begun mass shootings of communists and Jewish civilians, and by fall 1941, Hitler and the S.S.—the *Schutzstaffel*, or special security forces—were building a series of killing centers. Cattle cars shipped Jews from all over Europe to the extermination sites in the east where Nazis used the latest technology, including the arsenic-based poison gas Zyklon B, to kill men, women, and children. The largest facility, Auschwitz, combined an extermination center and work camp in a single complex.

The deliberate racial extermination of the Jews, known as the **Holocaust**, claimed around 6 million lives. About half of this number died in the gas chambers of death camps; the others were shot or gassed in mobile vans, or they succumbed to starvation or disease. The shift to a policy of extermination was both unimaginably brutal and rapid. At its core, the Holocaust was brief, intense mass murder. In mid-March 1942, roughly three-quarters of all victims of the Holocaust were still alive and one-quarter had been killed; within a year—by March 1943—the proportions were reversed, with three-quarters of the victims dead. The Nazis also turned their mass killing apparatus against gypsies, homosexuals, communists, and Slavs, with deportations to the death camps continuing to the very end of the war.

Nazi genocides—enormous in scale and reliant on modern, "enlightened" administrative practices—stood as a powerful challenge to European claims that science, technology, and an efficient bureaucracy would make life better for everyone. Lamenting connections between European culture and the Holocaust, German philosopher Theodor Adorno wrote: "[t]o write poetry after Auschwitz is barbaric" (1949). Nazi crimes, he suggested, defied human understanding.

THE PACIFIC WAR

Like the war in Europe, the conflict in the Pacific transformed the military and political landscape (see Map 20.2). The war broke out when Japan's ambitions to dominate Asia targeted American interests and might.

Japan's Efforts to Expand Japanese efforts to expand in Asia were already under way in the 1930s, but the outbreak of war in Europe opened opportunities for further expansion. Japan's military invaded and occupied Manchuria in 1931 and then launched an offensive against the rest of China in 1937. Although the Japanese did not achieve China's complete submission, the invaders exacted a terrible toll on the population. Most infamous was the so-called rape of Nanjing, in which Japanese aggressors slaughtered at least 100,000 civilians and raped thousands of women in the Chinese city between December 1937 and February 1938.

Meanwhile, Germany's swift occupation of western Europe left defeated nations' Asian colonies at the mercy of Japanese forces. After concluding a pact with Germany in 1940, the Japanese occupied French Indochina in 1941 and made demands on the Dutch East Indies for oil and rubber. The chief remaining obstacle to further expansion in the Pacific was the United States, which already had imperial interests in places like China and the Philippines, as well as other Pacific islands. Hoping to strike the United States before it was prepared for war, the Japanese launched a surprise air attack on the American naval base at Pearl Harbor in Hawaii on December 7, 1941.

Now Japan's expansion shifted into high gear. With French Indochina already under their control, the Japanese turned against the American colony of the Philippines and against the Dutch East Indies, both of which fell in 1942. By coordinating their army, naval, and air force units and using tactical surprise, the Japanese seized a huge swath of territory that included British-ruled Hong Kong, Singapore, Malaya, and Burma, while threatening the British Empire's hold on India as well.

Japan justified its aggression on the grounds that it was anticolonial and pan-Asian; Japan promised to drive out the European imperialists and to build a new order reflecting "Asia for Asians." In practice, however, the Japanese made oppressive demands on fellow Asians for resources, developed myths of Japanese racial purity and supremacy, and treated Chinese and Koreans with brutality.

MAP 20.2 | World War II: The Pacific Theater

Like Germany and Italy, Japan experienced stunning military successes in the war's early years.

- In what directions did the Japanese direct their military offensives?

- Analyzing this map, why do you think the Japanese were so concerned about an American presence in East Asia, when the United States was so geographically distant?

- According to your reading, how did the Allied strategies to defeat the Japanese Empire shape postwar relations in the region?

The Aftermath of the Atomic Bomb (*Left*) A view of Nagasaki less than half a mile from "ground zero" after the atomic bomb was dropped in August 1945. A few reinforced concrete buildings still stand. (*Right*) Thousands of people were immediately crushed or burned to death in the blast. Many died later from horrendous burns and radiation poisoning.

Allied Advances and the Atomic Bomb Like the Germans in their war against Russia, the Japanese could not sustain their military successes against the United States. By mid-1943, U.S. forces had put the Japanese on the defensive. Fighting from island to island, American troops recaptured the Philippines, and a combined force of British, American, and Chinese troops returned Burma to Britain. The Allies then moved toward the Japanese mainland. By summer 1945, American bombers had all but devastated the major cities of Japan. Yet Japan did not surrender.

Anticipating that an invasion of Japan would cost hundreds of thousands of American lives, U.S. president Harry Truman unleashed the Americans' secret weapon. It was the work of a team of scientists who were predominantly European refugees. On August 6, 1945, an American plane dropped an atomic bomb on the city of Hiroshima, killing or maiming over 100,000 people, and poisoning the air, soil, and groundwater for decades to come. Three days later, the Americans dropped a second atomic bomb on Nagasaki. Within days, Emperor Hirohito announced Japan's surrender, bringing the war to an official end. After the six years of World War II, much of East Asia and Europe lay in ruins; millions had died, and millions more were wounded, displaced, widowed, and orphaned. What the postwar world would look like, however, remained unclear. (See **Analyzing Global Developments: World War II Casualties**.)

The Beginning of the Cold War

The destruction of Europe and the defeat of Japan left a power vacuum, which the United States and the Soviet Union rushed to fill. Avoiding direct warfare, the Americans and Soviets vied for influence in postwar Europe and around the globe in a series of smaller conflicts.

REBUILDING EUROPE

Communism and liberal democracy offered competing approaches to rebuilding states and societies in Europe after World War II. The task of political rebuilding was daunting, for

COMPARISON

ANALYZE the roles that the United States and the Soviet Union played in the Cold War.

Analyzing Global Developments

World War II Casualties

World War II was the most destructive armed conflict in recorded history. It mobilized more than 120 million military personnel. More than 20 million died. The death toll on civilian populations was substantially greater. Civilian deaths from genocide, bombing, starvation, and disease were estimated to range from 30 million to 55 million, including the 6 million Jews killed in the Holocaust. Historians now put the total at roughly 60 million dead, more than double the number killed in World War I.

A total reordering of the globe was at stake from the outset of World War II. The war was a struggle not only for the control of resources and territory, as World War I had been, but it was also fought to decide which peoples would control the world's resources and which peoples would be destroyed because the aggressors decided that they were undesirable.

QUESTIONS FOR ANALYSIS

- Compare and contrast the casualties for World Wars I and II. (See the Analyzing Global Developments feature in Chapter 19.)
- Which countries endured the greatest loss of life in World War II and why? Which of the major participants in the war endured the fewest casualties and why?
- Contrast civilian and military casualties in World War II and explain why the civilian casualty rates were so much higher than military losses?
- Many historians, especially those specializing in modern European history, regard World War I as a greater turning point in European and Western history than World War II, with its extraordinarily high loss of life. Can you understand why these historians would hold to this view? What is your view of the relative global importance of the two wars?

NATION	POPULATION IN 1939	MAX. NO. MOBILIZED	MILITARY DEATHS	MISSING IN ACTION	CIVILIAN WAR-RELATED DEATHS	ESTIMATED TOTAL DEATHS
Belgium	8,386,000	800,000	22,651	55,513	76,000	88,000
Brazil	40,289,000	200,000		4,222		1,000
British Commonwealth		4,683,000	400,000	369,267	92,673	466,000
Australia	6,968,000	680,000	37,467	39,803		24,000
Canada	11,267,000	780,000	42,666	53,174		38,000
India	311,820,000	2,150,000	48,674	64,354		1,500,000
New Zealand	1,628,500	157,000	13,081	19,314		10,000
South Africa	10,160,000	140,000	8,681	14,363		7,000
UK	47,760,000	4,683,000	403,195	369,267	92,673	357,000
China	517,568,000	5,000,000	2,220,000	14,685,593		10,000,000
Czechoslovakia	15,300,000 (1938)	180,000	10,000	8,017	215,000	225,000
Denmark	3,795,000	15,000	6,400	2,000	2,000	4,000
France	40,000,000	5,000,000	245,000	390,000	350,000	563,000
Greece	7,221,900	414,000	88,300	42,290	325,000	413,000
Netherlands	8,729,000	500,000	7,900	2,860	200,000	208,000

Sources: Alan Axelrod (ed.), *Encyclopedia of World War II*, vol. 1. (2007); John Dower, *War without Mercy* (1986); Geoffrey Hosking, *Rulers and Victims: The Russians in the Soviet Union* (2006).

NATION	POPULATION IN 1939	MAX. NO. MOBILIZED	MILITARY DEATHS	MISSING IN ACTION	CIVILIAN WAR-RELATED DEATHS	ESTIMATED TOTAL DEATHS
Norway	2,944,900	25,000	3,000	364	7,000	10,000
Poland	34,775,700	1,000,000	597,320	766,606	5,675,000	5,800,000
Philippines	16,000,300	105,000	127,000		91,000	110,000
United States	131,028,000	16,353,659	292,000	671,801	6,000	298,000
USSR	108,377,000	12,500,000	8,700,000	14,685,593		27,000,000
Yugoslavia	5,510,100	500,000	305,000	425,000	1,200,000	1,505,000
Bulgaria	6,458,000	450,000	18,500	21,878	10,000	20,000
Finland	3,700,000	250,000	82,000	50,000	2,000	84,000
Germany	69,622,500	9,200,000	325,000	7,250,000	780,000	4,200,000
Hungary	9,129,000	350,000	200,000	89,313	290,000	490,000
Italy	44,394,000	4,000,000	380,000	225,000	152,941	395,000
Japan	71,380,000	6,095,000	1,740,955	326,000	672,000	2,700,000
Romania	19,933,800	600,000	300,000		200,000	500,000
Indonesia	69,435,000					4,000,000

Total World War II Deaths: 60 million (including 6 million Jews)

The Berlin Airlift In summer 1948, a new currency was issued for the united occupation zones of West Germany. It began to circulate in Berlin at more favorable exchange rates than the eastern zone's currency, and Berlin seemed poised to become an outpost of the West inside the Soviet occupation zone. The Soviets responded by blocking western traffic into Berlin; the West countered with an airlift, forcing the Soviets to back down in May 1949 but hastening the division of Germany into two countries.

the old order had been discredited. Liberal democrats had to distance themselves from their prewar predecessors. Communism, by contrast, gained new appeal. Many eastern Europeans, reacting to the horrors of fascism and not knowing the extent of Stalin's crimes, looked to the Soviets for answers.

Europe's leftward tilt alarmed U.S. policymakers. They feared that the Soviets would use their ideological influence and the territory taken over by the Red Army to spread communism. They also worried that Stalin might seize Europe's overseas possessions and create communist regimes outside Europe. But no one wished to fight another "hot" war. As President Truman began advocating a policy of containment to prevent the further advance of communism, an American journalist popularized the term *cold war* in 1946 to describe a new form of struggle in which both sides endeavored to avoid direct warfare.

Truman's containment policy was tested when the Soviets attempted to seize control of Berlin. Like the rest of Germany, Berlin had been partitioned into British, French, American, and Soviet zones of occupation; but the city itself was an island lying within the Soviet zone. In 1948, the Soviets attempted to cut the city off from western access by blocking western routes to the capital. The Allies responded with the Berlin Airlift, which involved transporting supplies in planes to western Berlin to keep the population from capitulating to the Soviets. This crisis lasted for almost a year, until Stalin allowed trucks to roll through the eastern zone in May 1949.

In that same year, occupied Germany was split into two hostile states: the democratic Federal Republic of Germany in the west, and the communist German Democratic Republic in the east. In 1961, leaders in the German Democratic Republic built a wall around West Berlin to insulate the east from capitalist propaganda and to halt a flood

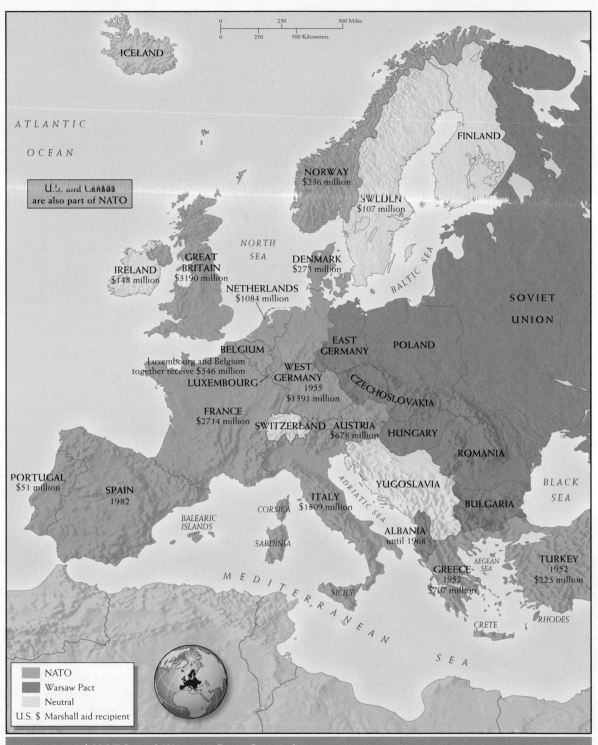

ICELAND

ATLANTIC

OCEAN

U.S. and Canada
are also part of NATO

FINLAND

NORWAY
$236 million

SWEDEN
$107 million

*NORTH
SEA*

GREAT
BRITAIN
$3190 million

DENMARK
$273 million

IRELAND
$148 million

NETHERLANDS
$1084 million

BALTIC SEA

SOVIET

UNION

BELGIUM

Luxembourg and Belgium
together receive $546 million

LUXEMBOURG

WEST
GERMANY
1955
$1391 million

EAST
GERMANY

POLAND

CZECHOSLOVAKIA

FRANCE
$2714 million

SWITZERLAND

AUSTRIA
$678 million

HUNGARY

ROMANIA

PORTUGAL
$51 million

SPAIN
1982

*BALEARIC
ISLANDS*

CORSICA

ADRIATIC SEA

ITALY
$1509 million

YUGOSLAVIA

BULGARIA

*BLACK
SEA*

SARDINIA

ALBANIA
until 1968

*AEGEAN
SEA*

TURKEY
1952
$225 million

MEDITERRANEAN

SICILY

GREECE
1952
$707 million

CRETE

RHODES

SEA

NATO
Warsaw Pact
Neutral
U.S. $ Marshall aid recipient

MAP 20.3 | **NATO and Warsaw Pact Countries**

The Cold War divided Europe into two competing blocs: those joined with the United States in the North Atlantic Treaty Organization (NATO) and those linked to the Soviet Union under the Warsaw Pact.

• Which nations had borders with nations belonging to the opposite bloc?

• Comparing this map with Map 20.1, explain how combat patterns in World War II shaped the dividing line between the two blocs.

• According to the map, where would you expect Cold War tensions to be the most intense?

of émigrés fleeing communism. The Berlin Wall became the great symbol of a divided Europe and of the Cold War.

U.S. policymakers wanted to shore up democratic governments in Europe, so Truman promised American military and economic aid. Containing the spread of communism meant securing a capitalist future for Europe, a job that fell to Truman's secretary of state, General George C. Marshall. He launched the Marshall Plan, an ambitious program that provided over $13 billion in grants and credits to reconstruct Europe and facilitate an economic revival. U.S. policymakers hoped the aid would dim communism's appeal by fostering economic prosperity, muting class tensions, and integrating western European nations into an alliance of capitalist democracies.

Stalin saw the Marshall Plan as a threat to the Soviet Union and rejected the offer of support. He felt the same about the formation in 1949 of the **North Atlantic Treaty Organization (NATO)**, a military alliance between countries in western Europe and North America. He believed that the Soviet Union, having sacrificed millions of people to the war against fascism, deserved to be dominant in eastern Europe. Soviet troops had occupied eastern European nations at the war's end, and both communists and leftist members of other parties formed Soviet-backed coalition governments there. In 1955, the Soviets formally allied themselves with these communist nations in the **Warsaw Pact**, a military alliance of their own (see Map 20.3). The tense confrontations between NATO and the Warsaw Pact countries in Europe and in other parts of the world in the 1950s and 1960s brought the world to the brink of an atomic World War III.

WAR IN THE NUCLEAR AGE: THE KOREAN WAR

The dropping of the atomic bombs on Japan in 1945 changed military affairs forever. Spurred by the onset of the Cold War, the Soviets worked hard to catch up to the Americans, and in 1949 tested their first nuclear bomb. Thereafter, each side rushed to stockpile nuclear weapons and update its military technologies. By 1960, the explosive power of these weapons had increased so greatly that nuclear war might lead to the world's destruction without a soldier firing a single shot. This sobering realization changed the rules of the game. Each side now possessed the power to inflict total destruction on the other, a circumstance that inhibited direct confrontations but sparked smaller conflicts in parts of Asia such as Korea, where the postwar settlement was murky.

In 1950, North Korean troops backed by the Soviet Union invaded U.S.-backed South Korea, setting off the Korean War (see Map 20.4). President Truman ordered American troops to drive back the North Koreans. The Security Council of the United Nations—established in 1945 to help prevent another world war—also sent troops from fifteen nations to restore peace. Within a year, the invaders had been routed and were near collapse. When U.N. troops advanced north to the Chinese border, however, Stalin maneuvered his communist Chinese allies into rescuing the communist regime in North Korea and driving the South Korean and U.N. forces back to the old boundary in the middle of the Korean peninsula. The fighting continued until 1953, when an armistice divided the country at roughly the same spot as at the start of the war.

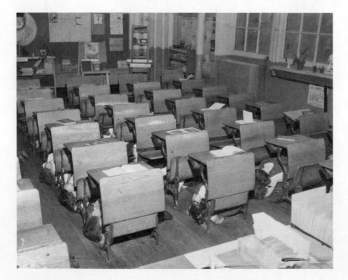

Atom Bomb Anxiety This photograph shows schoolchildren taking shelter under their desks during an A-bomb drill in Brooklyn, New York, 1951. The Soviets had exploded their first test bomb in 1949. Underground bomb shelters were built in many American urban areas as places in which to survive a doomsday attack.

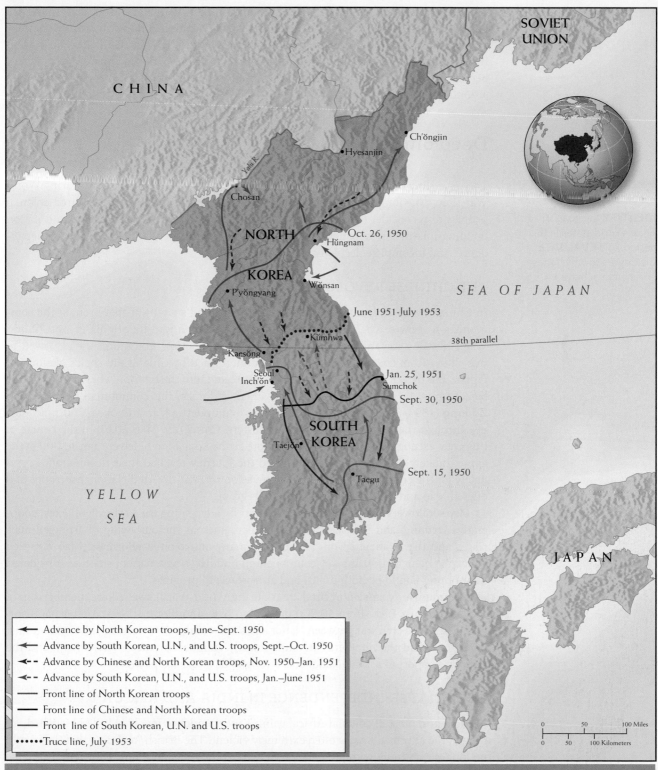

SOVIET UNION

CHINA

Ch'ŏngjin

Hyesanjin

Yalu R.

Chosan

NORTH

KOREA

Oct. 26, 1950

Hŭngnam

Wŏnsan

SEA OF JAPAN

P'yŏngyang

June 1951-July 1953

38th parallel

Kŭmhwa

Kaesŏng

Seoul

Inch'ŏn

Jan. 25, 1951

Sumchok

Sept. 30, 1950

SOUTH

KOREA

Taejŏn

Sept. 15, 1950

Taegu

YELLOW

SEA

JAPAN

← Advance by North Korean troops, June–Sept. 1950

← Advance by South Korean, U.N., and U.S. troops, Sept.–Oct. 1950

◄- - Advance by Chinese and North Korean troops, Nov. 1950–Jan. 1951

◄- - Advance by South Korean, U.N., and U.S. troops, Jan.–June 1951

— Front line of North Korean troops

— Front line of Chinese and North Korean troops

— Front line of South Korean, U.N. and U.S. troops

•••••• Truce line, July 1953

0   50   100 Miles

0   50   100 Kilometers

MAP 20.4 | The Korean War

The Korean War was an early confrontation between the capitalist and communist blocs during the Cold War era.

• What were the dates of each side's farthest advance into the other side's territory?

• Why was this peninsula strategically important?

• According to your reading, how did the outcome of the war shape political affairs in East Asia for the next several decades?

The Korean War energized America's anticommunist commitments and spurred a rapid increase in NATO forces. The U.S. now saw Japan as a bulwark against communism and resolved to rebuild Japanese economic power. Like West Germany, Japan went from being the enemy in World War II to being a valued U.S. ally as the Cold War rivalry between the United States and the Soviet Union spurred both sides to shore up alliances around the globe.

Decolonization

COMPARISON

IDENTIFY the goals of Third World states in this period, and **EVALUATE** the degree to which these goals were achieved.

The unsettling of empires, including those established by Japan before and during World War II and the longer-standing colonies belonging to European states, inspired colonial peoples to reconsider their political futures. The process of **decolonization** and nation building followed four patterns: civil wars, wars of independence, negotiated independence, and incomplete decolonization.

THE CHINESE REVOLUTION

In China, the ousting of Japanese occupiers intensified a civil war that brought the communists to power. The communist movement in China had its origins in post–World War I hostility toward the western powers. In this period, communists had vowed to free China from colonialism, but had been outgunned by Chiang Kai-shek's Nationalist regime and driven from China's cities; they retreated into the interior, where they founded base camps. In 1934, under attack by Chiang's forces, the communists, led by **Mao Zedong** (1893–1976), abandoned their bases and undertook an arduous 6,000-mile journey through the rugged terrain of northwestern China (see Map 20.5). In the course of this great escape, glorified in communist lore as the Long March, fewer than 10,000 of the approximately 80,000 people who started the journey reached their destination. Fortunately for the communists, the Japanese invasion in 1937 diverted Nationalist troops and offered Mao and the survivors a chance to regroup.

Mao's followers cultivated popular support by advocating the lowering of taxes, cooperative farming, and policies aimed at women, such as the outlawing of arranged marriages and the legalization of divorce. Like many anticolonial reformers, Mao regarded women's emancipation as a key component in building a new nation, since he considered their oppression to be both unjust and an obstacle to progress.

Communist expansion in rural areas during World War II swelled the membership of the Communist Party from 40,000 in 1937 to over a million in 1945. After Japan's surrender, China's civil war between Nationalists and communists resumed. But communist forces now had the numbers, the guns (mostly supplied by the Soviet Union), and the popular support to assault Nationalist strongholds and seize power.

NEGOTIATED INDEPENDENCE IN INDIA AND AFRICA

In India and most of colonial Africa, gaining independence involved little bloodshed, although the aftermaths were often extremely violent. The British, realizing that they could no longer rule India without coercion, bowed to the inevitable and withdrew. The same happened in Africa, where nationalists also succeeded in negotiating independence from European empires; although, as we shall see, there were notable exceptions.

India Unlike China, India achieved political independence without an insurrection. But it did veer dangerously close to civil war. The leadership of the Indian National Congress

Legend:

- Early Soviets (self-governing communist areas) 1927–1935
- Route of the main Chinese communist forces from Ruijin after Guomindang assaults on Jiangxi Soviet area
- Route of communist forces from other areas
- Main communist base area, governed from Yan'an 1935–1945
- "Liberated areas" dominated by local communist groups by 1945
- HUNAN Province

MAP 20.5 | The Long March, 1934–1935

During the Long March, which took place during the struggle for power between the Guomindang (Nationalists) and the communists within China, communist forces traveled over 6,000 miles to save their lives and their movement.

- What route did the communist forces take?
- Why did the communists take this particular route?
- How did this movement affect the outcome of this internal struggle in the long run?

retained tight control over the mass movement that it had mobilized in the 1920s and 1930s (see Chapter 19). Even Gandhi hesitated to leave the initiative to the common people, believing that they had not yet assimilated the doctrine of nonviolence. Gandhi and the leadership worked hard to convince the British that they, the middle-class leaders, spoke for the nation. At the same time, the threat of a mass peasant uprising with radical aims (like the communist revolution in China) encouraged the British to transfer power quickly.

As negotiations moved forward, Hindu-Muslim unity deteriorated. Whose culture would define the new nation? The Indian nationalism that had existed in the late nineteenth century reflected the culture of the Hindu majority. Yet this movement masked the multiplicity of regional, linguistic, caste, and class differences *within* the Hindu community, just as Muslim movements that arose in reaction to Hindu-dominated Indian nationalism overlooked divisions within their own ranks. Now the prospect of defining "India" created a grand contest between newly self-conscious communities. Riots broke out between Hindus and Muslims in 1946, which increased the mutual distrust between the Congress Party and Muslim League leaders. The specter of civil war haunted the proceedings, as outgoing colonial rulers decided to divide the subcontinent into two states: India and Pakistan.

On August 14, 1947, Pakistan gained independence from Britain; a day later, India did the same. The euphoria of decolonization, however, drowned in a frenzy of brutality. Shortly after independence, as many as 1 million Hindus and Muslims killed one another. Fearing further violence, 12 million Hindus and Muslims left their homes to relocate in the new countries where they would be in the majority. Although the British departed peacefully from India, the peoples inhabiting the subcontinent engaged in open warfare over differences that haunt the relationship between India and Pakistan to this day.

Africa for Africans Shortly after Indian independence, most African states also gained their sovereignty. Except in southern Africa, where minority white rule persisted, the old colonial states gave way to indigenous rulers.

The postwar years also saw Africans move to cities in search of a better life. As expanding educational systems produced a wave of primary and secondary school graduates, these educated young people and other new urban dwellers became disgruntled when attractive employment opportunities were not forthcoming. Three groups—former servicemen, the urban unemployed or underemployed, and the educated—led the nationalist agitation that began in the late 1940s and early 1950s (see Map 20.6).

Faced with rising nationalist demands and too much in debt to invest more in pacifying the discontented, European powers agreed to decolonize. The Soviet Union and the United States also favored decolonization. Thus decolonization in most of Africa was a rapid and relatively sedate affair. In 1957, the Gold Coast (renamed Ghana) under prime minister Kwame Nkrumah became tropical Africa's first independent state. Other British colonial territories followed in rapid succession, so that by 1963 all of British-ruled Africa except for Southern Rhodesia was independent.

Decolonization in much of French-ruled Africa followed a similarly smooth path, although the French were initially resistant. Instead of negotiating independence, they tried first to accord fuller voting rights to their colonial subjects, even allowing Africans and Asians to send delegates to the French National Assembly. In the end, however, the French electorate had no desire to share the privileges of French citizenship with African and Asian populations. Thus, France dissolved its political ties with French West Africa and French Equatorial Africa in 1960, having given protectorates in Morocco and Tunisia their independence in 1956. Algeria, considered an integral part of France, was a different

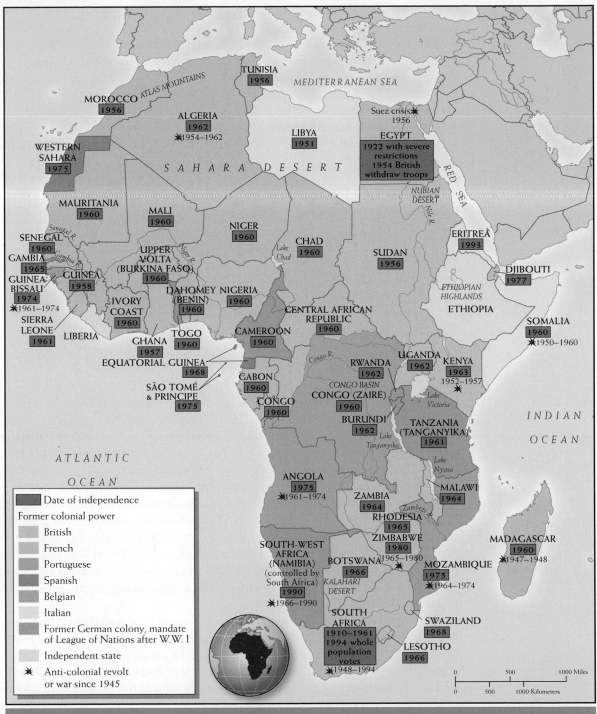

MAP 20.6 | Decolonization in Africa

African decolonization occurred after World War II, largely in the 1950s, 1960s, and 1970s.

- Find at least four areas that won independence in the 1950s, and identify which former colonial power had ruled each area.
- What areas took longer to gain independence?
- According to your reading, what problems and tensions contributed to this uneven process across Africa?

matter. Desperate efforts to hold onto French Algeria (see below) facilitated independence movements elsewhere in Africa.

The leaders of African independence believed that Africa's precolonial traditions would enable the region to move from colonialism right into a special African form of socialism, escaping the ravages of capitalism. Without rejecting Western culture completely, they praised the so-called African personality, exemplified by the idea of "Negritude" developed by Senegal's first president, Léopold Sédar Senghor. Negritude, they claimed, was steeped in common African traditions and able to embrace social justice and equality, while rejecting the unrestrained individualism that Africans felt lay at the core of European culture.

VIOLENT AND INCOMPLETE DECOLONIZATIONS

Although transfers of power in most of Africa and Asia ultimately occurred peacefully, there were notable exceptions. In Palestine, Algeria, Kenya, and southern Africa, the presence of European immigrant groups created violent conflicts that aborted any peaceful transfer of power—or left the process incomplete. In Vietnam, the process was also violent and delayed, partly because of France's desire to reimpose colonial control and partly from the power politics of Cold War competition.

Palestine, Israel, and Egypt In Palestine, Arabs and Jews had been on a collision course since the end of World War I. Before that war, a group of European Jews, known as Zionists, had argued that only a large-scale migration from existing states to their place of origin in Palestine could lead to Jewish self-determination. Zionism combined a yearning to return to the holy lands with a fear of anti-Semitism and anguish over increasing Jewish assimilation. Zionists wanted to create a Jewish state, and they won a crucial victory during World War I when the British government, under the Balfour Declaration, promised a homeland for the Jews in Palestine. But when the British took control of Palestine after 1918, they also guaranteed the rights of Palestinian Arabs.

As more Jews settled in Palestine, tensions rose between Zionists and Palestinian Arabs, and both grew dissatisfied with British rule. Arabs resented the presence of Jews, who displaced farmers who had lived on the land for generations and openly sought their own independent state. Zionists became especially enraged when British authorities wavered in supporting their demands for greater immigration. After World War II, the pressure to allow more immigration increased as hundreds of thousands of concentration camp survivors clamored for entry into Palestine, and Zionist militants began using force to attempt to gain control of the state.

In 1947, after the British announced that they would leave negotiations over the area's fate to the United Nations, that body voted to partition Palestine into Arab and Jewish territories. The Arab states rejected the partition, and the Jewish Agency, a non-governmental organization that supported the immigration of Jews from the diaspora to Israel, only reluctantly accepted it. Although the Jews were delighted to have an independent state, they were unhappy about its small size, its indefensible borders, and the fact that it did not include all the lands that had belonged to ancient Israel. For their part, the Palestinians were shocked at the partition, and they looked to their better-armed Arab neighbors to regain the territories set aside for the new state of Israel.

The ensuing Arab-Israeli War of 1948–1949 shattered the legitimacy of Arab ruling elites. Arab states entered the war poorly prepared to take on the well-run and enthusiastically supported Israeli Defense Force. By the time the United Nations finally negotiated a truce, Israel had extended its boundaries and more than 1 million Palestinians had become refugees in surrounding Arab countries.

Embittered by this defeat, a group of young army officers in Egypt plotted to overthrow the Egyptian regime, which they felt was corrupt and still under European influence. One of the officers, Gamal Abdel Nasser, became the head of a secret organization of junior military officers—the Free Officers Movement. These men had ties with communists and other dissident groups, including the Muslim Brotherhood, which favored a return to Islamic rule. They launched a successful coup in 1952, forcing the king to abdicate and leave the country. The new regime dissolved the parliament, banned political parties (including the communists and the Muslim Brotherhood), and stripped the old elite of its wealth.

In 1956, Nasser moved to nationalize the Suez Canal Company (an Egyptian company, mainly run by French businessmen and experts), inciting the Israelis, the British, and the French to invade Egypt and seize territory along the Suez Canal. Opposition by the United States and the Soviet Union forced the invading countries to withdraw, providing Nasser with a spectacular diplomatic triumph. As Egyptian forces reclaimed the canal, Nasser's reputation as leader of the Arab world soared. He became the chief symbol of a pan-Arab nationalism that swept across the Middle East and North Africa and especially through the camps of Palestinian refugees.

The Algerian War of Independence The appeal of Arab nationalism was particularly strong in Algeria, where a European settler population (the *colons*) of 1 million stood in the way of decolonization. Indeed, French leaders claimed that Algeria was an integral part of France. Although the *colons* were a minority, they held the best land and generally lived in the major cities near the coast. They controlled Algeria's finances and all of its major public institutions.

Anticolonial nationalism in Algeria gathered force after World War II. The Front de Libération Nationale (FLN) emerged as the leading nationalist party in the 1950s, using violence to provoke its opponents and to make the local population choose between supporting the nationalist cause or the *colons*. The full-fledged revolt that erupted in 1954 pitted FLN troops and guerrillas against thousands of French troops. Atrocities and terrorist acts occurred on both sides.

The war dragged on for eight years, at a cost of perhaps 300,000 lives. On the French mainland, the war came as a terrible shock, for many, though not all, French citizens had accepted the idea that Algeria was not a colonial territory but part of France itself. The *colons* insisted that they had emigrated to Algeria in response to their government's promises and that yielding power to the nationalists would be a betrayal. After an insurrection led by *colons* and army officers brought down the French government in 1958, the new French president, Charles de Gaulle, negotiated a peace accord. Shortly after handing over power to FLN leaders, 800,000 *colons* left Algeria. By late 1962, over nine-tenths of the European and indigenous Jewish population had departed.

Southern Africa The bloody conflict in Algeria highlights a harsh reality of African decolonization: the presence of European settlers often prevented the smooth transfer of power. South Africa, which held the continent's largest and wealthiest settler population (a mixture of Afrikaans- and English-speaking peoples of European descent), defied black majority rule longer than other African states. After winning the elections of 1948, the white Afrikaner–dominated National Party enacted an extreme form of racial segregation known as apartheid. Under apartheid, laws stripped Africans, Indians, and "colored" persons (those of mixed descent) of their few political rights. Racial mixing of any kind was forbidden, and schools were strictly segregated.

The ruling party tolerated no protest. Nelson Mandela, one of the leaders of the African National Congress (ANC) who campaigned for an end to discriminatory legislation, was repeatedly harassed, detained, and tried by the government, even though he had at first urged peaceful resistance. After the Sharpeville massacre in 1960, in which police killed demonstrators who were peacefully protesting the oppressive laws, Mandela and the ANC decided to oppose the apartheid regime with violence. A South African court sentenced Mandela to life imprisonment.

Women helped keep resistance flames burning. The most dynamic of these individuals was Winnie Mandela, wife of the imprisoned Nelson Mandela. Unlike many of the ANC leaders, who opposed the regime from exile, she remained behind and openly and courageously spoke out against the apartheid government. Nonetheless, whites retained external support. Through the 1950s and 1960s, Western powers (especially the United States) saw South Africa as a bulwark against the spread of communism in Africa.

Vietnam The same concern to contain communism also drew the United States into support for a conservative and pro-Western regime in South Vietnam. Vietnam had come under French rule in the 1880s, and by the 1920s approximately 40,000 Europeans were living among and ruling over roughly 19 million Vietnamese. To promote an export economy of rice, mining, and rubber, the colonial rulers granted vast land concessions to French companies and local collaborators, while leaving large numbers of peasants landless.

The colonial system also generated a new intelligentsia. Primarily schooled in French and Franco-Vietnamese schools, educated Vietnamese worked as clerks, shopkeepers, teachers, and petty officials. Yet they had few opportunities for advancement. Discontented, they turned from the traditional ideology of Confucianism to modern nationalism. Vietnamese intellectuals overseas, notably Ho Chi Minh, one of the original founders of the French Communist Party, took the lead in imagining a new Vietnamese nation-state.

When the French tried to restore their rule in Vietnam after Japan's defeat in 1945, Ho led the resistance. War with France followed (1946–1954), featuring guerrilla tactics to undermine French positions. The Viet Minh, the League for the Independence of Vietnam, were most successful in the north, but even in the south their campaign bled the French. Finally, in 1954, the anticolonial forces won a decisive military victory. At the Geneva Peace Conference, Vietnam (like Korea) was divided into two zones. Ho controlled the north, while a government with French and American support took charge in the south.

During the early 1960s, U.S. involvement escalated as Ho's support for Viet Cong communist guerrillas heightened American concerns about the spread of communism. In 1965, large numbers of American troops entered the country to fight on behalf of South Vietnam, while communist North Vietnam turned to the Soviet Union for supplies. Over the next several years, the United States sent some 500,000 soldiers to fight the Vietnam War, but peasant support enabled the Viet Cong, a term meaning Vietnamese communists, to continue fierce guerrilla fighting. Even the bombing of villages and the deployment of counterinsurgency forces failed to prevent the spread of communism in Southeast Asia. In 1975, two years after the final withdrawal of American troops, the South Vietnamese government collapsed.

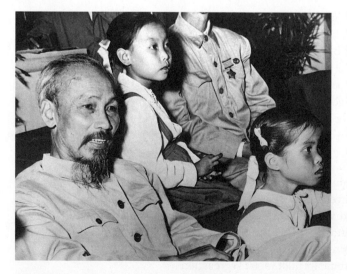

Ho Chi Minh Ho Chi Minh's formation of the League for the Independence of Vietnam, or Viet Minh, in 1941 set the stage for Ho's rise at the end of World War II. Here he attends a youth rally in October 1955, just over a year after the victory of his forces at Dien Bien Phu, which resulted in the ousting of the French from Vietnam.

Thus, the process of decolonization varied across regions. Although most of the lands in Asia and Africa had gained independence by the mid-1960s, there were significant exceptions in Africa—South Africa, Southern Rhodesia, and the Portuguese colonies—and Asia, notably Vietnam. Although the British and French realized that they no longer had the resources to stem the nationalist tide that was spreading through the Third World, they tried to use military might to support European areas of settlement, like Algeria and Kenya.

Three Worlds

World War II and postwar decolonization created a three-world order, in which the liberal-democratic and capitalist First World and the communist Second World competed for global influence, notably among the newly decolonized Third World states. The war had made the Soviet Union and the United States into superpowers. Possessing nuclear weapons, superior armies, and industrial might, they vied for global influence. As decolonization spread, the two Cold War belligerents offered new leaders their models for modernization. The decolonized, however, had their own ideas. With the communist takeover in 1949, China had shrugged off semicolonial status, but Mao soon broke from Soviet direction. Other decolonized nations in Asia and Africa had underdeveloped economies and could not leap into either capitalist or communist industrial development. They drew some elements from communist and capitalist models, but politically tended to favor single-party states. Moreover, in some places colonial rule persisted, and civilians were not allowed even relative autonomy, because the colonizers remained in place.

THE FIRST WORLD

As the Cold War spread in the early 1950s, western Europe and North America became known as the First World, or "the free world." Later on, Japan joined this group. First World states sought to organize the world on the basis of capitalism and democracy. Yet, in struggling against communism, the free world sometimes aligned with Third World dictators, thereby sacrificing its commitment to freedom and democracy for the sake of propping up pro-Western regimes.

Western Europe The reconstruction of western Europe after World War II was a spectacular success. By the late 1950s, most nations' economies there were thriving, thanks in part to massive American economic assistance. Improvements in agriculture were particularly impressive. As industrial production boomed and wages rose, goods that had been luxuries before the war—refrigerators, telephones, automobiles, indoor plumbing—became commonplace. Prosperity and the dismantling of national military establishments allowed governments to expand social welfare systems; by the late 1950s education and health care were within the reach of virtually all citizens.

Western Europe's economic recovery blunted the appeal of socialism and communism. At the same time, the Cold War slowed down efforts to punish fascists, Nazis, and collaborators. Although war crimes trials brought the conviction of a number of prominent Nazis, the fear was that a complete purge of former Nazis would deprive Germany of political and economic leaders, leaving it susceptible to communist subversion.

The United States While Europe lay in ruins in 1945, the United States entered a period of economic expansion and a rising standard of living. Americans could afford more consumer goods than ever before—almost always U.S. manufactures. Home ownership became more common, especially in the burgeoning suburbs.

Yet anxieties about the future of the First World abounded. Following the Soviet Union's explosion of an atomic bomb, the Communist Revolution in China, and the outbreak of the Korean War, fear of the communist threat prompted increasingly harsh rhetoric. Anticommunist hysteria led the Republican senator from Wisconsin, Joseph McCarthy, to initiate a campaign to uncover closet communists in the State Department and in Hollywood in the 1950s. Televised congressional hearings broadcast his views to the entire nation, compelling elected officials to support a strong anticommunist foreign policy and a large military budget.

Postwar American prosperity did not benefit all citizens equally. During the 1950s, nearly a quarter of the American population lived in poverty. But many African Americans, a group disproportionately trapped below the poverty line, participated in a powerful movement for equal rights and the end of racial segregation. The National Association for the Advancement of Colored People (NAACP) won court victories that mandated the desegregation of schools. Boycotts, too, became a weapon of the growing civil rights movement, with Martin Luther King Jr. (1929–1968) leading a successful strike against injustices in the bus system of Montgomery, Alabama. Here and in subsequent campaigns against white supremacy King borrowed his most effective weapon—the commitment to nonviolent protest and the appeal to conscience—from Gandhi. As the civil rights movement spread, the federal government gradually supported programs for racial equality.

The Japanese "Miracle" Japan reemerged as an economic powerhouse in this period. The war had ended with Japan's unconditional surrender in 1945, its dreams of dominating East Asia dashed, and its homeland devastated. But after 1945, in an attempt to

Civil rights movement The 1955 arrest of Rosa Parks (*left*), for refusing to give up her seat on a Montgomery, Alabama, bus, led to a boycott that brought Martin Luther King Jr. to prominence and galvanized the challenge to legal racial segregation in the American South. (*Right*) Borrowing from Gandhi's tactics of nonviolent civil disobedience, protesters staged "sit-ins" across the southern United States in the 1950s and early 1960s, as in this photograph of black and white students seated together at a segregated lunch counter in Jackson, Mississippi.

incorporate Japan into the First World, American military protection, investment, and transfers of technology helped to rebuild Japanese society. The Japanese government guided economic development through directed investment, partnerships with private firms, and protectionist trade policies. By the mid-1970s, Japan, formerly a dictatorship, became a politically stable civilian regime with a thriving economy, enjoying considerable American guidance and the replacement of the power of the emperor with a parliamentary system.

THE SECOND WORLD

The Soviet Union along with its eastern and central European allies as well as Mongolia and North Korea constituted the communist Second World. The scourge of World War II and the shadow of the Cold War fell heavily on the Soviets. Having suffered more deaths and more damage than any other industrialized nation, the Soviet Union was determined to insulate itself from future aggression from the West. That meant turning eastern Europe into a bloc of communist buffer states.

The Appeal of the Soviet Model The Soviet model's egalitarian ideology and success with rapid industrialization made it seem a worthy alternative to capitalism. Here, there was no private property and thus, in Marxist terms, no exploitation. Workers "owned" the factories and worked for themselves. The Soviet state promised full employment, boasting that a state-run economy would be immune from upturns and downturns in business cycles. Freedom from exploitation, combined with security, was contrasted with the capitalist model of owners hoarding profits and suddenly firing loyal workers when they were not needed.

The Soviet system touted protections for workers, inexpensive mass transit, paid maternity leave, free health care, and universally available education. Whereas under the tsarist regime less than one-third of the Russian Empire's population had been literate, by the 1950s the literacy rate soared above 80 percent. True, Soviet policies did not provide material abundance of the sort that First World nations were enjoying. But if consumer goods were often scarce, they were always cheap. Likewise, while it sometimes took ten years to obtain a small apartment through waiting lists at work, when one's turn finally came the apartment carried low annual rent and could be passed on to one's children.

Few Soviet citizens knew how people lived in the capitalist world, so it was easy to believe in the advantages of the Soviet system. Government censors skewed news about the First World and suppressed unfavorable information about the Soviet Union and the communist bloc. Critics did not typically seek to overthrow the system and restore capitalism. Rather, they wanted the Soviet regime to introduce reforms that would create "socialism with a human face."

Repression of Dissent Few people outside the Soviet sphere knew just how inhuman Soviet communism was, and few within knew the extent of the brutality. Under Stalin, anyone suspected of opposing the regime risked imprisonment, forced labor, and often torture or execution. By the time of Stalin's death in 1953, the vast Gulag (labor camp complex) confined several million people, who dug for gold and uranium and survived on hunks of bread and gruel.

In 1956, the new party leader, Nikita Khrushchev, delivered a speech at a closed session of the Communist Party Congress in which he attempted to separate Stalin's crimes from true communism. The speech was never published in the Soviet Union, but party members distributed it to party organizations abroad. The crimes that Khrushchev revealed came as a terrible shock.

Soviet Ecocide

Before the twentieth century, the spread of peasant agriculture, as well as settlement in the steppe and forest zones and the hunting of fur-bearing forest animals, brought profound changes in the Russian environment, including soil degradation, deforestation, and depopulation of species. But the environmental impact of Soviet-era industrialization was staggering. No other industrial civilization poisoned its land, air, water, and people so systematically and over so long a time. Scholars have deemed the Soviet environmental catastrophe an "ecocide."

Soviet economic planners and propagandists celebrated the plumes of purple and orange smoke in their skies as evidence of the huge quantities of industrial production. Pollution-control devices remained unheard of well after their 1950s introduction in Europe and the United States; even when installed in Soviet factories, they were rarely turned on so as not to depress output. Sulfur dioxide, hydrogen sulfide, and solid phenols in water, the food supply, and the air caused epidemic levels of respiratory and intestinal ailments, blood diseases, and birth defects. The giant steel plant at Magnitogorsk, once the pride of Stalin's industrial leap, became a zone of atmospheric and soil devastation 120 miles long and 40 miles wide; inside, chronic bronchitis, asthma, and cancers attacked the population.

In agriculture, the Soviet Union continued to use the fertilizer DDT long after its 1972 banning in the United States. Despite the socialist country's overall development, in the 1970s Soviet life expectancy began to decline and infant mortality to rise. By 1989, Soviet men lived an average of 63.9 years from birth, down from 66.1 in 1965. Infant mortality by the late 1980s rose to 25.4 per 1,000, roughly the same as in Malaysia, a developing country, and Harlem. Alcoholism also contributed mightily to adverse health trends.

The April 1986 Chernobyl nuclear disaster exposed 20 million people in Ukraine and Belarus to excess radiation. Although there was no bomb concussion, the accident spewed more radioactive material into the atmosphere than had been released in the atomic bombs over Hiroshima and Nagasaki. The Chernobyl cleanup claimed around 7,000 lives.

Few symbols of Soviet ecocide surpassed the Aral Sea. Because of dams built for wasteful power plants and excess irrigation for cotton production, the Aral's volume shrank by two-thirds, and gave way to huge white, lifeless salt marshes. Soviet cosmonauts, looking down from space in 1975, were astonished to see immense storms of dust and salt over Central Asia. Toxic salt rain wreaked enormous damage on human and animal lungs. Soviet Uzbekistan, with twice the population of Soviet Belarus, was served by only one-third the hospitals.

Lake Baikal, the largest fresh body of water, and once among the cleanest, suffered the construction from the 1950s

---

Repercussions were far-reaching. Eastern European leaders interpreted Khrushchev's speech as an endorsement for political liberation and economic experimentation. Right away, Polish intellectuals began a drive to break free from the communist ideological straitjacket. Hungarian intellectuals and students held demonstrations demanding an uncensored press, free elections with genuine alternative parties, and the withdrawal of Soviet troops. But the seeming liberalization promised by Khrushchev's speech proved short-lived.

Rather than let eastern Europeans stray, the Soviet leadership crushed dissent. In Poland, the security police massacred strikers. In Hungary, tanks from the Soviet Union and other Warsaw Pact members invaded and installed a new government that aimed to smash all "counterrevolutionary" activities. The Second World remained very much the dominion of the Soviet Union.

Despite its repressive policies, the Soviet Union's status surged after the launching of Sputnik, the first satellite, into space in 1957. Students from Third World countries flocked to the Soviets' excellent education system for training as engineers, scientists, army commanders, and revolutionaries. The updated 1961 Communist Party program predicted euphorically that within twenty years the Soviet Union would surpass the United

Aral Sea Catastrophe What was once one of the largest lakes in the world shrank to less than 10 percent of its original size, due to the aggressive Soviet construction of irrigation canals in the sixties to bolster cotton production. Here, a shipping vessel is moored in the field of the former Aral Sea, in present-day Kazakhstan.

people from all walks of life turned up at unsanctioned meetings and signed their names to petitions to stop the damage and protect the environment.

QUESTIONS FOR ANALYSIS

- Why do you think environmental degradation was so much more severe in the Soviet Union compared to Western countries?
- Why do you think environmental awareness developed much sooner in the United States than in the Soviet Union?

Explore Further

Murray Feshbach and Alfred Friendly Jr., *Ecocide in the USSR: Health and Nation under Siege* (1992).

Douglas R. Wiener, *A Little Corner of Freedom: Russian Nature Protection from Stalin to Gorbachev* (2002).

of factories on its perimeter, especially a cellulose cord plant (for tires on Soviet bombers) and pulp plant (for paper). The threat to Baikal, as well as the Aral Sea catastrophe, sparked grass-roots environmental groups in an otherwise tightly controlled Soviet society. Scientists led the way in breaking censorship taboos, and

States and eclipse the First World, but reckless industrialization left terrible scars both on the population and on the landscape. (See **Current Trends in World History: Soviet Ecocide**.)

THE THIRD WORLD

In the 1950s, the French demographer Alfred Sauvy coined the term **Third World** (*tiers monde*) to describe those countries that, like the "third estate" in the 1789 French Revolution, represented the majority of the population but were oppressed. By the early 1960s, the term characterized a large bloc of countries in Asia, Africa, and Latin America. All had experienced colonial domination and now aimed to create more just societies than those of the First and Second worlds.

Limits to Autonomy Charting a third way proved difficult. Both the Soviets and the Americans saw the Third World as "underdeveloped." The Western powers looked to two new instruments of global capitalism, the **World Bank** and the **International Monetary Fund (IMF)**.

Both raised capital from all participating nations, but the most from the United States, and provided economic guidance in the Third World. The World Bank funded loans for projects to lift poor societies out of poverty (such as providing electricity in India and building roads in Indonesia), while the IMF supported the new governments' monetary systems when they experienced economic woes (as in Ghana, Nigeria, and Egypt). Yet both institutions also intruded on these states' autonomy.

Another force that threatened Third World economic autonomy was the multinational corporation. In the rush to acquire advanced technology, Africans, Asians, and Latin Americans struck deals with multinational corporations to import their know-how. Owned primarily by American, European, and Japanese entrepreneurs, firms such as United Fruit, Firestone, and Volkswagen expanded cash-cropping and plantation activities and established manufacturing branches worldwide. But such corporations impeded the growth of indigenous firms. Although the world's nations were more economically interdependent, the West still made the decisions—and reaped most of the profits.

Whether dealing with the West or the Soviet Union, Third World leaders had limited options because they faced pressure to choose one side or the other in the Cold War. To create more subservient client states, the Soviet Union backed communist insurgencies around the globe, while the United States supported almost all leaders who declared their anticommunism. With the threat of nuclear war hanging over the United States and the Soviet Union, the two superpowers competed through proxy states that they armed to battle one another.

Nowhere was the militarization of Third World countries more threatening to economic development than in Africa. Whereas in the colonial era African states had spent little on military forces, this trend ended abruptly once the states became independent and were drawn into the Cold War. Civil wars, like the one that splintered Nigeria between 1967 and 1970, were opportunities for the great powers to wield influence. When the West refused to sell weapons to the Nigerian government so it could suppress the breakaway eastern province of Biafra, the Soviets supplied MIG aircraft and other vital weapons, contributing to a destructive conflict and the ultimate triumph of the federal government of Nigeria.

Revolutionaries and Radicals As postcolonial states increasingly found themselves mired in debt and dependency, dissatisfaction grew. While some radicals seized power in the 1950s and 1960s, revolutionary transformation of society proved elusive.

Third World revolutionaries drew on the pioneering writings of Frantz Fanon (1925–1961). While serving as a psychiatrist in French Algeria, Fanon (who was born in a French Caribbean colony) became aware of the psychological damage of European racism. He subsequently joined the Algerian Revolution and became a radical theorist of liberation. His 1961 book *The Wretched of the Earth* urged Third World peoples to achieve personal and national independence through violence against their European oppressors.

The Maoist Model While Fanon moved people with his writings, others did so by building political organizations and undertaking revolutionary social experiments. In 1958, Mao Zedong introduced the Great Leap Forward. Mao's program organized China into 24,000 social and economic units, called communes. Peasants took up industrial production in their own backyards. The campaign aimed to catapult China past the developed countries, but the communes failed to feed the people and the industrial goods were inferior. As many as 45 million people may have perished from famine and malnutrition, forcing the government to abandon the experiment.

The Cultural Revolution in China (*Left*) Young women were an important part of the Red Guards during the Cultural Revolution. Here female Red Guards march in the front row of a parade in the capital city of Beijing under a sign that reads "Rise." (*Right*) In their campaign to cleanse the country of undesirable elements, the Red Guards often turned to public denunciation as a way to rally the crowd. Here a senior provincial party official is made to stand on a chair wearing a dunce's cap, while the young detractors chant slogans and wave their fists in the air.

Fearing that China's revolution was losing spirit, in 1966 Mao launched the Great Proletarian Cultural Revolution. This time Mao turned against his associates in the Communist Party and appealed to China's young people. They enthusiastically responded. Organized into "Red Guards," over 10 million of them journeyed to Beijing to participate in huge rallies where they pledged to cleanse the party of corrupt elements and remake Chinese society.

With help from the army, the Red Guards set out to rid society of the "four olds"—old customs, old habits, old culture, and old ideas. They ransacked homes, libraries, museums, and temples. They destroyed classical texts, artworks, and monuments. With its rhetoric of struggle against American imperialism and Soviet revisionism, the Cultural Revolution also targeted anything foreign. Knowledge of a foreign language was enough to compromise a person's revolutionary credentials. The Red Guards attacked government officials, party cadres, or just plain strangers in an escalating cycle of violence. Even family members and friends were pressured to denounce one another; all had to prove themselves faithful followers of Chairman Mao.

Given the costs of the Great Leap Forward and the Cultural Revolution, many of Mao's revolutionary policies were hard to celebrate. But radicals in much of the Third World were unaware of these costs and found the style of a rapid and massive—if deeply undemocratic—appeal to the masses attractive.

Latin American Revolution Most Third World radicals did not go as far as Mao, but they still dreamed of overturning the social order. In Latin America, such dreams excited those who wished to throw off the influence of U.S.-owned multinational corporations and local elites.

Reform programs in Latin America addressed numerous concerns. Economic nationalists urged greater protection for domestic industries and sought to curb the multinationals. Liberal reformers wanted to democratize political systems and redistribute land, lest

Fidel Castro and Cuba's National Liberation The Cuban Revolution of 1958–1959 was a powerful model for many national liberation movements elsewhere in the world. No sooner did Cuban rebels force a break with the United States in 1959 than they discovered that they needed outside support to survive. The Soviet Union, eager to gain a toehold for communism close to the United States, began to provide economic and military help to their Caribbean ally. Here Castro grasps the hand of Nikita Khrushchev atop the Lenin Mausoleum in Moscow for the May Day parade in 1963.

discontent erupt into full-blown revolutions like China's. But when liberals and nationalists joined forces, as in Guatemala in the 1950s, their reforms met resistance from local conservatives and from the United States.

In Cuba, the failure to address political, social, and economic concerns spurred a revolution. Since the Spanish-American War of 1898, Cuba had been ruled by governments better known for their compliance with U.S. interests than with popular sentiment. In the 1930s, sugar planters, casino operators, and North American investors prospered, but middle- and working-class Cubans did not. In 1953, a group composed heavily of university students launched a botched assault on a military garrison. One of the leaders, a law student named **Fidel Castro**, gave a stirring speech at the rebels' trial, which made him a national hero. After his release from prison in 1955, he fled to Mexico. Several years later, he returned and started organizing guerrilla raids that brought him to power in 1959.

Castro then elbowed aside rivals and wrested control of the economy from the wealthy elite, who fled to exile. As his policies grew increasingly radical, American leaders began to plot his demise. It was over Cuba and its radicalizing revolution that the world came closest to nuclear Armageddon in the Cuban Missile Crisis of 1962. To deter U.S. attacks, Castro appealed to the Soviet Union to install nuclear weapons in Cuba—a mere ninety miles off the coast of Florida. When U.S. intelligence detected the weapons, president John F. Kennedy ordered a blockade of Cuba just as weapons-bearing Soviet ships were heading toward Havana. For several weeks, the world was paralyzed with anxiety as Kennedy, Khrushchev, and Castro matched threats. In the end, Kennedy succeeded in getting the Soviets to withdraw their nuclear missiles from Cuba.

By rejecting the power of capitalist industrial societies, Castro and his followers promoted revolution, not reform, as a way to achieve Third World liberation. The symbol of this new spirit was Castro's closest lieutenant, Ernesto "Che" Guevara (1928–1967). Shortly after receiving his medical degree in 1953, he arrived in Guatemala in time to witness the CIA-backed overthrow of the progressive Jacobo Arbenz government. Thereafter, Guevara became increasingly bitter about American influences in Latin America. He joined Castro's forces and helped topple the pro-American regime in Cuba in 1958. After 1959, he held several posts in the Cuban government but grew restive for more action. Latin America, he believed, should challenge the world power of the United States. Soon his casual military uniform, his patchy beard, his cigar, and his moral energy became legendary symbols of revolt.

To combat the germ of revolution, the Kennedy administration sent American advisers throughout Latin America to dole out aid, explain how to reform local land systems, and demonstrate the benefits of liberal capitalism. Working with American advisers, Latin American militaries were trained to root out radicalism. Even Salvador Allende's democratically elected socialist government in Chile was not spared; the CIA and U.S. policymakers aided General Augusto Pinochet's military coup against the regime in 1973 and looked the other way while political opponents were butchered. By 1975, protesters had been liquidated in Argentina, Uruguay, Brazil, Mexico, Bolivia, and Venezuela.

Tensions Within the Three Worlds

Each of the three "worlds" was beset by vulnerabilities and divisions. The United States experienced social unrest in this period on a scale not seen since the Great Depression, and other First World countries also experienced major protest movements. In the Second World, too, dissent challenged the Soviet Union's hold on world communism. In the Third World, the optimism generated at independence gave way quickly to discouragement and eventually despair. Finally, in the 1970s, the rising fortunes of oil-producing nations and of Japan introduced new problems in the relations within and among worlds.

TENSIONS IN THE FIRST WORLD

Although the First World enjoyed great prosperity in the decades after World War II, lingering inequality created friction within these societies and between allies.

Women's Issues, Civil Rights, and Environmental Concerns In the First World, groups that believed that they had been left behind in the surge of economic growth expressed deep unhappiness. One issue was women's economic and political opportunities. Women in Italy, France, and Belgium did not obtain the right to vote until the end of World War II. Although women made gains in employment outside the home, they still awaited a decrease in domestic responsibilities.

A second source of concern, especially articulated by students in Europe, was the deployment of nuclear weapons in their countries, as well as the rigid social and educational institutions that preserved power and high culture for the elite few. Protests reached their apex in Paris in 1968, when workers joined students in a general strike and clashed violently with police.

A rising crescendo of protests against racial discrimination in the United States propelled the U.S. federal government to enact civil rights legislation and to promote programs designed to end poverty. The Civil Rights Act of 1964 banned segregation in public facilities and outlawed racial discrimination in employment, and the Voting Rights Act of 1965 gave millions of previously disenfranchised African Americans an opportunity to exercise equal political rights. The Lyndon Baines Johnson administration also supported programs targeting social security, health, education, and assistance to the poor. Aided by impressive economic growth, the War on Poverty nearly halved the U.S. poverty rate.

But legacies of racism and inequality were not easy to overcome, and protest movements proliferated. In spite of Supreme Court decisions, most schools remained racially homogeneous not only in the South but across the United States, as "white flight" to the suburbs left inner-city neighborhoods and schools to minorities. Militant voices, like those of Malcolm X and the Black Panthers, became prominent. Instead of integration, these radicals advocated black separatism; instead of Americanism, they espoused embracing their African origins.

African American struggles inspired Native Americans, Mexican Americans, homosexuals, and women to initiate their own campaigns for equality and empowerment. Women now questioned a life built around taking care of home and family. In fact, the introduction of the birth control pill in 1960 and the publication of Betty Friedan's *The Feminine Mystique* in 1963 stand as watershed moments in American women's history. Because oral contraception allowed women to limit childbearing and to have sex with less fear of pregnancy, the resulting freedom helped unleash a sexual revolution. Moreover,

COMPARISON

COMPARE the civil rights issues in the First, Second, and Third worlds, and **ASSESS** the ways each "world" addressed these and other basic rights.

Friedan blasted the myth of middle-class domestic contentment, describing the idealized 1950s suburban home as a "comfortable concentration camp" from which women must escape. Despite rising numbers of married women and college-educated women in the workforce, their compensation and opportunity for advancement lagged far behind those of men.

A year before Friedan authored her challenge to the subordination of women, Rachel Carson published *Silent Spring*, a book that was equally revolutionary in its attack against long-held practices. In particular, Carson's book took on the use of synthetic pesticides such as dichlorodiphenyltrichloroethane (DDT), which she said caused cancer, devastated wildlife, and destroyed natural ecosystems. Although chemical manufacturers responded that pesticides had vastly multiplied agricultural yields, *Silent Spring* stirred opposition that ultimately led to the banning of DDT in the United States in 1972. More broadly, Carson's book spurred the development of an environmental movement that questioned many of the ideas about economic progress and material prosperity upon which the "American Dream" had rested.

The escalation of the Vietnam War prompted many white American college students to question the ideals of American society. As the United States increased troop levels there in the 1960s, it conscripted more and more men. After president Richard Nixon sent American troops into Cambodia in 1970 to root out North Vietnamese soldiers, students at over 500 campuses occupied buildings and closed down universities. At Kent State University in Ohio, National Guardsmen attempting to stop the protests killed four students. The United States withdrew from Vietnam in 1973, but not before the divisions created by the war had strained the country almost to the breaking point.

TENSIONS IN WORLD COMMUNISM

The unity of the communist world also came under increasing pressure. As early as 1948, Yugoslavia had broken free of the Soviet yoke and embarked on its own road to building socialism. Other satellite states within the Soviet bloc had more trouble freeing themselves. In 1956, Poland and Hungary were forced back in line. Twelve years later, Czechoslovakia experienced the Prague Spring, in which communist authorities experimented with creating a democratic and pluralist socialist world. Workers and students rallied behind the reformist government of Alexander Dubček, calling for more freedom of expression, more autonomy for workers and consumers, and more debate within the ruling party. Once again, Soviet tanks crushed what they branded a "counterrevolutionary" movement. As the tanks rolled into Prague, the Czech capital, one desperate student doused himself with gasoline and lit a match—his public suicide a gesture of defiance against communist rule.

Thereafter, the Prague Spring served as a symbol for dissenters, who were divided between those who still wanted to reform socialism and those who wanted to overturn it. Underground reading groups proliferated throughout eastern Europe, and many Russians renewed their faith in Orthodox Christianity, their prerevolutionary religion. Many dissidents were exiled from the Soviet Union. Most famous by the early 1970s was the Russian novelist Alexander Solzhenitsyn. His masterwork, *The Gulag Archipelago,* rejected the notion that socialism could be reformed by a turn away from Stalin's policies. Yet very few people in the Soviet Union could obtain copies of Solzhenitsyn's exposé, which had been published abroad and was a best-seller in the West. In 1974 the author himself was expelled from the USSR.

Still, there were important changes within the Second World. During the 1950s and 1960s, "national communism" became the rule throughout eastern Europe, even in countries that experienced Soviet invasions. National variations also arose within the Soviet

Hungarian Revolt Khrushchev's secret 1956 speech denouncing Stalin's crimes unintentionally destabilized the communist bloc. Tanks of the Soviet-led Warsaw Pact forces crossed into Hungary to put down a revolt that year, restoring the Soviet-style system but damaging Soviet prestige. Some American officials and especially American-supported radio had encouraged the Hungarians to rise up but then did nothing to support them, damaging U.S. prestige. The upshot was a turn to "national communism" in the Soviet satellites as a way to promote stability and loyalty.

Union, where Moscow conceded some autonomy to the communist party machines of its fifteen republics—in exchange for fundamental loyalty. Dissidents were still persecuted, but by the 1970s, many fewer were murdered outright, and the population of the gulags declined.

Widespread dislike of the United States created a Sino-Soviet alliance in the years just after the Chinese Revolution of 1949. By the late 1950s, the Soviet Union had contributed massive military and economic aid to China. But the Chinese increasingly sought to define their own brand of Marxism and criticized Khrushchev's efforts to reduce tensions with the United States and the West. The divide raised China's profile throughout Asia and even in eastern Europe. Indeed, Romania achieved a measure of autonomy in foreign policy by playing off China and the Soviet Union. Albania declared its allegiance to China. African nations, interested in Soviet aid, increased their demands with subtle hints that they might consider deepening ties with China instead. Clearly, the Second World was no monolith.

TENSIONS IN THE THIRD WORLD

In contrast to the First and Second worlds, the Third World was never unified by economic, military, or political alliances. The Cold War pushed Third World states to choose between alignment with the First World or the Second. Nonetheless, radicalism nourished new hopes for unifying and empowering the Third World.

One effort at collaboration was the formation in 1960 of an alliance of oil exporters. The Organization of Petroleum Exporting Countries (OPEC)—which included Algeria, Ecuador, Gabon, Indonesia, Iran, Iraq, Kuwait, Libya, Nigeria, Qatar, Saudi Arabia, the

United Arab Emirates, and Venezuela—had little impact in raising oil revenues through the 1960s, even though several members nationalized their oil fields. But after the fourth major Arab-Israeli war broke out in 1973, OPEC's Arab members decided to pressure Israel's First World allies by halting oil exports to them. Overnight, the embargo lifted oil prices more than threefold, a bonanza that enriched all oil producers and led to an oil crisis in the West. To many, the bulging treasuries of OPEC nations seemed like the Third World's revenge. Here were Saudi Arabian princes, Venezuelan magnates, and Indonesian ministers dictating world prices to industrial consumers.

But the realignment was not thorough. Third World producers of raw materials such as coffee and rubber tried unsuccessfully to duplicate OPEC's model, and OPEC itself had trouble controlling the world's oil market. During the 1970s, discoveries in the North Sea, Mexico, and Canada reduced pressures on the large oil-consuming states to be more fuel efficient. With supply up, prices fell. To compensate for lost revenue, various OPEC states raised their own production, putting further downward pressure on prices.

Nor did oil revenues help overcome poverty and dependency in the Third World as a whole. To the contrary, most revenue surpluses from OPEC simply flowed back to First World banks or were invested in real estate holdings in Europe and the United States. Some of these funds were in turn reloaned to the world's poorest countries in Africa, Asia, and Latin America, at high interest rates, to pay for more expensive imports—including oil! The biggest bonanza went to multinational petroleum firms whose control over production, refining, and distribution yielded enormous profits.

For all the talk in the mid-1970s of changing the balance of international economic relations between the world's rich and poor countries, fundamental inequalities persisted. Those few Third World nations that appeared to break out of the cycle of poverty, like South Korea and Taiwan, did not achieve success through free trade and private sector development. Rather, these states regulated domestic markets, nurtured new industries, educated the populace, and required multinationals to work with local firms.

Conclusion

The three-world order arose on the ruins of European empires and their Japanese counterpart. First, the Soviet Union and the United States became superpowers. Second, World War II affirmed the nation-state rather than the empire as the primary form for organizing communities. Third, in spite of the rhetoric of individualism and the free market, the war and postwar reconstruction enhanced the reach and functions of the modern state. In the Third World, too, leaders of new nations saw the state as the primary instrument for promoting economic development.

The organization of the world into three blocs lasted into the mid-1970s. This arrangement fostered the economic recovery of western Europe and Japan from the wounds inflicted by war. These nations' recovery grew out of a Cold War alliance with the United States, where anticommunist hysteria accompanied an economic boom. The Cold War also cast a shadow over the citizens of the Soviet Union and eastern Europe. Gulags and political surveillance became widespread, while the Soviets and their satellite regimes mobilized resources for military purposes. The Third World, squeezed by its inability to reduce poverty, on the one hand, and superpower rivalry, on the other, struggled to pursue a "third way." While some states maintained democratic institutions and promoted economic development, many tumbled into dictatorships and authoritarian regimes, marked by high levels of corruption. They also often suffered irreparable environmental damage.

In this context Third World revolutionaries sought radical social and political transformation, seeking paths different from both Western capitalism and Soviet communism. Though not successful, they energized considerable tensions in the three-world order. These tensions intensified in the late 1960s and early 1970s as Vietnamese communists defeated the United States, an oil crisis struck the West, and protests escalated in the First and Second worlds. Thirty years after the war's end, the world order forged after 1945 was beginning to give way.

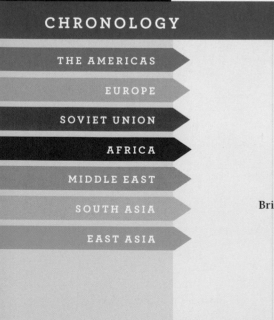

After You Read This Chapter

Go to INQUIZITIVE to see what you've learned—and learn what you've missed—with personalized feedback along the way.

FOCUS ON: *World War II and a New Global Order*

WORLD WAR II

- World War II grows out of unresolved problems connected to World War I, especially the aggressive plans of Germany and Japan to expand their political and economic influence.

- The war brings huge human and material costs and ushers in an age of nuclear weapons.

- At war's end, the United States, fearing the spread of communism and Soviet influence, rebuilds war-torn Europe and Japan and creates military and political alliances to contain Soviet expansionist ambitions.

A NEW GLOBAL ORDER

- The Soviet Union and the United States become superpowers.

- Japan emerges as an economic powerhouse and a U.S. ally.

- A weakened Europe cannot resist demands for independence from Asian and African nationalists.

- Chinese communists engineer a revolution, while Indian nationalists and many African leaders achieve independence through negotiations.

- Elsewhere, especially in territories with large settler populations, decolonization is violent (Palestine, Israel, Egypt, Algeria, and Kenya) or incomplete (southern Africa).

- Actions by Latin American reformers and revolutionary insurgents spark counterinsurgency efforts by the United States and its regional allies.

- An insecure three-world order emerges after most Asian and African states achieve independence.

CHRONOLOGY

THE AMERICAS		United States emerges as a global superpower 1945 ◆		
EUROPE		World War II 1939–1945	NATO formed 1949 ◆	
SOVIET UNION		Soviet Union emerges as a global superpower, creates client states in Eastern Europe 1945 ◆	Stalin dies 1953 ◆	
AFRICA				
MIDDLE EAST		Decolonization 1940s and 1950s		
		The United Nations partitions Palestine 1948 ◆		
SOUTH ASIA		British Raj ends, India and Pakistan declare independence 1947 ◆		
EAST ASIA		World War II 1937–1945		
		Communist victory in Chinese civil war 1949 ◆		
		Korean War 1950–1953		
		Vietnamese fight for independence 1950–1975		

1930	**1940**	**1950**

- ***Thinking about* Worlds Together, Worlds Apart *and the Three-World Order*** Explain how the collapse of a Europe-centered world changed how states interacted with one another. In what ways did the division of the globe into three rival worlds differ from the dominance of the European "great powers" that preceded it? Which world order do you think was more stable, the Europe-centered world or the three-world order that followed it? Do you think one system was more equitable than the other?

- ***Thinking about Changing Power Relationships and the Three-World Order*** Analyze Third World revolutionaries' ability to alter the dynamic of the Cold War. Where do you think power was located in this period? To what degree did Washington and Moscow determine the course of world affairs and to what degree were politicians in places like Havana, Ho Chi Minh City, or Cairo able to play the superpowers off against one another? How and to what degree were revolutionaries able to make claims on the First and Second worlds, in terms of economic, political, or military assistance?

- ***Thinking about Environmental Impacts and the Three-World Order*** In this period, for the first time, organized groups set out to defend the environment. What sparked their protests? Where were those organizations most fully developed? Where was ecological devastation most extreme? What force or forces opposed environmentalists?

1. Explain the relationship between the **Holocaust** and the Enlightenment tradition. In what sense were Nazi atrocities the result of modern technology, bureaucratic rationalization, and universalizing theories? To what extent did they violate the notions of tolerance, humanity, and justice that the *philosophes* promoted?

2. Compare and contrast the three worlds of the postwar order. What was each world attempting to achieve? How successful was each one in achieving these goals?

3. Analyze the roles played by OPEC, the **IMF**, and the **World Bank** in postwar economic competition.

4. Assess the impact of nuclear weapons on state rivalries and superpower relations during the **Cold War**, and evaluate the role played by **NATO** and the **Warsaw Pact**.

5. Evaluate the impact of **Third World** revolutionaries and radicals in transforming their societies. How successful were **Mao Zedong** and **Fidel Castro** in challenging the international status quo?

6. Analyze **decolonization**. Where and why did violence spiral out of control? Where and why did the process proceed smoothly?

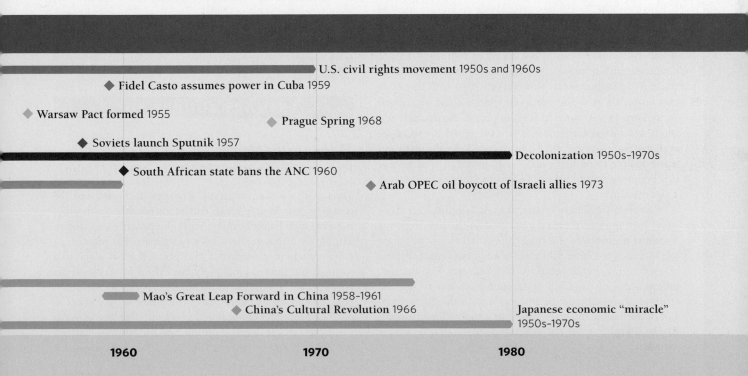

U.S. civil rights movement 1950s and 1960s

◆ Fidel Casto assumes power in Cuba 1959

◆ Warsaw Pact formed 1955

◆ Prague Spring 1968

◆ Soviets launch Sputnik 1957

Decolonization 1950s-1970s

◆ South African state bans the ANC 1960

◆ Arab OPEC oil boycott of Israeli allies 1973

Mao's Great Leap Forward in China 1958-1961

◆ China's Cultural Revolution 1966

Japanese economic "miracle" 1950s-1970s

1960　　　　**1970**　　　　**1980**

Competing Perspectives

Independence and Nation Building

Intellectuals and political activists in the Third World sought to expel foreign colonizers and build new societies. As their nations struck out on their own, the overwhelming majority of these thinkers and leaders wanted to borrow at least some elements from established traditions at home, on the one hand, and from foreign influences, on the other. The balance they proposed and the pace and nature of change they sought, however, differed widely. From a wide range of backgrounds, the authors represented here all drew inspiration in varying degrees from Marx and Lenin in their efforts to emancipate their countries and build new futures for their people.

In his "New Democracy" (1940), Mao Zedong set forth a new democratic culture—nationalistic, scientific, and mass-based—that he regarded as a transitional stage to the communist utopia of the future. Jawaharlal Nehru also celebrated science and technology in his "Note to the Members of the National Planning Committee" (1940), which sought a "third way" between capitalism and communism. Léopold Sédar Senghor presented a different "third way," in which he advocated a specifically African form of socialism in an essay from his *African Socialism* (1959) and a 1961 speech on the idea of "Negritude," or black civilization, different from but not inferior to European cultural forms. Frantz Fanon, inspired by Mao as well as Marx and Lenin, celebrated the power of violence to restore the self-respect of the colonized; only through violence and a rejection of all that the colonizers stood for, he thought, could the colonized ever truly free themselves.

PRIMARY SOURCE 20.1

"New Democracy" (1940), Mao Zedong

New-Democratic culture is national. It opposes imperialist oppression and upholds the dignity and independence of the Chinese nation. . . . China should absorb on a large scale the progressive cultures of foreign countries as an ingredient for her own culture; in the past we did not do enough work of this kind. We must absorb whatever we today find useful, not only from the present socialist or New-Democratic cultures of other nations, but also from the older cultures of foreign countries, such as those of the various capitalist countries in the age of enlightenment. However, we must treat these foreign materials as we do our food, which should be chewed in the mouth, submitted to the working of the stomach and intestines, mixed with saliva, gastric juice, and intestinal secretions, and then separated into essence to be absorbed and waste matter to be discarded—only thus can food benefit our body; we should never swallow anything raw or absorb it uncritically.

So-called wholesale Westernization is a mistaken viewpoint. China has suffered a great deal in the past from the formalist absorption of foreign things. Likewise, in applying Marxism to China, Chinese Communists must fully and properly unite the universal truth of Marxism with the specific practice of the Chinese revolution; that is to say, the truth of Marxism must be integrated with the characteristics of the nation and given a definite national form before it can be useful; it must not be applied subjectively as a mere formula. . . .

Communists may form an anti-imperialist and anti-feudal united front for political action with certain idealists and even with religious followers, but we can never approve of their idealism or religious doctrines. A splendid ancient culture was created during the long period of China's feudal society. To clarify the process of development of this ancient culture, to throw away its feudal dross, and to absorb its democratic essence is a necessary condition for the development of our new national culture and for the increase of our national self confidence; but we should never absorb anything and everything uncritically.

Source: Mao Zedong, *Selected Works*, in *Sources of Chinese Tradition*, 2nd ed., vol. 2, edited by Wm. Theodore de Bary and Richard Lufrano (New York: Columbia University Press, 2000), pp. 422–23.

PRIMARY SOURCE 20.2

"A Note to the Members of the National Planning Committee" (1940), Jawaharlal Nehru

The octopus of war grips and strangles the world and the energy of mankind is more and more directed to destroying what man has built up with infinite patience and labour. Yet it is clear that war by itself cannot solve any problem. It is by conscious, constructive and planned effort alone that national and international problems can be solved. In India many people thought, with reason, that it was premature to plan, so long as we did not have the power to give effect to our planning. The political and economic freedom of India was a prerequisite to any planning, and till this was achieved our national and international policy would continue to be governed, as heretofore, in the interests of the City of London and other vested interests. And yet we started, wisely I think, a National Planning Committee and we are trying, even in these days of world conflict and war, to draw up a picture of planned society in the free India of the future.

Our immediate problem is to attack the appalling poverty and unemployment of India and to raise the standards of our people. That means vastly greater production which must be allied to juster and more equitable distribution, so that the increased wealth may spread out among the people. That means a rapid growth of industry, scientific agriculture and the social services, all coordinated together, under more or less state control, and directed towards the betterment of the people as a whole. The resources of India are vast and if wisely used should yield rich results in the near future.

We do not believe in a rigid autarchy, but we do want to make India self-sufficient in regard to her needs as far as this is possible. We want to develop international trade, importing articles which we cannot easily produce and exporting such articles as the rest of the world wants from us. We do not propose to submit to the economic imperialism of any other country or to impose our own on others. We believe that nations of the world can cooperate together in building a world economy which is advantageous for all and in this work we shall gladly co-operate. But this economy cannot be based on the individual profit motive, nor can it subsist within the framework of an imperialist system. It means a new world order, both politically and economically, and free nations cooperating together for their own as well as the larger good.

Source: Jawaharlal Nehru, "A Note to the Members of the National Planning Committee," May 1, 1940, in *Jawaharlal Nehru: An Anthology*, edited by Sarvepalli Gopal (Delhi: Oxford University Press, 1980), pp. 306–7.

PRIMARY SOURCE 20.3

On Negritude (1959), Léopold Sédar Senghor

African Socialism

In the respective programs of our former parties, all of us used to proclaim our attachment to socialism. This was a good thing, but it was not enough. Most of the time, we were satisfied with stereotyped formulas and vague aspirations, which we called scientific socialism—as if socialism did not mean a return to original sources. Above all, we need to make an effort to rethink the basic texts in the light of the Negro African realities. . . .

Can we integrate Negro African cultural values, especially religious values, into socialism? We must answer that question once and for all with an unequivocal "Yes." . . .

We are not Communists for a practical reason. The anxiety for human dignity, the need for freedom—man's freedom, the freedoms of collectivities—which animate Marx's thought and provide its revolutionary ferment—this anxiety and this need are unknown to Communism, whose major deviation is Stalinism. The "dictatorship of the proletariat," which was to be only temporary, becomes the dictatorship of the part and state by perpetuating itself. . . .

The paradox of socialistic construction in Communist countries—in the Soviet Union at least—is that it increasingly resembles capitalistic construction in the United States, the American way of life, with high salaries, refrigerators, washing machines, and television sets. And it has less art and freedom of thought. Nevertheless, we shall not be won over by a regime of liberal capitalism and free enterprise. We cannot close our eyes to segregation, although the government combats it; nor can we accept the elevation of material success to a way of life.

We stand for a middle course, for a democratic socialism which goes so far as to integrate spiritual values, a socialism which ties in with the old ethical current of the French socialists. . . . In so far as they are idealists, they fulfill the requirements of the Negro African soul, the requirements of men of all races and countries. . . .

A third revolution is taking place, as a reaction against capitalistic and Communistic materialism—one that will integrate moral, if not religious, values with the political and economic contributions of the two great revolutions. In this revolution, the colored peoples, including the Negro African, must play their part; they must bring their contribution to the construction of the new planetary civilization.

What Is Negritude?

Assimilation was a failure; we could assimilate mathematics or the French language, but we could never strip off our black skins or root out black souls. And so we set out on a fervent quest for the "holy grail": our collective soul. And we came upon it. . . .

Negritude is the *whole complex of civilized values—cultural, economic, social, and political—which characterize the black peoples*, or, more precisely, the Negro-African world. All these values are essentially informed by intuitive reason, because this sentient reason, the reason which comes to grips, expresses itself emotionally, through that self-surrender, that coalescence of subject and object; through myths, by which I mean the archetypal images of the collective soul; and, above all, through primordial rhythms, synchronized with those of the cosmos. In other words, the sense of communion, the gift of mythmaking, the gift of rhythm, such are the essential elements of Negritude, which you will find indelibly stamped on all the works and activities of the black man.

Source: Léopold Sédar Senghor, excerpts from *African Socialism* (New York: American Society of African Culture, 1959), trans. Mercer Cook. Reprinted by permission of Moorland-Spingarn Research Center, Howard University, Washington, DC.

PRIMARY SOURCE 20.4

On Decolonization (1961), Frantz Fanon

In decolonization, there is therefore the need of a complete calling in question of the colonial situation. If we wish to describe it precisely, we might find it in the well-known words: "The last shall be first and the first last." Decolonization is the putting into practice of this sentence. That is why, if we try to describe it, all decolonization is successful.

The naked truth of decolonization evokes for us the searing bullets and bloodstained knives that emanate from it. For if the last shall be first, this will only come to pass after a murderous and decisive struggle between the two protagonists. That affirmed intention to place the last at the head of things, and to make them climb at a pace (too quickly, some say) the well-known steps which characterize an organized society, can only triumph if we use all means to turn the scale, including, of course, that of violence....

[E]very time Western values are mentioned they produce in the native a sort of stiffening or muscular lockjaw. During the period of decolonization, the native's reason is appealed to. He is offered definite values, he is told frequently that decolonization need not mean regression, and that he must put his trust in qualities that are well-tried, solid, and highly esteemed. But it so happens that when the native hears a speech about Western culture he pulls out his knife—or at least he makes sure it is within reach. The violence with which the supremacy of white values is affirmed and the aggressiveness which has permeated the victory of these values over the ways of life and of thought of the native mean that, in revenge, the native laughs in mockery when Western values are mentioned in front of him. In the colonial context the settler only ends his work of breaking in the native when the latter admits loudly and intelligibly the supremacy of the white man's values. In the period of decolonization, the colonized masses mock at these very values, insult them, and vomit them up. . . .

Source: Frantz Fanon, *The Wretched of the Earth*, trans. Constance Farrington (London: Penguin Books, 1967), 28, 33–4.

QUESTIONS FOR ANALYSIS

1. All of these authors came from overwhelmingly rural societies. Explain why they drew on the ideas of Karl Marx, who famously likened peasants to a "sack of potatoes" and thought modern industry essential to end oppression of all kinds.
2. Identify the balance between indigenous tradition and foreign influence in each selection. Which text draws most heavily on foreign sources and which rejects outside influences most completely?
3. Analyze the relationship between the individual and community in each of these readings.
4. Which of the readings do you consider most revolutionary and why? Do you think the idea of revolution was important to the authors?

Interpreting Visual Evidence

War and Propaganda

Both the Allies and the Axis powers made major efforts to mobilize consent and win support, not only among soldiers but on the home front as well. Governments used propaganda—information and ideas that are spread in order to promote a certain political point of view—to shape public opinion during World War II. While Joseph Goebbels and the Nazi Ministry for Public Enlightenment and Propaganda were the most famous for their efforts to demonize the enemy and foster a sense of solidarity at home and among Germany's allies, they had analogs from Washington, London, and Moscow to Tokyo. Propaganda offices around the world enlisted journalists, cartoonists and other visual artists, as well as radio and film to spread their messages.

The first image, "Victory or Bolshevism," a poster by Hans Schweitzer, known as Mjölnir (the name of the Norse god Thor's hammer), contrasts a wholesome German community with the bleak prospect of a Soviet occupation after the German defeat at Stalingrad (1942–1943). The next two images show European propaganda that celebrates the loyalty of colonial subjects in their war efforts. A recruitment poster for the British army shows seven uniformed soldiers from across the empire, prepared to fight for a common future. The photograph shows Free French troops—Resistance fighters who supported the Allies and opposed collaborationist Vichy France—marching in Bouar, French Equatorial Africa (today the Central African Republic). The final pair of images shows Japanese and American representations of one another. Ono Saseo's "Grieving Statue of Liberty" (1942) has Franklin Delano Roosevelt in the guise of a demon waving a banner of democracy while holding a club of dictatorship. When Japan surrendered in 1945, *The Detroit News* published a cartoon, republished to a wider audience by the Sunday *New York Times*, which presented American stereotypes of the Japanese as primitive, backward, and less than fully human.

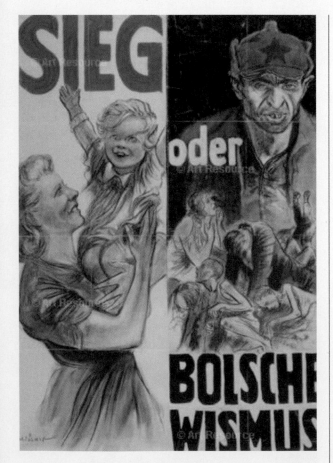

German poster, "Victory or Bolshevism."

British poster, "Together."

Free French troops train in Bouar.

Ono Saseo, "Grieving Statue of Liberty."

"Another Puzzler for World Scholars," cartoon from The Detroit News.

QUESTIONS FOR ANALYSIS

1. Contrast the stereotypes presented to celebrate cooperation with those that demonized enemies. Do they differ in any meaningful ways?
2. Does the medium—poster, cartoon, or photograph—shape the message these images convey? Is the photograph similar to or different from the posters and caricatures? Do the posters and caricatures appeal to audiences in the same way?
3. Analyze the role of gender in these images. How do the artists use masculine and feminine imagery, and to what effect?
4. Interpret the Saseo image. What do the figures in Liberty's crown represent?

Before You Read This Chapter

GLOBAL STORYLINES

- Following the collapse of the three-world order, new global markets and communications networks integrate the world but also create deep inequalities.
- New technologies and vast population movements make global culture more homogeneous.
- Globalization, supranational organizations (like the World Bank, the European Union, and the United Nations), and religious fundamentalism erode the power of the nation-state.

CORE OBJECTIVES

- **IDENTIFY** the transnational forces that eroded the power of the nation-state in the last third of the twentieth century, and **EXPLAIN** how they did so.
- **DESCRIBE** the relationship between global migration, new technologies, and the spread of cultural influences during and after the Cold War.
- **DESCRIBE** how globalization and population changes affected the environment, and vice versa.
- **EVALUATE** the degree to which globalization changed societies, and **COMPARE** globalization after the end of the Cold War to earlier forms of globalization.

Globalization

1970–2000

Consider the following comparison. In the thirteenth century, few people could imagine moving beyond their local regions. The Venetian explorer Marco Polo, who traveled through China, and the Arab scholar Ibn Battuta, who traversed the Islamic world, were rare exceptions. In contrast, by the late twentieth century people traversed in a matter of hours the distances that it took Marco Polo and Ibn Battuta years to cover. Many others staying at home could "travel" the world via the Internet, books, newspapers, and television.

But not all travelers moved about so comfortably. Many migrants—desperate to escape political chaos, persecution, or poverty—slipped across borders in the dark of night, traveled as human cargo inside containers, or fled their homelands on foot. Billions of others still had no access to the global age's technological wonders and economic opportunities. Thus, while **globalization** (the development of integrated worldwide cultural and economic structures) created possibilities for some, it also caused deeper inequalities.

The forces driving global integration—and inequality—were no longer the political empires of old. By the mid-twentieth century, the European empires had lost their sway. The Cold War and decolonization movements that had produced the three-world order no longer influenced world affairs. Power structures in the First World, under stress in the 1970s, did not crack. But those in the Second World did. Thus, the Cold War ended with the implosion of the Soviet bloc. The Third World also splintered, with some areas becoming highly advanced and others falling into deep poverty. To be sure, nation-states remained essential for establishing democratic institutions and protecting human rights, but supranational institutions—institutions that transcended nation-state borders, like the European Union and the International Monetary Fund (IMF)—often impinged on their autonomy. A new global order emerged with a unified marketplace and unhindered flows of capital, commerce, culture, and labor.

Removing Obstacles to Globalization

COMPARISON

IDENTIFY the transnational forces that eroded the power of the nation-state in the last third of the twentieth century, and **EXPLAIN** how they did so.

The collapse of the Soviet Union brought the Cold War to an end. At the same time, the capitalist First World gave up its last colonial possessions, and the remnants of white settler supremacy disintegrated. But as this occurred, the formerly colonized Third World's dream of a "third way" also vanished. As empires withdrew, they revealed a world integrated by markets for capital and labor, culture, and technology, rather than forced loyalties to imperial masters or rival superpowers.

ENDING THE COLD WAR

A world divided between two hostile factions limited the prospects for a global exchange of peoples, ideas, and resources. There was widespread exchange within the rival blocs, but for other countries the pressure from the Soviet Union and the United States to align with a superpower imposed limits to interaction, even with neighboring states. Pushing against the Cold War superpower framework, however, were strong nationalist aspirations and religious movements, which the Cold War order tried to control, or in some cases inflame, at great cost.

Mounting Costs Rivalry was enormously costly to the superpowers. The 1970s and 1980s saw the largest peacetime accumulation of arms in history. Despite myriad treaties and summits, the United States and the Soviet Union stockpiled nuclear and conventional weaponry. Furthermore, in 1983 U.S. president Ronald Reagan unveiled the Strategic Defense Initiative (nicknamed "Star Wars"), an elaborate and expensive plan to use satellites and space missiles to insulate the United States from incoming nuclear bombs. For both sides, these military spending sprees brought economic troubles.

Other pressures within and outside the United States and the Soviet Union also strained the Cold War order. The Soviet Union sent troops to prop up a puppet regime in Afghanistan, only to fall into a bloody war against insurgents financed and armed by the United States. The resulting stalemate undermined the image of the mighty Soviet armed forces, and mothers of Soviet soldiers protested their government's involvements abroad. In Europe and North America, the antinuclear movement rallied millions to the streets. Western industrialists worried about competition from Japan, which had been plowing money into rapid industrialization rather than arms. Political leaders also grappled with distressingly high unemployment rates. Thus, both sides shared a common crisis: fatigue from the Cold War, and an economic challenge from East Asia.

The Soviet Bloc Collapses In the end, the Soviet bloc collapsed (see Map 21.1). Even though planned economies employed the entire Soviet population, they failed to fill stores

NORTH SEA

DENMARK

BALTIC SEA

1989: Mass demonstrations, fall of the Berlin Wall
1990: Reunited with West Germany

1980 onward: Solidarity leads opposition
1981: Crackdown against Solidarity, driving it underground
1989: Solidarity wins 99 of the 100 seats in parliament that it is permitted to contest

SOVIET UNION

Gdansk

NETHERLANDS

EAST GERMANY
Berlin

POLAND

Warsaw

1989: Mass demonstrations
1990: Multiparty elections
1993: Czechoslovakia splits into Czech Republic and Slovak Republic

BELGIUM

Leipzig

LUX.

WEST GERMANY

Prague

CZECH REPUBLIC

CZECHOSLOVAKIA

SLOVAKIA

1989: Removal of barbed wire on border with Austria allows East German tourists to cross westward
1990: Multiparty elections

FRANCE

Bratislava

Budapest

1989: National uprising against Ceausescu
1992: First multiparty general election
1996: First non-Communist government

SWITZERLAND

AUSTRIA

HUNGARY

1990: Multiparty elections

SLOVENIA

ROMANIA

Timisoara

1990: Multiparty elections
1991–1992: War between Croats and Serbs

CROATIA

BOSNIA-HERZOGOVINA

Belgrade

Bucharest

BLACK SEA

1992: Fighting begins between Serbs and Bosnian Muslims
1995: Divided in two

ITALY

YUGOSLAVIA

SERBIA

Danube R.

MONTE-NEGRO

BULGARIA

1990: Multiparty elections
1991: Dissolved into warring states

KOSOVO

Sofia

MACEDONIA

1989: Demonstrations
1990: Multiparty elections

Tirana

ALBANIA

1990: Multiparty elections
2001: Fighting erupts between Macedonians and ethnic Albanians

1989: Loses autonomy from Serbia
1998–1999: Fighting between Serbs and ethnic Albanians
2000: First free elections

GREECE

TURKEY

1990: Demonstrations, civil war
1991: Multiparty elections

✳ Civil unrest

MEDITERRANEAN SEA

MAP 21.1 | Collapse of the Communist Bloc in Europe

The Soviet Union's domination of eastern Europe ended precipitously in 1989. The political map of eastern and central Europe took on a different shape under European integration.

• What significant event in many communist countries signaled the collapse of communism?

• In what part of eastern and central Europe did the most political instability and conflict occur?

• According to your reading, why did the end of communist rule cause the reshuffling of political boundaries in the region?

Lech Walesa A Polish electrician from the Lenin Shipyard in the Baltic port city of Gdansk, Walesa spearheaded the formation of Solidarity, a mass independent trade union of workers who battled the communist regime that ruled in their name. He later was elected president of post-communist Poland.

with sufficient consumer goods. Socialist health care and benefits lagged behind those provided by the United States and western European states. Authoritarian political structures relied on deception and coercion rather than elections and civic activism. Although communists had promised to beat capitalism by building socialism on the way to achieving full communism, the communist paradise was nowhere on the horizon. The gap between socialism and capitalism was growing.

Events in Poland were one catalyst in socialism's undoing. In 1980, the newly appointed Polish pope, John Paul, the first non-Italian pope in over 450 years, supported mass strikes at the Lenin Shipyard in Gdansk, which led to the formation of the Soviet bloc's first independent trade union, Solidarity. As Communist Party members in Poland defected to its side, the union became a society-wide movement; it aimed not to reform socialism (as in Czechoslovakia in 1968; see Chapter 20) but to overcome it. A crackdown by the Polish military and police put most of Solidarity's leadership in prison and drove the movement underground, but Soviet intelligence officials secretly worried that Solidarity could not be easily eradicated.

The most consequential factor in the collapse of the Soviet superpower was the reform effort launched by Mikhail Gorbachev, who became general secretary of the Soviet Communist Party in 1985. Under this effort (known as *perestroika*, meaning "reconstruction"), Gorbachev permitted competitive elections for Communist Party posts, relaxed censorship, allowed civic associations, legalized small nonstate businesses, granted autonomy to state firms, and encouraged the republics to be responsible for their own affairs within the Soviet Union. These reforms were linked with dramatic arms-control initiatives to ease the superpower burden on the Soviet Union. Gorbachev then began withdrawing troops from Afghanistan and informed eastern European leaders that they could not count on Moscow's armed intervention to prop up their regimes.

Having set out to improve socialism, however, Gorbachev instead destabilized it. Civic groups called not for reform of the system, but for its liquidation. Eastern European states declared their intention to leave the Soviet orbit, and some of the union republics began to push for independence. In response, disgruntled factions within the Communist Party and the Soviet military tried to preserve the destabilized old order by staging a coup attempt in 1991. However, the former Communist Party boss of Moscow and elected president of the Russian republic, Boris Yeltsin, rallied the opposition and faced down the hard-liners. Under Yeltsin, Russia, like Ukraine and the other Soviet republics, became a refuge for discontented Soviet elites. Thereafter, those elites abandoned the cause of the Soviet Union and divided up state property among themselves. The Soviet Union broke apart into independent states (see Map 21.2). The Cold War, which began as a tense standoff between World War II allies, ended when the eastern bloc failed to keep up with economic and technological development of its rivals.

AFRICA AND THE END OF WHITE RULE

Although the aftermath of World War II saw the dismantling of most of Europe's empires, remnants of colonial rule remained in southern Africa (see Map 20.6 on p. 737). Here,

MAP 21.2 | The Breakup of the Soviet Union

The Soviet Union broke apart in 1991. Compare this map with Map 17.6 (see p. 633), which illustrates Russian expansion in the nineteenth century.

▪ Which parts of the old Russian Empire remained under Russian rule, and which territories established their own states?

▪ In what areas did large migrations accompany the breakup, and for what reasons?

▪ According to your reading, how did the breakup of the Soviet Union change Russia's status in Europe and Asia?

whites clung to centuries-old notions of their racial superiority over non-Europeans. Final decolonization meant that self-rule would return to all of Africa. The end of colonialism also set the stage for former colonies to find new trading and investment partners and to become more integrated with the wider world.

The Last Holdouts The last African territories under direct European control were the Portuguese colonies of southern and western Africa. However, by the mid-1970s efforts to suppress African nationalist movements had exhausted Portugal's resources. As African nationalist demands led to a hurried Portuguese withdrawal from Guinea-Bissau, Angola, and Mozambique, formal European colonialism in Africa came to an end.

But white rule still prevailed elsewhere in Africa. In Rhodesia, a white minority resisted international pressure to allow black rule. In the end, independent African states helped support a liberation guerrilla movement under Robert Mugabe. Surrounded, Rhodesian whites finally lost control in 1979. The new constitutional government renamed the country Zimbabwe, erasing from Africa's map the name of the long-deceased British expansionist Cecil Rhodes (see Chapter 17).

South Africa and Nelson Mandela The final outpost of white rule was South Africa, where the European minority was larger, richer, and more entrenched than elsewhere in the region. Yet, in the countryside and cities, defiance of white rule was growing. Africans lobbed rocks and crude bombs at tanks and organized mass strikes against the multinational-owned mines.

At the same time, pressures from abroad to end the racist apartheid system were mounting. The International Olympic Committee banned South African athletes starting in 1970. American students insisted that their universities divest themselves of companies with investments in South Africa. As international pressures grew, foreign governments—even that of the United States, once South Africa's staunchest ally—applied economic sanctions against South Africa. A swelling worldwide chorus demanded that **Nelson Mandela**, the imprisoned leader of the African National Congress (ANC), be freed. The white political elite eventually realized that it was better to negotiate new

The End of Apartheid (*Left*) Nelson Mandela, running for president in 1994 as the candidate of the African National Congress, here casts a ballot in the first all-races election in South Africa. This election ended apartheid and saw the African National Congress take control of the Republic of South Africa. (*Right*) After the overwhelming electoral triumph of Mandela, F. W. de Klerk, leader of the once-powerful Afrikaner-dominated National Party, shakes hands with his successor.

arrangements than to endure international condemnation and years of internal warfare against a majority population. Ensuing negotiations produced South Africa's first free, mass elections in 1994. These brought an overwhelming victory to the ANC, with Nelson Mandela elected as president.

Still, African leaders faced immense problems in building stable political communities. Although they set out to destroy the vestiges of colonial political structures and to build African-based public institutions, those leaders struggled to find a third way between the superpower blocs. Ethnic and religious rivalries, held in check during the colonial period, now blazed forth. Civil wars erupted in many countries—most violently in Nigeria, Sudan, and Zaire—and military leaders were drawn into politics. By the 1990s, the continent was aflame with civil strife. Armed conflicts that started with the Cold War endured well after it ended even though white rule had finally come to an end throughout the entire continent.

Unleashing Globalization

As obstacles to international integration began to dissolve, capital, commodities, people, and culture crossed borders with ever-greater freedom. Even though these movements had occurred throughout history, the global age changed their scale. At the same time, never had there been such unequal access to the fruits of these exchanges. Several factors contributed to increasing integration and to new power arrangements: international banking, expanded international trade, population migrations, and technical breakthroughs in communications.

FINANCE AND TRADE

The increased international flow of goods and capital was well under way in the 1970s, but the end of the Cold War removed many impediments to globalization. During the 1990s, even the strongest nation-states felt the effects of economic globalization.

Global Finance and Deregulated Markets Major transformations occurred in the world's financial system in the 1970s. America's budget and trade deficits prompted president Richard Nixon to take the dollar off the gold standard, an action that enabled the yen, the lira, the pound, the franc, and other national currencies to cut their ties to the American dollar. Now international financiers enjoyed greater freedom from national regulators and found fresh business opportunities.

The primary agents of the heightened global financial activity were banks. Based mainly in London, New York, and Tokyo, big banks attracted large amounts of capital for lucrative ventures around the world. Revenues from oil producers provided a large infusion of cash into the global economy in the 1970s. At the same time, banks joined forces to issue mammoth loans to developing countries.

No international financial organization was more influential than the International Monetary Fund (IMF), which came into existence after World War II with a view to raising capital from all of the participating states so as to be able to lend funds to states in need. During the 1980s it emerged as a central player, especially in response to debt crises in what came to be called the **developing world**, a term that emerged as the prospect of finding a third way between the superpower blocs began to fade; it referred to poor countries in the Third World and eastern bloc. Throughout the 1970s, European, Japanese,

COMPARISON

DESCRIBE the relationship between global migration, new technologies, and the spread of cultural influences during and after the Cold War.

and North American banks had loaned money on very easy terms to cash-strapped Third World and eastern-bloc borrowers. But what was once good business soon turned sour. In 1982, a wave of defaults, in which governments and other borrowers found themselves unable to repay their loans, threatened to overrun Latin America in particular. Throughout the 1980s, international banks and the IMF kept heavily indebted customers solvent. The IMF offered short-term loans to governments on condition that recipients produce balanced budgets, compel civilian populations to give up subsidies on essential products, and cease to import far more than they exported. Latin Americans led the way in reorganizing their finances and thus pioneered the process of expanding domestic production while at the same time engaging in robust international trade. All across the world, tariffs and other barriers to foreign trade crumbled, state enterprises became private firms, and foreign banks and multinational companies took a great interest in investing in these newly reformed economies.

Effects of Integrated Networks New technologies and institutions enabled many more financial investors and traders to participate in the integrated networks of world finance. The Internet and online trading accelerated the movement of capital across borders. Rapid changes in financial and currency markets soon created problems, however. When the Mexican economy went into paralysis in 1994, the crisis was so extreme that not even the IMF could bail it out; the U.S. Treasury issued the largest international loan in history to pull Mexico out of its economic tailspin. Despite acting as the lender in that instance, the United States emerged in the new financial order as the world's largest borrower because it imported far more than it exported. Early in the new millennium, its net foreign debt soared past $2 trillion—a 700 percent increase since the early 1990s. Much of this debt was owed to China, which had a huge trade surplus with the United States.

Globalization increased commercial, as well as financial, interdependence. The total value of goods and services exchanged through world trade increased nearly tenfold between 1973 and 1998, and trade in Asia grew even faster. Where an American would once have worn American-made clothes (Levi's), driven an American car (a Ford), and watched an American television (made by Zenith), such was rarely the case by century's end. Increasingly, consumers bought foreign goods and services and sold a greater share of their own output abroad. This pattern had always been true of smaller regions like Central America and southern Africa. But in the 1980s it intensified as countries with cheap and skilled labor, like China, India, and Brazil, were able to undersell their competitors in world markets.

International trade also shifted the international division of labor. After World War II, Europeans and North Americans dominated manufacturing, while Third World countries supplied raw materials. But by the 1990s this was no longer the case. Brazil became a major airplane maker, South Korea exported millions of automobiles, and China emerged as the world's largest source of textiles, footwear, and electronics.

The most remarkable global shift involved East Asian industry and commerce. Manufactured goods, including high-technology products, now came from the eastern fringe of Afro-Eurasia as often as from its western fringe. Japan blazed the Asian trail: between 1965 and 1990 its share of world trade doubled to almost 10 percent. China, too, flexed its economic muscle. When Deng Xiaoping took power in 1978, China was already a growing economy. Under Deng, China started to become an economic powerhouse. For the next two decades, China chalked up astounding 10 percent annual growth rates, swelling its share of world GDP (Gross Domestic Product, the value of goods and services produced) from 5 percent to 12 percent.

For East Asia as a whole, its share of world exports doubled in the same period. Smaller countries using state support for economic development, like Singapore, Taiwan, South

Korea, and Hong Kong, became mini-powerhouses. By the early 1990s, these countries and Japan were also major investors abroad. As East Asia's share of world production quickly increased, the U.S. and European shares decreased.

Regional Trade Blocs and Growing Inequalities Industrialization of previously less developed countries, combined with lower trade barriers, increased the pressures of world competition on national economies. Some areas responded by establishing regional trade blocs in an effort to create larger markets for themselves and stay competitive in an ever more integrated world economy.

The most complete regional integration occurred in Europe, where states slashed trade barriers and harmonized their commercial policies toward the rest of the world. In 1993, the Maastricht Treaty established the **European Union (EU)** under its current name, and what had been conceived as a trading and financial bloc began to evolve into a political union as well, a supranational organization that encroached on the sovereignty of its member states. In 2002, a number of the European Union states deepened their economic interdependence by adopting a single currency, the euro. A few of them—most notably the United Kingdom—did not want to give up control of their own national currency. By 2012, the European Union had twenty-seven members, with seventeen members using the euro.

Although international trade then increased, it also became increasingly unequal. High-technology and high-value goods now occupied an ever-greater share of the manufacturing and exports of the world's richest countries. For "rich" countries as a whole, about half of total GDP reflected the production and distribution of such goods as computers, software, and pharmaceuticals, and services like insurance and banking, which, collectively, gave those countries a competitive advantage. Poor nations, by contrast, generally remained locked in the production of low-tech goods and the export of raw materials. Increasingly, technology and knowledge divided the world into affluent, technically sophisticated countries and poor, technically underdeveloped regions.

MIGRATION

Migration, a constant feature of world history, became more pronounced in the twentieth century (see Map 21.3). Although after 1970 fewer Europeans were on the move, many more Asians, Africans, and Latin Americans were, chasing jobs in the richer countries. By 2000, there were 120 million migrants scattered across 152 countries, up from 75 million in 1965.

Patterns of Migration Migratory flows often followed the contours of past colonial and political ties. Where North America and Europe had had colonies or dependencies, their political withdrawal left tracks for migrants to follow. Indians and Pakistanis moved to Britain; so did Jamaicans. Dominicans, Haitians, and Mexicans went to the United States. Algerians and Vietnamese moved to France. Where emerging rich societies cultivated close diplomatic ties, these relations opened migratory gates. This was true of Germany's relationship with Turkey, of Japan's with South Korea, and of Canada's with Hong Kong.

International migration was often an extension of regional and national migration from poorer, rural areas to urban centers. In Nigeria, for example, rural-urban migration intensified after 1970. In 1900, Nigeria's capital at the time, Lagos, had a population of 41,847. At the century's end, Lagos had more than 10 million people, with predictions that this number would double by 2025. The key to Lagos's boom in the 1970s was the existence of large oil reserves in the country and the high prices that

CANADA

UNITED STATES

East Europeans 1918–1919

East Europeans 1918–1919

Russian Jews to USA 1980s and 1990s

European Jews to USA 1930s

GREAT BRITAIN

SWITZ. FRANCE

Algerian colons to France 1962

SPAIN

1950–

West Indians to Britain

Spaniards to Mexico 1936

MOROCCO

TUNISIA ALGERIA

ATLANTIC OCEAN

1950–

1960–

Jamaicans, Haitians and Dominicans to USA 1990–

MEXICO

CUBA 1960–1980

BELIZE

HAITI

GUATEMALA NICARAGUA

COLOMBIA

NIGER

1970

1970

IVORY COAST NIGERIA

PACIFIC OCEAN

BRAZIL

1980

ARGENTINA

Foreign-born people as percentage of total population (latest available year)

Less than 1.5%
1.5%–2.9%
3.0%–7.5%
More than 7.5%
Data not available
Migration

0   1000   2000 Miles
0   1000   2000 Kilometers

The following labels appear on the map:

ARCTIC OCEAN

Poles and Baltic peoples to Siberia 1939–1940

RUSSIA

1930s and 1940s

GERMANY
POLAND
1918–1922
UKRAINE
AUSTRIA
1945
1922
ITALY
1950–
1945–
SYRIA
ISRAEL
JORDAN
EGYPT
1980–
LIBYA
Russian Jews to Israel 1980s and 1990s
GEORGIA
1922
TURKEY
2003
2003
IRAQ
1947–
AFGHANISTAN
1979
PAKISTAN
1970–
1947
BANGLADESH
INDIA
1972
1947
HONG KONG
CHINA
NORTH KOREA
1950–1954
SOUTH KOREA
JAPAN

1947–
Falasha to Israel 1991
SAUDI ARABIA
1970–

1970–
SUDAN
mid 1980s
ETHIOPIA
1980s
to Western Europe and USA

THAILAND
VIETNAM
to UK

to Canada and USA 1980–

PACIFIC OCEAN

to USA

to USA 1990–

1975
MALAYSIA
1975

1975
to France

Southeast Asians to Australia 1970s

INDONESIA

CONGO
RWANDA
1994
TANZANIA

INDIAN OCEAN

MOZAMBIQUE

BOTSWANA
1960–
1960–

SOUTH AFRICA

Europeans to Australia/New Zealand 1918–

AUSTRALIA

NEW ZEALAND

MAP 21.3 | World Migration, 1918–1998

The world's population continued to grow and move around in the twentieth century.

- Looking at this map, identify the countries that had the greatest increase in foreign-born people as a percentage of total population.

- Then compare the areas of most rapid population growth during the nineteenth century with those parts of the world that, according to this map, had the highest percentage of foreign-born people in the twentieth century. What are the similarities and differences?

- During the twentieth century, which parts of the world were the sending areas, and which were the receiving territories? See also Map 18.1, p. 649.

Lagos, Nigeria During the twentieth century, Lagos was one of the fastest-growing and most crowded cities in Africa.

oil fetched in international markets. When the Organization of Petroleum Exporting Countries (OPEC) sent oil prices soaring, money poured into Nigeria. The government kept most of it in its largest city. That, in turn, spurred people to move to Lagos. This rural-urban migration increased Lagos's population by 14 percent per year in the 1970s and 1980s. No government—least of all a new, weakly supported one like Nigeria's—could cope with such a huge influx. Electricity supplies failed regularly in and around Lagos. There were never enough schools, teachers, or textbooks. But the city burst with the vitality of new arrivals, prompting one immigrant to exclaim: "It's a terrible place; I want to go there!"

One of the biggest changes in world migration patterns took place in the United States. Having all but closed its coastal borders on the Pacific in the late nineteenth century and on the Atlantic in the 1920s, the United States enacted a major immigration reform in 1965. By 2000, 27 million immigrants lived there, accounting for almost 10 percent of the population—double the share in 1970 and approaching levels not seen since the early twentieth century. The profile of migration to the United States also changed. In 1970, there were more Canadians or Germans than Mexicans living in the United States. Over the next thirty years, the Mexican influx rose tenfold and by 2000 accounted for almost one-third of immigrants in the United States, with the flow of legal and illegal immigrants from Mexico and Central America having an especially dramatic impact on the border states. The numbers migrating from Asia also surged, accounting for over 40 percent of all immigrants to the United States in the 1990s.

Temporary Migrants Some migrants moved for temporary sojourns. At least that was the original intent. Into the 1950s and 1960s, southern Europeans moved northward; but when Spain, Portugal, Greece, and Italy also became wealthy societies, not only did the exodus decline, but these countries became magnets for Middle Eastern, North African, and then, later, eastern European migrants. The economic downturn in Europe in the 1970s and resulting high unemployment, however, made integration difficult. Most migrants from Asia and Africa went initially to Europe in search of temporary jobs as "guest workers." With time, they and their families who followed them settled in their host countries, often living in dilapidated public housing projects, isolated from city centers and public services. The existence of welfare programs made them less likely to leave and return "home" than earlier generations of labor migrants.

In Japan, too, immigrants were not easily incorporated. Tokyo's policy in the 1970s resembled guest-worker programs. Discouraging permanent settlement and immigration, Japan encouraged mainly itinerant workers to move to the country, yet its expanding economy required increasing numbers of these temporary migrants. Indeed, Japan's deep reluctance to recruit large numbers of minorities, for fear of their settling down, led to dire labor shortages. After Japan, the economic tigers of Hong Kong, Taiwan, and Malaysia all became hosts for temporary migrants. Millions of guest workers moved there, and ultimately the migrants sank deeper roots, especially once their children entered school.

Resident Noncitizens and Refugees Arguments in Los Angeles over schools and health care for resident noncitizens became part of a global debate over the rights and protections afforded to migrants. In Argentina, up to 500,000 undocumented Peruvians, Bolivians, and Paraguayans also lived without rights as citizens. Even more staggering, between 3 and 8 million migrants moved from Mozambique, Zimbabwe, and Lesotho to South Africa. In some Middle Eastern countries, like Saudi Arabia and Kuwait, foreign-born workers constituted over 70 percent of the workforce. In general, migrants were only partially accommodated, while many were fully excluded from host societies. Thus, even though population movements flowed across political, kinship, and market networks, demographic reshuffling heightened national concerns about the ethnic makeup of political communities.

Forced migrations remained a major problem. In contrast to earlier centuries' forced migration of slaves from Africa, recent involuntary flows involved refugees fleeing civil war and torture. Many suffered for weeks, months, or years in refugee camps on the periphery of violence. The greatest concentration of refugees occurred in the world's poorest region—Africa. Africans were often caught up in ethnic and religious conflicts that generated vast refugee camps, where survival depended on the generosity of host governments and international contributions.

Whether migrants traveled in search of work or fled persecution, they posed a series of challenges for host countries. If migrants crossed borders easily, they often struggled to receive basic rights. Especially during economic downturns, discrimination often led to violent conflicts among recent immigrants, long-time residents (often themselves of immigrant origin), and the state's security forces. Conflicts erupted over religion and culture, notably in French efforts to prevent women from wearing Muslim headscarves in public and the English-only movement in the United States. Governments in immigrant-receiving countries everywhere grappled with the challenge of extending citizenship to newcomers and then respecting their desires to dress, worship, and celebrate traditions from their families' homelands.

GLOBAL CULTURE

Migrations and new technologies helped create a more global entertainment culture. In this domain, globalization is often equated with Americanization. Yet American entertainments themselves reflected artistic practices from across the globe, as one mass culture met another. On the global scale, there was less cultural diversity in 2000 than in 1300; but in terms of individuals' everyday experience, the potential for experiencing cultural diversity, if one could afford the technology to do so, increased.

Current Trends in World History

Urbanization as a Global Phenomenon: Transforming Bombay to Mumbai

The city has played a pivotal role in world history since it first emerged thousands of years ago along the Tigris and Euphrates rivers in Mesopotamia (modern-day Iraq). People have ever since flocked to cities for the social and economic advantages that these locations offered. By the end of the twentieth century, the proportion of people living in cities, usually defined as having populations over 5,000 or 10,000, exceeded 50 percent in the wealthiest countries and was approaching that proportion in the less developed countries.

Of the burgeoning cities in the developing world, one of the most dynamic is Mumbai in India. Acquired in the sixteenth century by the Portuguese, who then transferred its control to the East India Company, Bombay (as it was named at the time)

developed as a port city for colonial commerce. It profited from the cotton trade, developed a vibrant textile industry, attracted migrants, and acquired a cosmopolitan image. India gained its independence from Britain in 1947, and in 1996 Bombay was renamed "Mumbai." Still, it epitomizes the modern face of the nation, and its increasingly heterogeneous population reflects the larger Indian melting pot.

Beginning in the 1980s, however, the nature of the city's relationship with the world economy started to change. The cotton textile industry, Bombay's economic backbone, went into a decline. Industrial employment fell sharply. Moreover, the share of informal household enterprises, small shops, petty subcontractors, and casual laborers rose, along with banking and insurance. Economic liberalization removed hurdles against foreign businesses and brought the city directly into the global economy.

Today Mumbai occupies a strategic place in transnational geography. This is evident in the increasing presence of financial institutions, trading organizations, insurance companies, telecommunications corporations, and information technology enterprises with worldwide operations. Even the city's vibrant film industry addresses a global, not just national, audience. Rather appropriately, Bombay cinema has been nicknamed "Bollywood." The city, however, still attracts a large number of poor migrants who live in slums or call the pavements their home. The gap between Bombay's rich and poor has grown alarmingly. Millions who eke out a miserable living stand in stark contrast to a tiny elite enriched by the global economy.

Globalization has also affected its residents' identity. In the 1990s, the political party then in power in Maharashtra was the Shiv Sena, a nativist regional party named after a seventeenth-century

New Media Technology was key in spreading entertainment. In the 1970s, for example, cassette tapes became the dominant medium for popular music, sidelining the long-playing record and the short-lived eight-track tape. Television was another globalizing force, as American producers bundled old dramas and situation comedies to stations worldwide. Brazilian soap operas began to appear in Spanish-language American TV markets in the 1980s, often inducing Mexican viewers to rush home from work to catch the latest episode. Latin American television shows and music were distributed in the United States in areas with large Spanish-speaking populations. Bombay also produced its fair share of programs for viewers of British television and today produces roughly twice as many films per year as Hollywood. (See **Current Trends in World History: Urbanization as a Global Phenomenon**.) In terms of box-office revenues, Hollywood remains the leading producer of films in the world, helped in no small measure by its ability to send movies across borders and also by the actors from around the world who star in its films.

Television's globalizing effects were especially evident in sports. Soccer (known as football outside the United States) became an international passion, with devoted national followings for national teams. Indeed, by the 1980s soccer was *the* world sport, with television ratings increasingly determining its schedule. Organizers of the 1986 World Cup in Mexico insisted that big soccer matches take place at midday so that games could be

Bollywood Bombay cinema, or Bollywood, has an increasing global presence. This is the poster for *Devdas*, a three-hour romance that won awards in India and around the world.

Maratha chieftain who opposed the Mughal Empire. As the industrial economy and trade unions gave way to the service sector and unorganized labor, the Shiv Sena utilized the social and political fluidity produced by globalization to win support for its nativist ideology. Mumbai's cosmopolitan image went up in smoke in 1992–1993, when the Shiv Sena led pogroms against the city's Muslim residents. In response, a Muslim underworld don, according to police investigations, engineered a series of bomb blasts in March 1993. Since then the city has experienced episodes of violence, none more gruesome than the terrorist attacks on two luxury hotels, a crowded railway station, and a Jewish center in November 2006. Ironically, the terrorists chose to attack Mumbai because of its economic importance and reputation as a cosmopolitan city.

Mumbai today illustrates the uneven effects of globalization. The society is sharply divided, economic disparities are great, and the city's politics is a cauldron of conflicting identities. These are the local forms in which this vast and influential city experiences globalization.

QUESTIONS FOR ANALYSIS

- Contrast the discussion of migration to Mumbai here with that to other parts of the world, notably western Europe and Japan, in the body of the chapter.
- How does Mumbai fit into the larger theme of "Worlds Together, Worlds Apart"?

Explore Further

Suketu Mehta, *Maximum City: Bombay Lost and Found* (2005).

Gyan Prakash, *Mumbai Fables* (2010).

televised live at prime time in Europe, although teams had to play under the scorching sun. In many parts of the globe, major American sports also made particularly deep inroads as more foreigners participated in them and as television broadcast American games in other countries. The National Basketball Association (and the athletic footwear firm Nike) was particularly successful in international marketing; in the process, it made Michael Jordan the world's best-known athlete in the late twentieth century.

Cultural Exchanges Technology was not the only driving force of world cultures; migration and exchange were also important. For example, as people moved around they brought their own musical tastes and borrowed others. Reggae, born in the 1960s among Jamaica's Rastafarians, became a sensation in London and Toronto, where large West Indian communities had migrated. Reggae lyrics and realist imagery invoked a black countercultural spirit and a call for a return to African roots. Soon, Bob Marley and the Wailers, reggae's flagship band, played to audiences worldwide. In northeast Brazil, where African culture emerged from decades of disdain, Bob Marley became a folk hero. In Soweto, South Africa, populated by black workers, he was a symbol of resistance.

Reggae propelled a shift in black American music. In broadcasting reggae, DJs often merged sounds and chant lyrics over a beat, a "talkover" form that soon characterized rap music as well. This was a disruptive concept in the late 1970s, but within ten years rap

Baseball Goes International The 1980s and 1990s saw an influx of ballplayers from Latin America and quite a few from Asia as well. (*Left*) Boston Red Sox slugger David Ortiz hails from the Dominican Republic. (*Right*) Ichiro Suzuki from Japan has been a top player for the Seattle Mariners and the New York Yankees.

had become mainstream. Rap lyrics emulated reggae realism by focusing on black problems, but they also opened a new domain of controversies involving gang worldviews. On the world stage, Latino rappers stressed multicultural themes, often in "Spanglish." Asian rap stressed the genre as a vehicle for cross-cultural sharing and epitomized the ability of new cultural forms to bring peoples together.

Local Culture World cultures may have become more integrated and homogeneous, but they did not completely replace national and local cultures. Indeed, technology and migration often reinforced the appeal of "national" cultural icons, as national celebrities gained popularity among immigrant groups abroad. Inexpensive new technology introduced these stars to more and more people. In Egypt, the most popular singer of the Nasser years was Umm Kalthum, who became the favorite of Arab middle classes via radio. In 1975 she was given a state funeral, the likes of which had rarely been seen.

Nonetheless, as the market for world cultures grew increasingly competitive, performers increasingly employed a wider array of styles and also challenged biases and conventions. Among the breakthroughs that have occurred since the 1970s is the triumph of black performers (Bob Marley, Dorothy Masuka), black athletes (Pelé, Michael Jordan), and black writers (Toni Morrison, Chinua Achebe). Competition also shattered some sexual biases. Female performers such as Madonna became popular icons. So did gay performers, starting with the Village People, whose campy multicultural anthem "YMCA" created a place for a new generation of homosexual or bisexual artists. Of course, beyond Europe and North America, flirting with sexual conventions had its limits. In the Middle East, female video artists continued to wear veils—but they still swung their hips. Relatively homogeneous national cultures, often dominated by men representing the ethnic majority, gave way to a wider variety of entertainers and artists who broke loose from confining local cultures.

COMMUNICATIONS

Computer technology drove a revolution in global communications networks. In the late 1980s, while working in Switzerland, the British physicist Tim Berners-Lee devised a way to pool data stored on various computers. Whereas previous electronic links had existed only between major universities and research stations, Berners-Lee made data more accessible by creating the World Wide Web. With each use and each connection, and as people entered more data, however, the Web grew unmanageably crowded and difficult to navigate. The early 1990s saw the first commercial browsers used in navigating the so-called Internet. Suddenly people were communicating across global networks more easily than with neighbors and more inexpensively than with local phone calls.

The change created a new generation of wealth. CEOs of top companies like General Motors, Royal Dutch Shell, and Merck had less net worth than Michael Dell (hardware maker), Bill Gates (software maker), and Jeff Bezos (creator of Amazon.com). Shares of Internet firms, known as dot-coms, swept the world's stock markets. Money from these companies flowed globally as they established offices worldwide. Software and Internet technologies developed enormous economies of scale and thus became prone to monopolization as they took over smaller companies.

Bob Marley In the 1970s, young Europeans and North Americans began to listen to music from the Third World. Among the most popular was Jamaican-based reggae, and its most renowned artist, Bob Marley. Marley's music combined rock and roll with African rhythms and lyrics about freedom and redemption for the downtrodden of the world.

While the Internet revolution provided new means to share and sell information, it also reinforced hierarchies between haves and have-nots. Great swaths of the world's population living outside big cities, especially in low-income countries, had no access to the Internet. The have-nots were poor not just from lack of capital but from lack of access to knowledge and new media.

Characteristics of the New Global Order

While providing access to an unimaginable array of goods and services, globalization also deepened world inequalities. Families changed, and life spans increased. Education and good health determined one's status in society as never before. Populations expanded dramatically, requiring greater industrial and agricultural output from all parts of the world. While many parts of the world consumed more than ever before, others struggled with famine and the consequences of environmental change.

THE DEMOGRAPHY OF GLOBALIZATION

It took 160 years (1800–1960) for the world's population to increase from 1 billion to 3 billion; over the next forty years (1960–2000) it jumped from 3 billion to over 6 billion. Behind this steepening curve were two important developments: a decline in mortality, especially among children, and a rise in life expectancy.

Population growth was hardly equal worldwide (see Map 21.4 and **Analyzing Global Developments: Globalization**). In Europe, population growth peaked around 1900, and it moved upward only gradually from 400 million to 730 million during the twentieth century, with little growth after the 1970s. North America's population quadrupled over the same period, mainly because of immigration. The other population booms in the twentieth century occurred in Asia (400 percent), Africa (550 percent), and Latin America (700 percent).

COMPARISON

EVALUATE the degree to which globalization changed societies, and **COMPARE** globalization after the end of the Cold War to earlier forms of globalization.

Analyzing Global Developments

Globalization: One World or Many?

People, funds, commodities and information move around the world with lightning speed. This rapid mobility has contributed to radical changes in population growth rates from one country to the next, and it has led to significant changes in the rate of economic growth worldwide. But do these kinds of changes dictate a growing uniformity in the world? In other words, is globalization creating a single world community? The following two tables reveal some striking demographic differences, by continent and country, with respect to rapid or not-so-rapid population growth rates, the age distribution of populations, and the Gross National Product (GNP) per person.

QUESTIONS FOR ANALYSIS

- Which of the continents has the fastest growing population? Why would this be the case?

- Although these tables do not provide data on the HIV/AIDS epidemic (see Map E.5 for that data), we know that Africa has been the most severely impacted continent. What impact is HIV/AIDS having on African population growth rates? Why do you think that its effects are so muted?

- According to these tables, Russia and Japan have negative population growth rates. What factors would account for these downward trends? What sorts of problems do you think that these countries are likely to encounter?

- Japan and Germany are the only countries that have smaller percentages of the populations under the age of fifteen than over the age of sixty-five. In contrast, the countries of sub-Saharan Africa have the largest proportion of their populations under age fifteen. What are likely causes for these developments in Japan, Russia, and sub-Saharan Africa? What problems are these countries likely to encounter as they move forward?

- Does this data suggest that the world is becoming more unified or integrated?

Table 1. Top 10 Most Populous Countries, 2012 and 2050

2012	POPULATION (MILLIONS)	2050	POPULATION (MILLIONS)
China	1,350	India	1,691
India	1,260	China	1,311
United States	314	United States	423
Indonesia	241	Nigeria	402
Brazil	194	Pakistan	314
Pakistan	180	Indonesia	309
Nigeria	170	Bangladesh	226
Bangladesh	153	Brazil	213
Russia	143	Democratic Republic of Congo	194
Japan	128	Ethiopia	166

Source: Population Reference Bureau, 2012: World Population Data Sheet, Washington, D.C., pp. 2, 6–9.

Table 2. World Population References for 2012 and Projection for 2050

CONTINENTS AND SELECTED COUNTRIES	POPULATION, 2012 (MILLIONS)	RATE OF NATURAL INCREASE (%)	PROJECTED POPULATION, 2050 (MILLIONS)	PERCENT OF POPULATION		GNP PER CAPITA (US $)
				UNDER AGE 15	OVER AGE 65	
World	7,058	+1.2	9,624	26	8	10,760
Africa	1,072	+2.5	2,339	41	3	2,630
Egypt	82.3	+2.0	135.6	32	4	5,760
Nigeria	170.1	+2.6	402.4	44	3	1,910
South Africa	51.1	+0.9	57.2	31	5	2,240
Democratic Republic of Congo	69.1	+2.8	194.2	46	3	320
The Americas	948	+1.0	1,212	25	9	23,870
United States	349	+0.5	471	20	13	47,310
Brazil	194.3	+1.0	213.4	24	7	11,000
Mexico	116.1	+1.5	143.9	29	6	14,400
Haiti	10.3	+1.8	14.2	36	4	1,180
Asia	4,260	+1.1	5,284	25	7	6,860
China	1,350.4	+0.5	1,310.7	16	9	7,640
India	1,259.7	+1.5	1,691.1	31	5	3,430
Japan	127.6	−0.2	119.8	13	24	34,610
Indonesia	241.0	+1.3	309.4	27	6	4,200
Europe	740	0.0	732	16	16	27,080
United Kingdom	63.2	0.4	79.6	18	17	35,840
France	63.6	0.4	78.4	19	17	34,750
Germany	81.8	−0.2	71.5	13	21	38,100
Russia	143.2	−0.1	127.8	15	13	19,240

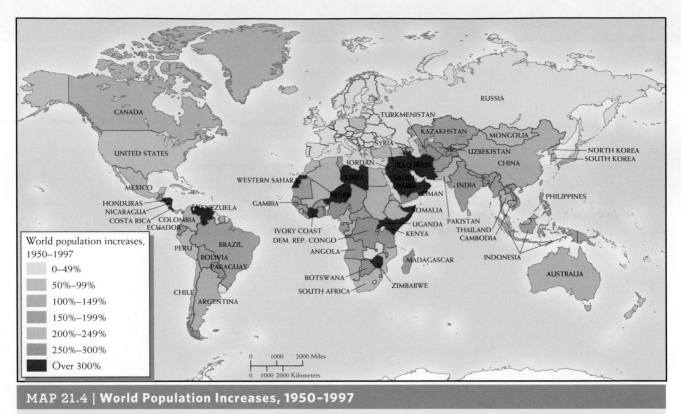

MAP 21.4 | World Population Increases, 1950–1997

The world's population more than doubled between 1950 and 1997, rising from approximately 2.5 billion to nearly 6 billion.

• Which countries had the largest population increases over these five decades?

• Why do you suppose these countries experienced such high population increases?

• According to your reading, why did western Europe and Russia have the lowest population increases?

China and India each passed the billion-person mark. Increases were greatest in cities. By the 1980s, the world's largest cities were Asian, African, and Latin American. Greater Tokyo-Yokohama had 30 million inhabitants, while Mexico City had 20 million, São Paulo 17 million, Cairo 16 million, Calcutta 15 million, and Jakarta 12 million.

Population growth slowed most dramatically in richer societies. For some, like Italy, the growth rate declined to zero, as the number of births no longer exceeded the number of deaths. More recently enriched societies like Korea, Taiwan, and Hong Kong also had fewer births. Societies that did not see their birthrates decline by the same rate (much of Africa, southern Asia, and impoverished parts of Latin America) had difficulty raising income levels. But even among poor nations, birthrates declined after the 1970s.

The most remarkable turnaround occurred in China, where the government instituted a "one-child family" policy in 1979 with rewards for compliance and penalties for transgression. The bias in favor of sons (long a feature of China's patrilineal system, which emphasized descent through the male line), together with the availability of ultrasound scanners, promoted the widespread—albeit illegal—practice of prenatal sex selection.

In general, however, declining family size resulted from choice. In rich countries, more women deferred having children as education, career prospects, and birth-control devices provided incentives and methods to postpone starting a family. In addition, love became a precondition to marriage and family formation in societies that had previously emphasized arranged marriages.

Families In many countries, the legal definition of families became more fluid in this period. Here again, the changes reflected women's choices and the relationship between love and marriage. First, couples chose to end their marriages at unprecedented rates. In Belgium and Britain late in the twentieth century, fewer than half of all marriages survived. China's divorce rate soared too. In Beijing, by century's end it approached 25 percent—double the 1990 rate. As of 2000, women initiated more than 70 percent of divorces.

As marriages became shorter-lived, new forms of child-rearing proliferated. Europeans, including the supposedly more traditional Italians and Greeks, abandoned nuclear family conventions. In those European countries where divorce remained difficult, more couples lived together without getting married. In the United States, out-of-wedlock childbirths constituted one-third of all births in the late 1990s, with only about half of American children living in households with both parents (compared with nearly three-quarters of children in the early 1970s).

Aging Longer life spans also affected families, as more infants survived childhood and lived to be old. The populations of industrialized nations "grayed" considerably as the median age increased and the percentage of the population over age sixty-five grew. In western Europe and Japan, graying rates were especially pronounced. Japan's birthrate plummeted, and the citizenry aged at such a rate that the country began to depopulate. From a population of 127 million in 2000, estimates forecast a decline to 105 million by 2050.

The aging population presented new challenges for families. For centuries, being a parent meant providing for children until they could be self-sufficient. Old age, the years of relatively unproductive labor, was brief. Communities and households absorbed the cost of caring for the elderly. Household savings became family bequests to future, not older, generations. But as populations aged, retirees needed their own and society's savings to survive. So public and private pension funds swelled to accumulate future pools of money for the retired. In Germany, over 30 percent of the government's social policy spending went into the state pension fund.

In Africa, where publicly supported pension funds were rare, the aged faced bleaker futures. Whereas in earlier times the elderly were respected founts of wisdom, colonial rule and the postcolonial world elevated the young—especially those with Western educations and lifestyles. Then, in the 1970s, as birthrates soared, the demand on family resources to care for infants and children rose at the very moment when society's resource base began to shrink. The elderly could no longer work, but neither could they rely on the household's support.

Health The spread of contagious diseases also reflected inequities in the globalized world. Although microbes have no respect for borders, the effects of public-health regulations, antibiotics, and vaccination campaigns reduced the spread of contagions. By the late twentieth century, not only did nutrition and healthy habits count (as they always had), but access to medicines did too.

What used to be universal afflictions in previous centuries now just affected certain peoples. Water treatment and proper sewerage, for example, had banished cholera from most urban centers by the mid-twentieth century. More recently, however, its deadly grip again reached across Asia and into the eastern Mediterranean, parts of Latin America and the Caribbean, and much of sub-Saharan Africa. Thus, diseases proliferated where urban squalor was most acute—in cities with the greatest post-1970s population growth.

In the 1970s, entirely new diseases began to devastate the world's population. Consider **AIDS (Acquired Immunodeficiency Syndrome)**, which in its first two decades killed 12 million people. First detected in 1981, AIDS was initially stigmatized as a "gay cancer" (it appeared primarily in homosexual men) and received little attention. But as it

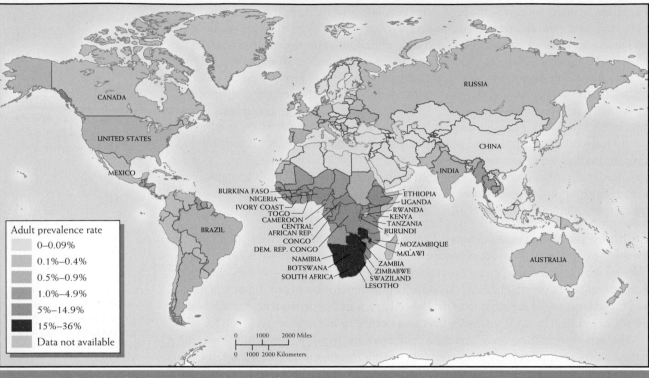

MAP 21.5 | HIV Infection across the World, 1999

HIV, which leads to AIDS, spread across the whole world, providing further evidence of global interconnectedness. The outbreak began in Africa.

• Where in Africa have the highest rates of HIV infection occurred?

• Which countries *outside* the African continent have had the highest rates of infection, and why is this so?

• Which countries have the lowest rates of HIV infection, and why is this so?

spread to heterosexuals and public awareness about it increased, a new campaign urged the practice of safe sex, control of blood supplies, and restrictions on sharing hypodermic needles. In Europe and North America, where the campaigns intensified and new drugs kept the virus under control, AIDS rates stabilized.

New treatments were very expensive, however, leaving the poor and disadvantaged still vulnerable to infection. By 2000, 33 million people had AIDS (the vast majority in poor countries) and even more were infected with HIV, the human immunodeficiency virus that causes AIDS (see Map 21.5). At least two-thirds of those with AIDS lived in Africa below the Sahara. In India, 7 million carried the virus; in China, the figure topped 1 million.

Education Access to education increasingly separated the haves from the have-nots. Moreover, because educational opportunities usually favored men, schooling shaped differences between males and females. In sub-Saharan Africa and in India, for example, literacy rates were, respectively, 63 and 64 percent for men and only 39 and 40 percent for women as of 2000. In the Arab world, the gap between men and women decreased somewhat by the end of the twentieth century. Yet low levels of literacy overall and the depressed levels for women continued to impede each region's efforts to combat poverty.

Gender bias also remained in rich societies. For decades, however, women and girls pressed for equal access to education, with some astounding results. In the United States, by the late 1980s, more than half of all college degrees went to women. Chinese women made even greater strides, although roadblocks persisted. Ironically, with China's recent market reforms women's access to basic education regressed, as families, particularly in rural areas, reverted to spending their limited resources on educating sons. Thus, in 2000, up to 70 percent of China's 140 million illiterates were female.

Women and Work Although more women held jobs outside the home, they lacked full equality at work. Limited by job discrimination and burdens of child-rearing, women's participation in the workforce reached a fairly stable level by the 1980s. The percentage of women at the top of the corporate pyramid was considerably smaller than their proportion in the labor force or their college graduation rates. Women worldwide had difficulties breaking through the "glass ceiling"—a seemingly invisible barrier to women's advancement. Consequently, while the difference between men's and women's incomes narrowed, a significant gap persisted.

African Women and Education Though women's education lagged behind that of men in Africa, a number of women, like Stella Kenyi, pictured here, graduated from African high schools and attended universities at home or abroad. Kenyi taught business skills to men and women in Sudan after completing an undergraduate degree at Davidson College in North Carolina.

Working outside the home led to problems inside the home. Who would take care of the children? Changing gender norms in rich countries sparked major migration streams. Jamaican and Filipino women, for example, migrated by the thousands in the 1970s and 1980s to Canada and Australia to work as nannies to raise money to send back home, where they had often left their own children. In South Africa and Brazil, local women served as domestic servants and nannies. They were doing the jobs that once belonged to middle- and upper-class homemakers, women who now wanted the same rights as men: to parent *and* to work.

The deeply ingrained inequality between men and women prompted calls for change. Feminist movements arose mainly in Europe and in North America in the 1960s and then became global in the 1970s. In 1975, the first truly international women's forum took place in Mexico City. But becoming global did not necessarily imply overturning local customs. What feminists called for was not the abolition of gender differences, but equal treatment—equal pay and equal opportunities for obtaining jobs and advancement. In general, then, in spite of rapid population growth, inequalities between and within societies remained in this period. The most glaring were between the rich and poor countries although well-to-do middle classes emerged everywhere in the world and tended to congregate in the big cities.

Agricultural Production The most immediate challenge facing many societies was how to feed their increasing populations. Yet, changing agrarian practices made a huge difference in increasing food production. Starting in the 1950s, the "green revolution," which relied on chemical fertilizers, herbicides, and pesticides, produced dramatically larger harvests. Then, in the 1970s, biologists began offering genetically engineered crops that multiplied yields at an even faster rate.

But these breakthroughs were not evenly distributed. American farmers, the biggest innovators, were the greatest beneficiaries. For example, by century's end they produced approximately one-ninth of the world's wheat and two-fifths of its corn. From this output, American exports accounted for about one-third of the world's international wheat trade and four-fifths of all corn exports. The most dramatic transformation occurred in China. Beginning in the late 1970s, the Chinese government broke up some of the old collective farms and restored

COMPARISON

DESCRIBE how globalization and population changes affected the environment, and vice versa.

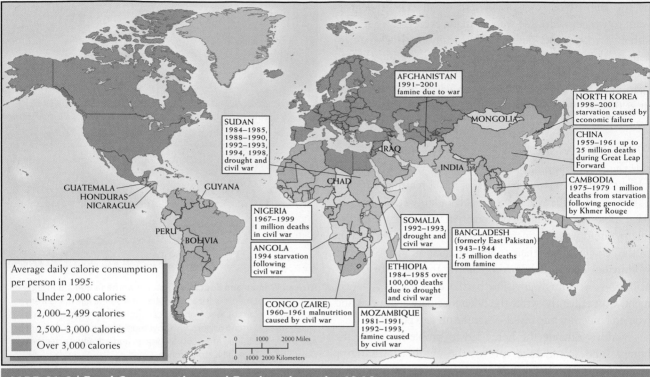

MAP 21.6 | Food Consumption and Famine since the 1940s

There is perhaps no better indicator of the division of the world into rich and poor, haves and have-nots, than this map on food consumption and famine.

• Which parts of the world have had the most difficulty in feeding their populations?

• What have been some of the causes of famine and malnourishment in these regions?

• How much have famine and malnourishment been due to human actions, and how much to climate and other matters over which human beings have little control?

the individual household as the basic economic unit in rural areas. Thereafter, agricultural output surged by roughly 9 percent per year and nearly doubled between 1978 and 1986.

While biology and chemistry allowed some farmers to get more out of their land, others simply opened up new lands to cultivation. The most notorious frontier expansion occurred in the Amazon River basin. Populations flocked to the Amazon frontier, largely from impoverished areas in northeastern Brazil. They cleared (by fire) cheap land, staked their claims, and, like nineteenth-century American homesteaders, tried to get ahead by cultivating crops and raising livestock. But the promise of bounty failed: the soils were poor and easily eroded, and land titles provided little security, especially once large speculators moved into the area. So the frontiersmen moved farther inland to repeat the cycle. By the 1980s, migrants to the Amazon River basin had burned away much of the jungle, contaminated the environment, reduced the stock of diverse plant and animal life, and fostered social conflict in the Brazilian hinterland.

Nor were "breadbasket" areas always able to feed exploding populations. This was especially true in Africa from the 1970s onward, when domestic food production could not keep pace with population growth (see Map 21.6). Food shortages increased in frequency and duration, wiping out large numbers of sub-Saharan peoples. The protruding ribs on African children became a clichéd image of the region.

Saving the Amazon The rise of an international environmental movement in the 1970s led to alliances with local indigenous and environmental leaders, especially in the Amazon. (*Left*) One of the most prominent advocates of the rights of indigenous people and the need to protect imperiled jungles was the British musician Sting. Here he is pictured alongside one of the Amazon's foremost Indian leaders, Bep Koroti Paiakan. (*Right*) Farmers and ranchers cut and burned the Amazon at a ferocious rate in pursuit of frontier lands. In these remote regions, it was hard for local authorities to enforce conservation laws.

What explained Africa's famines? As the Indian Nobel Prize–winning economist Amartya Sen observed, famines—and their increasing frequency—are not natural disasters; they are man-made. Food shortages in Africa stemmed largely from governments that ignored the rural sector and its politically unorganized farmers. Unable to persuade their governments to raise prices for their crops, the farmers lacked incentives to expand production. Food shortages were also by-products of global inequalities. At the urging of the IMF, African countries earmarked hefty chunks of their economies to agrarian exports to repay debts incurred in the 1970s. This left them without enough foodstuffs domestically, and thus they actually became food importers.

Natural Resources and the Environment The consumption of water, oil, and other natural resources became matters of international concern late in the twentieth century. So did pollution control and the disposal of waste products. Part of this internationalization reflected the recognition that individual nations could not solve environmental issues on their own. Air and water, after all, do not stop flowing at political boundaries.

Americans consumed a disproportionate share of the world's natural resources. By 2000, they were using water at a per capita rate three times the world's average. Indeed, extensive irrigation was crucial to California's agricultural sector, the most productive and profitable in the world. Gathering more water also allowed a desert metropolis like Los Angeles to grow.

In the United States and Canada, attempts to curb energy consumption saw little success, and the United States grew more dependent on imported oil. In the late 1990s, North American demand for fuel-guzzling sport utility vehicles intensified oil imports. Dependence on foreign sources locked oil importers into recurring clashes with oil exporters.

As Canadians saw their northern lakes fill up with acid rain (precipitation laced with sulfur, mainly from coal-fired plants), they urged their southern neighbor to curb emissions. Thus, reciprocal agreements between Canada and the United States took shape in the 1980s. Europeans, also beset by acid rain, likewise negotiated regional environmental treaties. But some polluters simply moved overseas to poorer and less powerful nations. As the West cleaned up its environment, the rest of the world paid the price.

Other problems crossed man-made borders as well. These included the greenhouse effect and **global warming** (release into the air of human-produced carbons that contribute to rising temperatures worldwide), ocean pollution, and declining biological diversity. International meetings in Rio de Janeiro and Kyoto in the 1990s urged restricting emission of gases that led to global warming, but a global accord proved impossible to achieve.

The response to environmental crises has been uneven at best. Where environmentalists acquired political power, they forced regulators to curb carbon emissions, a problem that grew with the rise in automobile traffic in cities like Tokyo, Mexico City, and Los Angeles. But controls on fossil-fuel emissions depended on power and wealth, for it was hard to impose restrictions in societies where high energy use seemed a necessity of economic life. Even the Japanese, pioneers of clean fuel as early as the 1960s, were polluters in other spheres long thereafter. With increasing controls at home, Japanese industrialists went abroad to unload hazardous waste. U.S. industrialists did the same, sending hazardous waste to Mexico. Argentina and Canada sent their nuclear waste not abroad, but to poor provinces desperate for jobs.

Even as some states enacted measures to protect the environment, environmental concerns did not observe boundary lines. At the end of the twentieth century, global guidelines for regulating the impact of human activities on the environment had eluded the world's leaders.

Citizenship in the Global World

Since the nineteenth century, nation-states were supposed to be key in defining the rights of citizens. But after the 1970s, people realized that international and supranational organizations often had more influence over their lives than did their own national governments, especially in the developing world. However, these organizations failed to stop the violence that erupted in many regions during this period. Religion also undermined the influence of nation-states, as religious groups often came into conflict with one another and with secular principles.

SUPRANATIONAL ORGANIZATIONS

New organizations with international responsibilities took shape after World War II for the purpose of facilitating global activities. These **supranational organizations** (organizations that transcend national boundaries) were intended to facilitate globalization and manage crisis situations; they impinged on the autonomy of all but the most powerful states.

Among the most prominent supranational organizations were the World Bank and the International Monetary Fund, which provided vital economic assistance to poorer nations. The World Bank, originally named the International Bank for Reconstruction and Development, was designed primarily to provide financial assistance for big development projects. In contrast, the IMF provided funds and technical assistance to countries whose economies were in trouble. A good example of the World Bank's agenda was the financial support that it gave to the government of Ghana in the 1960s for the Volta River project, which was intended to create an electrical grid for that country. Nonetheless, both the World Bank and the International Monetary Fund required that recipient governments implement far-reaching economic reforms, such as devaluation of the currency and the privatization of public sector companies; these reforms were often deeply unpopular and led to riots and charges that these international groups were agents of a new kind of imperialism.

Another set of supranational bodies, international nongovernmental organizations (NGOs), also stepped forward late in the twentieth century. Many championed human rights or highlighted environmental problems. Others, like the International Committee of the Red Cross, once dedicated to war relief, became more active in peacetime, sheltering the homeless or providing food for famine victims. What united NGOs was not so much their goals but the way they pursued them: autonomously, rather than through state power.

International NGOs reached a new level of influence in the 1970s because most nation-states at that time were still not democracies. Of the 121 countries in the world in 1980, only 37 were democracies, accounting for only 35 percent of the globe's population. People found it difficult to rely on authoritarians to uphold their rights as citizens. Indeed, despite adopting a Universal Declaration of Human Rights in 1918, the United Nations, (another international organization created after World War II and intended to provide a forum for settling international problems), was a latecomer to enforcing human rights provisions, largely because its own members were the self-same authoritarians.

NGOs, then, took the lead in trying to make the language of human rights stick. The brutality of military regimes in Latin America inspired the emerging network of international human rights organizations to take action. After the overthrow of Chile's Salvador Allende in 1973, political groups created by the Catholic Church protested the military junta's harsh repression. When the Argentine military began killing tens of thousands of innocent civilians in 1976 and news of their torture techniques leaked out, human rights movements again took action. Prominent among them was Amnesty International. Formed in 1961 to defend prisoners of conscience (detained for their beliefs, color, sex, ethnic origin, language, or religion), Amnesty International catalogued human rights violations worldwide. By 2000, an extensive network of associations was informing the public, lobbying governments, and pressuring U.N. member nations to live up to commitments to respect the rights of citizens.

VIOLENCE

International organizations and NGOs could play only a limited role in preserving peace and strengthening human rights. The end of the Cold War left entire regions in such turmoil that even the most effective humanitarian agencies could not prevent mass killings.

Consider the Balkans in the 1990s. In the territorial remains of Yugoslavia, groups of Serbs, Croats, Bosnians, ethnic Albanians, and others fought for control. Former neighbors, fueled by opportunistic leaders' rhetoric, no longer saw themselves as citizens of diverse political communities. Instead, demagogues trumpeted the superiority of ethnically defined states. Ethnic Serbians took up arms against their Croat neighbors, and vice versa. When international agencies moved in to try to bolster public authority, they failed as Yugoslavia's ethnic mosaic imploded into civil war.

Some of the most gruesome scenes of political violence occurred in Africa, where many nation-states struggled to uphold the rule of law for all citizens. Here, tension often erupted in conflict between ethnic groups. The failure of African agriculture to sustain growing populations, as well as unequal access to resources like education, made ethnic rivalries worse. Droughts, famine, and corruption ignited the rivalries into riots and killings—even into bitter civil war and the breakdown of centralized authority.

Events in Rwanda reflected Africa's horrifying experience with political violence. Friction grew between the majority Hutus (agrarian people, often very poor) and the minority Tutsis (herders, often with better education, wealthier, and chosen by the Belgians to rule over the Hutus) after the two peoples had intermarried and lived side by side for many generations. Some resentful Hutus blamed the Tutsis for all their woes. As tensions mounted, the United Nations dispatched peacekeeping troops. Moderate Hutus urged continued peaceful coexistence, only to be shouted down by government forces in command of radio

Rwandan Refugees Perhaps as many as 800,000 Tutsis were killed in 1994 as the Hutus turned against the local Tutsi population while Rwanda was being invaded by a Tutsi-led army from Uganda. Not surprisingly, the massacre led to an enormous refugee crisis.

stations and a mass propaganda machine. Although alerted to the impending problem, U.N. forces, fearing a clash and uncertain of their mandate, failed to prevent the violence.

The failure on the part of the international community, including the United States, which did not have troops on the ground and which had no clear policy toward Rwanda, gave the Hutu government a green light to wipe out opponents. In 100 days of carnage in 1994, Hutu militias massacred 800,000 Tutsis and moderate Hutus. This was not, as many proclaimed, the militarization of ancient ethnic rivalries, for many Hutus were butchered as they tried to defend Tutsi friends, relatives, and neighbors. Meanwhile, the ensuing refugee crisis destabilized neighboring countries. The Rwanda genocide sent riptides across eastern and central Africa, creating a whole new generation of conflicts.

Some societies, however, tried to put political violence behind them. In Argentina, El Salvador, Guatemala, and South Africa, the transition to democracy compelled elected rulers to establish inquiries into past rulers' human rights abuses. These **truth commissions** were vital for creating a new aura of legitimacy for democracies and for promising to uphold the rights of individuals. In South Africa, many blacks backed the new president, Nelson Mandela, but also demanded a reckoning with the punitive experience of the apartheid past. To avoid a backlash against the former white rulers, the South African leadership opted to record the past events rather than avenge them. The Rwandan catastrophe is the best example of the failure of international organizations to deal with a crisis, which eventually mushroomed into a genocide. Elsewhere, in famine areas and big development projects, the supranationals enjoyed more success.

RELIGIOUS FOUNDATIONS OF POLITICS

Secular concerns for human rights and international peace were not the only foundations for politics after the Cold War. In many regions, people wanted religion to define the moral fabric of political communities. Very often, religion provided a way to reimagine the nation-state, just as globalization was undermining national autonomy.

Hindu Nationalism In India, Hindu nationalism offered a communal identity for a country being rapidly transformed by globalization. In the 1980s, India freed market forces, privatized state firms, and withdrew from its role as welfare provider. Economic reforms under the ruling Congress Party sparked economic growth, thereby creating one of Asia's largest, best-educated, and most affluent middle class. But because these changes also widened the gap between rich and poor, lower classes and castes formed political parties to challenge the traditional elites. With established hierarchies and loyalties eroding, Hindu nationalists argued that religion could now fill the role once occupied by a secular state. Claiming that the ideology of *Hindutva* ("Hinduness") would bring the help that secular nationalism had failed to give, Hindu militants trumpeted the idea of India as a nation of Hindus (the majority), with minorities relegated to a lesser status. The chief beneficiary of the politics established by economic liberalization was a Hindu nationalist party, the Bhartiya Janata Party (BJP), or Indian People's Party. It was the political arm of an alliance of Hindu organizations devoted to establishing India as a Hindu state. By the late 1980s, a BJP coalition came to power and sought to transform the nation-state into a moral community, but without challenging the economic forces of globalization.

Islamic Conservatism In some cases, religion provided a way to resist seemingly American-dominated globalization. One of the most spirited challenges arose in the Islamic Middle East. Here, many people believed that modernizing and westernizing programs were leading their societies toward rampant materialism and unchecked individualism. Critics included traditional clerics and young western-educated elites whose job prospects seemed bleak and who felt that the promise of modernization had failed. Having criticized modernizing processes since the nineteenth century, Islamic conservatives flourished once more in the 1970s, as global markets and social tensions undermined secular leadership.

The most revolutionary Islamic movement arose in Iran, where clerics forced the shah, the country's ruler, from power in 1979. The revolt pitted a group of religious officials possessing only pamphlets, tracts, and tapes against the military arsenal and the vast intelligence apparatus of the Iranian state. Shah Mohammad Reza Pahlavi had enjoyed U.S. technical and military support since the Americans had helped place him on the throne in 1953. His bloated army and police force, as well as his brutally effective intelligence service, had crushed all challenges to his authority. The shah also had benefited from oil revenues, which soared after 1973. Yet the uneven distribution of income, the oppressive police state, and the royal family's ostentatious lifestyle fueled widespread discontent.

The most powerful critique came from the mullahs (Muslim scholars or religious teachers), who found in the Ayatollah Ruhollah Khomeini a courageous leader. Khomeini used his traditional Islamic education and his training in Muslim ethics to accuse the shah's government of gross violations of Islamic norms. He also identified the shah's ally, America, as the great Satan. With opposition mounting, the shah fled the country in 1979. In his wake, Khomeini established a theocratic state ruled by a council of Islamic clerics. Although some Iranians grumbled about aspects of this return to Islam, they prided themselves on having inspired a revolution based on principles other than those drawn from the West.

Religious Conservatism in the United States The search for religious foundations of politics in the global age reached beyond nonwestern societies. Indeed, in the United States, religion became a potent force after the 1970s as the membership and activism of conservative, fundamentalist Protestant churches eclipsed mainstream denominations. Insisting on a literal interpretation of the Bible, Protestant fundamentalists argued against secularizing trends in American society. This traditionalist crusade took up a broad range of cultural and political issues. Religious conservatives (predominantly evangelical Protestants, but also some Catholics and Orthodox Jews) attacked many of the social changes that had emerged from liberation movements of the 1960s. Shifting sexual and familial relations were sore points, but the religious conservatives especially targeted public leaders who, they felt, had abandoned the moral purpose of authority by legalizing abortion and supporting secular values.

ACCEPTANCE OF AND RESISTANCE TO DEMOCRACY

New sources of power and new social movements drastically changed politics in the global age. Increasingly, international organizations were decisive in defining the conditions of democratic citizenship. Perhaps most remarkable was how much democracy spread toward the end of the twentieth century. In South Africa, Russia, and Guatemala, elections now decided politicians' fate. In this sense, the world's societies embraced the idea that people had a right to choose their own representatives. Nevertheless, democracy did not triumph everywhere.

An important holdout was China. Mao died in 1976, and within a few years his successor, Deng Xiaoping, opened the nation's economy to market forces. But Deng and other Chinese Communist Party leaders resisted multiparty competition. Instead of capitalism and western-style democracy, they maintained that China should follow its own path to modernity. By the late 1980s, economic reforms had produced spectacular increases in production and rising standards of living for most of China's people. But the widening gap between rich and poor, together with increasing public awareness of corruption within the party and the government, triggered popular discontent. Worker strikes and slowdowns, peasant unrest, and student activism spread.

On April 22, 1989, some 100,000 people gathered in **Tiananmen Square** at the heart of Beijing in silent defiance of a government ban on assembling. The regime responded by declaring martial law. Two huge protest demonstrations followed, and residents erected barricades to defend the city against government troops. As the protest's momentum waned, a twenty-eight-foot icon, partly inspired by the Statue of Liberty, was unveiled at the square, capturing the imagination of the crowd and the attention of the cameras. But by then the government had assembled troops to crush the movement. In a night of terror that began at dusk on June 3, the People's Liberation Army turned their guns against the people.

In Mexico, democracy finally triumphed, as the single party that had dominated the country for seventy-one years fell after the election of Vicente Fox in 2000. Until that time, Mexican rulers had combined patronage and rigged elections to stay in office. By the 1980s, corruption and abuse permeated the system. The abuse of democratic rights fell hardest on poor communities, especially those with large numbers of indigenous people.

Mexico, South Africa, and China were powerful examples of how men and women in every corner of the earth yearned to choose their own leaders. In 1994, millions of previously disenfranchised South Africans lined up for hours to cast a vote for their new black African president, Nelson Mandela. In 2000, the Mexican electorate turned

Tiananmen Square This white plaster and styrofoam statue, inspired in part by the Statue of Liberty and dubbed the Goddess of Democracy, was created by students in Beijing in the spring of 1989. It was brought to Tiananmen Square and unveiled at the end of May in an attempt to reinvigorate the democracy movement and the spirits of the protesters. For five days it captured worldwide attention, until it was toppled by a tank on June 4 and crushed as the Chinese People's Liberation Army cleared the square of its democracy advocates.

Protests in Mexico (*Left*) After generations of oppression and exclusion, peasants of Chiapas, in southern Mexico, called for democracy and respect for their right to land. When Mexican authorities refused to bend, peasants took up arms. While they knew that they posed no military threat to the Mexican army, the Zapatista rebels used the world media and international organizations to embarrass the national political establishment into allowing reforms. (*Right*) Among the great Mexican muralists of the twentieth century, David Alfaro Siqueiros most advocated class struggle. In this 1957 mural image, *The People in Arms*, Siqueiros portrays Mexican peasants as they pick up arms in 1910 to fight for a new order. Paintings such as these provided inspiration for movements such as the Chiapas rebellion.

out the ruling party, while in China the ruling Communist Party had to call in the army to prevent regime change and democratic reforms.

Conclusion

In the thirteenth century (as long before), a few travelers like Ibn Battuta and Marco Polo ventured over long distances to trade, to explore, and to convert souls; yet communications technology was rudimentary, making long-distance mobility and exchange expensive, rare, and perilous. The world was much more a series of communities set apart than a world bound together by culture, capital, and communication networks.

By the late twentieth century, that balance had changed. Food, entertainment, clothing, and even family life were becoming more similar worldwide. To be sure, some local differences remained. In 2000, local cultures lived on, and in some cases were revived, through challenges to the authority of nation-states. No longer did the nation-state or any single level of community life define collective identities. At the same time, worldwide purveyors of cultural and commercial resources offered local communities the same kinds of products, from aspirin to Nike shoes. Exchanges across local and national boundaries became easier. For the first time, many of the world's peoples felt they belonged to a global culture.

New technologies, new methods of production and investment, and the greater importance of personal health and education created new possibilities—and greater inequalities. Indeed, the gaps between haves and have-nots in 2000 were astonishing. For as humanity harnessed new technologies to accelerate exchanges across and within cultures, an ever-larger gulf separated those who participated in global networks from those on the margins. This inequality produced a range of different political and cultural forms after the collapse of the three-world order. Thus, as the world became more integrated, it also grew apart along ever-deeper lines.

After You Read This Chapter

Go to INQUIZITIVE to see what you've learned—and learn what you've missed—with personalized feedback along the way.

FOCUS ON: *Globalization*

REMOVING OBSTACLES TO GLOBALIZATION

- Communism's fall and the end of the Cold War improve prospects for global exchange of peoples, ideas, and resources.

- Final decolonization in Angola, Mozambique, and Guinea-Bissau, and the end of apartheid in South Africa return self-rule throughout Africa.

UNLEASHING GLOBALIZATION

- Financial deregulation and the end of gold and silver standards allow money to move freely across borders but lead to a Third World debt crisis.

- Widespread migrations occur as people in Africa, Asia, and Latin America move to Europe and America, following the tracks of their former colonizers.

- Revolutions in culture and communications make cultural diversity more possible for those who can afford it.

THE NEW GLOBAL ORDER

- Globalization leads to dramatic population expansion, requiring greater agricultural and industrial output.

- Family structure changes, life spans increase, and more goods are available, yet inequalities deepen as education and good health determine social status as never before.

- As globalization erodes the power of the nation-state, greater violence occurs between and within states. Nongovernmental organizations (NGOs) and religion become resources for dealing with violence and inequality and for reimagining the nation-state.

CHRONOLOGY

THE AMERICAS		

U.S. announces Strategic Defense Initiative (SDI) 1983 ◆

EUROPE

SOVIET UNION

AFRICA

THE MIDDLE EAST

Khomeini establishes theocratic state in Iran 1979 ◆

SOUTH ASIA

EAST ASIA

Deng Xiaoping reforms China 1978–1992

1970   **1980**

- *Thinking about* **Worlds Together, Worlds Apart** *and Globalization* How did globalization shape patterns of inequality? After the Cold War standoff between superpower blocs, trade, migration, and communications reshaped the terms on which peoples interacted with one another around the world. Industry, agriculture, culture, and the arts all linked peoples and regions together in different ways. Consider differences in all these domains. What kinds of inequalities were most significant?

- *Thinking about Changing Power Relationships and Globalization* What kind of resistance movements did globalization generate, both within the core regions of the developed world and elsewhere? How did feminism, labor, and environmental reform movements resemble and differ from their predecessors? How did Hindu nationalism and religious conservatism differ from each other and from earlier nationalist and religious or pan movements?

- *Thinking about Environmental Impacts and Globalization* Explain the relationship between globalization, climate change, and the environment. The consumption of water, oil, and other natural resources became major national and international issues. How did the organization of agricultural and industrial production change, and what influence did those changes have on global warming, acid rain, and air pollution? Identify efforts to limit damage to the environment and evaluate their success.

1. Describe the new global order that replaced the so-called three-world order in the 1970s.

2. Analyze the role of the IMF in the **developing world**. On what terms did it provide assistance, who benefited, and what kind of sacrifices did it impose?

3. Explain the relationship between **supranational organizations** like the **European Union** and state sovereignty.

4. Explain the end of the Cold War. How, and to what degree, did U.S. policies contribute to the Soviet Union's demise?

5. Analyze how **globalization** transformed popular culture. To what extent does global popular culture reflect American culture and to what extent did it shape American culture?

6. Explain how **globalization** transformed world demography. What patterns emerged in terms of international migration?

7. Explain how environmentalists fought **global warming**. What kind of approach did they take? What kind of changes occurred, and how effective were they?

8. Explain trends in industrial production and consumption over the last several decades. Who produced the goods, and who consumed them?

9. Analyze both the spread of HIV/**AIDS** among geographic regions and socioeconomic groups around the world.

◆ North American Free Trade Association approved 1992
◆ Chiapas rebellion in Mexico 1994
◆ Eastern European communist regimes collapse 1989
Yugoslavia dissolves, ethnic cleansing ensues 1989–1995
◆ European Union formed 1991
Soviet war in Afghanistan 1979–1989
◆ Gorbachev assumes power 1985
◆ Chernobyl nuclear accident 1986 ◆ Dissolution of the Soviet Union 1991
◆ Mandela released from prison 1990
◆ Free elections in South Africa 1994
◆ Genocide in Rwanda 1998
BJP Party heads government in India 1998 ◆

◆ Chinese state cracks down on Tiananmen Square protesters 1989

1990

2000

Competing Perspectives

The Power of Grassroots Democracy

Despite the enormous economic and technological advances of the past 200 years, famine and dire poverty remain problems in many places. These problems have been particularly severe where unrepresentative, authoritarian leaders prevent foreign aid from reaching the needy and ordinary people from achieving self-sufficiency. Self-sufficiency has been further undermined by pervasive discrimination against women, which has limited their access to education and therefore compromised economic growth for everyone, men and women alike. The three selections presented here all call attention to the importance of grassroots democracy and equality in responding to economic and ecological disasters and achieving at least a measure of autonomy.

On January 1, 1994, a group of mostly Amerindians living in a jungle region in Chiapas, Mexico, took up arms against the government, calling for a restoration of the principles of the Mexican Revolution and protesting the confiscation of their land rights. The first document, from the General Council of the Zapatista Army for National Liberation (EZLN), sought international support for their conflict with Mexican authorities. In the second selection, "Using Subsidies to Close Gender Gaps in Education" (2000–2001), researchers for the World Bank found that better education, and especially better education for girls, improves economic development among the poor. The final selection, from the Nobel Prize–winning economist Amartya Sen, "Democracy as a Universal Value" (1999), argues that no major famine has occurred in a democratic country with a free press.

PRIMARY SOURCE 21.1

Declaration of War against the Mexican Government (1993), EZLN

We are a product of 500 years of struggle: first against slavery, during the War of Independence against Spain led by the insurgents; afterward to avoid being absorbed by American imperialism; then to promulgate our constitution and expel the French Empire from our soil; and later the Porfirista dictatorship denied us just application of the Reform laws, and the people rebelled, forming their own leaders; . . . we have nothing, absolutely nothing, not even a decent roof over our heads, no land, no work, no health care, no food, or education; without the right to freely and democratically elect our authorities; without independence from foreigners, without peace or justice for ourselves and our children.

But TODAY WE SAY, ENOUGH! We are the heirs of those who truly forged our nationality. We the dispossessed are millions, and we call on our brothers to join in this call as the only path in order not to die of hunger in the face of the insatiable ambition of a dictatorship for more than 70 years led by a clique of traitors who represent the most conservative and sellout groups in the country. They are the same as those who opposed Hidalgo and Morelos, who betrayed Vicente Guerrero, the same as those who sold over half our territory to the foreign invader, the same as those who brought a European prince to rule us, the same as those who formed

the dictatorship of the Porfirista "scientists," the same as those who opposed the Oil Expropriation, the same as those who massacred the railroad workers in 1958 and the students in 1968, the same as those who today take everything from us, absolutely everything.

To prevent this, and as our last hope, after having tried everything to put into practice the legality based on our Magna Carta, we resort to it, to our Constitution, to apply Constitutional Article 39, which says:

"National sovereignty resides essentially and originally in the people. All public power emanates from the people and is instituted for the people's benefit. The people have, at all times, the unalienable right to alter or modify the form of their government."

Therefore, according to our Constitution, we issue this statement to the Mexican federal army, the basic pillar of the Mexican dictatorship that we suffer. . . . In conformity with this Declaration of War, we ask the other branches of the Nation's government to meet to restore the legality and the stability of the Nation by deposing the dictator. . . .

PEOPLE OF MEXICO: We, upright and free men and women, are conscious that the war we declare is a last resort, but it is just. The dictators have been applying an undeclared genocidal war against our people for many years. Therefore we ask for your decided participation in support of this plan of the Mexican people in their struggle for work, land, housing, food, health care, education, independence, liberty, democracy, justice, and peace.

Source: General Council of the EZLN, Declaración de la Selva Lacandona, 1993 (www.ezln .org, January 1, 1994).

Why Gender Matters (2000), World Bank

Evaluations of recent initiatives that subsidize the costs of schooling indicate that demand-side interventions can increase girls' enrollments and close gender gaps in education. A school stipend program established in Bangladesh in 1982 subsidizes various school expenses for girls who enroll in secondary school. In the first program evaluation girls' enrollment rate in the pilot areas rose from 27 percent, similar to the national average, to 44 percent over five years, more than twice the national average. . . . After girls' tuition was eliminated nationwide in 1992 and the stipend program was expanded to all rural areas, girls' enrollment rate climbed to 48 percent at the national level. There have also been gains in the number of girls appearing for exams and in women's enrollments at intermediate colleges. . . . While boys' enrollment rates also rose during this period, they did not rise as quickly as girls'.

Two recent programs in Balochistan, Pakistan, illustrate the potential benefits of reducing costs and improving physical access. Before the projects there were questions about whether girls' low enrollments were due to cultural barriers that cause parents to hold their daughters out of school or to inadequate supply of appropriate schools. Program evaluations suggest that improved physical access, subsidized costs, and culturally appropriate design can sharply increase girls' enrollments.

The first program, in Quetta, the capital of Balochistan, uses a subsidy tied to girls' enrollment to support the creation of schools in poor urban neighborhoods by local NGOs. The schools admit boys as long as they make up less than half of total enrollments. In rural Balochistan the second program has been expanding the supply of local, single-sex primary schools for girls by encouraging parental involvement in establishing the schools and by subsidizing the recruitment of female teachers from the local community. The results: girls' enrollments rose 33 percent in Quetta and 22 percent in rural areas. Interestingly, both programs appear to have also expanded boys' enrollments, suggesting that increasing girls' educational opportunities may have spillover benefits for boys.

Source: Reproduced with permission of the World Bank from "Using Subsidies to Close Gender Gaps in Education," *World Development Report 2000–2001*, p. 122, Box 7.2. Copyright 2000 by World Bank. Permission conveyed through Copyright Clearance Center, Inc.

"Democracy as a Universal Value" (1999), Amartya Sen

[I]n the terrible history of famines in the world, no substantial famine has ever occurred in any independent and democratic country with a relatively free press. We cannot find exceptions to this rule, no matter where we look: the recent famines of Ethiopia, Somalia, or other dictatorial regimes; famines in the Soviet Union in the 1930s; China's 1958–61 famine with the failure of the Great Leap Forward; or earlier still, the famines in Ireland or India under alien rule. China, although it was in many ways doing much better economically than India, still managed (unlike India) to have a famine, indeed the largest recorded famine in world history: Nearly 30 million people died in the famine of 1958–61, while faulty governmental policies remained uncorrected for three full years. The policies went uncriticized because there were no opposition parties in parliament, no free press, and no multiparty elections. Indeed, it is precisely this lack of challenge that allowed the deeply defective policies to continue even though they were killing millions each year. . . .

Famines are often associated with what look like natural disasters, and commentators often settle for the simplicity of explaining famines by pointing to these events: the floods in China during the failed Great Leap Forward, the droughts in Ethiopia, or crop failures in North Korea. Nevertheless, many countries with similar natural problems, or even worse ones, manage perfectly well, because a responsive government intervenes to help alleviate hunger. . . . Even the poorest democratic countries that have faced terrible droughts or floods or other natural disasters (such as India in 1973, or Zimbabwe and Botswana in the early 1980s) have been able to feed their people without experiencing a famine.

Famines are easy to prevent if there is a serious effort to do so, and a democratic government, facing elections and criticisms from opposition parties and independent newspapers, cannot help but make such an effort. Not surprisingly, while India continued to have famines under British rule right up to independence (the last famine, which I witnessed as a child, was in 1943, four years before independence), they disappeared suddenly with the establishment of a multiparty democracy and a free press. . . .

When things go fine and everything is routinely good, this instrumental role of democracy may not be particularly missed. It is when things get fouled up, for one reason or another, that the political incentives provided by democratic governance acquire great practical value.

Source: Amartya Sen, "Democracy as a Universal Value," *Journal of Democracy* 10, no. 3 (1999): 3–17, passages from pp. 6–9.

QUESTIONS FOR ANALYSIS

1. On what basis do the authors of these documents claim authority? In whose name do they speak? What goals do they seek to attain?

2. What does justice mean from the perspectives of these three documents? Do the authors agree or disagree on what is just?

3. What is the relationship between individual and collective rights in these documents? To what degree does each text consider individual liberties essential or harmful to the common good? Pay special attention to differences between the first document and the next two.

Interpreting Visual Evidence

Chimerica

Coined by the historian Niall Ferguson and the economist Moritz Schularick, the term "Chimerica" refers to the idea that, beginning in the last two decades of the twentieth century and into the first decades of the twenty-first century, the People's Republic of China and the United States of America have made up a single, dominant economic entity. China began to open its economy in the early 1980s and export manufactured goods, especially to the United States—from $51.5 billion in 1996 to $102 billion in 2001—fueling the world economy. Combined, the two countries make up roughly 13 percent of the world's land surface, a quarter of its population, more than a third of all economic production, and, by some estimates, nearly half of all economic growth in the first decade of the new millennium. Chimerica is also a play on the word "chimera": a fire-breathing female monster in Greek mythology, or an unrealizable dream, an illusion.

Like Japan and Germany after World War II, China concentrated on export-led industrial growth. Unlike those countries, China refused to let workers' wages rise as the economy grew; leaders refused to apply international standards to workplace safety, intellectual property, or environmental protections. In developed economies, where those protections applied and wages were higher, production costs were higher. As a result, competition from China cost millions of jobs in developed countries, including 2.9 million jobs in the United States alone from 2001 to 2012. Chinese leaders instead invested the surplus revenues abroad, mostly in the United States, where the influx of Chinese investment kept interest rates low. U.S. consumers, in turn, used the easy credit to purchase homes, cars, and goods like tablets and mobile phones, many of them manufactured in China.

The images presented here portray different aspects of what Ferguson and Schularick call Chimerica. The first shows modern Beijing, with massive new buildings, roadways, and smog; it shows both the robust growth of the Chinese economy—notice how new the buildings are—but also the environmental costs. The second photograph shows protective nets around a Foxconn factory, one of Apple's leading suppliers in China, after a series of suicides in 2010 drew world attention to the company's labor practices; this case reflects some of the dire costs required to produce consumer goods at low prices. The third image shows a retirement community near Phoenix, Arizona, with its massive subdivisions filled with homes purchased at low interest rates, thanks to Chinese investment. The fourth image is of a Walmart superstore in Albany, New York, with inexpensive goods, many of them produced in China, and low-wage work for shop employees, much lower than the industrial jobs that have disappeared. The final image shows an unofficial Apple store in Tehran, Iran; it shows the dominance of global brands for consumer items.

Modern Beijing.

Foxconn factory with suicide nets.

Retirement community near Phoenix, Arizona.

Unofficial Apple Store in Tehran.

Walmart Supercenter.

QUESTIONS FOR ANALYSIS

1. Explain the relationship between China and the United States presented by these images. How has each country benefited from this relationship, and what sacrifices has each made?

2. Looking at the first two images, identify the sacrifices ordinary Chinese people made as a result of the policies that enabled their country to invest in the United States. What group or groups in China do you think benefited from these policies and how?

3. With the second, third, and fourth images in mind, analyze the tradeoffs for ordinary Americans that have resulted from Chinese investment in the United States.

4. Examine the final image and consider the likely consequences of the growth of Chimerica for ordinary consumers and workers around the world.

2001–The Present

On December 31, 1999, people worldwide celebrated the beginning of a new millennium. With the Cold War over, optimists hoped for an end to the history of ideological conflict that had bloodied the twentieth century. They looked forward to an era of peace and prosperity. But in the first decade of the new millennium, it became painfully clear that while the global economy and new technologies had brought the world together as never before, ideals that challenged the emerging world order dominated by the United States could still blow things apart. People across the world faced common challenges while also experiencing opportunities and challenges specific to their regions as they sought economic progress and true political independence.

Global Challenges

Less than two years into the twenty-first century, terrorist violence shattered the exuberance that had welcomed the new millennium. On September 11, 2001, nineteen hijackers commandeered four airplanes. The hijackers slammed two of the planes into the World Trade Center in

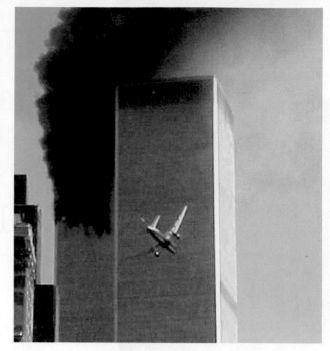

9/11 (*Right*) The North Tower already aflame, this photograph captures a second hijacked jet an instant before it crashes into the South Tower of New York's World Trade Center on September 11, 2001. (*Left*) Firefighters search for survivors in the smoldering ruins.

New York City and a third into the Pentagon building (home of the U.S. Department of Defense) in Washington, D.C. The fourth hijacked plane was diverted from its intended target—the White House or the Capitol—by the courageous actions of its passengers and crashed in a field in southwestern Pennsylvania. Television captured the event live for global viewers, recording the horrifying images of the Trade Center's twin towers engulfed in flames, then crumbling into a heap of ash and twisted metal. In the months and years that followed, countries grappled with a "war on terror," conflicts with militant Islamic groups, and a global economic crisis. The same globalizing forces that created new connections around the world also contributed to new challenges and conflicts.

WAR ON TERROR

The terrorist attack of 9/11 created outrage across the world. Anger focused on Osama bin Laden and al-Qaeda, the loosely organized militant network of Islamist groups that had organized the attack. The militants claimed that it was a response to the United States' imperialist policies in the Middle East. George W. Bush, who had become president after a close and disputed election the year before, gained broad public support for his tough talk about bringing terrorists to justice and for his insistence that the events of September 11 had introduced a divide between the "pre-9/11 world" and the "post-9/11" one. Domestically, Bush pushed for security measures to curb future terrorist violence and secure the American homeland.

Internationally, President Bush declared a "global war on terror." With the nearly unanimous backing of the American people, as well as strong support from many nations, Bush sent American forces to Afghanistan to hunt down bin Laden, destroy al-Qaeda training camps, and topple the Taliban government that had provided a haven for the terrorists. Expanding the battlefront in 2003, the Bush administration ordered an invasion of Iraq, falsely charging its brutal dictator, Saddam Hussein, with abetting the terrorist assault of 9/11 and producing weapons of mass destruction. As in Afghanistan, the initial offensive went well, but defeating the Iraqi army and finding Hussein proved easier than restoring order to the country.

Helped by a growing chorus of disapproval of the Iraq war, Barack Obama secured the American presidency in 2008. Following through on his campaign promise, President Obama announced plans to end the Iraq war and refocus attention on Afghanistan. The Democratic president ended the Iraq occupation in 2011 despite the fact that ethnic and religious tensions were still roiling the country, and announced that American troops would withdraw from Afghanistan in 2014. In 2011, U.S. forces finally succeeded in finding and killing Osama bin Laden, but terrorism remained a global concern.

ISLAMIC MILITANCY

In spite of the war on terror, Islamic militancy has gained a strong foothold in many parts of the world, and some radical Islamists were prepared to employ violence against secular governments in their regions as well as against western influences. Elections in Iraq under American occupation were won by sectarian and regionalist parties only partially committed to including other ethnic and religious groups in the government. In Afghanistan, American and NATO troops have weakened al-Qaeda, but the Taliban remains a significant force. In Pakistan, militant groups, long supported and used by the military in its proxy wars in Kashmir and Afghanistan, have grown, with some even turning against the regime itself in order to impose their radical agenda. Syria descended into a violent civil war, pitting the Assad regime against a variety of foes. Millions have been displaced and, as of summer 2014, at least 400,000 killed. Sunni militants, expelled from an alliance with al-Qaeda for excessive brutality, which they called Islamic State in Iraq and Syria (ISIS), took advantage of the United States withdrawal from Iraq and the civil war in Syria to dramatically increase the level of violence in the region. Unlike al-Qaeda, ISIS systematically targeted fellow Muslims, especially Shiites, and endeavored to control territory rather than promote global jihad. ISIS activities in Iraq necessitated increased military involvement of the United States and its allies in the region.

At the most general level, the appeal of radical Islam is connected to globalization. Confronting a world transformed and woven ever so tightly by economic, political, and cultural forces larger than the nation, the radical Islamists offer a return to the fundamental elements of the Muslim faith as a global alternative to what they consider as modern, Western, and un-Islamic influences.

Local conditions have conspired to lend traction to this global vision. In the Arab world, with the exception of oil-rich Persian Gulf states, poverty and economic insecurity are widespread. The long domination of the region by oppressive and dictatorial regimes has bred discontent that, in the absence of democratic institutions, finds an outlet in radical Islam. The continuing plight of Palestinians is a source of fury against Israel and its principal ally, the United States. Many in the Asian and African world see the recent actions of the United States and western powers through the memory of their previous colonial and imperial history. This is also true in Europe itself, where Muslim citizens see the exclusion and discrimination they endure as a continuation of the colonial past. Thus, in many ways, militant Islam has contributed to uncertainty in the global political environment in the twenty-first century.

CRISIS AND INEQUALITY IN THE GLOBAL ECONOMY

Beginning in 2007, the world economy fell into crisis. The problem began in the financial sector, the most globally interlinked of all. Seeking new sources of profits, investors from around the world poured their money into riskier and riskier investments—many of which were so complex that not even the regulators in charge of monitoring the financial sector could understand them.

One of the most enticing of these risky bets was real estate in the United States, where a frenzy of investment in the early 2000s created a "bubble" that drove real estate prices to

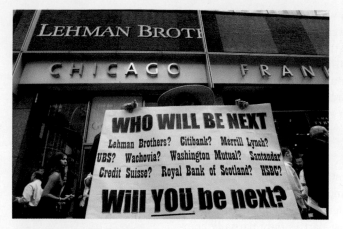

Global Financial Crisis When the major investment firm Lehman Brothers declared bankruptcy in September 2008, the world's increasingly integrated financial system teetered on the brink of collapse. Although massive government interventions kept the system afloat, they did not prevent severe downturns and sharply rising unemployment rates.

an unsustainable level. The bubble eventually burst, leading to a plunge in property values. This meant not only that banks and financial agencies were burdened with increasingly worthless assets but also that millions of homeowners could not afford to make their mortgage payments or sell their homes. Massive defaults on loans ripped through the world financial system. By the summer of 2008, there was a worldwide panic, and the banking system nearly collapsed. As it became more difficult to borrow money and consumers stopped spending, factories shut down and stores went bankrupt. Layoffs, higher taxes, and reduced consumption resulted in the contraction of developed economies and skyrocketing unemployment.

The financial crisis has brought signs of gathering discontent. In Europe, where, at last, economic and political integration within the EU had seemed to promise an end to conflict between states, the crisis created new tensions. In Greece, radical new parties arose to protest austerity measures or to take out frustrations on immigrants, and many blamed the richer nations, especially the Germans, for having profited from the creation of the eurozone at the expense of the poorer nations. For the first time in decades, vehement nationalist slogans came into wide circulation, and some commentators predicted that the common currency (the euro)—and perhaps even the European Union—in its current form would not last.

Even as economies emerged from the crisis, economic inequality among individuals and regions led to new challenges. The very same ongoing integration of the world economy that globalized the economic crisis also produced fresh wealth across the world. Brazil, Russia, China, India, Vietnam, Indonesia, and South Africa all became more prosperous than they were even just a decade before, leaving other states far behind economically. Capital, technology, and media brought the world together ever more closely. The movement of ideas and images across national borders accelerated. Social media like Facebook provided new lines of communication and connections, particularly among the young. New aspirations for employment, prosperity, consumption, and political expression appeared.

However, the growth of prosperity and wealth around the world was highly unequal and accompanied by an unprecedented rise in the power and influence of corporations and financial institutions. Even as a global middle class came into being, inequality deepened. The "Occupy" movement that emerged in 2011, first in New York (as "Occupy Wall Street," then in other cities in the United States and several other countries, protested the growing gap between the rich and everyone else. Claiming to speak on behalf of the "99 percent" against the richest 1 percent, the Occupy activists, consisting largely of young people, railed against the banks and financial institutions that had benefited from government help during the economic crisis. Although the movement ran out of steam by the end of the year, it succeeded in inserting the growing inequality into political discussions.

Occupy Wall Street Inspired by other stirrings around the world, this largely national movement was fueled by methods as novel as social media and as traditional as a sit-in. Here an Occupy Wall Street rally joins a labor union demonstration outside the New York County Courthouse in 2011.

GLOBAL WARMING

Global warming is just one of numerous environmental issues that have gained prominence in the new millennium. Leaders in Japan, Europe, and the United States acknowledge that humankind is contributing to, if not causing, the increase in temperatures and that climate change will bring catastrophic storms, severe droughts, famine, and flooding. In 2004, for example, an Indian Ocean earthquake, known as a tsunami, with its epicenter off the coasts of Indonesia, struck the west coast of Sumatra, Indonesia, bringing an estimated 168,000 deaths. In the United States, Hurricane Katrina in 2005 left much of New Orleans and the Mississippi Gulf Coast in ruins. Despite growing recognition that the planet needs healing, achieving a consensus on actions to address global warming has proved difficult.

The United States, the European Union, and Japan

While the global challenges of the twenty-first century touched virtually every corner of every region of the world, countries and regions experienced specific local changes, which were often related to globalizing forces. As we saw in the preceding section, the global political and economic crises of the early 2000s had a deep impact on the United States. Americans moved from supporting Bush to electing Barack Obama and tiring of the wars in Iraq and Afghanistan. The recession following the economic crisis resulted in soaring foreclosures, dwindling tax revenues, and millions thrown out of work. As the Obama administration sought to cope with the economic crisis, it encountered a conservative backlash. Europe and Japan also experienced internal divisions over social, economic, and political issues.

A CHANGING WESTERN EUROPE

Despite serious internal divisions, Europe's continuing integration was striking. By 2010, the European Union had widened its membership to twenty-seven countries, including ten nations that formerly had been part of the Soviet bloc. The process of EU unification did face some challenges and reversals. For example, as the European Union absorbed more and more of the territories that the Soviet Union had once controlled, the Russian president, Vladimir Putin, reacted by annexing Crimea in the Ukraine in 2014 and kept up constant pressure on eastern Ukraine, where many Russian-speaking and pro-Russian groups lived. In addition, voters in France and the Netherlands rejected the EU constitution. Still, viewed against the backdrop of twentieth-century total wars and genocides, it is remarkable that member states could bind themselves together in a union to which each relinquished significant degrees of sovereignty.

DEMOGRAPHIC ISSUES

One threat to future peace and prosperity in Europe—and the United States and Japan—is the interlocking set of issues posed by aging and immigration. Women in the European Union would have to bear 2 children on average to maintain its population of 500 million people, but women in the union now average only 1.5 offspring. Adding to demographic and labor pressures is the aging of the European population (see Chapter 21). With the percentage of elderly Europeans rising rapidly, sustaining the present workers-to-retirees ratio and paying for the region's burgeoning number of pensioners will require the European Union to attract and employ around 15 million immigrants annually.

That number has not been reached. European populations have been boosted by millions of immigrants, but sustainable economic growth has proven elusive. In prior generations, immigrants traveled from poor regions within Europe and farther afield to high-wage areas, and they left when work disappeared. After the oil crisis of the 1970s, however, the unemployed have stayed in Europe rather than returning "home," afraid of losing benefits and the right to return. A major part of immigration to Europe today consists of family reunifications, the arrival of dependents instead of workers, for whom there are no jobs. These immigrants, their children, and now grandchildren—many of them citizens—often live in impoverished circumstances; they face pervasive discrimination and periodic waves of xenophobic hostility directed especially against Muslims, who make up the majority of new arrivals. Islam now represents the fastest-growing religion in Europe, giving rise to anxiety over political disharmony based on ethnic and religious differences.

Europe is not alone in confronting the problems of an aging population and the integration of immigrants. As its baby-boom generation ages, the United States faces a similar imbalance between retirees and workers that endangers its Social Security system. Likewise, the flood of immigrants, particularly from Asia and Latin America, continues to shift the nation's ethnic composition. According to U.S. Census Bureau projections, in 2010 people of Latin American descent in the United States numbered nearly 48 million (about 15.5 percent of the population). The presence of so many Spanish-speakers troubles those who think the United States should remain an English-speaking country, and the degree to which immigrants should be required to assimilate remains a contentious issue. (For a global look at population growth and life expectancies, see Maps E.1 and E.2.)

In many respects, the dilemma of aging presses hardest of all today on Japan. Like Europeans and North Americans, the Japanese are marrying later and having fewer children. Japan's female population now averages barely 1.37 children, compared with nearly 3.7 in 1950. At the same time, Japanese life expectancy has reached eighty-five, the highest in the world, which further tilts the nation's age pyramid. In 1970 the elderly (those over age sixty-five) represented around 7 percent of the population; in 2005 it reached 20 percent, and is expected to hit 40 percent by 2050. Analysts surmise that Japan's population peaked at around 128 million and might decline to perhaps 90 million by 2050. Such a downturn bodes ill for Japan's dynamic economy, which is currently the world's third largest in terms of total GDP, China having moved into second place in 2012.

Like Europe and North America, Japan relies on immigrants to fill out its labor force. In the 1960s, the nation's booming economy experienced labor shortages, but neither the government nor major corporations chose to invite in foreign laborers. They preferred automation or recruitment of workers of Japanese descent from abroad. By the 1980s, however, deepening labor shortages and the yen's rising value led to an expanded dependence on immigrant workers. Recent estimates put the number of foreign nationals in Japan at nearly 2 million, or around 1.5 percent of the total population. Most of them hail from the Korean peninsula, the Philippines, Indochina, Brazil, and Iran, countries with a surplus of skilled workers.

ANTI-IMMIGRANT SENTIMENTS

In Europe, where unemployment rates remain higher than in Japan or North America, the political reaction against immigration has been sharpest. Far-right groups have demanded that immigration be halted or "foreigners" expelled. Support levels vary in each country, but across Europe the far right's electoral base appears to be around 15 percent; in some countries it is above 25 percent. The Freedom Party in Austria and the Northern

League and National Alliance in Italy regularly place cabinet representatives in coalition governments. Ultraright forces such as France's National Front, Denmark's People's Party, and the League of Polish Families sometimes pressure governing coalitions to slow EU integration and immigration, especially from Muslim countries.

In recent years, anti-immigrant sentiments in general and anti-Muslim ones in particular have risen in the wake of violent episodes. In Holland, the grisly murder of filmmaker Theo van Gogh by Mohammed Bouyeri in 2004 set off a national debate. Bouyeri claimed he was fulfilling his duty as a Muslim by killing van Gogh, who had made a film about the abuse of Muslim women. Following the assassination, many in Holland questioned the nation's traditional tolerance of diversity and expressed concern that Muslims were too alien in their values to ever fit in Dutch society. France confronted similar dilemmas after rioting rocked a series of poor neighborhoods in 2005, notably in Paris, protesting police brutality and the country's failure to offer equal opportunity to all. The riots also fed a nativist backlash that often blamed Muslims for the country's problems. Nicolas Sarkozy, France's interior minister at the time, spoke of power-scrubbing the "scum" from poor neighborhoods and ordered the deportation of immigrants convicted of rioting, while Jean-Marie Le Pen, leader of the far-right National Front, demanded that even naturalized citizens arrested as rioters be stripped of their citizenship.

Still more alarming to the Europeans' sense of well-being were several deadly terrorist attacks. A series of bombings of commuter trains in Madrid killed 191 people and wounded more than 2,000; in 2005, terrorists struck London's subways, leaving dozens dead and hundreds injured. In both cases, authorities pinned responsibility on al-Qaeda. But investigators also alleged that the operations were the work of Muslims who had resided in Spain or Britain for some time, which sparked doubts about the integration of all immigrants into European society. Those fears were exacerbated in May 2013 when a pair of British-born men who had converted to Islam ran down an off-duty soldier with a car, stabbed him, and hacked him to death with knives and a cleaver. Ever since the oil crisis of the 1970s, and especially since the economic crisis that began in 2007, all of the wealthiest countries in the world have struggled to compensate for aging populations with foreign migration and then dealt with xenophobic backlashes and conflict between entrenched, entitled citizens and unentitled immigrants.

China, India, and Russia

Fueling anti-immigrant fires in Europe, Japan, and North America is the increasing number of jobs being "outsourced" to China, India, and other countries. In the past, businesses had turned to immigrants to fill low-wage positions (and to keep all wages down). But at the end of the twentieth and the beginning of the twenty-first centuries, it has become more economical to relocate manufacturing to places where cheap labor is already available.

ECONOMIC GLOBALIZATION AND POLITICAL EFFECTS

In the new millennium, business mobility is not limited to low-skilled and low-wage jobs. Technological advances—particularly in computers and communication—have enabled all sorts of enterprises to operate from almost any point on the globe. No longer do educated workers have to leave India and China for employment in Europe or North America, because it is increasingly cost-effective for corporations to shift certain operations to those

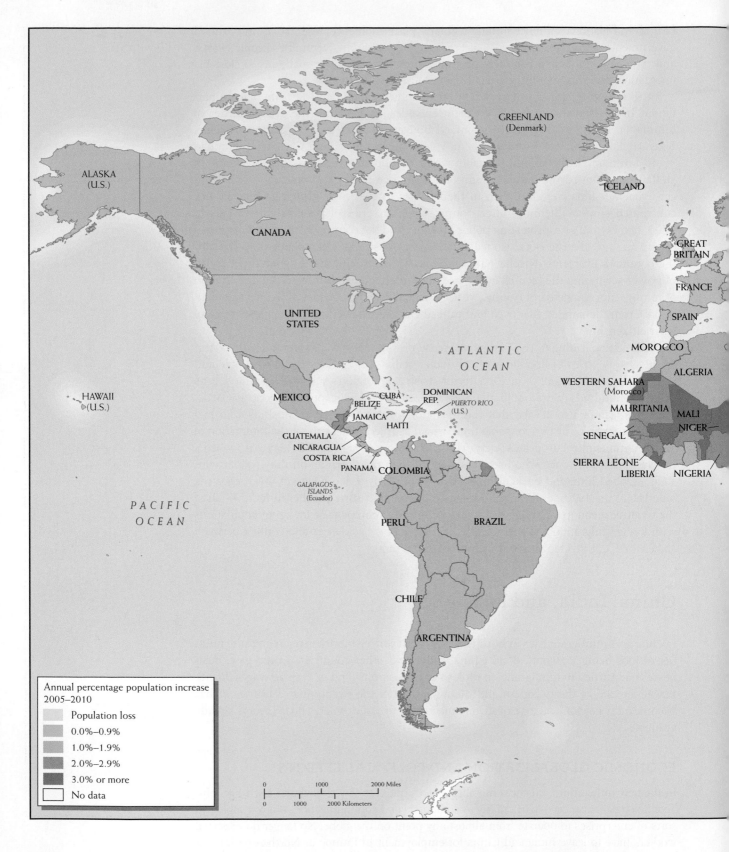

Annual percentage population increase
2005–2010

Population loss

0.0%–0.9%

1.0%–1.9%

2.0%–2.9%

3.0% or more

No data

MAP E.1 | Population Growth, 2005–2010

Strong demographic patterns at the beginning of the twenty-first century pose major problems for the industrialized societies of western Europe, North America, and Japan. As life expectancy increases and population growth slows, these regions' economies face labor shortages that have fueled immigration.

- According to this map and Map E.2, which regions of the world are prime candidates for sending migrants to the industrialized world?

- What cultural and political dilemmas does this phenomenon create?

- Which states within the industrialized world do you think have created the best environment for immigrant residents?

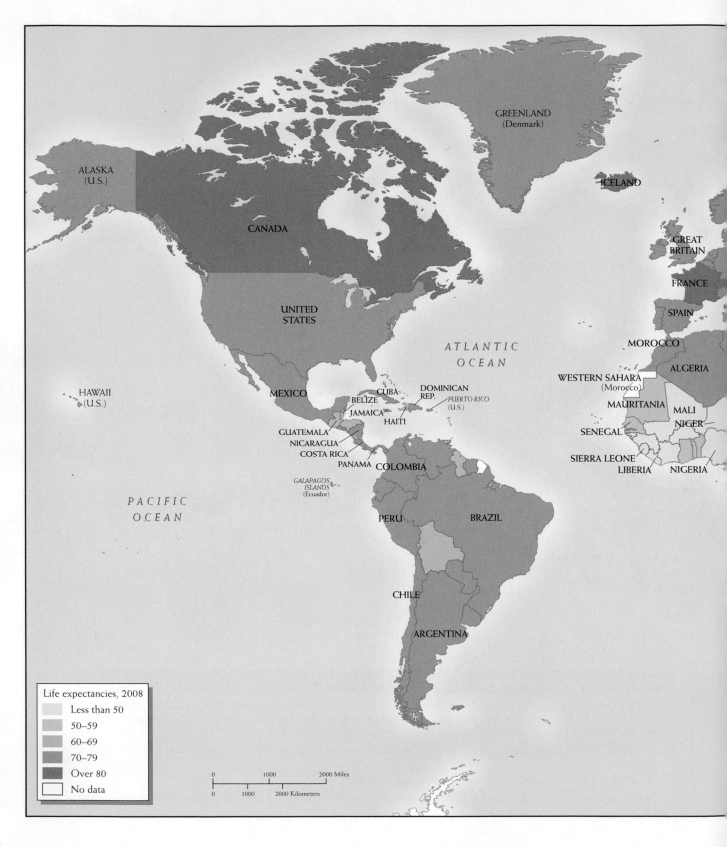

ALASKA
(U.S.)

GREENLAND
(Denmark)

ICELAND

CANADA

GREAT
BRITAIN

FRANCE

SPAIN

UNITED
STATES

ATLANTIC
OCEAN

MOROCCO

WESTERN SAHARA
(Morocco)

ALGERIA

HAWAII
(U.S.)

MEXICO

CUBA

BELIZE

JAMAICA

DOMINICAN
REP.

PUERTO RICO
(U.S.)

HAITI

MAURITANIA

MALI

NIGER

SENEGAL

GUATEMALA

NICARAGUA

COSTA RICA

PANAMA

COLOMBIA

SIERRA LEONE

LIBERIA

NIGERIA

*GALAPAGOS
ISLANDS*
(Ecuador)

PACIFIC
OCEAN

PERU

BRAZIL

CHILE

ARGENTINA

Life expectancies, 2008

Less than 50

50–59

60–69

70–79

Over 80

No data

0   1000   2000 Miles

0   1000   2000 Kilometers

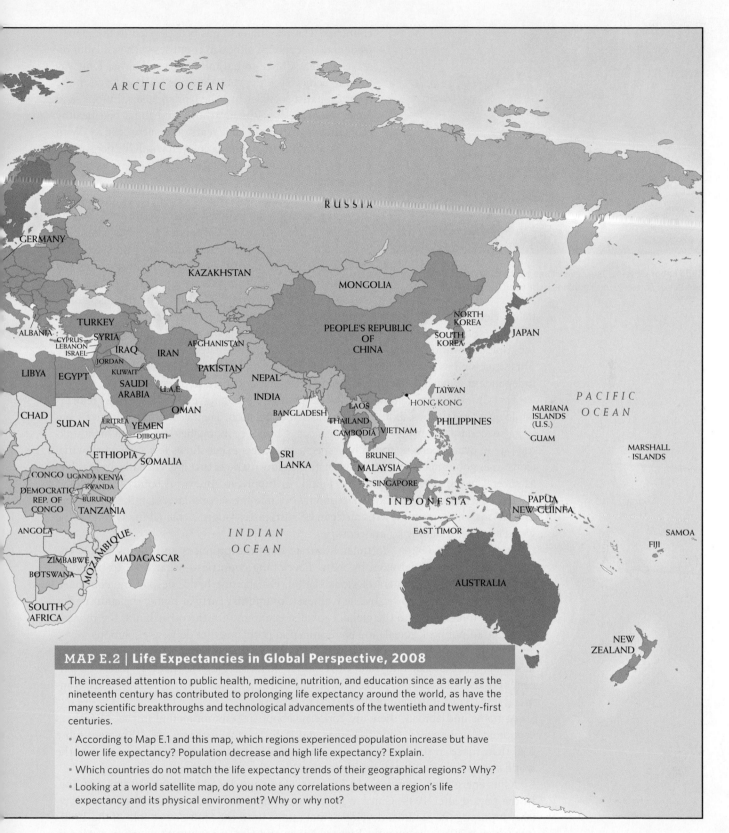

MAP E.2 | Life Expectancies in Global Perspective, 2008

The increased attention to public health, medicine, nutrition, and education since as early as the nineteenth century has contributed to prolonging life expectancy around the world, as have the many scientific breakthroughs and technological advancements of the twentieth and twenty-first centuries.

• According to Map E.1 and this map, which regions experienced population increase but have lower life expectancy? Population decrease and high life expectancy? Explain.

• Which countries do not match the life expectancy trends of their geographical regions? Why?

• Looking at a world satellite map, do you note any correlations between a region's life expectancy and its physical environment? Why or why not?

Child Labor Girls in a Javanese village work in a factory transferring bundles of cotton yarn to bobbins to be used in handlooms.

countries. The playing field has been leveled in the globalized market economy, although countries with vast labor reserves such as China, India, and Russia still have a long way to go to achieve the per capita income levels enjoyed in the older capitalist societies like the United States, Europe, and Japan. Nonetheless, Russia, China, and India had healthy economic growth in the first years of the new century. With oil prices running high, Russia enjoyed windfall energy revenues that boosted budget and trade surpluses and expanded personal incomes.

At the same time that Russia's economy is opening to the world, however, its political system seems to be closing in on itself. In addressing the anarchy of the Yeltsin era (see Chapter 21), president Vladimir Putin presided over the repossession of television stations from billionaires and the reassignment of other private properties to the state (or to his colleagues from the former KGB). He also eliminated elections for regional executives and restricted nongovernmental organizations receiving foreign financing. In short, Russia's economy is now more firmly connected to the capitalist world, but its political system remains dominated by the executive branch. This situation has dashed hopes for the eventual consolidation of a real legislature and an independent judiciary that the Gorbachev-Yeltsin era seemed to promise.

The Chinese have followed a similar path, encouraging market economic reforms while quashing the possibilities for political liberalization. Their economic strategies seem to be successful. Over the last three decades, China's economy has grown at a breathtaking rate of over 9 percent annually, a spectacular ascent that shows few signs of slowing. Consumer goods made in China dominate so many markets that it is virtually impossible, as several newspaper reporters have found, to supply an American family's needs on a "China-free" diet. In 2012 China's economy became the second largest in the world, and projections—if current growth rates can be sustained—suggest that China will have the world's largest economy by midcentury.

In many ways, China's fortunes illustrate both the promises and the pitfalls of the economic reforms undertaken by many developing countries—what used to be called the Third World—in the era of globalization. On the one hand, despite the continued monopoly of political power by the Chinese Communist Party at home, the country has been fully integrated into the global capitalist economy. On the other hand, the reforms have caused political, social, and environmental problems that defy easy solutions.

The gap between rich and poor in China's more economically developed urban areas has widened at an alarming rate. Government statistics indicate that the richest 10 percent of households own 45 percent of private urban wealth, while the poorest tenth command less than 1.4 percent of the wealth in the cities.

At home and abroad, there are concerns about the environmental impact of China's economic development. China's homes and factories, for instance, use 40 percent more coal than those in the United States, and Chinese city dwellers suffer from some of the world's worst smog and least healthy air quality.

As its energy consumption and economy have soared, so has China's global standing. In the period after 1949, China was the eager junior partner to the Soviet Union, slavishly imitating the Stalinist developmental model until the Sino-Soviet split of the 1960s (see Chapter 20). Subsequently, Richard Nixon and Henry Kissinger's courting of Mao in 1972 opened up a global option for China that Mao's successors have exploited. China's shift in foreign policy orientation from an alliance with the Soviet Union to better relations with the United States has arguably been the most important geopolitical realignment in the contemporary world.

Moreover, China has become the number one trading partner with almost every country in Asia, displacing the United States. It has even become the top trading partner with Brazil as well as many countries in Africa. China has also replaced the United States as the largest customer for Saudi Arabian oil. China-India economic relations have strengthened, too. Although China faces numerous challenges, from environmental degradation to an aging population, it has regained the enormous global weight it held for centuries up to the eighteenth century. In fact, commentators have begun to speculate that China's authoritarian capitalism could be a model for other countries seeking rapid economic development without political liberalization.

INTERNAL DIVISIONS, EXTERNAL RIVALRIES

Internal divisions and external rivalries threaten to undo many benefits of economic globalization in India, China, and Russia. For example, in India a coalition led by the Bharatiya Janata Party (BJP), the Hindu nationalist party, embraced market liberalization after coming to power in 1998 and again in 2014. Over the five years that followed the triumph of the BJP, the government opened India to the global market economy with spectacular economic results. Growth rates topped 7 percent annually, and India's stock market boomed. India is now a favorite destination for the flow of international capital, particularly in the information technology sector.

At the same time that the BJP-led government promoted market reforms, it also championed *Hindutva* (Hinduness) as the bedrock of Indian identity. The dark side of that nationalism erupted in February 2002 after sixty Hindus perished in a fire that consumed a train compartment. A rumor immediately spread, authenticated by the BJP government in Gujarat, that Muslims and a "foreign hand" were responsible. For the next few months, Hindu mobs went on a rampage, burning Muslim homes and hacking the residents to death. Newspapers reported that government leaders and the police force assisted in this carnage or looked the other way as over 2,000 Muslims lost their lives.

The ongoing tension with neighboring Pakistan poses additional problems. Flexing its nationalist muscle, the Indian government exploded a nuclear device in 1998. Pakistan responded by exploding its own bombs, casting an ominous shadow over the two nations' unresolved conflict over Kashmir. In Kashmir, terrorist violence repeatedly disturbed the peace and brought the nuclear-armed neighbors close to a potentially devastating war. The tension between the two countries escalated in 2008 when a small band of terrorists from Pakistan carried out raids in Mumbai, slaughtering many civilians and security personnel before being subdued.

India and Pakistan appear to have taken a step away from that brink, in part because national elections in 2004

Hindu-Muslim Tensions In 2002, Gujarat was consumed by sectarian riots set off by a train fire in which fifty-nine Hindu pilgrims died. Although an Indian government investigation concluded that the fire was accidental, the incident sparked an orgy of violence by Hindu mobs against Muslims. Shown here is an angry right-wing Hindu party activist.

returned a coalition headed by the Congress Party to power in India. Its victory represented a setback to the Hindu nationalist effort to define India's identity in singular terms—at least for the time being.

Projecting recent trends into the future, many observers forecast a rearrangement of the world's economic order, with China and India especially moving to the fore during the twenty-first century. Yet China, India, and Russia, like other parts of the world, have not escaped from their pasts. These societies too struggle with widening internal divisions and potentially devastating external rivalries. (For a global look at hunger and disparities in income, see Maps E.3 and E.4.)

The Middle East, Africa, and Latin America

In the Middle East and Africa, it is hard to find signs of enduring peace or general prosperity, and although some countries in Latin America have enjoyed strong economic performances, others are among the poor nations of the world.

THE ARAB SPRING

The trigger for what became known as the Arab Spring occurred on December 17, 2010, with a seemingly futile act of a twenty-six-year-old Tunisian vegetable vendor and father of eight who set himself on fire outside a provincial office to protest constant police harassment. This singular act aroused the entire population of Tunisia against the ruling elite. Not only had the police confiscated Mohammed Bouazizi's vegetable stand, and not for the first time, but a policewoman had slapped him in the face. In explaining his decision to take his life, his sister exclaimed, "[I]n Sidi Bouzidi [where he resided] those with no connections and no money for bribes are humiliated and insulted and not allowed to live." As the story circulated through the country, large numbers poured out into the streets, demanding an end to the long-term dictatorship of Zine al-Abidine Ben Ali, who had taken over from Habib Bourguiba, Tunisia's president from independence in 1956 until 1978. The catchword of the protesters was "*dégage*," get out. With the army refusing to suppress the dissenters and the security police overwhelmed, Ben Ali took the only way open to him. He departed for Saudi Arabia on January 14, 2011.

Young Egyptian radicals watched events in Tunisia with growing interest. After all, if the Tunisians could get rid of their dictator, why not the Egyptians? On January 25, 2011, ironically a holiday to honor Egypt's police forces, by now an object of people's hatred, Egyptians of all backgrounds and ages assembled in Cairo's major plaza, Midan al-Tahrir, or Liberation Square, to let Egypt's president, Hosni Mubarak, know that he was no longer wanted. Their watchword, *irhal*, meaning "scram" in Arabic, expressed the protesters' contempt for him and his rule. On February 11, 2011, just three weeks after the first mass demonstration, Hosni Mubarak left office, turning the reins of power over to the Supreme Command of the Armed Forces.

The ouster of Ben Ali and Mubarak sent shock waves of excitement throughout the Arab world. Decades of pent-up rage could no longer be contained. An outpouring of protests occurred in all of the Arab world's major cities. The demands were consistent—the end of repression, the establishment of democratic institutions, and the ousting of rulers who had stayed in power too long and who did not represent the will of the people. The results were astonishing. Monarchs in Jordan and Morocco promised new constitutions. Bahraini Shiites successfully demanded a new constitution from their Sunni king, and Ali Saleh, ruler of Yemen since 1978, fled the country. Even Muammar Qaddafi, the Libyan strongman, in power since ousting King Idris in 1969, felt the sting of protest, though his ouster and eventual execution on October 20, 2011, in the city of Sirte, owed as much to NATO air power as it did to the rebel army that rose up to unseat him.

Although much of the world had misunderstood the causes of these uprisings, they were not hard to discern after the fact. In the first place, Arab populations, 60 percent of whom were under thirty years of age and had known no other rulers, resented the fact that the wave of democratic reforms that had swept through Russia, much of eastern and central Europe, and large parts of sub-Saharan Africa had passed them by. They saw no reason why they, too, should not have leaders who represented their wishes rather than rigged elections and fraudulent referendums that supported the wishes of the ruling elites. The young came to be known as the generation in waiting—waiting for jobs that never seemed to appear; waiting to have enough money to move out of their parents' homes; and waiting to get married and start families. The fact that Hafez al-Assad had passed power to his son, Bashar al-Assad in Syria, and Hosni Mubarak was grooming his son, Gamal, heightened the rage. Although the uprisings often took names that suggested peaceful protest—the Jasmine Revolution in Tunisia followed by the White Revolution in Egypt—in reality these outbursts reflected deep-seated and long-standing fury at rulers who were repressive, corrupt, and unresponsive to their people.

The dictatorships and monarchies had lost control over the media. The Qatari television station and newspaper, Al Jazeera, founded in 1995, became an open forum for all kinds of opinions. One of its most dramatic and widely quoted programs featured an intense discussion about whether the Arab populations did not have the right like those in the West to criticize their leaders. In addition, mobile phones, Facebook, Twitter, and other social media all helped dissenters communicate with one another and enabled groups to organize large assemblies outside the purview of the state.

The early results led euphoric protesters to believe that they could create new and more open societies. Dictators were ousted, free elections were held, and new constitutions were promised. But the progress was hard to sustain. In Tunisia, which thus far has accomplished more than the other states, a moderate Muslim Brotherhood party, al-Nahda, won control of parliament. Egypt, too, held elections that were won by the Muslim Brotherhood party, Justice and Development, but nullified by the courts. It also elected a Muslim Brotherhood president, Muhammad Morsi, who in an effort to be seen as a ruler of all the people resigned from the Brotherhood. Yet President Morsi failed to establish an inclusive government and was ousted by Egypt's military leader, General Abdel-Fattah el-Sisi, who was commander in chief of the Egyptian army and minister of defense in the Morsi government. On June 4, 2014, el-Sisi was elected president, promising to restore order to Egypt and imprisoning a large number of Muslim Brothers.

By far the most lethal outcome of the Arab Spring has occurred in Syria, where protesters, seeking the ouster of president Bashar al-Assad, have formed a free Syrian army, gained international recognition for their movement, and led protests that have resulted in violent confrontation with Assad's forces. To date, more than 400,000 Syrians have lost their lives in the conflict.

Although Bashar al-Assad remains in power and another Egyptian general rules Egypt, the forces unleashed by the Arab Spring are still at work. The ideals enunciated by the protesters—open societies, representative of the people, promoting economic progress—are still vibrant in the region.

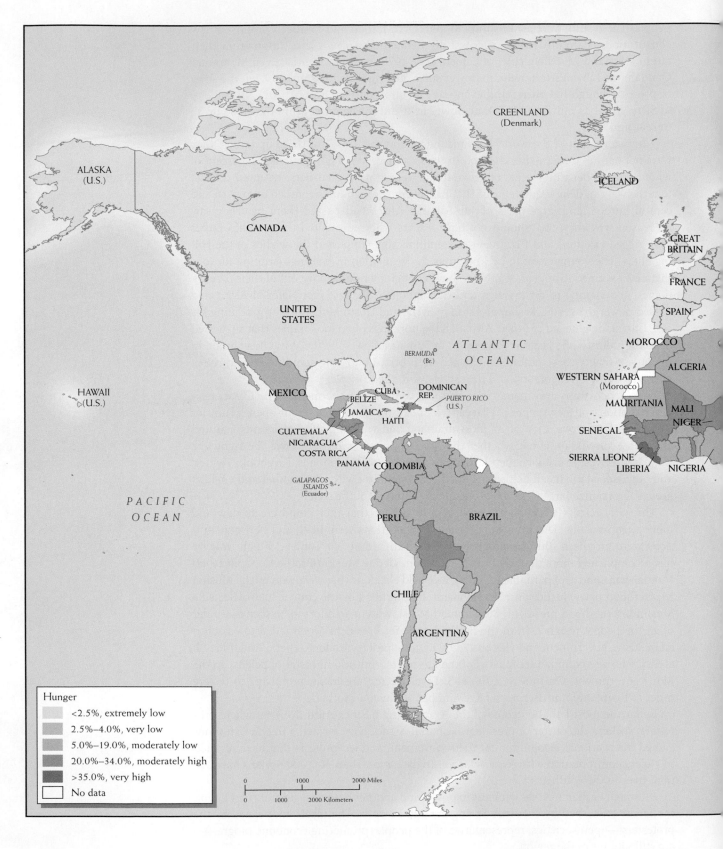

GREENLAND
(Denmark)

ICELAND

ALASKA
(U.S.)

GREAT
BRITAIN

FRANCE

CANADA

SPAIN

MOROCCO

UNITED
STATES

ATLANTIC
OCEAN

BERMUDA
(Br.)

WESTERN SAHARA
(Morocco)

ALGERIA

HAWAII
(U.S.)

MEXICO

CUBA

DOMINICAN
REP.

PUERTO RICO
(U.S.)

MAURITANIA

MALI
NIGER

BELIZE

JAMAICA

HAITI

SENEGAL

GUATEMALA
NICARAGUA
COSTA RICA
PANAMA

COLOMBIA

GALAPAGOS
ISLANDS
(Ecuador)

SIERRA LEONE
LIBERIA

NIGERIA

PACIFIC
OCEAN

PERU

BRAZIL

CHILE

ARGENTINA

Hunger

	<2.5%, extremely low
	2.5%–4.0%, very low
	5.0%–19.0%, moderately low
	20.0%–34.0%, moderately high
	>35.0%, very high
	No data

0   1000   2000 Miles

0   1000   2000 Kilometers

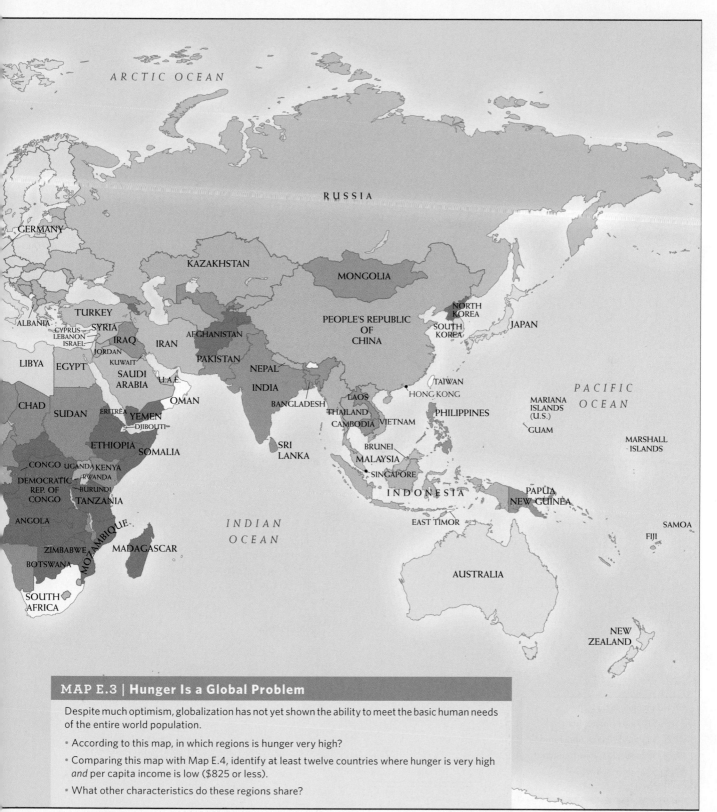

MAP E.3 | Hunger Is a Global Problem

Despite much optimism, globalization has not yet shown the ability to meet the basic human needs of the entire world population.

- According to this map, in which regions is hunger very high?

- Comparing this map with Map E.4, identify at least twelve countries where hunger is very high *and* per capita income is low ($825 or less).

- What other characteristics do these regions share?

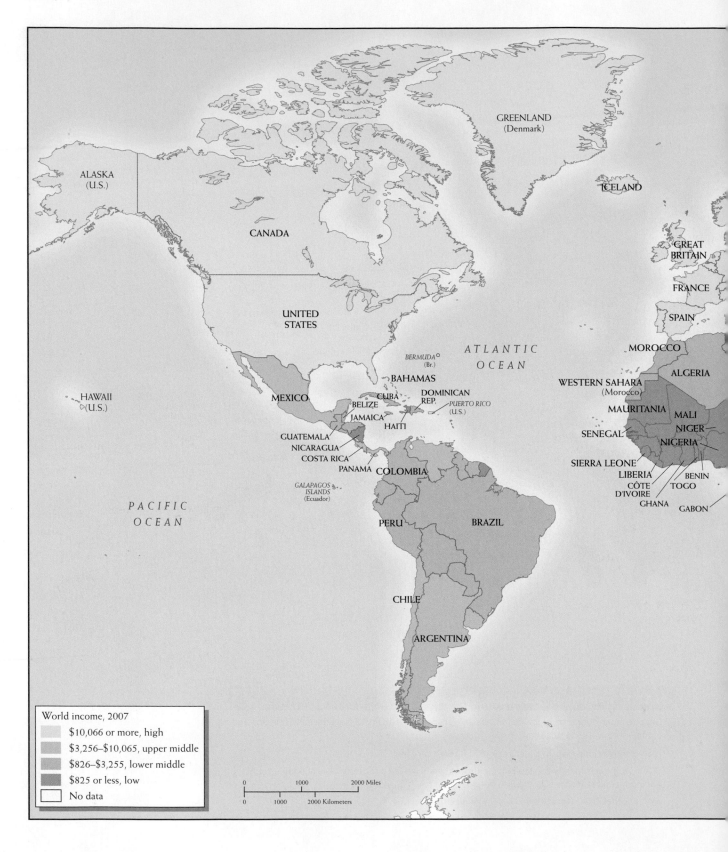

World income, 2007

$10,066 or more, high
$3,256–$10,065, upper middle
$826–$3,255, lower middle
$825 or less, low
No data

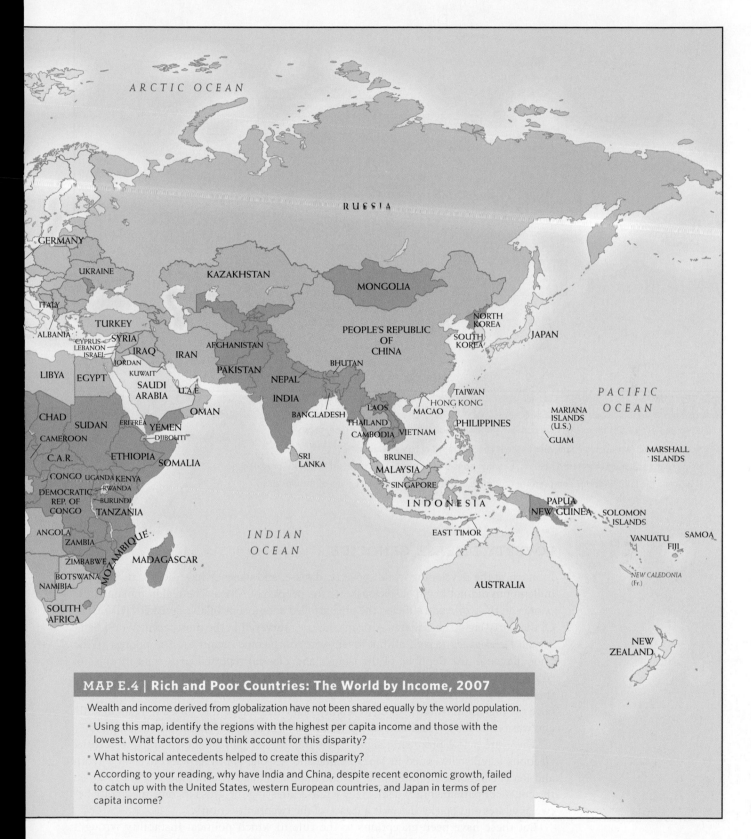

MAP E.4 | Rich and Poor Countries: The World by Income, 2007

Wealth and income derived from globalization have not been shared equally by the world population.

- Using this map, identify the regions with the highest per capita income and those with the lowest. What factors do you think account for this disparity?

- What historical antecedents helped to create this disparity?

- According to your reading, why have India and China, despite recent economic growth, failed to catch up with the United States, western European countries, and Japan in terms of per capita income?

MAP E.5 | The Number of HIV-Positive People Worldwide, 2007

The spread of HIV threatens the development of human capital in the twenty-first century.

• According to this map, which region has the highest amount of HIV infection?

• Using Maps E.3 and E.4 as reference, what connections do you see between poverty and HIV prevalence?

• How does the spread of HIV compromise economic development in poorer regions of the world?

POVERTY, DISEASE, GENOCIDE

In much of the developing world, poverty, disease, and violence have persisted. The new millennium did not begin auspiciously for the peoples of Africa. The region remained the poorest in the world and suffered the uncontrolled and uncontrollable spread of HIV/AIDS. Of the thirty-eight sub-Saharan African countries surveyed in the most recent World Bank *Annual Development Report,* all but seven were low-income countries. The poorest of the poor (Burundi, the Republic of the Congo, and Liberia) reported per capita incomes of $150 or less. Botswana, which enjoyed the second-highest per capita income level at $6,120 (behind only mineral-rich Gabon), was so devastated by HIV/AIDS that life expectancy, once the highest in Africa at close to seventy years, had tumbled to fifty-one years in 2007 and was one of the lowest in the world. (For a global look at HIV incidence, see Map E.5.)

There are a few promising signs. Ghana embraced parliamentary and presidential elections. Civil strife ended in Mozambique and Angola. South Africa convened a Truth and Reconciliation Commission to put the trauma of apartheid behind it and to stay on the course of parliamentary democracy while addressing the gross income inequality between whites and blacks that was a legacy of the twentieth century.

But these have been exceptions to the rule in which political instability wrought misery and devastation. Many of Africa's countries (Liberia, Sierra Leone, Mali, the Ivory Coast, and the Central African Republic) were torn asunder because of ethnic

AIDS Awareness (*Left*) A Gambian health worker offers AIDS awareness literature. (*Right*) Due in part to the high cost of medicines, AIDS has taken a deadly toll on Africans, prompting this memorial in the Netherlands on December 1, 2009, which was designated World AIDS Day. The crosses represented the millions of Africans unable to gain access to AIDS medications.

and personal rivalries and required foreign interventions. Nigeria finally rid itself of unwanted military dictatorial control and moved to a civil, parliamentary system. But Nigeria's democratically elected presidents have barely been able to hold the country together. The peoples of the Niger Delta in the south continue to rebel and to demand a larger share of the oil wealth that its region produces, while in the impoverished northeast a Muslim group calling itself Boko Haram (meaning no Western learning) has carried out acts of shocking violence.

In 2003, just when Africa's longest-running civil war, pitting the animist and Christian southern Sudanese against the northern Muslim peoples, had seemingly been resolved only to flare up again, a new dispute broke out in western Sudan. In the region of Darfur, the state allowed local horse-riding, nomadic tribesmen to carry out ethnic-cleansing campaigns against settled agriculturalists. This has led to perhaps the worst case of displaced peoples in the early twenty-first century, with over 2 million refugees fleeing government terror and civil war to huddle in vast, miserable camps. As in Rwanda in the 1990s (see Chapter 21), genocide has once more visited Africa. But there is some hope. In the West African country of Liberia, after years of pitiless civil war, the rival groups agreed to put down their guns in 2004. In 2005, remarkable elections swept Ellen Johnson-Sirleaf into office to become Africa's first woman president.

Liberia's President Ellen Johnson-Sirleaf after her inauguration at the Capitol Building in Monrovia, on January 16, 2006. Johnson-Sirleaf is Africa's first elected woman president; she enjoys strong U.S. support and has vowed to fight graft and rebuild her country after years of war.

DEEPENING INEQUALITIES

Globalization has contributed to economic inequality in some of the poorest parts of the world. Compared with sub-Saharan Africa, Latin America's situation is not so bleak. Globalization has had profound effects on Latin America, but it has not created an entirely new age. Across the region, the divide between haves and have-nots has widened in what has historically been the world's most

São Paulo, Brazil An aerial view of one of São Paulo's biggest slums, Favela Morumbi; Favela Morumbi borders one of the city's richest neighborhoods, also called Morumbi.

unequal region. The very rich in Buenos Aires live like the very rich in Boston; magnates of Mexico City drive the same cars, eat the same food, read the same books, and vacation in the same spots as their social cousins from New York. They send their children to private schools in the United States and the United Kingdom to join a cosmopolitan elite. For Latin American elites, globalization has been a boon to their wealth and has facilitated integration into the international circulation of goods, ideas, and people. Many, in fact, identify less and less with a particular place in the world.

Some of the same features hold for the social bottom. Being disadvantaged and poor in southern Mexico looks a lot like being on the losing end in southern Africa: In both cases, poor people cling to tiny parcels of land, migrate long distances for seasonal jobs, and fight against insensitive authorities for their basic needs. Globalization has offered few opportunities to make it at home. Old factories have closed in Rosario, Argentina, when faced with competition from Japan; maize farmers in Mexico have to contend with imports from Iowa. In many cases, thanks to globalization, the main solution to the problem is to leave—to move to the city or across borders in search of opportunities elsewhere.

Latin Americans have responded to these challenges in many ways. One sweeping trend is for voters to elect left-wing governments. Most of these are not like the rebel firebrands of the 1960s. Instead, in Brazil, Chile, Argentina, and Uruguay, left-wing governments offer policies designed to soften the blows of globalization and meet basic needs for land, schools, and decent housing. Here the same pressures of globalization that contribute to leftist electoral triumphs limit what these fledgling governments can do. Elsewhere a more nationalist and populist brand of politics has emerged, one that decries globalization altogether, including widespread protests by the poor about the vast expenditure of funds to bring the World Football Cup to Brazil. Rather than softening its effects, Brazilian leaders promise to reverse them. In Venezuela, Ecuador, and Bolivia, presidents criticize imperialism and challenge American influence. Their message is that Latin America is better off being a world apart; being together, especially if it means cozying up to the United States, implies a future of subservience and impoverishment. But as many of these leaders also stifle criticism at home, being apart does not ensure empowerment and prosperity for all, either.

The appeal of antiglobalist politics is not limited to Latin America, or even to the underdeveloped world. In the most advanced industrial societies, as well as in rapidly rising nations like China and India, programs to check globalization or buffer people from its destabilizing effects have found receptive audiences. Still, opposition to deeper global integration continues to be greatest in the poorest parts of the world, where globalization's benefits are least apparent and its costs are often lethal.

Historians are better at interpreting the past than at forecasting the future, but what seems certain is that economic, cultural, political, and environmental developments will continue to encourage exchange and interaction, fostering the integration of peoples and cultures in the new millennium. But cultural and religious diversity, local political institutions and prerogatives, economic competition and environmental particularities will also persist. Yet, the dynamic tensions that both link our worlds together and keep our worlds apart will continue to be a decisive theme in world history.

Further Readings

CHAPTER 10: BECOMING "THE WORLD," 1000–1300 CE

Allsen, Thomas, *Commodity and Exchange in the Mongol Empire: A Cultural History of Islamic Textiles* (1997). A study that uses golden brocade, the textile most treasured by Mongol rulers, as a lens through which to analyze the vast commercial networks facilitated by the Mongol conquests and control.

——, *Culture and Conquest in Mongol Eurasia* (2001). A work that emphasizes the cultural and scientific exchanges that took place across Afro-Eurasia as a result of the Mongol conquest.

Bartlett, Robert, *The Making of Europe: Conquest, Colonization and Cultural Change, 950–1350* (1993). The modes of cultural, political, and demographic expansion of feudal Europe along its frontiers, especially in eastern Europe.

Bay, Edna G., *Wives of the Leopards: Gender, Politics, and Culture in the Kingdom of Dahomey* (1998). A work that stresses the role of women in an important West African society and dips into the early history of this area.

Beach, D. N., *Shona and Zimbabwe, 900–1850: An Outline of Shona History* (1980). A good place to start for exploring the history of Great Zimbabwe.

Brooks, George E., *Landlords and Strangers: Ecology, Society, and Trade in Western Africa, 1000–1630* (1993). A survey assembled from primary sources of early West African history that stresses transregional connections.

Buzurg ibn Shahriyar of Ramhormuz, *The Book of the Wonders of India: Mainland, Sea and Islands*, ed. and trans. G. S. P. Freeman-Greenville (1981). A collection of stories told by sailors, both true and fantastic; they help us imagine the lives of sailors of the era.

Chappell, Sally A. Kitt, *Cahokia: Mirror of the Cosmos* (2002). A thorough and vivid account of the "mound people"; it explores not just what we know of Cahokia but how we know it.

Christian, David, *A Short History of Russia, Central Asia, and Mongolia*, vol. 1, *Inner Eurasia from Prehistory to the Mongol Empire* (1998). Essential reading for students interested in interconnections across the Afro-Eurasian landmass.

Curtin, Philip, *Cross-Cultural Trade in World History* (1984). A groundbreaking book on intercultural trade with a primary focus on Africa, especially the cross-Saharan trade and Swahili coastal trade.

Dawson, Christopher, *Mission to Asia* (1980). Accounts of China and the Mongol Empire brought back by Catholic missionaries and diplomats after 1240.

Foltz, Richard C., *Religions of the Silk Road: Overland Trade and Cultural Exchange from Antiquity to the Fifteenth Century* (1999). A study of the populations and the cities of the Silk Road as transmitters of culture across long distances.

Franklin, Simon, and Jonathan Shepherd, *The Emergence of Rus: 750–1200* (1996). The formation of medieval Russia between the Baltic and Black seas.

Gibb, Hamilton A. R., *Saladin: Studies in Islamic History*, ed. Yusuf Ibish (1974). A sympathetic portrait of one of Islam's leading political and military figures.

Goitein, S. D., *Letters of Medieval Jewish Traders* (1973). The classic study of medieval Jewish trading communities based on the commercial papers deposited in the Cairo Geniza (a synagogue storeroom) during the tenth and eleventh centuries; it explores not only commercial activities but also the personal lives of the traders around the Indian Ocean basin.

——, *A Mediterranean Society: An Abridgment in One Volume*, rev. and ed. Jacob Lassner (1999). A portrait of the Jewish merchant community with ties across the Afro-Eurasian landmass, based largely on the documents from the Cairo Geniza (of which Goitein was the primary researcher and interpreter).

——, "New Light on the Beginnings of the Karim Merchant," *Journal of Social and Economic History of the Orient* 1 (1958). Goitein's description of Egyptian trade.

Goitein, S. D., and Mordechai A. Friedman, *India Traders of the Middle Ages: Documents from the Cairo Geniza* (2008). Collection of documents (translated into English) and authoritative essays that explore the eleventh- and twelfth-century trade conducted by several prominent Jewish families along the Mediterranean and Indian Ocean routes.

Harris, Joseph E., *The African Presence in Asia: Consequences of the East African Slave Trade* (1971). One of the few books that looks broadly at the impact of Africans and African slavery on the societies of Asia.

Hartwell, Robert, "Demographic, Political, and Social Transformations of China, 750–1550," *Harvard Journal of Asiatic Studies* 42 (1982): 365–442. A pioneering study of the demographic changes that overtook China during the Tang and Song dynasties, which are described in light of political reform movements and social changes in this crucial era.

Historical Relations across the Indian Ocean: Report and Papers of the Meeting of Experts Organized by UNESCO at Port Louis, Mauritius, from 15 to 19 July, 1974 (1980). Excellent essays on the connections of Africa with Asia across the Indian Ocean.

Hitti, Philip, *An Arab-Syrian Gentleman and Warrior in the Period of the Crusades: Memoirs of Usāmah ibn-Munqidh* (1929). The Crusaders seen through Muslim eyes.

Hodgson, Natasha, *Women, Crusading, and the Holy Land in Historical Narrative* (2007). A book dealing with the Crusades and focusing on the place of women in them.

Holt, P. M., *The Age of the Crusades: The Near East from the Eleventh Century to 1517* (1984). The Crusades period as seen from the eastern Mediterranean and through the lens of a leading British scholar of the area.

Hymes, Robert, and Conrad Schirokauer (eds.), *Ordering the World: Approaches to State and Society in Sung Dynasty China* (1993). A collection of essays that traces the intellectual, social, and political movements that shaped the Song state and its elites.

Ibn Battuta, *The Travels of Ibn Battuta,* trans. H. A. R. Gibb (2002). A readable translation of the classic book, originally published in 1929.

Ibn Fadlan, Ahmad, *Ibn Fadlan's Journey to Russia: A Tenth Century Traveler from Baghdad to the Volga River,* trans. with commentary by Richard Frye (2005). A coherent summary of the observations of an envoy who traveled from Baghdad to Russia.

Irwin, Robert, *The Middle East in the Middle Ages: The Early Mamluk Sultanate, 1250–1582* (1986). Egypt under Mamluk rule.

Jeppie, Shamil, and Souleymane Bachir Diagne (eds.), *The Meanings of Timbuktu* (2008). New materials on the ancient Muslim city of Timbuktu by scholars who have been preserving its manuscripts and writing about its historical importance.

Lancaster, Lewis, Kikun Suh, and Chaishin Yu (eds.), *Buddhism in Koryo: A Royal Religion* (1996). A description of Buddhism at its height in the Koryo period, when the religion made significant contributions to the development of Korean culture.

Levtzion, Nehemia, and Randall L. Pouwels (eds.), *The History of Islam in Africa* (2000). A useful general survey of the place of Islam in African history.

Lewis, Bernard (trans.), *Islam: From the Prophet Muhammad to the Capture of Constantinople* (1974), vol. 2, *Religion and Society.* A fine collection of original sources that portray various aspects of classical Islamic society.

Lopez, Robert S., *The Commercial Revolution of the Middle Ages, 950–1350* (1976). An account focusing on the development around the Mediterranean of commercial practices such as the use of currency, accounting, and credit.

Lyons, Malcolm C. and D. E. P. Jackson, *Saladin: The Politics of the Holy War,* Cambridge (1984: reprint, 2001). The fundamental revisionist work on one of the more important historical figures of the time.

Maalouf, Amin, *The Crusades through Muslim Eyes,* trans. Jon Rothschild (1984). The European Crusaders as seen by the Muslim world.

Marcus, Harold G., *A History of Ethiopia* (2002). An authoritative overview of the history of this great culture.

Mass, Jeffrey, *Yoritomo and the Founding of the First Bakufu: The Origins of Dual Government in Japan* (1999). A revisionist account of how the Kamakura military leader Minamoto Yoritomo established the "dual polity" of court and warrior government in Japan.

McDermott, Joseph, *A Social History of the Chinese Book: Books and Literati Culture in Late Imperial China* (2006). The history of the book in China since the Song dynasty, with comparisons to the book's role in other civilizations, particularly the European.

McIntosh, Roderik, *The Peoples of the Middle Niger: The Island of Gold* (1988). A historical survey of an area often omitted from other textbooks.

Moore, Jerry D., *Cultural Landscapes in the Ancient Andes: Archaeologies of Place* (2005). The most recent and up-to-date analysis of findings based on recent archaeological evidence, emphasizing the importance of local cultures and diversity in the Andes.

Niane, D. T. (ed.), *Africa from the Twelfth to the Sixteenth Century,* vol. 4 of *General History of Africa* (1984). The general UNESCO history of Africa's volume on four centuries of African history. This work features the scholarship of Africans.

Oliver, Roland (ed.), *From c. 1050 to c. 1600,* vol. 3 of *The Cambridge History of Africa,* ed. J. D. Fage and Roland Oliver (1977). Another general survey of African history. This volume draws heavily on the work of British scholars.

Peters, Edward, *The First Crusade* (1971). The Crusaders as seen through their own eyes.

Petry, Carl F. (ed.), *Islamic Egypt, 640–1517,* vol. 1 of *The Cambridge History of Egypt,* ed. M. W. Daly (1998). A solid overview of the history of Islamic Egypt up to the Ottoman conquest.

Polo, Marco, *The Travels of Marco Polo*, ed. Manuel Komroff (1926). A solid translation of Marco Polo's famous account.

Popovic, Alexandre, *The Revolt of African Slaves in Iraq in the 3rd/9th Century*, trans. Leon King (1999). The account of a massive revolt against their slave masters by African slaves taken to labor in Iraq's mines and fields.

Scott, Robert, *Gothic Enterprise: A Guide to Understanding the Medieval Cathedral* (2003). The meaning and social function of religious building in medieval cities in northern Europe.

Shaffer, Lynda Norene, *Maritime Southeast Asia to 1500* (1996). A history of the peoples of the southeast fringe of the Eastern Hemisphere, up to the time that they became connected to the global commercial networks of the world.

Shimada, Izumi, "Evolution of Andean Diversity: Regional Formations (500 BCE–CE 600)," in Frank Salomon and Stuart Schwartz (eds.), *South America*, vol. 3 of *The Cambridge History of the Native Peoples of the Americas* (1999), Pt. 1, pp. 350–517. A splendid overview that contrasts the varieties of lowland and highland cultures.

Steinberg, David Joel, et al., *In Search of Southeast Asia: A Modern History* (1987). An account of the emergence of the modern Southeast Asian polities of Cambodia, Burma, Thailand, and Indonesia.

Tyerman, Christopher, *God's War: A New History of the Crusades* (2006). The balance of religious and nonreligious motivations in the Crusades.

Waley, Daniel, *The Italian City-Republics*, 3rd ed. (1988). The structures and culture of the new cities of medieval Italy.

Watson, Andrew, *Agricultural Innovation in the Early Islamic World: The Diffusion of Crops and Farming Techniques, 700–1100* (1983). An impressive study of the spread of new crops throughout the Muslim world.

CHAPTER 11: CRISES AND RECOVERY IN AFRO-EURASIA, 1300–1500

Bois, Guy, *The Crisis of Feudalism: Economy and Society in Eastern Normandy, c. 1300–1550* (1984). A good case study of a French region that illustrates the turmoil in fourteenth-century Europe.

Brook, Timothy, *Praying for Power: Buddhism and the Formation of Gentry Society in Late Ming China* (1994). An analysis of the role of a significant religious force in the political and social developments of the Ming.

Dardess, John, *A Ming Society: T'ai-ho County, Kiangsi, Fourteenth to Seventeenth Centuries* (1996). A work that covers the different changes and developments of a single locality in China through the centuries.

Dols, Michael W., *The Black Death in the Middle East* (1977). One of the few scholarly works to examine the Black Death outside Europe.

Dreyer, Edward, *Early Ming China: A Political History, 1355–1435* (1982). A useful account of the early years of the Ming dynasty.

Finkel, Caroline, *Osman's Dream: The Story of the Ottoman Empire, 1300–1923* (2005). The most authoritative overview of Ottoman history.

Hale, John, *The Civilization of Europe in the Renaissance* (1994). A beautifully crafted account of the politics, economics, and culture of the Renaissance period in western Europe.

Hodgson, Marshall, *The Venture of Islam: Conscience and History in a World Civilization*, vol. 3 (1974). A good volume on the workings of the Ottoman state.

Itzkowitz, Norman, *Ottoman Empire and Islamic Tradition* (1972). Another good book on the Ottoman state.

Jackson, Peter, *The Delhi Sultanate* (1999). A meticulous, highly specialized, political and military history.

Jackson, Peter, and Lawrence Lockhart (eds.), *The Cambridge History of Iran*, vol. 6 (1986). A volume that deals with the Timurid and Safavid periods in Iran.

Jones, E. L., *The European Miracle* (1981). A provocative work on the economic and social recovery from the Black Death.

Kafadar, Cemal, *Between Two Worlds: The Construction of the Ottoman State* (1995). A thorough reconsideration of the origins of one of the world's great land empires.

Karamustafa, Ahmed, *God's Unruly Friends: Dervish Groups in the Islamic Later Middle Period, 1200–1550* (1994). A book that describes the unorthodox Islamic activities that were occurring in the Islamic world prior to and alongside the establishment of the Ottoman and Safavid empires.

Levathes, Louise, *When China Ruled the Seas: The Treasure Fleet of the Dragon Throne, 1405–33* (1994). A book that provides a lively account of the Zheng He expeditions.

Lowry, Heath W., *The Nature of the Early Ottoman State* (2003). New perspectives on the rise of the Ottomans to prominence.

McNeill, William, *Plagues and Peoples* (1976). A pathbreaking work with a highly useful chapter on the spread of the Black Death throughout the Afro-Eurasian landmass.

Morgan, David, *Medieval Persia, 1040–1797* (1988). Contains an informative discussion of the Safavid state.

Peirce, Leslie, *The Imperial Harem: Women and Sovereignty in the Ottoman Empire* (1993). A work that describes the powerful place that imperial women had in political affairs.

Pirenne, Henri, *Economic and Social History of Medieval Europe* (1937). A classic study of the economic and social recovery from the Black Death.

Reid, James J., *Tribalism and Society in Islamic Iran, 1500–1629* (1983). A useful account of how the Mongols and other nomadic steppe peoples influenced Iran in the era when the Safavids were establishing their authority.

Singman, Jeffrey L. (ed.), *Daily Life in Medieval Europe* (1999). An introductory description of the social and material world experienced by Europeans of different walks of life.

Tuchman, Barbara W., *A Distant Mirror: The Calamitous Fourteenth Century* (1978). A book that shows, in a vigorous way, how war, famine, and pestilence devastated Europeans in the fourteenth century.

Wittek, Paul, *The Rise of the Ottoman Empire* (1958). A work that contains vital insights on the emergence of the Ottoman state amid the political chaos in Anatolia.

CHAPTER 12: CONTACT, COMMERCE, AND COLONIZATION, 1450–1600

Axtell, James, *Beyond 1492: Encounters in Colonial North America* (1992). A wonderfully informed speculation about Indian reactions to Europeans.

Brady, Thomas A., et al. (eds.), *Handbook of European History 1400–1600: Late Middle Ages, Renaissance, and Reformation, Structures and Assertions* (1996). A good synthetic survey of recent literature and historiographical debates.

Brook, Timothy, *Vermeer's Hat: The Seventeenth Century and the Dawn of the Global World* (2008). An interesting look at the connections forged across the globe through the works of a well-known European artist.

Cass, Victoria, *Dangerous Women: Warriors, Grannies, and Geishas of the Ming* (1999). An original study of Chinese female archetypes in memoirs, miscellanies, short stories, and novels.

Chaudhuri, K. N., *Trade and Civilisation in the Indian Ocean: An Economic History from the Rise of Islam to 1750* (1985). An excellent, comprehensive work that deals with the Indian Ocean economy and the appearance of European merchants there from the sixteenth century onward.

Clendinnen, Inga, *Aztecs: An Interpretation* (1991). Brilliantly reconstructs the culture of Tenochtitlán in the years before its conquest.

Crosby, Alfred W., *The Columbian Exchange: Biological and Cultural Consequences of 1492* (1972). A provocative discussion of the ecological consequences that followed the European "discovery" of the Americas.

———, *Ecological Imperialism: The Biological Expansion of Europe, 900–1900* (1986). Another important work on the ecological consequences of European expansion.

Curtin, Philip, *Cross-Cultural Trade in World History* (1984). A work stressing the role of trade and commerce in establishing cross-cultural contacts.

Febvre, Lucien, *The Problem of Unbelief in the Sixteenth Century: The Religion of Rabelais* (1982). A tour de force of intellectual history by the man who moved the study of the Reformation away from great men to the broader question of religious revival and mentalities.

Flynn, Dennis, and Arturo Giráldez (eds.), *Metals and Monies in an Emerging Global Economy* (1997). Contains several articles relating to silver and the Asian trade.

Frank, Andre Gunder, *ReOrient: Global Economy in the Asian Age* (1998). A reassessment of the role of Asia in the economic development of the world from around 1400 onward.

Glahn, Richard von, *Fountain of Fortune: Money and Monetary Policy in China, 1000–1700* (1996). Includes an excellent analysis of the history of silver in Ming China.

Gruzinski, Serge, *The Conquest of Mexico* (1993). An important work on the conquest of Mexico.

Habib, Irfan, *The Agrarian System of Mughal India* (1963). One of the best studies on the subject.

Hall, Richard Seymour, *Empires of the Monsoon: A History of the Indian Ocean and Its Invaders* (1996). A very engaging journalistic account with fabulous details.

Hodgson, Marshall, *The Venture of Islam*, vols. 2 and 3 (1974). A magisterial work that includes the Indian subcontinent in its careful study of the political and cultural history of the whole Islamic world.

Hulme, Peter, *Colonial Encounters: Europe and the Native Caribbean, 1492–1797* (1986). Presents an interesting interpretation of the encounters of Europeans and Native Americans.

Lach, Donald F., *Asia in the Making of Europe*, 5 books in 3 vols. (1965–). Perhaps the single most comprehensive and innovative guide to the European voyages of discovery.

Lockhart, James, and Stuart Schwartz, *Early Latin America* (1983). One of the finest studies of European expansion in the late fifteenth century.

McCann, James, *Maize and Grace: Africa's Encounter with a New World Crop, 1500–2000* (2005).

Melville, Elinor G. K., *A Plague of Sheep: Environmental Consequences of the Conquest of Mexico* (1994). A history of the transformation of a valley in Mexico from the Aztec period to the era of Spanish rule.

Mignolo, Walter D., *The Darker Side of the Renaissance: Literacy, Territoriality, and Colonization* (1995). Uses literary theory and literary images to present provocative interpretations of the encounter of Europeans and Native Americans.

Pagden, Anthony, *European Encounters with the New World* (1993). A complex look at the deep and lasting imprint of the New World on its conquerors.

Parker, Geoffrey, *The Military Revolution: Military Innovation and the*

Rise of the West, 1500–1800 (1996). Traces the changes in technology and tactics in the early modern period and discusses the political significance of this "revolution."

Pelikan, Jaroslav, *Reformation of Church and Dogma (1300–1700)* (1988). An important overview of major religious controversies.

Phillips, William D., and Carla Rahn Phillips, *The World of Christopher Columbus* (1992). One of the finest studies of European expansion in the late fifteenth century.

Russell-Wood, A. J. R., *The Portuguese Empire, 1415–1808* (1992). An important survey of early Portuguese exploration.

CHAPTER 13: WORLDS ENTANGLED, 1600–1750

Alam, Muzaffar, *The Crisis of Empire in Mughal North India* (1993). Represents the best of the new scholarly interpretations on the subject.

Bay, Edna, *Wives of the Leopard: Gender, Politics, and Culture in the Kingdom of Dahomey* (1998). A useful treatment of gender issues in Dahomey.

Blackburn, Robin, *The Making of New World Slavery: From the Baroque to the Modern, 1492–1800* (1997). A good place to begin when studying African slavery and the Atlantic slave trade, it compares the early expansion of the plantation systems across the Atlantic and throughout the Americas.

Calloway, Colin G., *One Vast Winter Count: The Native American West before Lewis and Clark* (2003). A sweeping survey of North American Indian histories prior to the nineteenth century.

Crossley, Pamela, *A Translucent Mirror: History and Identity in Qing Imperial Ideology* (1999). The author deals with the formation of identities such as "Manchu" and "Chinese" during the Qing period.

Eltis, David and Richardson, David, *Atlas of the Transatlantic Slave Trade* (2010). This work contains the most up-to-date data on the Atlantic slave trade, the numbers transported, where the captives came from, and where they landed.

Flynn, Dennis O., and Arturo Giraldez (eds.), *Metals and Money in an Emerging World Economy* (1997). A collection of articles about the place of silver in the world economy.

Forsyth, James, *A History of the Peoples of Siberia: Russia's North Asian Colony 1581–1990* (1992). A narrative overview of a violent history reminiscent of the western expansion of the United States.

Glahn, Richard von, *Fountains of Fortune: Money and Monetary Policy in China, 1000–1700* (1996). A discussion of the place of silver in the Chinese economy.

Halperin, Charles J., *Russia and the Golden Horde: The Mongol Impact on Medieval Russian History* (1985). A book on the rise of Muscovy, forebear of the Russian Empire, from within the Mongol realm.

Hämäläinen, Pekka, *The Comanche Empire* (2008). A book that inverts the conventional history of empires in North America by arguing that the Comanches were the most successful expansionist power in the middle of the continent during the eighteenth century.

Hattox, Ralph S., *Coffee and Coffeehouses: The Origins of a Social Beverage in the Medieval Near East* (1985). This work shows how widespread and popular coffee consumption and coffeehouses were around the world.

Huang, Ray, *1587, A Year of No Significance: The Ming Dynasty in Decline* (1981). An insightful analysis of the problems confronting the late Ming.

Lensen, George, *The Russian Push Toward Japan: Russo-Japanese Relations 1697–1875* (1959). A discussion of why and how Japan established its first border with another state and how Russia pursued its ambitions in the Pacific.

Lockhart, James, *The Nahuas After the Conquest* (1992). A landmark study of the social reorganization of Mesoamerican societies under Spanish rule.

Lovejoy, Paul, *Transformations in Slavery: A History of Slavery in Africa* (1983). An excellent discussion of African slavery.

Nakane, Chie, and Shinzaburo Oishi (eds.), *Tokugawa Japan: The Social and Economic Antecedents of Modern Japan* (1990). First-rate essays on Japanese village society, urban life, literacy, and culture.

Pamuk, Sevket, *A Monetary History of the Ottoman Empire* (2000). A discussion of the place of silver in the Ottoman Empire.

Parker, Geoffrey (ed.), *The Thirty Years' War* (1997). The standard account of the conflict and its outcomes.

Perdue, Peter C., *China Marches West: The Qing Conquest of Central Asia* (2005). This volume chronicles the expansion of the Qing Empire to its northwest, drawing comparisons to other colonial empires and their legacies.

Platonov, S. F., *Ivan the Terrible* (1986). Covers the controversies over Russia's infamous tsar.

Rawski, Evelyn, *The Last Emperors: A Social History of Qing Imperial Institutions* (1998). This volume explores the mechanisms and processes through which the Qing court negotiated its Manchu identity.

Reid, Anthony, *Charting the Shape of Early Modern Southeast Asia* (1999). A collection of articles by a leading historian of Southeast Asia.

Spence, Jonathan, and John Wills (eds.), *From Ming to Ch'ing: Conquest, Region, and Continuity in Seventeenth-Century China* (1979). Covers the various aspects of a tumultuous period of dynastic transition.

Taylor, Alan, *American Colonies: The Settling of North America* (2001). Brings together British, French, and Spanish colonial histories and shows how the fortunes of each were entangled with one another and with those of diverse Native American peoples.

Thornton, John, *Africa and Africans in the Making of the Atlantic World, 1400–1800* (1998). A wonderful discussion of how African slaves played a large role in the formation of the Atlantic world.

Thornton, John K., *The Kongolese Saint Anthony: Dona Beatriz Kimpa Vita and the Antonian Movement, 1684–1706* (1998). An excellent monograph on religious movements in the Kongo.

Toby, Ronald P., *State and Diplomacy in Early Modern Japan: Asia in the Development of the Tokugawa Bakufu* (1984). The author shows that the Japanese, far from being isolated from the outside world, engaged in vigorous and successful diplomacy.

Vilar, Pierre, *A History of Gold and Money* (1991). An excellent study of the development of the early silver and gold economies.

CHAPTER 14: CULTURES OF SPLENDOR AND POWER, 1500–1780

Axtell, James, *The Invasion of America: The Contest of Cultures in Colonial North America* (1985). Discusses the strategies of Christian missionaries in converting the Indians, as well as the success of Indians in converting Europeans.

Babaie, Sussan, *Isfahan and Its Palaces: Statecraft, Shi'ism and the Architecture of Conviviality in Early Modern Iran* (2008). An overview of the city of Isfahan, as the capital of the Safavid state.

Barmé, Geremie R., *The Forbidden City* (2008). A concise introduction to the history of one of the most important physical emblems of Chinese imperial power.

Berlin, Ira, *Many Thousands Gone: The First Two Centuries of Slavery in North America* (1998). Surveys the development of African-American culture in colonial North America.

Brook, Timothy, *The Confusions of Pleasure: Commerce and Culture in Ming China* (1999). An insightful survey of Ming society.

Clunas, Craig, *Superfluous Things: Material Culture and Social Status in Early Modern China* (1991). A good account of the late Ming elite's growing passion for material things.

Collcutt, Martin, Marius Jansen, and Isao Kumakura, *A Cultural Atlas of Japan* (1988). A sweeping look at the many different forms of Japanese cultural expression over the centuries, including the flourishing urban culture of Edo.

Darnton, Robert, *The Business of the Enlightenment: A Publishing History of the Encyclopédie, 1775–1800* (1979). The classic study of Europe's first great compendium of knowledge.

Dash, Mike, *Tulipomania: The Story of the World's Most Coveted Flower and the Extraordinary Passions It Aroused* (1999). A global perspective on and lively account of the spread of the tulip around the world as a flower signifying both beauty and status.

Elman, Benjamin A., *On Their Own Terms: Science in China, 1550–1900* (2005). A study of the development of "native" Chinese science and how the process interacted with the introduction of western science to China over the course of three and a half centuries.

Eze, Emmanuel Chukwudi (ed.), *Race and the Enlightenment: A Reader* (1997). Readings examining the idea of race in the context of the Enlightenment.

Fleischer, Cornell, *Bureaucrat and Intellectual in the Ottoman Empire: The Historian Mustafa Ali (1540–1600)* (1986). Offers good insight into the world of culture and intellectual vitality in the Ottoman Empire.

Grafton, Anthony, April Shelford, and Nancy Siraisi, *New Worlds, Ancient Texts: The Power of Tradition and the Shock of Discovery* (1995). A concise discussion of the impact of the New World on European thought.

Gutiérrez, Ramón, *When Jesus Came, the Corn Mothers Went Away: Marriage, Sexuality, and Power in New Mexico, 1500–1846* (1991). A provocative dissection of the spiritual dimensions of European colonialism in the Americas.

Harley, J. B., and David Woodward (eds.), *The History of Cartography*, vol. 2, Book 2: *Cartography in the Traditional East and Southeast Asian Societies* (1994). An authoritative treatment of the subject.

Horton, Robin, *Patterns of Thought in Africa and the West: Essays on Magic, Religion, and Science* (1993). Reflections on African patterns of thought and attitudes toward nature, which can help us understand African-American religious beliefs and resistance movements.

Keene, Donald, *The Japanese Discovery of Europe: Honda Toshiaki and Other Discoverers, 1720–1798* (1952). A study of the ways Japan managed to incorporate knowledge from the outside world with the development of national traditions.

Ko, Dorothy, *Teachers of the Inner Chambers: Women and Culture in Seventeenth-Century China* (1994). Explores the lives of elite women in late Ming and early Qing China.

Lewis, Bernard, *Race and Color in Islam* (1979). Examines the Islamic attitude toward race and color.

Morgan, Philip D., *Slave Counterpoint: Black Culture in the Eighteenth-Century Chesapeake and Lowcountry* (1998). Describes the development of African-American culture in colonial North America.

Munck, Thomas, *The Enlightenment: A Comparative Social History, 1721–1794* (2000). A wonderful survey, with unusual examples from the periphery, especially from Scandinavia and the Habsburg Empire.

Necipoglu, Gulru, *Architecture, Ceremonial, and Power: The Topkapi Palace in the Fifteenth and Sixteenth Centuries* (1991). A magnificently illustrated book that shows the enormous artistic talent that the Ottoman rulers poured into their imperial structure.

Publishing and the Print Culture in Late Imperial China (Special Issue), *Late Imperial China*, vol. 17, no. 1 (June 1996). Contains a collection of important articles with a foreword by the French cultural historian Roger Chartier.

Qaisar, Ahsan Jan, *The Indian Response to European Technology, AD 1498–1707* (1998). A meticulous, scholarly work on this little-studied subject.

Rizvi, Athar Abbas, *The Wonder That Was India*, vol. 2, *A Survey of the History and Culture of the Indian Sub-continent from the Coming of the Muslims to the British Conquest, 1200–1700* (1987). A deeply learned work in intellectual history.

Smith, Bernard, *European Vision and the South Pacific* (1985). An excellent cultural history of Cook's voyages.

Smith, Richard J., *Chinese Maps: Images of "All under Heaven"* (1996). Provides a good introduction to the history of cartography in China.

Welch, Anthony, *Shah Abbas and the Arts of Isfahan* (1973). Describes the astonishing architectural and artistic renaissance of the city of Isfahan under the Safavid ruler Shah Abbas.

Whitfield, Peter, *The Image of the World: Twenty Centuries of World Maps* (1994). A good introduction to the history of cartography in different parts of the world.

Wilks, Ivor, *Forests of Gold: Essays on the Akan and the Kingdom of Asante* (Athens, OH, 1993). A study that focuses on the Asante's drive for wealth.

Zilfi, Madeline C., *The Politics of Piety: The Ottoman Ulema in the Post-Classical Age (1600–1800)* (1988). Explores the cultural flourishing that took place within the Islamic world in this period.

CHAPTER 15: REORDERING THE WORLD, 1750–1850

Allen, Robert C., *The British Industrial Revolution in Global Perspective* (2009). The most recent and authoritative study of the industrial revolution in Britain and its implications around the world.

Anderson, Fred, *Crucible of War: The Seven Years' War and the Fate of Empire in British North America, 1754–1766* (2000). The best synthesis of the "great war for empire" that set the stage for the American Revolution.

Bayly, C. A., *Indian Society and the Making of the British Empire* (1998). A useful work on the early history of the British conquest of India.

Blackburn, Robin, *The Overthrow of Colonial Slavery, 1776–1848* (1988). Places the abolition of the Atlantic slave trade and colonial slavery in a large historical context.

Cambridge History of Egypt: Modern Egypt from 1517 to the End of the Twentieth Century, vol. 2 (1998). Volume 2 contains authoritative essays on all aspects of modern Egyptian history, including the impact of the French invasion and the rule of Muhammad Ali.

Chaudhuri, K. N., *The Trading World of Asia and the East India Company, 1660–1760* (1978). An authoritative economic history of the East India Company's operations.

Crafts, N. F. R., *British Economic Growth during the Industrial Revolution* (1985). A pioneering study that emphasizes a long-term, more gradual process of adaptation to new institutional and social circumstances.

de Vries, Jan, *Industrious Revolution: Consumer Behavior and the Household Economy, 1650 to the Present* (2008). A book on the lead-up to the industrial revolution, written by the leading economic historian who coined the term "industrious revolution."

Diamond, Jared, and James A. Robinson (eds.), *Natural Experiments of History* (2010). This book consists of eight comparative studies drawn from history, archaeology, economics, economic history, geography, and political science, covering a spectrum of approaches, ranging from a nonquantitative narrative style to quantitative statistical analyses.

Doyle, William, *The Oxford History of the French Revolution* (1990). A highly detailed discussion of the course of events.

Drescher, Seymour, *Abolition: A History of Slavery and Anti-Slavery* (2009). A recent and authoritative overview of slavery and its opponents.

Elvin, Mark, *The Retreat of the Elephants: An Environmental History of China* (2004). A study of the different ways in which China's natural environment was shaped.

Fick, Carolyn E., *The Making of Haiti: The Saint Domingue Revolution from Below* (1990). Provides a detailed account of the factors that led to the great slave rebellion on the island of Haiti at the end of the eighteenth century.

Findley, Carter, *Bureaucratic Reform in the Ottoman Empire: The Sublime Porte, 1789–1922* (1980). A useful guide to Ottoman reform efforts in the nineteenth century.

Geggus, David (ed.), *The Impact of the Haitian Revolution in the Atlantic*

World (2001). A lively effort to disentangle the effects of the Haitian Revolution from those of the French Revolution.

Hevia, James, *Cherishing Men from Afar: Qing Guest Ritual and the Macartney Embassy of 1793* (1995). Offers a definitive interpretation of the nature of Sino-British conflict in the Qing period.

Hobsbawm, Eric, *Nations and Nationalism since 1780* (1990). An important overview of the rise of the nation-state and nationalism around the world.

Howe, Daniel Walker, *What Hath God Wrought: The Transformation of America, 1815-1848* (2007). A Pulitzer Prize–winning interpretation of how new technologies and new ideas reshaped the economy, society, culture, and politics of the United States in the first half of the nineteenth century.

Hunt, Lynn, *Politics, Culture and Class in the French Revolution* (1984). Examines the influence of sociocultural shifts as causes and consequences of the French Revolution, emphasizing the symbols and practice of politics invented during the revolution.

Inikori, Joseph, *Africans and the Industrial Revolution in England* (2002). Demonstrates the important role that Africa and Africans played in facilitating the industrial revolution.

Isset, Christopher Mills, *State, Peasant, and Merchant in Qing Manchuria, 1644-1862* (2007). A study of the relationships between the sociopolitical structures and peasant lives in a key region during the Qing.

James, C. L. R., *The Black Jacobins: Toussaint L'Ouverture and the San Domingo Revolution* (1938). A classic chronicle of the only successful slave revolt in history, it provides a critical portrait of their leader, Toussaint L'Ouverture.

Jones, E. L., *Growth Recurring* (1988). Discusses the controversy over why the industrial revolution took place in Europe, stressing the unique ecological setting that encouraged long-term investment.

Kinsbruner, Jay, *Independence in Spanish America* (1994). A fine study of the Latin American revolutions that argues that the struggle was as much a civil war as a fight for national independence.

Landers, Jane, *Atlantic Creoles in the Age of Revolutions* (2011). A collection of fascinating and unique portraits of Atlantic world creoles who managed to move freely and purposefully through French, Spanish, and English colonies, and through Indian territory, in the unstable century between 1750 and 1850.

Mokyr, Joel, *Enlightened Economy: An Economic History of Britain, 1700-1850* (2009). Perspectives on the evolution of the British economy in the era that produced the industrial revolution.

———, *The Lever of Riches* (1990). An important study of the causes of the industrial revolution that emphasizes the role of small technological and organizational breakthroughs.

Naquin, Susan, and Evelyn Rawski, *Chinese Society in the Eighteenth Century* (1987). A survey of mid-Qing society.

Neal, Larry, *The Rise of Financial Capitalism* (1990). An important study of the making of financial markets.

Nikitenko, Aleksandr, *Up from Serfdom: My Childhood and Youth in Russia, 1804-1824* (2001). One of the very few recorded life stories of a Russian serf.

Pomeranz, Kenneth, *The Great Divergence: Europe, China, and the Making of the Modern World Economy* (2000). Offers explanations of why Europe and not some other place in the world, like parts of China or India, forged ahead economically in the nineteenth century.

Rudé, George, *Europe in the Eighteenth Century* (1972). Emphasizes the rise of a new class, the bourgeoisie, against the old aristocracy, as a cause of the French Revolution.

Wakeman, Frederic, Jr., "The Canton Trade and the Opium War," in John K. Fairbank (ed.), *The Cambridge History of China*, vol. 10 (1978), pp. 163-212. The standard account of the episode.

Wong, R. Bin, *China Transformed: Historical Change and the Limits of European Experience* (2000). Draws attention to the relative autonomy of merchant capitalists in relation to dynastic states in Europe compared to China.

Wood, Gordon S., *Empire of Liberty: A History of the Early Republic, 1789-1815* (2009). An excellent synthesis of the history of the United States in the tumultuous years between the ratification of the Constitution and the War of 1812.

Wortman, Richard, *Scenarios of Power: Myth and Ceremony in Russian Monarchy*, 2 vols. (1995-2000). Examines how dynastic Russia confronted the challenges of the revolutionary epoch.

CHAPTER 16: ALTERNATIVE VISIONS OF THE NINETEENTH CENTURY

Anderson, David M., *Revealing Prophets: Prophets in Eastern African History* (1995). Good discussion of the prophets in eastern Africa.

Beecher, Jonathan, *The Utopian Vision of Charles Fourier* (1983). A fine biography of this important thinker.

Boyd, Jean, *The Caliph's Sister: Nana Asma'u, 1793-1865, Teacher, Poet, and Islamic Leader* (1988). A study of the most powerful female Muslim leader in the Fulani religious revolt.

Clancy-Smith, Julia, *Rebel and Saint: Muslim Notables, Populist Protest, Colonial Encounter (Algeria and Tunisia, 1800-1904)* (1994). Examines Islamic protest movements against western encroachments in North Africa.

Clogg, Richard, *A Concise History of Greece* (1997). A good introduction to the history of Greece in its European context.

Dalrymple, William, *The Last Mughal: The Fall of a Dynasty: Delhi, 1857* (2007). A deeply researched and riveting account of Delhi during the 1857 revolt.

Danziger, Raphael, *Abd al-Qadir: Resistance to the French and Internal Consolidation* (1977). Still the indispensable work on this important Algerian Muslim leader.

Dowd, Gregory E., *A Spirited Resistance: The North American Indian Struggle for Unity, 1745-1815* (1992). Emphasizes the importance of prophets like Tenskwatawa in the building of pan-Indian confederations in the era between the Seven Years' War and the War of 1812.

Guha, Ranajit, *Elementary Aspects of Peasant Insurgency in Colonial India* (1983). Not specifically on the Indian Rebellion of 1857 but includes it in its pioneering "subalternist" interpretation of South Asian history.

Hamilton, Carolyn (ed.), *The Mfecane Aftermath: Reconstructive Debates in Southern African History* (1995). Debates on Shaka's *Mfecane* movement and its impact on southern Africa.

Hiskett, Mervyn, *The Sword of Truth: The Life and Times of the Shehu Usman dan Fodio* (1994). An authoritative study of the Fulani revolt in northern Nigeria.

Johnson, Douglas H., *Nuer Prophets: A History of Prophecy from the Upper Nile in the Nineteenth and Twentieth Centuries* (1994). Deals with African prophetic and charismatic movements in eastern Africa.

Keddie, Nikki, *An Islamic Response to Imperialism: Political and Religious Writings of Sayyid Jamal ad-Din "al-Afghani"* (1968). Definitive information on the Afghani's life and influence, coupled with a translation of one of his most important essays.

Michael, Franz, and Chung-li Chang, *The Taiping Rebellion: History and Documents,* 3 vols. (1966-1971). The basic source for the history of the Taiping.

Mukherjee, Rudrangshu, *Awadh in Revolt 1857-58* (1984). A careful case study of the Indian Rebellion.

Omer-Cooper, J. D., *The Zulu Aftermath: A Nineteenth-Century Revolution in Bantu Africa* (1966). A good place to start in studying Shaka's *Mfecane* movement, which greatly rearranged the political and ethnic makeup of southern Africa.

Ostler, Jeffrey, *The Plains Sioux and U.S. Colonialism from Lewis and Clark to Wounded Knee* (2004). Uses the lens of colonial theory to track relations between the Sioux and the United States, offering fresh insights about the Ghost Dance movement.

Peires, J. B. (ed.), *Before and After Shaka* (1981). Discusses elements in the debate over Shaka's *Mfecane* movement.

Pilbeam, Pamela, *French Socialists Before Marx: Workers, Women and the Social Question in France* (2001). Describes the development of a variety of socialist ideas in early nineteenth-century France.

Reed, Nelson, *The Caste War of Yucatan* (1964). A classic narrative of the Caste War of the Yucatan.

Restall, Matthew, *The Maya World* (1997). Describes in economic and social terms the origins of the Yucatan upheaval in southern Mexico.

Ruedy, John, *Modern Algeria: The Origins and Development of a Nation* (2005). Still the best overview of the modern political history of Algeria.

Rugeley, Terry, *Rebellion Now and Forever: Mayans, Hispanics, and Caste War Violence in Yucatán, 1800-1880* (2009). Explains the combination of economic and cultural pressures that drove the Mayans in the Yucatan to revolt in the Caste War.

Spence, Jonathan, *God's Chinese Son: The Taiping Heavenly Kingdom of Hong Xiuquan* (1996). A fascinating portrayal of the Taiping through the prism of its founder.

Wagner, Rudolf, *Reenacting the Heavenly Vision: The Role of Religion in the Taiping Rebellion* (1982). A brief but insightful analysis of the religious elements in the Taiping's doctrines.

White, Richard, *The Middle Ground: Indians, Empires, and Republics in the Great Lakes Region, 1650-1815* (1991). A pathbreaking exploration of intercultural relations in North America that offers a provocative interpretation of the visions of Tenskwatawa and the efforts of Tecumseh to resist the expansion of the United States.

CHAPTER 17: NATIONS AND EMPIRES, 1850-1914

Berry, Sara, *Cocoa, Custom and Socio-Economic Change in Western Nigeria* (1975), Innovative study based on interviews with local farmers that suggests that farmer enterprise and microeconomic theory better explain the spectacular growth in cocoa production than grand economic theory.

Cain, P. A., and A. G. Hopkins, *British Imperialism: Innovation and Expansion, 1688-1914* (1993). An excellent discussion of British imperialism, especially British expansion into Africa.

Cooper, Frederick, *Colonialism in Question: Theory, Knowledge, History* (2005). A collection of essays by one of the leading scholars of colonial studies.

Cronon, William, *Nature's Metropolis: Chicago and the Great West* (1991). Makes connections among territorial expansion, industrialization, and urban development.

Davis, John, *Conflict and Control: Law and Order in Nineteenth-Century Italy* (1988). A superb study of the north-south and other rifts after Italian political unification.

Frankel, S. Herbert, *Capital Investment in Africa: Its Course and Effects* (1938). A careful study based on a mass of detailed figures and statistics on the general economic development of states in sub-Saharan Africa.

Friesen, Gerald, *The Canadian Prairies* (1984). The most comprehensive account of Canadian westward expansion.

Gluck, Carol, *Japan's Modern Myths: Ideology in the Late Meiji Period* (1985). A study of how states fashion useful historical traditions to consolidate and legitimize their rule.

Headrick, Daniel R., *The Tools of Empire: Technology and European Imperialism in the Nineteenth Century* (1981). A useful general study of the relationship between imperialism and technology.

Herbst, Jeffrey, *States and Power in Africa: Comparative Lessons in Authority and Control* (2000). An overview of the impact of colonial rule on contemporary African states.

Hill, Polly, *The Gold Coast Cocoa Farmer: A Preliminary Survey* (1965).

Hine, Robert V., and John Mack Faragher, *The American West: A New Interpretive History* (2000). Presents an excellent synthesis of the conquests by which the United States expanded from the Atlantic to the Pacific.

Hobsbawm, Eric J., *Nations and Nationalism since 1780: Programme, Myth, Reality* (1993). An insightful survey of the origins and development of nationalist thought throughout Europe.

Hochschild, Adam, *King Leopold's Ghost* (1998). A full-scale, eminently readable study of Europe's most egregiously destructive colonial regime in Africa.

Lee, Leo Ou-fan, and Andrew Nathan, "The Beginnings of Mass Culture: Journalism and Fiction in the Late Ch'ing and Beyond," in David Johnson, Andrew Nathan, and Evelyn Rawski (eds.), *Popular Culture in Late Imperial China* (1985), pp. 360–95. An important article on the emergence of a mass-media market in late-nineteenth- and early twentieth-century China.

Lieven, Dominic, *Empire: The Russian Empire and Its Rivals* (2000). A comparison of the British, Ottoman, Habsburg, and Russian empires.

Mackenzie, John M., *Propaganda and Empire* (1984). Contains a series of useful chapters showing the importance of the empire to Britain.

Mamdani, Mahmood, *Citizen and State: Contemporary Africa and the Legacy of Late Colonialism* (1996). A survey of the impact of European colonial powers on African political systems.

McClintock, Anne, *Imperial Leather: Race, Gender and Sexuality in the Colonial Contest* (1995). A study of the imperial relationship between Victorian Britain and South Africa from the point of view of cultural studies.

McNeil, William, *Europe's Steppe Frontier: 1500–1800* (1964). An excellent study of the definitive victory of Russia's agricultural empire over grazing nomads and independent frontier people.

Mitchell, B. R., *International Historical Statistics: Africa, Asia, and Oceania, 1750–2005* (2007). This comparative volume provides data from over two centuries for all principal areas of economic and social activity in both eastern and western Europe.

Montgomery, David, *The Fall of the House of Labor: The Workplace, the State, and American Labor Activism, 1865–1925* (1987). An excellent discussion of changes in work in the late nineteenth century.

Myers, Ramon, and Mark Peattie (eds.), *The Japanese Colonial Empire, 1895–1945* (1984). A collection of essays exploring different aspects of Japanese colonialism.

Needell, Jeffrey, *A Tropical Belle Epoque: Elite Culture and Society in Turn-of-the-century Rio de Janeiro* (1987). Shows the strength of the Brazilian elites at the turn of the century.

Pan, Lynn (ed.), *The Encyclopedia of Chinese Overseas* (1999). A comprehensive coverage of the history of the Chinese diaspora.

Porter, Bernard, *The Absent-Minded Imperialists: What the British Really Thought about Empire* (2004). A careful dissection of the ways in which empire changed the British—and did not.

Stengers, Jean, *Combien le Congo a-t-il coûté à la Belgique* (1957). A detailed financial accounting of how much Leopold put into the Congo and how much he took out, underscoring just how ruthlessly he exploited this possession.

Topik, Steven, *The Political Economy of the Brazilian State, 1889–1930* (1987). An excellent discussion of the Brazilian state, and especially of its elites.

Walker, Mack, *German Home Towns: Community, State, and the General State, 1648–1871* (1971; reprint, 1998). A brilliant, street-level analysis of the Holy Roman Empire (the First Reich) and the run-up to the German unification of 1871 (the Second Reich).

Wasserman, Mark, *Everyday Life and Politics in Nineteenth-Century Mexico* (2000). Wonderfully captures the way in which people coped with social and economic dislocation in late-nineteenth-century Mexico.

Weeks, Theodore R., *Nation and State in Late Imperial Russia: Nationalism and Russification on the Western Frontier, 1863–1914* (1996). A good discussion of the Russian Empire's responses to the concept of the nation-state.

White, Richard, *Railroaded: The Transcontinentals and the Making of Modern America* (2011). A seering exposé of the corruptions and a startling critique of the economic and environmental costs associated with the expansion of railroad lines across Canada, the United States, and Mexico.

Yung Wing, *My Life in China and America* (1909). The autobiography of the first Chinese graduate of an American university.

CHAPTER 18: AN UNSETTLED WORLD, 1890–1914

Bayly, C. A., *The Birth of the Modern World, 1780–1914: Global Connections and Comparisons* (2004). A general study of the key political, economic, social, and cultural features of the modern era in world history.

Bergère, Marie-Claire, *Sun Yat-sen* (1998). Originally published in French in 1994, this is a judicious biography of the man generally known as the father of the modern Chinese nation.

Chatterjee, Partha, *The Nation and Its Fragments* (1993). One of the most important works on Indian nationalism by a leading scholar of "subaltern studies."

Conrad, Joseph, *Heart of Darkness* (1899). First published in a magazine in 1899, this novella contained a searing critique of King Leopold's oppressive and exploitative policies in the Congo and was part of a growing concern for the effects that European empires were having around the world, especially in Africa.

Esherick, Joseph, "How the Qing became China," in Joseph W. Esherick, Hasan Kayali, and Eric Van Young (eds.), *Empire to Nation: Historical Perspectives on the Making of the Modern World* (2006). A study of the processes through which the Qing Empire became the nation-state of China.

———, *The Origins of the Boxer Uprising* (1987). The definitive account of the episode.

Everdell, William R., *The First Moderns: Profiles in the Origins of Twentieth-Century Thought* (1997). A rich account of the many faces of modernism, focusing particularly on science and art.

Finnane, Antonia, *Changing Clothes in China: Fashion, History, Nation* (2008). An exploration of changing Chinese identities from the perspective of clothing.

Gay, Peter, *The Cultivation of Hatred* (1994). A provocative discussion of the violent passions of the immediate pre-Great War era.

Gilmartin, Christina, Gail Hershatter, Lisa Rofel, and Tyrene White (eds.), *Engendering China: Women, Culture, and the State* (1994). Analyzes politics and society in modern China from the perspective of gender.

Hochschild, Adam, *King Leopold's Ghost: A Story of Greed, Terror, and Heroism in Colonial Africa* (1998). A well-written account of the violent colonial history of the Belgian Congo under King Leopold in the late nineteenth century.

Katz, Friedrich, *The Life and Times of Pancho Villa* (1998). An exploration of the Mexican Revolution that shows how Villa's armies destroyed the forces of Díaz and his followers.

Keddie, Nikki, *An Islamic Response to Imperialism: Political and Religious Writings of Sayyid Jamal ad-Din "al-Afghani"* (1968). Definitive information on the Afghani's life and influence, coupled with a translation of one of his most important essays.

Kern, Stephen, *The Culture of Time and Space 1880–1918* (1986). A useful study of the enormous changes in the experience of time and space in the age of late industrialism in Europe and America.

Kuhn, Philip, *Chinese among Others: Emigration in Modern Times* (2008). An overview of the history of Chinese migration.

McKeown, Adam, *Melancholy Order: Asian Migration and the Globalization of Borders* (2008). An examination of global migration patterns since the mid-nineteenth century and how regulations designed to restrict Asian migration to other parts of the world led to the modern regime of migration control.

Meade, Teresa, *"Civilizing" Rio: Reform and Resistance in a Brazilian City, 1889–1930* (1997). A wonderful study of cultural and class conflict in Brazil.

Pick, Daniel, *Faces of Degeneration: A European Disorder, c. 1848–c. 1918* (1993). A study of Europe's fear of social and biological decline, particularly focusing on France and Italy.

Pretorius, Fransjohn (ed.), *Scorched Earth* (2001). A study of the Anglo-Boer War in terms of its environmental impacts.

Sarkar, Sumit, *The Swadeshi Movement in Bengal* (1973). A comprehensive study of an early militant movement against British rule.

Schorske, Carl E. *Fin-de-Siècle Vienna: Politics and Culture* (1980). The classic treatment of the birth of modern ideas and political movements in turn-of-the-century Austria.

Trachtenberg, Alan, *The Incorporation of America: Culture and Society in the Gilded Age* (1982). A provocative synthesis of changes in the American economy, society, and culture in the last decades of the nineteenth century.

Wang, David Der-wei, *Fin-de-Siècle Splendor: Repressed Modernities of Late Qing Fiction, 1849–1911* (1997). A fine work that attempts to locate the "modern" within the writings of the late Qing period.

Warren, Louis, *Buffalo Bill's America: William Cody and the Wild West Show* (2005). A superb portrait of William F. Cody, the person; of Buffalo Bill, the persona Cody (and others) created; and of the popular culture his Wild West shows brought to audiences in Europe and North America.

Warwick, Peter, *Black People and the South African War, 1899–1902* (1983). An important study that reminds readers of the crucial involvement of black South Africans in this bloody conflict.

Womack, John, Jr., *Zapata and the Mexican Revolution* (1968). A major work on the Mexican Revolution that discusses peasant struggles in the state of Morelos in great detail.

CHAPTER 19: OF MASSES AND VISIONS OF THE MODERN, 1910–1939

Bloxham, Donald, *The Great Game of Genocide: Imperialism, Nationalism, and the Destruction of the Ottoman Armenians* (2005). The definitive work on the Armenian genocide, set in a wide historical context.

Brown, Judith, *Gandhi: Prisoner of Hope* (1990). A biography of Gandhi as a political activist.

De Grazia, Victoria, and Ellen Furlough (eds.), *The Sex of Things: Gender and Consumption in Historical Perspective* (1996). Pathbreaking essays on how gender affects consumption.

Dumenil, Lynn, *The Modern Temper: America in the 1920s* (1995). A general discussion of American culture in the decade after World War I.

Fainsod, Merle, *Smolensk under Soviet Rule* (1989). The most accessible and sophisticated interpretation of the Stalin revolution in the village.

Friedman, Edward, *Backward toward Revolution: The Chinese Revolutionary Party* (1974). An insightful look at the failure of liberalism in early republican China through the prism of the short-lived Chinese Revolutionary Party.

Gelvin, James, *Divided Loyalties: Nationalism and Mass Politics in Syria at the Close of Empire* (1998). Offers important insights into the development of nationalism in the Arab world.

Horne, John (ed.), *A Companion to World War I* (2010). A collection of articles written by leading scholars of World War I; the most comprehensive and up-to-date work on this war.

———, *State, Society, and Mobilization during the First World War* (1997). Essays on what it took to wage total war among all the belligerents.

Johnson, G. Wesley, *The Emergence of Black Politics in Senegal* (1971). A useful examination of the stirrings of African nationalism in Senegal.

Kennedy, David M., *Freedom from Fear: The American People in Depression and War, 1929–1945* (1999). A wonderful narrative of turbulent years.

Kershaw, Ian, *Hitler*, 2 vols. (1998–2000). A masterpiece combining biography and context.

Kimble, David, *A Political History of Ghana* (1963). An excellent discussion of the beginnings of African nationalism in Ghana.

Kotkin, Stephen, *Magnetic Mountain: Stalinism as a Civilization* (1995). Recaptures the atmosphere of a time when everything seemed possible, even creating a new world.

LeMahieu, D. L., *A Culture for Democracy: Mass Communication and the Cultivated Mind in Britain between the Wars* (1988). One of the great works on mass culture.

Lyttelton, Adrian, *The Seizure of Power: Fascism in Italy, 1919–1929* (1961). Still the classic account.

Marchand, Roland, *Advertising the American Dream: Making Way for Modernity, 1920–1945* (1985). An excellent discussion of the force of mass production and mass consumption.

Mazower, Mark, *Dark Continent: Europe's Twentieth Century* (1999). A wide-ranging overview of Europe's tempestuous twentieth century.

McKeown, Adam, *Melancholy Order: Asian Migration and the Globalization of Border* (2008). A major study of the vast movement of peoples around the globe between the middle of the nineteenth and the twentieth centuries.

Morrow, John H., Jr., *The Great War: An Imperial History* (2004). Places World War I in the context of European imperialism.

Nottingham, John, and Carl Rosberg, *The Myth of "Mau Mau": Nationalism in Kenya* (1966). Dispels the myths in describing the roots of nationalism in Kenya.

Rosenberg, Clifford, *Policing Paris: The Origins of Modern Immigration Control Between the Wars* (2006). Explores the first systematic efforts to enforce distinctions of nationality and citizenship status in a major urban setting.

Taylor, Jay, *The Generalissimo: Chiang Kai-shek and the Struggle for Modern China* (2009). The first serious biographical study of Chiang Kai-shek in English, although its reliance on Chiang's own diary as a source does raise some questions of historical interpretation.

Thorp, Rosemary (ed.), *Latin America in the 1930s* (1984). An important collection of essays on Latin America's response to the shakeup of the interwar years.

Tsin, Michael, *Nation, Governance, and Modernity in China: Canton, 1900–1927* (1999). An analysis of the vision and social dynamics behind the Guomindang-led revolution of the 1920s.

Vianna, Hermano, *The Mystery of Samba* (1999). Discusses the history of samba, emphasizing its African heritage as well as its persistent popular content.

Wakeman, Frederic, Jr., *Policing Shanghai, 1927–1937* (1995). An excellent account of Guomindang rule in China's largest city during the Nanjing decade.

Winter, J. M., *The Experience of World War* (1988). A comprehensive presentation of the many sides of the twentieth century.

Young, Louise, *Japan's Total Empire: Manchuria and the Culture of Wartime Imperialism* (1998). An innovative case study of Japanese imperialism and mass culture with broad implications.

CHAPTER 20: THE THREE-WORLD ORDER, 1940–1975

Aburish, Said K., *Nasser: The Last Arab* (2004). An impressive look at Egypt's most powerful political leader in the 1950s and 1960s.

Anderson, Jon Lee, *Che Guevara: A Revolutionary Life* (1997). A sweeping study of the radicalization of Latin American nationalism.

Bayly, Christopher, and Tim Harper, *Forgotten Armies: Britain's Asian Empire and the War with Japan* (2004). A brilliant social and military history of the Second World War as fought and lived in South and Southeast Asia.

Chatterjee, Partha, *Nationalist Thought and the Colonial World: A Derivative Discourse?* (1986). An influential interpretation of the ideological and political nature of Indian nationalism and the struggle for a postcolonial nation-state.

Crampton, R. J., *Eastern Europe in the Twentieth Century and After,* 2nd ed. (1997). Comprehensive overview covering all Soviet-bloc countries.

Dikötter, Frank, *Mao's Great Famine: The History of China's Most Devastating Catastrophe, 1958–1962* (2010). A recent detailed account of one of the greatest man-made disasters in twentieth-century history.

Dower, John W., *Embracing Defeat: Japan in the Wake of World War II* (1999). A prize-winning study of the transformation of one of the war's vanquished.

Elkins, Caroline, *Imperial Reckoning: The Untold Story of Britain's Gulag in Kenya* (2005). Pulitzer Prize–winning study of the brutal war to suppress the nationalist uprising in Kenya in the 1950s that ultimately led to independence for that country.

Evans, Martin, *Algeria: France's Undeclared War* (2011). Gives the history of the Algerian nationalist movements and provides an overview of the Algerian war for independence.

Feshbach Murray, and Alfred Friendly Jr. (1992). *Ecocide in the USSR: Health and Nation under Siege.* A crucial study of ecological disasters in the Soviet Union.

Gao Yuan, *Born Red: A Chronicle of the Cultural Revolution* (1987). A gripping personal account of the Cultural Revolution by a former Red Guard.

Gordon, Andrew (ed.), *Postwar Japan as History* (1993). Essays covering a wide range of topics on postwar Japan.

Hargreaves, John D., *Decolonization in Africa* (1996). A good place to start when exploring the history of African decolonization.

Hasan, Mushirul (ed.), *India's Partition: Process, Strategy and Mobilization* (1993). A useful anthology of scholarly articles, short stories, and primary documents on the partition of India.

Iriye, Akira, *Power and Culture: The Japanese-American War, 1941–1945* (1981). A discussion that goes beyond the military confrontation in Asia.

Jackson, Kenneth T., *Crabgrass Frontier: The Suburbanization of the United States* (1985). An insightful and influential consideration of the movement of the American population from cities to suburbs.

Jalal, Ayesha, *The Sole Spokesman: Jinnah, the Muslim League and the Demand for Pakistan* (1985). A study of the high politics leading to the violent partition of British India.

Keep, John L. H., *Last of the Empires: A History of the Soviet Union 1945–1991* (1995). A detailed overview of the core of the "Second World."

Morris, Benny, *Righteous Victims: A History of the Zionist-Arab Conflict, 1881–1999* (2000). On the Arab-Israeli War of 1948.

Patterson, James T., *Grand Expectations: The United States, 1945–1974* (1996). Synthesizes the American experience in the postwar decades.

Patterson, Thomas, *Contesting Castro* (1994). The best study of the tension between the United States and Cuba. Culminating in the Cuban Revolution, it explores the deep American misunderstanding of Cuban national aspirations.

Roberts, Geoffrey, *Stalin's Wars: From World War to Cold War, 1939–1953* (2007). A reassessment of Stalin's wartime leadership that conveys the vast scale of what took place.

Saich, Tony, and Hans van de Ven (eds.), *New Perspectives on the Chinese Communist Revolution* (1995). A collection of essays reexamining different aspects of the Chinese communist movement.

Schram, Stuart, *The Thought of Mao Tse-tung* (1989). Standard work on the subject.

Tignor, Robert L., *W. Arthur Lewis and the Birth of Development Economics* (2006). An intellectual biography of the Nobel Prize–winning, West Indian–born economist, who proposed formulas to promote the economic development of less developed societies and then sought to implement them in Africa and the West Indies.

Wiener, Douglas R., *A Little Corner of Freedom: Russian Nature Protection from Stalin to Gorbachev* (2002). A groundbreaking book about Russian environmentalism.

Zubkova, Elena, *Russia after the War: Hopes, Illusions, and Disappointments, 1945–1957* (1998). Uses formerly secret archives to catalogue the devastation and difficult reconstruction of one of the war's victors.

CHAPTER 21: GLOBALIZATION, 1970–2000

Collier, Paul, *The Bottom Billion: Why the Poorest Countries Fail and What Can Be Done About It* (2007). Shows that despite the world's advancing prosperity, more than a billion people have been left behind in abject poverty.

Davis, Deborah (ed.), *The Consumer Revolution in Urban China* (2000). A look at the different aspects of the recent, profound social transformation of urban China.

Davis, Mike, *City of Quartz: Excavating the Future in Los Angeles* (1990). Offers provocative reflections on the recent history, current condition, and possible future of Los Angeles.

Dutton, Michael, *Streetlife China* (1999). A fascinating portrayal of the survival tactics of those inhabiting the margins of society in modern China.

Eichengreen, Barry, *Globalizing Capital: A History of the International Monetary System* (1996). An insightful analysis of how international capital markets changed in the period from 1945 to 1980.

Ferguson, Niall and Moritz Schularick, "'Chimerica' and the Global Asset Market Boom," *International Finance* 10, no. 3 (Winter 2007): 215-39. Coined the term "Chimerica" to designate a single, intertwined economic entity made up of a productive partner, China, and a consuming partner, the United States.

Gourevitch, Philip, *We Wish to Inform You That Tomorrow We Will Be Killed with Our Families: Stories from Rwanda* (1999). A volume that reveals the hatreds that culminated in the Rwanda genocide.

Guillermoprieto, Alma, *Looking for History: Dispatches from Latin America* (2001). A collection of articles by the most important journalist reporting on Latin American affairs.

Han Minzhu (ed.), *Cries for Democracy: Writings and Speeches from the 1989 Chinese Democracy Movement* (1990). A collection of documents from the events leading up to the incident in Tiananmen Square on June 4, 1989.

Herbst, Jeffrey, *States and Power in Africa: Comparative Lessons in Authority and Control* (2000). Explores the political dilemmas facing modern African polities.

Honig, Emily, and Gail Hershatter, *Personal Voices: Chinese Women in the 1980's* (1988). A record of Chinese women during a period of rapid social change.

Huang, Yasheng, *Capitalism with Chinese Characteristics: Entrepreneurship and the State* (2008). A sharp, unsentimental inside look at China's market economy and its future prospects.

Klitgaard, Robert, *Tropical Gangsters* (1990). On the intimate connections between corrupt native elites and international aid agencies.

Kotkin, Stephen, *Armageddon Averted: The Soviet Collapse, 1970–2000* (2001). Places the surprise fall of the Soviet Union in the context of the great shifts in the post–World War II order.

Mamdani, Mahmood, *When Victims Become Killers: Colonialism, Nativism, and the Genocide in Rwanda* (2001). Discusses the genocide in Rwanda in light of the legacy of colonialism.

Mehta, Suketu, *Maximum City: Bombay Lost and Found* (2005). Examines one of the great, and contradictory, cities in the era of globalization.

Mottahedeh, Roy, *The Mantle of the Prophet: Religion and Politics in Iran,* 2nd ed. (2008). Perhaps the best book on the 1979 Iranian Revolution and its aftermath.

Nathan, Andrew, and Perry Link, *The Tiananmen Papers* (2002). An inside look at the divisions within the Chinese elite in connection with the 1989 crackdown.

Portes, Alejandro, and Rubén G. Rumbaut, *Immigrant America,* 2nd ed. (1996). A good comparative study of how immigration has transformed the United States.

Prakash, Gyan, *Mumbai Fables* (2010). A spirited account of the rise of India's most modern city, a center of intellectual, commercial, and political vitality.

Prunier, Gerald, *Africa's World War: Congo, the Rwandan Genocide, and the Making of a Continental Catastrophe* (2009). A chilling discussion of the spillover effects of the Rwandan genocide on central, eastern, and southern Africa.

Reinhart, Carmen, and Kenneth Rogoff, *This Time Is Different: Eight Centuries of Financial Folly* (2009). Explains the latest financial crash using historical perspective.

Sen, Amartya, *Poverty and Famines: An Essay on Entitlement and Deprivation* (1982). A major study that reoriented the study of famines from a narrow concentration on food supply to broader questions of ownership, exchange, and democracy.

Van Der Wee, Hermann, *Prosperity and Upheaval: The World Economy, 1945-1980* (1986). Describes very well the transformation and problems of the world economy, particularly from the 1960s onward.

Westad, Odd Arne, *The Global Cold War: Third World Interventions and the Making of our Times* (2007). A genuinely global perspective on the cold war and its consequences.

Winn, Peter, *Americas: The Changing Face of Latin America and the Caribbean* (1992). A useful portrayal of Latin America since the 1970s.

Glossary

Abd al-Rahman III Islamic ruler in Spain who held a countercaliphate and reigned from 912 to 961 CE.

aborigines Original, native inhabitants of a region, as opposed to invaders, colonizers, or later peoples of mixed ancestry.

absolute monarchy Form of government where one body, usually the monarch, controls the right to tax, judge, make war, and coin money. The term *enlightened absolutists* was often used to refer to state monarchies in seventeenth- and eighteenth-century Europe.

acid rain Precipitation containing large amounts of sulfur, mainly from coal-fired plants.

adaptation Ability to alter behavior and to innovate, finding new ways of doing things.

African National Congress (ANC) Multiracial organization founded in 1912 in an effort to end racial discrimination in South Africa.

Afrikaners Descendants of the original Dutch settlers of South Africa; formerly referred to as Boers.

Agones Athletic contests in ancient Greece.

Ahmosis Egyptian ruler in the southern part of the country who ruled from 1550 to 1525 BCE; Ahmosis used Hyksos weaponry—horse chariots in particular—to defeat the Hyksos themselves.

Ahura Mazda Supreme God of the Persians believed to have created the world and all that is good and to have appointed earthly kings.

AIDS (Acquired Immunodeficiency Syndrome) Virus that compromises the ability of the infected person's immune system to ward off disease. First detected in 1981, AIDS was initially stigmatized as a "gay cancer," but as it spread to heterosexuals, public awareness about it increased. In its first two decades, AIDS killed 12 million people.

Akbarnamah Mughal intellectual Abulfazl's *Book of Akbar,* which attempted to reconcile the traditional Sufi interest in the inner life within the worldly context of a great empire.

Alaric II Visigothic king who issued a simplified code of innovative imperial law.

Alexander the Great (356–323 BCE) Leader who used novel tactics and new kinds of armed forces to conquer the Persian Empire, which extended from Egypt and the Mediterranean Sea to the interior of what is now Afghanistan and as far as the Indus River valley. Alexander's conquests broke down barriers between the Mediterranean world and Southwest Asia and transferred massive amounts of wealth and power to the Mediterranean, transforming it into a more unified world of economic and cultural exchange.

Alexandria Port city in Egypt named after Alexander the Great. Alexandria was a model city in the Hellenistic world. It was built up by a multiethnic population from around the Mediterranean world.

Al-Khwarizmi Scientist and mathematician who lived from 780 to 850 CE and is known for having modified Indian digits into Arabic numerals.

Allied powers Name given to the alliance between Britain, France, Russia, and Italy, who fought against Germany and Austria-Hungary (the Central powers) in World War I. In World War II the name was used for the alliance between Britain, France, and America, who fought against the Axis powers (Germany, Italy, and Japan).

allomothering System by which mothers relied on other women, including their own mothers, daughters, sisters, and friends, to help in the nurturing and protecting of children.

alluvium Area of land created by river deposits.

alphabet A new system of writing using relatively few letters (22) developed by the Phoenicians in the mid–second millennium BCE.

American Railway Union Workers' union that initiated the Pullman Strike of 1894, which led to violence and ended in the leaders' arrest.

Amnesty International Non-governmental organization formed to defend "prisoners of conscience"—those detained for their beliefs, race, sex, ethnic origin, language, or religion.

Amorites Name that Mesopotamian urbanites called the transhumant herders from the Arabian desert. Around 2300 BCE, the Amorites, along with the Elamites, were at the center of newly formed dynasties in southern Mesopotamia.

Amun Once insignificant Egyptian god elevated to higher status by Amenemhet (1991–1962 BCE). *Amun* means "hidden" in Ancient Egyptian; the name was meant to convey the god's omnipresence.

Analects Texts that included the teachings and cultural ideals of Confucius.

anarchism Belief that society should be a free association of its members, not subject to government, laws, or police.

Anatolia Now mainly the area known as modern Turkey; in the sixth millennium BCE, people from Anatolia, Greece, and the Levant took to boats and populated the Aegean. Their small villages endured almost unchanged for two millennia.

Angkor Wat Magnificent Khmer Vaishnavite temple that crowned the royal palace in Angkor. It had statues representing the Hindu pantheon of gods.

Anglo-Boer War (1899–1902) Anticolonial struggle in South Africa between the British and the Afrikaners over the gold-rich Transvaal. In response to the Afrikaners' guerrilla tactics and in order to contain the local population, the British instituted the first concentration camps. Ultimately, Britain won the conflict.

animal domestication Gradual process that occurred simultaneously with or just before the domestication of plants, depending on the region.

annals Historical records. Notable annals are the cuneiform inscriptions that record successful Assyrian military campaigns.

Anti-Federalists Critics of the U.S. Constitution who sought to defend the people against the power of the federal government and insisted on a bill of rights to protect individual liberties from government intrusion.

apartheid Racial segregation policy of the Afrikaner-dominated South African government. Legislated in 1948 by the Afrikaner National Party, it had existed in South Africa for many years.

Arab-Israeli War of 1948–1949 Conflict between Israeli and Arab armies that arose in the wake of a U.N. vote to partition Palestine into Arab and Jewish territories. The war shattered the legitimacy of Arab ruling elites.

Aramaic Dialect of a Semitic language spoken in Southwest Asia; it became the lingua franca of the Persian Empire.

Aristotle (384–322 BCE) Philosopher who studied under Plato but came to different conclusions about nature and politics. Aristotle believed in collecting observations about nature and discerning patterns to ascertain how things worked.

Aryans Nomadic charioteers who spoke Indo-European languages and entered South Asia in 1500 BCE. The early Aryan settlers were herders.

Asante state State located in present-day Ghana, founded by the Asantes at the end of the seventeenth century. It grew in power in the next century because of its access to gold and its involvement in the slave trade.

ascetic One who rejects material possessions and physical pleasures.

Asiatic Society Cultural organization founded by British Orientalists who supported native culture but still believed in colonial rule.

Aśoka Emperor of the Mauryan dynasty from 268 to 231 BCE; he was a great conqueror and unifier of India. He is said to have embraced Buddhism toward the end of his life.

Assur One of two cities on the upper reaches of the Tigris River that were the heart of Assyria proper (the other was Nineveh).

Aśvaghosa First known Sanskrit writer. He may have lived from 80 to 150 CE and may have composed a biography of the Buddha.

Ataturk, Mustafa Kemal (1881–1938) Ottoman army officer and military hero who helped forge the modern Turkish nation-state. He and his followers deposed the sultan, declared Turkey a republic, and constructed a European-like secular state, eliminating Islam's hold over civil and political affairs.

Atlantic system New system of trade and expansion that linked Europe, Africa, and the Americas. It emerged in the wake of European voyages across the Atlantic Ocean.

Atma Vedic term signifying the eternal self, represented by the trinity of deities.

Atman In the Upanishads, an eternal being who exists everywhere. The atman never perishes but is reborn or transmigrates into another life.

Attila Sole ruler of all Hunnish tribes from 433 to 453 CE. Harsh and much feared, he formed the first empire to oppose Rome in northern Europe.

Augustus Title meaning "Revered One," assumed in 27 BCE by the Roman ruler Octavian (63–14 BCE). This was one of many titles he assumed; others included *imperator*, *princeps*, and *Caesar*.

australopithecines Hominid species that appeared 3 million years ago and, unlike other animals, walked on two legs. Their brain capacity was a little less than one-third of a modern human's or about the size of the brain capacity of today's African apes. Although not humans, they carried the genetic and biological material out of which modern humans would later emerge.

Austro-Hungarian Empire Dual monarchy established by the Habsburg family in 1867; it collapsed at the end of World War I.

authoritarianism Centralized and dictatorial form of government, proclaimed by its adherents to be superior to parliamentary democracy and especially effective at mobilizing the masses. This idea was widely accepted in parts of the world during the 1930s.

Avesta Compilation of holy works transmitted orally by priests for millennia and eventually recorded in the sixth century BCE.

axial age Term often used to describe the pivotal period of the first millennium BCE when radical thinkers across the "second-generation societies" of connected Eurasia—including the Greek philosophers of the Mediterranean, Zoroaster in Southwest Asia, Buddha in South Asia, and Confucius and Master Lao in East Asia—offered dramatically new ideas that challenged their times.

Axis powers The three aggressor states in World War II: Germany, Japan, and Italy.

Aztec Empire Mesoamerican empire that originated with a league of three Mexica cities in 1430 and gradually expanded through the Central Valley of Mexico, uniting numerous small, independent states under a single monarch who ruled with the help of counselors, military leaders, and priests. By the late fifteenth century, the Aztec realm may have embraced 25 million people. In 1521, they were defeated by the conquistador Hernán Cortés.

baby boom Post–World War II upswing in U.S. birth rates; it reversed a century of decline.

bactrian camel Two-humped animal domesticated in central Asia around 2500 BCE. The bactrian camel was heartier than the one-humped dromedary and became the animal of choice for the harsh and varied climates typical of Silk Road trade.

Bactria A Hellenistic kingdom that broke away from the Seleucids around 200 BCE to establish a state in the Gandhara region modern Pakistan, which served as a bridge between South Asia and the Mediterranean Greek world.

Baghdad Capital of the Islamic Empire under the Abbasid dynasty, founded in 762 CE (in modern-day Iraq). In the medieval period, it was a center of administration, scholarship, and cultural growth for what came to be known as the Golden Age of Islamic science.

Baghdad Pact (1955) Middle Eastern military alliance between countries friendly with America who were also willing to align themselves with the western countries against the Soviet Union.

Balam Na Stone temple and place of pilgrimage for the Mayan people of Mexico's Yucatan peninsula.

Balfour Declaration Letter (November 2, 1917) by Lord Arthur J. Balfour, British foreign secretary, that promised a homeland for the Jews in Palestine.

Bamboo Annals Shang stories and foundation myths that were written on bamboo strips and later collected.

Bantu Language first spoken by people who lived in the southeastern area of modern Nigeria around 1000 CE.

Bantu migrations Waves of rapid population movement from West Africa into eastern and southern Africa during the first millennium CE that brought advanced agricultural practices to these regions and absorbed most of the preexisting hunting-and-gathering populations.

barbarian Derogatory term used to describe pastoral nomads, painting them as enemies of civilization; the term *barbarian* used to have a more neutral meaning than it does today.

barbarian invasions Violent migration of people in the late fourth and fifth centuries into Roman territory. These migrants had long been used as non-Roman soldiers.

basilicas Early church buildings, based on old royal audience halls.

Battle of Adwa (1896) Battle in which the Ethiopians defeated Italian colonial forces; it inspired many of Africa's later national leaders.

Battle of Wounded Knee (1890) Bloody massacre of Sioux Ghost Dancers by U.S. armed forces.

Bay of Pigs (1961) Unsuccessful invasion of Cuba by Cuban exiles supported by the U.S. government. The invaders intended to incite an insurrection in Cuba and overthrow the communist regime of Fidel Castro.

Bedouins Nomadic pastoralists in the deserts of the Middle East.

Beer Hall Putsch (1923) Nazi intrusion into a meeting of Bavarian leaders in a Munich beer hall; the Nazis were attempting to force support for their cause; Adolf Hitler was imprisoned for a year after the incident.

Beghards (1500s) Eccentric European group whose members claimed to be in a state of grace that allowed them to do as they pleased—from adultery, free love, and nudity to murder; also called Brethren of Free Speech.

bell beaker Ancient drinking vessel, an artifact from Europe, so named because its shape resembles an inverted bell.

Berenice of Egypt Egyptian "queen" who helped rule over the Kingdom of the Nile from 320 to 280 BCE.

Beringia Prehistoric thousand-mile-long land bridge that linked Siberia and North America (which had not been populated by hominids). About 18,000 years ago, *Homo sapiens* edged into this landmass.

Berlin Airlift (1948) Supply of vital necessities to West Berlin by air transport primarily under U.S. auspices. It was initiated in response to a land and water blockade of the city instituted by the Soviet Union in the hope that the Allies would be forced to abandon West Berlin.

Berlin Wall Wall built by the communists in Berlin in 1961 to prevent citizens of East Germany from fleeing to West Germany; torn down in 1989.

Bhakti Religious practice that grew out of Hinduism and emphasizes personal devotion to gods.

bhakti Hinduism Popular form of Hinduism that emerged in the seventh century. The religion stresses devotion (*bhakti*) to God and uses vernacular languages (not Sanskrit) spoken by the common people.

big men Leaders of the extended household communities that formed village settlements in African rain forests.

big whites French plantation owners in Saint-Domingue (present-day Haiti) who created one of the wealthiest slave societies.

Bilad al-Sudan Arabic for "the land of the blacks"; it consisted of the land lying south of the Sahara.

bilharzia Debilitating water-borne illness. It was widespread in Egypt, where it infected peasants who worked in the irrigation canals.

Bill of Rights First ten amendments to the U.S. Constitution; ratified in 1791.

bipedalism Walking on two legs, thereby freeing hands and arms to carry objects such as weapons and tools; one of several traits that distinguished hominids.

Black Death Great epidemic of the bubonic plague that ravaged Europe, East Asia, and North Africa in the fourteenth century, killing large numbers, including perhaps as many as one-third of the European population.

Black Jacobins Nickname for the rebels in Saint-Domingue, including Toussaint L'Ouverture, a former slave who led the slaves of this French colony in the world's largest and most successful slave insurrection.

Black Panthers Radical African American group in the 1960s and 1970s; they advocated black separatism and pan-Africanism.

black shirts Fascist troops of Mussolini's regime; the squads received money from Italian landowners to attack socialist leaders.

Black Tuesday (October 29, 1929) Historic day when the U.S. stock market crashed, plunging the United States and international trading systems into crisis and leading the world into the "Great Depression."

blitzkrieg "Lightning war"; type of warfare in which the Germans, during World War II, used coordinated aerial bombing campaigns along with tanks and infantrymen in motorized vehicles.

Bodhisattvas In Mahayana Buddhism, enlightened demigods who were ready to reach *nirvana* but delayed so that they might help others attain it.

Bolívar, Simón (1783–1830) Venezuelan leader who urged his followers to become "American," to overcome their local identities. He wanted the liberated countries to form a Latin American confederation, urging Peru and Bolivia to join Venezuela, Ecuador, and Colombia in the "Gran Colombia."

Bolsheviks Former members of the Russian Social Democratic Party who advocated the destruction of capitalist political and economic institutions and started the Russian Revolution. In 1918 the Bolsheviks changed their name to the Russian Communist Party.

Book of the Dead Ancient Egyptian funerary text that contains drawings and paintings as well as spells describing how to prepare the jewelry and amulets that were buried with a person in preparation for the afterlife.

bourgeoisie The middle class. In Europe, they sought to be recognized not by birth or title, but by capital and property.

Boxer Protocol Written agreement between the victors of the Boxer Uprising and the Qing Empire in 1901 that placed western troops in Beijing and required the regime to pay exorbitant damages for foreign life and property.

Boxer Uprising (1899–1900) Chinese peasant movement that opposed foreign influence, especially that of Christian missionaries; it was put down after the Boxers were defeated by an army composed mostly of Japanese, Russians, British, French, and Americans.

Brahma One of three major deities that form a trinity in Vedic religion. Brahma signifies birth. *See also* Vishnu *and* Siva.

Brahmans Vedic priests who performed rituals and communicated with the gods. Brahmans provided guidance on how to live in balance with the forces of nature as represented by the various deities. The codification of Vedic principles into codes of law took place at the hands of the Brahmans. They memorized Vedic works and compiled commentaries on them. They also developed their own set of rules and rituals, which developed into a full-scale theology. Originally memorized and passed on orally, these may have been written down sometime after the beginning of the Common Era. Brahmanism was reborn as Hinduism sometime during the first half of the first millennium CE.

British Commonwealth of Nations Union formed in 1926 that conferred "dominion status" on Britain's white settler colonies in Canada, Australia, and New Zealand.

British East India Company *See* East India Company.

bronze Alloy of copper and tin brought into Europe from Anatolia; used to make hard-edged weapons.

brown shirts Troops of German men who advanced the Nazi cause by holding street marches, mass rallies, and confrontations and by beating Jews and anyone who opposed the Nazis.

bubonic plague Acute infectious disease caused by a bacterium that is transmitted to humans by fleas from infected rats. It ravaged Europe and parts of Asia in the fourteenth century. Sometimes referred to as the "Black Death."

Buddha (Siddhartha Gautama; 563–483 BCE) Indian ascetic who founded Buddhism.

Buddhism Major South Asian religion that aims to end human suffering through the renunciation of desire. Buddhists believe that removing the illusion of a separate identity would lead to a state of contentment (*nirvana*). These beliefs challenged the traditional Brahmanic teachings of the time and provided the peoples of South Asia with an alternative to established traditions.

bullion Uncoined gold or silver.

Byzantium Modern term for the eastern Roman Empire (lasting from the fourth to the fifteenth century), centered at its "new Rome," Constantinople (founded by emperor Constantine in 324 on the site of a Greek city, Byzantium).

Cahokia Commercial center for regional and long-distance trade in North America. Its hinterlands produced staples for urban consumers. In return, its crafts were exported inland by porters and to North American markets in canoes. *See also* Mound people.

calaveras Allegorical skeleton drawings by the Mexican printmaker and artist José Guadalupe Posada. The works drew on popular themes of betrayal, death, and festivity.

caliphate Institution that arose as the successor to Muhammad's leadership and became both the political and religious head of the Islamic community. Although the caliphs exercised political authority over the Muslim community and were the head of the religious community, the *ummah,* they did not inherit Muhammad's prophetic powers and were not authorities in religious doctrine.

Calvin, Jean (1509–1564) A French theologian during the Protestant Reformation. Calvin developed a Christianity that emphasized moral regeneration through church teachings and laid out a doctrine of predestination.

Candomblé Yoruba-based religion in northern Brazil; it interwove African practices and beliefs with Christianity.

canton system System officially established by imperial decree in 1759 that required European traders to have Chinese guild merchants act as guarantors for their good behavior and payment of fees.

caravan cities Set of networks at long-distance trade locations where groups of merchants could assemble during their journeys. Several of these developed into full-fledged cities, especially in the deserts of Arabia.

caravans Companies of men who transported and traded goods along overland routes in North Africa and central Asia; large caravans consisted of 600–1,000 camels and as many as 400 men.

caravansarais Inns along major trade routes that accommodated large numbers of traders, their animals, and their wares.

caravel Sailing vessel suited for nosing in and out of estuaries and navigating in waters with unpredictable currents and winds.

carrack Ship used on open bodies of water, such as the Mediterranean.

Carthage City in what is modern-day Tunisia; emblematic of the trading aspirations and activities of merchants in the Mediterranean. Pottery and other archaeological remains demonstrate that trading contacts with Carthage were as far-flung as Italy, Greece, France, Iberia, and West Africa.

cartography Mapmaking.

caste system Hierarchical system of organizing people and distributing labor.

Caste War of Yucatan (1847–1901) Conflict between Mayan Indians and the Mexican state over Indian autonomy and legal equality, which resulted in the Mexican takeover of the Yucatan peninsula.

Castro, Fidel (1926–) Cuban communist leader whose forces overthrew Batista's corrupt regime in early January 1959. Castro became increasingly radical as he consolidated power, announcing a massive redistribution of land and the nationalization of foreign oil refineries; he declared himself a socialist and aligned himself with the Soviet Union in the wake of the 1961 CIA-backed Bay of Pigs invasion.

Çatal Hüyük Site in Anatolia discovered in 1958. It was a dense honeycomb of settlements filled with rooms whose walls were covered with paintings of wild bulls, hunters, and pregnant women. Çatal Hüyük symbolizes an early transition into urban dwelling and dates to the eighth millennium BCE.

cathedra Bishop's seat, or throne, in a church.

Catholic Church Unifying institution for Christians in western Europe after the collapse of the Roman Empire. Rome became the spiritual capital of western Europe and the bishops of Rome emerged as popes, the supreme head of the church, who possessed great moral authority.

Cato the Elder (234–149 BCE) Roman statesman, often seen as emblematic of the transition from a Greek to a Roman world. Cato the Elder wrote a manual for the new economy of slave plantation agriculture, invested in shipping and trading, learned Greek rhetoric, and added the genre of history to Latin literature.

caudillos South American local military chieftains.

cave drawings Images on cave walls. The subjects are most often large game, although a few are images of humans. Other elements are impressions made by hands dipped in paint and pressed on a wall or abstract symbols and shapes.

Celali revolts (1595–1610) Peasant and artisan uprisings against the Ottoman state.

Central powers Defined in World War I as Germany and Austria-Hungary.

Chan Chan City founded between 850 and 900 CE by the Moche people in what is now modern-day Peru. It had a core population of 30,000 inhabitants.

Chan Santa Cruz Separate Mayan community formed as part of a crusade for spiritual salvation and the complete cultural separation of the Mayan Indians; means "little holy cross."

Chandra Gupta II King who reigned in South Asia from 320 to 335 CE. He shared his name with Chandragupta, the founder of the Mauryan Empire.

Chandravamsha One of two main lineages (the lunar one) of Vedic society, each with its own creation myth, ancestors, language, and rituals. Each lineage included many clans. *See* Suryavamsha.

chapatis Flat, unleavened Indian bread.

chariots Horse-driven carriages brought by the pastoral nomadic warriors from the steppes that became the favored mode of transportation for an urban aristocratic warrior class and for other men of power in agriculture-based societies. Control of chariot forces was the foundation of the new balance of power across Afro-Eurasia during the second millennium BCE.

charismatic Person who uses personal strengths or virtues, often laced with a divine aura, to command followers.

Charlemagne Emperor of the West and heir to Rome from 764 to 814 CE.

chartered companies Firms that were awarded monopoly trading rights over vast areas by European monarchs (e.g., Virginia Company, Dutch East India Company).

Chartism (1834–1848) Mass democratic movement to pass the Peoples' Charter in Britain, granting male suffrage, secret ballot, equal electoral districts, and annual parliaments, and absolving the requirement of property ownership for members of the parliament.

chattel slavery Form of slavery that sold people as property, the rise of which coincided with the expansion of city-states. Chattel slavery was eschewed by the Spartans, who also rejected the innovation of coin money.

Chavín A people who lived in what is now northern Peru from 1400 to 200

BCE. They were united more by culture and faith than by a unified political system.

Chernobyl (1986) Site in the Soviet Union (in Ukraine) of the meltdown of a nuclear reactor.

Chiang Kai-shek (1887–1975) Leader of the Guomindang following Sun Yat-sen's death who mobilized the Chinese masses through the New Life movement. In 1949 he lost the Chinese Revolution to the communists and moved his regime to Taiwan.

Chimu Empire South America's first empire; it developed during the first century of the second millennium in the Moche Valley on the Pacific coast.

chinampas Floating gardens used by Aztecs in the 1300s and 1400s to grow crops.

China's Sorrow Name for the Yellow River, which, when it changed course or flooded, could cause mass death and waves of migration.

chinoiserie Chinese silks, teas, tableware, jewelry, and paper; popular among Europeans in the seventeenth and eighteenth centuries.

Christendom Entire portion of the world in which Christianity prevailed.

Christianity Religion that originated at the height of the Roman Empire and in a direct confrontation with Roman imperial authority: the trial of Yeshua ben Yosef (Joshua son of Joseph; we know him today by the Greek form of his name, Jesus). Jesus was condemned for sedition and crucified. His followers believed that he was resurrected and that his teachings were not that of a man, but a god who had walked among human beings. At first, the Roman Empire refused to recognize Christianity and persecuted its followers, but in the fourth century CE Christianity was officially recognized as the Roman state religion.

Church of England Established form of Christianity in England dating from the sixteenth century.

city Highly populated concentration of economic, religious, and political power. The first cities appeared in river basins, which could produce a surplus of agriculture. The abundance of food freed most city inhabitants from the need to produce their own food, which allowed them to work in specialized professions.

city-state Political organization based on the authority of a single, large city that controls outlying territories.

Civil Rights Act (1964) U.S. legislation that banned segregation in public facilities, outlawed racial discrimination in employment, and marked an important step in correcting legal inequality.

civil rights movement Powerful movement for equal rights and the end of racial segregation in the United States that began in the 1950s with court victories against school segregation and nonviolent boycotts.

civil service examinations The world's first written civil service examination system, instituted by the Tang dynasty to recruit officials and bureaucrats. Open to most males, the exams tested a candidate's literary skills and knowledge of the Confucian classics. They helped to unite the Chinese state by making knowledge of a specific language and Confucian classics the only route to power.

Civil War, American (1861–1865) Conflict between the northern and southern states of America; this struggle led to the abolition of slavery in the United States.

clan A social group comprising many households, claiming descent from a common ancestor.

clandestine presses Small printing operations that published banned texts in the early modern era, especially in Switzerland and the Netherlands.

Clovis people Early humans in America who used basic chipped blades and pointed spears in pursuing prey. They extended the hunting traditions they had learned in Afro-Eurasia, such as establishing campsites and moving with their herds. They were known as "Clovis people" because the arrowhead point that they used was first found by archaeologists at a site near Clovis, New Mexico.

Code of Manu Part of the handiwork of Brahman priests; a representative code of law that incorporated social sanctions and practices and provided guidance for living within the caste system.

codex Early form of book, with separate pages bound together; it replaced the scroll as the main medium for written texts. The codex emerged around 300 CE.

cognitive skills Skills such as thought, memory, problem-solving, and—ultimately—language. Hominids were able to use these skills and their hands to create new adaptations, like tools, which helped them obtain food and avoid predators.

Cohong Chinese merchant guild that traded with Europeans under the Qing dynasty.

coins Form of money that replaced goods, which previously had been bartered for services and other products. Originally used mainly to hire mercenary soldiers, coins became the commonplace method of payment linking buyers and producers throughout the Mediterranean.

cold war (1945–1990) Ideological conflict in which the Soviet Union and eastern Europe opposed the United States and western Europe.

colonies Regions under the political control of another country.

colons French settler population in Algeria.

colosseum Huge amphitheater completed by Titus and dedicated in 80 CE. Originally begun by Flavian, the structure is named after a colossal statue of Nero that formerly stood beside it.

Columbian exchange Movements between Afro-Eurasia and the Americas of previously unknown plants, animals, people, diseases, and products that followed in the wake of Columbus's voyages.

commanderies Provinces. Shi Huangdi (First August Emperor) divided China into commanderies (*jun*) to enable the Qin dynasty to rule the massive state effectively. The thirty-six commanderies were then subdivided into counties (*xian*).

Communist Manifesto Pamphlet published by Karl Marx and Friedrich Engels in 1848 at a time when political revolutions were sweeping Europe. It called on the workers of all nations to unite in overthrowing capitalism.

Compromise of 1867 Agreement between the Habsburgs and the peoples living in Hungarian parts of the empire that the Habsburg state would be officially known as the Austro-Hungarian Empire.

concession areas Territories, usually ports, where Chinese emperors allowed European merchants to trade and European people to settle.

Confucian ideals The ideals of honoring tradition, emphasizing the responsibility of the emperor, and respect for the lessons of history, promoted by Confucius, which the Han dynasty made the official doctrine of the empire by 50 BCE.

Confucianism Ethics, beliefs, and practices stipulated by the Chinese philosopher Kong Qiu, or Confucius, which served as a guide for Chinese society up to modern times.

Confucius (551–479 BCE) Influential teacher, thinker, and leader in China who developed a set of principles for ethical living. He believed that coercive laws and punishment would not be needed to maintain order in society if men following his ethics ruled. He taught his philosophy to anyone who was intelligent and willing to work, which allowed men

to gain entry into the ruling class through education.

cong tube Ritual object crafted by the Liangzhu. A cong tube was made of jade and was used in divination practices.

Congo Independent State Large colonial state in Africa created by Leopold II, king of Belgium, during the 1880s, and ruled by him alone. After rumors of mass slaughter and enslavement, the Belgian parliament took the land and formed a Belgian colony.

Congress of Vienna (1814–1815) International conference to reorganize Europe after the downfall of Napoleon. European monarchies agreed to respect each other's borders and to cooperate in guarding against future revolutions and war.

conquistadors Spanish military leaders who led the conquest of the New World in the sixteenth century.

Constantine Roman emperor who converted to Christianity in 312 CE. In 313, he issued a proclamation that gave Christians new freedoms in the empire. He also founded Constantinople (at first called "New Rome").

Constantinople Capital city, formerly known as Byzantium, which was founded as the New Rome by Constantine the Great.

Constitutional Convention (1787) Meeting to formulate the Constitution of the United States of America.

Contra rebels Opponents of the Sandinistas in Nicaragua; they were armed and financed by the United States and other anticommunist countries (1980).

Conversion of Constantine A significant political and religious turning point in the Roman Empire. Before the decisive battle for Rome in 312 CE, Constantine supposedly had a dream in which he was told to place a sign with the opening letters of Christ's name on his soldiers' shields. Constantine won the ensuing battle; he soon issued a proclamation giving privileges to Christian bishops. The edict spread Christianity through the institutions and across the byways of the Roman Empire.

conversos Jewish and Muslim converts to Christianity in the Iberian Peninsula and the New World.

Coptic Form of Christianity practiced in Egypt. It was doctrinally different from Christianity elsewhere, and Coptic Christians had their own views of Christology, or the nature of Christ.

Corn Laws Laws that imposed tariffs on grain imported to Great Britain, intended to protect British farming interests. The Corn Laws were abolished in 1846 as part of a British movement in favor of free trade.

cosmology Branch of metaphysics devoted to understanding the order of the universe.

cosmopolitans A development referring to the inhabitants of the multiethnic cities that thrived in the Hellenistic world; literally meaning "citizens belonging to the whole world," as opposed to a particular city-state.

Council of Nicaea Church council convened in 325 CE by Constantine and presided over by him as well. At this council, a Christian creed was articulated and made into a formula that expressed the philosophical and technical elements of Christian belief.

Counter-Reformation Movement to counter the spread of the Reformation; initiated by the Catholic Church at the Council of Trent in 1545. The Catholic Church enacted reforms to attack clerical corruption and it placed a greater emphasis on individual spirituality. During this time, the Jesuits were founded to help revive the Catholic Church.

coup d'état Overthrow of established state by a group of conspirators, usually from the military.

creation narratives Narratives constructed by different cultures that draw on their belief systems and available evidence to explain the origins of the world and humanity.

creed Formal statement of faith or expression of a belief system. A Christian creed or "credo" was formulated by the Council of Nicaea in 325 CE.

creoles Persons of full-blooded European descent who were born in the Spanish American colonies.

Crimean War (1853–1856) War waged by Russia against Great Britain and France. Spurred by Russia's encroachment on Ottoman territories, the conflict revealed Russia's military weakness when Russian forces fell to British and French troops.

crossbow Innovative weapon used at the end of the Warring States period that allowed archers to shoot their enemies with accuracy, even from a distance.

Crusades Wave of attacks launched in the late eleventh century by western Europeans. The First Crusade began in 1095, when Pope Urban II appealed to the warrior nobility of France to free Jerusalem from Muslim rule. Four subsequent Crusades were fought over the next two centuries.

Cuban Missile Crisis (1962) Diplomatic standoff between the United States and the Soviet Union that was provoked by the Soviet Union's attempt to base nuclear missiles in Cuba; it brought the world close to a nuclear war.

cult Religious movement, often based on the worship of a particular god or goddess.

cultigen Organism that has diverged from its ancestors through domestication or cultivation.

cuneiform Wedge-shaped form of writing. As people combined rebus symbols with other visual marks that contained meaning, they became able to record and transmit messages over long distances by using abstract symbols or signs to denote concepts; such signs later came to represent syllables, which could be joined into words. By impressing these signs into wet clay with the cut end of a reed, scribes engaged in cuneiform.

Cyrus the Great Founder of the Persian Empire. This sixth-century ruler (559–529 BCE) conquered the Medes and unified the Iranian kingdoms.

Daimyo Ruling lords who commanded private armies in pre-Meiji Japan.

dan Fodio, Usman (1754–1817) Fulani Muslim cleric whose visions led him to challenge the Hausa ruling classes, whom he believed were insufficiently faithful to Islamic beliefs and practices. His ideas gained support among those who had suffered under the Hausa landlords. In 1804, his supporters and allies overthrew the Hausa in what is today northern Nigeria.

Daoism School of thought developed at the end of the Warring States period that focused on the importance of following the Dao, or the natural way of the cosmos. Daoism emphasized the need to accept the world as it was rather than trying to change it through politics or the government. Unlike Confucianism, Daoism scorned rigid rituals and social hierarchies.

Dar al-Islam Arabic for "the House of Islam"; it describes a sense of common identity.

Darius I (521–486 BCE) Leader who put the emerging unified Persian Empire onto solid footing after Cyrus's death.

Darwin, Charles (1809–1882) British scientist who became convinced that the species of organic life had evolved under the uniform pressure of natural laws, not by means of a special, one-time creation as described in the Bible.

D-Day (June 6, 1944) Day of the Allied invasion of Normandy under General Dwight Eisenhower to liberate western Europe from German occupation.

Dear Boy Nickname of an early human remain discovered in 1931 by a team of archaeologists named the Leakeys. They discovered an almost totally intact skull. Other objects discovered with Dear Boy demonstrated that by the time of Dear Boy, early humans had begun to fashion tools and to use them for butchering animals and possibly for hunting and killing smaller animals.

Decembrists Russian army officers who were influenced by events in revolutionary France and formed secret societies that espoused liberal governance. They were put down by Nicholas I in December 1825.

Declaration of Independence U.S. document stating the theory of government on which America was founded.

Declaration of the Rights of Man and Citizen (1789) French charter of liberties formulated by the National Assembly that marked the end of dynastic and aristocratic rule. The seventeen articles later became the preamble to the new constitution, which the assembly finished in 1791.

decolonization End of empire and emergence of new independent nation-states in Asia and Africa as a result of the defeat of Japan in World War II and weakened European influence after the war.

Delhi Sultanate (1206–1526) Turkish regime of northern India. The regime strengthened the cultural diversity and tolerance that were a hallmark of the Indian social order, which allowed it to bring about political integration without enforcing cultural homogeneity.

democracy The idea that people, through membership in a nation, should choose their own representatives and be governed by them.

Democritus Thinker in ancient Greece who lived from 470 to 360 BCE; he deduced the existence of the atom and postulated that there was such a thing as an indivisible particle.

demotic writing The second of two basic forms of ancient Egyptian writing. Demotic was a cursive script written with ink on papyrus, on pottery, or on other absorbent objects. It was the most common and practical form of writing in Egypt and was used for administrative record keeping and in private or pseudo-private forms like letters and works of literature. *See also* Hieroglyphs.

developing world Term applied to countries collectively called the Third World during the cold war and seeking to develop viable nation-states and prosperous economies.

Devshirme System of taking non-Muslim children in place of taxes in order to educate them in Ottoman Muslim ways and prepare them for service in the sultan's bureaucracy.

Dhamma Moral code espoused by Aśoka in the Kalinga edict, which was meant to apply to all—Buddhists, Brahmans, and Greeks alike.

Dhimma **system** Ottoman law that permitted followers of religions other than Islam, such as Armenian Christians, Greek Orthodox Christians, and Jews, to choose their own religious leaders and to settle internal disputes within their religious communities as long as they accepted Islam's political dominion.

dhows Ships used by Arab seafarers; the dhow's large sails were rigged to maximize the capture of wind.

Dien Bien Phu (1954) Defining battle in the war between French colonialists and the Viet Minh that secured North Vietnam for Ho Chi Minh and his army and left the south to form its own government to be supported by France and the United States.

Din-I-llahi "House of worship" in which the Mughal emperor Akbar engaged in religious debate with Hindu, Muslim, Jain, Parsi, and Christian theologians.

Diogenes Greek philosopher who lived from 412 to 323 BCE and who espoused a doctrine of self-sufficiency and freedom from social laws and customs. He rejected cultural norms as out of tune with nature and therefore false.

Directory Temporary military committee that took over the affairs of the state of France in 1795 from the radicals and held control until the coup of Napoleon Bonaparte.

divination The interpretation of rituals used to communicate the wishes of gods or royal ancestors to foretell future events. Divination was used to legitimize royal authority and demand tribute.

Djoser Ancient Egyptian king who reigned from 2630 to 2611 BCE. He was the second king of the Third Dynasty and celebrated the Sed festival in his tomb complex at Saqqara.

domestication Bringing a wild animal or plant under human control.

Dominion in the British Commonwealth Canadian promise to keep up the country's fealty to the British crown, even after its independence in 1867. Later applied to Australia and New Zealand.

Dong Zhongshu Emperor Wu's chief minister, who advocated a more powerful view of Confucius by promoting texts that focused on Confucius as a man who possessed aspects of divinity.

double-outrigger canoes Vessels used by early Austronesians to cross the Taiwan Straits and colonize islands in the Pacific. These sturdy canoes could cover over 120 miles per day.

Duma Russian parliament.

Dutch learning Broad term for European teachings that were strictly regulated by the shoguns inside Japan.

dynastic cycle Political narrative in which influential families vied for supremacy. Upon gaining power, they legitimated their authority by claiming to be the heirs of previous grand dynasts and by preserving or revitalizing the ancestors' virtuous governing ways. This continuity conferred divine support.

dynasty Hereditary ruling family that passed control from one generation to the next.

Earth Summit (1992) Meeting in Rio de Janeiro between many of the world's governments in an effort to address international environmental problems.

East India Company (1600–1858) British charter company created to outperform Portuguese and Spanish traders in the Far East; in the eighteenth century the company became, in effect, the ruler of a large part of India.

Eastern Front Battlefront between Berlin and Moscow during World War I and World War II.

Edict of Nantes (1598) Edict issued by Henry IV to end the French Wars of Religion. The edict declared France a Catholic country but tolerated some Protestant worship.

Egyptian Middle Kingdom Period of Egyptian history lasting from about 2040 to 1640 BCE, characterized by a consolidation of power and building activity in Upper Egypt.

Eiffel Tower Steel monument completed in 1889 for the Paris Exposition. It was twice the height of any other building at the time.

eight-legged essay Highly structured essay form with eight parts, required on Chinese civil service examinations.

Ekklesia Church or early gathering committed to leaders chosen by God and fellow believers.

Ekpe Powerful slave trade institution that organized the supply and purchase of slaves inland from the Gulf of Guinea in West Africa.

Elamites A people with their capital in the upland valley of modern Fars who became a cohesive polity that incorporated transhumant people of the Zagros Mountains. A group of Elamites who migrated south and west into Mesopotamia helped conquer the Third Dynasty of Ur in 2400 BCE.

empire Group of states or different ethnic groups under a single sovereign power.

Enabling Act (1933) Emergency act passed by the Reichstag (German parliament) that helped transform Hitler from Germany's chancellor, or prime minister, into a dictator following the suspicious burning of the Reichstag building and a suspension of civil liberties.

enclosure A movement in which landowners took control of lands that traditionally had been common property serving local needs.

encomenderos Commanders of the labor services of the colonized peoples in Spanish America.

encomiendas Grants from European Spanish governors to control the labor services of colonized people.

Endeavor Ship of Captain James Cook, whose celebrated voyages to the South Pacific in the late eighteenth century supplied Europe with information about the plants, birds, landscapes, and people of this uncharted territory.

Engels, Friedrich (1820–1895) German social and political philosopher who collaborated with Karl Marx on many publications, including *The Communist Manifesto*.

English Navigation Act of 1651 Act stipulating that only English ships could carry goods between the mother country and its colonies.

English Peasants' Revolt (1381) Uprising of serfs and free farm workers that began as a protest against a tax levied to raise money for a war on France. The revolt was suppressed but led to the gradual emergence of a free peasantry as labor shortages made it impossible to keep peasants bound to the soil.

enlightened absolutists Seventeenth- and eighteenth-century monarchs who claimed to rule rationally and in the best interests of their subjects and who hired loyal bureaucrats to implement the knowledge of the new age.

Enlightenment Intellectual movement in eighteenth-century Europe stressing natural laws and reason as the basis of authority.

entrepôts Trading stations at the borders between communities, which made exchange possible among many different partners. Long-distance traders could also replenish their supplies at these stations.

Epicurus Greek philosopher who espoused emphasis on the self. He lived from 341 to 279 BCE and founded a school in Athens called The Garden. He stressed the importance of sensation, teaching that pleasurable sensations were good and painful sensations bad. Members of his school sought to find peace and relaxation by avoiding unpleasantness or suffering.

Estates-General French quasi-parliamentary body called in 1789 to deal with the financial problems that afflicted France. It had not met since 1614.

Etruscans A dominant people on the Italian peninsula until the fourth century BCE. The Etruscan states were part of the foundation of the Roman Empire.

eunuchs Loyal and well-paid men who were surgically castrated as youths and remained in service to the caliph or emperor. Both Abbasid and Tang rulers relied for protection on a cadre of eunuchs.

Eurasia The combined area of Europe and Asia.

European Union (EU) International body organized after World War II as an attempt at reconciliation between Germany and the rest of Europe. It initially aimed to forge closer industrial cooperation. Eventually, through various treaties, many European states relinquished some of their sovereignty, and the cooperation became a full-fledged union with a single currency, the euro, and with a somewhat less powerful common European parliament.

evolution Process by which the different species of the world—its plants and animals—make changes in response to their environment that enable them to survive and increase in numbers.

Exclusion Act of 1882 U.S. congressional act prohibiting nearly all immigration from China to the United States; fueled by animosity toward Chinese workers in the American West.

Ezo Present-day Hokkaido, Japan's fourth main island.

Fascism Mass political movement founded by Benito Mussolini that emphasized nationalism, militarism, and the omnipotence of the state.

Fascists Radical right-wing group of disaffected veterans that formed around Mussolini in 1919 and a few years later came to power in Rome.

Fatehpur Sikri Mughal emperor Akbar's temporary capital near Agra.

Fatimids Shiite dynasty that ruled parts of the Islamic Empire beginning in the tenth century CE. They were based in Egypt and founded the city of Cairo.

February Revolution (1917) The first of two uprisings of the Russian Revolution, which led to the end of the Romanov dynasty.

Federal Deposit Insurance Corporation (FDIC) Organization created in 1933 to guarantee all bank deposits up to $5,000 as part of the New Deal in the United States.

Federal Republic of Germany (1949–1990) Country formed of the areas occupied by the Allies after World War II. Also known as West Germany, this country experienced rapid demilitarization, democratization, and integration into the world economy.

Federal Reserve Act (1913) U.S. legislation that created a series of boards to monitor the supply and demand of the nation's money.

Federalists Supporters of the ratification of the U.S. Constitution, which was written to replace the Articles of Confederation.

feminist movements Movements that called for equal treatment for men and women—equal pay and equal opportunities for obtaining jobs and advancement. Feminism arose mainly in Europe and in North America in the 1960s and then became global in the 1970s.

Ferangi Arabic word meaning "Frank," which was used to describe Crusaders.

Fertile Crescent Site of the world's first agricultural revolution; an area in Southwest Asia, bounded by the Mediterranean Sea in the west and the Zagros Mountains in the east.

feudalism System instituted in medieval Europe after the collapse of the Carolingian Empire (814 CE) whereby each peasant was under the authority of a lord.

fiefdoms Medieval economic and political units.

First World Term invented during the cold war to refer to western Europe and North America (also known as the "free world" or the West); Japan later joined this group. Following the principles of liberal modernism, First World states sought to organize the world on the basis of capitalism and democracy.

Five Pillars of Islam The five tenets, or main aspects, of Islamic practice: testification or bearing witness that there is no God other than God (Allah, in Arabic) and that Muhammad is the messenger of God; praying five times a day; fasting from sunup to sundown every day during Ramadan (a month on the Islamic calendar); giving alms; and making a pilgrimage to Mecca.

Five-Year Plan Soviet effort launched under Stalin in 1928 to replace the market with a state-owned and state-managed economy, to promote rapid economic development over a five-year period of time and thereby "catch and overtake" the leading capitalist countries. The First Five-Year Plan was followed by the Second Five-Year Plan (1933–1937), and so on, until the collapse of the Soviet Union in 1991.

Flagellants European social group that came into existence during the bubonic plague in the fourteenth century; they believed that the plague was the wrath of God.

floating population Poor migrant workers in China who supplied labor under Emperor Wu.

Fluitschips Dutch shipping vessels that could carry heavy bulky cargo with relatively small crews.

flying cash Letters of exchange—early predecessors of paper cash instead of coins—first developed by guilds in the northwestern Shanxi. By the thirteenth century, paper money had eclipsed coins.

Fondûqs Complexes in caravan cities that included hostels, storage houses, offices, and temples.

Forbidden City Palace city of the Ming and Qing dynasties.

Force Publique Colonial army used to maintain order in the Belgian Congo; during the early stages of King Leopold's rule, it was responsible for bullying local communities.

Fourierism Form of utopian socialism based on the ideas of Charles Fourier (1772–1837). Fourier envisioned communes where work was made enjoyable and systems of production and distribution were run without merchants. His ideas appealed to the middle class, especially women, as a higher form of Christian communalism.

free labor Wage-paying rather than slave labor.

free markets Unregulated markets.

Free Officers Movement Secret organization of Egyptian junior military officers who came to power in a coup d'état in 1952, forced King Faruq to abdicate, and consolidated their own control through dissolving the parliament, banning opposing parties, and rewriting the constitution.

free trade Domestic and international trade unencumbered by tariff barriers, quotas, and fees.

Front de Libération Nationale (FLN) Algerian anticolonial, nationalist party that waged an eight-year war against French troops, beginning in 1854, that forced nearly all of the 1 million colonists to leave.

Fulani Muslim group in West Africa that carried out religious revolts at the end of the eighteenth and the beginning of the nineteenth centuries in an effort to return to the pure Islam of the past.

fur trade Trading of animal pelts (especially beaver skins) by Indians for European goods in North America.

Gandharan art Buddhist sculptures, particularly from the northern Kushan territory, that show a high degree of Greek and Roman influences.

Gandhi, Mohandhas Karamchand (Mahatma) (1869–1948) Indian leader who led a nonviolent struggle for India's independence from Britain.

garrisons Military bases inside cities; often used for political purposes, such as protecting rulers and putting down domestic revolts or enforcing colonial rule.

garrison towns Stations for soldiers originally established in strategic locations to protect territorial acquisition. Eventually, they became towns. Alexander the Great's garrison towns evolved into cities that served as centers from which Hellenistic culture was spread to his easternmost territories.

gauchos Argentine, Brazilian, and Uruguayan cowboys who wanted a decentralized federation, with autonomy for their provinces and respect for their way of life.

Gdansk shipyard Site of mass strikes in Poland that led in 1980 to the formation of the first independent trade union, Solidarity, in the communist bloc.

gendered relations A relatively recent development that implies roles emerged only with the appearance of modern humans and perhaps Neanderthals. When humans began to think imaginatively and in complex symbolic ways and give voice to their insights, perhaps around 150,000 years ago, gender categories began to crystallize.

genealogy History of the descent of a person or family from a distant ancestor.

Geneva Peace Conference (1954) International conference to restore peace in Korea and Indochina. The chief participants were the United States, the Soviet Union, Great Britain, France, the People's Republic of China, North Korea, South Korea, Vietnam, the Viet Minh party, Laos, and Cambodia. The conference resulted in the division of North and South Vietnam.

Genoa One of two Italian cities (the other was Venice) that linked Europe, Africa, and Asia as nodes of commerce in 1300. Genoese ships linked the Mediterranean to the coast of Flanders through consistent routes along the Atlantic coasts of Spain, Portugal, and France.

German Democratic Republic Nation founded from the Soviet zone of occupation of Germany after World War II; also known as East Germany.

German Social Democratic Party Founded in 1875, the most powerful socialist party in Europe before 1917.

Ghana The most celebrated medieval political kingdom in West Africa.

Ghost Dance American Indian ritual performed in the nineteenth century in the hope of restoring the world to precolonial conditions.

Gilgamesh Heroic narrative written in the Babylonian dialect of Semitic Akkadian. This story and others like it were meant to circulate and unify the kingdom.

Girondins Liberal revolutionary group that supported the creation of a constitutional monarchy during the early stages of the French Revolution.

global warming Release into the air of human-made carbons that contribute to rising temperatures worldwide.

globalization Development of integrated worldwide cultural and economic structures.

globalizing empires Empires, such as the Han and the Roman, that covered immense amounts of territory, included huge, diverse populations, exerted influence beyond their own borders, and worked to integrate conquered peoples.

Gold Coast Name that European mariners and merchants gave to that part of West Africa from which gold was exported. This area was conquered by the British in the nineteenth century and became a British colony; upon independence, it became Ghana.

Goths One of the groups of "barbarian" migrants into Roman territory in the fourth century CE.

government schools Schools founded by the Han dynasty to provide an adequate number of officials to fill positions in the administrative bureaucracy. The Imperial University had 30,000 members by the second century BCE.

Gracchus brothers Two tribunes, the brothers Tiberius and Gaius Gracchus, who in 133 and 123–21 BCE attempted to institute land reforms that would guarantee all of Rome's poor citizens a basic amount of land that would qualify them for army service. Both men were assassinated.

Grand Canal Created in 486 BCE, a thousand-mile-long connector between the Yellow and Yangzi rivers, linking the north and south, respectively.

grand unity Guiding political idea embraced by Qin rulers and ministers, with an eye toward joining the states of the Central Plain into one empire and centralizing administration.

"Greased cartridge" controversy Controversy spawned by the rumor that cow and pig fat had been used to grease the shotguns of the sepoys in the British army in India. Believing that this was a British attempt to defile their religion and speed their conversion to Christianity, the sepoys mutinied against the British officers.

Great Depression Worldwide depression following the U.S. stock market crash on October 29, 1929.

great divide The division between economically developed nations and less developed nations.

Great East Asia Co-Prosperity Sphere Term used by the Japanese during the 1930s and 1940s to refer to Hong Kong, Singapore, Malaya, Burma, and other states that they seized during their run for expansion.

Great Flood One of many traditional Mesopotamian stories that were transmitted orally from one generation to another before being recorded. The Sumerian King List refers to this crucial event in Sumerian memory and identity. The Great Flood narrative assigned responsibility for Uruk's demise to the gods.

Great Game Competition over areas such as Turkistan, Persia (present-day Iran), and Afghanistan. The British (in India) and the Russians believed that controlling these areas was crucial to preventing their enemies' expansion.

Great League of Peace and Power Iroquois Indian alliance that united previously warring communities.

Great Leap Forward (1958–1961) Plan devised by Mao Zedong to achieve rapid agricultural and industrial growth in China. The plan failed miserably and more than 20 million people died.

great plaza at Isfahan The center of Safavid power in the seventeenth century created by Shah Abbas (r. 1587–1629) to represent the unification of trade, government, and religion under one supreme political authority.

Great Proletarian Cultural Revolution (1966–1976) Mass mobilization of urban Chinese youth inaugurated by Mao Zedong in an attempt to reinvigorate the Chinese revolution and to prevent the development of a bureaucratized Soviet style of communism; with this movement, Mao turned against his longtime associates in the communist party.

Great Trek Afrikaner migration to the interior of Africa after the British abolished slavery in the empire in 1833.

Great War (August 1914–November 1918) A total war involving the armies of Britain, France, and Russia (the Allies) against those of Germany, Austria-Hungary, and the Ottoman Empire (the Central Powers). Italy joined the Allies in 1915, and the United States joined them in 1917, helping tip the balance in favor of the Allies, who also drew upon the populations and material of their colonial possessions. Also known as World War I.

Greek Orthodoxy Enduring form of Christianity that used the framework of the "Roman" state inherited from Constantine and Justinian to protect itself from Roman Catholicism and Muslim forces. The Greek Orthodox capital was Constantinople and its spiritual empire included the Russian peoples, Baltic Slavs, and peoples living in southwest Asia.

Greek philosophers "Wisdom-lovers" of the ancient Greek city-states, including Socrates, Plato, Aristotle, and others, who pondered such issues as self-knowledge, political engagement and withdrawal, and the order of the world.

Greenbacks Members of the American political party of the late nineteenth century that worked to advance the interest of farmers by promoting cheap money.

griots Counselors and other officials to the royal family in African kingships. They were also responsible for the preservation and transmission of oral histories and repositories of knowledge.

Group Areas Act (1950) Act that divided South Africa into separate racial and tribal areas and required Africans to live in their own separate communities, including the "homelands."

guerrillas Portuguese and Spanish peasant bands who resisted the revolutionary and expansionist efforts of Napoleon; after the French word *guerre*.

guest workers Migrants looking for temporary employment abroad.

Gulag Administrative name for the vast system of forced labor camps under the Soviet regime; it originated in a small monastery near the Arctic Circle and spread throughout the Soviet Union and to other Soviet-style socialist countries. Penal labor was required of both ordinary criminals (rapists, murderers, thieves) and those accused of political crimes (counterrevolution, anti-Soviet agitation).

Gulf War (1991) Armed conflict between Iraq and a coalition of thirty-two nations, including the United States, Britain, Egypt, France, and Saudi Arabia. It was started by Iraq's invasion of Kuwait, which it had long claimed, on August 2, 1990.

gunpowder Explosive powder. By 1040, the first gunpowder recipes were being written down. Over the next 200 years, Song entrepreneurs invented several incendiary devices and techniques for controlling explosions.

gunpowder empires Muslim empires of the Ottomans, Safavids, and

Mughals that used cannonry and gunpowder to advance their military causes.

Guomindang Nationalist Party of China, founded just before World War I by Sun Yat-sen and later led by Chiang Kai-shek.

Habsburg Empire Ruling house of Austria, which once ruled both Spain and central Europe but came to settle in lands along the Danube River; it played a prominent role in European affairs for many centuries. In 1867, the Habsburg Empire was reorganized into the Austro-Hungarian Dual Monarchy, and in 1918 it collapsed.

Hadith Sayings attributed to the Prophet Muhammad and his early converts. Used to guide the behavior of Muslim peoples.

Hagia Sophia Enormous and impressive church sponsored by Justinian and built starting in 532 CE. At the time, it was the largest church in the world.

Hajj Pilgrimage to Mecca; an obligation for Muslims.

Hammurapi's Code Legal code created by Hammurapi, the most famous of the Mesopotamian rulers, who reigned from 1792 to 1750 BCE. Hammurapi sought to create social order by centralizing state authority and creating a grand legal structure that embodied paternal justice. The code was quite stratified, dividing society into three classes: free men, dependent men, and slaves, each with distinct rights and responsibilities.

Han agrarian ideal Guiding principle for the free peasantry that made up the base of Han society. In this system, peasants were honored for their labors, while merchants were subjected to a range of controls, including regulations on luxury consumption, and were belittled for not engaging in physical labor.

Han Chinese Inhabitants of China proper who considered others to be outsiders. They felt that they were the only authentic Chinese.

Han Fei Chinese state minister who lived from 280 to 223 BCE; he was a proponent and follower of Xunzi.

Han military Like its Roman counterpart, a ruthless military machine that expanded the empire and created stable conditions that permitted the safe transit of goods by caravans. Emperor Wu heavily influenced the transformation of the military forces and reinstituted a policy that made military service compulsory.

Hangzhou City and former provincial seaport that became the political center of the Chinese people in their ongoing struggles with northern steppe nomads. It was also one of China's gateways to the rest of the world by way of the South China Sea.

Hannibal Great Roman general from Carthage whose campaigns in the third century BCE swept from Spain toward the Italian peninsula. He crossed the Pyrenees and the Alps mountain ranges with war elephants. He was unable, however, to defeat the Romans in 217 BCE.

Harappa One of two cities that, by 2500 BCE, began to take the place of villages throughout the Indus River valley (the other was Mohenjo Daro). Each covered an area of about 250 acres and probably housed 35,000 residents.

harem Secluded women's quarters in Muslim households.

Harlem Renaissance Cultural movement in the 1920s that was based in Harlem, a part of New York City with a large African American population. The movement gave voice to black novelists, poets, painters, and musicians, many of whom used their art to protest racism; also referred to as the "New Negro movement."

harnesses Tools made from wood, bone, bronze, and iron for steering and controlling chariot horses. Harnesses discovered by archaeologists reveal the evolution of headgear from simple mouth bits to full bridles with headpiece, mouthpiece, and reins.

Hatshepsut Leader known as ancient Egypt's most powerful woman ruler. Hatshepsut served as regent for her young son, Thutmosis III, whose reign began in 1479 BCE. She remained co-regent until her death.

Haussmannization Redevelopment and beautification of urban centers; named after the city planner who "modernized" mid-nineteenth-century Paris.

Hegira "Emigration" of Muhammad and his followers out of a hostile Mecca to Yathrib, a city that was later called Medina. The year in which this journey took place, 622 CE, is also year 1 of the Islamic calendar.

Heian period Period from 794 to 1185, during which began the pattern of regents ruling Japan in the name of the sacred emperor.

Hellenism Process by which the individuality of the cultures of the earlier Greek city-states gave way to a uniform culture that stressed the common identity of all who embraced Greek ways. This culture emphasized the common denominators of language, style, and politics to which anyone, anywhere in the Afro-Eurasian world, could have access.

hieroglyphs One of two basic forms of Egyptian writing that were used in conjunction throughout antiquity. Hieroglyphs are pictorial symbols; the term derives from a Greek word meaning "sacred carving"—they were employed exclusively in temple, royal, and divine contexts. *See also* Demotic writing.

Hijra Tradition of Islam, whereby one withdraws from one's community to create another, more holy, one. The practice is based on the Prophet Muhammad's withdrawal from the city of Mecca to Medina in 622 CE.

Hinayana (Lesser Vehicle) Buddhism Form of Buddhism that accepted the divinity of Buddha himself but not of demigods, or bodhisattvas.

Hinduism A refashioning of the ancient Brahmanic Vedic religion, bringing it in accord with rural life and agrarian values. It emerged as the dominant faith in Indian society in the third century CE. Believers became vegetarians and adopted rituals of self-sacrifice. Three major deities—Brahma, Vishnu, and Siva—formed a trinity representing the three phases of the universe (birth, existence, and destruction, respectively) and the three expressions of the eternal self, or *atma*.

Hindu revivalism Movement to reconfigure traditional Hinduism to be less diverse and more amenable to producing a narrowed version of Indian tradition.

Hiroshima Japanese port devastated by an atomic bomb on August 6, 1945.

Hitler, Adolf (1889–1945) German dictator and leader of the Nazi Party who seized power in Germany after its economic collapse in the Great Depression. Hitler and his Nazi regime started World War II in Europe and systematically murdered Jews and other non-Aryan groups in the name of racial purity.

Hittites The Hittites were a chariot warrior group of Anatolia, which spread east to northern Syria, though they eventually faced weaknesses in their own homeland. Their heyday was marked by the reign of the king Supiliulimua (1380 to 1345 BCE), who preserved the Hittites' influence on the balance of power in the region between Mesopotamia and the Nile.

Holocaust Deliberate racial extermination of the Jews by the Nazis that claimed around 6 million European Jews.

Holy Roman Empire Enormous realm that encompassed much of Europe and aspired to be the Christian successor state to the Roman Empire. In the time of the Habsburg dynasts, the empire was a loose confederation of principalities that obeyed an emperor elected by elite lower-level sovereigns. Despite its size, the empire never effectively centralized power; it was split into Austrian and Spanish factions when Charles V abdicated to his sons in 1556.

Holy Russia Name applied to Muscovy and then to the Russian Empire by Slavic Eastern Orthodox clerics who were appalled by the Muslim conquest in 1453 of Constantinople (the capital of Byzantium and of eastern Christianity) and who were hopeful that Russia would become the new protector of the faith.

home charges Fees India was forced to pay to Britain as its colonial master; these fees included interest on railroad loans, salaries to colonial officers, and the maintenance of imperial troops outside India.

hominids Humanlike beings who walked erect and preceded modern humans.

Homo A word used by scientists to differentiate between pre-human and "true human" species.

Homo caudatus "Tailed man," believed by some European Enlightenment thinkers to be an early species of humankind.

Homo erectus Species that emerged about 1.5 million years ago and had a large brain and walked truly upright. *Homo erectus* means "Standing man."

Homo habilis Scientific term for "Skillful man." Tool-making ability truly made *Homo habilis* the forerunners, though very distant, of modern humans.

Homo sapiens The first humans; they emerged in a small region of Africa about 200,000 years ago and migrated out of Africa about 100,000 years ago. They had bigger brains and greater dexterity than previous hominid species, whom they eventually eclipsed.

homogeneity Uniformity of the languages, customs, and religion of a particular people or place. It can also be demonstrated by a consistent calendar, set of laws, administrative practices, and rituals.

horses Animals used by full-scale nomadic communities to dominate the steppe lands in western Afro-Eurasia by the second millennium BCE. Horse-riding nomads moved their large herds across immense tracts of land within zones defined by rivers, mountains, and other natural geographical features. In the arid zones of central Eurasia, the nomadic economies made horses a crucial component of survival.

Huguenots French Protestants who endured severe persecution in the sixteenth and seventeenth centuries.

humanism The Renaissance aspiration to know more about the human experience beyond what the Christian scriptures offered by reaching back into ancient Greek and Roman texts.

Hundred Days' Reform (1898) Abortive modernizing reform program of the Qing government of China.

hunting and gathering Lifestyle in which food is acquired through hunting animals, fishing, and foraging for wild berries, nuts, fruit, and grains, rather than planting crops, vines, or trees. As late as 1500, as much as 15 percent of the world's population still lived by this method.

Hyksos A western Semitic-speaking people whose name means "Rulers of Foreign Lands"; they overthrew the unstable Thirteenth Dynasty in Egypt around 1640 BCE. The Hyksos had mastered the art of horse chariots, and with those chariots and their superior bronze axes and composite bows (made of wood, horn, and sinew), they were able to defeat the pharaoh's foot soldiers.

Ibn Sina Philosopher and physician who lived from 980 to 1037 CE. He was also schooled in the Quran, geometry, literature, and Indian and Euclidian mathematics.

ideology Dominant set of ideas of a widespread culture or movement.

Il Duce Term designating the fascist Italian leader Benito Mussolini.

Iliad Epic Greek poem about the Trojan War, composed several centuries after the events it describes. It was based on oral tales passed down for generations.

Il-khanate Mongol-founded dynasty in thirteenth-century Persia.

Imam Muslim religious leader and politico-religious descendant of Ali; believed by some to have a special relationship with Allah.

imperialism Acquisition of new territories by a state and the incorporation of these territories into a political system as subordinate colonies.

Imperial University University founded in 136 BCE by Emperor Wu, where important discoveries such as the rational diagnoses of the body's functions, the magnetic compass, and high-quality paper were developed; significant as a mechanism by which the Han state inculcated Confucian thought into the elite.

Imperium Latin word used to express Romans' power and command over their subjects. It is the basis of the English words *empire* and *imperialism*.

Inca Empire Empire of Quechua-speaking rulers in the Andean valley of Cuzco that encompassed a population of 4 to 6 million. The Incas lacked a clear inheritance system, causing an internal split that Pizarro's forces exploited in 1533.

Indian Institutes of Technology (IIT) Institutions originally designed as engineering schools to expand knowledge and to modernize India, which produced a whole generation of pioneering computer engineers, many of whom moved to the United States.

Indian National Congress Formed in 1885, a political party deeply committed to constitutional methods, industrialization, and cultural nationalism.

Indian National Muslim League Founded in 1906, an organization dedicated to advancing the political interests of Muslims in India.

Indo-Greek Fusion of Indian and Greek culture in the area under the control of the Bactrians, in the northwestern region of India, around 200 BCE.

Indu What we would today call India. Called "Indu" by Xuanzang, a Chinese Buddhist pilgrim who visited the area in the 630s and 640s CE.

indulgences Church-sponsored fund-raising mechanism that gave certification that one's sins had been forgiven in return for money.

industrial revolution Gradual accumulation and diffusion of old and new technical knowledge that led to major economic changes in Britain, northwestern Europe, and North America, catapulting these countries ahead of the rest of the world in manufacturing and agricultural output and standards of living.

industrious revolution Dramatic economic change in which households that had traditionally produced for themselves decided to work harder and longer hours in order to produce more for the market, which enabled them to increase their income and standard of living. Areas that underwent the industrious revolution shifted from peasant farming to specialized production for the market.

innovation Creation of a new method that allowed humans to make better adaptations to their environment such as the making of new tools.

Inquisition Tribunal of the Roman Catholic Church that enforced religious orthodoxy during the Protestant Reformation.

internal and external alchemy In Daoist ritual, use of trance and meditation or chemicals and drugs, respectively, to cause transformations in the self.

International Monetary Fund (IMF) Agency founded in 1944 to help restore financial order in Europe and the rest of the world, to revive international trade, and to support the financial concerns of Third World governments.

invisible hand As described in Adam Smith's *The Wealth of Nations*, the idea that the operations of a free market produce economic efficiency and economic benefits for all.

iron Malleable metal found in combined forms almost everywhere in the world; it became the most important and widely used metal in world history after the Bronze Age.

Iron Curtain Term popularized by Winston Churchill after World War II to refer to a rift, or an iron curtain, that divided western Europe, under American influence, from eastern Europe, under the domination of the Soviet Union.

irrigation Technological advance whereby water delivery systems and water sluices in floodplains or riverine areas were channeled or redirected and used to nourish soil.

Islam A religion that dates to 610 CE, when Muhammad believed God came to him in a vision. Islam ("submission"—in this case, to the will of God) requires its followers to act righteously, to submit themselves to the one and only true God, and to care for the less fortunate. Muhammad's most insistent message was the oneness of God, a belief that has remained central to the Islamic faith ever since.

Jacobins Radical French political group that came into existence during the French Revolution and executed the French king and sought to remake French culture.

Jacquerie (1358) French peasant revolt in defiance of feudal restrictions.

jade The most important precious substance in East Asia. Jade was associated with goodness, purity, luck, and virtue, and was carved into such items as ceremonial knives, blade handles, religious objects, and elaborate jewelry.

Jagat Seths Enormous trading and banking empire in eastern India.

Jainism Along with Buddhism, one of the two systems of thought developed in the seventh century BCE that set themselves up against Brahmanism. Its founder, Vardhamana Mahavira, taught that the universe obeys its own everlasting rules that no god or other supernatural being could affect. The purpose of life was to purify one's soul in order to attain a state of permanent bliss, which could be accomplished through self-denial and the avoidance of harming other creatures.

Janissaries Corps of infantry soldiers recruited as children from the Christian provinces of the Ottoman Empire and brought up with intense loyalty to the Ottoman state and its sultan. The Ottoman sultan used these forces to clip local autonomy and to serve as his personal bodyguards.

Jati Social groups as defined by Hinduism's caste system.

Jesuits Religious order founded by Ignatius Loyola to counter the inroads of the Protestant Reformation; the Jesuits, or the Society of Jesus, were active in politics, education, and missionary work.

Jihad Literally, "striving" or "struggle." This word also connotes military efforts or "striving in the way of God." It also came to mean spiritual struggles against temptation or inner demons, especially in Sufi, or mystical, usage.

Jih-pen Chinese for "Japan."

Jim Crow laws Laws that codified racial segregation and inequality in the southern part of the United States after the Civil War.

Jizya Special tax that non-Muslims were forced to pay to their Islamic rulers in return for which they were given security and property and granted cultural autonomy.

jong Large ocean-going vessels, built by Southeast Asians, which plied the regional trade routes from the fifteenth century to the early sixteenth century.

Judah The southern kingdom of David, which had been an Assyrian vassal until 612 BCE, when it became a vassal of Assyria's successor, Babylon, against whom the people of Judah rebelled, resulting in the destruction of Jerusalem in the sixth century BCE.

Julius Caesar Formidable Roman general who lived from 100 to 44 BCE. He was also a man of letters, a great orator, and a ruthless military man who boasted that his campaigns had led to the deaths of over a million people.

junks Trusty seafaring vessels used in the South China Seas after 1000 CE. These helped make shipping by sea less dangerous.

Justinian Roman or Byzantine emperor who ascended to the throne in 527 CE. In addition to his many building projects and military expeditions, he issued a new law code.

Kabuki Theater performance that combined song, dance, and skillful staging to dramatize conflicts between duty and passion in Tokogawa, Japan.

Kamikaze Japanese for "divine winds" or typhoons; such a storm saved Japan from a Mongol attack.

Kanun Highly detailed system of Ottoman administrative law that jurists developed to deal with matters not treated in the religious law of Islam.

Karim Loose confederation of shippers banding together to protect convoys.

karma Literally "fate" or "action," in Confucian thought; this is a universal principle of cause and effect.

Kassites Nomads who entered Mesopotamia from the eastern Zagros Mountains and the Iranian plateau

as early as 2000 BCE. They gradually integrated into Babylonian society by officiating at temples. By 1745 BCE, they had asserted order over the region, and they controlled southern Mesopotamia for the next 350 years, creating one of the territorial states.

Keynesian Revolution Post-Depression economic ideas developed by the British economist John Maynard Keynes, wherein the state took a greater role in managing the economy, stimulating it by increasing the money supply and creating jobs.

KGB Soviet political police and spy agency, formed as the Cheka not long after the Bolshevik coup in October 1917. Grew to more than 750,000 operatives with military rank by the 1980s.

Khan Ruler who was acclaimed at an assembly of elites and supposedly descended from Chinngis Khan on the male line; those not descended from Chinggis continually faced challenges to their legitimacy.

Khanate Major political unit of the vast Mongol empire. There were four Khanates, including the Yuan Empire in China, forged by Chinggis Khan's grandson Kubilai.

Kharijites Radical sect from the early days of Islam. The Kharijites seceded from the "party of Ali" (who themselves came to be known as the Shiites) because of disagreements over succession to the role of the caliph. They were known for their strict militant piety.

Khmers A people who created the most powerful empire in Southwest Asia between the tenth and thirteenth centuries in what is modern-day Cambodia.

Khomeini, Ayatollah Ruhollah (1902–1989) Iranian religious leader who used his traditional Islamic education and his training in Muslim ethics to accuse the shah's government of gross violations of Islamic norms. He also identified the shah's ally, America, as the great Satan. The shah fled the country in 1979; in his wake, Khomeini established a theocratic state ruled by a council of Islamic clerics.

Khufu A pyramid, among those put up in the Fourth Dynasty in ancient Egypt (2575–2465 BCE), which is the largest stone structure in the world. It is in an area called Giza, just outside modern-day Cairo.

Khusro I Anoshirwan Sasanian emperor who reigned from 530 to 579 CE. He was a model ruler and was seen as the personification of justice.

Kiev City that became one of the greatest cities of Europe after the eleventh century. It was built to be a small-scale Constantinople on the Dnieper.

Kikuyu Kenya's largest ethnic group; organizers of a revolt against the British in the 1950s.

King, Martin Luther, Jr. (1929–1968) Civil rights leader who borrowed his most effective weapon—the commitment to nonviolent protest and the appeal to conscience—from Gandhi.

Kingdom of Awadh One of the most prized lands for annexation and the fertile, opulent, and traditional vestige of Mughal rule in India.

Kingdom of Jerusalem What Crusaders set out to liberate when they launched their attack.

Kizilbash Mystical, Turkish-speaking tribesmen who facilitated the Safavid rise to power.

Knossos Area in Crete where, during the second millennium BCE, a primary palace town existed.

Koine Greek Common form of Greek that became the international spoken and written language in the Hellenistic world. This was a simpler everyday form of the ancient Greek language.

Koprulu reforms Reforms named after two grand viziers who revitalized the Ottoman Empire in the seventeenth century through administrative and budget trimming as well as by rebuilding the military.

Korean War (1950–1953) Cold war conflict between Soviet-backed North Korea and U.S.- and UN-backed South Korea. The two sides seesawed back and forth over the same boundaries until 1953, when an armistice divided the country at roughly the same spot as at the start of the war. Nothing had been gained. Losses, however, included 33,000 Americans, at least 250,000 Chinese, and up to 3 million Koreans.

Koryo dynasty Leading dynasty of the northern-based Koryo kingdom in Korea. It is from this dynasty that the name "Korea" derives.

Kremlin Once synonymous with the Soviet government; refers to Moscow's walled city center.

Kshatriyas Originally the warrior caste in Vedic society, the dominant clan members and ruling caste who controlled the land.

Ku Klux Klan Racist organization that first emerged in the U.S. South after the Civil War and then gained national strength as a radically traditionalist movement during the 1920s.

Kubilai Khan (1215–1294) Mongol leader who seized southern China after 1260 and founded the Yuan dynasty.

kulak Originally a pejorative word used to designate better-off peasants, the term used in the late 1920s and early 1930s to refer to any peasant, rich or poor, perceived as an opponent of the Soviet regime. Russian for "fist."

Kumarajiva Renowned Buddhist scholar and missionary who lived from 344 to 413 CE. He was brought to China by Chinese regional forces from Kucha, modern-day Xinjiang.

Kushans Northern nomadic group that migrated into South Asia in 50 CE. They unified the tribes of the region and set up the Kushan dynasty. The Kushans' empire embraced a large and diverse territory and played a critical role in the formation of the Silk Roads.

Labour Party Founded in Britain in 1900, the party that represented workers and was based on socialist principles.

laissez-faire The concept that the economy works best when it is left alone—that is, when the state does not regulate or interfere with the workings of the market.

"Land under the Yoke of Ashur" Lands not in Assyria proper, but under its authority; they had to pay the Assyrian Empire exorbitant amounts of tribute.

language System of communication reflecting cognitive abilities. Natural language is generally defined as words arranged in particular sequences to convey meaning and is unique to modern humans.

language families Related tongues with a common ancestral origin; language families contain languages that diverged from one another but share grammatical features and root vocabularies. More than a hundred language families exist.

Laozi Also known as Master Lao; perhaps a contemporary of Confucius, and the person after whom Daoism is named. His thought was elaborated upon by generations of thinkers.

latifundia Broad estates that produced goods for big urban markets, including wheat, grapes, olives, cattle, and sheep.

League of Nations Organization founded after World War I to solve international disputes through arbitration; it was dissolved in 1946 and its assets were transferred to the United Nations.

Legalism Also called Statism, a system of thought about how to live an ordered life. It was developed by Master Xun, or Xunzi (310–237 BCE). It is based on the principle that people, being inherently inclined toward evil, require authoritarian control to regulate their behavior.

Lenin, Nikolai (1870–1924) Leader of the Bolshevik Revolution in Russia and the first leader of the Soviet Union.

Liangzhu Culture spanning centuries from the fourth to the third millennium BCE that represented the last new Stone Age culture in the Yangzi River delta. One of the Ten Thousand States, it was highly stratified and is known for its jade objects.

liberalism Political and social theory that advocates representative government, free trade, and freedom of speech and religion.

limited-liability joint-stock company Company that mobilized capital from a large number of investors, called shareholders, who were not to be held personally liable for financial losses incurred by the company.

Linear A and B Two linear scripts first discovered on Crete in 1900. On the island of Crete and on the mainland areas of Greece, documents of the palace-centered societies were written on clay tablets in these two scripts. Linear A script, apparently written in Minoan, has not yet been deciphered. Linear B was first deciphered in the early 1950s.

"Little Europes" Urban landscapes between 1100 and 1200 composed of castles, churches, and towns in what are today Poland, the Czech Republic, Hungary, and the Baltic States.

Liu Bang Chinese emperor from 206 to 195 BCE; after declaring himself the prince of his home area of Han, in 202 BCE, Liu declared himself the first Han emperor.

llamas Animals similar in utility and function to camels in Afro-Eurasia. Llamas could carry heavy loads for long distances.

Long March (1934–1935) Trek of over 10,000 kilometers by Mao Zedong and his communist followers to establish a new base of operations in northwestern China.

Longshan peoples Peoples who lived in small agricultural and riverine villages in East Asia at the end of the third millennium BCE. They set the stage for the Shang in terms of a centralized state, urban life, and a cohesive culture.

lord Privileged landowner who exercised authority over the people who lived on his land.

lost generation The 17 million former members of the Red Guard and other Chinese youth who were denied education from the late 1960s to the mid-1970s as part of the Chinese government's attempt to prevent political disruptions.

Louisiana Purchase (1803) American purchase of French territory from Napoleon, including much of the present-day United States between the Mississippi River and the Rocky Mountains.

Lucy Relatively intact skeleton of a young adult female australopithecine unearthed in the valley of the Awash River in 1974 by an archaeological team working at a site in present-day Hadar, Ethiopia. The researchers nicknamed the skeleton Lucy. She stood just over three feet tall and walked upright at least some of the time. Her skull contained a brain within the ape size range. Also, her jaw and teeth were humanlike. Lucy's skeleton was relatively complete and at the time, was the oldest hominid skeleton ever discovered.

Luftwaffe German air force.

Luther, Martin (1483–1546) A German monk and theologian who sought to reform the Catholic Church; he believed in salvation through faith alone, the importance of reading Scripture, and the priesthood of all believers. His Ninety-five Theses, which enumerated the abuses by the Catholic Church as well his reforms, started the Protestant Reformation.

Maastricht Treaty (1991) Treaty that formed the European Union, a fully integrated trading and financial bloc with its own bureaucracy and elected representatives.

Ma'at Term used in ancient Egypt to refer to stability or order, the achievement of which was the primary task of Egypt's ruling kings, the pharaohs.

Maccabees Leaders of a riot in Jerusalem in 166 BCE; the riot was a response to a Roman edict outlawing the practice of Judaism.

Madhyamika (Middle Way) Buddhism Chinese branch of Mahayana Buddhism established by Kumarajiva (344–413 CE) that used irony and paradox to show that reason was limited.

madrassas Higher schools of Muslim education that taught law, the Quran, religious sciences, and the regular sciences.

Mahayana (Greater Vehicle) Buddhism School of Buddhist theology that believed that the Buddha was a deity, unlike previous groups that had considered him a wise human being.

Mahdi The "chosen one" in Islam whose appearance was supposed to foretell the end of the world and the final day of reckoning for all people.

maize Grains, the crops that the settled agrarian communities across the Americas cultivated, along with legumes (beans) and tubers (potatoes).

Maji-Maji Revolt (early 1900s) Swahili insurrection against German colonialists; inspired by the belief that those who were anointed with specially blessed water (*maji*) would be immune to bullets. It resulted in 200,000–300,000 African deaths.

Mali Empire West African empire, founded by the legendary king Sundiata in the early thirteenth century. It facilitated thriving commerce, with routes linking the Atlantic Ocean, the Sahara, and beyond.

Mamluks (Arabic for "owned" or "possessed") Military men who ruled Egypt as an independent regime from 1250 until the Ottoman conquest in 1517.

Manaus Opera House Opera house built in the interior of Brazil in a lucrative rubber-growing area at the turn of the twentieth century.

Manchukuo Japanese puppet state in Manchuria in the 1930s.

Manchus Descendants of the Jurchens who helped the Ming army recapture Beijing in 1644 after its seizure by the outlaw Li Zicheng. The Manchus numbered around 1 million but controlled a domain that included perhaps 250 million people. Their rule lasted more than 250 years and became known as the Qing dynasty.

mandate of heaven Ideology established by Zhou dynasts to communicate the moral transfer of power. Originally a pact between the Zhou people and their supreme god, it evolved in the first century BCE into Chinese political doctrine.

Mande A people who lived in the area between the bend in the Senegal River and the bend in the Niger River east to west and from the Senegal River and Bandama River north to south. Also known as the Mandinka. Their civilization emerged around 1100.

Mandela, Nelson (1918–2013) Leader of the African National Congress (ANC) who was imprisoned for more than two decades by the apartheid regime in South Africa for his political beliefs; worldwide protests led to his release in 1990. In 1994 Mandela won the presidency in South Africa's first free mass elections.

Manifest Destiny Belief that it was God's will for the American people to expand their territory and political processes across the North American continent.

manorialism System in which the manor (a lord's home, its associated industry, and surrounding fields) served as the basic unit of economic power; an alternative to feudalism (the hierarchical relationships of king, lords, and peasantry) for thinking about the nature of power in western Europe, 1000–1300.

Mao Zedong (1893–1976) Chinese communist leader who rose to power during the Long March (1934). In 1949, he defeated the Nationalists and established a communist regime in China. Although many of Mao's efforts to transform China, such as the industrialization program of 1958 (known as the Great Leap Forward) and the Cultural Revolution of 1966, failed and brought great suffering to the people, he did instill a new spirit of independence in China and a sense of purpose after many decades of political and economic failure.

maroon community Sanctuary for runaway slaves in the Americas.

Marshall Plan Economic aid package given by the United States to Europe after World War II in hopes of a rapid period of reconstruction and economic gain, thereby securing the countries that received the aid from a communist takeover.

martyrs People executed by the Roman authorities for persisting in their Christian beliefs and refusing to submit to pagan ritual or belief.

Marx, Karl (1818–1883) German philosopher and economist who created Marxism and believed that a revolution of the working classes would overthrow the capitalist order and create a classless society.

Marxism Form of scientific socialism created by Karl Marx and Friedrich Engels that was rooted in a materialist theory of history: what mattered in history were the production of material goods and the ways in which society was organized into classes of producers and exploiters.

mass consumption Increased purchasing power in the early twentieth-century prosperous and mainly middle-class societies, stemming from mass production.

mass culture Distinctive form of popular culture that arose in the wake of World War I. It reflected the tastes of the working and the middle classes, who now had more time and money to spend on entertainment, and relied on new technologies, especially film and radio, which could reach an entire nation's population and consolidate their sense of being a single state.

mass production System in which factories were set up to produce huge quantities of identical products, reflecting the early twentieth-century world's demands for greater volume, faster speed, reduced cost, and standardized output.

Mastaba Word meaning "bench" in Arabic; it refers to a huge flat structure identical to earlier royal tombs of ancient Egypt.

Mau-Mau Revolt (1952–1957) Uprising orchestrated by a Kenyan guerrilla movement; this conflict forced the British to grant independence to the black majority in Kenya.

Mauryan Empire Dynasty extended by the Mauryans from 321 to 184 BCE, from the Indus Valley to the northwest areas of South Asia, in a region previously controlled by Persia. It was the first large-scale empire in South Asia and was to become the model for future Indian empires.

Mawali Non-Arab "clients" to Arab tribes in the early Islamic Empire. Because tribal patronage was so much a part of the Arabian cultural system, non-Arabs who converted to Islam affiliated themselves with a tribe and became clients of that tribe.

Maxim gun European weaponry that was capable of firing many bullets per second; it was used against Africans in the conquest of the continent.

Mayans Civilization that ruled over large stretches of Mesoamerica; it was composed of a series of kingdoms, each built around ritual centers rather than cities. The Mayans engaged neighboring peoples in warfare and trade and expanded borders through tributary relationships. They were not defined by a great ruler or one capital city, but by their shared religious beliefs.

McCarthyism Campaign by Republican senator Joseph McCarthy in the late 1940s and early 1950s to uncover closet communists, particularly in the State Department and in Hollywood.

Meat Inspection Act (1906) Legislation that provided for government supervision of meat-packing operations; it was part of a broader "Progressive" reform movement dedicated to correcting the negative consequences of urbanization and industrialization in the United States.

Mecca Arabian city in which Muhammad was born. Mecca was a trading center and pilgrimage destination in the pre-Islamic and Islamic periods. Exiled in 622 CE because of resistance to his message, Muhammad returned to Mecca in 630 CE and claimed the city for Islam.

Medes Rivals of the Assyrians and the Persians. The Medes inhabited the area from the Zagros Mountains to the modern city of Tehran; known as expert horsemen and archers, they were eventually defeated by the Persians.

megaliths Literally, "great stone"; the word *megalith* is used when describing structures such as Stonehenge. These massive structures are the result of cooperative planning and work.

megarons Large buildings found in Troy (level II) that are the predecessors of the classic Greek temple.

Meiji Empire Empire created under the leadership of Mutsuhito, emperor of Japan from 1868 until 1912. During the Meiji period Japan became a world industrial and naval power.

Meiji Restoration Reign of the Meiji emperor, which was characterized by a new nationalist identity, economic advances, and political transformation.

Mencius Disciple of Confucius who lived from 372 to 289 BCE.

mercantilism Economic theory that drove European empire builders. In this economic system, the world had a fixed amount of wealth, which meant one country's wealth came at the expense of another's. Mercantilism assumed that colonies existed for the sole purpose of enriching the country that controlled the colony.

Mercosur Free-trade pact between the governments of Argentina, Brazil, Paraguay, and Uruguay.

meritocracy Rule by persons of talent.

Meroe Ancient kingdom in what is today Sudan. It flourished for nearly a thousand years, from the fifth century BCE to the fifth century CE.

mestizos Mixed-blood offspring of Spanish settlers and native Indians.

métis Mixed-blood offspring of French settlers and native Indians.

Mexican Revolution (1910) Conflict fueled by the unequal distribution of land and by disgruntled workers; it erupted when political elites split over the succession of General Porfirio Díaz after decades of his rule. The fight lasted over ten years and cost 1 million lives, but it resulted in a widespread reform and a new constitution.

Mfecane **movement** African political revolts in the first half of the nineteenth century that were caused by the expansionist methods of King Shaka of the Zulu people.

microsocieties Small-scale communities that had little interaction with others. These communities were the norm for peoples living in the Americas and islanders in the Pacific and Aegean from 2000 to 1200 BCE.

migration Long-distance travel for the purpose of resettlement. In the case of early man, the need to move was usually a response to an environmental shift, such as climate change during the Ice Age.

millenarian Believer in the imminent coming of a just and ideal society.

millenarian movement Broad, popular upheaval calling for the restoration of a bygone moral age, often led by charismatic spiritual prophets.

Millets Minority religious communities of the Ottoman Empire.

minaret Slender tower within a mosque from which Muslims are called to prayer.

minbar Pulpit inside a mosque from which Muslim religious speakers broadcast their message to the faithful.

Minoans A people who built a large number of elaborate, independent palace centers on Crete, at Knossos, and elsewhere around 2000 BCE. Named after the legendary King Minos, said to have ruled Crete at the time, they sailed throughout the Mediterranean and by 1600 BCE had planted colonies on many Aegean islands, which in turn became trading and mining centers.

mission civilisatrice Term French colonizers used to refer to France's form of "rationalized" colonial rule, which attempted to bring "civilization" to the "uncivilized."

mitochondrial DNA Form of DNA found outside the nucleus of cells, where it serves as cells' microscopic power packs. Examining mitochondrial DNA enables researchers to measure the genetic variation among living objects, including human beings.

Moche A people who extended their power and increased their wealth at the height of the Chimu Empire over several valleys in what is now Peru.

Model T First automobile, manufactured by the Ford Motor Company of Henry Ford, to be priced reasonably enough to be sold to the masses.

Modernists A generation of exuberant young artists, writers, and scientists in the late nineteenth century who broke with older conventions and sought new ways of seeing and describing the world.

Mohism School of thought in ancient China, named after Mo Di, or Mozi, who lived from 479 to 438 BCE. It emphasized one's obligation to society as a whole, not just to one's immediate family or social circle.

monarchy Political system in which one individual holds supreme power and passes that power on to his or her next of kin.

monasticism Christian way of life that originated in Egypt and was practiced as early as 300 CE in the Mediterranean. The word itself contains the meaning of a person "living alone" without marriage or family.

monetization An economic shift from a barter-based economy to one dependent on coin.

Mongols Combination of nomadic forest and prairie peoples who lived by hunting and livestock herding and were expert horsemen. Beginning in 1206, the Mongols launched a series of conquests that brought far-flung parts of the world together under their rule. By incorporating conquered peoples and adapting some of their customs, the Mongols created a unified empire that stretched from the Pacific Ocean to the shores of the eastern Mediterranean and the southern steppes of Eurasia.

monotheism The belief in only one god.

Moors Term employed by Europeans in the medieval period to refer to Muslim occupants of North Africa, the western Sahara, and the Iberian Peninsula.

mosque Place of worship for the people of Islam.

Mound people Name for the people of Cahokia, since its landscape was dominated by earthen monuments in the shapes of mounds. The mounds were carefully maintained and were the loci from which Cahokians paid respect to spiritual forces. *See also* Cahokia.

Mu Chinese ruler (956–918 BCE) who put forth a formal bureaucratic system of governance, appointing officials,

supervisors, and military captains to whom he was not related. He also instituted a formal legal code.

muckrakers Journalists who aimed to expose political and commercial corruption in late-nineteenth- and early twentieth-century America.

Muftis Experts on Muslim religious law.

Mughal Empire One of Islam's greatest regimes. Established in 1526, it was a vigorous, centralized state whose political authority encompassed most of modern-day India. During the sixteenth century, it had a population of between 100 and 150 million.

Muhammad (570–632 CE) Prophet and founder of the Islamic faith. Born in Mecca in Saudi Arabia and orphaned when young, Muhammad lived under the protection of his uncle. His career as a prophet began around 610 CE, with his first experience of spiritual revelation.

Muhammad Ali Ruler of Egypt between 1805 and 1848. He initiated a set of modernizing reforms that sought to make Egypt competitive with the great powers.

mullahs Religious leaders in Iran who in the 1970s led a movement opposing Shah Reza Pahlavi and denounced American materialism and secularism.

multinational corporations Corporations based in many different countries that have global investment, trading, and distribution goals.

Muscovy The principality of Moscow. Originally a mixture of Slavs, Finnish tribes, Turkic speakers, and many others, Muscovy used territorial expansion and commercial networks to consolidate a powerful state and expanded to become the Russian Empire, a huge realm that spanned parts of Europe, much of northern Asia, numerous North Pacific islands, and even—for a time—a corner of North America (Alaska).

Muslim Brotherhood Egyptian organization founded in 1938 by Hassan

al-Banna. It attacked liberal democracy as a cover for middle-class, business, and landowning interests and fought for a return to a purified Islam.

Muslim League National Muslim party of India.

Mussolini, Benito (1883–1945) Italian dictator and founder of the fascist movement in Italy. During World War II, he allied Italy with Germany and Japan.

Muwahhidin Term meaning "unitarians"; these were followers of the Wahhabi movement that emerged in the Arabian Peninsula in the eighteenth century.

Mycenaeans Mainland competitors of the Minoans; they took over Crete around 1400 BCE. Migrating to Greece from central Europe, they brought their Indo-European language, horse chariots, and metalworking skills, which they used to dominate until 1200 BCE.

Nagasaki Second Japanese city to be hit by an atomic bomb near the end of World War II.

Napoleon Bonaparte (1769–1821) General who rose to power in a post-Revolutionary coup d'état, eventually proclaiming himself emperor of France. He placed security and order ahead of social reform and created a civil legal code. Napoleon expanded his empire through military action, but after his disastrous Russian campaign, the united European powers defeated Napoleon and forced him into exile. He escaped and reassumed command of his army but was later defeated at the Battle of Waterloo.

Napoleonic Code Legal code drafted by Napoleon in 1804; it distilled different legal traditions to create one uniform law. The code confirmed the abolition of feudal privileges of all kinds and set the conditions for exercising property rights.

National Assembly of France Governing body of France that succeeded the Estates-General in 1789 during the French Revolution. It was composed of, and defined by, the delegates of the Third Estate.

National Association for the Advancement of Colored People (NAACP) Founded in 1910, the U.S. civil rights organization dedicated to ending inequality and segregation for black Americans.

National Recovery Administration (NRA) New Deal agency created in 1933 to prepare codes of fair administration and to plan for public works. It was later declared unconstitutional.

nationalism The idea that members of a shared community called a "nation" should have sovereignty within the borders of their state.

nation-state Form of political organization that derived legitimacy from its inhabitants, often referred to as citizens, who in theory, if not always in practice, shared a common language, common culture, and common history.

native learning Japanese movement to promote nativist intellectual traditions and the celebration of Japanese texts.

native paramountcy British form of "rationalized" colonial rule, which attempted to bring "civilization" to the "uncivilized" by proclaiming that when the interests of European settlers in Africa clashed with those of the African population, the latter should take precedence.

natural rights Belief that emerged in eighteenth-century western Europe and North America that rights fundamental to human nature were discernible to reason and should be affirmed in human-made law.

natural selection Charles Darwin's theory that populations grew faster than the food supply, creating a "struggle for existence" among species. In later work he showed how the passing on of individual traits was also determined by what he

called sexual selection—according to which the "best" mates are chosen for their strength, beauty, or talents. The outcome: the "fittest" survived to reproduce, while the less adaptable did not.

Nazis (National Socialist German Workers Party) German organization dedicated to winning workers over from socialism to nationalism; the first Nazi Party platform combined nationalism with anticapitalism and anti-Semitism.

Neanderthals Members of an early wave of hominids from Africa who settled in western Afro-Eurasia, in an area reaching from present-day Uzbekistan and Iraq to Spain, approximately 150,000 years ago.

needle compass Crucial instrument made available to navigators after 1000 CE that helped guide sailors on the high seas. It was a Chinese invention.

negritos Hunter-gatherer inhabitants of the East Asian coastal islands who migrated there around 28,000 BCE but by 2000 BCE had been replaced by new migrants.

Negritude Statement of the virtues of the black identity and the validation of African culture and the African past, even in a westernizing world. This idea was shaped by African and African American intellectuals like Senegal's first president, Léopold Sédar Senghor.

Nehemiah Jewish eunuch of the Persian court who was given permission to rebuild the fortification walls around the city of Jerusalem from 440 to 437 BCE.

Neo-Assyrian Empire Afro-Eurasian empire that dominated around 950 BCE. The Neo-Assyrians extended their control over resources and people beyond their own borders, and their empire lasted for three centuries.

Nestorian Christians Denomination of Christians whose beliefs about Christ differed from those of the

official Byzantine church. Named after Nestorius, former bishop of Constantinople, they emphasized the human aspects of Jesus.

New Deal President Franklin Delano Roosevelt's package of government reforms that were enacted during the 1930s to provide jobs for the unemployed, social welfare programs for the poor, and security to the financial markets.

New Economic Policy Enacted decrees of the Bolsheviks between 1921 and 1927 that grudgingly sanctioned private trade and private property.

New Negro movement *See* Harlem Renaissance.

New World Term applied to the Americas that reflected the Europeans' view that anything previously unknown to them was "new," even if it had existed and supported societies long before European explorers arrived on its shores.

nirvana Literally, nonexistence; *nirvana* is the state of complete liberation from the concerns of worldly life, as in Buddhist thought.

Nō drama Masked theater favored by Japanese bureaucrats and regional lords during the Tokugawa period.

Noble Eightfold Path Buddhist concept of a way of life by which people may rid themselves of individual desire to achieve *nirvana*. The path consists of wisdom, ethical behavior, and mental discipline.

Nok culture Spectacular culture that arose in what is today Nigeria, in the sixth century BCE. Iron smelting occurred there around 600 BCE. Thus the Nok people made the transition from stone to iron materials.

nomads People who move across vast distances without settling permanently in a particular place. Often pastoralists, nomads and transhumant herders introduced new forms of chariot-based warfare that transformed the Afro-Eurasian world.

non-governmental organizations (NGOs) Term used to refer to private organizations like the Red Cross that play a large role in international affairs.

nonviolent resistance (satyagraha) Moral and political philosophy of resistance developed by Indian National Congress leader Mohandas Gandhi. Gandhi believed that if Indians pursued self-reliance and self-control in a nonviolent way, the British would eventually have to leave.

North American Free Trade Agreement (NAFTA) Treaty negotiated in the early 1990s to promote free trade between Canada, the United States, and Mexico.

North Atlantic Treaty Organization (NATO) International organization set up in1949 to provide for the defense of western European countries and the United States from the perceived Soviet threat.

Northern Wei dynasty Regime founded in 386 CE by the Tuoba, a people originally from Inner Mongolia, that lasted one and a half centuries. The rulers of this dynasty adopted many practices of the earlier Chinese Han regime. At the same time, they struggled to consolidate authority over their own nomadic people. Ultimately, several decades of intense internal conflict led to the dynasty's downfall.

northwest passage Long-sought marine passageway between the Atlantic and Pacific oceans.

Oceania Collective name for the lands of Australia and New Zealand and the islands of the southwest Pacific Ocean.

Odyssey Composed in the eighth century BCE, an epic tale of the journey of Odysseus, who traveled the Mediterranean back to his home in Ithaca after the siege of Troy.

oikos The word for "small family unit" in ancient Greece, similar to the familia in Rome. Its structure, with men as heads of household over women and children, embodied the fundamental power structure in Greek city-states.

oligarchy Clique of privileged rulers.

Olmecs A people who emerged around 1500 BCE and lived in Mesoamerica. The name means those who "lived in the land of the rubber." Olmec society was composed of decentralized villages. Its members spoke the same language and worshipped the same gods.

Open Door Policy Policy proposed by American Secretary of State John Hay that would give all foreign nations equal access to trade with China. As European imperial powers carved out spheres of trade in late-nineteenth-century China, American leaders worried that the United States would be excluded from trade with China. To prevent this, Hay proposed the Open Door Policy.

Opium War (1839–1842) War fought between the British and Qing China over British trade in opium; resulted in granting to the British the right to trade in five different ports and the ceding of Hong Kong to the British.

oracle bones Animal bones used by Shang diviners. Diviners applied intense heat to the shoulder bones of cattle or to turtle shells, which caused them to crack. The diviners would then interpret the cracks as signs from the ancestors regarding royal plans and actions.

Organization of Petroleum Exporting Countries (OPEC) International association established in 1960 to coordinate price and supply policies of oil-producing states.

orientalism Genre of literature and painting that portrayed the non-western peoples of North Africa and Asia as exotic, sensuous, and economically backward with respect to Europeans.

orientalists Western scholars who specialized in the study of the East.

Orrorin tugenensis Predecessor to hominids that first appeared 6 million years ago.

Ottoman Empire Rulers of Anatolia, the Arab world, and much of southern and eastern Europe in the early sixteenth century. They transformed themselves from nomadic warrior bands who roamed the borderlands between Islamic and Christian worlds in Anatolia into sovereigns of a vast, bureaucratic empire. The Ottomans embraced a Sunni view of Islam. They adapted traditional Byzantine governmental practices but tried new ways of integrating the diverse peoples of their empire.

Pacific War (1879–1883) War between Chile and the alliance of Bolivia and Peru.

pagani Pejorative word used by Christians to designate pagans.

palace Official residence of the ruler, his family, and his entourage. The palace was both a social institution and a set of buildings. It first appeared around 2500 BCE, about a millennium later than the Mesopotamian temple, and quickly joined the temple as a defining landmark of city life. Eventually, it became a source of power rivaling the temple, and palace and temple life often blurred, as did the boundary between the sacred and the secular.

Palace of Versailles The palace complex, eleven miles away from the French capital of Paris, built by Louis XIV in the 1670s and 1680s to house and entertain his leading clergymen and nobles, with the hopes of diverting them from plotting against him.

Palmyra Roman trading depot in modern-day Syria; part of a network of trading cities that connected various regions of Afro-Eurasia.

pan movements Groups that sought to link people across state boundaries in new communities based on ethnicity or, in some cases, religion (e.g., pan-Germanism, pan-Islamism, pan-Slavism).

Pansophia Ideal republic of inquisitive Christians united in the search for knowledge of nature as a means of loving God.

papacy The institution of the pope; the Catholic spiritual leader in Rome.

papal Of, relating to, or issued by a pope.

Parthians Horse-riding people who pushed southward around the middle of the second century BCE and wiped out the Greek kingdoms in Iran. They then extended their power all the way to the Mediterranean, where they ran up against the Roman Empire in Anatolia and Mesopotamia.

pastoral nomadic communities Groups of people that moved their domesticated animals from place to place to meet the animals' demanding grazing requirements. Around 3500 BCE, western Afro-Eurasia witnessed the growth and spread of pastoral nomadic communities.

pastoralism Herding and breeding of sheep and goats or other animals as a primary means of subsistence.

paterfamilias Latin for "Father of the family," which itself was the foundation of the Roman social order.

patria Latin, meaning "fatherland."

patrons In the Roman system of patronage, men and women of wealth and high social status who protected dependents or "clients" of a lower class.

Pax Mongolica Term that refers to the political and especially the commercial stability that the vast Mongol Empire provided for the travelers and merchants of Eurasia during the thirteenth and fourteenth centuries.

Pax Romana Latin for "Roman Peace"; refers to the period between 25 BCE and 235 CE during which conditions in the Roman Empire were settled and peaceful.

Pax Sinica Period of peace (149–87 BCE) during which agriculture, commerce, and industry flourished in East Asia under the rule of the Han.

Peace Preservation Act (1925) Act instituted in Japan that specified up to ten years' hard labor for any member of an organization advocating a basic change in the political system or the abolition of private property.

Pearl Harbor American naval base in Hawaii on which the Japanese launched a surprise attack on December 7, 1941, bringing the United States into World War II.

Peloponnesian War War fought between 431 and 404 BCE between two of Greece's most powerful city-states, Athens and Sparta.

Peninsular War (1808–1814) Conflict in which the Portuguese and Spanish populations, supported by the British, resisted the French invasion under Napoleon of the Iberian Peninsula.

Peninsulars Spaniards who, although born in Spain, resided in the Spanish colonial territories. They regarded themselves as superior to Spaniards born in the colonies (creoles).

Peoples' Charter Document calling for universal suffrage for adult males, the secret ballot, electoral districts, and annual parliamentary elections. It was signed by over 3 million British between 1839 and 1842.

periplus Book that reflected sailing knowledge; in such books captains would record landing spots and ports. The word *periplus* literally means "sailing around."

Persepolis Darius I's capital city in the highlands of Fars; a ceremonial center and expression of imperial identity as well as an important administrative hub.

Peterloo Massacre (1819) The killing of 11 and wounding of 460 following a peaceful demonstration for political reform by workers in Manchester, England.

Petra City in modern-day Jordan that was the Nabataean capital. It profited greatly by supplying provisions and water to travelers and traders. Many of its houses and shrines were cut into the rocky mountains. *Petra* means "rock."

phalanx Military formation used by Philip II of Macedonia, whereby heavily armored infantry were closely arrayed in battle formation.

Philip II of Macedonia Father of Alexander the Great, under whose rule Macedonia developed into a large ethnic and territorial state. After unifying Macedonia, Philip went on to conquer neighboring states.

philosophes Enlightenment thinkers who applied scientific reasoning to human interaction and society as opposed to nature.

philosophia Literally "love of wisdom"; this system of thought originally included speculation on the nature of the cosmos, the environment, and human existence. It eventually came to include thought about the nature of humans and life in society.

Phoenicians Known as the Canaanites in the Bible, an ethnic group in the Levant under Assyrian rule in the seventh century BCE; they provided ships and sailors for battles in the Mediterranean. The word *Phoenician* refers to the purple dye they manufactured and widely traded, along with other commercial goods and services, throughout the Mediterranean. While part of wider Mesopotamian culture, their major contribution was the alphabet, first introduced in the second millennium BCE, which made far-reaching communication possible.

phonemes Primary and distinctive sounds that are characteristic of human language.

piety Strong sense of religious duty and devoutness, often inspiring extraordinary actions.

plant domestication Process of growing plants, harvesting their seeds, and saving some of the seeds for planting in subsequent growing cycles, resulting in a steady food supply. This process occurred as far back as 5000 BCE, when plants began to naturally retain their seeds. Plant domestication was practiced first in the southern Levant and spread from there into the rest of Southwest Asia.

Plato (427–347 BCE) Disciple of the great philosopher Socrates; his works are the only record we have of Socrates's teaching. He was also the author of formative philosophical works on ethics and politics.

plebs In Rome, term that referred to the "common people." Their interests were protected by officials called tribunes.

Pochteca Archaic term for merchants of the Mexicos.

polities Politically organized communities or states.

polyglot communities Societies composed of diverse linguistic and ethnic groups.

popular culture Affordable and accessible forms of art and entertainment available to people at all levels of society.

popular sovereignty The idea that the power of the state resides in the people.

populists Members of a political movement that supported U.S. farmers in late-nineteenth-century America. The term is often used generically to refer to political groups who appeal to the majority of the population.

potassium-argon dating Major dating technique based on the changing chemical structure of objects over time, since over time potassium decays into argon. This method makes possible the dating of objects up to a million years old.

potato famine (1840s) Severe famine in Ireland that led to the rise of radical political movements and the migration of large numbers of Irish to the United States.

potter's wheel Fast wheel that enabled people to mass-produce vessels in many different shapes. This advance,

invented at the city of Uruk, enabled potters to make significant technical breakthroughs.

pottery Vessels made of mud and later clay that were used for storing and transporting food. The development of pottery was a major breakthrough.

Prague Spring (1968) Program of liberalization under a new communist party in Czechoslovakia that strove to create a democratic and pluralist socialism.

predestinarian Belief of many sixteenth- and seventeenth-century Protestant groups that God had foreordained the lives of individuals, including their bad and good deeds.

primitivism Western art movement of the late-nineteenth and early twentieth centuries that drew upon the so-called primitive art forms of Africa, Oceania, and pre-Columbian America.

progressive reformers Members of the U.S. reform movement in the early twentieth century that aimed to eliminate political corruption, improve working conditions, and regulate the power of large industrial and financial enterprises.

proletarians Industrial wage workers.

prophets Charismatic freelance religious men of power who found themselves in opposition to the formal power of the kings, bureaucrats, and priests.

Prophet's Town Indian village that was burned down by American forces in the early nineteenth century.

Protestant Reformation Religious movement initiated by sixteenth-century monk Martin Luther, who openly criticized the corruption in the Catholic Church and voiced his belief that Christians could speak directly to God. His doctrines gained wide support, and those who followed this new view of the Christianity rejected the authority of the papacy and the Catholic clergy, broke away from the Catholic Church, and called themselves "Protestants."

Protestantism Division of Christianity that emerged in western Europe from the Protestant Reformation.

Proto-Indo-European The parent of all the languages in the Indo-European family, which includes, among many others, English, German, Norwegian, Portuguese, French, Russian, Persian, Hindi, and Bengali.

Pullman Strike (1894) American Railway Union strike in response to wage cuts and firings.

Punic Wars Three wars waged between the Romans and Carthage in the third and second centuries BCE that resulted in the defeat of the Carthaginian hegemony in the western Mediterranean and demonstrated the might of the Roman military (army and navy) and the beginnings of Rome's aggressive foreign imperialism.

puppet states Governments with little power in the international arena that follow the dictates of their more powerful neighbors or patrons.

Puritans Seventeenth-century reform group of the Church of England; also known as dissenters or nonconformists.

Qadiriyya Sufi order that facilitated the spread of Islam into West Africa.

Qadis Judges in the Ottoman Empire.

qanats Underground water channels, vital for irrigation, which were used in Persia. Little evaporation occurred when water was being moved through qanats.

Qing dynasty (1644–1911) Minority Manchu rule over China that incorporated new territories, experienced substantial population growth, and sustained significant economic growth.

Questions of King Milanda (Milinda-punha) Name of a second-century BCE text espousing the teachings of Buddhism as set forth by Menander, a Yavana king. It featured a discussion between the king and a sophisticated Buddhist sage named Nagasena.

Quetzalcoatl Ancient deity and legendary ruler of Native American peoples living in Mexico.

Quran The scripture of the Islamic faith. Originally a verbal recitation, the Quran was eventually compiled into a book in the order in which we have it today. According to traditional Islamic interpretation, the Quran was revealed to Muhammad by the angel Gabriel over a period of twenty-three years.

radicals Widely used term in nineteenth-century Europe that referred to those individuals and political organizations that favored the total reconfiguration of Europe's old state system.

radiocarbon isotope C^{14} Isotope contained by all living things, which plants acquire directly from the atmosphere and animals acquire indirectly when they consume plants or other animals. When living things die, the C^{14} isotope they contain begins to decay into a stable nonradioactive element, C^{12}. The rate of decay is regular and measurable, making it possible to ascertain the date of fossils that leave organic remains for ages of up to 40,000 years.

raj British crown's administration of India following the end of the East India Company's rule after the Rebellion of 1857.

raja "King" in the Kshatriya period in South Asia; could also refer to the head of a family, but indicated the person who had control of land and resources in South Asian city-states.

Ramadan Ninth month of the Muslim year, during which all Muslims must fast during daylight hours.

Rape of Nanjing Attack against the Chinese in which the Japanese slaughtered at least 100,000 civilians and raped thousands of women between December 1937 and February 1938.

Rashtriya Swayamsevak Sangh (RSS) (1925) Campaign to organize Hindus as a militant, modern community in India; translated in English as "National Volunteer Organization."

Rebellion of 1857 Indian uprising against the East India Company to bring religious purification, an egalitarian society, and local and communal solidarity without the interference of British rule.

rebus Probably originating in Uruk, a representation that transfers meaning from the name of a thing to the sound of that name. For example, a picture of a bee can represent the sound "b." Such pictures opened the door to writing: a technology of symbols that uses marks to represent specific discrete sounds.

Reconquista Spanish reconquest of territories lost to the Islamic Empire, beginning with Toledo in 1061.

Red Guards Chinese students who were the shock troopers in the early phases of Mao's Cultural Revolution in 1966–1968.

Red Lanterns Female supporters of the Chinese Boxers who rebelled against foreign intrusions in China at the turn of the twentieth century. Most were teenage girls and unmarried women and dressed in red garments.

Red Turban movement Diverse religious movement in China during the fourteenth century that spread the belief that the world was drawing to an end as Mongol rule was collapsing.

Reds Bolsheviks.

Reich German empire composed of Denmark, Austria, and parts of western France.

Reichstag The German parliament.

Reign of Terror Campaign at the height of the French Revolution in the early 1790s that used violence, including systematic execution of opponents of the revolution, to purge France of its enemies and to extend the revolution beyond its borders; radicals executed

as many as 40,000 persons who were judged enemies of the state.

Renaissance Term meaning "rebirth" that historians use to characterize the expanded cultural production of European nations between 1430 and 1550. Emphasized a break from the church-centered medieval world and a new concept of humankind as the center of the world.

republican government Government in which power and rulership rest with representatives of the people—not a king.

Res publica Literally "public thing"; this referred to the Roman republic, in which policy and rules of behavior were determined by the Senate and by popular assemblies of the citizens.

Restoration period (1815–1848) European movement after the defeat of Napoleon to restore Europe to its pre-French revolutionary status and to quash radical movements.

Rift Valley Area of northeastern Africa where some of the most important early human archaeological discoveries of fossils were found, especially one of an intact skull that is 1.8 million years old.

river basin Area drained by a river, including all its tributaries. River basins were rich in fertile soil, water for irrigation, and plant and animal life, which made them attractive for human habitation. Cultivators were able to produce surplus agriculture to support the first cities.

riverine Term denoting an area whose inhabitants depend on irrigation for their well-being and whose populations are settled near great rivers. Egypt was, in a sense, the most riverine of all these cultures, in that it had no hinterland of plains as did Mesopotamia and the Indus Valley. Away from the banks of the Nile, there is only largely uninhabitable desert.

Roman army Military force of the Roman Empire. The Romans devised a military draft that could draw from a huge population. In their encounter with Hannibal, they lost up to 80,000 men in three separate encounters and still won the war.

Roman Catholicism Branch of Christianity established by 1000 CE in western Europe and led by the Roman papacy. In contrast to ancient Greek Orthodoxy, western Catholics believed that their church was destined to expand everywhere, and they set about converting the pagan tribes of northern Europe. Western Catholics contemptuously called the eastern Romans "Greeks" and condemned them for their "Byzantine" cunning.

Roman law Roman legal system, under which disputes were brought to the public courts and decisions were made by judges and sometimes by large juries. Rome's legal system featured written law and institutions for settling legal disputes.

roving bandits Large bands of dispossessed and marginalized peasants who vented their anger at tax collectors in the waning years of the Ming dynasty.

Royal Road A 1,600-mile road from Sardis in Anatolia to Susa in Iran; used by messengers, traders, the army, and those taking tribute to the king.

Russification Programs to assimilate people of over 146 dialects into the Russian Empire.

S.S. (*Schutzstaffel*) Hitler's security police force.

Sack of Constantinople Rampage in 1204 by the Frankish armies on the capital city of Constantinople.

sacred kingships Institutions that marked the centralized politics of West Africa. The inhabitants of these kingships believed that their kings were descendants of the gods.

Sahel region Area of sub-Saharan Africa with wetter and more temperate locations, especially in the upland massifs and their foothills, villages, and towns.

St. Bartholomew's Day Massacre (1572) Roman Catholic massacre of French Protestants in Paris.

St. Patrick Former slave brought to Ireland from Britain who later became a missionary, or the "Apostle of Ireland." He died in 470 CE.

Salt March (1930) A 240-mile trek to the sea in India, led by Mohandas Gandhi, to gather salt for free, thus breaking the British colonial monopoly on salt.

Samurai Japanese warriors who made up the private armies of Japanese daimyos.

Sandinista coalition Left-leaning Nicaraguan coalition of the 1970s and 1980s.

Sanskrit cosmopolis A cultural synthesis based on Hindu spiritual beliefs and articulated in the Sanskrit language that served to unify South Asia in place of a centralized empire.

Santería African-based religion, blended with Christian influences, that was first practiced by slaves in Cuba.

Sargon the Great King of Akkad, a city-state near modern Baghdad. Reigning from 2334 to 2279 BCE, Sargon helped bring the competitive era of city-states to an end and sponsored monumental works of architecture, art, and literature.

Sasanian Empire Empire that succeeded the Parthians in the mid-220s CE in Inner Eurasia. The Sasanian Empire controlled the trade crossroads of Afro-Eurasia and possessed a strong armored cavalry, which made them a powerful rival to Rome. The Sasanians were also tolerant of Judaism and Christianity, which allowed Christians to flourish.

sati Hindu practice whereby a woman was burned to death on the pyre of her dead husband.

satrap Governor of a province in the Persian Empire. Each satrap was a relative or intimate associate of the king.

satyagraha See nonviolent resistance.

scientific method Method of inquiry based on experimentation in nature. Many of its principles were first laid out by the philosopher Sir Francis Bacon (1561–1626), who claimed that real science entailed the formulation of hypotheses that could be tested in carefully controlled experiments.

Scramble for Africa European rush to colonize parts of Africa at the end of the nineteenth century.

scribes Those who wield writing tools; from the very beginning they were at the top of the social ladder, under the major power brokers.

Scythian ethos Warrior ethos that embodied the extremes of aggressive mounted-horse culture, c. 1000 BCE. In part the Scythian ethos was the result of the constant struggle between settlers, hunter-gatherers, and nomads on the northern frontier of Europe.

Sea Peoples Migrants from north of the Mediterranean who invaded the cities of Egypt and the Levant in the second millennium BCE. Once settled along the coast of the Levant, they became known as the Philistines and considerably disrupted the settlements of the Canaanites.

SEATO (Southeast Asia Treaty Organization) Military alliance of pro-American, anticommunist states in Southeast Asia from 1954 to 1977.

Second World Term invented during the cold war to refer to the communist countries, as opposed to the West (or First World) and the former colonies (or Third World).

second-generation societies Societies that expanded old ideas and methods by incorporating new aspects of culture and grafting them onto, or using them in combination with, established norms.

Seleucus Nikator Successor of Alexander the Great who lived from 358 to 281 BCE. He controlled Mesopotamia, Syria, Persia, and parts of the Punjab.

Self-Strengthening movement In the latter half of the nineteenth century, a movement of reformist Chinese bureaucrats that attempted to adopt western elements of learning and technological skill while retaining their core Chinese culture.

Semu Term meaning "outsiders" or non-Chinese people—Mongols, Tanguts, Khitan, Jurchen, Muslims, Tibetans, Persians, Turks, Nestorians, Jews, and Armenians—who became a new ruling elite over a Han majority population in the late thirteenth century.

sepoys Hindu and Muslim recruits of the East India Company's military force.

serfs Peasants who farmed the land and paid fees to be protected and governed by lords under a system of rule called feudalism.

settled agriculture Application of human labor and tools to a fixed plot of land for more than one growing cycle. It entails the changeover from a hunting-and-gathering lifestyle to one based on agriculture, which requires staying in one place until the soil has been exhausted.

Seven Years' War (1756–1763) Worldwide war that ended when Prussia defeated Austria, establishing itself as a European power, and when Britain gained control of India and many of France's colonies through the Treaty of Paris.

sexual revolution Increased freedom in sexual behavior, resulting in part from the advances in contraception, notably the introduction of oral contraception in 1960, which allowed men and women to limit childbearing and to have sex with less fear of pregnancy.

shah Traditional title of Persian rulers.

shamans Certain humans whose powers supposedly enabled them to commune with the supernatural and to transform themselves wholly or partly into beasts.

shamisen Three-stringed instrument, often played by Japanese geisha.

Shandingdong Man A *Homo sapiens* whose fossil remains and relics can be dated to about 18,000 years ago. His physical characteristics were close to those of modern humans, and he had a similar brain size.

Shang state Dynasty in northeastern China that ruled from 1600 to 1045 BCE. Though not as well defined by borders as the territorial states in the southwest of Asia, it did have a ruling lineage. Four fundamental elements of the Shang state were a metal industry based on copper, pottery making, standardized architectural forms and walled towns, and divination using animal bones.

Shanghai School Late-nineteenth-century style of painting characterized by an emphasis on spontaneous brushwork, feeling, and the incorporation of western influences into classical Chinese pieces.

sharecropping System of farming in which tenant farmers rented land and gave over a share of their crops to the land's owners. Sometimes seen as a cheap way for the state to conduct agricultural affairs, sharecropping often resulted in the impoverishment and marginalization of the underclass.

sharia Literally, "the way"; now used to indicate the philosophy and rulings of Islamic law.

Sharpeville Massacre (1960) Massacre of sixty-nine black Africans when police fired upon a rally against the recently passed laws requiring nonwhite South Africans to carry identity papers.

Shawnees Native American tribe that inhabited the Ohio valley during the eighteenth century.

Shays's Rebellion (1786) Uprising of armed farmers that broke out when the Massachusetts state government refused to offer them economic relief.

Shi Huangdi *See* Zheng.

Shiism One of the two main branches of Islam, practiced in the Safavid Empire. Although always a minority sect in the Islamic world, Shiism contains several subsects, each of which has slightly different interpretations of theology and politics.

Shiites Group of supporters of Ali, Muhammad's cousin and son-in-law, who wanted him to be the first caliph and believed that members of the Prophet's family deserved to rule. The leaders of the Shiite community are known as "Imam," which means "leaders."

Shinto Japan's official religion; it promoted the state and the emperor's divinity. The term means "the way of the gods."

shoguns Japanese military commanders. From 1192 to 1333, the Kamakura shoguns served as military "protectors" of the ruler in the city of Heian.

Shotoku Prince in the early Japanese Yamoto state (574–622 CE) who is credited with having introduced Buddhism to Japan.

shudras Literally "small ones"; workers and slaves from outside the Vedic lineage.

Siddhartha Gautama Another name for the Buddha; the most prominent opponent of the Brahman way of life; he lived from 563 to 483 BCE.

Sikhism Islamic-inspired religion that calls on its followers to renounce the caste system and to treat all believers as equal before God.

Silicon Valley Valley between the California cities of San Francisco and San Jose, known for its innovative computer and high-technology industries.

silk Luxury textile that became a vastly popular export from China (via the Silk Roads) to the cities of the Roman world.

Silk Roads Trade routes linking China with central Asia and the Mediterranean; it extended over 5,000 miles, land and sea included, and was so named because of the quantities of silk that were traded along it. The Silk Roads were a major factor in the development of civilizations in China, Egypt, Persia, India, and even Europe.

Silla One of three independent Korean states that may have emerged as early as the third century BCE. These states lasted until 668 CE, when Silla took control over the entire peninsula.

Silver Islands Term used by European merchants in the sixteenth century to refer to Japan, because of its substantial trade in silver with China.

Sino-Japanese War (1894–1895) Conflict over the control of Korea in which China was forced to cede the province of Taiwan to Japan.

Sipahi Urdu for "soldier."

Siva The third of three Vedic deities, signifying destruction. *See also* Brahma *and* Vishnu.

slave plantations System whereby labor was used for the cultivation of crops wholly for the sake of producing surplus that was then used for profit; slave plantations were a crucial part of the growth of the Mediterranean economy.

small seal script Unified script that was used to the exclusion of other scripts under the Qin, with the aim of centralizing administration; its use led to a less complicated style of clerical writing than had been in use under the Han.

social contract The idea, drawn from the writings of British philosopher John Locke, that the law should bind both ruler and people.

Social Darwinism Belief that Charles Darwin's theory of evolution was applicable to humans and justified the right of the ruling classes or countries to dominate the weak.

social hierarchies Distinctions between the privileged and the less privileged.

Social Security Act (1935) New Deal act that instituted old-age pensions and insurance for the unemployed.

socialism Political ideology that calls for a classless society with collective ownership of all property.

Socrates (469–399 BCE) Philosopher in Athens who encouraged people to reflect on ethics and morality. He stressed the importance of honor and integrity as opposed to wealth and power. Plato was his student.

Sogdians A people who lived in central Asia's commercial centers and maintained the stability and accessibility of the Silk Roads. They were crucial to the interconnectedness of the Afro-Eurasian landmass.

Solidarity The communist bloc's first independent trade union, it was established in Poland at the Gdansk shipyard.

Song dynasty Chinese dynasty that took over the mandate of heaven for three centuries starting in 976 CE. It ruled an era of many economic and political successes, but it eventually lost northern China to nomadic tribes.

Song porcelain Type of porcelain perfected during the Song period that was light, durable, and quite beautiful.

South African War (1899–1902) Conflict between the British and Dutch colonists of South Africa which resulted in bringing two Afrikaner republics under the control of the British. Often called the Boer War.

Soviet bloc International alliance that included the east European countries of the Warsaw Pact as well as the Soviet Union but also came to include Cuba.

Spanish-American War (1898) War between the United States and Spain in Cuba, Puerto Rico, and the Philippines. It ended with a treaty in which the United States took over the Philippines, Guam, and Puerto Rico; Cuba won partial independence.

speciation The formation of different species.

specie Money in coin.

species Group of animals or plants possessing one or more distinctive characteristics.

spiritual ferment Process that occurred after 300 CE in which religion touched more areas of society and culture than before and touched them in different, more demanding ways.

Spring and Autumn period Period between the eighth and fifth centuries BCE, during which China was ruled by the feudal system. Considered an anarchic and turbulent time, there were 148 different tributary states in this period.

Stalin, Joseph (1879–1953) Leader of the communist party and the Soviet Union; sought to create "socialism in one country."

steel A metal more malleable and stronger than iron that became essential for industries like shipbuilding and railways.

stoicism Widespread philosophical movement initiated by Zeno (334–262 BCE). Zeno and his followers sought to understand the role of people in relation to the cosmos. For the Stoics, everything was grounded in nature. Being in love with nature and living a good life required being in control of one's passions and thus indifferent to pleasure or pain.

Strait of Malacca Seagoing gateway to Southeast and East Asia.

Strategic Defense Initiative ("Star Wars") Master plan, championed by U.S. president Ronald Reagan in the 1980s, that envisions the deployment of satellites and space missiles to protect the United States from incoming nuclear bombs.

stupa Dome monument marking the burial site of relics of the Buddha.

Suez Canal Channel built in 1869 across the Isthmus of Suez to connect the Mediterranean Sea with the Red Sea and to lower the costs of international trade.

Sufi brotherhoods Mystics within Islam who were responsible for the expansion of Islam into many regions of the world.

Sufism Emotional and mystical form of Islam that appealed to the common people.

sultan Islamic political leader. In the Ottoman Empire, the sultan combined a warrior ethos with an unwavering devotion to Islam.

Sumerian King List Text that recounts the making of political dynasties. Recorded around 2000 BCE, it organizes the reigns of kings by dynasty, one city at a time.

Sumerian pantheon The Sumerian gods, each of whom had a home in a particular floodplain city. In the Sumerian belief system, both gods and the natural forces they controlled had to be revered.

Sumerian temples Homes of the gods and symbols of Sumerian imperial identity. Sumerian temples also represented the gods' ability to hoard wealth at sites where people exchanged goods and services. In addition, temples distinguished the urban from the rural world.

Sun Yat-sen (1866–1925) Chinese revolutionary and founder of the Nationalist Party in China.

Sunnis Orthodox Muslims. The majority sect of Islam, Sunnis originally supported the succession of Abu Bakr over Ali and supported the rule of consensus rather than family lineage for the succession to the Islamic caliphate. *See also* Shiism.

superior man In the Confucian view, a person of perfected moral character, fit to be a leader.

superpowers Label applied to the United States and the Soviet Union after World War II because of their size, their possession of the atomic bomb, and the fact that each embodied a model of civilization (capitalism or communism) applicable to the whole world.

supranational organizations International organizations such as non-governmental organizations (NGOs), the World Bank, and the International Monetary Fund (IMF).

survival of the fittest Charles Darwin's belief that as animal populations grew and resources became scarce, a struggle for existence arose, the outcome of which was that only the "fittest" survived.

Suryavamsha The second lineage of two (the solar) in Vedic society. *See* Chandravamsha.

Swadeshi movement Voluntary organizations in India that championed the creation of indigenous manufacturing enterprises and schools of nationalist thought, in order to gain autonomy from Britain.

syndicalism Organization of workplace associations that included unskilled labor.

tabula rasa Term used by John Locke to describe the human mind before it begins to acquire ideas from experience; Latin for "clean slate."

Taiping Heavenly Kingdom (Heavenly Kingdom of Great Peace) Religious sect established by the Chinese prophet Hong Xiuquan in the mid-nineteenth century. Hong Xiuquan believed that he was Jesus's younger brother. The group struggled to rid the world of evil and "restore" the heavenly kingdom, imagined as a just and egalitarian order.

Taiping Rebellion Rebellion by followers of Hong Xiuquan and the Taiping Heavenly Kingdom against the Qing government over the economic and social turmoil caused by the Opium War. Despite raising an army of 100,000 rebels, the rebellion was crushed.

Taj Mahal Royal palace of the Mughal Empire, built by Shah Jahan in the seventeenth century in homage to his wife, Mumtaz.

Tale of Genji Japanese work written by Lady Murasaki that gives vivid accounts of Heian court life; Japan's first novel (early eleventh century).

talking cures Psychological practice developed by Sigmund Freud whereby the symptoms of neurotic and traumatized patients would decrease after regular periods of thoughtful discussion.

Talmud Huge volumes of oral commentary on Jewish law eventually compiled in two versions, the Palestinian and the Babylonian, in the fifth and sixth centuries BCE.

Talmud of Jerusalem Codified written volumes of the traditions of Judaism; produced by the rabbis of Galilee around 400 CE.

Tang dynasty (608–907 CE) Regime that promoted a cosmopolitan culture, turning China into the hub of East Asia cultural integration, while expanding the borders of their empire. In order to govern such a diverse empire, the Tang established a political culture and civil service based on Confucian teachings. Candidates for the civil service were required to take examinations, the first of their kind in the world.

Tanzimat Reorganization period of the Ottoman Empire in the mid-nineteenth century; modernizing reforms affected the military, trade, foreign relations, and civilian life.

tappers Rubber workers in Brazil, mostly either Indian or mixed-blood people.

Tarascans Mesoamerican society of the 1400s; rivals to and sometimes subjects of the Aztecs.

Tatish Ruler of Chan Santa Cruz during the Mexican Caste War. The term means "father."

Tecumseh (1768–1813) Shawnee who circulated Tenskwatawa's message of Indian renaissance among Indian villages from the Great Lakes to the Gulf Coast. He preached the need for Indian unity, insisting that Indians resist any American attempts to get them to sell more land. In response, thousands of followers renounced their ties to colonial ways and prepared to combat the expansion of the United States.

Tekkes Schools that taught devotional strategies and the religious knowledge for students to enter Sufi orders and become masters of the brotherhood.

temple Building where believers worshipped their gods and goddesses and where some peoples believed the deities had earthly residence.

Tenskwatawa (1768–1834) Shawnee prophet who urged disciples to abstain from alcohol and return to traditional customs, reducing dependence on European trade goods and severing connections to Christian missionaries. His message spread to other tribes, raising the specter of a pan-Indian confederacy.

Teotihuacán City-state in a large, mountainous valley in present-day Mexico; the first major community to emerge after the Olmecs.

territorial state Political form that emerged in the riverine cities of Mesopotamia, which was overwhelmed by the displacement of nomadic peoples. These states were kingdoms organized around charismatic rulers who headed large households; each had a defined physical border.

Third Estate The French people minus the clergy and the aristocracy; this term was popularized in the late eighteenth century and used to exalt the power of the bourgeoisie during the French Revolution.

Third Reich The German state from 1933 to 1945 under Adolf Hitler.

Third World Nations of the world, mostly in Asia, Latin America, and Africa, that were not highly industrialized like First World nations or tied to the Soviet bloc (the Second World).

Thirty Years' War (1618–1648) Conflict begun between Protestants and Catholics in Germany that escalated into a general European war fought against the unity and power of the Holy Roman Empire.

Tiananmen Square Largest public square in the world and site of the pro-democracy movement in 1989 that resulted in the killing of as many as a thousand protesters by the Chinese army.

Tiers monde Term meaning "Third World," coined by French intellectuals to describe countries seeking a "third way" between Soviet communism and western capitalism.

Tiglath Pileser III Assyrian ruler from 745 to 728 BCE. This leader instituted reforms that changed the administrative and social structure of the empire to make it more efficient and introduced a standing army.

Tiwanaku Another name for Tihuanaco, the first great Andean polity, on the shores of Lake Titicaca.

Tlaxcalans Mesoamerican society of the 1400s; these people were enemies of the powerful Aztec Empire.

Tokugawa shogunate Hereditary military administration founded in 1603 that ruled Japan while keeping the emperor as a figurehead; it was toppled in 1868 by reformers who felt that Japan should adopt, not reject, Western influences.

Toltecs A Mesoamerican people who, by 1000 CE, had filled the political vacuum created by the decline of the city of Teotihuacán.

tomb culture Warlike group from northeast Asia who arrived by sea in the middle of the third century CE and imposed their military and social power on southern Japan. These conquerors are known today as the tomb culture because of their elevated necropolises near present-day Osaka.

Topkapi Palace Political headquarters of the Ottoman Empire, located in Istanbul.

total war All-out war involving civilian populations as well as military forces, often used in reference to World War II.

transhumant migrants Nomads who entered settled territories in the second millennium BCE and moved their herds seasonally when resources became scarce.

Trans-Siberian Railroad Railroad built over very difficult terrain between 1891 and 1903 and subsequently expanded; it created an overland bridge for troops, peasant settlers, and commodities to move between Europe and the Pacific.

Treaty of Brest-Litovsk (1918) Separate peace between imperial Germany and the new Bolshevik regime in Russia. The treaty acknowledged the German victory on the Eastern Front and withdrew Russia from the war.

Treaty of Nanjing (1842) Treaty between China and Britain following the Opium War; it called for indemnities, the opening of new ports, and the cession of Hong Kong to the British.

Treaty of Tordesillas (1494) Treaty in which the pope decreed that the non-European world would be divided into spheres of trade and missionary responsibility between Spain and Portugal.

trickle trade Method by which a good is passed from one village to another, as in the case of obsidian among farming villages; the practice began around 7000 BCE. Also called "down-the-line trade."

Tripartite Pact (1940) Pact that stated that Germany, Italy, and Japan would act together in all future military ventures.

Triple Entente Alliance developed before World War I that eventually included Britain, France, and Russia.

Troy Important site founded around 3000 BCE in Anatolia, to the far west. Troy is legendary as the site of the war that was launched by the Greeks (the Achaeans) and that was recounted by Homer in the *Iliad*.

Truman Doctrine (1947) Declaration promising U.S. economic and military intervention, whenever and wherever needed, for the sake of preventing communist expansion.

Truth and Reconciliation Commission Quasi-judicial body established after the overthrow of the apartheid system in South Africa and the election of Nelson Mandela as the country's first black president in 1994. The commission was to gather evidence about crimes committed during the apartheid years. Those who showed remorse for their actions could appeal for clemency. The South African leaders believed that an airing of the grievances from this period would promote racial harmony and reconciliation.

truth commissions Elected officials' inquiries into human rights abuses by previous regimes. In Argentina, El Salvador, Guatemala, and South Africa, these commissions were vital for creating a new aura of legitimacy for democracies and for promising to uphold the rights of individuals.

tsar/czar Russian word derived from the Latin *Caesar* to refer to the Russian ruler of Kiev, and eventually to all rulers in Russia.

Tula Toltec capital city; a commercial hub and political and ceremonial center.

Uitlanders British populations living in Afrikaner republics; they were denied voting rights and subject to other forms of discrimination in the late nineteenth century. The term means "outsiders."

ulama Arabic word that means "learned ones" or "scholars"; used for those who devoted themselves to knowledge of Islamic sciences.

Umayyads Family who founded the first dynasty in Islam. They established family rule and dynastic succession to the role of caliph. The first Umayyad caliph established Damascus as his capital and was named Mu'awiya ibn Abi Sufyan.

Umma Arabic word for "community"; used to refer to the "Islamic polity" or "Islamic community."

Universal Declaration of Human Rights (1948) U.N. declaration that laid out the rights to which all human beings are entitled.

universalizing religions Religions that appeal to diverse populations; are easily adaptable across various cultural and geographical areas; promote universal rules and principles to guide behavior that transcend place, time, and specific cultural practices; are proselytized by energetic and charismatic missionaries; foster a deep sense of community felt by their converts; and are supported by powerful empires.

universitas Term used from the end of the twelfth century to denote scholars who came together, first in Paris. The term is borrowed from the merchant communities, where it denoted the equivalent of the modern "union."

Untouchables Caste in the Indian system whose jobs, usually in the more unsanitary aspects of urban life, rendered them "ritually and spiritually" impure.

Upanishads Vedic wisdom literature collected in the first half of the first millennium BCE. It took the form of dialogues between disciples and a sage.

urban-rural divide Division between those living in cities and those living in rural areas. One of history's most durable worldwide distinctions, the urban-rural divide eventually encompassed the globe. Where cities arose, communities adopted lifestyles based on the mass production of goods and on specialized labor. Those living in the countryside remained close to nature, cultivating the land or tending livestock. They diversified their labor and exchanged their grains and animal products for necessities available in urban centers.

utopian socialism The most visionary of all Restoration-era movements.

Utopian socialists like Charles Fourier dreamed of transforming states, workplaces, and human relations and proposed plans to do so.

Vaishyas Householders or lesser clan members in Vedic society who worked the land and tended livestock.

Vardhamana Mahavira Advocate of Jainism who lived from 540 to 468 BCE; he emphasized interpretation of the Upanishads to govern and guide daily life.

varna Caste system established by the Vedas in 600 BCE.

vassal states Subordinate states that had to pay tribute in luxury goods, raw materials, and manpower as part of a broad confederation of polities under the kings' protection.

Vedas Rhymes, hymns, and explanatory texts composed by Aryan priests; the Vedas became their most holy scripture and part of their religious rituals. They were initially passed down orally, in Sanskrit. Brahmans, priests of Vedic culture, incorporated the texts into ritual and society. The Vedas are considered the final authority of Hinduism.

Vedic people People who came from the steppes of Inner Asia around 1500 BCE and entered the fertile lowlands of the Indus River basin, gradually moving as far south as the Deccan plateau. They called themselves Aryan, which means "respected ones," and spoke Sanskrit, an Indo-European language.

veiling Practice of modest dress required of respectable women in the Assyrian Empire, introduced by Assyrian authorities in the thirteenth century BCE.

Venus figures Representations of the goddess of fertility drawn on the Chauvet Cave in southeastern France. Discovered in 1994, they are probably about 35,000 years old.

Versailles Conference (1919) Peace conference between the victors of World War I; resulted in the Treaty of Versailles, which forced Germany to pay reparations and to give up its colonies to the victors.

Viet Cong Vietnamese communist group committed to overthrowing the government of South Vietnam and reunifying North and South Vietnam.

Viet Minh Group founded in 1941 by Ho Chi Minh to oppose the Japanese occupation of Indochina; it later fought the French colonial forces for independence. Also known as the Vietnamese Independent League.

Vietnam War (1965–1975) Conflict that resulted from concern over the spread of communism in Southeast Asia. The United States intervened on the side of South Vietnam in its struggle against peasant-supported Viet Cong guerrilla forces, who wanted to reunite Vietnam under a communist regime. Faced with antiwar opposition at home and ferocious resistance from the Vietnamese, American troops withdrew in 1973; the puppet South Vietnamese government collapsed two years later.

Vikings A people from Scandinavia who replaced the Franks as the dominant warrior class in northern Europe in the ninth century CE. They used their superior ships to loot other seagoing peoples and sailed up the rivers of central Russia to establish a trade route that connected Scandinavia and the Baltic with Constantinople and Baghdad. The Vikings established settlements in Iceland and Greenland and, briefly, North America.

Vishnu The second of three Vedic deities, signifying existence. *See also* Brahma *and* Siva.

viziers Bureaucrats of the Ottoman Empire.

Vodun Mixed religion of African and Christian customs practiced by slaves and free blacks in the colony of Saint-Domingue.

Voting Rights Act (1965) Law that granted universal suffrage in the United States.

Wafd Nationalist party that came into existence during a rebellion in Egypt in 1919 and held power sporadically after Egypt was granted limited independence from Britain in 1922.

Wahhabism Early eighteenth-century reform movement organized by Muhammad Ibn abd al-Wahhab, who preached the absolute oneness of Allah and a return to the pure Islam of Muhammad.

Wang Mang Han minister who usurped the throne in 9 CE because he believed that the Han had lost the mandate of heaven. He ruled until 23 CE.

war ethos Strong social commitment to a continuous state of war. The Roman army constantly drafted men and engaged in annual spring military campaigns. Soldiers were taught to embrace a sense of honor that did not allow them to accept defeat and commended those who repeatedly threw themselves into battle.

War of 1812 Conflict between Britain and the United States arising from U.S. grievances over oppressive British maritime practices in the Napoleonic Wars.

War on Poverty President Lyndon Johnson's push for an increased range of social programs and increased spending on social security, health, education, and assistance for the disabled.

Warring States period Period extending from the fifth century to 221 BCE, when the regional warring states were unified by the Qin dynasty.

Warsaw Pact (1955–1991) Military alliance between the Soviet Union and other communist states that was established in response to the creation of the North American Treaty Organization (NATO) alliance.

Weimar Republic (1919–1933) Constitutional Republic of Germany that was subverted by Hitler soon after he became chancellor.

Western Front Military front that stretched from the English Channel through Belgium and France to the Alps during World War I.

White and Blue Niles The two main branches of the Nile, rising out of central Africa and Ethiopia. They come together at the present-day capital city of Sudan, Khartoum.

White Lotus Rebellion Series of uprisings in northern China (1790–1800s) inspired by mystical beliefs in folk Buddhism and, at times, the idea of restoring the Ming dynasty.

White Wolf Mysterious militia leader, depicted in popular myth as a Chinese Robin Hood whose mission was to rid the country of the injustices of Yuan Shikai's government in the early years of the Chinese Republic (1910s).

Whites "Counterrevolutionaries" of the Bolshevik Revolution (1918–1921) who fought the Bolsheviks (the "Reds"); included former supporters of the tsar, Social Democrats, and large independent peasant armies.

witnessing Dying for one's faith, or becoming a martyr.

Wokou Supposedly Japanese pirates, many of whom were actually Chinese subjects of the Ming dynasty.

Works Progress Administration (WPA) New Deal program instituted in 1935 that put nearly 3 million people to work building roads, bridges, airports, and post offices.

World Bank International agency established in 1944 to provide economic assistance to war-torn and poor countries. Its formal title is the International Bank for Reconstruction and Development.

World War I *See* Great War.

World War II (1939–1945) Worldwide war that began in September 1939 in Europe, and even earlier in Asia, and pitted Britain, the United States, and the Soviet Union (the Allies) against Nazi Germany, Japan, and Italy (the Axis).

Wu or **Wudi** Chinese leader known as the "Martial Emperor" because of his many military campaigns during the Han dynasty. He reigned from 141 to 87 BCE.

Wu Zhao Chinese empress who lived from 626 to 706 CE. She began as a concubine in the court of Li Shimin and became the mother of his son's child. She eventually gained power equal to that of the emperor, and named herself regent when she finagled a place for one of her own sons after their father's death.

Xiongnu The most powerful and intrusive of the nomadic peoples; originally pastoralists from the eastern part of the Asian steppe in what is modern-day Mongolia. They appeared along the frontier with China in the late Zhou dynasty and by the third century BCE had become the most powerful of all the pastoral communities in that area.

Xunzi Confucian moralist whose ideas were influential to Qin rulers. He lived from 310 to 237 BCE and believed that rational statecraft was more reliable than fickle human nature and that strict laws and severe punishments could create stability in society.

Yalta Accords Results of the meeting between President Roosevelt, Prime Minister Churchill, and Premier Stalin that occurred in the Crimea in 1945 to plan for the postwar order.

Yavana kings Sanskrit name for Greek rulers, derived from the Greek name for the area of western Asia Minor called Ionia, a term that then extended to anyone who spoke Greek or came from the Mediterranean.

yellow press Newspapers that sought a mass circulation by featuring sensationalist reporting.

Yellow Turbans One of several local Chinese religious movements that emerged across the empire, especially under Wang Mang's officials, who considered him a usurper. The Yellow Turbans, so called because of the yellow scarves they wore around their heads, were Daoist millenarians.

Yin City that became the capital of the Shang in 1350 BCE, ushering in a golden age.

Young Egypt Antiliberal, fascist group that gained a large following in Egypt during the 1930s.

Young Italy Nationalist organization made up of young students and intellectuals, devoted to the unification and renewal of the Italian state.

Yuan dynasty Dynasty established by the Mongols after the defeat of the Song. The Yuan dynasty was strong from 1280 to 1368; its capital was at Dadu, or modern-day Beijing.

Yuan Mongols Mongol rulers of China who were overthrown by the Ming dynasty in 1368.

Yuezhi A Turkic nomadic people who roamed on pastoral lands to the west of the Xiongnu territory of central Mongolia. They had friendly relationships with the farming societies in China, but the Yuezhi detested the Xiongnu and had frequent armed clashes with them.

Zaibatsu Large-scale, family-owned corporations in Japan consisting of factories, import-export businesses, and banks that dominated the Japanese economy until 1945.

Zamindars Archaic tax system of the Mughal Empire where decentralized lords collected tribute for the emperor.

Zapatistas Group of indigenous rebels that rose up against the Mexican government in 1994 and drew inspiration from an earlier Mexican rebel, Emiliano Zapata.

Zheng King during the Qin era who defeated what was left of the Warring States between 230 and 221 BCE. He assumed the mandate of heaven from the Zhou and declared himself Shi Huangdi ("First August Emperor"), to distinguish himself from other kings.

Zheng He (1371–1433) Ming naval leader who established tributary relations with Southeast Asia, Indian Ocean ports, the Persian Gulf, and the east coast of Africa.

Zhong Shang Administrative central complex of the Shang.

Zhongguo Term originating in the ancient period and subsequently used to emphasize the central cultural and geographical location of China in the world; means "Middle Kingdom."

ziggurat By the end of the third millennium BCE, the elevated platform base of a Sumerian temple had transformed into a stepped platform called a *ziggurat*.

Zionism Political movement advocating the reestablishment of a Jewish homeland in Palestine.

Zoroaster Sometimes known as Zarathustra, thought to have been a teacher around 1000 BCE in eastern Iran and credited with having solidified the region's religious beliefs into a unified system that moved away from animistic nomadic beliefs. The main source for his teachings is a compilation called the Avesta.

Zoroastrianism Religion based on the teachings of Zoroaster that became the dominant religion of the Persian Empire.

Zulus African tribe that, under Shaka, created a ruthless warrior state in southern Africa in the early 1800s.

Credits

CHAPTER 10

Photo Credits Pages 340–341: HIP/ Art Resource; p. 342: Granger Collection; p. 343: Nik Wheeler/Corbis; p. 345: Alamy; p. 351: Keren Su/Corbis; p. 355 (top): Granger Collection; p. 355 (bottom): Christophe Loviny/ Corbis; p. 359: The Art Archive; pp. 360 & 361: Snark/Art Resource; p. 364: Werner Forman/Art Resource; p. 366 (top): Charles & Josette Lenars/Corbis; p. 366 (bottom): Otto Lang/Corbis; p. 369: akg-images; p. 380: Giraudon/Art Resource; p. 381 (top): Wikimedia Commons; p. 381 (bottom): Art Resource.

Text Credits Primary Source 10.1 (p. 376): *The Monks of Ḳûblâi Khân, Emperor of China, or, The history of the life and travels of Rabban Şâwmâ, envoy and plenipotentiary of the Mongol khans to the kings of Europe, and Markôs who as Mâr Yahbh-Allâhâ III became Patriarch of the Nestorian Church in Asia.* Edited and translated by E.A. Wallis Budge (London: Religious Tract Society, 1928). Reprinted by permission of the Lutterworth Press. Primary Source 10.3 (p. 377): *Ibn Battuta: Travels in Asia & Africa, 1325-1354* translated by H. A. R. Gibb, pp. 55–56. Copyright © 1929 George Routledge & Sons. Reprinted by permission of Taylor & Francis Books (UK).

CHAPTER 11

Photo Credits Pages 382–383: Snark/ ArtResource; p.385: GrangerCollection; p. 389: Wikimedia Commons; p. 393: Album/Art Resource; p. 394: Yann Arthus-Bertrand/Corbis; p. 395: Sta-pleton Collection, UK/Bridgeman Art Library; pp. 398 & 399: Giraudon/Art Resource; p. 401: Granger Collection; p. 403 (left): Scala/Art Resource; p. 403 (right): Scala/Art Resource; p. 405: Granger Collection; p. 406: Réunion des Musées Nationaux/Art Resource; p. 409: The Jan Adkins Studio; p. 416 (left): Bridgeman Art Library; p. 416 (right): Library of the Topkapi Palace Museum folio 31b, photograph courtesy of Talat Halman; p. 417: Granger Collection.

Text Credits Primary Source 11.1 (p. 414): Ahmet Karamustafa, "Dervish Groups in the Ottoman Empire 1450-1550" from *God's Unruly Friends: Dervish Groups in the Islamic Later Middle Period*, pp. 6–7 (Oneworld Publications, 2006). Copyright © 1994 by the University of Utah Press. Used by permission of the University of Utah Press. Primary Source 11.2 (pp. 414–415): Robertus de Avesbury, "The Flagellants in England" from *The Black Death*, Rosemary Horrox, trans./ed., pp. 153–154. Copyright © Rosemary Horrox 1994. Reprinted with permission of Manchester University Press.

CHAPTER 12

Photo Credits Pages 418–419: Wychwood Editions; p. 420: Reunion des Musees Nationaux/ Art Resource, NY; p. 421: akg-images/Cameraphoto; p. 422: De Agostini/Getty Images; p. 423: Bildarchiv Preussischer Kulturbesitz/Art Resource, NY; p. 427: Granger Collection; p. 428 (left): Granger Collection; p. 428 (right): Mireille Vautier/Paris; pp. 432 & 433 (top): Francois Guenet/Art Resource; p. 433 (bottom): Granger Collection; p. 439: Bridgeman Art Library; p. 444: The Art Archive/Maritime Museum Kronborg Castle Denmark/ Gianni Dagli Orti; p. 450 (left): Scala/ Art Resource, NY; p. 450 (right): Granger Collection; p. 451: Réunion des Musées Nationaux/Art Resource.

Text Credits Primary Source 12.1 (p. 448): "The Florentine Codex," *from Victors and Vanquished: Aztec Spanish and Nahua Views of the Conquest of Mexico*, 2000. Reprinted from Bedford/ St. Martin's Press. Primary Source 12.3 (p. 449): Basil Davidson (trans.) "Letters to the King of Portugal," from *The African Past: Chronicles from Antiquity to Modern Times*, 1964. Reprinted by permission of Curtis Brown, Ltd. Primary Source 12.4 (p. 449): T'ien-Tsê Chang, from *Sino-Portuguese Trade From 1514 to 1644: A Synthesis of Portuguese and Chinese Sources* (Leyden: E.J. Brill, 1934), pp. 51-52. Reprinted by permission of Brill Academic Publishers.

CHAPTER 13

Photo Credits Pages 452–453: Reunion de Musees Nationaux/Art Resource; pp. 454 & 455 (right): British Museum, London/E.T. Archives, London/SuperStock; p. 455 (left): Chester Beatty Library and Gallery of Oriental Art, Dublin/ Bridgeman Art Library; p. 460: Granger Collection; p. 461: MPI/Getty Images; p. 462: MPI/Getty Images; p. 467 (left): © 1989 North Wind Picture Archives; p. 467 (right): Private Collection/Bridgeman Art Gallery; p. 468: The Newberry Library; p. 469: Mary Evans Picture Library/The

Image Works; p. 471: The Art Archive/ Museum der Stadt Wien/Dagli Orti; p. 473: © The Metropolitan Museum of Art/Art Resource; p. 477: Gianni Dagli Orti/The Art Archive at Art Resource; p. 482: Anne S. K. Brown Military Collection, Brown University Library/ Wikimedia Commons; p. 485: Chateau de Versailles, France/Bridgeman Art Library; p. 494 (left): Metropolitan Museum of Art; p. 494 (right top): Bridgeman Art Library; p. 494 (right bottom): Wikimedia Commons; p. 495: Metropolitan Museum of Art.

Text Credits Primary Source 13.5a (page 492, top): Katherine Holt, "Population by Racial Classification, Santiago de Iguape 1835." From The Bahian History Project, www.mappingbahia.org. Reproduced with permission from Katherine Holt. Primary Source 13.5b (page 492, bottom): Katherine Holt, "Free and Freed Population by Racial Classification, Iguape 1835." From The Bahian History Project, www .mappingbahia.org. Reproduced with permission from Katherine Holt. Primary Source 13.5c (page 493): Katherine Holt, "Enslaved Population by Place of Birth, Santiago do Iguape, 1835." From The Bahian History Project, www .mappingbahia.org. Reproduced with permission from Katherine Holt.

CHAPTER 14

Photo Credits Pages 496–497: Scala/ Art Resource; p. 500 (left): Topkapi Palace Museum, Istanbul; p. 500 (right): Victoria & Albert Museum, London/Art Resource; p. 502: By permission of the trustees of the Chester Beatty Library and Gallery of Oriental Art; pp. 504 & 505: Werner Forman/Art Resource; p. 506 (left): Underwood & Underwood/ Corbis; p. 506 (right): Underwood & Underwood/Corbis; p. 508: British Library/Bridgeman Art Library; p. 510: © The Metropolitan Museum of Art/Art Resource; p. 515 (top): Private

Collection/Bridgeman Art Library; p. 515 (bottom): Private Collection/ Bridgeman Art Library; p. 518 (left): Museo de America, Madrid; p. 518 (right): Museo de America, Madrid/ Bridgeman Art Library; p. 520 (left): E.T. Archives, London/Superstock; p. 520 (right): The Granger Collection, New York; p. 528 (top left): The Needham Research Institute; p. 528 (bottom left): Wikimedia Commons; p. 528 (top right): British Library; p. 528 (bottom right): Private Collection, courtesy of the owner and D.A. King, contributor; photo by Christie's of London; p. 529 (top): Private Collection/ Bridgeman Art Library; p. 529 (bottom left): Wikimedia Commons; p. 529 (bottom right): Rare Books Division, The New York Public Library.

Text Credits Primary Source 14.1 (p. 526): Immanuel Kant, "What is Enlightenment?," from *Practical Philosophy (The Cambridge Edition of the Works of Immanuel Kant)*, edited by Mary J. Gregor (Cambridge University Press, 1999). Primary Source 14.4 (p. 527): Jean-Jacques Rousseau, from *Rousseau's Political Writings: A Norton Critical Edition*, edited by Alan Ritter and Julia Conaway Bondanella, translated by Julia Conaway Bondanella. Copyright © 1988 by W.W. Norton & Company, Inc. Used by permission of W.W. Norton & Company, Inc. Primary Source 14.5 (p. 527): Jean-Jacques Rousseau, from *Rousseau's Political Writings: A Norton Critical Edition*, edited by Alan Ritter and Julia Conaway Bondanella, translated by Julia Conaway Bondanella. Copyright © 1988 by W.W. Norton & Company, Inc. Used by permission of W.W. Norton & Company, Inc.

CHAPTER 15

Photo Credits Pages 530–531: Stefano Bianchetti/Corbis; p. 536: Library of Congress; p. 538: Hulton

Archive/Getty Images; p. 541: North Wind Picture Archives; pp. 542 & 543: Granger Collection, NY; p. 547: Granger Collection; p. 549: Granger Collection; p. 556: National Army Museum, London/Bridgeman Art Library; p. 558 (left): British Library/ Bridgeman Art Library; p. 558 (right): North Wind Picture Archives; p. 568 (left): Louvre, Paris, France/ Giraudon/Bridgeman Art Library; p. 568 (right): Wikimedia Commons; p. 569 (left): © The Metropolitan Museum of Art/Art Resource; p. 569 (right): © The Metropolitan Museum of Art/Art Resource.

Text Credits Primary Source 15.3 (p. 565): Abd al-Rahman al-Jabarti, From *Napoleon in Egypt: al-Jabarti's Chronicle of the French Occupation*, 1798, translated by Shmuel Moreh, pp. 24–29. (Princeton: Markus Wiener Publishing, 1993).

CHAPTER 16

Photo Credits Pages 570–571: Harvard-Yenching Library, Harvard University; pp. 574 & 575: Wikimedia Commons; p. 578 (left): British Library; p. 578 (right): National Archives, Zimbabwe; p. 581: Granger Collection; p. 582: Corbis; p. 585: Granger Collection; p. 586: Alamy; p. 590 (left): Granger Collection, New York; p. 590 (right): Granger Collection; p. 591: Wikimedia Commons; p. 594: Getty Images; p. 604 (left): Wikimedia Commons; p. 604 (right): Wikimedia Commons; p. 605 (left): Public Domain; p. 605 (right): Wikimedia Commons.

Text Credits Primary Source 16.2 (p. 601): Beverly Mack & Jean Boyd, "Gikku Bello" from *One Woman's Jihad* by Beverly Mack & Jean Boyd. Copyright © 2000 by Beverly B. Mack and Jean Boyd. Reprinted with permission of Indiana University Press. Primary Source 16.4 (pp. 602–603): From "The

Principles of the Heavenly Nature," in *Sources of Chinese Tradition*, 2nd Edition, Volume 2, pp. 229-30. Edited by Wm. Theodore de Bary and Richard Lufrano. Copyright © 2000 Columbia University Press. Reprinted with permission of the publisher.

CHAPTER 17

Photo Credits Pages 606–607: Granger Collection; p. 611 (left): Granger Collection; p. 611 (right): Granger Collection; p. 613: Time & Life Pictures/Getty Images; p. 619: Bettmann/Corbis; p. 620 (top): Illustrated London News/Mary Evans Picture Library; p. 620 (bottom): Nizamps Good Works Project - Famine Relief: Road Building, Aurangabad 1895–1902, from Judith Gutman, "Through Indian Eyes," Private Collection; p. 623 (left): Hulton/Getty Images; p. 623 (right): Private Collection/Bridgeman Art Library; pp. 624 & 625: Roger-Viollet, Paris/Bridgeman Art Library; p. 626: The Art Archive; p. 628: Erich Lessing/Art Resource; p. 630: The Art Archive; p. 642: Wikimedia Commons; p. 643 (left): From Encyclopedia of the Ottoman Empire, by Gabor Agoston and Bruce Alan Masters; p. 643 (right): Library of Congress.

CHAPTER 18

Photo Credits Pages 644–645: Super-Stock; p. 647 (left): Hulton Archive/Getty Images; p. 647 (right): LL/Roger Viollet/Getty Images; p. 653: ullstein bild/Granger Collection; p. 655: Super-Stock; p. 660 (left): akg-images; p. 660 (right): Hulton-Deutsch Collection/Corbis; pp. 662 & 663: Wikimedia Commons; p. 664 (left): © National Gallery, London/Art Resource; p. 664 (right): Erich Lessing/Art Resource; p. 665 (left): Erich Lessing/Art Resource; p. 665 (right): Scala/Art Resource; p. 669: Schalkwijk/Art Resource; p. 672: Gianni

Dagli Orti/The Art Archive at Art Resource; p. 680 (left): © Estate of Pablo Picasso/Artists Rights Society (ARS), New York. Digital Image © The Museum of Modern Art/Licensed by Scala/Art Resource; p. 680 (right): The Palace Museum, Beijing/Wikimedia Commons; p. 681: Wikimedia Commons.

Text Credits Primary Source 18.2 (pp. 676–677): Maria Eugenia Echenique: "The Emancipation of Women." From Brians. *Reading About the World, Vol. 2.* 1E. © 1999 Custom Solutions, a part of Cengage Learning, Inc. Reproduced by permission. www.cengage.com/permissions. Primary Source 18.3 (p. 677): Qui Jin, "An Address to Two Hundred Million Fellow Countrywomen." Reprinted with the permission of Simon & Schuster Publishing Group, a division of Simon & Schuster, Inc. from the Free Press edition of *Chinese Civilization: A Sourcebook*, 2nd Edition by Patricia Buckley Ebrey. Copyright © 1993 by Patricia Buckley Ebrey. Copyright © 1981 by The Free Press. All rights reserved. Primary Source 18.4 (pp. 677–678): Margot Badran & Miriam Cooke (eds.), "Industrialization and Women's Freedom in Egypt" from *Opening the Gates: An Anthology of Arab Feminist Writing*, 2nd edition. Copyright © 1990. Reprinted with permission of Indiana University Press.

CHAPTER 19

Photo Credits Pages 682–683: The Illustrated London News Picture Library; p. 685: The Imperial War Museum; p. 687: Hulton-Deutsch Collection/Corbis; p. 689 (left): Sovfoto/Eastfoto; p. 689 (right): SuperStock; p. 694: ©SF Palm/Stageimage/The Image Works; p. 695: Granger; p. 697: Marion Post Wolcott/Library Of Congress; p. 698: Granger Collection; p. 704: Genevieve Naylor/Corbis; pp. 706 & 707: Granger Collection; p. 708 (left): The Illustrated London News Picture Library; p. 708 (right): Private Collection/Bridgeman Art Library; p. 718:

Getty Images; p. 719 (top): Detroit Institute of Arts, USA/Gift of Edsel B. Ford/Bridgeman Art Library; p. 719 (bottom left): Granger Collection; p. 719 (bottom right): © Everett Collection Inc/Alamy.

Text Credits Primary Source 19.2 (pp. 714–715): M. K. Gandhi, From *Hind Swaraj and Other Writings*, edited by Anthony J. Parel, pp. 26–91. Copyright © 1997 Anthony J. Parel. Reprinted by permission of Cambridge University Press. Primary Source 19.3 (pp. 715–716): Jomo Kenyatta, Excerpt from *Facing Mount Kenya* by Jomo Kenyatta, published by Vintage Books, a division of Random House LLC. Used by permission of Alfred A. Knopf, an imprint of the Knopf Doubleday Publishing Group, a division of Random House LLC. All rights reserved.

CHAPTER 20

Photo Credits Pages 720–721: F.D.R. Library; p. 723 (left): The Illustrated London News Picture Library/Mary Evans Picture Library; p. 723 (right): Sovfoto/Eastfoto; p. 727 (left): Official U.S. Air Force Photo/TRH Pictures; p. 727 (right): U.N. Photo 149446 by Yosuke Yamahata/TRH Pictures; p. 730: NATO Photo/TRH Pictures; p. 732: Bettmann/Corbis; p. 740: © Hulton-Deutsch Collection/Corbis; p. 742 (left): AP Photo; p. 742 (right): State Historical Society of Wisconsin Visual Materials Archive; pp. 744 & 745: Wikimedia Commons; p. 747 (left): Roger-Viollet/The Image Works; p. 747 (right): Li Zhensheng/Contact Press Images; p. 748: Itar-Tass/Sovfoto; p. 751: Hulton-Deutsch Collection/Corbis; p. 760 (left): Art Resource; p. 760 (right): Wikimedia Commons; p. 761 (top left): George Rodger/Magnum Photos; p. 761 (bottom left): Courtesy of Ono Saseo estate; p. 761 (top right): Reprinted by permission of the Detroit News, a division of Evening News Association, copyright 1985.

Text Credits Primary Source 20.3 (p. 757): Léopold Sédar Senghor, Excerpts from *African Socialism* (New York: American Society of African Culture, 1959), trans. Mercer Cook. Reprinted by permission of Moorland-Spingarn Research Center, Howard University, Washington, DC. Primary Source 20.4 (p. 758): Frantz Fanon, "On Violence." From *The Wretched of the Earth*, translated by Constance Farrington (Grove Press, 1963), pp. 27, 43. Used by permission of Grove Press.

CHAPTER 21

Photo Credits Pages 762–763: AP Photo/Anat Givon; p. 766: Hulton Archive/Getty Images; p. 768 (left): Peter Magubane/TimePix; p. 768 (right): David and Peter Turnley/Corbis; p. 774: George Esiri/Reuters/Corbis; pp. 776 & 777: Mary Evans/EROS INTERNATIONAL/Ronald Grant/Everett Collection; p. 778 (left): Getty Images; p. 778 (right): AFLO/Nippon News/Corbis; p. 779: Jeff Albertson/Corbis; p. 785: Vanessa Vick/Redux; p. 787 (left): © Susan I. Cunningham/Panos Pictures; p. 787 (right): Douglas Engle/Corbis; p. 790: Peter Turnley/Corbis; p. 792: Jeff Widener/AP/Wide World Photos; p. 793 (left): Clive Shirley/Panos Pictures; p. 793 (right): Schalkwijk/Art Resource, © Estate of David Alfaro Siqueiros/Licensed by VAGA, New York, NY; p. 798 (left): Getty Images; p. 798 (right): Corbis; p. 799 (top left): Getty Images; p. 799 (bottom left): Wikimedia Commons; p. 799 (top right): Wikimedia Commons.

Text Credits Primary Source 21.2 (p. 797): The World Bank, From "Using subsidies to close gender gaps in education," World Bank. 2001. *World Development Report 2000-2001: Attacking Poverty*, p. 122, Box 7.2. © World Bank. https://openknowledge.worldbank.org/handle/10986/11856 License: Creative Commons Attribution license (CC BY 3.0). Primary Source 21.3 (p. 797): Amartya Kumar Sen, "Democracy as a Universal Value." *Journal of Democracy* 10:3 (1999), 6–9. © 1999 National Endowment for Democracy and the Johns Hopkins University Press. Reprinted with permission of Johns Hopkins University Press.

Epilogue

Photo Credits Pages 800–801: AP Photo/Jason DeCrow; p. 802 (left): Matt McDermott/Corbis Sygma; p. 802 (right): AP Photo/Carmen Taylor; p. 804 (top): AP Photo; p. 804 (bottom): AP Photo/Jason DeCrow; p. 812: Dean Conger/Corbis; p. 813: Sebastian D'Souza/AFP/Getty Images; p. 821 (top left): Liba Taylor/Corbis; p. 821 (top right): Herman Wouters/Hollandse Hoogte/Redux; p. 821 (bottom): Jason Reed/Reuters/Landov; p. 822: AP/Wide World Photos.

Index

monarchies (*continued*)
    and political uses of space, 504–5
    and revolutions in Caribbean and
        Iberian America, 542–43
    see also specific monarchs and
        monarchies
Monet, Claude, *664*
money, monetary system:
    between 1600–1750, 470–71, 473, 480
    between 1890–1914, 656–58
    between 1910–1939, 695, 696
    in China, 420–21, 473
    and commerce and colonization
        between 1450–1600, 420–21
    and Great Depression, 695, 696
    and Ottoman Empire, 470–71
    "protection," 421
    in Russia, 480
    and worldwide insecurities, 657
    see also banking
Mongke Khan, 369
Mongolia, Mongols, *375*, 376, 377, 474, 476
    between 1600–1750, 480
    in Afro-Eurasia, 368–73, *370–71*,
        383–84
    and alternative visions of nine-
        teenth century, 578
    Baghdad sacked by, 369, 391
    Black Death brought by, 383–84,
        391, 414
    Caffa besieged by, 383
    China conquered by, 369, *369*, 372,
        385
    gender and, 368
    and immigration, 650
    in Islamic world, 391–92
    Korea invaded by, 369
    Persia ruled by, 372
    spread of disease by, 391
    waning power of, 389
Montenegro, 688
Montgomery, Alabama, 742, *742*
Moors, 400, 402
Morgan, J. Pierpont, 611, 657
Morocco, 400, 736, 815
Morrison, Toni, 778
Morsi, Muhammad, 815
Moscow, Russia, 480, *481*, 482, 484
Mosque of Shaykh Lutfolla, 505
mosques, *see specific mosques*
Mozambique, 768, 775, 820
Mubarak, Gamal, 815
Mubarak, Hosni, 814, 815
Mugabe, Robert, 768
Mughal Empire, *413*, 549, 680
    between 1600–1750, 454, 455, 469,
        472–73, 477, 479, 487
    between 1750–1850, 556
    agrarian resources of, 391
    and alternative visions of nine-
        teenth century, 573, 592–96, 600

authority in, 472
and colonial reordering in India, 556
and commerce and colonization
    between 1450–1600, 440, *441*,
    442, 450, *451*
and culture between 1500–1780,
    501–2
and culture between 1600–1780,
    498, 499, 501–2
diversity in, 440
economy in, 442, 454, 455, 472
elites in, 472, 502
end of, 455
expansion of, 440, *441*, *447*, 472, *488*
and Indian rebellion of 1857, 592–96
and insurgencies against colonizing
    and centralizing states, 592–96
Islam in, 440
population of, 440
revenue system in, 442
and Safavid Empire, 470
Turkish warriors in, 392
unrest in, 454, 455, 472, 487, 777
wealth of, 440
zenith and decline of, 472–73
Muhammad, prophet of Islam, 573, 575,
    600
mulattoes, *518*, 542
multinational corporations, 746, 747, 752
Mumbai, India, 776–77, 813
Murad II, Ottoman emperor, 393
Muscovy, 480
    see also Moscow, Russia; Russia,
        Russians
Muslim Brotherhood, *713*, 739, 815
Muslim League, 708, 736
Muslims:
    between 1600–1750, 463
    between 1750–1850, 556
    between 1850–1914, 624, 670, 671–72
    between 1910–1939, 707, 708, 710–11
    and alternative visions of nine-
        teenth century, 572–77, 594–96,
        597, 600, 601
    and anti-colonialism, 707, 708,
        710–11
    and China, 670
    and commerce and colonization
        between 1450–1600, 422, 440
    and culture between 1600–1780,
        499–502
    in Europe, 806, 807
    Fulani people, 574–77, 600
    and globalization, 777, 791
    and imperialism, 624
    in India, 556, 594–96, 671, 707, 708,
        736, 813, *813*
    and insurgencies against colonizing
        and centralizing states, 594–96
    and mass politics, 707, 708, 710–11
    and Mughal Empire, 440
    and Muslim Brotherhood, 711, *713*

and nationalism, 671–72, 707, 708
in Nigeria, 600, 821
and pan movements, 671–72
and revival of trade, 421, *421*
and slave trade, 436, 463
and spread of corn in Africa, 432
    see also Islam; Shiites; Sufis, Sufism;
        Sunnis; *specific ethnicities,*
        nations and regions
Mussolini, Benito, 694, 700–701, *712*
Muteferrika, Ibrahim, 499
Mutsuhito, emperor of Japan, 629
Myanmar, *see* Burma (Myanmar)
Mysore, India, *556*

Nagasaki, Japan, 479, 508, 727, *727*
Namibia, 653
Nanjing, China, 404, 405, 406, 420, 442,
    560, 581, 709, 725
Nanjing, Treaty of (1842), 560
Napoleon I, emperor of the French, 531,
    539–451, *540*, 542, *549*, 553, 558, *563*,
    564, 565
    see also Napoleonic Wars
Napoleon III, emperor of the French, 617
Napoleonic Code, 539
Napoleonic Wars, 531, 539–41, *540*, 543,
    545, 553, 554, 582, 646, 657, 695
Nasser, Gamal Abdel, 739
Natal, 621, 651
"nation":
    between 1850–1914, 608–17, 621,
        667–72
    and consolidation of nation-states in
        Europe, 614–17
    and expansion and nation-building,
        608–17
    and imperialism, 621
    and race, 667–72
    reimagining concept of, 667–72
    see also nation-states
National Alliance (Italy), 807
National Assembly, French, 537, 538, 736
National Association for the Advancement
    of Colored People (NAACP), 742
National Basketball Association, 777
National Convention, French, 541
National Forest Service, 667
National Front, 807
nationalism:
    between 1750–1850, 532, 554
    between 1850–1914, 608–11, 614–17,
        629–30, 645–46, 667
    between 1910–1939, 700–702, 704,
        705, 706, 708, 709–10
    in Africa, 736, 768
    and alternative visions of nineteenth
        century, 582–84
    and anti-colonialism, 709–10, 734
    in China, 669–70, 709

NORTH POLAR REGION

GLOBAL SATELLITE MOSAIC

The beauty and complexity of Earth's landscapes—above and below the oceans—is revealed with the Global Satellite Mosaic. The mosaic was created for the National Geographic Society by NASA's Jet Propulsion Laboratory, using more than 500 satellite images from the National Oceanic and Atmospheric Administration. The cloud-free images show Earth in its natural colors as it would be seen from space. One can easily identify the world's major glaciers, deserts, mountain ranges, and rain forests. For example, follow the green ribbon of lush vegetation along the Nile into the stark, dry Sahara. The mountain ranges seem to rise off the map thanks to digital elevation databases from the Department of Defense. The deepest areas of the ocean realm are colored dark blue in contrast to the light blue areas highlighting continental shelves, submarine ridges, and underwater mountains.

BIOSPHERE

Thousands of satellite images combined to show a picture of biosphere productivity. In the oceans, red, yellow, and green indicate waters rich in phytoplankton. On land, green areas show high potential plant productivity, tan areas suffer from productivity limitations due to aridity and temperature.

THE W
SATE